THE DIVINE GRACE
OF
SRI SHIRDI SAI BABA

THE DIVINE GRACE
OF
SRI SHIRDI SAI BABA

**Experiences of a cross section
of contemporary
and post-samadhi beneficiaries**

SATYA PAL RUHELA

PARTRIDGE

To order additional copies of this book, contact
Partridge India
000 800 10062 62
orders.india@partridgepublishing.com

www.partridgepublishing.com/india

ALSO BY THE SAME AUTHOR

- Thus Spake Sri Shirdi Sai Baba
  (By: B. Umamaheswar Rao; Ed. by S.P. Ruhela, 1997)
- Shirdi Sai: The Supreme
- Sri Shirdi Sai *Bhajanavali* (In Roman, 1998)
- The Immoral Fakir of Shirdi, 1998
- The Divine Glory of Sri Shirdi Sai Baba
  (By: Chakor Ajgaonkar; Ed. by S.P. Ruhela, 1998)
- Communications from the Spirit of Sri Shirdi Sai Baba
  (By: B. Umamaheswar Rao; Ed. by S.P. Ruhela, 2008)
- Sai Grace and Recent Predictions
  (By: Acharya Purshottamanda; Ed. by S.P. Ruhela, 2000)
- Truth in Controversies on Sri Shirdi Sai Baba, 2000
- Shirdi Sai Baba's Mother and her Present Re-incarnation
  (Interview with Seethammal 'Baba Paatti' of Chennai)
- New Light on Sri Shirdi Sai Baba, 1999
- Sai Ideal and the Sai World, 2000
- The Spiritual Philosophy of Sri Shirdi Sai Baba
  (By: B. Umamaheswar Rao; Ed. by S.P. Ruhela, 1997)
- Sri Shirdi Sai Baba, 2000
- New Researches on Sri Shirdi Sai Baba *2000*
- *Sri Shirdi Sai Baba: Jeevan* aur *Darshan* (in Hindi), 2004
- Sri Shirdi Sai Baba: The Universal Master, 2007
- *Sri Shirdi Sai Baba ke Divya Chamatkar* (in Hindi), 2007
- How I Found God:- *Roles played by Fakir Shirdi Sai Baba and Spirit Masters in my Spiritual Training resulting in my God-realization*
  (By: Yogi M.K. Spencer; Ed. by S.P. Ruhela), 2011
- *Maine Ishwar ko kaise paya* (Hindi version of the above),2915
- Triple Incarnations of Sai Baba,2015
- Shirdi Sai Speaks to Yogi Spencer in His Vision, 2015
- Select Spiritual Writings of Yogi M.K.Spencer,2015
- Shirdi Sai Baba: The Universal Master,2015
- Unique Spiritual Philosophy of Sri Shirdi Sai Baba (*Forthcoming*)

This painting of Shri Sai Baba was painted in his life time and is now hung in the Dwarakamayee, Shirdi.

PRAYER TO GURU

Salutations to the real Guru who is the embodiment of the Bliss of *Brahman* (Divinity) who bestows supreme bliss of *Brahman* (Divinity) who bestows supreme happiness and is detached, knowledge personified, beyond duality, who is like the sky and is indicated by such Vedic dicts as 'Thou art That', and who is the One, eternal, pure, immovable, the witness of all the workings of the intellect, beyond all states and devoid of the three *Gunas*.

Sri Shirdi Sai Baba's *Samadhi* in Shirdi

Sri Shirdi Sai Baba's marble statue in *Samadhi Mandir* in Shirdi

SWAMI PRAGYANAND
Founder/Patron

सांई प्रज्ञा धाम
SAI PRAGYA DHAM
(Vishwa Mata Gayatri Trust Delhi)
PRAGYA MISSION INTERNATIONAL ● PRAGYA MITRA PARIWAR
PRAGYA YOGA FOUNDATION ● PRAGYA PRAYAVARAN PRATISTHAN

SAI PRAGYA DHAM
PRAGYA MARG, SAKET
NEW DELHI - 110017
TEL : 685 6666, 6866889
FAX (019111) 6852828

Date 27-8-97

To

Shree Satyapal Ruhelaji

May Satchidanand Sadguru Shirdi
Sai Baba Bless you for your
noble effort to bring out the holy
book DIVINE GRACE OF SHREE SHIRDI
SAI BABA "

With prayerful heartiest Love
& Blessings

Yours in the Service
of Divine Wisdom

Message   27.9. 1997

Sai Pragya Dham
Pragya Mission International
Sai Pragya Dham
(Vishwa Mata Gayatri Dham)
Pragya Marg, Saket
New Delhi-110017

*"Om Shirdi Vasaya Vidmsye Sachidandaya
Dheemahi Sanno Sai Pachodayat."*

*"Anant Koti, Brahmad Nayak, Rajadhiraj, Yogiraj, Parabrahma Sadguru
Shri Sai Nath Maharaj* is spreading consciousness like *sanjivani* medicine to
all these afflicted with worldly maladies. He is a unique Incarnation of God
in their modern age. Universally known as *Sabka Malik Ek* or *Fakir*, He is the
true representative of the God Almighty. He is the Incarnation of Lord Datta,
the Trinity of Brahma, Vishnu and Mahesh, the adopted son of Sati Anusuya.

Shri Hemadpant has enabled all of us to taste the divine nectar of his *leelas*
through *'Shri Sai Satcharita'*;

The word 'SAI' appears in many highly venerated religious composition of
Sant Tulsidas and Sant Kabir – the immortal saint poets of the Bhakti age in
the medieval history of our country, as the name of the Divine Incarnation of
the Lord of Universe. In *Bal Kaand, Ayodhya Kaand, Aranya Kaand, Kishkindha
Kaand, Lanka Kaand* and *Uttar Kaand* of Rmaayna by Tulsidas, we find many
couplets in which 'Sai' name has been used for Lord Rama.

In Kabir's *Sakhis*, the word 'Sai' has been used for the Master or the Supreme Soul who is the indweller of every heart:

"Tera Sai tujh mein jyon upvan mein baas,
Kasturi ka mraga jyon phir sunghe ghas."
"Your Sai is within you as is the scent in the flowers of
the garden, the *Kasturi* (musk) is within the deer's body
yet he runs searching for the scent in grass."
"Kon chuega uski parchayee jisko bachane wala Sai"
"Who can touch even his shadow whom Sai protects?"
"O Sai, give me as much that may fulfil my household's need, Neither
I may go hungry, nor the Sadhu asking for alms may have to go hungry."
"Sai itna deejiye jame kutumb samaya,
Mein bhi bhuka na rahun sadhu na bhukha jaya."

Indeed, our SAI is the same Sai whose bounties and virtues Tulsi Das and Kabir so eloquently extolled and sang in their immortal devotional verses.

The *Leela bhoomi* of our Lord Sai, Shirdi, has now become the greatest pilgrimage in the whole world. Sai Baba had changed the bitter taste of the *neem* tree there to sweetness by His divine touch. He had transformed the lives of countless devotees by a mere glance of His compassionate eyes. Even now He rushes forward towards all those who cry and pray to receive His divine help, protection or cure, howsoever near or far they may be stationed. His love and compassion for every one, irrespective of any differentiation, is the same and are readily available to all. How fortunate are we to have such a unique and compassionate divine Master as our Lord, the sole object of our prayers and love.

I am indeed happy to learn that in this book *'Divine Grace of Sri Shirdi Sai Baba'* compiled and edited by Professor Satya Pal Ruhela, the thrilling experiences of so many Sai devotees of Baba's Grace have been presented, and also some valuable articles on how His grace can be obtained and what His divine attributes are, have been included. I congratulate and bless the editor Prof. S.P. Ruhela for rendering such a noble service to the Sai world. I pray to Lord Shri Shirdi Sai Baba to shower His choicest blessings on the editor and its contributors and on all the readers of this unique book. This book will be an important milestone on the man kind's journey to the *Satyuga* the new era of truth which will be Sai Age.

The International Pragya Mission cordially welcomes the coming *Satyuga* or the *Sai Yuga* in this daily welcome song:

> *"Satyuga aa raha hai, swagtam, swagatam, swagatam,*
> *Sai Yuga aa raha hai; swagatam, swagatam, swagatam."*
> (Satyuga is coming, welcome, welcome, welcome,
> *Sai Yuga* is coming, welcome, welcome, welcome.)

Let us all join in singing this welcome song and pray to our dearest Sai to bestow His choicest blessings on us, develop *'Sraddha'* and *'Saburi'* in us, and make our lives full of Sadhna, *Siddhis*, joy and enlightenment.

> *"Om Sai, Sri Sai, Jaya Jaya Sai"*
> Swami Pragyanand
> Founder & Patron
> SAI PRAGYA DHAM
> Pragya Mission International
> Pragya Marg, Saket, New Delhi-110017

RAJ RAJESHWARI DEVI
Mobile: 9818322334
Sevamurti Gurumaa
Peethadheeshwar
Shirdi Sai Vatsalya Dham
Sainagar, Mawae, Greater Faridabad
(HARYANA)

Respected Prof. S.P.Ruhela ji

As requested by you, I am sending this message for your new book "*Divine Grace of Shirdi Sai Baba*".

Shirdi Sai Sai Baba was a unique prophet who throughout His life helped and genuinely served the unhappy people and gave the great messages;

- Allah, Bhagavan or Ahura Mazda (God), the Supreme Soul, is omnipresent, omnipresent, omnipotent and omniscient; He is One and for all. He is present hidden in the form of soul in every creature.
- All the creatures are linked to one another by rinanubandh (bonds of give and take); no one comes to us without our connections in past births which you do not remember now. So we should always be kind, compassionate and helpful to whosoever – human beings, animals or birds you come in your contact with. Treat all with due courtesy and truth.
- Always remembering this real fact that I (Self) am in each one
  of them. You should do selfless service. Give food, clothes and shelter to the needy. This only pleases Me and thereby you earn My grace.

- Have shraddha(devotion) and saburi (patience). Have faith, I am with you here and now and always. Just keep on reciting 'Sai', 'Sai'.
- If you walk one step towards me, I will walk ten steps towards you.
- You must meditate and converse with Me. I will help you

No one ever goes disappointed with Me, none will ever

These valuable teachings are well known to Sai devotees throughout the world. But many of them do not know how to converse with Him. Let me advise them on this crucial point.

Close your eyes, be relaxed and silent. Have no thought, imagination and just recite 'Om Sai' 11 or 21 or more times. Then thank Sai Baba for giving you this beautiful morning and the full day to be spent happily. Then humbly and sincere pray to Him for a few minutes to solve your problem. He will surely respond. Try to listen to the inner voice of Sai Baba. Then after some time you yourself will experience the grace of Sai Baba.

This is the easiest, simplest and sure shot method of obtaining His grace. I have been doing so and am getting all my problems miraculously solved. We in the Shirdi Sai Vatsalya dham in this small Maval village have been able to do a lot for the educare and welfare of rural poor children of special needs, poor old people and women and also have built Sri Shirdi Sai Baba Ashram. Since 2012 I have further been asked by Baba to spiritually educate public by doing Srimad Bhagwat katha, Hari-katha, Gita pravachan etc. Help from many unknown people has been coming to us for all our modest services instantly. I do not have to worry for them as I keep on remembering the sacred name of Sai Baba every moment in my heart and trying my best to do as per His wishes and directions. I am convinced that Sai Baba is always present to guide, protect, help me and solve all problems. You have been seeing me, my small family and the steady progress and the expanding circumference of the welfare activities of Shirdi Sai Vatsalya dham. Everyday Sai miracles are happening with us. This is no self-praise but only a concrete proof of Sai grace as rightly mentioned in a popular Sai Bhajan '...karta tu hindu tere more nigam ho raha hai' (Sai, You only are doing all this and the credit for it is being given to me) sung by Sai devotees around the world.

So my message to all the readers of your book is to surrender to Sai Baba and earnestly tell Him 'ab sara kam mera jeevan ka sab bhar tuhare hathon mein'. Everyday morning thank Sai Baba for giving the beautiful morning and for providing full day to discharge his/her duties and serve others. Sit in silence, meditate for some time and then submit your problem before Him emerging out of your conscience or antar-sujhav asking you to do what and how. Thus you yourself will experience the grace of Sai Baba.

I am sure your book will help the readers throughout the world in solving their problems of many kinds and uplifting them materialistic and spiritually.

With kind regards and Om Sai Ram.

Raj 19·11·2015

RAJ RAJESHWARI DEVI

www.saivatsalyadham.com

facebook: sevamurti gurumaa

email.: saibabakiagya@gmail.com

FOREWORD

I have been requested by my Sai devotee friend Prof.S.P.Ruhela to write Foreword to this book. My modesty does not permit me to accept this challenge, but as the request originates from an earnest quarter I venture to make a modest attempt and exercise my limited talents. The state anything about the great saint of Shirdi, the greatest Universal Spiritual Master of this era, is just equivalent to showing a small torch against the Sun. Truly confessing, to realize Him and His spiritual powers only one birth is certainly not enough. A number of births with the same carried over mission or purpose of life are essential.

Remember one thing once for all: the Saint is one but the followers are in thousands seeking His divine grace. But how many ultimately succeed? How many are rewarded? Those making half-hearted attempt totally lacking in strong determination, are, automatically, weeded out. Only a few headstrong, obstinate, staunch of purpose, cling to His feet. They are kicked off number of times, but again and again they promptly rush back to kiss the Lotus feet of Sai Baba. Thus subsequently filtered, tested, moulded, they finally earn the real divine grace of Sri Shirdi Sai baba. Astonishingly, at times Sri Sai Himself on his own picks up some out of the millions and showers His divine grace on them, which is known all in this world.

No country in the world is so famous for saints, *sadhus* and sages as our country Bharat. We are the inheritors of the richest cultural inheritance in the world. Sai Baba himself, had said, when living, "I shall speak to My devotees though My tomb." He has withstood the test of time and tides of this era. This is indeed been being found true since His body was interned in the the Sai *Samadi Mandir* in Shirdi in 1918.

Every human surviving today is banking upon one spiritual power or the other. Our living is such that some day or the other we step into some difficulty. At such we remember a His importance as *Jagat Guru* (The Universal Master).

He is now the Supreme Ascended Spirit Master. He appears before His ardent devotees in their dreams and in person to guide, inspire, save and help them in their problems instantly on remembering Him. His *Dwarka Mai masjid* mosque) and *Samadhi Mandir* (temple) in Shirdi are known as to billons of people of all religions and nations and are visited by thousands of people daily and even more than 100 thousand pilgrims from al lover the world to seek His blessings and none ever returns from Shirdi disappointed by the most merciful saint there

Sri Sai is one unique force who is approached at the time of difficulties. One cardinal point of His functioning is His promptness of response. With those who have built up their links with Him, His response comes tothem like a flash. Believe it, I am one who has well experienced it not once but a number of times in my life.

Now you will ask me how to build up link with Sri Sai. The only thing required between Him and us is a strong building up of Supreme faith in His unseen powers, total surrender at His Lotus Feet. Nothing can convince you better than your personal experiences. My experiences have been incorporated elsewhere in this book. I can thoughtfully assert that no amount of money, no amount of flowery offerings or shows can bring Sri Sai close to you. Your total, absolute faith in him, your absolute surrender unto him, your deep concentration, remembering His immortal spirit are a few very effective ways and essential requirements and you can find the Sai spirit in front of you, any time you want.

This is my personal experience and this can be the experience of anybody else. We must have that much of power intrinsically in you first. He is our caretaker, our mother and our savior sprotector. He forms a ring around us which no evil force can pierce. He develops an aura around our personality, which goes a long way in every walk of life in this world. His flash point response protects us from accidents, steering us out of our difficulties or difficult situations, and granting us exactly what we have in our He is the Universal Master with *lakhs* and *lakhs* of devotees visiting His Shirdi shrine and His temples not only in India but throughout the world, seeking His blessings and His divine response.

For the benefit of those who desire to seek him and His power, I have certain points in mind which if you apply will help you to get close to that Supreme Power. First, convince yourself well, beyond my doubt, that Sri Sai is a responsive spirit which can be contacted by you. Have absolute faith in Him. Surrender yourself totally to him. Tell him "I am at your feet, Baba, kindly Everything of mine is Yours. You are my Saviour and you are my God and beneficiary. You take care of me, my activities, my family and children, my service or business." One thing is sure. You are under the umbrella of His protective powers. From this day He will have an unseen hand in manipulating your entire affairs. He has the sole power to reduce the impact of any damage or injury caused in your sphere.

Out of my own personal experience, I have no hesitation to apprise you that whenever He comes in your home, when He personally welcomes you, He will make you cry, you will cry like a babe. That feeling will be so imperative that you will not be able to suppress it in any way. This is one concrete indication that His divine Soul, or Spirit you may call, is in contact with yours. Be assured of that, I am speaking out of my intimate experience, not once but numerous times any day outside or within my own house. Meditation on His name is yet another approach to him, but it requires life-long practice and time also. Morning hours from 3 A.M. to 5 A.M. are most suitable for meditation on His name.

Sri Sai Baba has assured said "With good faith if you come to Me one step, I come to you ten steps". He has also said "Why fear when I am near". This one assurance imbibed in me has given me personally one confidence that I do not fear anybody. I always move with my head up in the world. This is not conceit. Do not misunderstand. It is my strong point. He also rightly said, "You will never look to Me in vain". He is ever merciful, ready to pardon our ill-doings if only we sincerely pray and acknowledge our mistakes. Assure him that such mistakes will not be repeated. He pardons us. Its indication is that you at once start feeling light. That obsession of error is erased in full. Your life and living must be on pure lines. Your intentions must be good. Your bad karmas are burnt up by unseen spiritual power which He (Shirdi Sai Baba) Himself possesses.

Our Sri Sai has on record cases where he had given new lease of life to the ones already departed. *Sri Sai Satcharita* gives us many examples of this type, and His unseen and unlimited powers. One who has realized Him with all His powers, has realized God-powers. Just imagine that you are facing some impossible task and you are entrusted to make it achievable. Do not feel despair. Impossible situations have been converted into possible ones.

If we look back in the annals Indian history we know that a *'Miya'* (Muslim) and *'Madhav'* (Hindu) never lived in harmony but that discord was purely political. Muslims and Hindus were always kept fighting among themselves. This was the design and style of the British rule. Sri Sai of Shirdi never indulged in the political life in Shirdi or elsewhere, but He well realized that He should work for good harmony between Muslims and Hindus. In *Dwarka Mai masjid* (mosque) Muslims sat together at the same place with Baba, dined together and prayed together. Sri Sai Baba had as many Hindu disciples as Muslims. He treated all very lovingly. Baba also gave medicines to the sick. He used the *udhi* (sacred miraculous ash) of the *Dhuni* fire place) at His *Dwarka Ma*i as medicine. Whoever used it with full faith was invariably cured of his illness. I myself apply his *Udi* received from His *Mandi*r every time on the forehead before I step out of my house. I also put on His ring or kept His small photo around my neck when I move out. Fortunate are we, the readers and the listeners who have developed this interest and link with such a great Spiritual Master of the century. Under the umbrella of his blessings everywhere, every time we are protected by Him. I am a Zoroastrian. In our religion we call God *Ahura Mazda*, I staunchly believe that Sri Shirdi Sai Baba is *Ahura Mazda*. The famous Zoroastrian lady (Late) Mrs.Manager of Bombay was a contemporary devotee of Sri Shirdi Sai Baba. She had written her thrilling experience of witnessing Sri Shirdi Sai Baba's penetrating eyes and unique power of immediately reading what is going on in any devotee's mind. You should read hr thrilling account how Sai Baba had stunned her by asking her to eat a piece of *peda* (milk toffee) brought to Him by a stinking old leper in *Dwaka Mai masjid* which He had then most eagerly and gladly taken out from his dirty cloth packet and eaten half of it and asked her to t the rest, which terribly disgusted Mrs.Manager sitting in thevked courtyard the Dwarka Mai. That incident taught her many invaluable moral and spiritual teachings.

You must be knowing that a Zoroastrian lady Mrs.Zarina Taraporewala is an ardent devotee of Sai Baba, she has translated the immortal prayer song books of Sai Baba's famous *kitanka*r Das Ganu Maharaj. The world renowned *Avata*r Meher Baba was a Zoroastrian, who as a young boy had seen Sai Baba at Shirdi and he later on became the foremost devotee of Sai Baba's most favourire devotee Sri Upasani Baba of Kanya Kumari Sansthan, Sakori near Shirdi. He in his book on hirdi awrote' "You will never be able to understand thoroughly how great Sai Baba was. He was the personification of perfection. If you know him as I knew him, you will call him the Master of Creation." Meher Baba's contemporary spiritualist Minocher K. Spencer of Karachi, the author of the great spiritual work 'How I Found God' too was a Zorostrian. He had received 77 rare spiritual messages from the spirit of Sri Sai Baba as Godin1954. Thus It is to be underlined that not only many Hindus and Muslims but Zoroastrians and followers of other religions were then and are now Sri Shirdi Sai Baba's devotees and recipients of His grace. This fact testifies the universal appeal and firm faith that Sai Baba has been evoking inin the hearts of millions of people.

With these observations, I am happy to recommend this new book by the eminent scholar Prof. S.P. Ruhela to Sai devotees and spiritual seekers. He has prepared it with great love, efforts, sacrifice, labour and dedication. May Sai Baba bless him profusely for this unique Sai service.

Jal Mani Chinoy

PREFACE

Sri Shirdi Sai Baba (1838-1918) is well known all over the world today as the most loving compassionate and caring incarnation of God. Apart from his unique simplicity, divinity and charismatic magnetism of personality, what attracts countless people throughout the world towards Him is His unparalleled genuine standing all-time assurances such as: "If you look to Me, I look to you"; If you cast your burden on Me, I will surely bear it"; "Whoever puts his feet on Shirdi soil, his sufferings would come to an end"; "The wretched and miserable would rise to plenty of joy and happiness as soon as they climb the steps of My mosque"; "I am ever willing to help and guide all who come to Me, who surrender to Me and who seek refuge in Me."

Nowhere else throughout this vast earth planet which is full of countless saints and centres of pilgrimage such unique assurances have ever been given by any God man or saint. Millions of people - devotees as well as non-devotees of all faiths, have for the last ten decades been finding these assurances of Sai Baba invariably coming true in their own lives, just on remembering Sai Baba earnestly in their hearts at the hour of their need and on visiting His sacred *Dwarkamai masjid* and *Samadhi Mandir* at Shirdi.

About 80 years back, Sri Narasimha Swamiji, the Founder President of All India Sai Samaj and the first great propagator of Baba's divine name and message throughout the world, had compiled a unique book *"Devotees Experiences of Sai Baba"* (1936) after personally contacting and interviewing as many as 80 foremost devotees and visitors who had personally known and benefitted from Sai Baba during his *Avataric* career at Shirdi till 1918. That wonderful book contains the most thrilling memories of those blessed souls about the rarest of the rare kind of divine charisma of Sri Shirdi Sai Baba, his breathtaking miracles and most penetrating teachings and invaluable message to mankind. Baba is still active even after his Mahasamadhi on 15th October, 1918, As per His grand assurances highlighted above, millions or people have been and area still receiving Sri Shirdi Sai Baba's grace in innumerable ways, instantly and mysteriously.

I have compiled this book "DIVINE GRACE OF SRI SHIRDI SAI BABA" – *Thrilling Experiences of Sai Devotees in the* Post-*Samadhi Period* (1918--1997) in order to highlight the real experiences of a sample of such beneficiaries who have received Baba's grace. Also I have tried to focus on the theme *'How Sai Baba's grace can be obtained'*. Everyone who has heard of Sai Baba is naturally eager for enlightenment on this theme.

We all know that Sri Shirdi Baba is approachable very easily. A sincere cry in one's heart at the moment of crisis instantly moves Sai Baba and His benevolent mysterious help or solution is soon forthcoming. Even then, many ways or approaches to get Baba's grace have been advocated by many ardent Sai devotees and learned authors of books on Baba. I have felt it necessary to collect l, review and present of them in all seriousness. While a number of books on Sri Shirdi Sai Baba have been published highlighting his divine life as *Avatar* and His unique teachings and messages, very few books focusing on this central or crucial theme, *'How Sai Baba's Grace can be obtained'* are available. Some very thought-provoking and revealing articles by perceptive devotees and intellectuals have appeared in the past 30 years in Sai journals. This book is solely focused on this very crucial theme of Sri Sai Baba's Grace. I have compiled critical incidents showing how it was actually obtained or experienced by a cross section of devotees in the last ten decades.

Being a social science researcher, I had also sent a questionnaire by post to many Sai devotees throughout India and abroad and also met many of them imploring them to share with me their own experiences of Sri Shridi Sai Baba's divine grace in their lives.. I was fortunate to receive very encouraging response from some of them. Also I have carefully chosen many experiences of devotee from Sai journals especially Shri *Sai Leela* (Shirdi), *Sai Padananada* (Bangalore), *Sai Kripa* (New Delhi), and other publications.

The famous spiritualist Sri Pragyananda Ji, the Founder of Prgya Mision Internationsl, Saket, was invited to came to Faridabad to deliver his spiritual discourse in *Gita Mandir in* Ashoka Enclave near my colony. I heard his learned discourse in which he spoke very eloquently and forcefully on Sri Shirdi Sai Baba's grace. I was very impressed with his learned discourse. After a few days I drove to his Pragya Temple, Saket, New Delhi and gave my self- typed manuscript requesting him to kindly go through it. He was very pleased and kept the manuscript for reading for a few days. After a week he telephoned me to come and collect the Message from him personally..I was very happy to meet him and get his valuable Message, blessings and encouragement. Then I got this book manuscript computerized by DataPro Co., Jamia Nsgar New Delhi at my own cost, corrected it and gave it to Diamond Pocket Books, New Delhi for publishing it. They readily published it in 19997 and sold it throughout the world. I immediately received appreciation letters from many readers, One of them, Mr.Mukund Raj. Web Site Administrator,'Shirdi Sai Website,182, West Melrose Streeet, Suite No,1, South Elgin,IL 60177, U.S.A.(web:http.www.saibaba.com) wrote to me on 14.7.1948:" I want to thank you for your efforts in compiling and publiszhing this wonderful boon….. "I want to thank you for your efforts in compiling and publishing this wonderful book" Mr. Chakor Ajgaonkar, the eminent Maharastrian Sai devotee from Thane –the former editor of *Shree Sai Leela* monthly magazine of Shirdi i Sai Baba Trust appreciated this book in these words;" The book is a compilation of divine and thrilling experiences of Sai devotees ranging from 1918 to 1977. The book reflects in a nutshell the benevolence, philanthropic and humanitarian working of Sai Baba's. Omniscience, Omniscience and Omnipotence of the Shirdi *avata*r operating in all times and at every place. I appeal to my Sai brothers to benefit themselves from the rich treasure of Sai knowledge contained in Dr.Ruhels's great literary works,.,"

This book has been reprinted and published in a number of new editions from 1997 till 2013 and it has continued to be the only book on Sri Shirdi Sai Baba,s divine grace worldwide advertised Amazin, in website till now, Ithas been repubkushed n 2014.

Unfortinately, the publisher Diamond Pocket Books proved to be a cheat, they did niotgiveme my due royalty on this books alsobesideson my over 30 druing the last17 years despite many requests and remainders.

This s evident from the following details:

DIVINE GRACE OF SRI SHIRDI SAI BABA
ISBN 81-7182-047-6 First published in 1997 Rs.150

- Royalty on 1000 copies only in 1998 was paid   Rs 7,500/-
- Royalty on 1000 copies only in 2001-02 was paid   Rs.7,500/-

Ref. Ledger A/c of Diamond (April 2003-31 Mar.2004)

- No Royalty on internationally reputed book has been paid after to the author/petitioner who is its copyright holder, after F.A.2001-02 till no i.e,.2013.
- No. details of further reprints were ever given and no royalty paid after Year 2001-02 but this book has been still selling world wide as a very popular book. ItS 2012 New Edition is being sold by *web@mlbd..om* throghtoutn the world.

Proofs (A): Advertisements in '*Diamond Pustak Samachar*':-
1999: Rs.150/-; Oct. 2001 Rs.150/-; July 2002 Rs.150/-; June 2004 Rs.150/-; Aug.2005 Rs.150/-; Oct.2005 Rs. 150 April (II)2009 Rs. 150/-;Sept.(I)2008; Sept.(II)2008;Oct.(II)2008;;Sept.(First)2009;

- ISBN 81-7182-04-6 was printed for the first time on this new edition in 2009 which proved that its NEW EDITION had been published in July (II)2009.

....

Proofs: INTERNET:
- Countless unknown no. of the reprints of its First Edition and further Editions were published and sold during 1999 -2005.
- Information about its New Edition/Reprint done in March 2006 was discovered from the following international book distributor's website: (Proof: www.alwebstores.com/search all.com (p.2) Date Wed,29 Mar 2006)

- INFORMATION ABOUT ITS New Edition of 2010 has been discovered from the following

    1. Divine Grace of Sri Shirdi Sai Baba Rs.150(9788171820474)817 16204762010 Proof: Advt: *www.alibris.com/seach/booksisbn/878 8171820474*
    2. Divine Grace of Sri Shirdi Sai Baba Rs.150(9788171820474) 8171620476 Pub.dt.30.3.2010 Proof: Advt.*www.mightyape.co,oz*
    3. Divine Grace of Sri Shirdi Sai Baba Rs.150(9788171820474) Pub. dt. 30 March 2010 Proof: Advt:*www.deastore.com*

4. Divine Grace of Sri Shirdi Sai Baba
    Pub.dt. 30 March 2010:
    Proof: Advt.: *www..bookdepository.co,uk.)*
5. Divine Grace of Sri Shirdi Sai Baba pub.in 2012
    Proof: *www.web@mlbd.com*

CLAIMS:

(A) The publisher had verbally told me that only 1000 copies has been printed in each of these years1997 and 2001 which was surprisingly questionably very low and false and what could I do then. At least 3000 copies were printed in each of these years, otherwise how can it be believed that they did not publish many reprints of this book for so many years, Their own self –admitted further prints/ editions expose their dishonesty, it is proved by the fact they are still selling through some distributors like New Age Books the copies of books printed in the earlier edition of over 12years back. Evenly they had printed thousands of copies in those early editions and thus cheated me. Therefore, the publisher is liable to pay royalty on the undisclosed no. of copies (30001000=2000 copies) in the first two editions of 1999-2000 and 2001-02:

For 1999-2000   on 2000 copies:@Rs.7.50 = 15,000/-
For 2000--2001;   on 2000 copies:@Rs.7.50 = 15,000/-
                                          Total (A) Rs.30,000/-

It has been discovered from the Internet that International booksellers like *deastoress* in Italy and *bookdepository* in UK have advertised that its new edition was published by DiamoPocket Books on 30 March 2010.

I believe that this world famous book must have been sold in very large numbers throughout the worl5- and so the publisher iliable to pay the underpaid royalty t leasrt for my moderately estimated minimum average annual sale of 3000 copies from F.Y.2002-03 to F.Y.2014-15 i.e. for 13 years: on 33,000 copies @ 5% on its price of Rs.150/- i.e.Rs.7.50 each= About rs.,3,00000/-Actually it might have been sold in far more number of copies in the world.

GRAND TOTAL: (A) +(B) = Rs. only in the 17 years. So uchifs theirhighhasndedness and bunglinmg.

This is not only in case of this book. The same sort of gross unfairness, high handedness and exploitation of me as author has been done by the Diamond Pocket Books publisher in case of all my other pocket books.

After being thus cheated and severely exploited by the dishonest publisher for so long, I ultimately decided to fight out against the grave injustice of the publisher. Despite my old age and my being surrounded by so many health, financial, social problems and lack of material help and even moral supportfrom anybody, but having total faith in the identical great teachings of LordKrishna and Sri Sai Baba, I mustered courage and decided toagainst THE Co. in the High Court of Delhi in 2012. The High Court inAugust 2013 appointed a Sole Arbitrator to settle this royalty dispute. I then filed my claim petition with all concrete proofs with the Sole Arbitrator in May2014. The arbitration proceedings are now going on and the judgment will be known in near future. My experiences with some other Indian publishers also have been unhappy. I had such sad experience with the dishonest publishers of India who camein my life, they only exploited me by not paying the due royalties on my very important and popular spiritual books in English and Hindi for long.

When I was so disappointed, I providentially, mysteriously and unexpectedly received a phone call from Mr.Nelson Cortez, Senior Publishing Consultant of the renowned American publishing Co. - Partridge India of the world renowned Partridge Random Penguin group of internationally reputed publishing companies. He was very courteous and encouraging and he assured me that his publishing Co. would like to publish my books underany of their self-publishing packages. I prayed to Sai Baba for His direction. and as guided by Him in 2013 I approached Mr.Nelson Cortez with my book proposals three in 2013 and two in early 2014. They have by now published.

In July 2015, Mr,Franco Martinez of the same publishing Co. enquired of me if I had still more books and was thinking to get them published byPartridge India publishing Co. I wanted to publish my two most important and well known books. and so I agreed to give them also to Partridge India Co.. Thus they are now publishing the revised and updated editions of my two books 'Sri Shirdi Sai Baba: The Universal Master'and this one 'Divine Grace of Sri Shirdi Sa Baba'. All these books are being publishe under their Amethyst Self-publishing package.'They will be available inboth paperback and e mail formats throughout the world.. May Sri Shirdi Sai Baba shower His grace on all the readers as He been kind to me. My life has been saved many times by

His grace and I have beenable to continue pursuing my spiritual writing work even at this advanced age of 80. Although I cannot walk, stand, travel and speak legibly and doany physical activity and have been greatly suffering from economic, health and many problems yet I am able to work on my personal computer for sometime daily and maintain poise and peace by following Sri Sai Baba's two commands – *shraddha* (devotion) and *saburi* (patience, contentment). This is the concrete evidence of Sai Baba's grace and mercy on me.

2015   Satya Pa Ruhela

ACKNOWLEDGEMENTS

I mmost sincerely acknowledge the precious illumination and help received from:

- Sri shirdi Sai Baba
- Many Sai devotees and friends, Sai journals and books and the learned authors of the am grateful to them from the core of my heart. I am really grateful to the Editor of *Shri Sai Leela* from which some highly valuable articles have been reproduced in this book.
- II am especially grateful to these most eminent and highly inspiring senior Sai devotees –my esteemed Zoroastrian elderly friend (Late) Sri Jal Mani Chinoy (Nagpur), Sri T.R. Naidu (Hyderabad), Sri V.B. Kher (Mumbai), (Late) Smt. Seethammal *'Baba Paatti'* (Chennai), (Late) Sri B. Umamaheswara Rao (Guntur), Prof. Subhash Chowfla (Solan), Sri T.R. Ram Nathen (Sarangabad), Sri G. Meenakshi Sundaram (Chennai), Sri Radha Krishnan 'Sai Jeevi' (Hubli), Sri Janak Raj Laroria (NOIDA), Sri S.M. Bannerjee (Calcutta), Dr. K.V. Raghav Rao (Hyderabad), Sri H.D. Lakshman Swami (Bangalore), Sri Chakor Aajgaonkar (Thane), Sri C.M. Sehgal (Fridabad), Dr. G.R. Vijay Kumar (Hosur), Sri S. Seshadri (Bangalore), my spiritual Guru (Late) Sri A.Somasundaram (Markapur) and Sri Dinesh Dosajh (Nairobi, Kenya), for their encouragement and help in this book.
- My grateful thnks are due to Swam iPragayanananda Ji and Sai Maa RajRajesrri Devi for their inpriring Messages and (late) Shri Jal Mani Chnow for hisbrillianyt Foreword to this book
- Guru Ji C.B. Sathpathy, the eminent Sai prachark.(propagator)
- My esteemed friend (Late) Prof. Adhya Prashad Tripathi, PrasanthiNilyam
- All the Sai devotees whose experiences of Sai Babs's grace hsvr been recorded in this book.
- Dr.Zebnof Gerrmny and Mr.Angira Desai of U.S.A..

- Mr. Frano Martinez, Supervisor, Mr. Jeric Fraco, Author Advisor. and Mr. Pohar Baruah, Publishing Services Associate, Partridge India Publishing Co., Bloomington (USA) for their kind cooperation, efficiency and remarkable help due to which my ardent wish and dream to see this book published.

- I would be failing in my duty if I forget to acknowledge the variouskinds of assistance given to me by my wife Mrs.Sushila Devi Ruhela, my sons Vinod Ruhela and Arvind Ruhela and my grand children Deepali and Akshya.. I fall short of adequate words to thank my ideal wife. I am happy to rcall that she my wife in one of my past births also as was revesled by *Sukanandi (*palm leaf ecords) astrologer Gunjur Narayan Shastri of Banglore on 18.12.1979. She has been not only my great support but most caring and sef-sacrificing guardian and sole caretaker in this tumultuous. All my higher education after my marriage with her in 1955 and achievements have been possible only due to her. I am grateful to Sai Baba His great blessing for giving me such an ideal Hindu wife so hard to find these days.

(Dr) Satya Pal Ruhela
Christmas, 2015 Retired ProfessoEducation (Sociology)
Jamia Mllisa Islamia University.
Residence 126, Sector 37,
Faridabad – 121003 (India)
E-mail: spruhela@gmail.com
M.:9910494110

Contents

Chapter - I

Know This About My *Avatar*

(Sri Shirdi Sai Baba)

❖ Those who love Me most, they see Me always before them. Without Me they are desolate. They have only My stories on their lips. They meditate on Me ceaselessly they have My name on their tongue and chant repeatedly and they sing of My deeds wherever they come or go when they are so merged in Me and forget all about their actions and omissions and where there is reverence for service to be rendered to MeI dwell there always He who constantly remembers Me after completely surrendering to Me I owe him a debt which I will repay by uplifting him I am in bondage to him who does not eat or drink anything without offering it to me first and who constantly meditates upon me. I act according to his wishes

❖ I constantly care for him who only longs for Me and for him no one is equal to me I act according to his wishes. He who has turned away from mother, father, kinsmen, friends, relatives, wife and son alone is attached to My feet. During the rainy season many rivers in flood meet the sea and forget that they are rivers. They become one with the ocean. The form as well as the name has disappeared. The water has mixed with sea. The river and the sea are enjoined. Duality is lost in on achieving such oneness the mind forgets the name and the form it will begin to see Me with its natural disposition because there is no other place for it out with Me. Discarding all pride surrender to Me who dwells in the heart. Ignorance will be destroyed immediately and there will be no need to listen any instructions about knowledge. Due to ignorance body consciousness is born which leads to sickness and sorrow. It is this which leads to the disregard of the code of conduct that becomes the obstacle for self realization.

❖ You may ask where I am now and how I can meet you now. But I am within your heart and we can meet without any effort. You may ask who is in the heart and how? What are his attributes? And what is his identity by which he can be recognized?

❖ Be completely attentive, listen to the clear description to whom one should surrender, and who is the dweller in the heart. The creation is filled in plenty with object of different names and forms which on one has been able to count. They are all the forms of the one embedded in the heart.

❖ The creation is filled in plenty with objects of different names and forms which no one has been able to count. They are all the forms of *Maya*. In the same way indeed that throbbing of reality which goes beyond the three aspects viz Satva, Rajas and Tamas are really the form of the One embedded in the heart. One has to appreciate that I alone am 'He and Thou" On extending this very idea of identity in the world of beings, there appears the weighty essence of one's own self.

❖ There is no room for anything or anyone besides Myself. With continuous practice you will experience my all – pervasiveness.. Then you will become one with ME and experience that there is nothing beyond me. You will be one with the Supreme Spirit and your heart will be pure. Without even having the waters of the Ganges you will have had a Ganga bath (that is you will be purified). "Believe Me, though I pass away, My bones in My tomb will give you hope and confidence. Not only Myself but My Tomb would be speaking, moving and communicating with those who would surrender themselves wholeheartedly to Me. Do not be anxious that I would be absent from you. You will hear My bones speaking and discussing your welfare, But remember Me always, believe in Me heart and soul and then you will be most benefitted.

❖ There will never be any dearth or scarcity regarding food and clothes in my devotees' home. It is my special characteristic that I look always to and provide for the welfare of those devotees who worship me whole-heartedly with their mind ever fixed on Me." Believe Me, though I pass away. My bones in My tomb will give you hope and confidence. Not only Myself but My tomb would be speaking, moving and communicating with those who would surrender themselves whole-heartedly to Me."

❖ "If a man utters My name with love, I shall fulfil all his wishes, increase his devotion. If he sings earnestly My life and My deeds, him I shall beset in front and back and on all sides. "it is my special characteristic to free any person, who surrenders completely to Me and mediates on Me constantly.

❖ "I shall draw My devotees from the jaws of death."

❖ "If My stories are listened to, all the disease will be got rid of. So hear My stories with respect and think and mediate on them, assimilate them. This is the way of happiness and contentment."

❖ "The simple remembrance of My Name as *"Sai, Sai"* will do away sins of speech and hearing." Says Sai Baba "It is enough if you keep me in your heart and make your heart harmonise with the head."

❖ I am you, You are I. There is no difference between you and Me."

❖ "You must always adhere to truth and fulfil all the promises you make. Have faith and patience. Then I will be always with you wherever you are and at all times."

CHAPTER - 2

Who is Sai Baba?

(Dr. S.P. Ruhela)

I

There are three views regarding the question 'Who is Sai Baba?'
According to Gunaji, the English translator of 'Shri Sai Satcharitra' – the
original and most authentic biography of Sri Sai Baba of Shirdi.

1. Many persons who are accustomed to see things and persons
   superficially said that Sai Baba was a mad Fakir who lived for many
   years in a wornout and dilapidated masjid at Shirdi, who talked at
   random and extracted money in the form of *Dakshina* (cash offering)
   from people who went to see him.
   This view is quite wrong. To a friend of Mr. R.A. Tarkhadkar who was
   full of tears when he was taking Sai Baba's leave at the time of leaving
   for Bombay. Baba said, "Why do you behave like a madman? Am I not
   with you there in Bombay?" The friend said, "I know that, but I have
   no experience of your being with me there in Bombay." Thereupon
   Sai Baba said that the person who thinks that Baba is in Shirdi only,
   has not at all seen Baba (does not know him really).
2. Some persons said that Sai Baba was a saint. The Muslims took him
   for one of their *Pirs* and the Hindus regarded him as one of their saints.
   The managers of the festivals annually celebrated at Shridi refer to
   Sai Baba in their announcements as the crest jewel-best of the saints.
   The view is also not correct for
3. Those who knew Sai Baba intimately and really regarded him as God
   incarnate. We give below a few instances:

(i) Hon. Mr. Justice M.B. Rege, B.A., High Court Judge, Indore in his foreword to "Sai Baba's Saying and Characters" by B.V. Narasimha Swami says:

"Baba in the flesh was, to his devotees, the embodiment of the Supreme spirit lighting the *Sadhakas* (spiritual seakers) path by his word and action." The mortal body has passed away but the 'Baba' once in it now lives in the Spirit Eternal, helping in the silent way. He often did in the flesh, the myriads of his devotees who seek solace in him.

(ii) A High Court Judge of a state in the north in his statement, recorded in *"Devotees Experiences"* by B.V. Narasimha Swam, i says:

"I look upon Shri Sai Baba as the creator, preserver and destroyer. I did so before his *Mahasamadhi* (passing away) in 1918 and do also now. To me, he is not gone. He is active even now.

"To me, he had no limitations. Of course when he was with us, there was the fleshy tabernacle. That was prominently brought to our notice at times. But mostly the infinite aspect of his was what remained before me. I thought of him as a mental or spiritual image, in which the finite and infinite blended very perfectly – yet allowing the finite to appear before us at times. Now that the body has been cast off, the infinite alone remains as "Sai Baba".

(iii) Professor G.G. Narke of the College of Engineering, Poona in his statement on page 19-20 in *"Devotees Experiences"* by B.V. Narsimha Swami says:

"I have placed Sai Baba amongst the household gods we worship daily at home. Sai Baba is God, not an ordinary *Satpurusha* (great soul). My father-in-law, Mr. Buti, my wife and my mother were all great devotees of Sai Baba and worshipped him as God.

"At an *Aarti* (worship) in my early visit, Sai Baba was in a towering passion. He fumed, cursed and threatened for no visible cause. I doubted if he was a mad man. That was a passing thought. The *Aarti* was completed in the usual way. In the after-noon (of that day) I went and massaged his feet and legs. Then he stroked my head and said "I am not mad". Lo! He is seeing my heart. Nothing is concealed from him. He is my *Antaryami* – the inner soul of my soul. I thought. Thence forward, numerous instances occurred in my own experience of his Omniscience. When he talked, he spoke as one seated in Rama, knowing all its thoughts and all its wishes etc. This is God within. I had no hesitation in deciding that he was God. I tested him at times. Each test produced the same conviction that he was all knowing and able to mould all things to his will."

(iv) The Dadasaheb Khaparde – the famous and learned Advocate of Amraoti-Berar in his introduction to *'Shri Sai Baba of Shirdi'* by R.B.M.W. Pradhan (Page 3) says:

"He appeared to know the innermost thoughts of everybody, relieved their wants and carried comforts to all. He fulfilled my idea of God on earth."

(v) Shri Das Ganu Maharaj in his *Stavanmanjari* (*ovi* 17) refers to Sai Baba as the Primary Cause of the universe, the Pure Consciousness, the Ever Merciful etc.

(vi) His biographer Hemadpant first referred to Sai Baba as a wonderful Saint who ground wheat, but after coming in closer contact he referred to him as God or Brahman, (18-41, 21-126).

(vii) Shirdi devotees, especially Madhav Rao Deshpande alias Sharma who was very intimate with Sai Baba and other devotees from outside always addressed Sai Baba as *Deva* (God).

We agree with all these devotees and think that they are perfectly right.

The Doctrine of the Immanence of God

Our ancient Rishis, the Seers of the Upanishads propounded the doctrine of the Immanence of God. They declared in various passages of *Brihadaranyak, Chhandogya, Katha and Shwetashwatara Upanishads* that the whole of Nature including all things and beings which is God's handiwork is filled and inspired by the *Antaryamin*, i.e., the Inner Controller and Ruler. If any illustration of proof be needed to prove this doctrine, it is Shri Sai Baba. If the reader reads carefully the *Sai Satcharitra* and other Sai Literature that is being published, he will no doubt be convinced of this doctrine and know 'The Real Sai Baba'.

During his life time (1838-1918) Sai Baba preferred not to disclose his social background and the facts and circumstances of his early life. Only to his very few close devotees he had given some hints about his background – that he was a Brahmin, his family belonged to Pathri village in Maharashtra, he was brought up for a few years by a Muslim Fakir (mendicant) and his wife, Guru Venkusha was his Guru with whom he had lived for twelve years, and he had countless births in the past and in one of them he had been Kabir – the famous saint of medieval India.

'Shri Sai Satcharitra', Sri Shirdi Sai Baba's authentic biography written originally in Marathi by Anna Saheb Dabholkar 'Hemadpant' (which was later on translated into English by Gunaji and published by Sai Baba Saunsthan, Shirdi in early 19th century) gave thrilling account of the innumerable miracles, teachings and graces of Sri Shirdi Sai Baba. To all Sai devotes, this book is the most sacred scripture – their Holy Bible. In 1910 Hemadpant had sought Sri Shirdi Sai Baba's permission and blessings to compile this book and he had materials from many people who had been Baba's devotees, visitors to him and his contemporaries.

Besides this treasure house of information on Sri Shirdi Sai Baba, four more books by Baba's three close devotees – *Shirdi Diary* (Khaparde), *Shri Sai Baba of Shirdi* (Pradhan) and *Shri Sai The Superman* and *Shri Sai Baba* (in Gujarati language by – Sai Shsaranananda), published in 1918, 1943, 1962 and 1966 respectively, gave thrilling accounts of the life, miracles and teachings of this unique saint of Shirdi. Sri Narasimha was Swami ji, a doyen among the propagators of Sri Shirdi Sai Baba's divine life and teachings, after Baba's *Mahasamadhi*, took up on himself the task of gathering the memories of Baba's devotees and visitors in 1936, and he brought the testimonies of about 80 such persons in his book *'Devotees Experiences of Shri Sai Baba'* in the late 1930s. He also brought out *'Life of Sai Baba'* (in four volumes) and *'Sri Sai Baba's Charter & Sayings'* in the late 1930s.

All these precious books have given very authentic and inspiring account of Sri Shirdi Sai Baba's divine incarnation. A very interesting big book *'Shri Saiche Sathya Charitra'* (in Marathi language) published in 1993 by M.B. Nimbalkar is based on *Sai Satcharitra* and some other original Marathi sources.

All these books have presented the life of Sri Shirdi Sai Baba in a rather traditional way; they have by and large, not tried to go beyond the limits of *'Sri Sachcharitra'* and not ventured to discover Baba's background and throw light on Baba's workings and his place in the Spiritual Plane or his incarnation.

II

Information on Sai Baba Emerging Since 1974

Since 1974, a number of thrilling new pieces of information on Sri Shirdi Sai Baba have come to light. They may very briefly be summarized as under:

(i) In 1974, Sri Sathya Sai Baba, the saint of Puttaparthi (Andhra Pradesh), who had as a boy of 14 in 1940 claimed himself to be the re-incarnation of Sri Shirdi Sai Baba, first of all revealed that Sri Shirdi Sai Baba was a Brahmin, his parents were Ganga Bhavadia, a hoatman of Pathri, and Devagiriamma, and that he was born due to the blessings of LOrd Shiva who had come to test the devotion and integrity of Devagiriamma, that he was born in a forest near Pathri and was forsaken by his mother who followed the foot prints of her husband who had become a recluse, that he was picked up by a Muslim Fakir and his childless wife and brought up by them in their house or Manwat till the age of 4, and after the Fakir's death his wife, disgusted by the strange religious behaviours of the boy 'Babu' took him to Guru Venkusha of Selu; the latter brought him up till the age of 16, that one of the jealous *Ashramites* (dwellers of Guru Venkusha's hermitage) hit him with a brick, and then the Guru immediately transferred all his spiritual powers to Babu and asked him to leave the ashram for good, and thus he ultimately come to Shirdi and later on became Sai Baba of Shirdi.

In his three discourses specially focused on the life of Sri Shirdi Sai Baba on 28 September, 1990, 27 September, 1992 and 6 October, 1992 Sri Sathya Sai Baba made further revelations about Sri Shirdi Sai Baba – that he was born on 27 September 1838.

This claim of Sri Sathya Sai Baba is not acceptable to most of the devotees of Sri Shirdi Sai Baba and these running Sri Shirdi Sai Baba's organization – 'Sai Baba Sansthan, Shirdi', but all the devotees of Sri Sathya Sai Baba throughout the world, firmly believe in this claim of their Guru.

Sri Sathya Sai Baba revealed also that Sri Shridi Sai Baba had told his devotee Abdul that he would be reborn after 8 years assuming the name of 'Sathya' in Madras Presidency.

(ii) V.B. Kher in his book *'Sai Baba of Shirdi: A Unique Saint'* (1991) claimed that in course of his field research in Pathri village and Selu in 1975-76 he discovered that Sri Shirdi Sai Baba was a high caste Yajurvedi Desahatha Brahmin, his family was known as Bhusari family whose family deity was Hanuman of Kumharbawdi on the outskirts of Pathri and his parental hosue was No. 4-423-61 in Pathri.

(iii) The famous spiritual Guru Meher Baba who was the disciple of Sri Upansani Maharaj of Sakori fame, the only disciple of Sri Shirdi Sai Baba, who had seen Sri Shirdi Sai Baba, has revealed in his book *'Sai Baba: The Perfect Master'*, published by Meher Era Publication, Avatar Meher Baba Poona Centre, Poona in 1991 that:

"Sai Baba was not only a *Qutab*, but was the *Qutab-e-Irshad*, meaning the Chuief of Spiritual Hierarchy of the Age, who brought the Formless God into form and gave him power."

A Sufi saint Zar-Zari-Zarbaksh, who lived about 700 years back at Khuldabad village near Ellora Caves in Maharashtra, had been the Master of Sri Shirdi Sai Baba in one of his past incarnations. Sufi Saint Sheikh Nizamuddin Auliya had sent Zar-Zari-Baksh with 700 followers to Decan for spreading doctrines of Sufism in 1300 A.D. – he had died in 1302, a foot note in the book states.

Gopal Rao Deshmukh of Selu, who was popularly known as Guru Venkusha, was a *Jagirdar* (Feudal Lord) of Selu (Shelwadi village); the intensity of his religious temperament can be gauged from an incident related about him. One day while going out for a walk he looked at a beautiful woman, which gave rise to lustful thoughts in him. He at once returned home and standing before the households deity Venkatesh, pierced both the eyes with an iron poker. He lost the light of the external world. But it enhanced the inner light in him.

The widow of the fakir who had brought up the infant Shirdi Sai Baba begging from door to door and suffering insults and refusal often, sometime receiving sufficient to sustain themselves, at last arrived at the door of blind saint Gopal Rao Deshmukh (Venkusha). Evidently, the saint was waiting for the mother and son. With great respect and love he prepared a room in his own house for them to live with him permanently. When the boy was twelve years old, his mother died. All parental connection being snapped, the boy was drawn closer to the saint and he lived with him in the same house for several years.

During this period the saint slowly unveiled to the boy the mysteries of the spiritual world and the boy became Gopal Rao's chief disciple. Seeing their close association, the Saint's Brahmin disciples became resentful and envious of the boy. One of them threw a brick at the boy's head; and hit him and blood flowed; but instead of hitting the boy, the stone hit Gopal Rao.

Soon after Gopal Rao's *icchamaran* (self desired death) the very next day, the young man (young Sai Baba of 16 years of age) left Shelwadi (Selu).

Sai Baba was a *'ghouse'* type of spiritual personality. . . he was in charge of World War I. As the Head of the Spiritual Hierarch of his time, Sai Baba controlled World War I. As the war was ending, on September 28th, 1918, Sai Baba, then said to be eighty years old, had an attack of fever which lasted for two days. After seventeen days with no food, Sai Baba leaning of the shoulder of a close disciple breathed his last at 2.30 in the noon uttering *'Ah, Deva!'* (Oh God! The day was Thursday, October 15, 1918, the important Hindu holiday of Dassera.

"Sri Baba had several strange personal habits. He was a very heavy smoker and the *chillum* (Indian earthen pipe) he would pass around amongst his devotees sitting around him. . ."

(iv) According to (Late) A. Somasundaram, Founder and Honorary Secretary of Divine Centre, Markapur (District Prakasam) Andhra Pradesh, after his passing away in 1918, Sri Shirdi Sai Baba reached the spiritual plane and became the Guiding Spirit controlling the universe. IN 1941 his spirit merged in God, and his mental fell on the spirit of Rishi Ram Ram who remained as the spirit controlling the universe till May 1967, and after his spirit's merger in Lord Srinivasa (Lord Vishnu), his mental fell on the Spirit of Swami Amritanandaji, who is still controlling the world from the spiritual personality Mrs. Anne Besant of the Theosophical Society was quoted by Somasundaram in his book *'The Dawn of New Era: The Vision of Master Rishi Ram Ram'* (1970).

"In a message delivered on 17.04.1942, Mrs. Annie Besant speaks about Ram Ram thus:

"Good morning. I am now happy having seen the Masters who guided us unerringly for many years. Ram Ram is the greatest of Master, gentle as Jesus Christ, all knowing and pure, his resplendent presence is an inspiration. He is guiding humanity into the higher paths of spiritual life and he is guiding many denizens of the visible worlds into the right path of the evolving souls. You do not and cannot Ram Ram's greatness by human comparison. He stands head and shoulders above many masters, and guides your vision to see unity amidst the diversities of life.

Sri Sai Baba after achieving the spiritual regeneration of a considerable cross-section of the people of India, having realized the universal self merged himself with the universal consciousness the necessary sequel. His mental fell in 1941 on Rishi Ram Ram, who was elected as the spirit guide of the world." (pp. 5-6)

In his other book *'The Dawn of a New Era and The Need For Universal Religion'* (1970) also, Somasundaram disclosed the following spiritual secret which has been unknown to most of the people so far:

"The spiritual guides are disembodied spirits belonging to higher plane. Their duties are to guide the lower plane spirits in the spirit world and also persons in the earthy plane along the spiritual path. Their activities are controlled by a highly evolved spirit who is called 'the Spirit Guide of the World'. A highly evolved spirit, usually belonging to the sixth plane is nominated by the Cosmic Greatness (God) and the Fourth Plane Spirits, who will benefit the most by this guide, are asked to signify their approval. According to eh spiritual sources, the recent Spirit Guides of the World were Sai Baba and Ram Ram. Apart from their arranging for religious instructions to the spirits of different spiritual planes, they have also to arrange for the spiritual education of persons in the earthly plane." (For more details, readers are referred to the interesting book *'Twenty-Six Years of Contact With The Spirit World'* by Sri V.S. Krishnaswami, I.F.S. Retired, Madras.

(v) Zoroastrian Yogi M.K. Spencer (1888-1958), a great spiritualist was some eyars attached to The Spiritual Healing Centre, Coimbatore during the 1950s. He was being guided by the Spirit Man Rishi Ram Ram since he was in his cradle, According to A. Somasundaram, who too was attached to The Spiritual Healing Centre, Coimbatore in those years, on reaching higher stages in his spiritual evolution, his (Spencer's) progress we was taken over by Sri Shirdi Sai Baba's Spirit till the last stage – God realization.

In his autobiography *'Romance of a Soul'* (1954) published by the Spiritual Healing Centre, Coimbatore, M.K. Spencer wrote as under: ". . . God ordered Ram Ram to take the soul under his special protection. . . It was Ram Ram who made him pay visits to two God-realized souls on the earth plane, viz., Meher Baba and Sri Ramana Maharishi. He took to solitude and deep contemplation and meditation connect with his Master Ram Ram and the study of Scriptures, which enabled him to write a series of books on Spiritual Philosophy and Religion published by the Spiritual Healing Centre of Coimbatore – an institution founded under the guidance of the same Master, Ram Ram – developed the soul to such an extent that Ram Ram was ordered by Ahura Mazda to relax his teaching and to hand over the aspirant for further training and guidance to God himself." (pp. 50-51)

Let us recall that Sri Shirdi Sai Baba, having relinquished his charge as the Spirit Guide of the World in 1941 had himself merged into God – he was that God who had ordered Ram Ram to hand over the further spiritual training to himself.

Sri Shirdi Sai Baba appeared before M.K. Spencer in his meditations during 1952-53 and gave him 77 rare discourses which he recorded. Under the guidance of Sri Shirdi Sai Spirit, M.K. Spencer wrote a 2000 page typed manuscript *'How I Found God'*. One hundred copies of that manuscript were printed by the Spiritual Healing Centre, Coimbatore in 1953, but before that interesting, illuminating book could be released for the benefit of the devotees, God (Sai Baba) ordered Spencer that all the copies of that book, which had been written by Spencer be burnt. This shocking incident was God's test to judge whether there had remained any grain of egoism in Spencer. The latter withstood the trust, and finally was able to achieve salvation – the highest goal of his soul, in 1957.

(vi) In July 1995 an unknown person M.R. Raghunathan, A Sai devotee from Madras (resident of 22, Venkatachala Naicken Street, Komaleeswarapet (Pudupet), Madras 600002) conveyed to me the thrilling news that from ancient *Naadis* (Palm leaf records) preserved in Madras and Kanchipuram he had just discovered Shirdi Sri Sai Baba's horoscope which revealed that Sri Shirdi Sai Baba's mother Devagiriamma had been reborn as Smt. R. Seethammal 'Baba Patti",

('Bba Patti' menas 'Grandmother' or elderly lady connected with Sai Baba in Tamil), Shirdi Sai Baba's elder sister had been reborn as Smt. P. Rajeswari, daughter of Smt. Seethammal (who at that lived in House No. 22, III Trust Cross Street, Mandavelipakkam, Madras 600028) and Sri Shirdi Sai Baba's elder brother Ambadass has been reborn as himself (M.R. Raghunathan). He wrote to me as under on 27 July, 1995:

"I started going to Little Kanchipuram (about 80 kms from here) since March 1992 and visited the *Naadi* readers quite often for getting my predictions from Sri *Agasthya Naadi* there, also for the sake of my friends and relatives. I have been in close contact with another established Naadi Reader here at Madras ('Jothida Ratna' Dr. A. Karunakaran, Sri Sughar Agasthiyar Naadi Jothida Nilayam, 14 Mannar (Reddy) Street, T. Nagar, Madras 600017: Tel. 4348094). I was already moving close with Smt. P. Seethammal, called 'Baba Patti' (Grandmother) aged 84 years and her 54 year old daughter Smt. P. Rajeswari (wife of A.V. Padmanabhan, a retired employee of Electricity Board, Madras, living at 22, III Trust Cross Street, Mandavelipakkam, Madras 600028) (as my mother and sister) (Brahmins and both staunch devotees of both Shirdi Sai Baba and Sathya Sai Baba).

Only then I got my first *Gnaana Kaandam* (Canto) as written by Sri Agasthiya Muni (thousands of years back), on 15.02.1993 wherein the Rishi tells that I was born to Smt. Devagiriamma, the mother of Sri Shirdi Sai Baba as her first son (Ambadass), then Smt. Rajeswari (as Balwan Bai) was born after me, and Sri Shirdi Sai Baba was born to her thirdly as our younger brother. I only informed these revelations to the above mother and her daughter and their own individual predictions taken by me later on their behalf have also proved the above Sri Agasthiyar's words as true.

I have been consulting the *Naadi* centre here is Madras and I have consulted almost all different *Naadis* – *Maha-Siva-Vakya* (Elaborate); *Vashista, Vishwamithra, Suka Muni* (son of the great Guru Veda Vyas), *Bhoga, pul; Plani, Koushika, Koumara* – all these are different *naadis*, and all of them confirm the things as above as true and correct. . ."

Sri M.R. Raghunathan also sent me the horoscope ofSri Shirdi Sai Baba prepared by him, based on the *naadi* revelations, in which it was mentioned that Sri Shirdi Sai Baba was born in a forest near Pathri village on 27 Sept., 1838 on Thursday, Tamil year *Vilambhi*, *Vikrama* year 1895, *Hijri* 1254 (J. Akhir), Month – Tamil *Purattasi*, *Kanya*; 13th (Tamil Date in month *Kanya*), and his parents were Sri Ganga Bhavadia (Brahmin) and Smt. Devagiriamma.

Horoscope of Sri Shirdi Sai Baba discovered by M.R. Raghunathan in 1994

```
-------------------------------------------------
        Ketu          Mangal          Shani
         4        5        6            7
         3                              8
                       Rasi
                      Shukra
         2                              9
       Lagna                          Ravi
      Chandra              Rahu       Budha
                                      Guru
         1        12       11         Guru
                                       10
-------------------------------------------------
```

Star	*Pooraadam* (20th star, 3rd part)
Rasi	*Dhanus* (Sagittarius)
Lagna	(Ascendant): *Dhanus* (Sagittarius)
Exact Time of Birth	12 Hrs. 5 MIn. 25 Sec. (12-5-25 PM in a Forest near the village Pathri of Aurangabad District of Maharashtra)
Date	27-09-1838, Thursday (Tamil Year *Vilambhi*; *Vikrama* Year 1895; *Hijri* 1254 (*J. Akir*; Month Tamil *Purattaasi*)
Rashi	*Kanya*
Month	13th Tamil date in the month of Kanya
Father	Shri Ganga Bhavadia (Brahmin)
Mother	Smt. Devagiriamma (in this birth Smt. R. Seethamal, Madras)
Brother	Elder brother Shri Ambadass (in this birth, the writer, M.R. Raghunaathan, Pudupet, Madras-600 002)
Sister	Elder sister Smt. Balwanth Bai (in this birth Smt. P. Rajeshwari, D/o above Seethammal called as "Baba Paatti")

III

Thrilling Life Story of Sri Shirdi Sai Baba

Sri Shirdi Sai Baba once disclosed his true identity in these words:
"I am all-pervasive, all-engulfing spirit of the world and all its manifestations
are none else than me. My divine nature will be revealed to the entire humanity
with lightening speed. I am a nutshell, I am the Goal, Abode, Refuge, Friend,
Origin, Dissolution, Foundation, Treasure-house and imperishable seed of
things. I am existence and non-existence, aught and naught, is and is-not, I
am the ineffable cosmic mystery."

- A keen researcher on the Baba, B.V. Kher had discovered by his field
  research in the 1970s that Sri Shirdi Sai Baba most probably belonged
  to the Bhusari Family of the Brahmins of Pathri village and his parental
  house (No. 4-438-61) was situated in Vaishnav Gali. That house was later
  on bought by B.V. Kher and donated to the local people who formed *"Shri
  Sai Smarak Mandir Samiti"*. This Samiti has erected a shed and temple
  for local Sai Devotees to perform *aarti* (worship) of Sri Shirdi Sai Baba.
- According to the revelations discovered by (Late) M.R. Raghunathan
  from the ancient *Naadi* (palm leaf records) in Tamil authored by the
  sages like Agusth Suka and others, Sai Shuirdi Sai Baba was actually
  born near the present Pathri village, in a jungle at 14 Hrs. 5 Mts. 25
  Sec., in noon time of Thursday, the 27th September 1838. His father
  was Sri Ganga Bhavadia and his mother was Srimati Devagiriamma.
  His elder brother was Sri Amba Das and his elder sister was Srimati
  Balwant Bai. Smt. Devagriamma and Balwant Bai have been reborn
  and are living in Chennai as Smt. R. Seethammal (88 year old lady
  known as 'Baba Paatti), Mr. M.R. Raghunathan was Sai Baba's elder
  brother Amba Das in his previous life.
- Pathri is now an important place. There are two trains on Central
  Railway line from Bombay to Selu. They halt at both Selu (Sailu) and
  Manwat. Pathri is about 15 kms from Selu and about 10 kms from
  Manwat. Tapovan Express does not halt at either of these but only at
  Parabhani from which Pathri is 40-45 kms distant. One can catch
  these trains at Manwat also if one is at *Shirdi*. There are direct State
  Transport buses from Bombay to Pathri, a *taluka* town.

- Sri Shirdi Sai Baba's father was a boatman. It was a poor family. Baba's parents were religious people who worshipped Hanuman, Shiva, Shakti and other gods of the Hindus. They did not have any child. Once when Ganga Bhavadia had gone to the riverside to save his boat in rainy and stormy night and Devagiriamma was alone in the house, at about 9 p.m. at first, Lord Shiva, Disguised as an old man came to her house and asked for shelter and food, then Goddess Shakti (Lord Shiva's Consort), also came there in the form of a village woman of low caste for massaging the legs of the old man. Being happy with the hospitality, good character and pity of Devagiriamma, the old man and the woman gave *darshan* as the divine couple Shiva and Parvati, and blessed her that she would have three children – one son, then a daughter and then one son, adding further, that the third child would be the incarnation of Shiva.

This divine blessing materialized in course of a few years. First, a son was born and then a daughter. When the third child was going to be born, suddenly Ganga Bhavadia developed *vairagya* (detachment with the worldly life) and decided to leave the house and family to become a renunciate. Devagiriamma, being a devout wife, decided to follow her husband's path; she sent both her children to her mother's home and accompanied her husband. On 27 September 1838, they left Pathri early in the morning. While they were passing through a forest, a few miles away from their village, birth pangs set in. Devagiriamma implored her husband to wait till the child was born, but he would not heed and went ahead. So Devaririamma gave birth to her third child all alone in the forest. Placing the child on the ground and covering him with *peepal* leaves near the forest path around mid-day, she hastened after her husband. This child was later known as the famous Sri Sai Baba of Shirdi.

After some time, an elderly Muslim Fakir, named Patil and his wife, called Fakiri, who were returning from his in-law's house in a *tonga* (horse carriage), reached the spot where the new born baby was lying. Fakiri alighted the tonga to answer the short call of nature and then she heard the cries of the new born baby. Exited at this, she called her husband to the spot. As they were a childless couple, they thought that *Allah* (God) had sent that child for them. They took the child to their village Manwat. They named the child as 'Babu'. They brought uup the child as their own. Unfortunately, the Fakir died after four years, i.e. in 1842. The child was uncontrollable. He was doing very strange and offensive acts like visiting Hindu temples to recite the Quran and visiting the mosque to install stone *Lingam*. He sang songs in praise of and worshipped *Allah* in Hindu temples. Disgusted with the daily complaints of neighbours against her son, *Fakiri* ultimately decided to carry Babu to Sailu village and leave him there in the ashram of a Hindu saint, Gopal Rao 'Venkusha' who looked after a number of abandoned, orphaned and poor boys. He had been the ruler of that place and so his ashram was in a big building and there was no dearth of food and clothing for the inmates.

- In one of his lives, Venkusha had actually been Guru Ramanand, the teacher of the eminent saint poet Kabir. It is said that Venkusha had a dream one night in 1842 in which Lord Shiva appeared before him and told him that he would himself be coming to his ashram at 11 A.M. the next day. So when Fakiri carrying the four year child Babu on her back all the way travelling on foot for miles, they were readily welcome and given shelter in the Guru Venkusha's ashram. She was given a room to live in. She dued after some years. The Guru loved Babu very much being highly impressed by his love, devotion and service, later on when Babu came to be known as a great saint Shirdi Sai Baba once he mentioned about his guru Venkusha's great love for him in his *ashram* to one lady devotee Radhabai Deshmukh. His glowing words in praise of his guru are recorded at length in chapter 18-19 of his official biography *Shri Sai Charitra*.

"I had Guru. He was great saint and most merciful. I served him long, very long; still be would not blow any *mantra* in my ears. I had a keen desire, never to leave him but to stay with him and serve him and at all cost receive some instruction from him . . . I resorted to my Guru for 12 years. He brought me up. There was no dearth of food and clothing. He was full of love, nay, he was love incarnate. How can I describe him? When I looked at him, he seemed to be in deep meditation and then, we both were filled with bliss. Night and day, I gazed at him with no thought of hunger or thirst. Without him, I felt restless. I had no other object to mediate, nor any other thing than my Guru to attend. . . He always protected me by his glance, just as the tortoise feeds her younger ones whether they are near or away on the other side of the river bank, by her loving looks."

Because of Venkusha's great love for Babu (the original name of Shri Sai Baba) the other boys of the ashram grew jealous of him. In 1854, one day, when Babu had been sent by his Guru to the forest to bring bilva leaves for worship, a group of the ashram boys beat him there and one of them hit his forehead with a brick and Babu bled profusely. The boys ran to the *ashram*; Babu came to the *Guru* with that brick. Venkusha tore his loin cloth and bandaged Babu's forehead wound. He was deeply grieved. He shed tears. He told Babu: "Now, the time has come for me to part with you. Tomorrow at 4 p.m., I shall leave this body. I shall vest my full spiritual personality in you. For that purpose, bring milk from a black cow." Young Babu went to Hulla, the Lambadi (herdman). He had only one black cow but she was not giving milk. Babu, nevertheless, came with the cow to the Guru. The Guru touched the cow from horns to tail and sasked the Lambadi, "Now pull at the tears". The Lambadi's pull drew out plenty of milk and the whole of that milk was given by Venkusha to Babu and he drank it then and there. The Guru's blessings and full spiritual powers immediately were thus passed on to the 16 years old Babu.

At the same time, the boy whose brick had hurt Babu, fell dead. His friends ran to Guru Venkusha to request him to revive the dead boy. Venkusha asked them to request Babu for this, as all his powers had already been transferred by Venkusha to him. Babu touched the dead body and immediately he came back to life. This was the first great miracle that Sri Shirdi Sai Baba performed in his life.

Thereafter, Babu was asked to leave the ashram and go towards the Godavari river. The Guru gave Babu his old sheet of cloth and the brick which had hit him. Carrying these two things as gifts from his Guru, the young Baba (Saint) traveled on foot for several days and ultimately reached the Shirdi village, which is a few miles away from the Godavari river.

He quietly reached Shirdi and stayed under a big *nee)* tree outside the village. It was the same neem tree which we now find at *Gurusthan* at Shirdi – the place of Shirdi Sai Baba's Guru in one of his previous births. An old woman of Shirdi, the mother of Nana Chopdar, then saw the young Baba and she the portrait of him:

"This young lad, fair, smart and very handsome, was first seen under the *neem* (margosa) tree, seated in an *asana* (yogic posture). The people of the village were wonderstruck to see such a young lad practicing hard penances, not minding heat and cold. By day he associated with none, by night he was afraid of none . . . Outwardly he looked very young but by action, he was really a great soul. He was the embodiment of dispassion and an enigma to all . . ."

After about two months, one day he suddenly left Shirdi. For about four years shrouded in mystery, he wandered without disclosing his identity. During these four years, he visited a number of places, lived in some mosques, and influenced a number of people.

"I grew up in Meurgad (a place sanctified by the presence of Lord Dattatreya). When people pestered me, I left for Girnar; there too people pestered me much and I left for Mount Abu (a hill station in Rajasthan). There too the same thing happened. Then I came to Akkalkot and from there, to Daulatabad. Then I went no Pandarpur, from there came to Shirdi."

But prior to this, as per his own revelation, he walked on foot for eight days on the path from Pathri (his parental village) via Selu (Sailu), Mannoe (Manwat, where he had spent the first four years of his life in the Muslim Fakir's house), and Jalnapur "trotting over the grass and sleeping at night in the grass", he reached Paithan, Aurangabad, where he stayed in an old mosque and guided and begged for an old Muslim Fakir for some years.

- The Baba once disclosed to Upasani Maharaj's elder brother, Balkrishna Govind Upasani that he had seen the battle in which the Rani Laxmi Bai of Jhansi took part, as he was then in her army. (Rani Laxmi Bai was one of the foremost freedom fighters in the first Battle of Independence of the Indians with the then British rulers in 1857 sand she was killed in the battle in late June in that year). It is likely that soon after her death in 1857, the Baba might have left the army service and reached Meurgad and later to Girnar, Mt. Abu Akkalkot, Daulatabad and Pandarpur as mentioned above.

From Paithan, the young Baba went towards the twin villages Sindhon – Bindhon. One noon, he was sitting in the forest near these twin villages when a Muslim landlord of Dhoopkhera village Chand Bhai Patil was passing. Seeing him sad, the young Baba addressed him by his name, called him near, did the miracles of calling Chand Bhai's lost mare and of materializing live amber and water by thrusting his tongs in the ground. These miracles of the young Baba greatly thrilled Chand Bhai Patil. He invited the Baba to his house. The Baba did not go with him, but he reached his village a few days later. At Dhoopkheda, the curious villagers crowd became unruly and started pinching and pestering the young Baba. So, Baba became furious and started pelting stones at the crowd. Two stones hit a mad adolescent girl (who used to roam about naked) and a lame boy. They were immediately cured of their ailments by the miraculous hitting. These miracles immediately impressed the villagers. Baba stayed at Chand Bhai's house for a few days. He accompanied Chand Bhai's nephew's marriage party on bullock carts to Shirdi where the bridegroom was going to be married to Chand Bhai's sister's daughter. The carts of the marriage party halted near the Khandoba temple outside Shirdi. Baba was the first one to alight from the cart. He moved a few steps towards the Khandoba temple.

The priest of the Khandoba temple, Mhalsapati, who was somewhat friendly with the Baba when he had first come to Shirdi in 1854, welcomed him with these words, *"Ya Sai"* (Welcome Sai). This new name 'Sai' (which means Saint, Divine Father) given by MHalsapati, was accepted by the Baba, and from that memorable day in 1858, he became known as Sai Baba.

Although Sai Baba moved to a nearby village for a few weeks, he soon returned to Shirdi and permanently settled down here. He made an old discarded mosque his home. Throughout his life, till his *Maha Samadhi* on 15 October 1918, he lived in this mosque which he had named as 'Dwarkamayi'. In the beginning, he was considered to be a cynical, half-mad *Fakir* and children used to pelt stones at him, but gradually he became the favorite of all the villagers of Shirdi and the neighboring villages.

- In his early years, he used to cure people with herbal medicines but when one patient, who was a leper, died due to the violation of food and other precautions (he indulged in sexual relations with his wife during treatment which was prohibited by Sai Baba), Sai Baba stopped giving medicines. Gradually, Dwarkamayi *masjid* (mosque) became the heart of Shirdi and the Baba did all his *leelas* (miracles), teaching and spiritual transformation of his devotees there for six decades.

He used to live on alms collected from only five specific families. He shared his food freely with his devotees as well as other creatures like dogs, cats, birds etc. His external appearance of a simple, modest, illiterate, moody, very indulgent, at times very fiery and sometimes abusive in speech and an aggressive fakir. All this was, in fact, the mask of *maya* (illusion) put on by him just to hide his real identity as God Incarnate.

However, the villagers of Shirdi and nearby places soon discovered (by experiences of his thrilling miracles and compassionate instant mysterious help) that he was no ordinary saint, but was, in fact, a divine personality of a very high order. Rarely did he declare publicly that he was God. Mostly, he uttered the name of *Allah* and advised people to remember, depend on and venerate whatever God or Goddess they had been worshipping in their families. He demonstrated that he was the incarnation fo Shiva, Dattatreya (the Incarnation of the Trinity of Brahma, Vishnu and Mahesh) and that all other Gods and Goddesses were within him.

- He incessantly worked for Hindu-Muslim unity in Shirdi. Despite the then prevailing fundamentalism and opposition on the part of Muslims and Hindus, he was ultimately successful in making them appreciate and tolerate each other's faith. He taught them spirituality and morality in very simple words. During 1885, he died for three days, but again came back to life. During his sixty year stay at Shirdi, he performed many thrilling miracles. His fame spread fast from 1910 and people from far and near started coming in crowds and presenting *dakshina* (cash gifts) as demanded by him from whomsoever he wanted. During the last 10-15 years of his life, he daily received hundreds of rupees as *dakshina*, but by evening he would distribute all of it among his devotees, beggars and poor people. Before his *Maha Samadhi* in 1918, he had assured that all his miracles and grace would be available to those who would remember him and visit his *Samadhi* and *Masjid* complex at Shirdi. And rightly so, innumerable people have actually been benefitting by praying to Sri Shirdi Sai Baba and visiting Shirdi and many have witnessed the miracle of seeing him in person even now, in different forms or in his usual attire and in their dreams.
- The name of Sri Shirdi Sai Baba has been spreading very fast throughout the world.

  Now there are hundreds of Shirdi Sai Temples not only in India, but even in London, Los Angeles, Loredo (U.S.A.), Canberra, (Australia), Durban (South Africa), Logos (Nigeria), Mauritius, Nepal, Japan, China and recently in Russia. Some other countries may be having Shirdi Sai Temples.

  He has staunch devotees not only amongst Indians but also among Germans, Americans, Australians, Africans, Britishers, Italians,

Japanese etc. The name of Sri Shirdi Sai Baba and the Sai movement has been are spreading like wildfire in the world for the last thirty years. The simple village Fakir of Shirdi, which lived till 1918, has now become the object of deep veneration and adoration of countless seekers of peace, bliss and spirituality.

- The eminent mystic Meher Baba, the disciple of Upasani Maharaj, (the only disciple of Sri Shirdi Sai Baba) had seen Sri Shridi Sai Baba in 1915. His testimony is very valuable and revealing. According to him." You will never be able to understand thoroughly how great Sai Baba was. He was the personification of perfection. If you know him as I knew him, you will call him the Master of Creation."

- Sri Sathya Sai Baba revealed about Sri Shirdi Sai Baba as under: "Shirdi Sai was a *Brahma-jnani*. He was the embodiment of Universal Consciousness, *Gyanswaroopa*. He was also the *Sadguru* teaching his devotees the reality and guiding them along the path of truth. He was a *Poornavatar* (Full or Integral Incarnation of God) and possessed the attributes of Divine *Shakti* (Power) but he held them in check and did not reveal them fully. He was like a learned musician who exhibits his musical skills occasionally; he was like a gifted poet who gave voice to his verse only rarely. He was like a skilled sculptor who revealed his artistry some times. *Siddhis* (miraculous power) and *Leelas* (sport) were merely outpourings of his love for his devotees. They were not meant to attract but only to safeguard and protect. He did not use them like visiting cards. He used his *Shakti* (power) only to save the devotees from distress and trouble; from sorrow and pain . . . His advent was for revealing divinity."

- Sri Shirdi Sai Baba's miracles were of many kinds – miraculous cures, removal of poverty, barrenness, warding of disease, lighting lamps with water, saving lives, forecasting future calamities, giving blessings for prosperity, his own thrilling yogic exercise like *Khand yoga*, removing his intestines and drying them in the sun and granting all kinds of boons. He would often tell people about the number of past births in which some of his close devotees had been associated with him.

His devotees and followers belonged to all religions, castes, social classes and occupational groups. Even some foreigners came for his *darshan* and they held him in high esteem. There were then about fifty contemporary saints in Maharashtra and other adjoining states.

They interacted with Sri Shirdi Sai Baba by paying visits to him and many of the did so mysteriously, remaining at their places. Baba remained a celibate all his life. Although he was loving and calm, yet, at times he became furious and abusive, and sometimes he beat people. He was fond of smoking his *chillum* (pipe). He often danced and sang some bhajans. All kinds of village entertainers, dancing girls, musicians, acrobats, circus men, jugglers etc., often exhibited their skills at this Dwarkamayi mosque. Although he was very kind and sympathetic towards everyone in Shirdi, yet he had a towering personality and none except two very close devotees Tatya and Shama dared to take liberties with him. Sometimes he was humorous. Daily, he told parables and stories to instruct his devotees as also to reveal the working of spiritual laws like *Rinanubandha* (Bondage of give and take), *Sambhava* (principle of equality), *Karma* and *Punarjanma* (Action and Rebirth), unity of the souls of all creatures etc. He disliked castesm, practice of untouchability, dowry, religious conversion, religious fundamentalism, and the traditional bar on women in matters of worship and social life.

- He was a mild and tolerant incarnation of mediaeval rebel saint Kabir who boldly criticized rituals and superstitions of both the Hindus and Muslims and taught spirituality pure and simple. He once disclosed that he was Kabir in one of his past Births. But as Shirdi Sai instead of attacking the so-called superstitious beliefs and practices of the Hindus and the Muslims, he liberally allowed and encouraged each one of them to continue following his or her traditional belifs and religious modes or worship. Thus, he promoted intrinsic and genuine communal tolerance and emotional and national integration by allowing both the Hindus and Muslims to worship him according to their respective modes of worship in the Dwarkamayi mosque. The wonderful miraculous *Udi* (Holy Ash) of his *dhuni* (fireplace) in Dwarkamayi was his regular gift to all his visitors and devotees. It was and is still considered to be a unique miraculous and beneficial substance much sought after by all devotees.

- His image as an *Avatar* (Incarnation) – a *Fakir* (mendicant) clad in rags, begging alms for his sustenance and wishing well of all creatures, his austerity and superb poise and spiritual attainments have for decades been turning millions of people into his devotees. Each day,

23

the number of his devotees is increasing in astronomical proportions. When he breathed his last, the only property he had, consisted of 16 rupees in his pocket, some of his clothes and shoes, *chillums* and *sadka* (a wooden stick), a *chakki* (hand mill) to grind grain and a tin pot. Although, during the later years of his life, he had been daily getting hundreds of rupees as *dakshina*, so much that the British Government Income Tax department once considered to tax his daily income which, during 1916-18, was more than that of the Governor General of India. In all wisdom, they did not tax him for he was giving away all his daily income in charity, but they did tax some of the regular beneficiaries of his charity.

- B.V. *Narsimhaswamyi*, the foremost *pracharak* (propagator) of Sri Shirdi Sai Baba, wrote these apt words on the Baba's greatness: "Baba, however, is not a mere worker of miracles. He is a *Samartha Sadguru* (All powerful Guru). He applies miracles or miraculous means to fill with faith and gratitude the hearts of devotees. Gratitude soon turns into love and then Baba's real work is seen. Baba purifies the hearts of all the dross of low attachments and their consequences, and gradually raises the devotee's souls to loftier and still loftier states of being, till they finally merge into him."

IV

Information on Sri Shirdi Sai Baba (Wikipedia)

Full Name: Sai Baba of Shirdi
Died: October 15, 1918 (age 80)
Era: 19th to 20th Century
Region: India
School:(H(induism *(Advaita Vedanta)* and Islam (Sufism)

Sai Baba of Shirdi (Unknown – October 15, 1918), also known as Shirdi Sai Baba, was an Indian *guru, yogi* and *fakir* who is regarded by his Hindu and Muslim devotees as a saint. Hindu devotees consider him an incarnation of Lord Dattatreya. Many devotees believe that he was a *Sadguru*, an enlightened *Sufi Pir* or a *Qutub*. He is a well-known figure in many parts of the world, but especially in India, where he is much revered.

Sai Baba's real name is unknown. The name "Sai" was given to him upon his arrival at Shirdi. No information is available regarding his birth and place of birth. Sai Baba never spoke about his past life. Sai is of Sanskrit origin, meaning *"Sakshat Ishwar"* or the divine. The honorific "Baba" means "father; grandfather; old man; sir" in Indo-Aryan languages. Thus Sai Baba denotes "holy father" or "saintly father".

Sai Baba had no love for perishable things and his sole concern was self-realization. He remains a very popular saint, and is worshiped by people around the world. He taught a moral code of love, forgiveness, helping others, charity, contentment, inner peace, and devotion to God and guru. Sai Baba's teaching combined elements of Hinduism and Islam: he gave the Hindu name Dwarakamayi to the mosque he lived in, practiced Hindu and Muslim rituals, taught using words and figures that drew from both traditions, and was buried in Shirdi. One of his well known epigrams, *"Sabka Malik Ek"* ("One God governs all"), is associated with Islam and Sufism. He always uttered *"Allah Malik"* ("God is the Owner, Master or King of all).

Sai Baba is revered by several notable Hindu religious leaders. Some of his disciples became famous as spiritual figures and saints, such as Mhalsapati, priest of Kandoba temple in Shirdi, Upasani Maharaj, Saint Bidkar Maharaj, Saint Gangagir, Saint Jankidas Maharaj, and Sati Godavari Mataji.

Early years:

Little has been documented on the early life of Shirdi Sai Baba. Baba reportedly arrived at the village of Shirdi in the Ahmednagar district of Maharashtra, British India, when he was about 16 years old. It is generally accepted that Sai Baba stayed in Shirdi for some times and * disappeared for a year, and returned permanently around 1858 'long hair flowing down to the end of his spine' when he arrived in Shirdi, and that he never had his head shaved. It was only after Baba was defeated in a wrestling match with one Mouniddin Tamboli that he took up the *kafni* (long shirt) and cloth cap, articles of typical Sufi clothing. This attire contributed to Baba's identification as a Muslim fakir, and was a reason for initial indifference and hostility against him in a predominantly Hindu village. According to B.V. Narasimha Swamyji, a posthumous follower who was widely praised as Sai Baba's "apostle", this attitude was prevalent up to 1954 even among some of his devotees in Shirdi.

In India, it's a common sight to find a Sai Baba temple in any city or town, in every large city or town there is at least one temple dedicated to Sai Baba.

There are even some in towns and cities outside India. In the mosque in Shirdi in which Sai Baba lived, there is a life-size portrait of him by Shama Rao Jaykar, an artist from Mumbai. Numerous monuments and statues depicting Sai Baba, which serve a religious function, have also been made. One of them, made of marble by a sculptor named Balaji Vasant Talim, is in the Samadhi Mandir in Shirdi where Sai Baba was buried. In Sai Baba temples, his devotees play various kinds of devotional religious music, such as *aarti*.

Indian Postal Service released a Sai Baba commemorative stamp in May 2008.

On July 30, 2009, the New and Renewable Energy Minister Farooq Abdullah inaugurated what has been acclaimed as the largest solar steam system in the world, at the Shirdi shrine. The Shri Sai Baba Sansthan (Trust) paid an estimated Rs.1.33 crore for the system, Rs. 58.4 lakh of which was paid as a subsidy by the renewable energy ministry. It is said the system can cook 20,000 meals per day for pilgrims visiting the temple.

Film and television:

Sai Baba has been the subject of several feature films in many languages produced by India's film industry.

Year	Film	Title role	Director	Language	Notes
1977	*Shirdi Ke Sai Baba*	Sudhir Dalvi Bhushan	Ashok V.	Hindi	Also featuring Manoj Kumar, Rajendra Kumar, Hema Malini, Shatrughan Sinha, Sachin, Prem Nath
1986	*Sri Shirdi Sai Baba*	Vijayachander	K. Vasu	Telugu Dubbed into Hindi as Shirdi Saibaba *Sai Baba Ki Kahani*, into *Mahathyam* Tamil as *Sri Shirdi Saibaba*.	Also featuring Chandra Mohan, Suthi Veerabhadra Rao, Sarath Babu, J.V.Somayajulu, Rama Prabha, Anjali Devi, Raja.
1989	*Bhagavan Sai Baba*	Sai Prakash	Sai Prakash Brahmavar	Kannada	Also starring Ramkumar, Vijaylakshmi
1993	*Sai Baba Fattelal*	Yashwant	Babasaheb S.	Marathi	Also featuring Lalita Pawar Dutt

2001	*Shirdi Sai Baba*	Sudhir Dalvi	Deepak Balraj	Hindi		Also featuring Dharmendra, Rohini Hattangadi, Suresh Oberoi
2005	*Ishwarya Avatar Sai Baba*	Mukul Nag	Ramanand Sagar	Hindi		Composite movie drawn from Sagar's *Sai Baba (TV Series)*
2010	*Malik Ek*	Jackie Shroff	Deepak Balraj	Hindi		Also featuring Manoj Vij, Hattangadi, Zarina, Wahab and Anup Jalota as Das Ganu

v

Sri Shirdi Sai Baba:: A Brief Profile
S..P.Ruhela

The eminent God's incarnation Sri Shirdi Sai Baba was born on 27 September, 1838 in the forest near Pathri village in Aurangabad District of the Maharashtra State of India. His parents were high caste Brahmins belonging to Bhardwaja Gotra (Lineage). His father's name was Ganga Bhavadia and his mother was Devagiriamma. His father was a boat man. This was a poor family. The parents were religious people who worshipped Hanuman, Shiva, Shakti and other Gods of the Hindus. They did not have any child. One night when Ganga Bhavadia had gone to the riverside to save his boats in the rainy and stormy night and Devagiriamma was alone in the house, at about 9 P.M., first Lord Shiva disguised as an old man came to her house and asked for shelter and food, and then Goddess Shakti (Lord Shiva's Consort) also came there in the form of a village woman of low caste to massage the legs of the old man. Being happy at the hospitality and good character and piety of Devagiriamma, the old man and the woman they gave their *darshan* (glimpse) as the divine couple and blessed Devagiriamma that she would have three children – one son, then a daughter and then one son, adding further that the third child would be the incarnation of Shiva himself. Indeed this blessing materialized in course of a few years. First a son was born and then a daughter. When the third child was going to be born, suddenly Ganga Bhavadia developed *vairagya* (detachment from the worldly life) and decided to leave the house and family and become a

27

enunciate. Devagiriamma, as a devout wife too decided to follow her husband's path. She sent both her children to her mother's home, and accompanied her husband. On 27 September, 1838 they left Pathri village very early in the morning. While they were passing through a forest, a few miles away from their village, birth pangs set in. Devagiriamma implored her husband to wait for a while till the child could be born, but he would not heed and went ahead. So Devagiriamma gave birth to her third child all alone in the forest. Placing the child on the ground and covering him with *peepal* leaves near the forest path around mid day, she hastened after her husband.

After a few minutes, an elderly Muslim Faqir named Patil and his wife, called Faqiri, who were returning from his in-law's house in *tonga* (horse carriage), reached near the spot where the new born baby was lying. Faqiri alighted from the *tonga* to answer the short call of nature, and there she heard the cries of the new born baby. Excited at this, she called her husband to the spot. As they were a childless couple, they thought that *Allah* had sent that child for them in response to their prayers. They took the child to their village Manwat. They named the child as 'Babu'. They brought up the child as their own son. Unfortunately, the Faqir died after four years, i.e., in 1842. The foster mother of Babu soon got tired of him as he was becoming uncontrollable. He was doing very strange and offensive acts like visiting Hindu temples and reciting the Quran there, visiting the mosque and installing a stone Lingam there and worshipping it, singing songs in praise of Allah in Hindu temples and saying that *"Rama Allah hai"*, *"Shiva Allah hai"* etc. etc. This irritated the people of Manwat. Disgusted with the daily complaints of neighbours against her son, Faqiri ultimately decided to take the child Babu to Sailu village and leave him there in the *ashram* (heritage) of a famous Hindu saint Gopal Rao 'Venkusha' who looked after a number of abandoned, orphaned and poor boys. Venkusha had been the ruler of that place and so his ashram was in a big building and there was no dearth of food and clothing for the inmates. He was loved very much by Venkusha due his great devotion for the Guru.

Because of Venkusha's great love for Baba, other boys of the *ashram* grew very much jealous of him. In 1854 one day when Babu had been sent by his Guru to the forest to bring *Bilva* leaves for worship, a group of the *ashram* boys beat him there and one of them hit his forehead with a brick and Babu bled profusely. The boys ran to the *ashram; Babu* came to the Guru with that brick. Venkusha tore his loin cloth and bandaged Babu's forehead wound. He was deeply grieved. He shed tears. He told Babu: "Now the time has come for me to part with you. Tomorrow at 4 p.m. I shall leave this body. I shall bestow my full spiritual powers on you. For that purpose, bring milk from a black cow." Young Babu went to Hulla, the *Lambadi* (herdman); he had only one black cow, but she was barren and therefore could not yield milk. The *Lambadi* and Babu, nevertheless, came with the cow to the Guru. The Guru touched the cow from horns to tail and asked the *Lambadi*, "Now pull at the teats." The Lambadi's pull drew out plenty of milk, and the whole of this milk was given by Venkusha to Babu to drink then and there. The Guru's blessings and full spiritual powers immediately were thus passed on to the young 16 year old Babu.

At the same time, the boy, whose brick had hurt Babu, fell dead, his friends ran to Venkusha to request him to revive the dead boy. Venkusha asked them to request Babu for this as all his powers had already been transferred by Venkusha to him. Babu touched the dead body, and immediately it came back to life. This was the first great miracle that Sri Shirdi Sai Baba did in his life.

Thereafter, *Babu* was asked to leave the ashram and to go towards Godavari river. The Guru gave Babu his old sheet of cloth and the brick which had hit him. Carrying these two precious gifts from his Guru Venkusha, the young Baba travelled on foot for several days and ultimately reached Shirdi village, which is a few miles away from Godavari river.

The Guru waved his hand westward towards the young Babu had now become a *fakir*.

He stayed under a *neem* tree in an isolated corner outside the village. It was the same *neem*

After about two months, one day he suddenly left Shidi and for four years shrouded in mystery he wandered without disclosing his identity to any one. During these four years, he visited a number of places, lived in some mosques, worked for some time.

Baba once disclosed to his disciple Upasani Maharaj's elder brother Balkrishna Govind Upasani that he had seen the battle in which the Rani Laxmi Bai of Jhansi took part as he was then in her army. We know that Rani Laxmi Bai was one of the foremost freedom fighters who fought the first battle of India's Independence with the then British colonial masters in 1857 and she was killed in that war in late June 1857.

It appears that from Paithan the young Baba went towards the twin Sindhon-Bindhon villages. In the forest near these twin villages, one noon he was sitting, and just then a Muslim Jagirdar of Dhoopkheda village Chand

Bhai Patil passed that side. Seeing him depressed, the young Baba addressed him by his name, called him near, and performed the miracles of calling Chand Bhai's lost mare there and of materializing live amber and water by thrusting his tongs in the ground. These miracles of the young Baba greatly impressed Chand Bhai Patil. He invited Baba to his house; Baba did not go with him, but He reached his village a few days later. At Dhoopkheda, the curious villagers crowd became unruly and started pinching and pestering the young Baba. So Baba became furious and started pelting stones at the crowd. Two stones hit a mad adolescent girl (who used to roam about naked) and a lame boy. They were immediately cured of their ailments by the miraculous hitting of Baba's stones. These miracles immediately impressed the villagers. Baba stayed at Chand Bhai's house for some days. Then he accompanied Chand Bhai's nephew's marriage party on bullock carts to Shirdi where the bridegroom was going to be married. The marriage party halted near the Khandoba temple outside Shirdi village. Baba was the first one to alight from the cart. He moved a few steps towards the Khandoba temple.

The priest of the Khandoba temple Mhalsapati, who was somewhat friendly with Baba when He had first come to Shridi in 1854, welcomed him with these spontaneously spoken words. *"Ya Sai"*. (Come Sai). This new name *'Sai'* (which means Saint, Divine Father) was then accepted by Baba and so in 1858 he begun to be called as *'Sai Baba'*..

Although Sai Baba moved to a nearby village for a few weeks, yet He returned to Shirdi and permanently settled here. He made an old discarded mosque his home. Till his Maha Samadhi on 15th October, 1918, for sixty years he lived in this mosque which he had named as *"Dwarkamai"*. In the beginning, He was considered to be a cynical, half-mad Fakir and children used to pelt stones at him, but gradually He became the favourite of all the villagers of Shirdi and the neighboring villagers.

In his early years, he used to cure people by his herbal medicines, Dwarkamai masjid became the heart of Shirdi, and Baba did all his activities, miracles, teachings and spiritual transformation of his devotees there for six decades.

He used to live on alms begged from five specific families. He shared his food freely with his devotees as well as other creatures like dogs, cats, birds etc. His external appearance as a simple, modest, illiterate, moody, very indulgent, yet at times very fiery and sometimes abusive in speech and aggressive kind of fakir was in fact his mask of *maya* (illusion) put up by him just to hide his real identity as God incarnate.

However, the villagers of Shirdi and nearby places soon came to discover by their experiences of his thrilling miracles and compassionate instant mysterious help that he was no ordinary saint but was in fact a divine personality of a very high order. Most of the time he uttered the name of Allah and advised people to remember, depend on and venerate whatever God or Goddess they had been worshipping in their families. He announced and actively demonstrated that He was the incarnation of Shiva, Dattatreya, (the Incarnation of the Trinity of Brahma, Vishnu and Mahesh) and that all other Gods and Goddesses were within Him.

He ceaselessly worked for bringing about Hindu-Muslim unity in Shirdi. Despite the then prevailing fundamentalism and opposition on the part of some Muslims as well as Hindus he was ultimately successful in making them appreciative and tolerant of each other's faith. He taught them spirituality and morality in very simple words, During 1878 he died for three days, but again came back to life. During his sixty years stay at Shirdi he performed many thrilling miracles. His fame spread fast from 1910 onwards; people from far and near started coming in crowds, presenting *dakshinas* (cash gifts) as demanded by him from whomsoever he liked. During the last 10-15 years of his life, he daily received hundreds of rupees as *dakshina*, but by evening he would distribute all of it among his devotees, beggars and poor people. Before his *Maha Samadhi* (passing away) in 1918, he had assured that his grace would be available to all those who would remember him and visit his *Masjid* at Shirdi. And rightly so, innumerable people have actually been benefitting from remembering Sri Shirdi Sai Baba and visiting Shiridi, and many have witnessed the miracle of seeing Him in person even now in different forms and even in his usual attire, and also in their dreams.

Now there are hundreds of Shirdi Sai Temples not only in India, but also in USA, U.K., Australia, South Africa, Mauritius, Nigeria, Hong Kong, Canada, Japan and many foreign countries. Not only the Indians are his devotees, even many Germans, Americans, Australians, Africans, Britishers, Italians etc. are deeply impressed by Him and have become His devotees. The name of Sri Shirdi Sai Baba has been spreading like wild fire in the world The simple village *Fakir* of Shirdi in the *, has now become the object of deep veneration and adoration of billion seekers of peace, bliss, spirituality and happiness.

Sri Shirdi Sai Baba's miracles were of many kinds – miraculous cures, removal of poverty and barrenness in women, warding of disease, lighting lamps with water, saving lives, forecasting future calamities, giving blessings for prosperity, his own thrilling yogic exercises like *Khandyoga* and removing his intestines and drying them in sun, and granting all kinds of boons to people. He would sometimes reveal to people about the number of past births in which some of his close devotees had been associated with him.

His devotees and followers belonged to all religions, castes, social classes, and occupational groups. Even some foreigners came to see him and they held him in high esteem. There were then about forty contemporary saints in Maharashtra and other adjoining states, and they interacted with Sri Shirdi Sai Baba, some paying visits to Him and many of them interacting mysteriously while remaining

His memory as an *Avatar* (Incarnation) - a fakir clad in rags, begging alms for his sustenance and wishing well of all creatures, his austerity and superb poise and spiritual attainments have been turning millions of people into his devotes and each day the number of his devotees is increasing in astronomical proportions.

CHAPTER - 3

Bliss Aspect of Sai Baba

(P.S.V. Aiyer)

Sai Baba commands universal esteem and regard on account of his innate compassion and boundless grace. Fault finding is the work of small minds, forgiving is a sign of divinity. But loving because of weakness and flaw in another is the glorious part of divinity. Herein lies the maternal touch of Baba. "Will I frown on my children?" says Baba.

When people get into scrapes, they alone are to blame, for by their acts in the past they have created the present situation for themselves. Still, they cry for relief, they run to Baba, swear and complain. He bears with them and like a loving mother he helps them out. It is this earnest solicitude for any one that may accost him, which wins for Sai Baba the devotion of so many.

Now, why should Baba do so much for every one of his devotees? Simply stating that it is his nature to sympathise and to help is no answer. It is begging the question. Sai Baba is ever in bliss, and he wishes to share his bliss with us all. There is a theory of creation that because God wished to share his bliss, He caused the universe to come into being. At our level we can neither make out nor experience the nature of the bliss which is Baba's. It may be experienced by one nearest to Baba's level, but it can never be reported. All that we can say is that this bliss is inseparable from Divine Love or Grace or whatever you may call it. Baba can help us have some idea of this at our level only by letting us have fulfillment of our wants. In this momentary satisfaction we cease to desire for what we wanted. That is to say, if we intensely desire for something, our desire for that object leaves us as soon as we get it. This desirelessness lasts for a flicker. From this we are led on to higher stages of evolution where we come in for superior kinds of joys – from sensual pleasure to cultural delights, from cultural satisfaction to spiritual ecstasy and from ecstasy to divine joy or bliss and so on. We get these as we move to different planes of consciousness, from the emotional to the mental, from mental to Buddhic, then to spiritual and then to still higher planes. Baba's grace percolates from the level first to the lowliest level distributing bliss in its finer or cruder forms at particular steps, and thus is fulfilled his wish to share his bliss. A favour shown to a devotee is a token of Baba's grace and fulfillment of Baba's wish to share his bliss with that devotee at his level. This mission of Baba is universal and it is functioning ceaselessly.

If relief or joy is delayed in any case, the recipient and not Baba's to blame for it. The devotee should focus all attention on Baba and hold fast to him and should not allow any other force to interfere.

"Hold on to my *daman*", says Meher Baba, the very embodiment of Divine love. That is what Sai Baba expects of his devotees too. Says Lord Krishna *"Ananya chintayanto mam"* (Have no thought save what you have for me), *"Mamekam saranam vraja"* (Surrender into Me alone). Krishna, Sai Baba, Meher Baba all say the same thing. Tune yourself up with the divine melody and then you sing the right note.

While Sai Baba is eager to reach out to us, we profess to be devoted to him getting ourselves mixed up in thousand preoccupations. Our own accumulated tendencies called *samskaras*, undesirable associations and other distractions are sure to disturb us, our senses, emotions and above all our vanity may conspire against us and confound us. Disinterested service, meditations, *Satsang*, devotional reading and merciless self-examination are prescribed by our seers and sages to overcome these troublesome elements.

Let us pray Baba to help us in getting single-hearted devotion to him that we all may come in for his grace and share in the bliss which he is so eager to bestow on us.

Bliss Aspect of Sai Baba calls for further discussion for the purpose of clearing up some points raised previously. The term *"bliss"* needs to be properly understood. Bliss is unmixed and unceasing happiness in its highest form. *Anand* (Sanskrit name for bliss) is graded in the Taitriya Upanished in accordance with our evolution, as the bliss of a perfect human being, higher than that of the bliss of a *manushya* and *gandharva*; superior to that the bliss of the *devas*, and next to that of *Indra*, and again of his *guru*, then of the *Pithras* and so on. Bliss necessarily lie beyond our conception because we, with the limitations of our physical bodies and senses, cannot follow the experiences of those who belong to planes higher than ours.

Bliss has a place in our life according to the Vedantic classification of our constitution. Man has *Annamaya Kosha* (Physical body), *Pranamaya Kosha* (body of vital force), *Manomaya Kosha* (mental body), *Vigyanamaya Kosha* (intellectual body) and *Anandamaya Kosha*, bliss, which remains inseparable from the *atman*. The other four Kosha, or sheaths disintegrate in physical death but *Anandamaya Kosha* leaves the body together with the *atman* (Sanskrit term for soul). This classification makes it clear that bliss is within every one of us and that it is upto us to discover its existence in ourselves.

The *Bhagvad Gita* holds that the soul is uncreated, indestructible and immortal. It is luminous like God, and so it has to possess *ananda* (Bliss) in the same way as God Himself. This theoretical understanding is to be realized by each one for oneself. No one can share with another in that task of *atma vichar* or enquiry into Self. When we say Sai Baba wants to share his bliss with us, we mean He is ready to help us in making this discovery, in getting at this self realization.

Just as infants are taught with the help of toys, pictures and games, and sometimes they are presented with sweets as incentive to make them learn, so also Baba favours his immature devotees with material benefits showing them a taste of bliss at the lowest level and then, step by step, he takes them on to higher places in the Path.

It is regrettable that we stop short of temporal gains, committing the same fault as is done by his uninformed critics who hold that Sai Baba has nothing more to give than temporal favours, and thereby we confuse the means for the end.

This error that we commit is clearly pointed out by Baba when he says "Some want wealth, some woman, some sons, but what I have none wants."

People do not aspire to higher life and higher forms of happiness because they are unable to see anything beyond what their senses convey to them. We have got used to look only outward. But the door is to be opened within, the gaze to be turned inward, as the way to higher life exists inside of us. Said Jesus Christ "The Kingdom of Heaven is with you". This is what Baba wants us all to understand and to aspire to, namely, "DIVINE WISDOM" and bliss along with it by enquiring within, Says Sai Baba:

"Think who you are" (Verse 121, *Charters and Sayings*).

Naturally he should deplore that, what he has, no one wants to take.

We trust that it is now made clear that the statement that Sai Baba wishes to share his bliss with us all has sufficient authority and arguments.

Bliss Aspect of Sai Baba was discussed in regard to its nature and how it came to us. In the first section it was recommended that maximum benefit of this bliss could be obtained only by the devotee focusing all attention of Baba and holding fast to him, without allowing any other force to interfere. In the next section. Self enquiry was recommended by turning the gaze inward. Only one thing can be attempted, namely, meditate on Baba or meditate on the self. One can not do more than one thing at a time. A reconciliation is, therefore, felt to be necessary.

It is possible to achieve both points if Yoga is properly understood and practiced. Now what is *Yoga*? *Yoga* is controlling the mind. We learn from the Ramayana that Anjaneya or Hanuman was a Yogi. Taking the sea by a leap, reducing oneself to the size of a mustard seed or magnifying one's form to an enormous size, and uprooting a hill and carrying it in the air, are *Yoga siddhis* or fruits of *Yoga*. How could Hanuman achieve these powers? The secret is disclosed to us from the words of that astute *Yogi*. In his report to Sri Ramachandra about his meeting with Sita, Hanuman had columns to speak about her alone and he mentioned nothing about himself. Sita filed his mind so much that there was no room in it for any thought about himself or anything else. This absence of any reference to self became nature to him, as he was a perfect Yogi. The first lesson to learn in Yoga or meditation is to forget the self and pin-point attention on the object of meditation. Poets and artists create masterpieces, and scientists make notable discoveries and brilliant inventions in selfless moments. We never talk of Sai Baba without reference to our experiences, our sadhanas, our own achievements and what we are doing to serve the cause of Sai Baba. The highest form of devotion is, according to Prahlad, *atma nivedan* (surrendering the self).

Next, meditation does not mean looking forward and outward, but it means looking inward. As we concentrate on Sai Baba in this way and set aside all other thoughts including our little self, the Master reveals himself in our hearts in all his glory as a lovely picture on the silver screen and then comes the realization that Sai Baba alone exists and he alone matters and nothing else. This discovery is bliss. Here we find no conflict between meditating on the Self and meditating on Sai Baba. Let us understand that Sai Baba is our Higher Self.

CHAPTER - 4

Sai Baba's Immortal Gospel

(R. Radha Krishnan 'Sai Jeevi')

I

Saints & God men

A saint is an elder brother of human beings and younger brother of gods and angels and liberated souls *(Mukta Purushas)* who are always in bliss and await the commandments of the most high (God). The functions of a saint are stated clearly in scriptures in felicitous terms:

"In the case of saints like Sri Sai Baba the relation is generally that of a beneficent superior entirely dealing with inferiors that may crave contact with a view to protection, etc. In developing one's contact with externals it is not merely one's nature that decides but also functions. Any entity along with others forms part of a joint whole or a system and functions are assigned by providence to each part. So the saint has some functions to fulfil in society and that question what these functions are, naturally arises. These functions are clearly connected with and, in fact, dependent upon the nature of the saint and his surroundings and as a rule the greater the power, the greater and wider are the responsibilities and functions."

In fact in the Brahma Sutras (Chap. IV, p. 4) the penultimate sutra shows that the rulership of the world and the assignments of the fruits of human actions belong to God and God alone. Sometimes he comes himself as an Avatara Purusha or incarnation like Shirdi Sai Baba, Sometimes he commissions a god, a guru, an angel or a liberated soul like Shri Ramana Maharishi or Shri Ramakrishna Paramahamsa, to do so and sometimes he inspires some human beings (great and ardent devotees of God) and authorizes them to do so. That is why, it is said that the ways of providence are mysterious, inscrutable, inconceivable and beyond the reach of our mind and thought. He need not and will not take orders from anybody.

37

II
Gospel of Sri Sai Baba

Sai Baba's following words guarantee the welfare of the devotees:

"There will never be any dearth or scarcity regarding food and clothes in My devotees home. It is my special characteristic that I look always to and provide for the welfare of those devotees ever fixed on Me". Lord Krishna has also said the same in Bhagvat Gita (Chapter IX verse 22). Therefore, strive not much for food and clothes. If you want anything, beg of the Lord, Leave worldly honour, try to get the Lord's grace and blessings and be honoured in His court. Do not be deluded by worldly honours. The form of the deity should be firmly fixed in the mind. Let all the senses and mind be ever devoted to the worship of the Lord. Let there be no attraction for any other thing; fix the mind in remembering Me always so that it will not wander elsewhere towards body, wealth and home. Then it will be calm, peaceful and carefree. This is the sign of the mind being well engaged in good company. If the mind be vagrant, it cannot be called well merged." (*Shri Sai Sat Charita*, Chapter VI).

Now, I will relate the life story of two ardent devotees namely, Das Ganu Maharaj and Balaram Mankar, who implicitly obeyed Baba's orders and got all the benefits (both material and spiritual) from him which bears the testimony to Baba's words stated above.

Shri Ganpatrao Sahasra-buddhe alias Das Ganu Mahraj was a police constable and orderly of Baba's ardent and great devotee, Shri Nana Saheb Chandorkar (Deputy Collector). Once Das Ganu visited Shridi along with Nana and had Darshan of Baba. Baba (looking to his future bright spiritual prospects), told him to resign from the constable's post, come to Shirdi and stay with him. But, Das Ganu replied that he would do it after becoming Fouzdar (Sub-Inspector). Although Baba repeatedly told him to resign, he did not. But, finally Baba created a grave situation for him; he was to be killed by a notorious dacoit by name Kanha Bhil in Ram Mandir, when he took the oath as follows: "Baba, I will resign this time if I am now saved." Wonder of wonders! the decoit warned him not to try to catch him and hand over to the police and let him go scotfree.

This happened in the year 1903 and Das Ganu finally left the job, went to Baba, prostrated before him and said with tears in his eyes "Baba, I am without any property and I have no income. Unless there is some provision, myself and my wife have to starve". (No children was born to him). Then Baba said, "Do not fear. I will provide for you, Ganu". Baba did provide. He told him, "Go to Nanded in Nizam's state. Attend to your Braminical duties *(Swadharma)* of reading 'Puran', explaining them and conducting *keertan*, etc." Das Ganu did so. He had an excellent voice and had a good mastery of the art of keertan singings. He used to keep Baba's photo by his side while doing keertan and used to draw thousands of devotees through his melodious voice. His name was a "household word" throughout Maharashtra. It was said in those day that Dasganu Maharaj by his inimitable keertans and Nana Saheb Chandorkar by his talks and discourses on Baba to his friends spread Baba's name and fame and glory throughout Maharashtra. Ganu was a great devotee of Lord Panduranga and he used to do *"Vari"* trip to Pandharpur every year. He died at the ripe age of about 90 at Pandharpur itself as per his wish. Thus Baba made him to cast his mortal coil and fulfilled his wish to attain *"Sadgati"* at the above of Lord Panduranga. In fact, Baba and Panduranga are one and the same. It may not be out of place if I say that His Samadhi is at *'Umri'* near Nanded and hundred of his disciples even now flock there (Umri) every year to participate in the Samadhi *Utsav* (function).

It is also to be mentioned here that Das Ganu, after becoming Baba's devotee, never had to starve for want of food and clothes, always someway or other money was pouring in and later he began to own land in Nanded, which he gave to his adopted son. Baba's undertakings for his *bhaktas* are never left unperformed.

Let us see what was Das Ganu (Police Constable Dattatreya Ganpatrao Sahasra Budhe) before becoming Baba's ardent devotee. He was leading a sinful life and he used to take pleasure in composing *"Lavanis"* (Marathi poems in vulgar language) and the same was sung by groups of Nautch girls (Dancing girls) during the performance of *"Tamashas"* (popular stage dramas) in villages throughout Maharashtra arousing passion in the minds of viewers. How great our Lord Sai is. He turned such a sinner into a great saint par excellence.

Then again is the case of Balaram Mankar, who attached himself to Baba with intense love solely for spiritual purposes. His relatives complained to Baba that he was the only earning member in his family and by his sticking on to Baba at Shridi there was utter damage done to the family welfare. They said that Mankar had a number of sons who would be left destitute by his neglecting business. Baba then said, "I will provide for Mankar's sons". Mankar was sent away to Machindragad for spiritual meditation and especially for learning the fact that Baba was as much with him at Machindragad as he was at Shirdi.

One day Baba appeared to him at Machindragad and told him that the object of his being sent there was to demonstrate to him that Baba who was at Shirdi was at the same time at Machindragad also and could talk to him and guide him. Mankar had very great spiritual advancement and it was one time hoped that he would be the successor to Baba's "Gadi" (Seat). So high was his spiritual position. But, unfortunately he died in the year 1913 long before Baba attained Mahasamadhi in 1918. As for provision, for his family, all the four sons of Mankar are now well placed and are in high positions drawing incomes mostly in seven to eight figures (in 1913). Baba's statement that He would provide for Mankar's sons *(Yoga kshemam Vahamiaham)* has proved to be absolutely true.

In conclusion, it is to be stated that Baba had also provided well being to hundred of his devotees when he was living; to mention a few, Abdul Baba, Madhava Rao Despande (alias School Master Shama), Annasaheb Dabholkar (alias Hemadpant), Mahalsapathi, Appa Shinde, Kashiram, Megha etc. Even now He is providing to every sincere and ardent devotee who has completely surrendered to him with *"Tan, Man, Dhan"* (body, mind and wealth) and worships him with whole-hearted devotion.

Therefore, let us always remember Baba's leelas and stories, meditate on them and chant his "Taraka mantra", *(Om Sai Sri Sai Jaya Jaya Sai)*, so that we may easily cross over the sea of *Samsara* (mundane existence and finally merge in the eternity of Baba (Self-realization).

III
Sai Baba's Parable of Nine Balls of Stool

One gentleman from Pune by name Anantrao Patankar came to Shirdi and took Baba's *darshan*. His eyes were appeased and he was much pleased. He said to Baba, "I have read a lot, studied *Vedas. Vedanta* and *Upanishads* and heard all the *Puranas*, but still I have not got any peace of mine; so I think that all my reading was useless. Simple ignorant, devout persons are better than myself. Unless the mind becomes calm, all book-learning is of no avail. I have heard from many people that you easily give peace of mind to so many people by your mere glance and playful words. So I have come here. Please take pity on me and bless me."

Then, taking pity on him, Baba told him a parable, which was a follows:

"Once a *'Saudagar'* (merchant) came here. Before him a mare passed nine balls of stool. The merchant intent on his quest, spread the end of his *'dhotar'* and gathered all the nine balls in it and thus got concentration and peace of mind."

Mr. Patankar could not make out the meaning of this story and humbly requested Ganesh Damodar alias Dada Kelkar to explain its meaning. Dada Kelkar replied, "I too do not know all that Baba says and means, but at his inspiration I say what I came to know. The mare is God's grace and the nine balls excreted are the nine forms or types of *bhakthi*. If any of these is faithfully followed and practiced by the devotees, Lord Hari will be pleased and manifest himself in the hearts of such devotees."

Next day when Patankar went to Baba for salutation, he was asked by him whether he collected the 'nine balls of stool', for which Patankar replied that his (Baba's) grace was required and then they would be easily collected. Then Baba blessed and comforted him, saying that he would attain peace and welfare. Hearing this, Patankar became overjoyed and happy (*Sri Sai Sat Charita*, Chapter XXI).

Let us now analyse in detail the nine types of devotion *(Navavidha Bhakti)*. Devotion holds a special appeal to a very large section of aspirants. In the Holy Trinity, Maha Vishnu is believed to foster devotion among his votaries in the same way Lord Shiva helps in dawning of wisdom. Of all the devotees of Maha Vishnu sage Narada and bhakta Prahalad hold the highest place and they have prescribed for our guidance the technique of devotion. There is much to be gained in this field of knowledge from the *Narada Pancharatha* and the *Narada Bhakthi sutras*. To Prahald belongs the credit of having favoured, with his formula of the nine fold devotion *(Navavidha Bhakthi)* in a couplet addressed to Maha Vishnu as follows:

"(1) *Sravanam*, (2) *Keerthanam*, (3) *Vishnoho: Smaranam*, (4) *Pada Sevanam*, (5) *Archanam*, (6) *Vandanam*, (7) *Dasyam*, (8) *Sakhyatvam* and (9) *Atmanivedanam*." Their meaning is as follows: (1) Listening to sacred works or accounts of god, avatars and saints; (2) reciting the name of god and saints; (3) remembrance and meditation; (4) prostration at god's or gurus' feet; 95) Worship of objects representing him; (6) paying respect to saints; (7) service to god and his devotees; (8) fellowship & (9) self-surrender.

Devotion, properly so called, is spontaneous and starts with the urge to know all about the fine and noble qualities of the object of devotion. Listening to discourses by the enlightened devotees on the numerous *"Kalyana Gunas"* (auspicious qualities) of the lord, saints and their *leelas* (sports) form the first stage in devotional practice. This is followed by joining in the singing and chanting the *'keerthi'* (glory) of the Lord or saints called *'keerthanam'.*

The next step is the chanting of the holy name with single-hearted devotion. It should be borne in mind that the holy name of the lord and saints (Sadgurus) in charged with mystical power and the one that chants it with full faith, love and devotion in its efficacy comes into possession of extraordinary power for working in the Lord's (Guru's) service. Legend has it that the celestial Rishi Narada has accepted the challenge of the Lord of the Kali age saying that he would enable the people of this age to resist evil temptations by chanting the holy name. Acknowledging the lord is shown by offering prostrations (Namaskarams) at his lotus feet and this termed as *"Padasevanam"*. The devotee is now no longer satisfied with loving the Lord in secret, but he is eager to translate that love into action by acts of worship and this is called *'Archana'* which is performed as often privately as in public. The devotee takes the next step in meeting fellow devotees and paying respects to them, thereby recognizing their devotion and also sharing with them in the bliss arising from spiritual association *(Sat Sang)*. This act of paying respect to saints is termed as *'vandanam'.*

An indissoluble bond is thus created between the Lord and his devotee, who is his servant. This bond of union is strengthened by the devotees engaging in the laudable act of spreading far and wide spiritual culture by making the people understand the Lord's glory and his *leelas* through music, *Bhajan* (Community singing), public worship, discourses etc. This service is called *'Daasyam'*. Realizing the intimate relationship with the Lord, certain indulgences came to be claimed by the devotee, as in the case of a wife who had lived with her husband for many long years. The devotee no longer looks upon Lord as the master, but treats him as a partner in life and indulges in frolicsome sports and even in reviling him for his seeming defects.

Some of the saints who have attained to this stage of devotion have composed poems which pass for criticism, but they are actually deftly covered compliments and are called *"Ninda-Sthuthi"* (Hymns in the garb of criticism of the Lord). The 'Gopis' of Brindavan cultivated this *'Madhurya Bhava'* (Pleasant attitude) and enjoyed, in rich measure, the 'Bliss' arising from their association with the Lord in that delectable diversion called *'Rasa Kreeda'* in the happy groves of Brindavan. The pastoral life in Goverdhana, the handsome player of the enchanting flute, the sports in the river Yamuna and revels in the groves of Brindavan afford inexhaustible themes for devotional poetry to many a saint as Jayadeva, Surdas, Meera Bai, Chaitanya Mahaprabhu, etc. The boyhood of Krishna is a Glorious chapter in Srimad Bhagavata Purana. The aspect of the devotion discussed above is called *'Sakhyam'* (Fellowship with the Lord).

Devotion which started with fellowship with the saints *(Sadgurus)* and ascended to the fellowship with the Lord himself leads eventually to absolute self-surrender *(Atma Nivedan)*. This is also called *'Prapatti'*. This is the final stage in devotion and it is based upon complete renunciation of all earthly possessions and attachments and it is self-abnegation. This is the unmistakable goal to which devotion leads the aspirant.

Lord Sai Nath has, out of compassion, recommended the *'Nava Vidha Bhakthi'* as laid down in our scriptures and chanting of his Taraka Nama Mantra *"Om Sai Sri Sai Jaya Jaya Sai"* constantly is the easiest path to attain salvation in this Kali age for Baba's devotees.

IV

Sai Baba's Method

The subject of Sai Baba of Shirdi is an extremely interesting one and at the same time one of great complexity and difficulty. Sai Baba is a living force and the Sai movement is growing, expanding, and developing in its nature as time goes on. Though Sai Bab passed away in 1918, it is quite correct to say that we are too near the trees to see the forest. Sai Baba's movement is growing around us and we can not feel sure that we have seen most of it, much less of it. Baba's life is also so full of mystery that one can not be sure that one gives an accurate account of Baba. Yet we shall follow the legacy, the unearthed treasure, stored up by our Sri Narasimha Swamiji.

In the first place, Sai Baba is absorbing the attention of an increasingly large number of people, and that is the meaning of the growth of the Sai movement. The subject of Baba's life and the history of his movement are of romantic interest and far surpasses the interest which we have in reading fiction like Arabian Nights, etc. The off-quoted saying that truth is stranger than fiction is best illustrated here. Taking the mere question of the life of the Saint that itself is incredible and marvelous.

When he got into Shirdi, he was ripening his process of love in solitude. *Vairagya, Dhriti* and interest in all creatures were developed unnoticed and in obscurity by Baba, and the benefit to the world came through the intrepid courage of a goldsmith (Mahlsapathy) who was anxious to get the best of the saints for his Guru. Mlasapathy, a highly devout and dispassionate worshipper of Khandoba found that Baba who had come as an unknown fakir was really a remarkable gem of the highest virtues and was most fitted to be his own Guru. So he started the worship of Baba in the mosque itself where Baba was living. His example was followed by others slowly. Now it has developed so vastly in all parts of the country and Baba's worship is going on individually and collectively. This is a well known fact.

In Sai's system, as Sri Narasimha Swamiji puts it, the *Guru* undertakes every responsibility for the devotee that surrenders himself. The devotee is there styled as the *Ankita* i.e. the stamped child of the Guru. Everything concerning that pupil is looked after by the Guru, with his wonderful superhuman powers. For a time, the circle of his worshippers and admirers was extremely limited and in the close proximity of Shirdi. You can not conceal the Sun by convering it with the back of your hand. Murder will be out, truth will be out, and greatness of Saints will be out also. Baba's powers of achieving objects by mere blessings were so well known to many now. Without any education or training, he dared to give medicines for highly advanced cases of tuberculosis, leprosy, rotting eyes, bone, rot etc. and effected most remarkable cures. The devotees discovered that Baba knew everything of their present condition and the innermost thoughts that lay hidden in their hearts, their entire past history, their previous births and also that Baba could definitely state what the future was going to be for each person that came to him.

Those wonderful powers were employed by Baba not for purposes of show or for getting wealth or plaudits but merely to promote the best interests of those people who confined themselves entirely to his care. Naturally, the advantages of having such a Guru to worship was highly esteemed and the worship of Baba went on from the neighbourhood of Shirdi to distant outlying areas and reached practically the confines of Maharashtra by the time of his Mahasamadhi in 1918 And it has spread all over our country and abroad.

We shall remember now one of Baba's eleven sayings: "I am ever living to help all who come to me, who surrender to me and who seek refuge in me." Thus Baba is living and helping us, his devotees, in every respect, temporal and spiritual, not for one moment but for the entire life of the devotees that He takes charge of, Baba's methods are unconventional. He insisted upon the essence of all religions viz. love, intense, unselfish love evidenced by devotion and service to all mankind and all creatures. This love begins with the Guru but grows and covers up every creature. Hatred is inconsistent with Baba's faith and the more this doctrine of love gathering momentum under the Sai Baba Movement spreads, the more chances there will be for people's love to grow and for this unfortunate tendency of mutual jealousy and hatred which now threatens world peace to get absorbed. That hatred ceases not by hatred but by love, is demonstrated in individual lives and will also be demonstrated more and more in the history of groups of nations and of the world.

V

How to achieve Sri Shirdi Sai Baba's divine great

In order to achieve the grace of Sri Shirdi Sai Baba, great and powerful *tarak* salvation *mantra "OM SAI, SRI SAI, JAYA"* is a very unique magnet to realize the true nature of one's self (self-realization). *Vishnu Purana* says that which is attained through *Tapasya* (Penance) in *Krita Yuga,* through, sacrifice in *Treta Yuga* through *nama japa* and for this purpose the *tarak mantra* was chanted by Sai devotee in His life time and it befitted them like the old popular *mantras* of Goddesses *Gayatri*, Lord Shiva, Lord Rama,. Lord, Krishna, Allah etc.*agnas*, I am chanting them, but, as Lord Krishna said:" Right rules and austerities have to be observed by the *sadhakas* in doing other *japa."* But in the case of chanting Sai *Nama Japa*, no formalities are necessary. It can be done at all times - while sitting, eating, walking etc., only qualification required is "*Shradha* and *Bhakti"* in the Divine Name. It is prescribed in the *Upanishads Vedas* etc. that any *Maha mantra* is to be repeated a minimum number of "three and a half Crores" of times by a *sadhaka* to achieve his object. But in the case of Sai Mantra, let us remember what Sai says, "If you simply say "*Sai, Saiz'*, I will take you over the seven seas", that is to say we can easily cross over the mundane existence by chanting His name, (according to our convenience and conditions of life) by *Japa, Kirtan, Nama Sankirtana* at our houses or Sai temples or in public places, streets, *Nagara Sankirtana* etc

It is highly advisable not to allow a *sadhaka* or group of singers of the name to be disturbed by his/their friends or relations for ordinary worldly purposes..

CHAPTER - 5

How to Obtain Sri Shirdi Sai Baba's Grace

(Compiler: Dr. S.P. Ruhela)

"To those in urgent need of help and guidance, Sai Baba appears in dreams and visions, prayers area answered, hopes and wishes fulfilled, sicknesses and diseases cured and all manner of problems solved so effectively, that His following continues to multiply. People experience strange and inexplicable happenings, many of which are nothing short of miracles. Nor are such phenomena confined and restricted to those who have heard about Him or believe in Him. People from all walks of life and from all parts of the country continue to be drawn to Shirdi and Sai Baba, in exactly the same manner as people and been drawn during His life time. Except that the names of the experiences are different; there is virtually no dissimilarity in happening prior to October 15, 1918 and those reported even today."

-Perin Bharucha

I

Countless people in the world have been receiving Sri Shirdi Sai Baba's unique and instant grace in their lives during the last 80 years since He achieved Mahasamadhi in 1918. If one were to ask: "How to get Sri Shirdi Sai Baba's Grace?" what reply should be given? This question gripped my mind while compiling this book 'Divine Grace of Shirdi Sai Baba'.I searched for the appropriate answer to this central or crucial question in *'Shri Sai Satcharita'* and other books on Baba and in several Sai devotees articles published in *'Shri Sai Leela'* (Shirdi) and other journals devoted to Sri Shrdi Sai Baba during the last ten years or so, besides carefully going through all the 150 or so experiences of devotees relating of Baba's grace which have been collected by me and included in this book during the last few years.

A broad review of all these books, articles and memories has enabled me to identify the following various ways or approaches advocated by Sai devotees to secure Baba's grace.

(1) Reposing complete faith in Baba and remembering Him earnestly at the time of one's calamity.

(2) Chanting repeatedly 'Sri Sai Baba's *Tarak Mantra*' – *"Om Sai, Sri Sai, Jaya Jaya Sai"*.

(3) Visiting Shirdi and praying there in Baba's *Samadhi Mandir* and *Dwarka Mai Masjid*.

(4) Sending *Dakshina* (Cash offering) to Shri Sai Baba Samadhi, Shirdi or Sai Baba Sansthan, Pathri Karati (Baba's home village in Maharashtra).

(5) Taking Baba *Udi* (Holy Ash) obtainable from Baba's dhni located in Dwarka Mai Masjid or any other Sai Temple, or Sai devotees.

(6) Feeding hungry people, animals, birds and insects.

(7) Helping the orphans, destitute, old people etc. with clothes, money etc.

(8) Providing medicines and medical help to patients.

(9) Organizing *Sai Sankeertans* or *'Nama Japa'* sessions in homes, or in public places.

(10) Writing and articles on Baba's divinity and miracles.

(11) Installing Baba's statues and helping in building and furnishing Sai Baba temples.

(12) Organizing *bhandaras* (community feeding) in Sai Baba's Name.

(13) Doing silent introspection on Baba's divinity and his touchings.

(14) Introspction, meditation. self-purification.

(15) Fasting on Thursday in Baba's Name.(Baba did not like His devotees to go on for Fasts on other days.)

(16) Helping *Sai Pracharaks* in collection of funds for Sai Temples, *bhandaras*, seminars, conventions and the like.

All these are the desirable ways to earn Baba's grace.

In various writings, I have found the merits of these different ways or approaches to get Sai Baba's divine grace r advocated forcefully.

Let us seriously go through the following sample of valuable inspirational or suggestive writings which we discovered and collected from Sai journals.

1. Surrender Before Sai

   (a) Sweet fruits of absolute surrender

   In Shri Baba's *Marga,* study of *Vedanta* and its mechanical application to *Sadhana* is of no avail, for He takes full responsibility for granting ultimate spiritual welfare to His chosen devotees by changing them inwardly. In this context, it is interesting to cite the example of Shri Narasimhaswamiji who did *taaps* at Arunachalam while Shri Ramana Maharshi was in flesh and blood. After three years of arduous *Sadhana* Swamiji realized the emptiness of mere *jnana* obtained through" "Who am I?" inquiry. He therefore set out in search of a *Guru* who could make the disciple perfect so that the latter would not feel he was wanting in anything. He met Shri Upasani at this time at Sakori who directed him to Shridi. It is astonishing but true that Shri he he did feel at Shirdi that it was his *tapas* that had led him to Shri Baba who was then not in flesh and blood. The powerful presence of the eternal spirit gripped his soul and though no details of his apprenticeship with Shirdi Sai Baba are available, it can be surmised that Swamiji made absolute surrender of his life at the lotus feet of Sai Baba.

   What is the thing that Shri Sai Baba gave to Swamiji which led to his absolute surrender? The answer is simple. That is mere *Jnana* without intense *bhava* is of no use. For, in Baba's course of Sadhana as Swamiji himself said, "Love is the beginning, the middle and the end.". In Baba's *Marg,* spoken words are of no use, spontaneous outpouring of Love from the *Sad-guru* to the devotee and vice-versa lead a seeker to the goal. The surrender of Narasimhaswamiji was complete. He questioned nothing, asked nothing from *Guru,* but experienced in the stillness of silence the eloquent ripeness, richness and fullness of Sad-guru's Grace which changed him inwardly. Outwardly it would appear to disciples that Shri Baba is acting harshly but the intention is to mould the devotee so thoroughly that the latter remains firm even while the world goes topsy-turvy. Even if the so-called adversities or prosperities befall, a disciple, being a surrendered soul, experiences eternal joy through detachment. And this is the sweetest grace of this Spiritual Master. Perfect surrender leads to perfect joy and peace. Such a soul becomes a magnet of Shri Baba to lead others in the path, for he becomes one with Shri Baba and can safely guide others.

-Shri Anil Keshavrao Rasal
21/382, B.P.T. Staff Quarters,
Wadala, (E) Bombay 400 037
(*Shree Sai Leela*, April 1987)

(b) Lord Krishna, the *Gitacharya* says:

"Whosoever offers to Me with love, a leaf, a flower, a fruit, or even water, I appear in person before that disinterested devotee of purified intellect and delightfully partake of that article offered by him with love."

He. further advises:

"Fix your mind on Me, be devoted to Me, worship Me, and bow to Me, so shall you without doubt Me. This I truly promise to you for you are dear to Me."

"Surrendering all duties to Me seek refuge in Me alone. I shall absolve you of all sins; grive not."

Sai krishna reiterates the same and wants us not to fan our ego by boasting. 'I have done this marvelous thing… I have done that etc.' All that we enjoy is Sai's gift to us a result of our implicit faith in Him and our surrendering completely heart and soul, without even a tinge of ego. So, *Saibandhus*, what an easy and simple way to get rid of all our sins committed knowingly or unwittingly and attain Supreme Grace by entering Kingdom of Sai.

Sai Sewak

(c) Sai Ways to Beat the Blues

Once, at a time of great sorrow, I found it difficult to overcome the feelings of loneliness, grief and depression that kept enveloping me. Finally, though, I discovered some ways to beat the blue moods. I believe that they can work for other *Sai-bandhus* (brothers0 too:

1. It may seem to simple, but ask Lord Sainath to give you the strength to overcome your sad mood.
2. Say to yourself: "I have felt this way before. It will pass. It did so the other times." The grief may not leave, but the present mood often does.
3. Deliberately "Turn off" your mind from your unhappiness in place of sad memories, force yourself to inject pleasant things into your thoughts.
4. If the weather permits, take a walk or engage in some exercise. If that is not possible, sit in a corner and go on chanting *'Om Sri Sai, Jia Jai Sai'* without keeping a count or looking at the clock.
5. Be grateful to Lord Sainath for all the happiness you have had. List your present blessings.
6. 'Be not overcome of evil, but overcome evil with good'. Remember these words o f Lord Sainath. Help someone, may be a stranger even, if you can.
7. Realize that this mood may have a physical basis. Try to find out its cause, Sainath is there to help us; 'Hari will protect him who has got *Sraddha* and *Saburi*'.
8. Be confident that if you are really willing to place yourself in Lord Sainath's hands, Sainath will come along in some form or the other and will help you bear the unbearable.
9. Remember that every person at some time in his or her life must make the same adjustments, many with fewer 'tools' with which to work better than you have.
10. Believe in tomorrow!

-Mrs. Seetha Vijayakumar,
W/o Dr. G.R. Vijayakumar,
Kil-Kotagiri Estate,
Kil-Kotagiri-643 216,
Nilgiris, Tamil Nadu
(*Shree Sai Leela*, April 1988)

(d) **Introvert Thyself and Rest with Sai**

Mind like a monkey, already drunk and stung by a scorpion, jumps from one thing to another. Mind is the hunting ground for all the five senses of *Kama*, *Krodha*, *Mada*, *Moha* and *Matsara*. Like the unbridled horse it goes its own way unchecked and quite unaware of the consequences of getting strayed into this wide world and unning after mundane affairs. The initial and partial success that may greet, is only temporary, which is not at al l realized. This achievement which thrills one as though achieved by his own effort, makes him blind to the fact that this is due to his good deeds performed in the previous birth *(Poorva Karma)*. The unseen power, the *Sootradhari* – Omnipotent and Omniscient, is absolutely forgotten. We gloat over our success and slide away from Him; forgetting utterly that we are trekking towards doom.

To avoid the pitfalls in life and to have a smooth sailing in the *Samsara Sagar*, Hemadpant, the author of 'Shri Sai Satcharita' has given us the golden path to attain Sai's Grace and merge with Him.

"Let us" Hemadpant says: "Worship our Sai *Sadguru* and pray to Him to give us the true vision which is nothing but God-Vision.

Let us use hot water in the form of tears of joy to wash Sai's Feet.

Let us besmear His body with sandal-paste of pure love.

Let unalloyed *Saburi* (Faith) be the cloth with which we adorn Him.

Let us perform *Archana* with the Eight *Sattwik* emotions and fruit of the concentrated mind as Lotuses.

Let our pure devotion adorn His head as *Bukka*.

Let his waistband comprise of our fervent *Bhakti*.

Let us bow and do *Sashtanga Namaskar* at His Feet.

Decorating Sai with all those *"Manasik Kriya"*, let us surrender our all to Him which He has been so good to give us and pray fervently: "Oh! Sai, introvert my mind, give me discrimination between the real and the unreal; help me to be swayed not by pleasures and pain and aid me to become a *Sthitapragnya*, by making my turbulent mind rest at Thy Holy Feet. What a simple and Golden path! That is all Sai wants from us.

(*Shri Sai Leela*, March 1990)

(*Shri Sai Leela*, Dec. 1988)

(a)   Our *Loka Guru* is Lord Maheshwara. He is also a Sidha Guru from whom the *Moola Mantra* (Panchakshri the original mantra *"Om Namah Shivaya"* has originated. Accordingly to the taste of different kinds of devotees many *mantras* for *Nama Japan* are in popuolar such as '*Shri Ram Jai Ram, Jai Jal Ram*', '*Hare Ram, Hare Rama, Rama Rama Hare Hare, Hare Krishna Krishna KrihnaKrishna Hare Hare*', or '*Om Namo Bhgwat Vasudevaya.* In this connection, I may mention at Hubli in 'Sddhartidath DharmaDMutt' the non-stop chanting of the five syallabled mantra "Om, NamahShivaya is going on Day & Night without break for the past more than 120 years. I wish and pray to Lord Sainath that similar arrangements may kindly be make in our Shirdi also, so that Sai and other devotees from all over the world visiting Shirdi may avail this opportunity of chanting the Sai *Taraka Mantra* "Om Sai, Sri Sai, Jaya Jaya Sai*'in any part of day and night and get immense benefit thereby, both materially and spiritually..."

(*Shree Sai Leela*, July 1988)

(b)   **Constant Repetition of Baba's Name**
Ceaseless repetition of the Lord Sai's name is prayer to Him to reveal Himself. One can practice repeating the Name always, whether sitting down or walking, whether when one is sitting quiet or working, when bathing or taking food. If one repeats the Name while taking food, the food becomes offering to God. If, when bathing the Name is repeated the waters become holy, the water of the Ganga. If one repeats it while walking, the walking becomes 'Pradakshina'. To bear the shocks and bumps of life there is no remedy equal to repetition of His Name. When the body is ailing repeat the Name and you get relief. In distress repeat the Name you will either get relief or strength to endure the trouble. If one abuses you or injures you repeat the Name, you will soon forget the injury and your anger against that person will vanish. By constant repetition of the Name one conquers one's passion like lust, anger and jealousy.

The practice takes such a hold on you that you feel you cannot do without it. The Name grips the mind. Even during sleep the mind keeps repeating it. Before actually sleeping, if one sits on the bed and repeats the Name silently, one slides into sleep and the character of the sleep itself will be changed.

The name has the capacity to reveal the personality which it represents. This is not all. Uninterrupted repetition passes soon, from the lips to the heart. Then there is an urgent inclination to sit down and repeat the name mentally (without moving the tongue and lips). In the process both the name and the mind and the name sink down into the depths of your being and you enjoy blissful absorption.

In the course of practice one feels one's body become light. Sometimes flashes or dots of light appears, and sometimes celestial music is heard.

One begins to love birds and beasts, insects, animals and all human beings as one's kith and kin.

A good and kind thought of one who repeats the name always, directed towards an ailing person, or a person in distress soothes and comforts the afflicted person.

All talk without experiences is Babble. The Lord abides in the heart of the person who takes the Name, and the devotee abides in Him *(para)*. Om Sri Sai, All glory is yours. Blessed is He whose hairs stand on end, who sheds tears of joy and trembles with joy whose voice is chocked repeating Thy Name.

-C.S. Ramaswamy,
C/II/4, Tata Housing Centre,
Andheri, Bombay – 400058

(c) *Sankeertan* is infectious. NOt only the Sankeertankaar but others also experience it. When Sri Chaitanya Prabhu used to sing in all ecstasy even animals used to enjoy the *Sankirtan.*
Baba was very fond of *Naama Sankeertan.* Daily, Bhajan used to be conducted in his *Durbar.* Sri Dasganu Maharaj used to do *Harikatha Sankeer*tan. Sankeertan was very dear and pleasing to Lord Sai Baba. Hence, O Sai *Bhaktaas* (devotees)! Whatever be

the form please do *Sankeertan* sharing with others the pleasure of *Sankeertan*.

R.V.V.L., Narasimha rao,

"Saipaada Ranu"

(d)   Shri Baba used to tell His intimate friend disciple Shama that he could never tell a lie in front of the *Dhuni*. The real fact is that Baba held fast to his heart the dearest devotees who forgot themselves in the loving presence of Baba, who surrendered to Baba as *Guruj*i and tried to practice the tenets preached by Baba and sing the *Mahima* or glory of Baba untiringly. As Lord Lord Krishna has said in the 12th Chapter of *Gita,* Baba as said:

"I am the *Kalpataru* (wish-fulfilling tree) for my devotees. I am compassion incarnate, I am the nectar like mantra, I am the yonder bank of liberation for my devotees."

Surrender: Baba used to say to Nana Ssaheb Chandorkar:

"Nana, you have to cast lust, desire, ego and attend to your assigned duties without shirking. You have to see the entire world with a balanced mind and equipoised intellect. There is no difference between gold and dust in principle. You have to understand the ultimate truth and act detachedly." This ios indeed the version of message of Gita in Sai language. Baba says that one should not forget presence of God in every being and observe the world round himself as the product moulded from the substance "Vasudeo". Baba desires that His *bhakta*s should ask for the gift of grace from the *kalpavruksha* (i.e. Guru). Baba used to say that His Government's treasure lies abundantly in the field outside. But people who come to him do not want this immortal wealth. Lord Dattatreya was His Government and the treasure was nothing else but *Moksha*. Baba alerted His devotees that on this playground of Destiny where the *sanchita* and *prarabdha* are from Guru will not come again. This was the moment when we should be consciously living right and purposeful life. When Baba appears before our door for receiving alms, we should not treat Him as a beggar. He is the Shri Guru who was asking for your mind, intellect, ego and self-surrender. You cannot give anything which is not your own to Baba. You have to gift your ego itself. This is a rare occasion when God has appeared at your door as a beggar!

(*Shri Sai Leela*, July 1989)

(e) Meditation of *Sai Kripa* or Grace through *Gurudhyan*

The consultant fixing of mind on the form of Guru leads us into instant link with the Guru principles. The aspirant looks at the Guru as a moth fixes his mind on the bee. The moth becomes bee itself one day and flies away. Similarly the disciple assimilates the principle of *Gurutwa* in him and one day becomes Guru himself. The *Guru* lights the lamp of realization. Shri Guru protects the disciple as the female tortoise protects its off springs with the sheath of its sight. The faith protects him during his sadhana and further lifts him upwards towards the goal. The walls between the Guru and disciples fall. Sai enters the body of His disciple. The *Bhakti* turns in to *Bhavavastha*, the *Karma* becomes *Naishkarmaya*, The *dnyana* reaches the stage of *Sahajavastha*. The mind enters the *Turiya* stage crossing the borders of the gross body, the subtle body and the causal body. When the mind enter *turiya*, it is slowly merges into *Unmani Awastha*. The grace of Sai and the *Jivas* is transformed into Shiva. The consciousness is further led towards cosmic consciousness. This is the stage of *Samarasya* and is even higher than *Samadhi*-stage. The *Kripa* renders all exercises like *japa-tapa*, *mantra-tantra* unnecessary. The intense devotion, balanced discrimination, surrendered Karma and the merger of yoga become a common disposition of the realized once.

Baba says:

"I am the fragrance in the *Sahasradal* lotus,

I am the supreme ambrosial drop of *para bhakti*,

I am the bliss untainted and unshackled by external mattes."

(*Sai Geetayan*)

SADHANA – The culmination of Natha and Kabir *sadhana* is full of *Ananda*. The devotee achieves fulfillment which is blissful state. The chakor bird becomes the moon. *Bhakta* merges in Sai.

The life turns into a song of glory and light mixed with *amrita*. Even the pain is tinged with joy and the *sahaja* stage abides. The disciple merged in Guru and His grace makes his entire existence a song of love and joy divine. The world gains merits through the praise words of such evolved soul!

-Chakor Ajgaonkar,
(*Shri Sai Leela*, July 1989)

2. PRAYER BEFORE BABA'S PICTURE

(a) Baba's Picture is Baba Himself in Living Presence

Baba is in His picture of worship. He sees, listens and knows through His picture. Those eyes of him are living ayes. They are powerful and all pervading; several stories in the *Sri Sai Satcharitha* illustrate the actual presence of Baba in his picture of worship. Therefore it is of paramount importance that we should guard and protect His pictures always.

When Balabuva Sutar went to Shirdi for the first time and bowed before Baba, Baba said, 'I know this man since four years'. But actually, he had only prostrated before Baba's picture four years back. He says, "I merely bowed to His picture. This fact was however known to Baba and in due course He made me realize that seeing His picture is equal to seeing Him in person" (*Shri Sai Satcharita*, Page 185).

(b) Enriching your life through Prayer

"The uncultured man always blames others; the semi-cultured man blames himself and the fully cultured man blames neither."

As a doctor, I work as a spiritual counselor, and I have seen lives transformed through prayer to Shirdi Sai Baba. As your prayer power is enriched, so will be every other aspect of life.

Here are some suggestions, that I have seen work for Sai-devotees and which can enrich your prayer life. Try them during the four stages of communion with Sai Baba. I have outlined here, for at least 15 minutes a day for the next three months. I guarantee, that you will have an increasing sense of Sai Baba's presence in your life and be in a better relationship with yourself and others.

STAGE 1 – Be Still

The goal of the first stage of prayer is to become aware of Sai Baba's presence before you begin to pray to Sai Baba. Try to calm your mind.

Most people will be helped to achieve a state of stillness. If they try to follow these points, when they pray:

- When possible, sit in front of Sai Baba's photograph and let His peaceful face make you receptive.
- Allow your body to relax; it will help to clear your mind.
- Realize, that Sai Baba is there with you. Sai-brother N.M. Yusuf Ali Khan of Hyderabad taught me that when I pray, whether alone or in a temple, I should say the following: "Oh, my Sai Baba, we are here." This strengthens your awareness, that you are with Sai Baba and He is with you.
- Don't pray immediately, but sit in silence for a minute or two.
- Begin your prayer by reciting this Vedic Prayer, which was dear to H.H. Saipadananda Radhakrishna Swamiji:
  "May everybody be happy; May everybody be free from disease.
  May everybody have good luck; May none fall on evil days,
  May the wicked turn good; May the good attain peace,
  May the peaceful be free from all bondage, and May the liberated redeem others.

STAGE II – Get Rid of Stumbling Blocks

As you pray, ask Lord Sainath to help you, get rid of all the excess baggages of fears, resentments, jealousies, hidden guilt or unworthy desires, that may be encumbering your mind and heart. Remember, that Sai Baba said to forgive anyone, whom you resent before you begin to plead your case before Him.

Try these simple block-removing steps:

- If there is someone you dislike, picture the person and yourself together, then pray for this individual and imagine Sai Baba lifting the resentment off your heart, until your relationship is transformed: "Your heart must be so broad..." This is why Sai Baba said, "...He, who clasps and cavils at others pierces

Me in the heart and injures Me, but he that suffers and endures pleases Me most.

- Review the activities of the day. Is there anything you should or should not have done? If there is any shadow of omission or commission, tell Sai Baba.
- Ask for forgiveness. No matter, what you have done, Sai Baba will surely forgive you.
- Accept it… and then forgive yourself. Remember Sai Baba's words: "He, who loves most, always sees Me… I feel indebted to him, who surrenders himself completely to Me and ever remembers Me."

STAGE III – Ask with Confidence

Once you have accepted Sai Baba's forgiveness, be confident. 'Claim His aid, comfort and mercy for others and for yourself. Sai Baba knows what we need; but still this is the stage of prayer, in which we make our petitions and needs knows to Lord Sainath. Don't be afraid t bring small concerns or material and monetary problems before Sai Baba. He is interested in all your needs. The following suggestions will be helpful:

- Prepare your list of concerns beforehand. Write out if necessary.
- Pray for others first not in false humility, but because there are so many, that need your aid Sai Baba's Blessing. "A true *Ramdasi* should have no *Mamata*, but have *Samata* (equanimity) towards all."
- Visualize some specific person with a problem or need and visualize him helped or healed. Rely on the promise of Sai Baba: "Our karma is the cause of our happiness and sorrow. Therefore put up with whatever comes to you. Allah is the sole dispenser and protector, always think of Him. He will take care of you. Surrender to His feet with body, mind, wealth and speech: and then see, what He does."
- As you start to pray for yourself, pray for your spiritual health first, then for your physical well-being, and finally for material things.

STAGE IV – Listen

Once you have asked Sai Baba for help, begin tuning your mind and heart for His answer. Remember the lines; "Sweet is Ram in the heart sweet with love. *"Mite Mamme MItai Ram"*.

Don't let your prayer life cease, when you open your eyes or unclasp your hands. Love is the binding thread of all life and all the works of Sai Baba. It is the work, you can do – a touch of the hand, a friendly glance, a comforting remark, a selfless action, a constructive suggestion, a sharing of grief, a going out of your way. An act of love is a prayer in itself.

Try these follow up exercises.

- Recommit yourself to Lord Sainath at the end of each prayer.
- Make a contract in each prayer to do something in the Name of Sai Baba that very day.
- Keep a follow-up diary. What did you do to help a certain prayer to work? How did Sai Nath respond to that prayer.
- Keep your eyes and ears open for the hand of Lord Sai Nath is daily events.
- Read *'Shri Sai Satcharita'* daily. The word found therein, gives you concrete foundation, on which to build your life. The *Shri Sai Satcharita* is perhaps the greatest tool in preparing for a communion with Sainath and enriching your life – the goal, which is gaining closer union with Lord Sainath.

If I had, but one gift to give to my children, it would be for them t know with certainty, that at any moment each of us can reach out and be with Lord Sainath in prayer. When this happens, you are in Him and He is in you. And your life is enriched beyond all measures.

-Dr. G.R Vijay Kumar,
Ashok Leyland Ltd.,
175, Hosur Industrial
Complex, Hosur – 635126
(*Shri Sai Leela*, Dec. 1989)

3. READING OF *SHRI SAI SATCHARITA*

(a)   A Unique Experience

I cannot call myself as devotee of Sai Baba of Shirdi because unless He himself recognize, no one can claim so. At the same time, I can't resist my temptation to share with the Sai devotees the experience that I had and which changed my life completely. On June 13, 1985, I had a very bad time of my life and on 14th June I left for Shirdi and reached there on 15th. I had been going earlier but this was the time when I was completely dejected with the life itself.

By chance, after reaching Shirdi; I went to the Library Casually I picked up a book written by a South Indian, whose name I do not recollect today. But see the Leela of Sai, the Chapter that I opened in that book said "If anybody is in the whirlpool of life and does not find a way, he should then finish *'Sai Sai Sat Charita'* in 7 days by reading in front of *dhuni* of Baba in Shirdi." Immediately I went to the Book Stall and wanted to buy the book but I did not have sufficient money to buy English Edition because I am fluent in English. Hence I bought Hindi Edition. I did not have enough money to last for 3 days stay at Shirdi. Therefore, I chose to complete the reading in just 3 days. Accordingly I started with the prayers that with the end of the reading, my problems should also end, and luckily by the grace of Sai, I did complete the book in 3 days but as I progressed in the reading. I was so much moved that every word shook me to the bottom of my heart. On the final day, as I completed the last Chapter and offered one coconut, sugar candy and flowers in the *Dhun*i, I felt as if a very heavy burden had been removed from my body and I was fairly composed. The same evening I felt for my house and reached the next day, the 18th June, 1985. Wonder of wonders, one of the persons who met me in U.S.A. in 1984, had called at my house and left a word that I should contact him in Hotel Siddhartha. On 19th morning I called him up and he asked me to meet him in the hotel, where he offered me a job with handsome position. The 19th June, 1985 changed my life completely and all my financial domestic and health problems were solved and thereupon. I had responded that it was the grace of Sai only that had helped me when I could not help myself. Hence, I feel Shri Sai Baba is alive to a sincere call from his devotee even today and He responds favourably if only the devotee is earnest in his desire and faithful to Sai.

-Amar Nath Bararia
R/K 40, Old Roshanpura,
Najafgarh
New Dedlhi – 110043

(b) **_Shri Sai Satcharita_ – Its Miracles**

In our Indian culture we have get certain invaluable books which are not only to be read, not only to be chewed and digested, but also to be placed on the esteemed 'Alter of our heart' so that our lives can be sanctified. Our heart is a seat for the admixture of good and evil feelings and impulse. By reading these books our hearts are cleaned; and purified. This one category of books is called in Sanskrit as _"Ashirvachana granths"_, i.e. book which are capable of blessing not only peace and prosperity, but also the rarest transformations and spiritual achievements in the life of ordinary persons, which are otherwise impossible. These are the books for all the times and for all the people of all the places of earth. They transform miseries into merries; perils into pearls; sighs and sobs into songs. This is called as _"Shstr Kripa',_.

"DurgashasatiI", the 13-chaptered book of Markandeya Purana is an _"Ashirvachana Grantha"_, and similarly the saluted 'Guru Charita,.'. In this order comes 'ShriI Sai Satcharita. _The value of reading these books is established beyond doubt by the hoary past generations after generations These books are the divine manifestations of the Almighty Lord in the fashion of letters and lines; script and scripture._ To bow down to this book of 'Shri Sai Satcharta' is to bow down before the Holy Feet of Sri Sai Baba. Reading such books is called 'Swadhyaya' or _"Parayana"_. What happens when we read this 'Shri Sai Satcharta'? On the screen of our consciousness, the divine image of Sai Baba acts and plays, so that the mind's eyes can visualize the living presence of Sai Baba within Oneself. Sri Sai Baba says that His path is the path of cleanliness. We know that cleanliness is next to

Godliness! Generally our transformations is only through books like Shri Satcharta' I read this Holy-Book, for the first time in my father-in-law's house during 1958 after my marriage. Its impact is so profound on my life that I have been steadily followwing this arduous path of spiritual evolution, despite the gloomy, gruesome, degrading, degenerating, polluted and profane environments of our modern life. By its miraculous influence, my spiritual exodus remains secure and safe. Another wonder! Whomsoever I meet in my life's journey, are also metamorphosised into the crystal pure aspirants! This contact with 'Shri Sai Satcharitra' is really a satsang for us.

Several relatives and innumerable friends of mine have derived this benediction from it when I gave it to them in their testing times! Recently, my friends, Sri Rama Tulasi Rraju, was in the state of Cognitive dissonance puzzle and unrest His son wasxin need of a job and his daughter was to be married. What a wonder! I was instrumental in giving him my loving book 'Shri Sai Satcharta' of on 20-10-1988 i.e. on Sri Sai Baba's Maha Samadhi Day, i.e., Vijayadasami Day. I somehow or other, could convince his boy to read it. After all, our modern boys are sceptics to begin within these matters. I told the young man to read the book even without faith, so that Divine faith is generated by reading it. The result was stupendous! Soon after his reading the 'Shri Sai Charita', even without faith, he got an appointment in a Private Firm. Subsequently, within a short period he got another posting order in a State Government Department. My friend, Sri Raji and his family were much elated, and a tiny lamp of faith in Sai Baba is lit in the sanctum sanctrorum of their hearts! Getting a job for his son may not be of much surprise. What my beloved friend Sri Raju experienced was really a miracle! He said that some Udhi and Ashaktas also have got materialized in the Holy book of Satcharita in the course of his reading it.

Sai Baba always gives Udhi for the material and spiritual well being of His Devotees. Now, Sai Baba gave the Udhi through Satcharita, only to prove, that the book is not different from His Divine Incarnation Sri Raju returned back the Book to me; and again the book was demanded by my daughter's friend Miss

Lalita; who is a student of M.Sc. After her prolonged persuasion only, I could be able to spare the Holy book to her, with a clear advice to respect the book and read it with devotion, since she is already a devotee. While returning the book with a sense of gratitude, the young lady says "Uncle! Baba materialized some *Kumkum*-applied *Akshatas* from this book!" How is it possible? There is no explanation! We all had the blessed *Akshatas* over our heads!" I told her "Madam! The days of miracles are not over. With Sai, every day is a day of miracle; because we live in Him; and He lives in us! What young lady says "Uncle! Baba materialized some *Kumkum*-applied her. Reading of *Shri Sai Satcharita* gives relief to the persons who get tired in their life's journey, and reading the book itself becomes a miracle with them."

Sai Grace is eternal and everlasting. The only requirement is to keep our hearts open to the Divine influence, by rendering ourselves as His Temples in Human Form. For us, reading Sai Satcharitra is the topmost spiritual sadhana, which is not only a means for Sai Grace, but also an end by itself?

-Paturi Prasannam,
24-143/29, Vishnu Puri,
Malkajgiri, Hyderabad – 500 047
(*Shri Sai Leela*, May 1989)

(c) Reading of *Sai Sat-Charita* or Baba's *Charters and sayings* is not a dull chore. I read these holy books daily because they tell me so much about the character and ways of Sai Baba. I find myself eager to know how Sai Baba dealt with men and women in every: maginable circumstances, so that I can have some idea how He might deal with me.

This has made me understand that Sai Baba means that all lives be lived in co-operation with Him, His friendship, His plans for us; His grace is awaiting each of us, provided we want Him in our lives.

And then the point of the claiming prayer become clearer; The rcihes of His grace must be claimed. Its very easy for Baba has assured us.– 'You look to Me: I look after you'.

The process goes like this:

- Sai Baba had given the standing assuance of promise.
- If conditions are attached to it, we should do our best to meet them.
- We do an act at a specific time and place of claiming this promise.
- Sai Baba fulfills the promise in His own time and way.

How practical the Claiming Prayer can be was illustrated by a Sai-sister, who is a young Bank Manager's wife at Coimbatore.

Before marrying Sri P.J. Narasimhulu in 1980, Smt. Umadevi had been a happy-go-lucky girl. Being the youngest daughter of a rich business-magnate, she had a comfortable and glamorous life. Upon marriage, Smt. Umadevi made the decision to give up her glamorous life and be a good housewife and a loving mother. In the years since, she has never compromised with that decision. But little did Smt. Umadevi know how difficult the transition would be. By 1983, Smt. Umadevi was a proud mother of a bonny son and a chubby daughter. Soon she felt herself at the end of all physical resources. Always tired, she could never see over the top of the mountain of home chores and social obligations. Nor could she find time even for a few minutes of quietness and prayer. She was near a nervous collapse.

Smt. Umadevi's first opportunity to think through the situation came during a visit to 'Naga-Sai Temple' of Coimbatore. At the august presence Lord Saij, she determined to pray her way through to some answers. She placed before Lord Sainath three acute problems:

- There was simply too much work. She felt like a servant in own home. How could one woman be a maid, laundress, mother, wife?
- Constant interruptions from friends and relatives through visits and telephone calls.
- The need for a daily quiet time. How could she manage all that?

"That evening Sai Baba gave me an insight into every problem", Smt. Umadevi told me. "Sai Baba answered me in His Eleven

Charters. He did not take away my difficulties, but he showed me how to handle each situation by claiming His strength..."

Here is the guidance Smt. Umadevi feels she received from Sai Baba:

For too much work and feeling like a servant in her own home:

"Accept your role. If you give Me your willingness, I will do the rest. Above all do not feel sorry for yourself."

(*Shri Sai Leela*, Feb., 1988)

(d) In the chapter 52 of *Shri Sai Sai Charita* it is stated that "If you hear or read a chapter daily, Sai will ward off all calamities and you will reap fruit according to your faith. If you read with reverence your ignorance will be destroyed. It is efficacious to complete the reading of Shri Sai Sat Charita in one *Sapthaha* (week) If it is not possible to read a chapter daily, by reading atleast Chapter XI and XV daily, all of our miseries will be removed by the grace of Sadguru and all our desires fulfilled."

-K. Venkata Ramaiah,
Deputy Registrar of Co-op. Society. (Rtd.)
Sudarsan, Krishna Nagar, 2nd Line,
Guntur 522 006
Shri Sai Leela, Feb. 1988

(e) Shri Sai Wisdom
Sai Satcharita is a splendid tonic
Have full trust in Shirdi Sai Baba
It is egoism which is responsible for manifold troubles
Repeat constantly Shri Sai Manthram
Do you part and be sure that Shri Sai will do His part
If you want divine grace free yourself from egoism
Sins flung off by the strength of Shri Sai faith
Aspire for attaining Shri Sai wisdom
Idleness deserves no consideration.
Be ever straight, good and loving
All actions in the world are His own
All actions in the world are His own

Be fearless and develop your will power
Above all know that Shri Sai is dwelling within you.

-P.J. Reddy,
C-3, P & T Colony,
Ashoknagar
Hyderabad 500 020

(f) *Shri Sai-Sat-Charita* and Sacred *Udhi*
     (The Gold I found In My Life)
     Dear Sai Brothers and Sisters, I had visited the Holy Land of Sai
     Baba, Shirdi in 1983 and the greatest book I found was the holy
     'Shri Sat Charita' and the greatest gold I found was the sacred *Udi*
     (holy ash) of Sai Baba, by His divine inspiration.

     After leaving the Shirdi, while travelling by bus to Bombay,
     something inspired me to read the *Sai Satcharita* and I started
     with chapter one. As I began reading, I felt like keeping on
     reading for I began to know more about Sai Baba's love for me,
     and He captured me with his string of love and took me closer
     to Him. I read daily one chapter before going to my regular job
     and believe me, not I but Sai Baba works out everything for me
     all through each day of my life. The sacred *Udi* of Sai Baba has
     cured me and my family from various difficulties and troubles.
     Whenever any member of my family has any pain, or fever or
     whatever be the suffering, we do not apply Vicks or any pain
     reliever, but, the gold we found in our lives – The Sacred *Udi* of
     Sai Baba and believe me, we are a happy and healthy family, with
     Sai Baba's Grace. My Greatest experience reading a chapter of Sai
     Satcharita a day and having *Udi* with water keeps the doctor away
     and Sai Baba to stay with us for ever and ever.
     BOW TO SHRI SAI – PEACE TO ALL

-E. Pereira,
32 Kevni, 1ˢᵗ Floor,
Andheri, Bombay – 400 050
(*Shri Sai Leela*, Jan. 1988)

4. SELF-PURIFICATION APPROACH

R. Subramanian of Madras, in his write up 'Who is Lord Sainath?' published in *Shri Sai Leela*, April 1988, has emphasized on self-purification approach in these words:

WHO IS LORD SAINATH?
WHO IS LORD SAINATH?

The centre of my life, the centre of existence – of all that is.

To know Him, I must deny myself.

Attachment of the earth must end before Sai life begins,

In the mirror of the heart – the image of myself must no longer be reflected –

If indeed, the knowledge of Sai is to shine upon me.

The "EGO", the 'I', must go.

When I lose myself, I find Sai.

To lose myself, I must be lifted above myself I must turn from the transient.

And this is not possible, until the gate of my heart is opened to receive the richest gift life can give – the Sai Grace.

What must I do to receive Sai Grace?

1. I must seek Sai every day.
2. I must have no worldly ambitions.
3. I must accept all suffering.
4. I must welcome what comes to me – joy or pain, love or hate.
5. I must realize that I am but a Sai-child and must ever strive to do Sai-Will.
6. I must love silence in the midst of the world's noises and strife. Gradually, I shall grow in the presence of Sai, seeing Sai all around – and beyond Sai nothing.

-R. Subramanian
Shri Sai Leela, April 1988,3, Lakshmipuram,
High Court Colony,
Villivakkum,
Madras – 600 049
(*Shri Sai Leela*, April 1988)

(a)   Link with Sai Baba

Let us establish a link of love and devotion with Sai Baba who to us, is God Himself. Every day let us strengthen this link of love and devotion. Everyday, let us pray to Him, let us kiss His holy feet, let us offer all our work to Him, let us in moments of silence commune with Sai Baba in love and intimacy. Be this link grow from more to more, until we feel that wherever we are, we are not from Him a far, we are over shadowed by His radiant presence so that when this body drops down, Sai Baba will be by us and He will lift us in His loving arms and will lead us on.

Let Us Accept Sai-Will

Many things happen in life; we are unable to understand the reasons. A calamity befalls us, a misfortune overtakes us. Instead of wasting our time and energy in enquiring as to why we faced such a bitter experience, let us greet every incident and accident, every illness and adversity, every misfortune and calamity as 'Sai-will'. Let us accept that everything happens for our good. Everything that happens to us comes to bless us and lead us onward in our way.

Be A Blessing To Others

Let us be a blessing to others. Those that lead selfish lives on earth, those that harm others to get little advantages for themselves find no favour from Lord Sainath. Therefore live unselfishly, be a blessing to others. Lord Sainath has blessed you with wealth and abundance, with position and power that you may be a blessing to others. Give out the best in you, in Lord Sainath's name, for the good of others. Lend your helping hand to those who need it. Try to lighten the load of others. Bring joy into the lives of those that are joyless. Give comfort to those in need of comfort. Be ready to serve those that require your service.

Dear Sai-brothers and Sai-sisters: Will Lord Sainath like me? He knows best. I only know that wherever He takes me, He will keep me close to Himself – and that is all I need. For in Him is peace and joy – the peace that passed understanding, the joy that no ending knows.

-M. Rama Rao,
497, IX, Block East,
Jayanagar, Bangalore – 650 069
(*Shri Sai Leela*, April, 1988)

(b) Sweet and Sour of Life

"Our *karma* is the cause of our happiness and sorrow. Therefore put up with whatever comes to you. Allah is the sole dispenser and protector. Always think to Him. He will take care of you. Surrender to His feet with body, mind, wealth and speech and then see what He does." *Sai Baba of Shridi.*

Sai Baba of Shirdi was a divine phenomenon. His methods were unique. Unlike the sages of the past or even of modern India, He influenced those whom He drew Himself, not merely through intellectual arguments and spiritual prescriptions, but by the direct awareness of His comnipresence. The granting of succour to devotees in distress the timely warning He gave in dreams, the assumption of different forms (and the latter confirmations that it was He who helped in that particular form), all these demonstrated that He is the immanent being in all. He also demonstrated that He is immanent not only in humans but in animals as well; the dog that took away the *roti* offered to Him, and the fly that tested the food set apart for Him is He! Shirdi Sai Baba thus proved beyond doubt that the phenomenal world is as valid as the Absolute Reality.

Hundreds and thousands forms all over the world have been drawn by Sai Baba's powers to cure and console, and often out of sheer curiosity. To each one who visits Shirdi, the truth that Sai Baba is immanent in all is evidenced. Sai Baba knows us through and through and He floods us in divine love and blesses us with His grace, even after so many years of His *Mahasamadhi.*

Inspite of Sai Baba's assurance 'Why fear when I am here'? many of us put the blame on others for our own shortcomings and misfortunes. Sai Baba wants us to learn that we are ourselves responsible for our troubles and difficulties. Sai Baba teaches us – 'Your sorrows are your own making'. We are our own jailors and we are our own liberators.

Dear Sai *Bandhus*: You must learn to shoulder the responsibilities of your life and admit your own weakness without blaming or disturbing others. Remember the old saying: "The uncultured man always blames others; the semi-cultured man blames himself and fully cultured man blames neither". This is in short Sai-philosophy.

Man's mind is given to so much self-deceit that man does not want to face his own weakness. If he happens to see his weakness he will try to find some excuse to justify his action and to create an illusion. You must have the course to face your weakness. Sai Baba say; "Easily seen are other's faults; hard indeed to see one's own faults". You must have the courage to face your weakness.

Sai Baba is watching us in every moment of our lives. Remember that you may fool some of the people some of the time but not Sai Baba. Lord Buddha said: "The fool who does not admit he is a fool is a real fool. And the fool who admits he is a fool, is wise to that extent."

You are responsible for our relationship with others:

Shri Sai Satcharita teaches us that whatever happens one should not feel hurt if he knows how to keep a balanced mind. You are hurt only by the mental attitude that you adopt yourself and towards others. If you try to see Sai Baba in every individual, no one can hurt you. Remember that no one can hurt you unless you allow him to hurt you. If another person blames or hurts you, remember Sai's words: "He who clasps and cavils at others, pierces Me in the heart and injures Me, but he that suffers and endures pleases Me most". Whoever harms a harmless person, one pure and guiltless, upon that very fool the evil recoils like fine dust thrown against the wind – according to Buddhist philosophy.

Accept responsibility – Don't blame others:

You must not blame circumstances when things go wrong. Try to solve your problems without showing a sour face. In times of difficulty think that you are soaked in Sai-grace and work cheerfully under the most trying circumstances. Be courageous enough to change if change is necessary. Be serene enough to accept what you cannot change. Be wise enough to know the difference. Sai Baba has sent you these difficulties to help you overcome them.

You are responsible for your inner peace:

Sai Baba is the Master of peace and not of confusion. If you surrender totally to Sai Baba, you can maintain your inner peace. You must know when to throw away your price, when to subdue your false ego and when to change you false conviction. You can allow others to take away your inner peace, or you can preserve your inner peace – it is upto you!

The correct attitude towards criticism:

You must look objectively at the criticism that others give to you. If the criticism that comes to you is just well-founded and given with good intention, then accept that criticism and put it to use. However, if the criticism that comes to you is unjust and ill founded, you are under no obligation to accept this kind of criticism. Just remember the way Sai Baba dealt with Javar Ali, or when a person criticized how Sai Baba showed him a pig eating the night soil. If you know that your attitude is correct and appreciated by wise and cultured people, then do no worry about the ill-founded criticism.

Expect nothing and nothing will disappoint you:

You can protect yourself from disappointments by not having any undue expectations. If you expect nothing, then nothing can disappoint you. Do not expect reward for the good that you have done. Then you might ask: "If good begets good and bad begets bad, why should I have to suffer when I am completely innocent? Why should I have to undergo so many difficulties? Why should I get blamed by others despite my good work?" Sai Baba gives a simple answer – "You are facing a past bad karma that is ripening in the present. Continue with your good work and you will soon be free such troubles". Remember Mhalsapathy – he had a miserable life but Sai Baba granted him salvation.

Gratitude is a rare virtue:

Sai Baba considered gratitude to be a great blessing; however, gratitude is a virtue that is rare in any society. Sai Baba wants us to be happy whether people are grateful or ungrateful for our help; we need only think whether we have done our duty s human beings to our fellow-beings. Ramana points out: "Brotherhood based on equality is the supreme goal of human society."

Compare not with others:

Sai Baba has give us several instances of His knowledge of His devotees through several births. "So long as you regard others as your 'equal' or as your 'superior' or as you inferior, you will continue to have problems to worry about." If you think you are better than others, you may become proud. If you are inferior to others you may become useless to yourself and to others.

Try to realize that equality, inferiority and superiority are all changing relative states – at one time you may be a beggar; at other time you may be a rich men. In the endless souls within the realm of life and death, we are all equal, inferior and superior to each other at different times. So why worry?

Tolerance, patience and understanding:

Sai Baba insists on two-*paise 'dakshina'* from us – faith and patience. When others do wrong to you, you must take their action as an opportunity for you to get rid of your defilements and to develop your virtues. Forget and forgive the faults of others. "The more evil that comes to me, the more good will radiate from me" must be our attitude.

How to reduce mental pain:

Sai Baba wants us to learn the nature of world where we live. We can never expect everything in the world to be perfect and to run smoothly. There is no world and no life without problems. The physical pain and mental agony can be equated to the payment of rental for the 'house' occupied by you – 'rental' being the 'physical pain and mental agony' the 'house' being your physical body occupied by you on a temporary basis.

We must always count our blessings whenever we face problems. When Sai Baba is there to solve our problems, we should not worry unnecessarily. The Chinese have a useful saying for resolving problems "If you have a big problem, try to reduce it to a small problem, if you have a small problem try to reduce it to 'no problem'."

Why do good people suffer in life? Take the example of 'good and careful driver' and the 'bad and wreck less driver'. Even the good drivers meet with accidents, through he fault of bad one…"

It is a fact that:

➢ The grace of SaI Baba is his who asks for it.
➢ The grace of SaI Baba is found by him who seeks i.t
➢ The grace of SaI Baba is on him who knocks at His door..

5. Guru Ji C.B.Sathpathy has released the folllowing exhaustive questionnaire fore the Sai devotees worldwide on the internet to help them to self analyze and correct themselves to be able to achieve the divine grace of Sri Shirdi SaI Baba:

1. **Why do you come to the temple of Sri Shirdi Sai Baba?**
   a) Is it because you love Baba so much that at least without His symbolic presence, life seems meaningless to you?
   b) Is it because you take some time out of your busy schedule and come to Baba's temple for generating a nobler state of mind by praying, singing *aarti* and doing *pooja* etc?
   c) Is it because you have too many problems around you in the practical world surrounding you and cannot fight and therefore run to the temple for getting blessings of Baba?
   d) Is it because you have problems and want to solve it through Baba's grace within the desired period in the desired method?

2. Do you remember Baba having said that all seeds planted need not necessarily become trees. Are you prepared to believe that you may not get as much results as you wish by coming to the temple?

3. Whatever you offer to Baba, are they out of your honest income?

4. Do you think it is proper to make presents to Baba out of your dishonest income?

5. Don't you remember that Baba had refused to take gold and silver presents from a Queen who had come in a palanquin but, had accepted a single *chapaati* with an onion from an old lady offered out of love?

6. Are you coming to temple to satisfy your sentimental requirements at the cost of your family members and other dependents? Don't you remember Baba had forced Mahalsapati to go and stay with family because he was coming and staying at Dwarkamai. Are you doing your family duties perfectly?

7. Do you come to temple to socialize because you have known people there and to gossip about things. Don't you think it is a useless wastage of time to talk, discuss topics pertaining to issues other than that of Baba, religion and spiritualism.

8. Don't you think that it is better to spend your time in meditating on Baba, praying, participating in aarti or by reading books like Sai Satcharitra etc.

9. Since no one is perfect, don't you think it is improper to think of the imperfections of others or gossip bout them In the temple? Don't you remember that Baba had told one person that talking ill of other person is like a pig eating dirty food, just as some find fault in others.

10. Do you think that your devotional level is higher than that of others and therefore criticize about others way of worshipping. Don't you think that it is highly negetive approach.

11. Don't you agree with Sri Sai saying that we meet people and face problems because of Rinanubandha I.e debt of the past life. If we believe in this saying of Baba then isn't it required of us to accept our own problems and not always cry and fret about them. Do you think that anyone is so specially chosen by God that He will have no pain and problem but only happiness?

12. Do you have the amount of patience (Saburi) and faith (Shraddha) needed to come closer to Baba. Do you think that your Shraddha is constant or it changes with problems and situations? Do you change your mentors frquently?

13. Baba always advised people to develop qualities of kindness, impartiality, sympathy, tolerance and sacrifice to others. How much sacrifice do you do for others at your cost? Do you think that whatever little sacrifice you think you do is enough?

14. Do you remember Baba having said that when two persons are fighting, the person that doesn't hurt the others or tolerates the negetives is dearer to me.. Do you do so?

15. Do you think that unbridled sentimentality, which includes crying and wailing etc are required in spiritual path? Don't you know by such sentiments, you, at times, cause harm to others and contaminate good atmosphere. Is it not better to contain your emotionality within yourself, and not make a public display of it to establish your devotional fervour?

16. You want yourself to be sympathetically dealt by others and also to be understood. Don't you think that others, also would be expecting the same from you. Do you do so?

17. Do you think that by being jealous about others improvements even in the devotional field, you gain anything?

18. Whatever work you do for Baba, are you doing it honestly and with intensity I.e purity of thought, or do you do it in a casual manner?

19. We want Sri Sai to take care of all your problem but do we equally try to even do a fraction of His work perfectly for His cause?

20. Do you think the blessings of God will come to you when you don't qualify for it, breaking the law of Karma I.e action and reaction syndrome?

21. Don't you think it is proper that you first work for His cause which qualifies for His blessings. Good resultd do follow ultimately in accordance with the 'Law of Karma'. If you really want to have the blessings of Baba and live peacefully along with your fellowmen, first improve your own qualities on the lines indicated in the preceding paragraphs. THINK, THINK AND THINK

22. **Everything happening in this universe is mystically systematical. Every action /word has a meaning ans a purpose behind it. Is it true?**

    Law of Nature is highly precise and scientific. Nothing is meaningless and unsystematic in nature no matter how so ever small. Just remember that 'Man is God fooling himself'. Those human beings who strived and knew the laws of nature, to them there are no mysteries. They are saints, ypgis and Perfect Masters.

23. **If there is one God, then why are there so many religions on this earth?**

    It is only God, the Almighty or the Divine force that is responsible to create the human beings, sustain them and also to bring about their physical end which we term as death. All this is true for the living and non-living. All these beings carrying human souls are scattered all over this earth. They are born in different social, cultural and geographic situations. Each one has certain level of conciosness, and a series of experience. The experiences and levels of conciouisness may be similar but cannot be the same. God creates different religions for the evolution of different group of souls who are required to follow the path which one religion prescribes. In fact, religions have been created differently through different Incarnations to evolve different groups of souls. Any person who is born in one religion should, therefore, stick to it because without experience of the path prescribed by that religion, he cannot further evolve. So Geeta clearly tells us 'Swadharme nidhana shreyah, Parodharma Vayavaha' which means it is better to die for one's own religion, than accept any other religion.

24. **If all religions have came out of God, then why do people fight on religion?**

If human beings were that perfect, there was no need for God to incarnate and establish so many religions. Only because human beings naturally have tendency to differ and antagonise each other, therefore, religions try to show them different ways to get out of their self created problems and limitations. The main problem is that after the departure of the Incarnations, interpretation of His sayings or commands rae doneby some religious leaders, who are imperfect. Some of them, even if possessing some spiritual power interpret the original sayings of thof the Incarnationin a limited way. History shows that at times, such interpretations are totally contradictory to what the founder of any religion had said. Common people, not knowing the difference between the real incarnations and these leaders, follow them blindly. This lead to fanaticism, rivalry and even wars. Whenever situation becomes bad and people suffer due to wrong interpretation of religion, God again incarnates and re-stabalizes Dharma, the rules of nature. This has been going on since long and will also continue in future.

25. **Religions are different but is there anything common in them, Imean are there any common parameters?**

'Dharma' is from a Sanskrit root (Dhaa) which means to hold and also to think. Religions therefore try to hold together not only different human beings or group of people but also the other aspects of nature like plants, animals, birds and all living aspects. As ordained by nature they live together and are interdependent, therefore these must be held in a fine balance. The principles for holding them for the greatest goodof them for the longest period of time is known as Dharma. The concepts of Hindu universalism, the Muslim brotherhood, the Christian service, the Buddhist tolerance are nothing but attempts to bring out and establish the common denominators of togetherness. Human beings are aware of these but lose their path from time to timewhen these Incarnations again come and reestablish these concepts of love, tolerance, sacrifice, unity and simplicity. I would like to know whether Sai Baba is coming as Maitreya Buddha in future. If so, how can I make sure He and coming Buddha .

26. **All incarnations are the human forms of God, playing different roles at different places and a different points of time. Are they not the. ame?**

I love Sai Baba a lot and have a great faith in Him. ever reappear in the same body. Only highly evolved souls can know about an incarnation. Unless He reveals it Himself others cannot know. Believe that Baba is same as Buddha. Your thinking, even if you do not know the inner truths of nature, is correct.

27. **I just learned about Sai Baba today. Is He the reincarnation of Jesus on earth?**

Shri Shirdi Sai is an incarnation. His role on earth has been like that of Jesus,-kindness personified, the most merciful man to redeem humanity of its misery.

28. **I would like to know what is the relationship between Baba and Jesus? And if I believe in Jesus, can All incarnations are manifestation of God. The Almighty works differently at different times and in different societies as per the prevailing conditions. I believe in Baba too?**

There is a lot common between Baba and Christ I.e love, self -sacrifice, living like ordinary people among their disciples etc Go Step by Step. Always pray to Him to give you the direction. Even I believe in Jesus as the kindest redeemer of millions of human beings.

29. **I want to start a "Sai movement" in a foreign land but have no idea or contacts to do that. How should I go about it?**

First action to start a Sai movement is to make oneself mentally, morally and financially strong. The immediate steps you can take at this stage are:-

a)   Get His Photograph, pictures for free distribution.

b)   Get books on Him and magazines for circulation.

c) Call the devotees on a Sunday and do prayers .

30. **I am in search of my spiritual destiny at the moment. I would like to preach for Sai Baba but I have no resources for that. Please advice?**

To have a desire to work for Shri Sai is a noble idea. But, first one must create a ground by his own hard work and patience. Such work can be done if one has pue emotions supported by intelligence, knowledge and material support. One has to create these assets for himself/herself before taking a plunge. The growth will be slow and one has to face this reality with forbearance. There is no shortcut to spiritualism. Pray to Baba to build you up for His cause.

31. **What should be the role of patrons of Sai Temples towards the people who come to temples?**

The patrons should let the people come forward, to see and worship Baba.. They had special blessings of Baba when they got an opportunity for construction of a temple. Now it is important for them that they should not pose a hindrance to the devotees. They have already been blessed by Baba's grace now they should let others also benefit by His grace. Temple belongs to all. They should work with utmost humility with a service - oriented mind.

32. **Please tell me one mantra to pray to Shri Sai Baba?**

Sai Mantra for you is "Aum Shri SaiNathay Namah". Be steadfast in your devotion to Baba.

33. **How to win Sai's love?**

Though I do everyday *pooja, Shri Sai Sacharitra parayana* and His namsmarana still I am not feeling His presence as I used to do in the past. I want His assurance like He used to give me before, there is nothing but silence. Please help. Baba's assurances cover this, "If you take one step towards Me, I will take ten steps towards you". Baba's love never stops or changes with situations. He is constantly there with you. Your faith is being tested. Very soon He will assure you in a certain way provided you are honest and steadfast in your prayer. Don't worry over temprory

34. **I feel that smoking is not all that bad. Am I correct?**

Baba was in the Beyond state whom no material aspect including smoking affected. If he offered Chillum to any one, he saw to it that it did not adversely affect the person. Rather, some people got cured of disease as it is mentioned in Shri Satcharitra. Through group Chillum habits, he tried to breakdown the barriers of high, low castes and religions. An ordinary person knowing the hazards of smoking cannot afford to continue because this habit is for his pleasure and does not have a greater social significance. Pray to Baba to get you out.

35. **What should be our prayer towards Baba?**

We should pray to Baba that first of all, He should free us from the bad actions I.e paap, and the debts generated through many of our past lives. Before we ask for Baba's grace we should say that "O Baba make us worthy of your grace". It is necessary to become worthy of His grace before receiving it, no matter how much one has to suffer for it.

36. **Please teach me how to do prayers to Shirdi Sai Baba?**

Begin by concentrating on His photograph from feet to head and vice versa as Baba has told in *Shri Sai Satcharitra*. Either pray through your normal language, or Aarti of Baba or through any *Mantra* you know. What is necessary is a feeling of love towards Him. Silent and concentrated prayer is the best.

37. **I very much want to get closer to Baba, both through prayers and meditation. Although, things go smoothly at most of the times, Living amidst the worldly situations termed as Maya, one cannot avoid this situation unless one decides to leave the worldly activities. I am often afflicted by attacks of Maya, and this repeatedly disheartens me because I feel that all the progress that I have made upto that point is lost. What is the way to be more steadfast inone's principles?**

Totally and become a yogi or Sanyasi. Simultaneously, if one holds on to Baba always in some form say, taking His name, speaking about Him to others, reading about Him, thinking about Him etc, the mind gets His support to sustain or develop the inner power to resist the attacks of Maya. More strong the attraction towards Baba develops less strong will be the attraction towards the illusory worldly aspects.

38. **What is the best method of praying? Is it the mental prayer conducted silently before Lord Sai or praying aloud to the Lord?**

Mental Prayer with concentration is better, in case mind has developed that capacity or otherwise, pray aloud individually or in congregations.

39. **What does Shri Sai Baba require of His devotees, does He expect them to sing His *Aartis* etc or are the Those who remember Him with equanimity both in happiness and sorrow, thinking Him to be the only refuge in their life will be closer to Him. Keeping devotees like us who keep remembering Him in both happiness and sorrow, are also dear to Him?**

Him in conciousness always by singing Aarti or remembering Him in happiness and sorrow or even while doing any kind of service, these are all interlinked spontaneosly.

40. **While praying I go into a tunnel, some forces try to stop me while others help me to continue going further. Is it coming from within you, your imagination or having read anywhere about it?**

If it is coming from within you, such a tunnel means one is going in the correct path. Analyse your At the end of this tunnel I see bright light. What is the significance of this? mind to find the origin of this thought. Many questions will get answered if we analyse and understand our own thought. disturbances.

41. **I want to perform *pooja* two or three times a day for Baba, which I was doing till some months back when I was not working?**

Do not worry if you cannot do formal pooja. If a small *pooja* before going out and before sleep is done it is fine. You can even do mental pooja.

42. **I want Baba to be in each and every activity of mine?**

Though at the back of mind He is always there but still I 'm not satisfied, I want to do much more. I am working married woman through concentration. Constant and loving rememberance of Baba through whatever support system is the best path. Read Sai Satcharitra regularly. and remain at work most of the times.

43. **How do I manage my time for Baba's worship?**

    It is said that all prayers reach Baba and Sadgurus. Many times in my life Baba listened to my prayers instantly and has been helping me in various forms. Though I firmly believe that all my prayers and feelings reach Baba and Guru, sometimes I feel like having a feedback whether God and my Guru received my prayers.

44. How do I know their response?

    All prayers even the unspoken ones, the moment they are thought reach Baba instantly. Continue to remember Him and pray to Him. Be patient and pray Him continuously. You will get what you call 'feedback' in some manner some day. Thousands of devotees of Baba experience Baba's grace.

45. **May I know the meaning of 'OM SAI SRI SAI JAYA JAYA SAI'?**

    'Hail *Sai, Oh Sai*, Let you *be there always!'*

    - GuruJ C,B.Satpathy (From the Internet)

CHAPTER - 6

Sai Way To Salvation

(Dr. G.R. Vijay Kuma)

One of my colleagues died in March, 1968 at a tender age of 37. During his short tenure as a doctor, he had earned the respect and admiration of both professionals and patients, especially for his love and compassion for the sick and disable. This doctor had reached the pinnacle of success in his chosen field and enjoyed the status and financial rewards that accompany such accomplishment. He had tasted every good thing, by the standards of the world. At the staff meeting following his death, a five minute eulogy was read by a member of his department. Then the Chairman invited the entire staff to stand for one minute of silence in memory of the fallen colleague. I have no idea what the other staff members contemplated during that pause, but I can tell what went through my mind at this time.

I was asking Lord Sainath, "Is this what it all comes down to? We sweat and worry and labour to achieve a place in life, to impress our fellow-men with our competence. We take ourselves so seriously, over-reacting to the insignificant events of each passing day. Then finally, even for the brightest amongst us, all these experiences fade into history and our life is summarized within a five-minute eulogy and sixty seconds of silence. It hardly seems worth the effort Lord."

I was also struck by the collective inadequacy of that staff meeting to deal with the questions raised by our friend's death. Where had he gone? Would he live again? Will we see him on the other side? Why was he born? Were his deeds observed and recorded by a loving God? Is there meaning to life beyond our investigative research and expensive automobiles? The silent response by learned men and women in that staff meeting symbolized our inability to cope with these issues.

Then a wave of relief swept over me as I thought about the message of Sai Baba:

"Wherever you are, if you think of me, I am there at any time you please. Believe Me, though I pass away, My bones in My tomb will give you hope and confidence. Not only Myself but My tomb would be speaking, moving and communicating with those, who surrender themselves whole heartedly to Me."

It provides the only satisfactory explanation for why we are here and where we are going to. The final heart-beat for a Sai-devotee is not the mysterious conclusion to a meaningless existence. It is, rather the grand beginning to a life that will never end. Is that why we can proclaim even thy sting? In fact Sai Baba told Shama that they were together for 72 births.

How extremely important it is for the man of the house to know the answer to these perplexing questions, and to be able to lead his family in the path of righteousness. When he accepts that spiritual responsibility as Sai Baba intends, the entire family is likely to follow his example, Sai asked: "Give me two-pice 'dakshina' – 'Nishta' and 'Saburi', i.e. faith and patience." This issue is of such significance that I feel compelled to set down here my convictions regarding the basic plan of salvation.

I used to ponder over a difficult question. It seemed strange that God would incarnate as Sai Baba and live amidst us for eighty years and undergo suffering for the benefit of His devotees. I reasoned that God, as Creator of the universe, was in charge of everything. That entitled Him to make His own rules and establish His own boundaries. It seemed to me that God could have provided any plan of salvation. He chose anything that suited.

Sai Baba's aid was received by hundreds of people. He said to G.S. Khaparde that constant attention to the thousands that sought his aid ruined his system and would continue to ruin it till the fleshy tabernacle should break; and that he did not mind the trouble and loss, as he cared more for his devotees, than for decades and the cross he was nailed to From that cross, his soul has ascended and regained its spiritual perfection and is blessing all devotees.

I could not comprehend why He would put Himself through such grief and sorrow on our behalf when He could have offered a less costly plan of salvation, I struggled with this issue as a Sai-child and was perplexed by the questions it raised H.H. Narasimha Swamiji provided me the answer in one of His 'Mahasamadhi' message's:

The central truth of Sai Baba's life is: 'A life spent in sacrifice and loving service is life; And that a life spent in indulgence and other ways is death': If all of us do but strive to reach this ideal, our individual and natural goals are sure to be achieved. "Deserve and you will get it", so said Sai.

It is interesting to look back on the things that troubled me in earlier days. I now have a better understanding of Sai Baba's plan of salvation and what motivated it. And the explanation is of great significance for me, because it deals with the very essence of Sai philosophy. Here, then, is my concept of the plan of salvation and why Sai's physical death was necessary. It begins, as it should, with an understanding of Sai Baba's nature', throughout 'Sai Satcharita', the Almighty is represented by two uncompromising characteristics "His love and His justice". Both of these aspects are reflected in everything God does, and none of His actions will ever contradict the other one.

Love and justice of God were especially evident when He created us human beings. Obviously, he could have programmed us to love Him and obey His laws. This could have been accomplished by creating us as highly sophisticated robots or puppets. He did in fact, program the brains of lower animals, causing birds to build a certain kind of nest and wolves to kill wounded deers. They have no choice in the matter. My pet dog plays an assortment of wired-in behaviour about which neither of us has a choice. For, example, he can help barking when the front-bell rings. Nor can he keep from gobbling his food as though he would never get another meal. God has imposed instinctual behaviour in him, which operates without learning.

But Lord Sainath chose to put no instructive behaviour in mankind and left it free to learn. This explains the utter helplessness of human infants, who are the most dependent of all creatures at birth. They lack the initial advantages of unlearned responses, but will later run circles around the brightest animals with 'lock-in' reactions. Such is the nature of our humanness.

By granting us freedom of choice, therefore, Lord Sainath gave meaning to our love. He sought our devotion, but refused to demand it. However, the moment He created this choice, it became inevitable that He would eventually be faced with man's sin. Sai Baba told people that if they quarreled and hurt each other his heart was burning within and that if they endured each other's faults and attacks with patience, his heart was rejoicing. In His own mosque the Hindus. Christian, Muslims, Parsis stand side by side in their adoration of Him. Far from destroying each other, they are building each other's temples, mosques and sacred structures, and helping each other to have unmolested celebrations in the same building. The Hindus rebuilt his mosque and a Brahmin devotee of his, Upasani Baba, built a mosque next to his own temple. The Muslims perform their 'Id' in the same mosque without noise and when the turn for the Hindu worship in the same place comes up, the Muslim brother beats the drum in the mosque to help the Hindu in his worship.

In spite of Sainath's advocating *'Saburi'* (Patience) we do come across stray instances wherein Sai devotees lose their calmness and confront each other, with the most serious dilemma of all time. Sai Baba's love for His devotees is unlimited and He forgives His disobedient children. The Bible say "A father pitieth his children, so the Lord pitieth them that fear Him."

(*Psalm* 103:13)

That is an analogy I can comprehend. I know how I pity my children when they have done wrong. My inclination is to forgive them.

Lord Sainath is close behind our thoughts. In every moment of our life his declaration comes true; "Wherever you may be, you may remember this always: "I ever know whatever you do or say."

In spite of Sai Baba's great love, His justice required complete obedience. It demanded repentence and punishment for disobedience. So herein was a serious paradox or conflict within Sai Baba's nature. If he destroyed the human race, as his justice would require in response to our sinful disobedience, his love would have been violated; but if he ignored our sins, his justice would have been sacrificed. Yet neither aspect could he compromise.

But Sai Baba, in his marvelous wisdom, proposed a solution to that awful dilemma. "Do not try to get *Mantra* or *Upadesh* from anybody. Make Me the sole object of your thought and actions and you will no doubt attain *'Paramartha'*. Look at Me whole-heartedly and I, in turn, look at you similarly." Years after His Mahasamadhi, when Kaka Dixit had a doubt as to how he could attain the 'devotional status' of *Nava-nathas*, Sai Baba cleared his dilemma through a dream-vision to Anand Rao Pakhade. "...Devotion in the form of a bow to or worship of Guru's feet is sufficient."

This understanding of the plan of salvation is not based on guesses and suppositions, of course. it is drawn from the literal interpretation of Sai's word.

Isn't that a beautiful explanation of Sai Baba's purpose here on earth? It makes clear why Sai Baba's plan necessarily involve his own exchange of life with Tatya Patil. Only by paying this incredible price could He harmonize the potential contradiction between love and justice, and provide a 'why of escape' for mankind. It also explains why there is no other means. Sai Baba said: "Simple remembrance of my name as SAI, SAI will do away with sins of speech and hearing".

Just how does a person proceed, now to accept this plan and follow the risen Lord? Prof. G.G. Narke in 1936 said: "We are aware that there is no change in Sai BabaHe was, He is and will ever be an *Aparntaratrna*". The Bible says: "Anyone who calls upon the name of the Lord will be saved (Romans 10:13)."

As I understand the Sai philosophy, there is a second responsibility. "Are there still some among you who hold that 'only believing' is enough? "Well, remember that the demons believe this too so strongly that they tremble in terror. When will you ever learn that 'believing' is useless without doing what God wants you to do? Faith that does not result in good deeds is not real faith (*James*: 2: 12-20)." So something else is required. While it is true that you could 'work' your way to salvation, you cannot do enough good deeds to earn it; repentence is still an important part of the process.

'Repentance' is a word that is often misunderstood. What does it really mean? Sapatnekar's incident in Chapter 48 of *Shri Sai Satcharita* defined repentence as having three parts to it. "The first is conviction. You have to know what is right before you can do what is right; and you have to know what's wrong in order to avoid those misbehaviours." Repentance also involves a deep awareness that you stand guilty before the Lord. When Sapatnekar went and placed his head at the holy feet of Sai Baba, he seemed to have no real awareness of his own sin and guilt. He had no 'contrition' of heart. That is why Sai Baba rebuked him saying "Get out".

But where does this spirit of repentance originate from? It must come through the teaching 'Look to me, I look after you'. We should have this relationship with Lord Sainath. Sainath must be so important that you will allow Him to turn your life around and change your behaviours. In summary, then, repentence includes conviction, knowing right from wrong, then contrition, being aware of your guilt and sin, and finally, a resulting change of mind and heart and behaviour. We are aware that Sapatnekar led a blissful life after Sainath ultimately blessed him.

I think it would be helpful to give an example of the kind of prayer that a person might pray if he understands what I have been writing and wants to accept Sai Baba as his own Lord and Saviour. Let me express it in this way.

"Lord Sainath: I do not have anything valuable to offer except myself and my love. I accept your control of my life, and intend to serve you, obey you and follow you. You have my past, my future, my family, my money and my time. Nothing will I withhold. Thank you for loving me and forgiving

Courtesy:: *Shri Sai Leela,* Sept.-Oct., 1996.

CHAPTER - 7

The Great Miraculous Grace
of Shri Shirdi Sai Baba

D.N. Jagtap Baba Ji

I am at the Lotus Feet of Shri Shirdi Sai Baba. Without His grace, I am not able to do anything. As Shri Hemadpant i.e., Shri Govind Raghunath Dabholkar has rightly mentioned that because of Shri Sai Baba's blessings only he could write '*Shri Sai Satcharita*', I too have been blessed by Shri Sai Baba to do spiritual healing which I have been doing for a number of years. Only with His blessings and that too instantly He gives *darshan* to some devotees in right hand palm and or in my both eyes or sometimes He changes my face into His own face and many devotees are blessed and cured. It is said in '*Shri Sai Satchatrit'a*I that whosoever because of his or her *poorvajanma karmas* (past good actions) is able to have the Sri Shirdi Sai Baba's *darshan* will not have rebirth but will get *Moksh or Mukti (Mukti)*. With His blessings and mighty powers He is spreading His Healing touch messages all over the world through the quarterly magazine 'SHiRDI SAI LEELAMRUT, a quarterly magazine published from, "SAI DEEP", No. 1, Lognathan Street, Tambaram, (West), Chennai-600045, Tel. No. 044-22261670 by Shri E. Radhakrishnan Ji who is an ardent devotee of Shirdi Sai Baba.

Here, I like to tell to the devotees that it is because of our *poorvajanma karma* and also the devotion and f surrender to our God - *Shri Sai Nath* we are ultimately able to reach Him and get His blessings HIM and some may get *Mukti* or *Moksh* (libratio). I have been blessed by our *Guru*, Shri Sai Baba on many occasions. He came to my house on 4 to 5 times and asked only Rs. 3/- as *Dakshina* which I gave to Him. He travelled with me on my motor cycle, on 7 times, as pillion rider. He was stopping my motor cycle and was requesting me for the lift to travel for the short journey. On the way, He was asking me to stop the vehicle and He was asking to give Rs. 3/- as *Dakshna* which I was to give to Him. After getting Rs. 3/- He has blessed me on all the 7 times of His accompanying me. On 21/03/2001, when I went to Shirdi to have the *darshan*, Shri Sai Baba came before me after entering the main gate of *Sansthan*. He was very dark in colour and beard and hair grown about 3-4 inches long and may be aged about 90 to 95 years old. He stopped me and asked my help to sit down. I helped Him to sit Him down comfortably and I offered some mixture to eat which He accepted. Then He asked me to help for change of place as some hot rays of sunlight was troubling Him. I helped Him for change of place as some hot rays of sunlight was troubling Him. I helped Him for change of place and took Him to other place near to PRO's pass issue counter in *Sansthan* in Shirdi. Then, He sat there comfortably and advised me to go and have the *darshan* in *Samadhi Mandir, Dwarkamai* and *Chavad*i. I left that place and walked about 5 steps only and turned back (out of curiosity) to see whether He is sitting comfortably, and to my surprise nobody was there. A person aged about 90 to 95 years age cannot get up in 1/2 seconds and disappear so sudden! He was Shri SAI BABA only. ON 21/06/2001, again it, so, happened other Miracle. I was travelling to SHirdi by state bus from Ahmednagar to Shirdi, and there was a woman with her grandson next to my seat. She was suffering from the incurable pain in her calf of both the legs * 7 years, despite consulting good Doctors/specialists with their medicines. I did the free service of healing touch to her and Shri Sai Baba cured her instantly inside the bus during travelling. She was to go to Surat. I advised her to pay *thanks to Sai Baba and continue her* *journey afterwards. So we both sat in Dwarkamai.* A cat suddenly appeared there in crowded people who were sitting there and came to us and sat on my lap for some time. I told that woman, "Please see this cat" but may be Sai Baba as no cat 'suppose' to enter in *Dwarkamai*. And to our surprise the cat disappeared suddenly. He was Shri Sai Baba. Again, on 21/09/2001, after my free services opf healing touch at Mumbai and Navi Mumbai and Kalyan I came to Shirdi to get blessing from Sai Baba, with my nephew named Mr Sekhekhar Shingare (Mob. No. 9967822924). While taking tea at Sansthan (Trust), tea canteen, a person aged about 45-50 years asked me by holding my right hand, to get one cup of tea. We bought 3 cups of tea and I offered a cup to Him and we drank the tea by talking to each other. Afterwards the person who took tea with us put the empty cup in waste bin, and paid thanks to us and wanted to leave. We thanks him for giving company. He walked just 5 steps and disappeared. My nephew Mr. Shekhar asked me about Him and how He had disappeared. I told him that, he was SAI BABA. Here I want to tell that, because of Mr. Shekhar's *poorvajanma karma* only he got darshan of Shri Sai Baba on 21/09/2009 in Shirdi Sai *Sansthan* premises inside the canteen. With the *darshan* Mr. Shekhar got married within 2 months and within few months his wife delivered and got a child. It is said that devotee who can get *Darshan* of God can get *Moksh/Mukti* (libration). So, Mr. Shekhar is a blessed soul. In November, 2003, I * buy some flowers to offer to Sai Baba during my prayers. I went to market at Mahalakshmi Nagar but stop, Selaiyur, Chennai. I was paying the money to the vendor, suddenly somebody touched my back, I turned and saw Shri Shirdi Sai Baba in real form with *satka*, *jholi*, begging bowl and head covered with cloth as usual. He asked me to give *dakshina* of *. I got some change from the flower vendor and gave rupees five as no change was available, and Sai Baba accepted it. Then He blessed me. I requested Him to come to my house to bless my wife as she was sick. He told me that He had already visited my wife and blessed her. After blessing me He disappeared. After reaching my house my wife told me that Sai Baba had come and blessed her. On 2ⁿᵈ December, 2011, I was in my morning walk at about 5.30 AM, in Air Force Road, near Indira Nagar bus stop, Selaiyur, Chennai (Tamil Nadu). Suddenly an old man with a pant and half sleeves shirt came before me and asked me that how to go Shri Sai Baba temple. I told him the way of a particular Sai Baba temple. But He said that I do not like to go to that temple (as I also avoid). Then I told the way of another temple. But one has to go by bus or by auto as the distance in quite far away. He said that He did not have money. I requested Him to sit over the bridge and I came back to my residence and took 108/- and went to him and given all the Rs. 108 to Him. He paid thanks to me and assured me that he would come back to my house. Then He walked few steps and disappeared. Then who was He! He was Shri Sai Baba only.

On an advise from Shirdi Shri Sai Baba and on a strong request from Sai Baba devotee shri Sai Ravi, we had arranged a Free Service Camp of HealingTouch at Avadi, Chennai (T.N.). We started the service after the Sai Baba's Aarti and also ended the free service after eh Aarti. Many devotees came to receive the blessings of Shri Sai Baba through me. All the devotees were sitting in an orderly manner and the Sai Baba volunteers were guiding them to control the crowd. So many chairs were arranged for the devotees to sit. All the devotees, were registered and the numbers were allotted. Some senior citizens and very sick people were given the priority to attend Healing Touch and to receive the blessings through me. Some devotees those who were suffering severely and not able to get down from the cars/autos/ambulance were, attended by me by going to them and undertaking the free services of healing. Devotees were suffering from the various problems viz: kidney, cancer, body pain, arthritis, heart problems, BP, diabetes, skin problems, gastric problems, headache, knee pain, piles, gall stone, spondylitis, weak memory, insomnia, acidity, constipation, flatulence, not getting married, married but no issue (no child), all physical problems of women, no expected yield from land cultivation, evil spirit, black magic, no proper education, educated but no job, promotion, court litigation, not able to speak/deaf and dumb, blindness, and many more, problems were faced by these devotees and after blessing them all the problems, were taken care by Shri Sai Baba and some of them, were, cured instantly by Shri Sai Babathrough me, and these miracles were witnessed by these devotees..

My Encounter with Shirdi Sai Baba

Here, I like to tell to the devotees that it is because of our poorvajanma karma and also the devotion to our God-Shri Sai Nath with self surrender, is ultimate to reach to HIM and get the blessings by worshiping HIM and some may get Mukti/Moksh. I have been blessed by our Guru, shri Sai Baba on many occasions. He came to my house on 4 to 5 times and asked only Rs. 3/- as dakshina which I gave to HIM. HE traveled with me on my motor cycle, on 7 times, as pillion rider. HE was stopping my motor cycle and was requesting me for the lift to travel for the short journey. On the way, He was asking me to stop the vehicle and He was asking to give Rs. 3/- as dakshina which I was to give to Him. After getting Rs. 3/- He blessed me on all the 7 times of His accompanying me. On 21/03/2001, when I went to Shirdi to have the darshan, Shri Sai Baba came before me after entering the main gate of Sansthan. He was very dark in colour and beard and hair grown about 3-4 inches long and may be aged about 90 to 95 years old. He stopped me and asked my help to sit down. I helped Him to sit Him down comfortably and I offered some mixture to eat which He accepted. Then He asked me to help for change of place as some hot rays of sunlight was troubling Him. I helped Him for change of place and taken Him to other place near to VIP's pass issue counter in Sansthan. Then, He sat there comfortably and advised me to go and have the darshan in Samadhi mandir and dwarkamai and chavadi. I left that place and walked about 5 steps only and turned back to see whether He is sitting comfortably, and to my surprise no body was there. A person aged about 90 to 95 years age can not get up in 1/2 seconds and disappear so sudden! HE was SHRI SAI BABA only. On 21/06/2001, again it so happened other Miracle. I was traveling to Shirdi by state bus from Ahmednagar and there was a woman with her grandson next to my sit. She was suffering from the incurable pain in her calf of both the legs since last 7 years despite of consulting good Doctors/ specialists with their medicines. I did the free service of healing touch to her and Shri Sai Baba cured her instantly. She was to go to Surat. I advised her to pay thanks to Sai Baba and continue your journey afterwards. So we both sat in Dwarkamai. A cat came to us and sat on my lap for some time. I told that woman please see this cat but may be Sai Baba as no cat suppose to come in Dwarkamai. And to our surprise the cat disappeared suddenly. He was Shri Sai Baba. Again, on 21/09/2001, after my free services of healing touch at Mumbai and Navi Mumbai and Kalyan I came to Shirdi for blessing with my nephew named Mr. Shekhar Shingare (Mob. No. 9322096866). While taking tea at Sansthan tea canteen, a person aged about 45-50 years asked me by holding my right hand, to get one tea. We bought 3 cups of tea and I offered a cup to him and we drank the tea by talking to each other. After wards the person who took a tea with us put the empty cup in waist bin, and paid thanks to us and wanted to leave. We told him thanks for giving company and you can go. He walked just 5 steps and disappeared. My nephew Mr. Shekhar asked me about Him and how He had disappeared. I told him that, He was SaiI Baba.. Here I want to tell that, because of Mr Shekhar's *poorvajanma karma* only he got *darshan* of Shri Sai Baba on 21/09/2009 in Shirdi Sai *Sansthan* premises inide the canteen. With that *darshan* Mr. Shekhar got married within 2 months and within few months his wife delivered and got a child. It is said that devotee who can get Darshan of God can get *Moksh/Mukti*. So, Mr. Shekar is a blessed soul.

I used to buy some flower garland (*mala*) every day in evening time to offer to Shri Sai Baba on the next day at morning hours during the pooja/archana. On one occ) for the Sai Baba's idol, I was tapped by a person from behind and when I turned and seen who was it, I was just shocked by seeing Shri Sai Baba in His real form with green colour long shirt, a begging bowl and a stick about 2 and half to 3 feet called *sataka* (stick), a bag on HIS shoulder called zoli with beard and moustache and head was covered with green color cloth as usual, as we see in photo. He asked me to for *daksina* which I was not having a change. He told me that He got the change but I wanted to get it from the vendor only. After getting two five rupee coins, I gave Him one coin, and He blessed me. I requested Him to come to my house and have a cup of tea. He told me that He had a cup of tea which was offered by my wife some time back about 9 months before during His visit to my house. After blessing me, suddenly He disappeared from there. I can not explain in words about my feelings at that moment.

Magazine - *Shirdi Sai Leelamrut*

Shirdi Sai Leelamrut - I
Shirdi Sai Leelamrut - II
Shirdi Sai Leelamrut - III July - Sept 2009
Shirdi Sai Leelamrut - IV Oct-Dec 2010
Shirdi Sai Leelamrut - V Jan-Mar 2011
Shirdi Sai Leelamrut - VI Jan-Mar 2011
Shirdi Sai Leelamrut - VII Jul-Sep 2011
Shirdi Sai Leelamrut - VIII Oct-Dec 2011
Shirdi Sai Leelamrut - XI JUL-SEPT-2012.
Shirdi Sai Leelamrut - X APL-JUN-2012
SHIRDI SAI LEELAMRUT-IX
JAN-MAR-2012
Shirdi Sai Leelamrut - XII OCT- DEC -2012.
Shirdi Sai Leelamrut XIII JAN -MAR -2013.
Shirdi Sai Leelamrut XIV APR -JUN -2013.
Shirdi Sai Leelamrut XV JUL - SEP 2013.

Shirdi Sai Leelamrut XVI OCT - DEC 2013.
Shirdi Sai Leelamrut XVII JAN - MAR 2014.
Shirdi Sai Leelamrut XVIII APL - JUN 2014.
Shirdi Sai Leelamrut XIX
JUL - SEP 2014.
Shirdi Sai Leelamrut XX OCT - DEC 2014.
Shirdi Sai Leelamrut XXI JAN - MAR 2015.
Shirdi Sai Leelamrut XXII APR - JUNE 2015.
Shirdi Sai Leelamrut XXIII JULY - SEP 2015.

[Sri D.H.JAGTAPJI, (BABAJI), is an advent and revered devotee of Shirdi Sai Baba in Chennai. He prays and invokes the blessings of Sri Shirdi Sai Bab and does spiritual healing for the benefit of the devotees, who are suffering from various problems or diseases like: education, job, promotion, not getting married, married but no issue (child), court cases, litigation, black magic, possession of evil spirit, agricultural cultivation, house construction, headache, spondylitis, backache, skin diseases, heart problems, blood pressure, kidney diseases, gall bladder stone, arthritis, lumbago, acidity, asthma, cancer, colic, constipation, deafness, diabetes, flatulence, paralysis, insomnia, tonsillitis, vertigo, etc and other worldly miseries, problems,. He chants 'OM SAI RAMA'- 9 times and does the spiritual touch healing. the devo He may be contacted on telephone or by e mail <jagtapsai@ redifmail.com and invited by Sai devotees of any place in India and abroad.]

Sri *D.H.Jagtap Baba jIJI)*
Addresss:
"SAINIVAS" NO. 14, SRIRAM NAGAR LAYOUT,
AIR FORCE ROAD,
POST- SELAIYUR,
CHENNAI-600073.
Mob No. 09841586849
E Mail<jagtapsai@rediffmail.com>

_____

_____

Permission email from Sri Jagtap Ji received on Saturday, 28.11.2015

<jagtapsai@rediffmail.com>   12:37 (2 hours ago)
to me

To,

Shri S.P. Ruhela ji,
Shri Shirdi Sai Baba's Grace,

Respected Sai Ram ji,

I am Sai Devotee and residing at Chennai since long. Shri Sai Baba has blessed me and with His blessings I do the service of Healing Touch to all irrespective of religion or caste or creed. This service is FREE to ALL. I do go all over the India and abroad. I visited Jammu/ Jalander/ Ludhiana/ Kharad/ Chandigarh/ Delhi/ Shamali/ Deharadun/ Mawana/ Meerut/ Baroda/ Mumbai/ Aurangabad/ Nashik/ Pandhrpur/ Satara/ Kolhapur/ Kanpur/ Lucknow/ Ranchi/ Bokaro/ Kolkatta/ Salem/ Trichy/ Madurai/ Pondichery/ Thanjavur/ Bangalore/ Belgaum/ Hyderabad/ Vizag and many places. Also I visited Malaysia-10 times/ U.S.A.-2 Times/ Australia/ Singapore - 5 times. This is purely service of HEALING TOUCH. This is FREE service to ALL. Any body is suffering from cancer/ kidney or any diseases or any problems I do this service to them with vibhuti. And many miracles have been witnessed by devotees that in minutes they have been cured.

You may visit: www.jagtapbabaji.com and see the TESTIMONY and also some video clips and Magazine etc.

Out of those 2 TESTIMONIES are forwarded to you which may be published in your book so that many people can read and they may get benefits by contacting me and solving their problems.

Thanks.

Regards,

Shri D H JAGTAP. Mob. No. +91 9841586849

TESTIMONY- A GREAT MIRACLE---?

I am Mrs. Nandita Madhav, aged 48 years, from Maleswaram, Bangalore, Karnataka. I was suffering from sciatica with hernia and disc problems since last one and half years. I did all types of medication through the renowned doctors but still I was suffering from this pain and all in vain. On 20/04/2014, there was a free service of healing touch camp at Maleswaram, Bangalore, and I came to seek the blessing from Shri Jagtap Babaji. Babaji blessed me and what a miracle! I was cured instantly. All my pain disappeared. My thanks to Sai Baba and Shri Jagtap Guruji.

TESTIMONY- A GREAT MIRACLE---?

I am Mrs. Kalawati Bharti, aged 54 years, from Ambedkar Nagar, Ujjain, M.P. I was suffering from the severe pain in my stomach due to tumor since last 10 years. I was suffering from stomach pain due to a tumor since last 10 years. I consulted doctors and I was under their medication but all in vain. I came to know about the free service camp of healing touch that has been organized by Shri Sai Baba devotees at Ujjain from 24/04/2010 to 26/4/2010. So I went there and registered my name and was waiting for my turn. When I was called upon, I went to Shri Jagtap Babaji to get the blessings of Shri Sai Baba through him. Shri Jagtap Babaji did the service of healing touch to me and what a miracle! I was cured instantly and all my pain was completely vanished. My tumor in my stomach vanished. Thanks to Shri Sai Baba and Shri Jagtap Babaji. (MRS. KALAWATI BHARTI)

Get your own **FREE** website, **FREE** domain & **FREE** mobile app with Company email. **Know More >**
3 Attachments

Preview attachment 1__1_.jpg2
Preview attachment LEELA_48__8_.jpg
LEELA_48__8_.jpg
Preview attachment e1__23_.jpg
e1__23_.jpg

CHAPTER - 8

Evidences of Sri Shirdi Sai Baba's Global popularity

(S.P.Ruhela)

Since Sri Shirdi Sai Baba attained *Maha Samadhi* in 1918, His nameand fame as a very great and highly benevolent and merciful saint, God'sincarnation of a very high stature, have been spreading throughout the world. In a miraculous manner, thousands of people of different religions andnationalities are becoming His devotees each day having come under the foldof His agnanimous grace and experiencing some sort of thrilling miracle intheir lives. Temples devoted to Him have been coming uin different places, cities, towns and villages in India as well as in far off lands Like USA, UK, Australia and African countries, Singapore, etc., due to the efforts of highlydevoted self-motivated people. Innumerable devotees and rich donors vie witheach other in providing funds and material for building and furnishing ShirdiSai temples that are coming up throughout the world as inspired by Him inmany invisible and mysterious ways. Many charitable hospitals are run sidesthese temples and many welfare services and other charitable activities arebeing carried out by enthusiastic people in the name of Sri Shirdi Sai Baba. The number of devotees visiting Shirdi is ever increasing. In a nutshell, thedevotional cult of Sri Shirdi Sai Baba is fast spreading throughout the world.

It is only because of Baba's mysterious divine wish and design that allthese unique things are happening and Baba's eminence is fast spreading inconcentric circles in all lands and all ommunities. Why is it that the appealof Shirdi Sai Baba's charismatic personality is so irresistible to people?

Sai devotee, B. Ramanatha Rao of Sai Kutir, Madras, has advanced the following reasons for it:

1. First and foremost because, in the words of Hemadpant, the author of *Shri Sai Sat Charita*, He (Shirdi Sai Baba) had taken a vow to giveyou what you want.

2. And that too immediately cash down; you ask with sincere devotion (*Shraddha*) and patience *(saburi)* and there is the result.

3. He is so easily pleased. No hard penance, no unbearable fasts, not even difficult concentration and control of senses. In His words, "You lookto Me and I will look to you." Can there be anything simpler than this?

4. He left His mortal body years ago and even today thousands of devotees have experienced His presence, having met their demands. What more guarantee is required.

5. Not being bodily present as a human being today, there is no danger of being cheated in His worship. In the case of so many *avatars*, *Bhagawans*, and *yogis* who have cropped up at present in the country, one is not sure if one is following the real preceptor *(Sadguru)*.

6. No money is required to worship Baba. He is pleased even with flowers, fruits, leaves or even water, devotionally offered. You do not even have to spend for travelling up to Shirdi. He is available even where you are "even beyond the seven seas".

7. Ashes *(udi)* from the fire burning eternally in His *Dwarka Mai* is thecheapest and most infallible medicine for all diseases. The cost is only two -paise – faith and patience.8. His life history written by Hemadpant contains all the wisdom of the *Vedas*, the *Upanishsads* and the *Gita* in the form of simple stories and anecdotes. Reading them alone and following the advice, therein, one can reach the goal of liberation without fail.

8. Repetition of His name *'Sat'* is so short, so sweet and so easy to pronounce; no twisting of tongue and difficult accents.10. Last but not least, He on fulfilling your demands in this world, ensuresthat you do not get caught up in the dangerous web of this *sansar*, so He slowly moulds you, guides you and takes you step by step toliberation which is the key to eternal and everlasting bliss.

Shirdi Sai Baba's main insistence was on morality and simple and essentiallaws of spirituality which are universally emphasized by all religious scriptures, moral leaders and great personalities of all races and nations not on ritualisticreligion as such. In matters of religion, He preached integration or unity ofthe genuine kind. He emphasized that all human beings and creatures have the same *atma* and, therefore, all are one and everyone in the living world is entitled to receive our love, care, hospitality, concern and help. The world, as it is, is full of so many dissensions and social, cultural, economic and political conflicts, jealousies and immoral, disjunctive and dysfunctional tendencies which have made the life of human beings all over the world very insecure. Religions have disappointed humanity through the doings of many fundamentalist, fanatics, hypocrites and wealth loving and power-nkering Godmen, *yogis* and *acharayas* who rarely see eye to eye among themselves and do not feel shy in openly condemning each other. In such a social and religious context of the contemporary world, Shirdi.

Sai Baba alone comes up to the expectations of the masses of the world asthe ideal God man who epitomizes simplicity, spirituality, love and genuine concern for all creatures, of the highest order. He combined in Him all thefinest traits of the Vedic gods, Adi Shankara, Christ, Buddha, Zoroaster, Mohammed, Nanak and all other great spiritual and religious personalities born in the world. Shirdi Sai Baba's charisma based on Hissimplicity, unconventionality lack of diehard ritualism, love and stress on unity and harmony is in utter contrast of the affluent and controversial lifestyles of many of the contemporary God men, *yogis* and *acharyas* captivates the hearts of people and is more than thereof anyone of the modern world. The world is fed up with all those who teach religion, morality, spirituality and yoga and the like in enchanting words but crave for worldly properties, publicity, political patronage and all the pleasures and luxuries of modern life. Sri Shirdi Sai Baba, therefore, impresses us most. It is also true that generally the modern educated people do not have much fascination for die-hard ritualism. They do not have patience to do any kind of elaborate penance, *yagna*, *dhyana* or the like. They crave for simple, easy, readymade, andt benefits even in spiritual matters. They are cosmopolitan, secular and universal in their outlook and, therefore, do not wish to be confined to the narrow walls of their traditional religion and complicated incomprehensible rituals and customs. They crave for a broader, more sublime and easier-to understand kind of spiritual experience. Shirdi Sai Baba's simple teachings are without any trappings of a complicated philosophy and His grace can be available to them just on remembering Him without any kind of difficulty or special effort.

Sri Shirdi Sai Baba had given eleven assurances of protection and wish fulfillment to all the worshippers -contemporary as well future ones. They have proved true to all believers le throughout have faith in then and so they have been coming in hordes every day. On an average about 20,000 people visit Shirdi daily and on Thursday and every Hindu festival the number of visitors invariably swells up to more than1 00000 and even more. Even some foreigners come here to receive sai Baba's legendary grace, It is because of these solid reasons that Shirdi Sai Baba's name and fame have been spreading so fast throughout the world during the preceding nine tdecades and it continues to spread with ever growing tempo.

How Baba's name is spreading

Sri Shirdi Sai *Sansthan* (Trust), Shirdi, has been publishing valuable booksand pictorial albums on Baba which have been spreading Baba's name and message throughout the world. Besides this, a number of organizations and voluntary bodies have come up to spread Baba's message. Sri NarasimhaSwamiji established the All India *Sai Samaj* at Madras (now called Chennai) and authored a number of valuable books on Bbaa and spread His name and message throughout India. Sri Sai Sharananadji, Baba's noted contemporarydevotee, authored a book '*Shri Sai Bab,* in Marathi and, *Sri Sai The Superman'.* which have made Baba known throughout the world. Swami Karunananda had his son Shri Narayana Swami of Bhagawati Sai Sansthan, Panwel (Maharashtra) have been instrumental in spreading the teachings of Baba through their books, lectures and pioneering efforts to establish Sri Shirdi Sai Temples in U K, USA, Africa, Australia, etc. Sri Sai Samaj, Picket, Secundrabad (Andhra Pradesh), Sai Bhakta Samaj, Delhi (Shirdi Sai Temple, 17, Institutional Area, LodhiRoad, New Delhi), Shirdi Sai Sabha, Chandigarh and other organizations have for years been doing remarkable service in the propagation of the message of Shirdi Sai Baba. In Karnataka, a number of Shirdi Sai Temples have been established by the individual efforts of a highly devoted soul, Sri H.D. Laxman Swami, Shivamma Thayee of Bangalore, a contemporary devotee of Shirdi Sai Baba inaugurated a number of Sri Shirdi Sai Temples and herself established a temple in her a*shram* Agrahara, Maliwada, Bangalore.

A great Sai devotee Guru Ji Dr.Chandra Bhanu Sathpathi, a senior Police officer, has during the last two decades motivated the establishment of over 200 Shirdi SaiTemples throughout India and in UK. His profile and the list of Sai temples established and inaugurated by him are amiable on the interne.

To me it seems that the hundreds of Shirdi Sai Baba teples that have come up during the last 97 years, i.e. since Baba's casting His morta l coils on 18.10.1818 have been built only due to the divine will and the miraculous help of Sri Shird Sai Baba. This is not my superstitious belief or exaggeration but my information about many Sai temples. I have come across many mysterious real stories of the coming up of a number of Shirdi Sai Temples.

In Bangalore, Shivama Thayee, a contemporary beneficiary of Sai Baba's graceand whobecame a greatsaint, had built three Sai temples in her Ropopen Agraham *ashram* and had installed a marblestature of Baba[1]in standing posture with His timpot for begging, as told by Baba in her vision, in the first half of the 19th century. She inaugurated many Sai temples in Karnataka State in her 104 years long life; l had the blessed opportunity. of interviewingher on 5.7.1992 and then writing a book on her *"My Life wiith Sri Shirdi Sai Baba'*;(1993). She had seen Baba in 1906 and visited Him in Shirdi a number of times, her lastvisit was in1917 when Baba directed her to become a *sanysin*,. settle in Bangalore. do hard penance and assured her that would have her *ashram* in due course

In Rajasthan, an old devotee, Kailash Chandra Bakiwala of Jaipur established Shirdi Sai Temple at village Kukas, 17 Kms from Jaipur on the Jaipur-Delhi roadI imert him in 1993 and learnt from him that he possessed the rare –the only - original, letter in Hindi, dictated by Sai Baba to the close ealkest devotee and helper school master Shama and sdent by posdt by Baba to the Thakur at Mount Abu, the famous hill station in south Ra\jasthan in 1857some months before his (they young 20 years old *fakir*(then he was not called Sai Baba) before his second coming to Shirdi and acceopting the name of Sai Baba from Mahlasapthy and settling in Dwarka Mai *masjid* in 1858. Bakiwal providentially happened to get that rarest of the rare original letter of Sai Baba, which was gifted by his brother- in-law who happened to purchase it from a *kabadi* (junk dealter) of Jaipur city who had bought the old materials, books, files. letters etc. as *raddi* (waste or junk) from the family of of the decased e Thankr of Achrol.

Being an ardent old Sai devotee and collection of Sai Baba;s pictures,. being his hobby, Bskiwa overjoyed and inspiteredby this uniuque find decided to build a Shirdi Sai temple near Achrol at the village kukas where he could purchase land for ithe temple. He very kindly gave methe Photostat copy of

1

that leter and prermiitterdc me to publish in my books. I published that letter in my book' *What Researchers Say on Sri Shirdi Sai Baba* (1993)

Due to this rare letter ot Sai Baba the r the SaI Temple was built at Kukas about 40 yesars back.

The English version of the letter is as follows:

SRI RAM JI ALLAH

Welcome to SrI Thakur from Sri Sai Baba.. this is to infom you that SaI Baba has arrived, we are happy.. we go out for walking daily. Be happy,. be prosperous.
ThIs is s the blessinmg of Baba fakir toyou and all..

In Moradabad (Uttar Pradesh) *'ai Surya Mandir'* on. Delhi Road was built by Mr.Paras an old ardent Sai devotee/. I had visited that temple many years back. I was thrilled to learn from Mr. Paras that Sai Baba sent a number of unknown liberal donors who unexpectedly came at different stages of the temple construction, without Mr. Paras, requesting for any kind of help, voluntarily and persistently with great humility supplied freely all the required building materials and funds. One stranger came and left a big cloth bag full off gold ingots covered with sand. That gold (which might be of several kilograms in weight) was not used but was just placed in a deep pit immediately dug in the temple courtyard for future need if any..

I have come across many more such mysterious real stories of the coming up of a number of Shirdi Sai temple. Several years back at Coimbatore a cobra had appeared and stayed there at a *bhajan* session for several hours. People were convinced that it was nothing else but Sri Shirdi Sai Baba Himself and hen a huge Nag Sai Temple was built on that very spot which has been attracting thousands of visitors every year. On the Internet anyone find details of this great snake miracle, the temple and Sri Nag Sai Trust in Coimbatore.

This temple was inaugurared by Sri Sathya Sai Baba. I had also visited it inCoimbatore many years back,

A brief write up on this miracle available on theintrernet is as under: 'In 1943 on the evening of the 7th of January, *Guru-vara* (Thursday) sacred for worship of Baba, a miracle happened! A shining and lustrous *naga* (Cobra) small in size but posessing an unusually big hoad with divine marksof *Tripundra, Shankh*a and Chakra appeared before Baba's picture when the*Bhajan* was going on in full swing to the accompaniment of drum cymbals etc., with all the lights on. The *Naga* (cobra) stood there in a pose of worshipfullness entranced in Baba music! Waving of lights, *aratis* etc had no effect onthe nerves of the Cobra. People around who had swelled into a crowd of a fewhundred stood there in awe and wonder at the wondrous sight of the *Naga* with spread head. There was no fear for the snake; the proverb that even a battalionof soldiers of valour shiver at the sight of a cobra was falsified- young and old, women and children in thousands began to pour into the spacious land of the*Bhajan maidan* to witness the *Naga* that lingered in the same spot for full 48 hours Baba *bhaktas* (devotees) began to shower baskets after baskets of flowers in worshipful reverence for the *Naga*. The Cobra was virtually submerged ina mound of flowers but even then, he was unmobile. Arti was performed for the *Naga.*

On the second day of *Naga*'s advent, a photographer came to take a pictureof the Naga in its majesty but the latter was immersed under heaps of flowers. No one had the courage of go near the spot where the cobra ws lodged and clear the flowers. The only course open to them was to pray ho! the *Naga*jumped out of the flowers heaps and posed for the photograph as if in answer to the prayers of the multitude. One and all were sure for the first time that itwas all the work of Sai Baba. The devotees then prayed with fervour and faith to the *Naga* to clear out and enable them to resort to their routine worship of Baba in the *maidan*. Then the immobile Naga showed signs of movements, itwent around Sri Sai Baba's picture and slowly marched out into the open anddisappeared into bush where later an ani-hill (snake's natural habitat) appearedThe place where the Naga disappeared in held as a 'Holy Ground' by devoteesand from that day onwards Shirdi Sai Baba in Coimbatore is worshipped as "*Sri Nagasai*"

Miracles have indeed happened and every day happening with countlesspeople at many places in India and broad. Many Sri Shirdi Sai Temples havesprung up throughout India and in many foreign countries. Guru ji C.B.Satpathy Ji has motivated the establishment of over 200 Shirdi Sai temples. The name and fame of Baba and His universal message have thus beenspreading all over. Instances like these compel even the extreme rationalists and iconoclasts among the modernites to believe in the mysterious supernaturalpowers and divine will of Shirdi Sai Baba which makes such things possible inthe materialistic and selfish world of today.

There are many self-inspired and self-motivated devotees of Sri Shirdi SaiBaba belonging to Hindu, Jain, Christian, Zoproastrian, Sikh and major andtribal religions who on their own havenbeen writing and publishing books onBaba, doing social welfare activities for the poor and organizing Sai *kirtans* and *bhajan* sessions for moral and spiritual uplift of mankind. Considerationsof religion, race, caste, nationality, class, etc., do not come in the way ofanyone becoming a Sai devotee and propagator of Baba's message. Thus, forinstance, Zarine Taraporewalla, the English translator of Das Ganu's famous.'*Stavan Manjari* and K.J. Bhishma's '*Sainath Sagunopasana*'is a Parsee;Kailash Chandra Bakiwala of Jaipur, the founder of Sri Shirdi Sai Temple at Kukas (near Achrol, Jaipur district, Rajasthan) is a Jain; Bashir Baba, a great followerand propagator of Sri Shirdi Sai Baba (some believe that He Himself was Baba's incarnation) was a Muslim. There are many other such examples of devotees belonging to other religions who are great devotees of Baba. There are also some foreign Christians of Austria, Australia and Canada who are great devotees of Shirdi Sai Baba. At Shirdi, one could during 1990s see a middle aged African lady attired in a white robe like a nun moving about *Gurusthan*, *Chavadi* and *Dwarka Mai* constantly or sitting with Sri Shivnesh Swami Ji at *Gurusthan* and singing Kabir's songs at the *bhajan* sessions at *Chavadi*.

All these concrete examples testify to the fact that the universal nature of Shirdi Sai Baba and the greatness and uniqueness of his divine message of fatherhood of One God and the brotherhood of all men have indeed been understood by many enlightened people of different racial, religious and national backgrounds. Baba's Spiritual Socialism has won the hearts of many people and the impact of His magnetism is thus going to attract more and more people's souls towards Him.

Prominent Shirdi Sai Temples & Centrrs in the World

Sri Shirdi Sai Baba's name and fame has spread all over the world. Thereare countless Shirdi Sai Baba temples and centres in India and in a number offoreign countries. Given below are the prominent ones among as far as I could learn about:

- Shirdi Sai Baba Temple, Shirdi (Maharashtra)
- Nag Sai Temple, Coimbatore (Tamil Nadu)
- Shirdi Sai Baba Temple, Bharat Nagar, Chennai
- Shirdi Sai Baba Temple, Kolhapur (Maharashtra)
- Shidi Sai Baba Temple, Sholapur (Maharashtra)
- Shirid Sai Baba Temple, Khar (West) Mumbai (Maharashtra)
- Shirid Sai Baba Temple, Mylapore, Chennai
- Shirid Sai Baba Temple, Bharat Nagar, Chennai
- Shirid Sai Baba Temple, Lodhi Road, New Delhi
- Shirid Sai Baba Temple, Shirdi (Maharashtra)
- Shirid Sai Baba Temple, Sector 16A, Faridabad
- Shirid Sai Baba Temple, Chandigarh
- Shirid Sai Baba Temple, Sector 25, NOIDA (U.P.)
- Shirid Sai Baba Temple, Sector 40, NOIDA
- Shirid Sai Baba Temple, Gurgaon (Haryana)
- Shirid Sai Baba Temple, Agra, Chippitola, Agra (U.P.)
- Shirid Sai Baba Temple, Aligarh (U.P.)
- Shirid Sai Baba Temple, Jaipur (Rajasthan)
- Shirid Sai Baba Temple, Kukas, Jaipur (Rajasthan)
- Shirid Sai Baba Temple, Bank Colony, Hyderabad
- Shirdi Sai Baba Temple, Moradabad (U.P.)
- Shirdi Sai Baba Temple, Bareilly (U.P.)
- Shirdi Sai Baba Temple, Sapnawat (U.P.)
- Shirdi Sai Baba Temple, Shirdi Sai Temple, Shastri Nagar, Meerut
- Shirdi Sai Baba Temple, Illford, (U.K.)
- Shirdi Sai Baba Centre, Forida, Inverness (U.S.A.)
- Shirdi Sai Baba Temple, 45-16, Robinson Street, Flushing, New York
- Shirdi Sai Baba Temple, Bronswick, New Jersey (U.S.A.)
- Shirdi Sai Baba Ambers Creek, Flushing, Pittsberg (U.S.A.)
- Shirdi Sai Baba Temple, Chicagoland, Hampshire (U.S.A.
- Shirdi Sai Baba Temple, Hurlington House, Nathan Road, Tsim Tsa Tsui, Kowloon, Hongkong
- Shirdi Sai Baba Temple, Toronto
- Shirdi Sai Baba Temple. Ontrio,.Canada
- Shirdi Sai Baba Temple, Blutaser, Canada.
- Shirdi Sai Baba Temple., Seathe
- Shirdi Sai Baba Temple., Ohio

- Shirdi Sai Baba Temple, ChicaommDalas (USA).
- Shirdi Sai Baba Temple, Piano,.Dallas (USA).
- Shirdi Sai Baba Temple, Mapleg.
- Shirdi Sai Baba Temple. Mauritis.
- Shirdi Sai Baba Web Site Organization 182, West Melrose Street, Suite No. 4, South Elgin,
  1L 60177, U.S.A.
  Phone: 847-931-4058
  Fax: 847-931-4066
  Web: http://www.saibaba.org
  E-mail: maildrop@saibaba.org

- Shirdi Sai Temple
  46-16 Robinson Street, Flushing,
  New York (U.S.A.)
  Tel: (718) 3219243
- Shirdi Sai Baba Sansthan of America,
  625, Summerset Country,
  Richwater Township, New Jersey-08807 (U.S.A.)
  Tel.: (908) 3061420
- Shirdi Sai Foundation Centre,
- 4901, Pleasant Grove, Inverness,
  Florida – 34452 (U.S.A.)
  Tel.: (352) – 8602181
- Sai Foundation, Kenya (Africa)
  P.O. Box 41409, Nairobi, Kenya
- E-mail: ushmid@africaonline.com

There are many Sai temples in like these in many countries,

There are many Shirdi Sai Baba temples in Himachal Pradesh, U.P Andhra Pradesh, Tamil Nadu, Odesa and other states in India.

Many of these (about 200) temples have been started by the efforts of Guruji C.B.Satpathi, who is a highly inspired *pracharak* of Sri Shirdi Sai Baba.

Important Shirdi Sai Baba Organizations

- All India Sai Samaj Mylapore, Chennai. (T.N.)
- Sai Publications, Red Cross Road, Civil Lines, Nagpur (Maharashtra)
- Dwarakamayi Publications, Hyderabad-500033 (A.P.)
137
Sri Shirdi Sai Baba
- Shri Bhagwati Sai Sansthan, Panvel-410206 (Maharashtra) (Sai Sevak Narayan Baba, Spiritual Head).
- Sai Foundation India, New Delhi-110060: H-353, New Rajinder Nagar.
- Sai Prachar Kendra, S.C.F. 18, Sector 19-D, Chandigarh-160 019.
- Sri Sai Spiritual Centre, T. Nagar, Bangalore-560 028.
- Sri Sai Samaj, Picket, Secunderabad (A.P.)
- Sri Sai Baba *Sansthan*, Shirdi (Maharashtra)
- Sri Sai Samaj Calcutta, P-113, Lake Terrace, Calcutta-700 029
- Sai Sudha Trust, Shirdi Sai Bab Mandir, Garkhal, Kausauli
- Sri Bhakta Parivar, 91, Napier Town, Jabalpur (M.P.)
- International Pragya Mission, Saket, New Delhi-110017.
- Akhil Bhartiya Shirdi Sai Bhakti Mahasabha, Hyderabad.
- Akhanda Sainama Saptaha Samithi, B/3/F-15, Krupa Complex, Ananda Bagh, Hyderabad- 500 047. (A.P.) (D. Shankariah, Secretary).
- Shri Shatha Shruga Vidhya Samasthe ®
Magadi Main Road,
Bangalore – 560079, (Phone: 3486044)
- Shirdi Sai Baba Satsang,
KBRS Bldg., Near Velu Mudaliar Dispensary,
Kamaraj Road, Bangalore – 560042
Phone Off.: 5300225, Res.: 5300116 Shri Saibaba *Sansthan* (Trust), P.O.: Shirdi -258500 (30 lines) Fax No.: +91-2423-258870, P.R.O. Office: +91-2423-258770
E-mail: saibaba@sai.org.in
URL: http://www.shrisaibabasansthan.org/ & http://www.sai.org.in
- "International Sri Sai Consciousness Foundation Centre".Venue: "Sri Sai Sharanalaya"
Premises II Main, Nagarabhavi Main Road, Sanjeevini Nagar, Moodalapalya'Bangalorehirdi

- Sai Baba Old Age Home Educational Trust, Plot No. 124, 4th Main Road, Sundara Babu Nagar, Veppampattur, Thiruvallur Dist. Ph.: 044-27620950, Cell: 9840081877
- All India Akhanda Sai Nama Seva Samithi A.K.S. Shruthi, Flat No. S-18, Second Floor, 63, K.K. Road, Venkatapuram, Ambattur, Chennai-600 053, Tel.: 044-2657-3496 R. Radhakrishna (Sai Jeevi) Chief Patron

Journals Devoted to Sri Shirdi Sai Baba

1. *Sai Chetna* (English), Chennai, Sri Sai Baba Spiritual & Charitable Trust, Injambakkam, Chennai-600 041.
2. *Sai Kripa* (English & Hindi). New Delhi-110003) Shri Sai Bhakta Samaj, 17, Institutional Area, Lodhi Road, New Delhi.
3. *Sai Kripa*: (Hindi) New Delhi: Sai Kripa Sansthan, A-16, Naraina II New Delhi-110 028, (Editor: Dipli Tuli).
4. *Sai Padananda*, Bangalore-560 028: Sri Sai Spiritual Centre, T. Nagar, (Editor: R. Seshadri).
5. *Sai Prabha* (English & Telugu). Hyderabad-500 027: H. No. 3-5-697/A, Telugu Academi Lane, Vittalwadi, Narayanguda.
6. *Sai Sudha*, All India Sai Samaj, Mylapore, Chennai (T.N.).
7. *Sai Sugam* (English & Tamil), Sri Shirdi Bhairava Sai Bbaa Temple Trust, 6 Bharath Nagar, Neel Kattabi Road, Madipakkarm, Chennai-600091.
8. *Shri Sai Leela* (English & Hindi), Bombay-400 014: 'Sai Niketan', 804-B, Dr. Ambedkar Road, Dadar.
9. *Sri Sai Avatars*, (English & Bengali). Calcutta-700 029: Sri Sai Samaj, Calcutta, P-113, Lake Terrace, (Editor: S.M. Bannerjee).
10. *Sri Sai Divya Sandesh*, (English & Hindi). (Distt. Raigarh): Sri Bhagawati Sai Sansthan Plot No. 400/I, Near Railway Station. Panvel-410 206.
11. *Sri Sai Spandan*, Hyderabad-500 872: Self-Analysis Institute, 402 Raj Apartments, B.H. Society, Kulkatpally (A.P.)
12. *Shradha suburi* (English & Hindi). 702, 7th Floor, Plot No. 9, Yash Apartment, Sector 11, Dwarka, New Delhi (Editor: Ruby Sharma)

Sri Shirdi Sai Baba Websites

- Annababa.com
- Baba's Eleven Promises
- From Shirdi Sai to Sathya Sai
  By Sharada Dev
- Life History of Shirdi Sai Baba
  By Sri Ammula Sambasiva Rao – Online book
- My Meeting with Baba of ShirdiBy Shivamma Thayee
- O Sai Baba
- Reincarnation of Shirdi Sai Baba
- *Sab-ka-malik-ek*
- *Sai Aarati* and *Bhajans*
- Sai Baba of Shirdi
- Sai Baba Temple, Shirdi
- Sai Bharadwaja
- www.Saidrbarusa.org
- Shri Sai Baba Sansthan, Shirdi
- Shree Shirdi Sai Sansthan. Sydney Australia (The first Sai temple inAustralia)
- Shri Saibaba Sansthan, Shirdi
- Shirdi Sai and Sathya Sai are One and the samez; By Arjan D. Bharwani
- Shirdi Sai Baba.com
- Shirdi Sai Baba Website
- Shirdi Sai Baba Site
- Shirdi Sai Baba on the World Wide Web
- Sai Bab Guru Srinath
- Shirdi Sai Organization
- Shirdi Sai Baba – Hindi Literature
- Shirdi Sai Jalaram Mandir
- Shri Saibaba Sansthan, Shirdi
- Sri Gurucharitra
- Sri Sai Baba of Shirdi
- Sri Shirdi Sai Baba Temple
- The Sai Baba of Shirdi
- The Shirdi Sai Avatar
- http://www.saibaba.website.org

- http://www.saibaba.org
- http://www.admn@saibaba.org
- http://www.saijanmasthan.com
- http://www.floridashirdisai.org
- http://www.saidarbarusa.org
- http://www.saimukthi.com
- http://www.saipatham.com
- http://www.saibaba.org
- http://www.shirdisaitemple.com
- http://www.saileela.org
- http://www.saisamadhi.org
- http://www.saimandir.org
- http://www.shirdi.org
- http://www.shirdisaibaba.com
- http://www.templeofpeace.org
- http://www.srisaimarggam.org
- http://www.theshirdisaimandir.com
- http://www.shrishirdisaicanada.org
- http://www.shirdisainath.org
- http://www.saisamsthanusa.org
- http://www.baba.org
- http://www.saibaba.us

108 Divine Names of Sri Shirdi Sai Baba
(*Om* is the name of God)

1. *Om Shri Sainathaya namah.*
   (*Om* obeisance to Shri Sai Nath)
2. *Om Shri Sai Lakshminarayanays namah.*
   (*Om* obeisance to Shri Sai Nath who is Narayana, Consort of Goddess Lakshmi)
3. *Om Shri Sai Krishna-Rama-Shiva-Maruityadirupaya Namah.*
   (*Om* obeisance to Shri Sai Nath, the manifestation of Lord Krishna, Ram, Shiva, Maruti & others)
4. *Om Shri Sai Shes-shayine Namah.*
   (*Om* obeisance to Shri Sai Nath, the Manifestation of Lord Vishnu resting on the thousand headed snake)

5. *Om Shri Sai Godavri-tata-sidhi-vasnih namah.*
(*Om* obeisance to Shri Nath, who made Shirdi on the banks of river Godavari his abode)

6. *Om Shri Sai Bhakta-hridalayaya Namah.* (*Om*, obeisance to Shri Sai Nath who dwell in his devotees hearts)

7. *Om Shri Sai Sarva-hrinnilayaya Namah.*
(*Om* obeisance to Shri Sai Nath who dwells in the hearts of all beings)

8. *Om Shri Sai Bhuta-vasaya namah.*
(*Om* obeisance to Shri Sai Nath who is in the hearts of all living creatures)

9. *Om Shri Sai Bhuta-Vhavishyad-bhava varjitaya namah.*
(*Om* obeisance to Shri Sai Nath who does not allow the thoughts of past and future to torment the mind)

10. *Om Shri Sai Kata-teetaya namah.*
(*Om* obeisance to Sri Sai Nath who is beyond the limitations of time)

11. *Om, Shri Sai Kataya namah.*
(*Om* obeisance to Shri Sai Nath who is time incarnate)

12. *Om Shri Sai kalkalaya namah.*
(*Om* obeisance to Shri Sai Nath who is the Lord of eternity)

13. *Om Shri Sai Kal-darpa-damanaya namah.*
(*Om* obeisance to Shri Sai Nath, who has destroyed the pride of death)

14. *Om Shri Sai Mrtyunjayaya namaha.*
(*Om* obeisance to Shri Sai Nath who has conquered death)

15. *Om Shri Sai Amartyaya namah.*
(*Om* obeisance to Shri Sai Nath who is immortal)

16. *Om Shri Sai Martyabhaya-pradaya namah.*
(*Om* obeisance to Shri Sai Nath who grants freedom from the fear of death)

17. *Om Shri Sai Jivadharaya namah.*
(*Om* obeisance to Shri Sai Nath who is the support of all living beings)

18. *Om Shri Sai sarydharyaya namah.*
(*Om* obeisance to Shri Sai Nath who is the support of the Universe)

19. *Om Shri Sai Bhaktavana-samarthaya namah.*
(*Om* obeisance to Shri Sai Nath who grants power to his devotees)

20. *Om Shri Sai Bhaktavana-pratigyaya namah.*
(*Om* obeisance to Shri SaiNath who has vowed to protect his devotees)

21. *Om Shri Sai Anna-Vastra daya namah.*

(*Om* obeisance to Shri Sai Nath, the bestower of good health and freedom from diseases)

22. *Om Shri Sai Dhana-mangalya-pradaya namah.*
    (*Om* obeisance to Shri Sai Nath, who grants wealth and happiness)

23. *Om Shri Sai Riddhi-Siddhi-daya namah.*
    (*Om* obeisance to Shri Sai Nath who bestows psychic and spiritual powers).

24. *Om Shri Sai Putra-mitra-kalatrabandhu-daya namah.*
    (*Om*, obeisance to Shri Sai Nath who grants sons, friends, spouse and relatives)

25. *Om Shri Sai Yoga-kshaema-vahya namah.*
    (*Om* Obeisance to Shri Sai Nath who undertakes the responsibility of providing for and sustaining the devotees)

26. *Om Shri Sai Apad-bandhavaya namah.*
    (*Om* obeisance to Shri Sai Nath who protects his devotees like friends)

27. *Om Shri Sai Marga-bandhava namah.*
    (*Om* obeisance to Shri Sai Nath who is a companion on life's path)

28. *Om Shri Sai Bhukti-mukti-svargapavarga-daya namah.*
    (*Om* obeisance to Shri Sai Nath who is the bestower of worldly pleasure, salvation, heavenly bliss and ultimate beatitude)

29. *Om Shri Sai Priyaya namah.*
    (*Om* Obeisance to Shri Sai Nath, the beloved)

30. *Om Shri Sai Priti-vardhanaya namah.*
    (*Om* obeisance to Shri Sai Nath who provides capacity for boundless love)

31. *Om Shri Sai Antaryamine namah.*
    (*Om* Obeisance to Shri Sai Nath who is familiar with the innermost secrets of heart)

32. *Om Shri Sai Sahhidatmane namah.*
    (*Om* obeisance to Shri Sai Nath who is symbol of truth and pure consciousness)

33. *Om Shri Sai Nityanandya namah.*
    (*Om* obeisance to Shri Sai Nath who is the embodiment of eternal bliss)

34. *Om Shri Sai Parama-sukha-daya namah.*
    (*Om* obeisance to Shri Sai Nath who bestows supreme happiness)

35. *Om Shri Sai Parmeshwaraya namah.*
    (*Om* obeisance to Shri Sai Nath, the Supreme Lord)

36. *Om Shri Sai Bhakti-Shakti-Pradaya namah.*
(*Om* obeisance to Shri Sai Nath who grants strength for devotion)

37. *Om Shri Sai Gyana-vairagya-daya namah.*
(*Om* obeisance to Shri Sai Nath who is the bestower of knowledge and freedom from worldly desires)

38. *Om Shri Sai Prema-Pradaya namah.*
(*Om* obeisance to Shri Sai Nath, who grants love)

39. 39. *Om Shri Sai Sanshaya hirdaya-daurbalyapapa-karma-vasana kshaya namah.*
(*Om*, obeisance to Shri Sai Nath who removes doubts, human weakness and inclination to sinful deeds and desire)

40. *Om Shri Sai Hridaya-granthi-bhedkaya namah.*
(*Om* obeisance to Shri Sai Nath who unbinds all the knots in the heart)

41. *Om Shri Sai karma-dhvansine namah.*
(*Om* obeisance to Shri Sai Nath who destroys the effects of past evil deeds)

42. *Om Shri Sai Shuddha-sattvasthitaya namah.*
(*Om* obeisance to Shri Sai Nath who inspires pure and pious thoughts)

43. *Om, Shri Sai Gunatita-gunatmane namah.*
(*Om* obeisance to Shri Sai Nath who attributes is endowed with all wirtues and yet transcends them all)

44. *Om Shri Sai Ananta-kalyana-gunaya namah.*
(*Om* obeisance to Shri Sai Nath who has limitless virtuous attributes)

45. *Om Shri Sai Amita-parakramaya namah.*
(*Om* obeisance to Shri Sai Nath who has unlimited Supreme power)

46. *Om, Shri Sai Jayine namah.*
(*Om* obeisance to Shri Sai Nath, who is the personification of victory)

47. *Om Shri Sai Durdharshakshobhyaya namah.*
(*Om* obeisance to Shri Sai Nath who is unchallengeable and impossible to defy)

48. *Om Shri Sai Aparajitaya namah.*
(*Om* obeisance to Shri Sai Nath who is unconquerable)

49. 49. *Om Shri Sai Trilokeshu Avighata-gataye namah.*
(*Om*, obeisance to Shri Sainath, the Lord of three worlds whose actions there are no obstructions)

50. 50. *Om Shri Sai Ashakya-rahitaya namah.*
(*Om* obeisance to Shri Sai Nath for whom nothing is impossible)

51. *Om Shri Sai Sarva-Shakti-Murtaye namah.*
    (*Om* obeisance to Shri Sai Nath, who is the Almightly, the Omnipotent)

52. *Om Shri Sai Suroopa-sundaraya namah.*
    (*Om* obeisance to Shri Sai Nath who has a beautiful form)

53. *Om Shri Sai Sulochanaya namah.*
    (*Om* obeisance to Shri Sai Nath whose eyes are beautiful and whose glance is auspicious)

54. *Om Shri Sai Bahurupa-vishva-murtaye namah.*
    (*Om* obeisance to Shri Sai Nath who is of various form, and is manifest in the form of Universe itself)

55. *Om Shri Sai Arupavyakatya namah.*
    (*Om* obeisance to Shri Sai Nath who is formless and whose image cannot be bound in mere word)

56. *Om Shri Sai Achintaya namah.*
    (*Om* obeisance to Shri Sai Nath who is inconceivable and incomprehensible)

57. *Om Shri Sai Sookshmaya namah.*
    (*Om* obeisance to Shri Sai Nath who dwells within every minute creature)

58. *Om Shri Sai Sarvantaryamine namah.*
    (*Om* obeisance to Shri Sai Nath who dwells in all souls)

59. *Om Shri Sai Manovagatitaya namah.*
    (*Om* obeisance to Shri Sai Nath who is the familiar with the thoughts, speech and past of the devotees)

60. *Om Shri Sai Prema-murtaye namah.*
    (*Om* obeisance to Shri Sai Nath who is the embodiment of love and affection)

61. *Om Shri Sai Sulabha-durlabhaya namah.*
    (*Om* obeisance to Shri Sai Nath who is easily accessible to his devotes but inaccessible to the wicked)

62. *Om Shri Sai Asahaya-sahayaya namah.*
    (*Om* obeisance to Shri Sai Nath who is the supporter of the helpless)

63. *Om Shri Sai Anathanatha-decna-bandhave namah.*
    (*Om* obeisance to Shri Sai Nath who is the protector of the unprotected and the kinsman of the destitute)

64. *Om, Shri Sai Sarva-bhara-bhric namah.*
    (*Om* obeisance to Shri Sai Nath who takes over entire burden of all)

65. *Om Shri Sai Akannaneka-karma-sukannine namah.*
(*Om* obeisance to Shri Sai Nath who himself is the non-doer yet inspires others to perform numberless virtuous deeds)

66. *Om Shri Sai Punya-shravana-keertanaya namah.*
(*Om* obeisance to Shri Sai Nath hearing about whom and speaking of whose glories, is an act of religious merit)

67. *Om, Shri Sai Tirthaya namah.*
(*Om* obeisance to Shri Sai Nath who is the embodiment of all holy places)

68. *Om Shri Sai Vasudevaya namah.*
(*Om* obeisance to Shri Sai Nath who is the incarnation of Lord Krishna i.e. Vasudeva)

69. *Om Shri Sai Satam gataya namah.*
(*Om* obeisance to Shri Sai Nath who guides the devotees on the noble and cirtuous path)

70. *Om Shri Sai Sat-parayanaya namah.*
(*Om* obeisance to Shri Sai Nath, who is fully dedicated to truth)

71. *Om Shri Sai Loknathaya namah.*
(*Om* obeisance to Shri Sai Nath who is the Lord of the Universe)

72. *Om, Shri Sai Pavananghayanamah.*
(*Om* obeisance to Shri Sai Nath whuo is pure and free form sins)

73. *Om Shri Sai Amritanshave namah.*
(*Om* obeisance to Shri Sai Nath who is ambrosial)

74. *Om Shri Sai Bhaskara-prabhaya namah.*
(*Om*obeisance to Shri Sai Nath who is lustrous like the sun)

75. *Om Shri Sai Brahmacharya-tapashcharyadi-suvrataya namah.*
(*Om* obeisance to Shri Sai Nath who has adopted celibacy, sceticism, devout austerity and other spiritual disciplines)

76. *Om Shri Sai Sathya-dharma-parayanaya namah.*
(*Om* obeisance to Shri Sai Nath who has taken to truth and righteousness)

77. *Om Shri Sai Siddhesvaraya namah.*
(*Om* obeisance toi Shri Sai Nath who is the incarnation of Shiva i.e. Siddheswar)

78. *Om Shri Sai Siddha-sankalpaya namah.*
(*Om* obeisance to Shri Sai Nath whose determination prevails)

79. *Om Shri Sai Yogeshvaraya namah.*
(*Om* obeisance to Shri Sai Nath who is Yogeshwar i.e. incarnation of Lord Shiva & Lord Krishna)

80. *Om Shri Sai Bhagavati namah.*
(*Om* obeisance to Shri Sai Nath who is the Divinity)

81. *Om Shri Sai Bhakta-vatsalaya namah.*
(*Om* obeisance to Shri Sai Nath who is full of love for his devotees)

82. *Om Shri Sai Satpurushaya namah.*
(*Om* obeisance to Shri Sai Nath the virtuouos, pious & venerable one)

83. *Om Shri Sai Purushottamaya namah.*
(*Om* obeisance to Shri Sai Nath who is the incarnation of the Supreme i.e. Lord Rama)

84. *Om Shri Sai Sathya-tattva-bodhakaya namah.*
(*Om* obeisance to Shri Sai Nath who is the preceptor of the essence of truth)

85. *Om Shri Sai Kamadi-sad-vair-dhvansine namah.*
(*Om* obeisance to Shri Sai Nath who destroys all worldly desires i.e. lust, nager, greed, delusion, ego and envy)

86. 86. *Om Shri Sai Abhed-anand-anubhav-pradaya namah.*
(*Om,* obeisance to Shri Sai Nath to the bestower of the bliss arising from oneness with God)

87. *Om Shri Sai Sama-Sarva-mata-sammmataya namah.*
(*Om,* obeisance to Shri Sai Nath who preaches that all religions are equal)

88. *Om Shri Sai Dakshina-murtayenamah.*
(*Om* obeisance to Shri Sai Nath who is himself Lord Dakshinamurti i.e. Shiva)

89. *Om Shri Sai Venkateshharamanaya namah.*
(*Om* obeisance to Shri Sai Nath who is remains merged in Lord Venkateshwara i.e. Vishnu)

90. *Om Shri Sai Adbutananta-charyayanamah.*
(*Om* obeisance to Shri Sai who is Divine and is ever engrossed in blissful meditation)

91. *Om Shri Sai Prapannarti-haraya namah.*
(*Om* obeisance to Shri Sai Nath who eradicates the distress of those who take refuge in him)

92. *Om Shri Sai Sansara-sarva-duhkha-kshaya-karaya namah.*
    (*Om* obeisance to Shri Sai Nath who destroys all the calamities of the world)
93. *Om Shri Sai Sarvavit-sarvato-mukhaya namah.*
    (*Om* obeisance to Shri Sai Nath who is omniscient and omnipresent)
94. *Om Shri Sai Saravantar-bahih-sthitaya namah.*
    (*Om* obeisance to Shri Sai Nath who exists everywhere and in everything)
95. *Om Shri Sai Sarva-mangala-karaya namah*avde.
    (*Om* obeisance to Shri Sai Nath who is the bestower of auspiciousness)
96. *Om Shri Sai Sarvabhista-pradaya namah.*
    (*Om* obeisance to Shri Sai Nath who established amity and harmony amongst followers of diverse religions leading to a common path of virtue)
97. *Om Shri Sai Samarth Sadguru Sainathaya namah*h.
    (*Om* obeisance to Shri Sai Nath who is the most powerful and the Supreme Guru in Spiritual life).
98. *Om Shri Sai Dakshina-murtayenamah.*
    (Om obeisance to Shri Sai Nath who is himself Lord Dakshinamurti i.e. Shiva)
99. *Om Shri Sai Venkateshharamanaya namah.*e
    (Om, obeisance to Shri Sai Nath who remains merged in Lord Venkateshwara i.e. Vishnu)
100. *Om Shri Sai Adbutananta-charyayanamah.*
    (Om, obeisance to Shri Sai who is Divine and is ever engrossed in blissful meditation)
101. *Om Shri Sai Prapannarti-haraya namah.*
    (Om obeisance to Shri Sai Nath who eradicates the distress of those who take refuge in Him).
102. *Om Shri Sai Sansara-sarva-duhkha-kshaya-karaya namah.*l
    (Om obeisance to Shri Sai Nath who destroys all the calamities of the world)
103. *Om Shri Sai Sarvavit-sarvato-mukhaya namah.*
    (Om obeisance to Shri Sai Nath who is Omniscient and Omnipresent)
104. *Om Shri Sai Saravantar-bahih-sthitaya namah.*ro
    (Om obesisance to Shri Sai Nath who exists everywhere and in everything)

105. *Om Shri Sai Sarva-mangala-karaya namah.*
     (Om obeisance to Shri Sai Nath who is the bestower of auspiciousness)
106. *Om Shri Sai Sarvabhista-pradaya namah.*
     (Om obeisance to Shri Sai Nath who grants all desires)
107. *Om Shri Sai Samarasa-sanmarya-sthapanaya namah.*
     (Om, obeisance to Shri Sai Nath who established amity and harmony amongst followers of diverse religions leading to a common path of virtue).
108. *Om Shri Sai Samarth Sadguru sainathaya namah. and*
     (Om obeisance to Shri Sai Nath who is the most powerful and the Supreme Guru in Spiritual life).

BIBLIOGRAPHY
ON SRI SHIRDI SAI BABA

1. Agaskar, P.S., *Sri Sai Leelamrita*. Shirdi: Shri Sai Baba Sansthan, 1989. (In Hindi).

2. Aiyer, P.S.V., *Perfect Masters*. Calcutta: Author, 1973.

3. Ajgaonkar, Chakor, *The Divine Glory Sri Shirdi Sai Baba*. New Delhi: Diamond Pocket Books, 1998, pp. 126. (Ed. S.P. Ruhela).

4. _____, *Tales From Sai Baba's Life*. New Delhi: Diamond Pocket Books, 1998, pp. 183 (Ed. S.P. Ruhela)

5. _____, *What Saints & Maters Say on the Realm of Sadhna*. New Delhi: Diamond Pocket Books, 1998, pp. 88 (Ed. S.P. Ruhela)

6. _____, *Foot Prints of Shirdi Sai*. New Delhi: Diamond Pocket Books, 1998. (Ed. S.P. Ruhela)

7. _____, *Sri Shirdi Sai Baba Ki Divya Jeevan Kahani*. New Delhi: Diamond Pocket Books, 1998, pp. 164. (Trans. J.P. Srivastava; Ed. S.P. Ruhela). (In Hindi)

8. _____, *Sri Sai Geetayan*. New Delhi: Diamond Pocket Books, 1998, pp. 93, (Trans. J.P. Srivastava, (Ed. S.P. Ruhela): (In Hindi).

9. Anand, Sai Sharan, *Sri Sai Baba*. Bombay: Dinpushpa Prakashan, 1989. (In Marathi/Gujarati).

10. _____, *Sri Sai Baba*. New Delhi: Sterling Publishers, 1997. (Trans. V.B. Kher) (In English)

11. _____, *Sai; The Supeman*. Shirdi: Shri Sai Baba Sansthan, 1991.

12. _____, Awasthi, Dinesh & Blitz Team of Investigators, "Sai Baba The Saint of Shirdi", *Blitz* (Bombay Weekly), Nov. 6 & 13, 1976. (Article)

13. Balakrishna, V.V., Sri *Sayee Smaromstroram*.

14. Balse, Mayah, *Mystics and Men of Miracles in India*. New Delhi: Orient Paper backs, 1978.

15. Bharadawaja, Acharya, E., *Sai Baba The Master*. Ongole: Sri Guru Paduka Publications, 1991. (III Ed.)

16. Bharati, Sushil, *Sai Darshan Sagar*: Sai Prakashan, 1995, p. 62, (In Hindi).

17. _____, *Sai Upasana*. Sagar, Sai Prakashan, 1995, pp. 36, (In Hindi).

18. _____, *Sai Kripa Ke Pawan Kshan*. Sagar: Sai Prakashan, 1995. (in Hindi).

19. _____, *Sai Dham*. Sagar: Sai Prakashan, 1996. (In Hindi).

20. _____, *Sai Sukh Chalisa*, Sagar, Sai Prakasthan.

21. _____, *Sai Sandesh*. Sagar: Sai Prakashan.

22. _____, *Sai Mahima*. Sagar: Sai Prakashan.

23. _____, *Bachchon Ke Sai*. Sagar: Sai Prakashan.

24. _____, *Sai Geetmala*. Sagar: Sai Prakashan.

25. _____, *Sai Chintan*. New Delhi: Diamond Pocket Books, 1998, pp. 110.

26. _____, *Sai Sri Ke Adbhut Devdoota*. New Delhi: Diamond Pocket Books, 1998, pp. 216.

27. _____, *Sai Kripa Ke Pavan Kshan*. New Delhi: Diamond Pocket Books, 1998, pp. 126.

28. _____, *Sai Sarita*. New Delhi: Diamond Pocket Books, 1998, 1998, pp. 227.

29. Bharucha, Perin S., *Sai Baba of Shirdi*. Shirdi: Shri Sai Baba Sansthan, 1980.

30. Bharvani, A.D. & Malhotra, V., *Shirdi Sri Baba and Sathya Sai Baba are One and Same*. Bombay: Sai Sahitya Samiti, 1983.

31. Bhisma, K.J., *Sadguru Sai Nath Sagunopasama*. Shirdi: Shri Sai Baba Sansthan, 1986. (Marathi).

32. Chatturvedi, B.K. Sai Baba of Shirdi. New Delhi: Diamond Pocket Books, 1998. (Revised Ed. S.P. Ruhela).

33. Chopra, Parveen, 'Shirdi Sai Baba: Beacon of Hope', *Life Positive* (Monthly), New Delhi; Magus Pvt. Ltd. S-487, Greater Kailash, Part I, Jan. 1998, pp. 16-21 (Article).

34. Das, M. Machinder, *Sai-The God on Earth*.

35. Ganu, Das, *Shri SaiNath Stavan Manjari*. Shirdi: Shri Sai Baba Sansthan, (English Trans. Zarine Taraporewala, Bombay: Sai Dhun Enterprises, 1987).

36. _____, *Sai Harkathas*. Madras: All India Sai Samaj, Mylapore.

37. *Gems of Wisdom*, Nagpur: Sri Publicatins.

38. *Guide to Holy Shirdi*. Shirdi: Shri Sai Baba Sansthan.

39. Gunaji, N., Shri Sai Satcharita, Shirdi: Sai Baba Sansthan, 1944.

40. Harper, Marvin Henry, 'The Fakir: Sri Sai Baba of Shirdi' in *Gurus, Swamis, and Avataras: Spiritual Masters and Their American Disciplines*. Philadelphia: Westminister Press, 1972. (Article).

41. Hattingatti, Shaila, *Sai's Story*. Bombay: India Book House, 1991.

42. Hemadpant, *Shri Sai Satcharita*, Shirdi: Shri Sai Baba Sansthan, (In Marathi, Hindi, Gujarati, Telugu, etc.)

43. *Is Sai Baba Living and Helping Now?* Madras: All India Sai Samaj. Mylapore.

44. Jha, Radhanandan *Sai Baba: Sab Ka Malik Ek Hai*. Patna, Sri Sai Baba Trust, I-A, Aney Marg, 1997, pp. 65. (In Hindi).

45. Joshi, H.S., *Origin and Development of Dattatreya Worship in India*. Baroda: M.S. University of Baroda, 1965. (Chapter 12).

46. Kakade, R.C. & Veerbhadra. A., *Shirdi to Puttaparthi*. Hyderabad: Ira Prakastha, 1989. (In English & Hindi).

47. Kamath, M.V. & Kher, V.B., *Sai Baba of Shirdi: A Unique Saint*. Bombay: Jaico Publishing House, 1991.

48. Karunanada, Swami, *The Uniqueness of the Significance of Sri Sai Baba*. Panvel: Sri Bhagwati Sai Sansthan.

49. Kevin, Shephered, R, D., *Gurus Discovered* (Biographies of Sai Baba & Upasani Maharaj) Cambridge: Anthropoprahia Publicatiuon 1984.

50. Khaparde, G., *Sources of Sai History*. Bangalore: Jupiter Press, 1956.

51. _____, *Shirdi Diary*. Shirdi: Shri Sai Baba Sansthan.

52. Krishna, Indira Anantha, Sai Baba of Shirdi. (Adarsh Chitra Katha-Pictorial).

53. Krishna, S. Gopala K., *Understanding Shirdi Sai*. Hyderabad: Shirdi Sai Mandiram, Chikkadpalli, 1997, pp. 227.

54. Kumar, Anil, *Doctor of Doctors Sri Sai Baba*. Nagpur: Sri Sai Clinic.

55. Kumar: Sudhir, *Shirdi Ke Sai Baba: Chalisa aur Bhajan*. New Delhi: Author, (In Hindi).

56. Maneey, S., *The Eternal Sai*. New Delhi: Diamond Pocket Books, 1997.

57. Mani, Amma B., *Sai Leela Taranagini*. (Parts 1 & 2). Guntur: Authoress.

58. Mehta, Rao Bahadur Harshad B., *The Spiritual Symphony of Shree Sainath of Shirdi*. Baroda: Rana & Patel Press. 1952.

59. Mehta, Vikas, *Hridaya Ke Swami Shri Sai Baba*. New Delhi: Siddartha Publicatins, 10 DSIDC, Scheme 11. Okhla Industrial Area Part 11, 1995. (In Hindi).

60. _____, *Karunamaya Shri Sai Baba*. New Delhi: Siddartha Publications, 1996. (In Hindi).

61. Mittal, N., *World Famous Modern Gurus and Guru Cults*. New Delhi: Family Books, F 2/16, Darya Ganj.

62. Monayan, S.V.G.S., *Sai the Mother and Ansuya, the Amma*. Masulipattanm, Sai Ma Gurudatta Publications, 18/286, Ambani Agraham.

63. Munsiff, Abdul Ghani, "Hazrat Sai Baba", *The Mehar Baba Journal* (Ahmednagar): Vol. 1 1938-39 (Article.)

64. Murthy, G.S., *Understanding Shirdi Sai Baba*. Hyderabad: Sri Shirdi Sai Prema Mandiram, 1977.

65. Narasimhaswamy ji, *Who is Sai Baba of Shirdi?* Madras: All India Sai Samaj, 1980.

66. _____, *Sri Sai Vachnamrita*. Madras: All India Sai Samaj.

67. _____, *Sai Baba's Charters, and Sayings*. Madras: All India Sai Samaj, 1980.

68. _____, *Devotees' Experiences of Sai Baba*. Madras: All India Sai Samaj, 1965. Hyderabad: 1989.

69. _____, *Glimpses of Sai Baba*. Madras: All India Sai Samaj.

70. _____, *Life of Sai Baba*. Madras: All India Sai Samaj.

71. Narayan, B.K., *Saint Shah Waris Ali and Sai Baba*. New Delhi Vikas Publishing House, 1995, pp. 112.

72. Narayanan, C.R., *A Century of Poems on Sri Sai Baba of Shirdi*. Madras: Author, 1994 (11 Ed.)

73. Nimbalkar, M.B., *Sri Sai Satya Charitra*. Poona: Author, 1993 (In Marathi).

74. 108 Names of Sri Shirdi Sai Baba. New Delhi: Sterling Publishers, 1997. Pp. 108. (Pocket Book).

75. Osburne, Arthur. *The Incredible Sai Baba*. Delhi: Orient Longmans, 1970.

76. Paranjape, Makarand, 'Journey to Sai Baba', *Life Positive*, New Delhi: Magus Media Pvt. Ltd. Jan. 1998, pp. 22-23 (Article).

77. Parchure, D.D., *Children's Sai Baba*, Shirdi: Shri Sai Baba Sansthan, 1983. (In English, Hindi)

78. Parchure, S.D., *Shree Sai Mahimashstra*. Bombay: Tardeo Book Depot, 1990.

79. Parthsarthi, R., *Gold Who Walked on Earth*. New Delhi: Sterling Publishers, 1996.

80. _____, *Apostle of Love: Saint Saipadananda*, New Delhi: Sterling Publishers, 1997.

81. *Pictorial Sai Baba*. Shirdi: Sai Baba Sansthan, 1968.

82. Pradhan, M.V., Sri *Sai Baba of Shirdi*: Shirdi Sri Sai Baba Sansthan, 1973.

83. Ramalingaswami, *The Golden Words of Shri Sai Baba*. Shirdi, 1983.

84. _____, *Ambrosia in Shirdi*. Shirdi: Shri Sai Baba Sansthan, 1984.

85. Ramakrishna, K.K., *Sai Baba The Perfect Master*. Pune: Meher Era Publications, Avatar Meher Baba Poona Centre, 441/1, Somwarpeth, 1991.

86. Rao. A.S., *Life History of Shirdi Sai Baba*. New Delhi: Sterling Publishers, 1997, pp. 228 (Eng. Trans. Thota Bhaskar Rao).

87. Rao, A.S., *In Search of the Truth*, New Delhi: Sterling Publishing, 1998.

88. Rao, B. Umamaheswara, Thus Spoke Sri Shirdi Sai Baba. New Delhi: Diamond Pocket Books, 1997. (Ed. S.P. Ruhela)

89. Rao, B. Umamaheswara, *Communications From the Spirit of Shri Shirdi Sai Baba*. New Delhi: Diamond Pocket Books, 1998, pp. 160 (Ed. S.P. Ruhela).

90. _____, *The Spiritual Philosophy of Sri Shirdi Sai Baba*. New Delhi: Diamond Pocket Books, 1998. (Revised edition of *Bhava Lahari: Voice of Sri Sai Baba,* 1993) Ed. S.P. Ruhela.

91. _____, *Sai Leela Tarangini*. Guntur: Author, Flat 12, 'Sai Towers', 4th Line, Brindavan Gardens, Guntur-522006). (In Telugu).

92. _____, *Sai Tatwa Sandesham* (Part I & II). Guntur: Author, (In Telugu).

93. _____, *Sai Tatwa Sandesham*. Guntur: Author. (In English)

94. Rao, evata Sabhe, *Baba Sai*. Hyderabad: 76, N.H.I., Type Ramchandrapuram.

95. Rao, M.S., *Divine Life Story of Sri Sudguru KrishnaprIyaji*. Burla: Author, 1995.

96. Rao, Devata Sabha, *Baba Sai* Hyderabad: 76 N.H.I., Type 5, Ramchandrapuram (BHEL).

97. Rao, K.V. Raghva, *Message of Sri Sai Baba*. Madras: All India Sai Samaj, 1984. (Ed. By Dwarkamai Trust, Hyderabad, 1995).

98. _____, *Message of Shri Sai Baba*. Hyderabad: Shri Shirdi Publications Trust, 1992

99. _____. *Enlightenment From Sri Baba on Salvation of Soul*. Hyderabad: Dwarkamai Publications, 1994.

100. _____. *Golden Voice and Divine Touch of Sri Sai Baba*. Hyderabad: Dwarkamai Publications, 1997.

101. Rao, M. Rajeswara, *Shri Shirdi Sai Baba and His Teaching*. New Delhi: Diamond Pocket Books, 1998, pp. 76 (Ed. S.P. Ruhela) (Mini Book).

102. Rigopoulos, Antonio, *The Life and Teachings of Sri Sai Baba of Shirdi* (Ph. D. Thesis) New York: State University, 1992. (Delhi—110007):

Sri Sadguru Publications, Indian Book Centre 40/5, Shakti Nagar 1995).

103. Ruhela, Sushila Devi, *Sri Shirdi Sai Bhajan Sangraha (Samprna)*. New Delhi: Diamond Pocket Books, 1998, pp. 287. (In Hindi)

104. ——, *Sri Shirdi Sai Bhajan Sangraha*. New Delhi: Diamond Pocket Books, 1998. Pp. 96.

105. ——, *Sri Shirdi Sai Bhajanmala*. New Delhi Diamond Pocket Books, 1998, pp. 135. (Mini Book)

106. Ruhela, S.P., My Life with Shirdi Sai Baba—*Thrilling* Memories of Shivamma Thayee. Faridabad: Sai Age Publications, 1992. (New Delhi-110002: M.D. Publications, 11, Darya Ganj, 1995).

107. ——, *Sri Shirdi Sai Baba Avatar.* Faridabad: Sai Age Publications, 1992.

108. ——, *What Researchers say on Sri Shirdi Sai Baba*. Faridabad: Sai Age Publications, 1994. (II Ed. New Delhi-110002: M.D. Publications, 1995).

109. ——, *Sri Shirdi Sai Baba: The Universal* Master. New Delhi; Sterling Publishers, L-10, Green Park Extension, 1994. (Reprint 1995, 1996).

110. ——, *The Sai Trinity*—Sri Shirdi Sai, Sri Sathya Sai, Sri Prema Sai Incarnations, New Delhi-110014; Vikas Publishing House, 1994.

111. ——, *Sai Puran*, Delhi: Sadhna Pocket Books, 1996.

112. ——, Shirdi Sai Baba Speaks to Yogi Spencer in Vision, New Delhi: Vikas Publishing House, 1998.

113. ——, *Sant Shiromani Sri Shirdi* Sai Baba, New Delhi: Sterling Publishers, 1997.

114. ——, (Ed) *Divine Revelations of a Sai Devotee*. New Delhi: Diamond Pocket Books, 1997, pp. 270.

115. ——, (Ed.) *Sri Shirdi Sai Bhajan-mala*, (In Roman) New Delhi: Diamond Pocket Books, 1998, pp. 111.

116. ——, *Shirdi Sai Baba's Mother and Her* Re-*incarnation*. New Delhi: Aravali Books International (W-30, Okhla Industrial Area, Phase-II, New Delhi-110020). 1998, pp. 45. (Pocket Books).

117. ——, (Ed.) New Light on Sri Shirdi Sai Baba. New Delhi: Diamond Pocket Books, 1998.

118. ——, (Ed.) *Shirdi Sai Ideal and The Sai World*. New Delhi: Diamond Pocket Books. 1998.

119. (Ed.), *The Immortal Fakir of Shirdi*, New Delhi: Diamond Pocket Books, 1998.

120. ——, My *Life with Sri Shirdi Sai Baba*. (In Japanese).

121. *Sai Amritvani* (By:B.K. Bassi, 1/42, Panchsheel Park, New Delhi An excellent melodious prayer to Sri Shirdi Sai Baba. This very impressive impressive and highly elevasting prayer is mmost attentatively listened by countless Sai devotee throughout the world on Thursday—Sai Baba's favorite day. It may bedowsnloaded from: http://groups.yahoo.com/group/ mysaiu baba20

122. *Sadguru Nityananada Bhagavan The Eternal Entity*. Kanhangad Pin Code 671315. Kerala: Swami Nityananda Ashram, 1996 (IIEd.)

123. *Sai Ma Ki Kripavrasti*—Souvenir, Mussorie, Sai Darbar, 2, Garden Reach. Kulri, 1997. (In Hindi)

124. *Sai Sandesh* (Sri Shirdi Sai Messages give to Devotee). (Parts I & II Hyderabad: Sai Prabha Publications (3050697/87. Telugu Academy Lane, Vithalwadi)

125. Seshadri, H., *Glimpses of Divinity—A Profile of Shri Saidas Babaji*, Bombay: Shri Bhopal Singh Hingharh. (It shows that Sri Shirdi Sai Baba and Sri Sathya Sai Baba are one and the same.)

126. *Sai Sudha*. Magazine—Golden Jubilee Issue, Special Number, Madras: All India Sai Samaj.

127. Savitri, Raghnath, *Sai Bhajanmlal*. Mumbai: Balaji Bagya, Sudarshan Art Printing Press, 5 Vadla Udhyog Bhavan, Mumbai-400031, 1995 (24th Ed. 1986) (In Marathi). (It contains folk songs and Bhajans on Sri Shirdi Sai since his lifetime.)

128. Shepherd, R.D. *Gurus Rediscovered*. Cambridge: Anthropological Publications, 1985. Biographies of Sri Shirdi Sai Baba and Sri Upasani Maharaj).

129. *Shirdi Darshan*, Shirdi, Shri Sai Baba Sansthan, 1966, 1972. (Pictorial).

130. Shirdi Ke Sai Baba. Delhi: Ratna Book Co. (In Hindi)

131. Shivnesh Swamiji, *Sri Sai Bavani*, Shirdi.

132. *Shree Sai Leela: Sachitra Jeevandarshan*. 1939.

133. *Shree Sai Leela*, March—April 1992. (First Convention of Sai Devotees).

134. *Silver Jubilee Souvenir*. Madras: All India Sai Samaj, 1996.

135. *Spiritual Recipes*, Bangalore: Sri Sai Baba Spiritual Centre, Sri Sai Baba Mandir Marg, T. Nagar.

136. Singh. I.D, *Gagar Main Sai Kshir Sagar*. Faridabad; Sai Age Publications, 1996. (In Hindi). (New Delhi: Diamond Pocket Books, 1997)

137. Somsundaram, A., The *Dawn of a New Era: The Message of Master Ram Ram And the Need for Universal Religion*. Markapur (A.P.): Divine Centre, 1970.

138. Somsundaran, A., *The Dawn of New Era: The Vision of Master Rishi Ram Ram*. Markapur: Divine Centre, 1969.

139. *Souvenir: Maha Samadhi Souvenir*. Madras: All India Sai Samaj, 1966.

140. *Souvenir*, Delhi: Shri Sai Bhakta Samaj, 1972.

141. *Souvenir*. Secunderabad: Sri Sai Baba Samaj, 1975.

142. *Souvenir*: Secunderabad: Sri Sai Baba Samaj, 1990.

143. *Souvenir*: 26th All India Sai Devotees Convention: Golden Jubilee Year, 1991.

144. *Sri Harikatha—Special Number on Shirdi Ke Sai Baba*. New Delhi: Srikath, B-5/73, Azad Apartments, Sri Aurobindo Marg (Bilingual).

145. Sri *Sainath Mananan*. (Sanskrit with English). A Symposium: All India Sai Samaj, Mylapore.

146. *Sri Sai Spiritual Centre and The Trinity* (Sai Baba, Sri Narasimha Swamiji, Sri Radhakrishna Swamiji). Bangalore: Sri Sai Spiritual Centre, Sai Baba Mandir Road, Ist Block, Thyagraja Nagar, Bangalore-560028), pp. 36.

147. Steel, Brian, *Sathya Sai Baba Compendium*. York Beach (USA): Samuel Weisner, 1997. Pp. 244-248.

148. Subramaniam, C.S., *The Life and Teachings of Great Sai Baba*.

149. *Tales of Sai Baba*. Bombay: India Book House, 1995. (Pictorial)

150. Tanavde, S.V. May Sai Baba Bless Us All. Bombay: Taradeo Book Depot.

151. Taraporewala, Zarine, *Worship of Manifested Sri Sadguru Sainath*. (English translation of K. J. Bhismas Sri Sadguri Sainath Sahunopasan). Bombay: Saidhun Enterprses 1990.

152. Towards *Godhood*—Messages *Revieved by Autowriting at the Centre* (Third Annual Number). Coimbatore: The Spiritual Healing Centre, 1945. Pp. 6-8 (It contains some Spirit Message on and from Sai Baba received in 1940).

153. Uban, Sujan Singh, 'Sai Baba of Shirdi', *The Gurus of India*. London: 1977.

154. *Verma, Subha, "Shirdi, Sab Boom Sai Ki . . ." Saptahik* Hindustan, Nov. 12, 1992, pp. 17-25. (In Hindi). (Article).

155. Verma, Subha, *Sri Das Ganukrita Char Adhyaya*. New Delhi: Ansh Media Expression. Subha Verma, A-35, Chittaranjan Park, New Delhi-110019), 1997, pp. 46.

156. White, Charles, S. J., 'The Sai Baba Movement: Approaches to the Study of India, Saints', *The Journal of Asian Studies*, Vol. XXXI, (Article) No. 4, August 1972.

SECTION II

BENIFICIARIES' EXPERIENCES OF BABA'S GRACE

"Whoever thinks of Me (looks to Me) with undivided
Bhakti, I will protect him. It is my duty to do so."

-Sri Shirdi Sai Baba

Many thrilling experiences of Sri Shirdi Sai Baba's miraculous grace during Hs life time (1838-1918) were recorded by His devotes and beneficiaries like Hemadpant, Swami Sharananda, etc, and in some books by other writers of the post-*Samnadhi*. Period. In January 2005, a book *'Sai Baba's 261 Leelas: A Treasure House of Miracles'* (ISBN-10: 8120727274. ISBN-13: 978-8120727274) by Balkrishna Panday was published by Sterling Publishers, New Delhi, in which Sai Baba's life time miracles have been very briefly and scientifically compiled. That book should be read by all Sai devotees.

In 2007 I had compiled 122 incidents of Sai grace experienced by many post-*samadhi* period beneficiaries.. They were published. Many such experiences of the beneficiaries of the post-*samadhi* have been and and are still being reported in various Sai journals and on the internet

Here about 200 incidents are being mentioned;

1. BABA'S BLESSING GOT HER A SON (1921)

Smt. Chandrabai w/o late Sri Rama Chandra Borkar was visiting Shirdi and Sai Baba since 1898. She had innumerable instances of help from Baba before his *Mahasamadhi*. The one to follow, is an instance of Sai Baba's miraculous grace after his Mahasamadhi. It may be noted that she was one of the persons who was near Baba when He breathed His last. She gave water to Sai Baba in His last moments. In 1918, she was 48 years old and had not conceived. She yearned for a child, even at that age. The people and doctors around her ignored her desire, as conception at that age was inconceivable. In 1918, Baba asked her what her desire was, She replied that she need not mention, as He knew it. In 1921, her menses stopped. Dr. Purandhare examining her diagnosed that she was suffering from internal tumor and proposed operation. Her faith in Baba was such that she told her husband and other relatives, that she would wait for ten months and then decide. In her 51st year, three years and two days after Baba's *Mahasamadhi*, she gave birth to a son at Chembur in Bombay. At the time of delivery she had neither the services of a doctor nurse or any medicine.

2. BABA'S HELP TO DEVOTEE'S FAMILY (1922, 1934)

When Baba accepts a person as His devotee. He takes full responsibility for his welfare. Sri S.B.N. Dahanukar visited Sai Baba at Shirdi and had His *darshan* in 1912. He had lot of experiences when Baba was alive. His parents were arranging for his second marriage. Two girls were offered, one a wealthy one and another, a girl from a poor family. An ignorant man, naturally, is attracted to wealth. But Baba knows better. Baba appearing in his mother's dream in 1922, showed the girl to be married, who happened to be the girl from the poor family. They were married in 1922.

In 1934, Shri Dahanuhar's son had measles, pneumonia and abscess in the chest. As the child was weak, the doctor was hesitant to operate on the abscess. Sri Dahanukar applied anti some thing over the abscess and the abscess opened up. The doctor was still hesitant. So Sri Dahanukar relied on his own doctor, Sri Sai Baba. He applied Baba's *udhi* on the wound and prayed to Sai Baba. His friend one Vasanth Rao Jadhav, who later become D.C. of Poona, who was watching, asked him, whether *udhi* could cure the would. "Yes" replied Dahanukar. "In what time?" asked his friend. "In just 24 hours", said Dahanukar. That night Baba appearing in his dream chided Dahanukar. "Why did you say 24 hours, you should have said immediately. Your faith should be such". Dahanukar apologized to Baba in the dream. The next morning the wound was healed.

3. BABA SAVED DEVOTEE'S WIFE FROM UNDER RUNNING TRAIN (1927)

In 1927, a couple was returning to Bombay by train after participating in the Ramanavami celebrations in Shirdi. The wife alighted from the train to fetch water. As she was getting into the compartment with the jug of water she slipped and fell down under the carriage. The train had started. The train could be stopped only after it had moved some distance. Everyone thought that the woman had been crushed under the wheels of the train. But the woman, amazingly was back on the platform, unhurt, and smiling. As she fell down she remembered Baba. She said that Baba appeared from nowhere, held her tight in the space between the wheels and the platform till the train passed. Incredible! but it has come from the horse's mouth!

4. BABA'S GRACE IN DAKSHINESWAR (1922)

In 1928 I went to Dakshineswar to see the places and things of interest. I got the service of a local man to act as my cicerone and he showed me the Kali figure that Paramahamsa worshipped and other images. I looked at Kali standing outside the worship room and passed on. I was anxious to see the tiny image of Ramlal that sported as a living boy with Paramahamsa, and told my guide to show me Ramlal. He took me to one of the temples and showed me a huge image and said "This is Ramlal". I said it could not be. The man replied that he, as the local man should know and that I, as a stranger, could not possibly be better informed. I had to apologize and I wondered what to think of the Ramlal. I had read about in Paramahansa's life. Just at this juncture, a *pujari* (priest) of these temples came and inquired if I was from Deccan. I replied I was. Then he said he would show me real Kali and every other image at close quarters with full detail. I said I had just seen them. He Insisted. He did not take any money from me. The reason for his persistent request was that he has been instructed in a dream overnight that a devotee from Deccan would be coming on the following day and that he was to take him to all the images and help him to worship them. Thus assured, I followed him. He took me inside the *Garbhagrah*, the holy of holies of Kali and said I was free to touch the image and worship as I liked. Next he said that he would show me Ramlal. I said I had been shown a huge figure as Ramlal by my guide. The Pujari chided my cicerone for deceiving me and then took up the tiny image of Ramlal that Paramahansa had played with and placed it on my lap. Thus all my expectations were fulfilled beyond measure all through the grace of Sai who is no other than Ramkrishna.

-*(Sri M.B. Rege, Retd. High Court Judge, Indore)*
From: Devotees, Experiences Sai Baba (Part I)

5. BABA CURED AN ECZEMA PATIENT (1929)

In 1929, one Appaji Sutar of Shirdi had been suffering from Eczema. He found no cure. He went to the nearby Kopergaon Government Hospital and was admitted as an in-patient. He spent Rs. 200 there, but got no cure. He went to Nasik and was hospitalized again there. He had already been there for eight days. On the eight night Baba appeared in his dream and said "Go back to Shirdi nad read Purana". Appaji said he had been hospitalized for cure of Eczema. But Baba insisted that he go back to Shirdi, read Purana and apply *udhi*. Accordingly, he came away from the hospital and began reading Purana everyday at 4 pm before Baba's photo and began applying *udhi*. In seven days he was completely cured. There was no trace of Eczema, which had troubled him for so long.

The same Appaji had another experience in 1932. He owed Rs. 350 to one Multan Fatehehand Marwadi of Shirdi, who was threatening to sue him and get him arrested. The frightened and worried Appaji turned to Baba for help Baba appeared in his dream and asked him to recite certain stanzas of the Gita. His debt would be cleared. Sri Appaji followed Baba's instruction. The creditor came to appaji's House and Appaji was naturally frightened, but the Marwadi came to tell appaji to build a house for him, and on the completion of the house, he would write off the debt. Appaji gratefully accepting the offer and completed the construction in a month's time. The bond was returned. Appaji tore away the bond, expressing heartfelt thanks to Baba.

6. HOW BABA TESTED DEVOTEE'S FAITH (1936)

After Sri Narasimha Swami JI, the famous Sai *pracharak*, realized Sri Sai Bai in 1936, he called upon Sri Upasani Baba, in Sakori, to pay his respects. At that time, another devotee of Sri Sai Baba, who later came to be called as Sri Ram Baba, who lived for more than 140 years, was also present there. Sri Upasani Baba arranged for an open feast. As the feast was about to end, an old man suffering from leprosy came along. He had a frightening appearance. He had only one eye, blood and pus were oozing from his disfigured lips, nose and eyes. He had open ulcers all over his body; an awful stench was also emanating from him. One can imagine Sri Ram Baba's bewilderment, when Sri Upasani Baba said Baba said "Feed the old man with your own hands, as he is not able to eat himself." Sri Ram Baba pulled himself up as best as he could and started feeding the leper. He, however, took great care to see that his hand did not touch the bleeding lips of the leper. As a result of this, some of the food kept spilling.

After the leper had eaten and walked away, Sri Upasani Baba now asked Sri Narasimha Swamiji "Pick up the food and eat it". For the onlookers, to eat the food that had been contaminated by the bleeding lips of the leper looked horrendous. But a realized soul that he was Sri Narasimha Swamiji took the food and ate up all the remnants without any hesitation. Every one was amazed. Sri Upasani Baba then told the onlookers "Did you see how swiftly the old man walked away? Is it possible for one so terribly afflicted to walk like that? Do you know who came to you in the garb of the repulsive leper? It was none other than the Lord Sai Baba Himself."

7. BABA'S INVISIBLE HELP IN TEMPLE CONSTRUCTION (1940)

Sri Ramanaiah of Gudur was, in 1940, directed by Baba in a dream that he should build His temple in the site north to his house. The site did not belong to Ramanaiah but to another person, laborer by name Pichivadu. Ramanaiah was a devotee of Baba but the other person had not heard of Baba. Soon after Ramanaiah's dream Pichivadu saw in the jungle where he was working, a fakir, who told him to hand over his site to Ramanaiah for the construction of Baba's temple. The direction was repeated a second time. Pichivadu confronted Sri Ramanaiah with these facts, and when asked how the fakir looked, he showed him Baba's picture in Ramanaiah's house. Pichivadu soon after gifted his plot of land to Ramanaiah. Baba told Ramanaiah in his dream the dimensions and specifications of the temple to be built. When people came to know about these happening, some people gave bricks for the walls, some for the foundations and terrace, some provided rafters, some provided wood for doors etc. Pichavadu also contributed with his labour, with the help of the people a small temple of the size of 10 feet × 8 feet was built in less than four weeks time. Dr. M.K. Rajagopalachari of Nellore contributed a Baba portrait. Sri Narasimha SwamIJi, Sri Panini Rao and others attended the temple opening ceremony. This is the first temple of Sai Baba in South India.

8. BABA'S MYSTERIOUS GRACE EXPERIENCED BY A BENGALI SAI DEVOTEE (1940-1969)

The way of showering Lord Sai's blessings on His devotees is miraculous beyond any expectations. Sometimes he used to say that 'I am Allah *(Mein Allah Hu)*, some time He used to say *'Allah Malik'* (Allah is Almighty). The following accounts will prove how the blessings are showered by Him on His devotees:

Introductory (1940-41 onward) – How Sai Puja was initiated and *Bangiya Sai Sadguru Sangha* was established?

The Bangiya Sai Sangha was established in 1940 as an inevitable sequel to the miraculous recovery of late Himadri Bose, the thirteen year old son of Sri J.N. Bose, from a critical illness with the help of holy '*Udhi*' presented by the Calcutta Sai Bhakta Samaj, to Sri Bose. This incident instilled firm faith in Baba in the minds of members of the family of Sri Bose who started a small association in his house at 15A, Rajani Gupta Row, Calcutta, with the photo presented by Sri Naidu along with the members of the Calcutta Sai Samaj. In accordance with the instructions of Sri Naidu, daily puja commended in our house in a very humble way.

In 1941, His Holiness B.V. Narasimha Swami came to Calcutta and graced Sri J.N. Bose's house and formally opened the Sangha at the above address by worshipping the coloured photo of Sri Baba (Dwarka Mai type) presented by Sri Naidu on the "Mahasamadhi Day". This photo is being worshipped daily in the Puja Mandir of our Sangha for more than three decades.

9. GUIDANCE TO SHIRDI VISIT IN A DREAM IN A MIRACULOUS WAY (1942)

In this yea I got a dream one night that Sri Baba has been guiding me to Shirdi by holding my hand up the staircases of Dwarkamayi. I had no idea where Dwarkamai was and in my busy preoccupations in the office work during the four years, I forgot all about it. But the dream was still vividly remembered by me.

Visit to Shirdi in 1943.

But wonder of wonders Sri Baba did not forget it. While staying on my long official tour in Bombay for a month the same S.P.R. Naidu, who was transferred from Calcutta to Bombay exactly at the time, arranged for our trip to Shirdi along with some other devotees in April 1943. Before we started for Shirdi, I met Rao Bahadur M.W. Pradhan, one of the most favorite personal associates of Sri Baba at his Santa Cruz residence who embraced me and made all arrangements of our comfortable stay at Shirdi which was at the time, a village of mud houses with no facility for food and accommodation. We had wonderful experience during our trip to Shirdi. We met Sri Narayan Maharaj, an *Avatar,* and Sri Baba's devotee who blessed us at a road side station; In the night with storms and rain at the Kopergaon Station – we were accommodated at the station by one Sri Naidu, the Station Master an receptionist of Sri Baba, of course without any food. In the next morning we came to the Kopergaon town and met one advocate, a friend of one (Mr. D.K. Deshpande) of the members of our party, who gave us tea and enquired about our object of Shirdi trip. He called me 'a fool' for coming all the way from Calcutta for visiting Shirdi and advised me to go back to Calcutta."

Test of His Devotee by Baba

This is usual first test of faith of devotees by Baba. Anyhow we did not pay any heed to the advocate's advice and went straight to Shirdi and offered our Puja in the Samadhi Mandir where I placed a big picture drawn up in black chalk by an inspired devotee of Sri Baba working under Sri Baba's instruction at B.B. Dadar, and a silver idol (presented by Sri. S.P.R. Naidu) which are being daily worshipped in our Mandir since 1943.

Then I went up the steps of Dwarkamayee in the same way as I saw in my dream a year back and prostrated at Sri Baba's feet in the sitting position of photo the type of which was installed in my house in 1941. Naturally I felt a thrill in my mind and remembered Sri Baba's prophetic saying "He who steps up "DwarkamayI" will have no wants in his life". We visited the Holy *Neem* tree under which Sri Baba used to sit and were amazed to taste the leaves of one branch as sweet and then of another branch of the same tree as bitter.

Then we saw His daily associate, Abdulla Bhai who embraced us and blessed us in answer to his query that we were coming from Calcutta. But this visit besides being a profound source of inspiration of Sai faith, had struck me with remarkably wonderful experience by noticing the synthesis of all religions in one place and one floor of the same Dwarkamai – the Hindus are worshipping freely with bells and cymbals, the Muslims were saying their Namaj in the opposite wall, the Parsis were offering their prayers before the ever-burning *Dhuni*. This Dwarkamai is a place of synthesis of all castes and creeds in the same way as Dakhineswar of Sri Ramakrishna Paramahans Dev. We had good fortune to meet and dine with Sri Baba's one of the most favourite associates, Sri Tatiya Patel who blessed us profusely.

We were accommodated as VIPs in the upstairs of *Samadhi Mandir* and took our meals with the Secretary, Mr. Karkar. At the time of our departure from Shirdi, Mr. Karkar foretold me, "Mr. Bose, you will visit Shirdi next with your family", as if Sri Baba spoke through him. I laughed mentally at this apparently impracticable suggestion for the reason that it was physically impossible for me to come again to Shirdi with family. Then afterwards I forget all about this miraculously memorable pilgrimage to *Maha Tirtha*, Holy Shirdi *Pith*, the permanent abode of God Sri Shri Sai Baba for more than six and a half decades upto December 1968.

10. FULFILMENT OF PREDICTION OF SRI KARKAR – HOW IT HAPPENED?

Once of my sons who is a most earnest and sincere devotee of Sri Baba made a suggestion to me from his professional Headquarters at Dundee (Scotland) in November 1968 in a casual way that during our anticipated and prolonged stay in Bombay in December 1968, we might arrange for a trip to Shirdi. Then in the following month (December 68) almost all the members of my family, including my Dundee boy who returned to India on leave by that time, assembled by chance at Bombay under unforeseen circumstances in connection with an All India Conference and other cognate matters. In the meantime, I remembered my son's suggestion and started inquires about how to go over to Shirdi by car from Bombay. On conclusion of the sessions of our meetings I suggested 25th December but Sri Baba willed it otherwise. Transport consisting of two cars could only be arranged for the 26th December the holy *Guru* Day for Sri Baba's *Puja* and all preliminary arrangements for our journey to Shirdi were completed without any difficulty.

Our Actual Trip to Shirdi

We left for Shirdi in the very early morning of the 26th December in two cars along with my wife, daughter-in-law, grand children, my Dundee boy, other friends and relatives who were also staunch devotees of Sri Baba. We expected to reach Shirdi before 12 noon, the noon *Arati* time. In the likely event of our possible detention in our journey and consequent arrival after 12 noon.

We went fully prepared for stay overnight as a contingent measure. Our cars were actually held up for more than an hour as two Railway level crossings and also for our stoppage in the way for our tea and filling up of petrol. We started from Nasik at about 10:30 A.M. and hoped to reach before twelve the time of the noon Arati, but the road was uneven, undulated hilly with resultant slower movement of our vehicles and we were looking at our watches in breathless suspense. After 12 A.M. we felt disheartened but mentally prayed to Baba. This is one of the usual trials of His devotees by Sri Baba about which I had got some personal experience in the past. At the same time I felt an intuition in my mind as if Sri Baba was telling me "Come on, I am waiting for you all". We drove our cars at break-neck speed and reached Shirdi exactly at half past twelve quite broken-hearted. Lo and behold! we were informed by the shop-keepers that the noon *Arati* was held at 12:30 P.M. I remembered Sri Baba's call felt by me intuitively. offering *Puja* to our Heart's Content:

There was a tremendous rush of hundreds of visitors at that time, many of whom came by a large number of cars. Without wasting a single moment after getting down from our cars, my daughter-in-law purchased gorgeous garlands, flowers and sweets arranged nicely by the shop-keepers in *thalies*. We all rushed in a frantic hurry to the Holy *Samadhi Mandir* where in spite of awful crowd all round at the time, all of us entered the Samadhi Hall with great difficulty by over-coming several barriers put up by the Darwans asking for tickets from us the purchase for which we had no time. All of us offered *Puja* to Sri Baba quietly with awful reverence, made our obeisance and bowed down to Sri Baba's Samadhi and to the gorgeously decorated, flower bedecked and drowned marble statue of Sri Baba which I felt that Sri Baba has been sitting there as a crowned Maharaja for the protection and well being of all His devotees, irrespective of caste, creed or religion.

In our very presence, the much coveted Holy noon *Arati* was performed by two priests with grandeur. *Bhajan* was also held in a divinely mysterious and solemn atmosphere with enchantingly melodious songs in which we unconsciously took part, joined chorus and also clapped our hands along with other devotees. This wonderful *Bhajan* rings into my ears even now. *Bhog* was held and we were fortunate enough to share the Holy *Prasad*, some of the garlands which were taken off from Baba's body and thrown away by the priests on the floor from both the sides. The flowers strewn ever Baba's *Samadhi* were collected by me. At 2 O'clock the *Puja* was completed. It took us an hour more in the *Sansthan* office to pay money for *Puja* an behalf of all the members of my family, numerous friends and relatives and our humble contribution to the *Mahasamadhi* Golden Jubilee Celebration Fund. We then bowed down to the Holy *Neem* tree and to the holiest of holy, Dwarkamai which is associated with Sri Baba's Biblical well-known precept:

"Those who step into my Dwarkamai will have no wants, no distress."

We bowed down to *Chavadi* and the *Samadhi* of Sri Abdul Baba whose loving and affectionate embrace and blessings of 1943 were well-remembered by me. We collected *Udhi* and made various purchased like lockets, plastic idols of Baba, etc.

Return Journey to Bombay

We left Shirid at 4 P.M. with expectation of returning to Bombay by 10 P.M. as it took six hours in our onward journey. But Baba willed it otherwise. Immediately after starting, one of our cars developed trouble. The nearest repair shop was 30 miles away. But we remained undaunted. After frantic driving with earnest prayer to Sri Baba, we reached a small town (30 miles from Shirdi) in which the repair shop was located. It took us 3 hours to get the dynamo repaired. then we commenced our return journey at 7 P.M. and reached Bombay quite hale and hearty at 12 A.M. in the next morning after mysteriously and safely meeting the challenge of hundreds of loaded trucks coming from Bombay from the opposite side. Had our car not developed trouble in the jungle in the pitch dark night, we would have had every chance of being crushed to death by probable collision with the loaded trucks in the dark midnight, and the condition of our party consisting of 12 people including children might better be imagined than described. Every devotee of Baba who has got firm faith in Him will agree that only through wonderful grace of Baba, we easily overcame all hurdles and difficulties in our way. Thus with fatherly care Baba unknowingly and mysteriously piloted us in the memorable journeys and through insuperable dangers and difficulties without a scratch on our body and we were back to our normal work on the 27th quite hale and hearty.

I sincerely feel that my account of our pilgrimage to Shirdi Sansthan in December 1968 will be incomplete without communicating to His devotees in brief, only four instances of miracles experienced by us in course of this Holy pilgrimage, in which all concerned will assuredly be interested:

Two days prior to our proposed departure for Shirdi the forefingers of my right hand was tightly squeezed under the new spring clutch door of a big Mercedes Benz car. Nothing serious happened except a sprain in my finger. The pressure of the clutch was so serious and painful as to necessitate amputation of my finger with consequent cancellation of our trip to Shirdi. But Sri Baba protected me miraculously by holding out His Hand at the time.

Just after *Puja* in the *Mandir* Hall there was so much frantic rush for exit by pilgrims from the Hall that my little grand daughter and the grand son were going to be crushed to death in Sri Baba's presence, it was beyond my power to help them. But lives of the kiddies were wonderfully saved by Sri Baba without a scratch.

The trouble in the car in our return journey as indicated above was got over only through His grace actually before we commenced our long journey.

My gold ring unconsciously fell down from my left hand without my knowledge due to uncommon excitement at the time of our arrival. When I returned from the *Samadhi Mandir* after the Puja was over I was amazed to find back my ring in my coat's pocket and discovered the finger without the ring, I am still unaware how it happened.

Conclusion

The brief summary of my mysterious pilgrimage will, I hope, inspire all Sai devotees about His Omnipotence and Omnipresence like all other Sad Gurus.

We therefore prostrate before Him and pray to Him with reverence at our command for the well-being of all men in general health and happiness of all devotees in particular, in the beginning of the New Year.

'OM NAMA BHAGAVATE SRI SAI NATHAYAM'

-J.N. Bose, eminent Botanist. Scientist, Calcutta
(Courtesy: Sri A. Somsunderam,
Founder & Secretary: Divine Centre,
7/.250, Nehru Street, Markapur (A.P.) – 523316

11. BABA'S GRACES ON A DOCTOR (1942-53)

Dr. A.R. Govind Rao, MBBS, M.S. (Yale) was posted as Medical officer of Civil/Military centre at Anantapur (A.P.) during world war II in 1942. His search for a house for himself and his family led him to the house of one Ramaswamy, an advocate and an ardent devotee of Baba. The time was 7 P.M. On that eventful day, Sri Ramaswamy's wife and other members of the family were crying loudly. On enquiry he doctor was informed that Ramaswamy's daughter Pramila, 6 years old had sustained severe burns all over the body upto neck, Her *pavadai* (clothes) had caught fire while she was doing *Pradakshina* to Tulsi Brindavan, where oil lamps were lit. It was Dwadeshi festival (festival of Sri Krishna at Brindavan). The girl's body had received burns ten days back. Her body was full of foul smelling pus, havin lots of maggots (young worms of flies). She was being treated at the local government hospital. She was unconscious for the last six days with high temperature and could not take a drop of water. As her condition deteriorated, the doctors in the hospital advised her parents to take the patient home as nothing more could be done from their side. The girl was brought to her home and that was the condition that prevailed when the doctor entered the house, accompanied by his brother-in-law. His brother-in-law who was also a lawyer, introduced the doctor as having come from Madras and that he was in search of a house. Sri Ramaswamy who immediately came out of the pooja room, exclaimed that Sri Baba has sent the medical aid at the critical time. The doctor was requested to examine the patient and treat her suitably. The doctor was dumb-founded as he had not heard of Sai Baba before and it appeared to him that the condition of the patient was beyond human help. However, being a doctor he had to face the emergency. He went back to the travelller's bungalow where he was camping with his family to bring his medical kit, and informed his wife the predicament in which he was, and told her not to worry if he returned late in the night.

The patient had 104°C temperature, the pulse was rapid and feeble. She was not responding to any kind of stimuli. The pus was smelling badly. After protecting his nose with a cloth, he cleaned the whole body, removed manually with forceps a number of maggots (about 180) and applied gauze soaked in cod liver oil over the wound. The girl did not show any sign of life during whole process which took nearly three hours. As only Sulphar drugs were available then, the doctor gave Mand B 693 tablets, powdered them and asked the mother to give it with honey in case the girl woke up in the night. Ramaswamy, the girl's father, applied Baba's *udhi* on the girl's forehead.

The doctor went home with no hopes what-so-ever. Next morning the doctor returned to see the patient, with great trepidation in his heart, whether the girl would be alive. There he saw the miracle of Sai Baba for the first time in his life. The girl was awake, had asked for water in the night, had asked for milk, which were given. Her condition was very much improved. The temperature a had touched normal and the pulse was full. She answered the doctor's questions clearly and fluently.

Every day the doctor would visit their house and dress the wounds. At the end of six months the burnt area had fully healed up, covered with healthy skin, with no trace of scar. Baba used the doctor as an instrument for saving the girl from the jaws of death.

Soon after the doctor was transferred from Anantapur to Madras. Sri Ramaswamy while giving a farewell dinner to the doctor gave him a photo of Sai Baba and a packet of *udhi*, and asked him to worship Baba. But the doctor's mind was not receptive to such things at that time. He forgot about Baba entirely for nearly a decade, when Baba reminded him again.

Pramila had grown up. She was of marriageable age. When her marriage was fixed she personally came to invite the doctor for her marriage. The young wife and husband are now settled at Hyderabad.

Here is the Doctor's second experience. The doctor had forgotten Sai Baba for more than a decade. Baba re-established the faith in Him, by His own initiative. The doctor was posted as Professor, Andhra Medical College, Vishakapatnam in the year 1950. In the period 1952-1953, the now Andhra Pradesh was in the midst of political turmoil, for creation f separate state from the composite state of Madras. In order to escape the turbulence and insecurity to life and property, The doctor went to Mysore on two month's leave.

One evening while he had his brother-in-law were walking in Thyagaraja Road, Mysore, there was a sudden down pour of rain. They went and took shelter in the nearest building, which happened to be a beautiful temple of Sai Baba, the existence of which the doctor was unaware of. At that time, the evening pooja and arati were going as and the doctor was reminded of the evening *puja* and *arati* in Sri Ramaswamy's house in Anantapur. After *arati,* they were given *Prasad* and *udhi.* An old man of about 95 years was sitting in the sanctum sanctorum of the temple. He beckoned the doctor to come near him. When he went near the old man, he gave the doctor a beautiful photo of Sai Baba.

The doctor thinking that the old man was entrusted with selling photo of Sai Baba, asked him the price. The old man retorted at once that the photo was not for sale. "Baba has asked me to give it to you. It seems you have forgotten Him. You take the photo and put it in your own house and that done He will ever be with you." The doctor was taken aback. With humble devotion he accepted the photo and offered his gratitude to the old man and to Baba.

The doctor had saved only Rs. Five Thousand, and hence he could not imagine how he would be able to own a house and install Baba's photo there.

The above incident took place in 1953 and within a year thereof, a miracle really happened. A co-operative house construction society in Madras accepted Rs. Five Thousand only and allotted the doctor a big plot of land (Five grounds) in Adyar, a posh locality in Madras. The society also constructed a fine spacious house on the plot, costing nearly thirty thousand rupees. The doctor was given possession of the house in 1954, with a stipulation that be should pay the cost of the land and the house on moderate monthly installments spread over a period of twenty years. He and his wife were immensely happy. After house warming ceremony, they put up Sai Baba's photo in the hall facing the main entrance.

12. SAI BABA BEGAN TO MAKE HIS PRESENCE FELT

A well was dug to supplement the corporation water which was inadequate. The experience of the neighbors who had also dug wells were discouraging. The wells had saltish water. The doctor also got the same saline water. The doctor and his wife were much disappointed. In the evening both of them prayed before Baba and told Him "This is your house, not ours. So if you want us to drink salt water, we are ready. So kindly give us the solution to the salt water problem".

It rained throughout the night, the wall of the well partially collapsed. The contractor told the doctor that if he were prepared to spend a little more money, he would remove the mud and dig a few feet deeper. The doctor agreed. After digging three or four feet deeper, a fresh water underground stream was seen oozing out from the side of the well. In summer, which is very severe in Madras, the neighbors well go dry, but the doctor's well has at least 8 to 9 feet of sweet water.

13. BABA'S HELP IN CURE OF ILLNESS (1943)

V.N. Murthy Rao of Basavanagudi, Bangalore, was suffering from fits for 17 years from his 19th year. All kinds of treatments and charms were of no avail. About 1943, a friend of his gave him a little *udhi* of Sai Baba, advised him to leave all other medicines, cast all his burden and anxieties on Sai Baba and worship Him. He began to worship Sai Baba, not with any faith but with the hope that he would get relief from his fits. He began to get relief immediately. First he would get fits only when he was in the office or in the house and never while outside, or on roads. The attacks became milder and milder. Murthy Rao was content to be cured gradually. But his mother and brothers, were anxious for cure immediately. They approached some tantriks, without the knowledge of Murthy Rao. Every time it was done, the attacks increased, until one day Sai Baba came upon him and in that condition, told his mother "Why did you go elsewhere? Never has any of My devotees been thrown to despondency. He is not having any of his previous attacks. Within another three or four months, he will be completely the alright. Be content with having the complaint cured slowly." Murthy Rao became alright as told by Baba.

14. THE TOMB THAT RESPONDS AND THE BONES THAT SPEAK (1944)

For the first time I visited Shirdi in the year about 1944. Then my father was employed in Poona and I was schooling in a convent institution. I do not remember much about the trip that we made then to Shirdi specially the route that we traversed. The only incident that I recall to my memory is that while I was playing outside the room provided to us by authorities, an old man with long white Kurta (like one worn by Fakirs and Christian priests) lifted me into his arms, carried me to his abode, made me sit on a wooden box and put holy ashes *(Vibhuti)* into my mouth, poured holy water *(teertham)* saying that it was given to him by Shirdi Sai and blessed me profusely and brought me back to the room. I did not understand anything of what he did and indeed neither the ash nor the water that he gave me tasted differently. My people told me that the Fakir was Abdul Baba, a great soul. It all mattered very little to me except that I thought the Fakir to be a very kind-hearted man. All this happened four decades ago.

In the years that followed I did not visit Shirdi again nor had I any strong inclination to do so. For reasons unknown to me I respected Sai and on a few occasions in casual talks with friends I used to narrate to them the incident that took place early in life. Devotees of Baba rather attached importance to the subject while that looked add to me rather than attractive or thrilling.

Then in the years that rolled by, I passed through several rissitudes of life. I witnessed several thrilling people's movements. In some I participated and till recently I was involved in political movements which in correct parlance, is knows as mass movements covering all the cross sections of people, most of whom belong to petty bourgeoisie class. I spent over a decade in this arena of life almost breathing in insecure conditions or threats each day and more than this leading tension-built-in life. God or Divinity or Providence just did not bother me. In fact I did not have time to reflect on any of these except my own problems of keeping the hearth burning and work on the problems posed before the organization that I belonged to.

After long time, I returned to picking up threads that I left over a decade ago, and determined to take a fresh look at things. A few years ago I went to Tirupati with all the members of my family and had pleasant moments of surprise that kindled a hope in me to take a few steps more towards things spiritual without losing balance of vision. A word about this may interest the readers. In Tirupati, I walked straight into the Sanctorum, I stood face to face with the deity and said to myself "Well, well this is nothing but a block of stone and indeed it it no God." I hastened to my room, picked up the baggage and ran to station to catch the next immediate train. To the surprise of everyone in the house I returned home in less than two days. Since then I did not go to Tirupati till quite recently. Now the same block of stone seem to convey to me a different thing than its mere looks. I do not know what to call this and I am still thinking along the lines that I am trained in, earlier.

The next in order of my visit was Mantralayam of Sri Raghavendraswami fame. There are enough stories about him to attract and engage our attention. Whatever be the credibility of those stories in circulation, I bent my head down for the enormous amount of scholarship that the great saint was said to have had and lived up to the letter and spirit of it. To top it all, He entered 'Jiva Samadhi', something that sounds to strange in the present day world and to a person like me in whom 'suspicion' takes the better of reasoning. I felt thoroughly enlivened.

After my visit to Mantralayam I and my family member decided to visit Shirdi, a programme fixed and cancelled twice before. A couple of days before the scheduled program my bosom friend Sri E. Bharadwaja, a lecturer of Vakadu college dropped in. He always commands respect and demands nothing Mr. Bharadwaj, a great devotee of Sai, gave us send off at station.

My second daughter Sow Prafulla who proficially read the life history of Baba, poured out her knowledge of Baba and the importance of the spots at Shirdi. My mind again recalled to its memory the incidents that occurred to me nearly four decades ago. I went about visiting the place 'Dwarakamai'. 'Chavadi', the 'Shrine' and 'Lendi Bagh' followed by other members of my family. My son who is better placed on the spiritual plane brought a nice-looking garland to decorate the statue of Baba. He was greatly elated when the priest called him out to make his offering. As if Baba desired the garland it remained around his neck almost for the whole of the day and for some part of the next day too. This my son took as a blessing of Baba. His simple understanding was while a series of garlands offered by devotees remained on Baba hardly a few minutes why should the garland offered by him (my son) remain for so many hours. Though all the members of my family also thought so, I accepted the fact but doubted whether it could be taken for as the grace of Baba.

I gazed at the beautiful statue of Baba chiseled by the deft hands of a renowned sculptor. Surely as one looks on, one would definitely begin to fix his focus on the inwardly drawn sharp looks of Baba, I touched the tomb of Baba and inquired "Is it true that you said 'the tomb' will respond and the bones of your body speak?" Was it a statement of fact or words of consolation to calm down the anguished minds of his devotees who surrounded him when he left his mortal coil? Such and several other thoughts flooded my mind. We remained for the day and attended some of the programs like 'Arati'. I made it a point to pay a visit to Abdulla Baba's son was seated on a cot praying to Allah. I spoke to him and reminded him of my meeting his great father years ago.

While leaving Secunderabad Mr. Vikram, a young and dynamic associate of Sri Bharadwaja had requested me to place his 'visiting card', at the feet of Sri Sai. I remembered that and told my daughter to pass on the visiting card. She took my visiting card also and gave it to the priest. He took the cards. He threw my card as he would do to any other's. My card went in small circles and landed. I went near to see the position of my card – an obvious inquisitiveness of persons like me. I was thrilled to see my card at the feet of Sri Sai and a beautiful flower lying over the card. Did it signify anything? Whether it did or not, certainly I was happy to know that the card thrown so casually by the priest did not fall aside as a cast-away ship! This thought did touch the chord of my heart immediately, but slowly melted away under the weight of another 'thought' that it could be an accident. Before returning to my native cit, I went around Shirdi and visited a couple of places and paid my respects to those octogenarians, the contemporaries of Sri Sai. One gentleman showed me a few articles given to him by Sri Sai, so carefully treasured by him and from the clothes worn by Sai he gave us a small piece of cloth. If one attaches any value to it, it is an invaluable gift otherwise it is merely a piece of rag. I asked the old gentleman "You served Baba so devotionally and faithfully; what has he given you?" The old man smiled and said with a twinkle in his eyes' "what Baba has given me? He gave me everything; this house, daily I hear the name of Sri Sai chanted in the shrine and food to eat… What else I need? Nothing." In fact, the house in which he was living was nothing better than a hut and his belonginess a few vessels and an old and small wooden cot. This is what Baba gave him. I said to myself that what Baba gave him was the greatest gift of 'contentment', a gift that can not be purchased by all the wealth in the world. The object is so handy but so difficult to hold on to.

We made all preparations to return home. All the bags and baggages were arranged. The one fact that I missed to mention is that Mr. Vikram who turned up in the morning stayed back at Shirdi for some reason of his own.

We all went to the shrine for taking leave of Sri Sai. I said to my family members that I did not have any thinking experience to treasure or cherish and everything was quite natural.

For the return journey, we got into a bus at Shirdi at 4.15 p.m. which is expected to reach Manmad by 6.00 p.m. or at the latest by 6.30 p.m. The bus startd at the right time but halted at Kopargaon station, for nearly an hour for the flimsy reason that the conductor and driver went for tea and returned late. I was told that such things do not take place but on that day it did. The bus was expected to reach Manmad well in advance to enable the passengers to board the train at 7.00 p.m. for Hyderabad. Obviously the bus that had to travel long stretch of route reached Manmad bridge at 7.00 p.m. As we were hurriedly alighting from the bus, the train snailed out of the station. I lost all sense of proportion and got into a mood to hurl out the *prasadams* collected at Shirdi. Indeed my anger had no reason. Probably I thought that Sri Sai let us down! Why did I think so? Frankly, I have no rational explanation of offer. Did I pin my hopes on Sri Sai who left his mortal coil decades ago to come to my succour? Did my anger arise out of my faith in the promise made by Sri Sai that his tomb would respond to the call and bones would speack? May be it was. I am not in a position to explain the turbulent thoughts that tormented my mind then. Left with no alternative, we all went to the station to think of what next. I approached the Station Master with the woeful tale. He advised me to surrender the tickets and try to make the journey by next train. I cancelled the tickets and mercilessly the official slashed the cost of the tickets by 60 per cent. The authorities told me that the next train was at 1 a.m. (after midnight) and that would go only upto Nizamabad; from there I should take a bus. Another passenger train would start at 3.00 a.m. and that would take minimum, twenty four hours to reach its destination. I thoroughly became a bundle of nerves. My wife and children were sitting in the station which was almost like a thorough-fare. On the bench that we were sitting a Sardarji was lying with folded legs. He suddenly woke up and started abusing someone and was a nuisance. He would not question himself in spite of my protests. All the money that we had, except a few rupees, was spent out by us at Shirdi. After the cut of return fare all the money that we gathered from purse was alarmingly too less to take a long travel back to our home town. I and my son went to Bus stop to try a bus in the hope that we might reach home faster. My son suggested to sell away his wrist watch and I protested that I would not allow him to do that and instead I would raise money by selling away my gold ring. At the bus stop I was informed that there was no through bus to Hyderabad. I had been a patient with cardiac ailment for some years. I was utterly frustrated. I and my son returned to station to discuss the situation with my wife. Meanwhile the Sardarji who was under the influence of liquor created enough nuisance and my wife and children had moved to the opposite bench. When I returned to the station from bus stop my wife was talking to two gentlemen who were also sitting on the same bench. The two gentlemen smiled at me and said, "Why should you sell anything when we are here to help you? How much money you need?" Hesitating I whispered to my wife that we needed Rs. 1000/- to make up for the journey. The two gentlemen readily obliged me with Rs. 1000/-. They did not even ask me about my status or even as to when would repay it and how I would do it at all. I gave the gentlemen my visiting card. They looked at it and said that they might require my help at any time. I collected their address. The two gentlemen advised me to stay in a hotel for the night and travel the next day by the same train at 7 a.m. They hurried us out of the station and insisted that we should go and have rest. When we raised the question of getting reservations for the next day, they affirmatively said that everything could be had. I did not understand as to how they could say that when the persons at the railway counters were doubtful.

As a result of this development, we all breathed a sigh of relief. We got into a hotel. My son retorted now saying that "Daddy, you wanted an experience, an experience that you could cherish, well, you have had it now. Henceforth do not seek experience."

From: *Shri Sai Leela*,
August 1987, pp. 24-29

15. BABA'S *DARSHAN* CURED A DUMB GIRL

This narration appeared in *"Swadeshamitran"*, a Tamil magazine dated 15-9-1944. Sri T.R.S. Mani Iyer of Kumbakonam was an ardent devotee of Sai Baba. He had a daughter Rajalakshmi who was dumb since birth. When she was 9 years old, Sri Iyer was directed by Sai Baba to visit his Samadhi at Shirdi Sri Iyer visited Shirdi on 28-3-1942 along with his daughter. They worshiped the Lord before His Samadhi with all devotion, and lo! the girl began to cry "Sai Baba, Sai Baba", the first words uttered by her. The girl is a student and Sri Iyer is gratefully worshiping Sai Baba at his house. In may 1944, Sri Iyer went to Shirdi during Ramanavami celebrations, presented a Banaras Silk

Shawl, and silver lamp of the height of his daughter to Baba. A photo of the girl Rajalakshmi was also published in the said news magazine of that date.

16. BABA SAVED DEVOTEE'S LIFE (1947)

In the year 1947, there was not much electricity in the interior countryside of India. It was so in the residence of Ravalu Devendra, Perala, Chirala. He lived with his daughter Indra and other members of the family in a big house. Indira had a separate room for herself. She had the walls well whitewashed and roof covered with *tatty* to which paper was plastered so as to prevent insects from falling. As Baba's photo next to the lamp. It was a Saturday and eight o'clock in the night. In her place there was Hanuman temple and on Saturdays Hanuman Puja was performed and prasad distributed. She was reading a religious book, lying on her cot, when she was roused suddenly by her father's unusually loud voice "Indra, Indra"; she felt irked at the disturbance. But she went out and found the *Pujari* with a plate of *prasadam*, which she took and brought inside the house. When she returned to continue her reading, she was shocked to find that a big snake had fallen on her cot in her absence. She shouted "Snake Snake" and her father and others gathered, caught the snake and left it on the outskirts. Indra had requested them not to harm the snake. The benevolent grace of Baba was on Indra. At the appropriate time. He made her to leave her cot, which saved her from mishap.

17. MIRACLES WORKED BY SHIRDI SAI BABA IN MY LIFE (1948)

My ancestral background and the environment in which I was born and bred up had cast me into a philosophic mould and conditioned me to believe that 'There is a destiny that shapes our ends. Rough-hew them how we may." After the advent of Baba into my life, my experiences with Him amply confirmed and ratified this belief. Rather it became an axiom in due course proving itself again and again in a remarkably incredible manner. I gave no thought for the morrow. The unsettled war-years found a large number of us employed willy-nilly in some establishment connected with the war-effort. With the ending of the war, however, most of these units were closed down one by one. I was functioning as an Administrative Officer in the Embarkation HQ. Visakhapatnam at that time. Of course, I knew I had to seek a job elsewhere. But then what is Baba for? Does he not provide the impetus to act, leading us into 'fresh fields and pastures new?' Has He not assured His devotees that there would be no want in their houses? Is He not ever ready and willing to take over our burdens if only we cast them on Him with full faith? So why worry? Such were my thoughts and I was as unconcerned as I could be. Accordingly, one fine morning my boss, one Capt. Boohariwallah, a man of sterling character and independence, who had recently taken over asked me whether I had been recommended for a permanent position as an Administrative Officer in the army. On my replying in the negative, he forthwith put up a letter to the GHQ strongly recommending me for the job. He followed it up by phoning the Staff Officer concerned at intervals to make sure the proposal received due consideration. This spontaneous action of the Officer only underlined my belief in Baba's solicitude for the welfare of those who put their entire faith in Him. On this note of hope I found myself discharged on the closing down of our establishment in July '48.

Months dragged on but nothing was heard from Delhi. I had saved nothing and had to begin selling things to fend for the family. First it was the furniture. Then it was my wife's jewelry one by one till by December '48 we came to the end of our resources except for just one chain around her neck. I kept in touch with the GHQ through one of the officers still available. I had every reason to be hopeful. However, in retrospect I wonder at my seeming stupidity in my failure to seek an alternative job. But, then it never occurred to me I should try. As luck would have it, reducing my hopes to ashes, came the government's declaration of the 'Hyderabad Action' against the Nizam. The whole army was geared overnight to achieving success in their effort and chances of my appointment vanished into thin air.

It was a terrible shock. I sat before Baba and cried. My wife who was convalescing after confinement and whose matchless devotion to Baba has always been exemplary told me it was needless for me to cry or lose heart. Baba was actually testing her faith not mine, she exclaimed. "Let this last piece too go. Let us see what He does afterwards", so saying, she practically tore the chain off her neck and threw it. "Please take and sell this away and let Him take over", She concluded. For a long while I could not bring myself to pick it up. I felt like a heartless robber. Having no alternative, I steeled myself to take it and sell it. Within a week after this, I got my first permanent appointment as a higher grade Office Assistant in the Royal Indian Navy through the good offices of Capt. Krishnaswamy who happened to be a former student of mine. I was past 40. I think it was the first as well as the last exemption from such over-age ever granted. It could happen that way because the Navy was still under the British Admiralty manned by Britishers at the top and an Englishman had strongly recommended it in my favor. In the ultimate analysis, it was Baba fulfilling Himself in His own wonderful way.

-Dr. P.S.R. Swami,
D-9, P&T Qrtrs., Hyderabad
From: *Shri Sai Leela*, August 1988

18. BABA SAVED K.M. MUNSHI'S FAMILY FROM RAZAKARS CRUEL HANDS (1948)

I am a lawyer by profession and I have been trained to accept a fact only when it is conclusively proved. It was with this background and training that my association with the name of Shirdi Sai Baba first started.

In May 1948, my wife and I were travelling in a first class compartment of the train going from Bangalore to Bombay. There were six of us in the compartment, including an old couple and two youngsters. Having nothing else to do, the two youngsters, my wife and I was playing cards. The old man was obviously praying and his wife was watching us. We had been advised not to travel by this particular route because of the Razakar trouble then prevailing in the erstwhile Hyderabad state. As youngsters, we thought, it was our privilege not to heed to such advice which we believed was borne out of undue apprehensions and fear.

The train had left the last station in Hyderabad territory and was fast approaching Sholapur station in the Indian union. Suddenly the train was forced to stop at a station called Gangapur. There was a large crowd of Razakars on this station, armed with rifles, lathsi, and other lethal weapons. As soon as the train stopped, a cry was raised by the Razakars. "All Muslims get down. Kill all Hindus". The old man immediately ordered us to pull down the shutters and to lock the door. We promptly carried out his orders. For nearly five hours we could hear screams and wailings of passengers who were pulled out of the train, beaten and robbed. Third class passengers fled into the nearby fields and their belongings were looted. The Razakars repeatedly tried to force open our compartment but failed to do so. Even in the midst of this cacophony and panic, we would observe the old man praying. Queer enough from the reports confirmed at the Sholapur station, our compartment was the only one in the entire train that had escaped the marauders.

After nearly five hours, the train crawled towards Sholapur station. Once we reached the shores of safety, the old man's wife explained to us that the old man had been suffering from blood pressure and heart disease and that they were fleeing from the Hyderabad territory with all their money and belongings because of the

Razakar trouble. Once we reached Sholapur station, the military officers took down our statements and the incident came to an end. Although we had escaped untouched by the Razakars, this incident left such an indelible scar in our memory that for a long time my wife and I suffered from night-mares arising out of it.

A few days after this incident a friend of mine read out to me, in Bombay an article in a magazine, obviously written by the old man wherein he had related this incident and had claimed that it was because of his prayers to Shirdi Sai Baba, that the entire compartment of the train escaped unscathed by the Razakars. As witness to this incident, he had cited my name in the article.

My friend saw me with this article for corroboration of this incident. I told him that the facts stated in the article were all true. It was also true that our compartment was the only one which had escaped unhurt. It was also true that the old man was frantically praying all the time. I, however, told him that I had never before heard of Shirdi Sai Baba and that whether this incident was a miracle or a mere co-incidence was for him to judge for himself.

While this incident remained embedded in my memory except in the course of stray discussion with frien ds. Shridi Sai Baba was more or less forgotten for a long time. In the early part of 1953, I again came in close association with the name of Shirdi Sai Baba. This was a bad period for my wife and myself. My wife had been seriously ill and because of her long stay in the hospital she was feeling very miserable. I was having some trouble in my office and had threatened to leave my partners. Life in general, was fraught with problems, for which no solutions were in sight.

On the way to my office there was a small photo frame-maker's shop. Outside his shop was hung a picture of Shirdi Sai Baba. Below the picture was his message 'If you look to me, I shall look to you'. I do not remember how long this picture was hung there, but it was during early 1953 that my attention got first focused on this picture and the message.

It was then that I was suddenly reminded of the oldman's assertion during the Razakar incident, that Shirdi Sai Baba had saved him. Gradually I got so obsessed by this picture of Shirdi Sai Baba and the message, that one day I told my wife about my obsession and my desire to acquire the said picture and to perform the pooja of Baba. My wife readily agreed to my proposal.

We purchased Baba's picture, brought the picture home, lit a lamp before the photo and prayed that we looked to him for solution of our problems. Within a few days thereafter, all our problems got settled to our reasonable satisfaction and life ran smooth again.

Was this another co-incidence? Was this Pooja a weakness of our minds? or could the solution of our problems be the working of that indefinable, mysterious phenomenon called Shirdi Sai Baba? Well, let each one judge for himself. For us since the time Shirdi Sai Baba entered our home and heart. Not only the two of us, but our near relations, as also the domestic servants, accepted Him as an essential part of our existence.

As the *pooja* continued daily, we gradually got used to look to Shirdi Sai Baba for his blessings, particularly in times of distress. Many things big and small did happen which ostensibly appeared co-incidental but which one could in all humility attribute to the phenomenon called Shirdi Sai Baba.

A few years thereafter, I was once travelling by the night train from Surat to Bombay. After the train left Surat station, I suddenly developed severe pain which later was diagnosed as being on account of stone in the bladder. Within a couple of hours the pain aggravated to such an extent that I could neither lie down on my berth nor sit down. The only choice for me was to keep standing writhing in pain, while my co-passenger was fast asleep on the adjoining berth. I also began passing blood through the bladder.

When the train reached Palghar station, at 2 A.M., the pain became severe that I had to shake my co-passenger out of his slumber and urge him to call the guard and to see whether he could find a doctor travelling by the train who could relieve me of the pain. My co-passenger there upon called the guard and explained the situation to him. No doctor could be located in the train at that time of the night. The guard therefore advised me to get down at Palghar so that I could receive treatment from a local doctor and proceed to Bombay by subsequent train. The guard called the station master and under their joint advice, I got down at Palghar and the train left the station.

The advice given by the guard and the station master was however not at all sound. For nearly an hour, I waited at the Palghar station for the doctor who had been summoned by the station master. I was virtually howling in pain, and taking the name of Baba. No doctor was however forth-coming. The station master then told me that the doctor summoned by him was refusing to come to the station at that time of the night. He suggested that instead I should be taken to the doctor. There was no taxi available at the time and the only available conveyance was a bullock-cart.

So the station master and his associates lifted me into the bullock-cart and directed the driver to take me to the doctor. One can imagine my mental state travelling alone in a bullock-cart in that condition at that time of the night, in a town I had never visited before and where I knew no one. I was not sure whether I was going to survive this predicament. The only thing I could do in the circumstances was to look upon Shirdi Sai Baba for aid and assistance.

The doctor diagnosed my ailment, administered morphine injection and I was soon immersed into oblivion. At my request, he had sent a call to my relations at Bombay. The next day my relations arrived and I was taken to Bombay.

But the most important experience of my life was yet to come. It was this incident which shook the lawyer out of me and converted me into a humble devotee recognizing the work of the Master.

In October 1959, my one month old daughter got seriously dehydrated and was admitted to the Breach Candy Hospital. Over three weeks of treatment, including blood transfusion, could not bring her round. Leading doctors were attending on her. The child had been running high temperature for many days and the doctors were not sure whether she should pull through. My wife and I were on the verge of a complete breakdown.

On the early morning of November 14th 1959, we were informed by two leading doctors that the child was so serious that her chances of survival were remote. She was being administered oxygen as her breathing had been difficult. With tears, agony and deep dejection, my wife and I came home from the hospital at about 9 a.m. for a short while, so that we could get ready and again ruskback to the hospital. As soon as we reached our home, I told my wife about a decision which I had reached. My decision had arisen out of sheer desperation. I said to my wife "We have been worshiping Shirdi Sai Baba for several years." It has been said that if we looked to Him. He would look to us. The survival of our only child means a lot to us. My decision is that if the child survives, our faith that Shirdi Sai Baba looks to us in times of distress, would become conclusive. If on the other hand, the child does not survive, we would end our worship as He would have failed us".

The sequence of events, after this decision, is interesting. At 10 a.m. we were again at the hospital. Another senior doctor was attending on the child. He too came to the conclusion that the childe was dying and there was hope of survival. Suddenly a comparatively junior doctor, who was also there said "Doctor, I have been observing this child for sometime, while she is running very high temperature, she has not lost consciousness. Could it be that the child is not suffering from septianaemia but from malaria?"

The senior doctor laughed and said, "How do you expect malaria in Beach Candy Hospital. Anyway, there is not much left in the child. You may try a shot of quinine".

As stated above, this talk took place at 10 a.m. On that day the temperature of the child came down to 101 degrees after several days. At 4 p.m. the temperature came further down to 99 degress and by 7 p.m. the temperature was 97.5 degrees. Oxygen and blood transfusion were no longer called for. The eminent doctors, who during the earlier part of the day had certified her as dying, left baffled.

The temperature of the child remained at normal ever since. Within three months, the child was in the pink of health. Those who saw her at the age of five months could hardly believe our description of the crisis that she had passed through a few months earlier. Consistent with our promise we took our daughter to Shirdi In March 1960 by car. Strange and dramatic though it may appear, on our way to Shirdi, during a halt, our daughter gazed at the world around her, spread out both arms, and made her first utterance *"ba, ba, ba, ba"*.

These are facts of my life as they stand. The sequence of events is also in the above order. The conclusion is for each individual to make for himself. For myself I felt convinced of the existence of that power which assists us, if we, in all humility look to it.

Today, with all the above mentioned and other experiences, my entire family, near relations, and servants, have got completely used to looking upto Shirdi Sai Baba for succour in times of distress. I must admit in all humility that He has never failed us. Many things big and small, have happened in our lives which have made us acknowledge the existence of this indefinable sterious power or my phenomenon, whose only message is that if one looks, to Shirdi Sai Baba, the Baba will look to him.

So far as I am concerned, the Baba has now become the very part of my existence. He has been my guide, philosopher and friend. In different occasions, depending on my variable moods, I have prayed to Him, beseeched Him, implored Him, begged of Him, argued with Him, and sometimes even quarreled with Him, for not solving the knotted problems of my existence. Whatsoever the mood, the problems have been ultimately solved.

J.M. Munshi, Advocate, Bombay
Son of (Late) K.M. Munshi, Statesmen
From Maneey, *The Eternal Sai*
(Courtesy: Author)

19. BABA'S INSTANT HELP TO PILGRIMS SURROUNDED IN FLOOD WATER (1948)

In the *Ashad* month of 1948, a batch of devotees left for Shirdi from Hyderabad. It was rainy season. From Kopergaon, in those days there were no buses to Shirdi. One had to cross river Godavari and then catch a bus to Shirdi. The present road over the bridge was under construction. The devotees found that the low level bridges across Godavari was almost submerge in water. A boat was plying to enable people to cross to the other shore. The Hyderabad devotees also wanted to do the same. But the cart man, who had brought them from the Kopergaon station, suggested that he would take them through the low level bridge, and the party devotes agreed, to avoid trans-shipment by boat. When the cart was half-way through, there was a heavy downpour of rain; the river which was already swelling became furious. The bullocks were virtually in water, and the cart man lost his control. In addition one of the cart wheels got stuck to a boulder. There was no parapet wall to the low-level bridge, and the water had engulfed the cart. The party chanted the name of Sai Baba in chorus and had almost made up their mind to meet the watery grave with Lord's name on their lips.

Suddenly from nowhere a middle aged man appeared in from of the bullock cart, and assumed control of steering the cart of his own accord. The cart man removed the boulder and the stranger piloted the cart. Soon after, the rains stopped, clouds cleared and there was some sunshine. The crowds of people who were watching from the other shore at the party's plight rejoiced with shouts of *"Sat Bbaa ki jai"*. Mr. Baliah, the head of the group of devotees, was so immensely happy, that he took out a ten rupee note to offer as a presentation to the stranger. But lo! the stranger was not there!

After evening "darshan" of the shrine, the party returned to their cottage and everyone including Sri Baliah fell asleep. IN his dream, a certain person appeared and told him that he has erred in accounting the *"hundi"* money to be given to Sai Baba, and also told him the extent of the error. Sri Baliah immediately got up, took his pencil and paper and began calculations. To his surprise, he found the error exactly, as the gentleman in the dream had said.

20. BABA'S TIMELY HELP (1948)

I had to take my second daughter to Bangalore to leave her at her father-in-law's house for the first time. Her father-in-law occupied a high place in the Government. To suit the new environment I had to provide proper dress for her and I required at least Rs. 50/- for other expenses. I had not a pie in my purse. Praying to Baba before going to bed I slept. Early morning Baba appeared in dream with two letters one in each hand. I could read the letters. They appeared to be in my writing. One was addressed to a cloth merchant requesting him to send a saree for my daughter on credit and the second letter to a friend of mine requesting a loan of Rs. 50/-. In the morning soon after waking up I wrote these very letters and sent them to the persons concerned by a messenger. The cloth merchant knew my relation at Bangalorre and to suit their status, sent me a saree more costly than I thought of and later on entrusted me professional work and adjusted the fees towards the cost of the saree etc. The other friend to whom applied for loan, knowing the situation sent me Rs. 75/- while I asked for Rs. 50.

Another instance, after coming in touch with Sri B.V. Narasimha Swamy I gave up doing *japa* of a mantra which I had received from an adopt previously. One night Baba appeared and scolded me for not repeating that Mantra and in addition commanded that I should repeat '*Stotra*' also concerning that particular Deity.

On several occasions he asked me to visit different saints. I was asked t go to Ramana Maharshi in 1949, and Baba said "You will have to regret if you fail to go now". I stayed with the Maharshi for a long time, spoke to him and received his blessings. Four months after my visit the Sage shuffled off his mortal coil.

In innumerable ways Baba helped and guided my spiritual evolution till I felt that I need nothing more either materially or spiritually.

-C.S. Ramaswamy
C/II 14 Tata Centre, Andheri, Mumbai – 80
(Courtesy – T.R. Naidu, Hyderabad)

21. BABA SAVES A SAINT FROM COMMITING SUICIDE (1949)

This incident happened in 1949. Sri Shantavanji was a great saint of Gujarat and a disciple of Pujya Ramsharmji. He was a worshipper of Bhagwathi Gayatri.

After leaving home, in his early years, he stayed on that bank of the river Ganga for doing *Gayatri Sadhana*. Not being able to concentrate, he started roaming and reached Balaram, a holy place near Palampur, where the atmosphere is serene and spiritual. He spent three or four days there in meditation.

Thereafter for reason unknown, he began to feel discouraged, and could not concentrate. He was upset with himself and decided to commit suicide by jumping into the river. He offered his last prayer in a Shiva temple. Reaching the river bank, chanting the Gayatri mantra, and ascertaining that there was nobody around, he was about to jump into the flowing river. A Fakir caught hold of him, smiled gently and enquired why he was doing that act. He bade Shantavanji to follow Him, the Fakir's words were so forceful and magnetic that Shantavanji just followed Him like a dumb creature. The Fakir got Shantavanji a railway ticket to his home town, and disappeared there after.

Sri Shantavanji did not know who the Fakir was, and after roaming the Himalayas frequently for meditation, Sri Shantavanji finally settled at Karnali on the banks of the Narmada, Baroda District. In 1979, thirty years after the incident, Sri Shantavanji was invited to Sai temple of Surat, on the day of Dutta Jayanthi, and for Gayatri Yagna.

Sri Shantavanji had not visited any Sai temple, nor Shirdi, nor was he a devotee of Sai Baba. On the night before the pooja celebrations, Sri Shantavanji, who used to meditate every night before going to bed, prayed for the reason why he was selected for performing pooja. In the night Sai Baba appeared in his dream and asked him "Have you forgotten me, who saved you thirty years ago in Balram?... "On hearing these words Sri Shantavanji immediate got up, taking a bath, sat in meditation. In his meditation he saw Sai Baba in the place of Gayatri, he experienced bliss beyond description. He related this incident when he went to the Sai temple for the *Yagna* and *Puja*.

22. BABA'S MYSTERIOUS HELP IN THE ESTABLISHMENT OF A SAI TEMPLE AT KURNOOL (1951)

Shri Veeraswamy, a resident of Madras before independence, came to Kurnool as a Jeep Driver. One day while he was sleeping on the banks of river Tungabadra, Sai Baba appeared in his dream and directed him to construct a temple for Baba. When he awoke, thinking of Sai Baba, he saw immediately one Cobra (small) spreading its hood in the vicinity underneath the shade where an Aswatha tree intertwined by a Neem tree (the symbol of Lakshmi Narayana) was situated. Afterwards this cobra glided away into the ant hill situated nearby.

Since then, he became a Sai devotee and from that day onwards he spread no pains to secure funds and firmly resolved to construct the temple. He managed by the grace of Sai Baba to purchase a bus and by the windfull of fortune he became a owner of 16 buses and named 'Sri Sai Baba Bus Service' and still these bus services are running and managed by his children.

In between the years 1949-51 Sai Baba temple in Star shape, on the banks of Tungabadra river, was constructed by him with an expenditure of 4.5 lakhs. A pure beautiful marble stone Statue of Sai Baba was installed it. It has 16 rooms. Sri Veeraswamy left his body in 1953 and his body is interred in a tomb in the premises of the temple. Here, as in South Indian temples, regular pooja, Archana & Bhajana is conducted and grand functions on all important festive days celebrated with huge mass poor feedings. This temple is thronged with surging crowds on all Thursdays.

(Transisted from the article 'Sri Sai Baba' by Sri A.V.V. Narasimha Rao, published in *Andhra Pradesh Illustrated Weekly* on 14.7.1974).

Courtesy: T.R. Naidu

Hyderabad (A.P.)

23. BABA'S TIMELY HELP (1956)

I am a native of Coimbatore (Tamil Nadu). Long ago, I made it a vow to visit Sai Baba temple here and worship Baba just before leaving on tour to outstations whenever occasion arose. I appeared at the Intermediate (Arts) Examination conducted by the Central Board of Secondary Education, Ajmer at Bhopal centre during July 1956. I left Coimbatore for Bhopal on 2nd July 1956 duly fulfilling my vow.

About 25 candidates including me were accommodated in a big hotel next to Lakshmi Theatre, Bhopal. Everything went on well during our stay. As usual, we all left the hotel at 1 P.M., attended the last examination on 25th July 1956, and returns back at 6 P.M. in order to leave for Railway station. To our utter disappointment and dismay we saw that the front door of the hotel was locked and sealed by the Court authorities. Our money, railway concession tickets etc., were kept inside the hotel. Our sorrow and agony knew no bounds. We were told by the neighbours that the door could be opened by the Court only after the Civil case against the hotel was disposal of. We all cried aloud, but in vain. I, on my part, prayed to Sai Baba to help us in that unforeseen distress. The time was running out.

Suddenly, two Sardarjis (hailing from Punjab and who had stayed at the hotel the previous day) came to the scene and they also completely broke down, since they had to leave for Delhi and Bombay respectively by flight scheduled at

P.M. on that fateful day. The Sub-Inspector stationed at the Lakshmi Theatre advised us to contact personally the District Magistrate. We all went to him, explained our case in detail and pleaded to help us at any cost. He obliged and immediately contacted the police authorities by phone and the latter instructed the Sub-Inspector to open the door and also keep it open till 10 A.M. the next day so that the people who stayed there might take back their belongings by that time. Filled with joy and happiness we all went inside the hotel and retrieved all our belongings (we had already paid all the dues in advance) and rushed to Bhopal Railway Station to catch the G.T. Express coming from New Delhi. The moral of this experience is: "Dedicate all actions to the Almighty".

-C.R. Balasundaram
No. 9 Muthuswamy Layout,
Barathi Park Road No. 2
Coimbatore – 641043

24. MIRACLE EXPERIENCED BY A SAI DEVOTEE (1949-1981)

(i) Date: Feb 1978 place: Vilasavalli, East Godavari, (A.P.)

God is love and love is God. Those who cleanse their hearts of the battering poison of selfishness, hate greed, etc., shall find God as their own "TRUE SELF". Love has to originate naturally from within. It is in no way responsible to any form of inner or outer force. Humanity will attain the new life through the free and unhampered interplay of pure love – love from heart to heart and man to man. This kind of love will establish peace, harmony and happiness in social, natural and international spheres and shine in its purity and beauty. Truth and lie are beyond the reach of mind. If one practices to tell lies, his mind will entertain telling lies only. Hence, everybody should try to tell truth under any circumstances. Where there is truth, peace and cleanliness, there is God. Mere intellectual understanding does bring God near to us. Love is the nearest means to reach God. I will say that God and eternal love are identical and one who has divine love has realized God.

In 1949, when I was 10 years old my father Sri Tatapudi Bhyravarama Murthy Bhagavathar was seriously bed-ridden for 40 days with double typhoid. My father was a *Hari Das* i.e., Bhagavathar who read Ramayana and Bharatham as *Hari Kathas*. On the 40th day he was at his death bed. For the whole day he was unconscious and in hopeless condition which brought him to be kept on the ground. But surprisingly my father woke up at 4.00 a.m. and surprised the curiously attending people. He told us that Baba had appeared in his dream. So gracefully, he appeared and assured him saying "Why fear when I am here. Don't worry." Saying this, he disappeared. A thunder like sound was heard by my father, which made him to get up from the bed. With this great blessing of Sai Baba my father remained alive upto 63 years and passed away on Vijayadasami Festival day on 8.10.1981 which is the auspicious day as Lord Sai Baba who also attained Mahasamathi on that day. I feel how Baba saves the life of his devotees. I was astonished at this *leela* of Baba and became his Devotee even from my childhood i.e., since 1949.

Visit to Shirdi (1978)

I became a Sai Devotee since my childhood i.e., since 1949. I had as earnest desire to visit Shirdi, but I could not go there. My desire was, however, fulfilled during Feb. 1878 at the age of 40 without any prior programme. One of my friends Sri V. Narayana Rao (Retired Dy. Pay And Accounts Officer), who was going to Shirdi, wanted me to accompany him, but I had no reservation for the Railway journey in the Ajanta Express in which he was travelling. But by the grace of Baba and due to my good fortune, he secured me a seat even at the last hour in the same compartment in which he was travelling. We got a very good room for our stay at Bhaktha Nivas. In Shirdi we entered the Bootiwada where the Samadhi and Shrine of Sai Baba are located. This made me shed tears before Him, thinking of His love towards me. Sometime later I could know that He had made me enter His chamber through the other door near Samadhi though it was not open for everybody to go through it. This was the miraculous love He showed towards me. I was not stopped by anybody while entering. I was really lucky for this opportunity. We stayed there for three days and returned safely. At the bus stand at Shirdi there was a weighing machine. In the name of Sai Baba, I put a 10 paise coin in it and took the ticket from the machine. The following caption was inscribed there on "CULTIVATE CLEAN HABITS, YOU WILL ENJOY DEVOTION OF RECIPROCATED LOVE". This I took as a direction and advice of Baba. He is at my back and watching me to see how I am following his directions.

Date: 3.8.78 at Hyderabad

I started for going to Osmania General Hospital at Hyderabad on 3.8.78 undergoing Hydrocel Operation, but had some bad omens when I started from the house. Half way on the road I saw a lorry proceeding in my direction;

on the front mirror of which I could read the words "GURU KRIPA" which immediately struck me as his Grace and his permission to me to even though I had encountered bad omens. I safely returned to my house after one week with the operation having been successfully done. Even now also Baba is with me and guiding my life in a peaceful and devotional manner.

Date: 30-10-1982 Place: Hyderabad

Sri Sai Baba declared this to His staunch devotee Shama, "If a man utters my name with love, I shall fulfil all his wishes, increase his devotion. It is my special characteristics to free any person who surrenders completely to me and who does worship Me faithfully and who remembers me and meditate on me constantly. The simple remembrance of my name as "Sai Sai will do away with since of speech and hearing (Chapter III of *Sai Satcharita*).

Only the simple remembrance of His name "Sai Sai" in my mind, at all times, saved me from the danger of death on 30.10.1982. I pray to Baba every day while leaving my residence to enable we reach my destination safely and to bring me back home safely. On that day, I went to my office (Pay and Accounts Office, Hyderabad) and worked till the evening. Thereafter, I went to Radio Station (A.I.R. Hyderabad) all the way to meet my friends as usual as I used to write articles viz, playts, talks, dramas etc., and after meeting my friends, I started to go to my home. While crossing a road junction near the Radio Station (Gun Park) all the way on my Cycle, a car un-noticeably rushed up and dashed at the back side of my bicycle. I fainted due to sudden shock and fell down before the car bumper. Nothing this the driver of the car suddenly applied the brakes. I would have died on the spot, but Baba very kindly saved me from the unnatural death.

Date: 29.3.80

In March 1980, I had high blood pressure. I was suffering from mental torture due to giddiness and feeling sensation. I took so many injections. In the meanwhile a Sai *bhakta* advised me to study: *Shri Sai Leelamrutham*" (as *Parayan*) of Shri Ekkirala Bharadwaja Vidyanagar, Nellore Dist (A.P.) I started parayana on 29.3.80; but I could not complete the *parayana* within one week. Suddenly I had to go to my native place for the settlement of the marriage of my sister. So I took *Shri Sai Leelamrutham* with me there for completing the *parayan*. I started for my native place on 7.4.80 in the same unhealthy condition with medicines of course. After reaching my native & place, the giddiness increased and I was in a perturbed position. One day I thought came in my mind with the grace of Shri Sai Baba to stop taking the medicines and to complete the *parayan*. I also prayed to Baba to control my trouble immediately or at least till the time I could return to Hyderabad. I completed or at least till the time I could return to Hyderabad. I completed the *parayan* on 14.4.80 and returned to Hyderabad on 22.4.80. To my surprise my trouble had vanished by that time.

One niece of my officer, Sri Surendranath (now retired Assistant Secretary to Govt.) suffered from ill health. They took her to the doctor, who stated that T.B. symptoms were visible and that her one lung was effected. The doctor directed her to have the X-ray done on the every next day. On hearing that, the Officer prayed to Baba with much pain in his heart, saying "Baba you will have to help her." On the next day they went to the doctor for X-Ray. When the X-Ray was taken, to the surprise of the doctor and other attendants on her, there were no tuberculosis symptoms in the X-Ray. The doctor then concluded that she was only suffering from weakness.

Date: 20.01.1981 At Kakkkaparru

When I was on leave in connection with my youngest sister Sitha Rama' marriage which was held on 8.2.81 and with the thread function of my son Sai Kumar, myself and my family and went to Rajahmundry my brother-in-law, Sri. M. Bapannavadhanulu to purchase clothes for the bride groom. After the purchase was made, we returned by bus from Rajahmundry to Kakaraparru my mother-in-law's place. While getting down from the bus at Kakaraparru (West Godavari District) we forgot one packet containing a saree in the shelf of R.T.C. Bus. In the meanwhile, the bus had gone. Then what to do? We prayed Baba to save us from the loss. Luckily a lorry came there. I followed the bus in the lorry. The bus was going towards Tanuku side. Again I caught another lorry at Paravali and at last I caught the bus at the bus stop of Tanuku. Luckily the *saree* was found there.

In connection with the above on 27.2.81 I went to Amalapuram which is a nearby town to my native place Nangavaram, Bheemanpalli Post Office, East Godavari, for the registration of the land sale which was sold to perform my sister's marriage. On that occasion, I forgot my bag with money which was paid to us by the land purchaser in a Hotel at Amalapuram Bus stand. The Same was got back by Baba's grace.

(DATE 01.03.1981 AT HYDERABAD

Sri Sai Baba appeared before me in a dream as an old Man. In that dream my ulcer trouble was repeated. I asked the old Man what should I do as I was suffering from severe pain. Then He told me "Operation has to be done and I will do it". The dream was over. After I woke up, there was nothing. After some day my ulcer disappeared.

-Tatapudi Brahmananda Sastry
SRI SAI NILAYAM
Plot No. 16 (H 4-54) Santhinagar,
Vanasthalipuram (P.O.)
Hyderabad – 500 070 (A.P.)

25. BABA CURED A LAME BOY (1956)

Swami Sai Sharan Anandthecontemporary devotee of Sai Baba has, recorded in his book that a school mistress, a widow, had an only son. In 1956, he appeared for SSLC with a bad attack of fever. Medicines cured him of fever, but the fever left him lame. The boy had to be lifted for being taken from place to place. As all medicines were tried and found ineffective, the school mistress having heard of Sai Baba of Shirdi, took her son to Shirdi. The boy felt they of being taken to Samadhi Mandir on the shoulders of others. So he remained in his room. The mother alone went to pray for two days. On the third day she was to leave Shirdi, and before taking leave, she offered her obeisance to Baba. In the meanwhile Baba appeared before the boy and told him "Have courage". He then lent His hand and led him to the *Samadhi Mandir* and kept him standing against the pillar of the Mandir. On return the mother did not find the son in the room. Worried, she again rushed to Baba. Her eyes fell on the boy standing against the pillar. Surprised, she enquired, how he had managed to come there. The mother heard the boy's accounts in disbelief. She was highly pleased when she found that the boy was able to walk with her support. The boy fully recovered in a month and was able to move and walk freely.

SAI THE OMNIPRESENT (1957)

26. I first heard about Sri Shirdi Sai Baba in 1938 while I was working in Madras. People used to tell stories about him that He was a Brahmin boy, bought up by a Muslim fakir, again brought into a fold of a Brahmin Maharashtrian ruler for 12 years, then settled at Shirdi and lived there for about 60 years etc. etc. He was a great saint, why a saint, God incarnate I had

not seen either Sri B.V. Narasimha Swamy or Sai Baba *Mandir* and also Sai Baba at Shenoy Nagar started by Swami Kesavayyaji, sever all times after 1958.

In December 1957, when I was working at Donakonda, I had to go to Hyderabad on leave. The Post-master who was my relative advised me to avail of this leave and passes to visit Shirdi also which I had not done till then. It was a good suggestion. Accordingly, I proceeded to Aurangabad from Hyderabad, saw Ajanta and Ellora caves and reached Shirdi at about 10 A.M. I saw *Samadhi Mandir, Dwaraka Mai, Chavadi* etc. and left Shirdi in the evening itself. On my way back to Donakonda I meet one driver Sri Vankateshawar Rao at Vijayawada Railway Station. He was promoted as foreman and transferred to Donokonda but he wanted to go on leave. He was advised to join first at the new station and then to avail leave after my joining duty and also he too was on his way to Donakonda. On hearing from me that I was just returning for Shirdi, he asked from Shirdi *Prasad.* But I was sorry that I did not bring either Prasad or *udhi* or even a photo. In turn I asked him to get a big Photo of Baba for me. We both went to Donakonda. I relie*ved him to avail of leave. He was kind enough to get me Shri Baba's photo, Udhi and Prasad.*

From now on climax began. It was Wednesday that I got Baba's photo. I got it framed and hung it on the wall in my Railway Quarter. In the night I had a dream that: I was in Shirdi. Baba was sitting in the Masjid. I was one among about 200 visitors there. I offered two plantains to Baba while others offered nothing. Baba asked me to cut the two fruits into bits and distribute the piece to all present there. I told Baba that the two fruits might not be sufficient for all. Baba said: "When you have no faith in me, why have you come here all the way from a very long distance?" Immediately cut the two fruits into bits and distribution them to all including Baba. A wonder, of wonder the plate was full as if I had not distributed anything to anyone.

Thus the dream ended. The next morning was Thursday. I went to foreman Sri Venkateswara Rao and narrated to him about my dream. He was wonderstruck and said, "Though I have been visiting Shirdi for the last 14 years, I have had no such experiences. You are very fortunate to have a wonderful experiences within a few days after your first visit". I wanted to perform Baba's Puja but I had no book on it. He searched his old book-shelf and picked up one on Baba's Puja in Telugu. He gave it to me. It was from that day I commenced Thursday Puja and after a few years daily Puja was also commenced in my house.

Second Vision:- Again on the following Wednesday night when I was fast asleep I felt that somebody was knocking at the doors of my house (in dream only). I went and opened the door and found Sri Sai Baba in flesh and blood standing at the door with his usual *kafni* (long roe) ead-gear, *Satka*. I invited Baba into the house. He come in and sat on a sofa and I was standing in front of his with folded hands. Baba asked me to sit with him on the same sofa by his side. With amazement and fear I sat. He exhorted me to cast off all my fears and told me that he was on his way to Bhadrachalam (where there is a very big temple for the Lord Sai Rama) to give darshan to all the devotees there, as He and Rama were the same and on his way came to our house to see us. Then I asked him why he should be going to Bhadrachalam, leaving Shirdi, to the disappointment of all the devotees coming from all over the country to have darshan and take his blessing. I requested Baba to go back to Shirdi, to the pleasure and welfare of all the people going there. He was silent for a minute or two as I did not approve of his going to Bhadrachalam. He told me that he was not going either to Bhadrachalam or to Shirdi. Then I picked up some courage as Baba spoke softy, and I asked what he wanted to do. He told me that He was going to stay in our house as one of the members of my family. I was very much afraid of his proposal and told him that I was a *grihastha* (householder) with so many avocations and how could I accommodate a saint like Him as there might be so many drawbacks in the family and sometimes we may not be in a position to do full justice to His supernatural spiritually and we may be subjected to his rase. Then he called me saying that he would adjust with the family in all respects and assured to take the burden of looking after all our needs and we would not have to take care of Him. The dream ended at about 5 A.M. with the calling by the milkmaid. From that day we intensified our devotion and *puja* regularly and are feeling His presence at all times.

My third son Chi. K. Raghuram [B. Tech, now Engineer, NTPC, Salem] was 5 months old in February, 1958. I fixed my program to celebrate 'Kesakhandana' (hair removing) ceremony at Shirdi before the end of his fifth month. I wrote to one of my relatives who owed me Rs. 300/- to send the amount through M.O. at an early date as had fixed my ShIrdi trip to perform on the Sunday of Feb. 1958 He remitted the amount accordingly. The M.O. was received in the Post-Office on Saturday [i.e.] the preceding day of my journey. But the post-man came to my house and informed that there was no such large amount available-since it was a small Post-Office and payment would be made on Monday after getting the amount from Vinukonda, the nearest big Post-Office. I rushed to the Post-Office and there the Post-Master informed me that since it was Saturday the M.O.s and saving bank account would not be operated in the evening and chances wear bleak to get Rs. 300/- by 11 A.M.

I told my wife: "Baba used to advice the devotees not to incur debts for pilgrimages or festivals. So I did not wish to raise a loan from any body for our Shirdi trip. We would go to Shirdi if the money order was received today only, otherwise there shall be no Shirdi trip. It is upto Baba whether to take us there or not". She asked me not to utter such words. I attended my office. Again I went to the Post-Office at 2 P.M. The Post Master told that there were no money transactions either in S.B. accounts or money orders. I went back to office with utter disappointment and all hopes of going to Shirdi the next day [i.e.] Sunday were shattered.

At about 4 P.M., I was called by the post-man to come to the Post Office. Hurriedly I went there. The Post Master paid Rs. 300/- asked to me sign on the money order. for without putting the date. When asked how he could pay the amount, he replied "A Muslim merchant whom I know came here at about 3:30 P.M. for depositing Rs. 300/- in his S.B. account. When I told him to come on Monday as the transactions were closed at 11 A.M. he requested me to deposit the money as Monday only, as he was going on a trip. So don't put the date on the M.O. from. I shall regularize both your transactions on Monday". My joy knew no bounds. We left for Shirdi on Sunday as per our scheduled programme. Thus Sri Sai proved his omnipotence and brought us to Shirdi. We stayed there for a few days visiting all the important place including Sakori. Our wish to remove hair of our third son at Shardi was fulfilled before his 5th month. Thereafter, almost every year we have been visiting Shirdi. I have numerous such experiences.

"May Sri Sai Baba Bless Us All"
-K.V.S. Subramanyam,
'SAI VIHAR' 46/18/10,
Danavaipeta, Rajahmundry-3
[Andhra Pradesh]
(From: *Shree Sai Leela*, May 1987)

27. SAI *DARSHAN* (1959)

My professor G.S. Paramasivayya (Principal, P.I.Sc. Institute, Belgaum) Initiated me to worship lord Sai Baba of Shirdi in 1551. So I followed in my own humble way. I was posted to Loni Engineering College during the period 1983-86, just near Shirdi to have Darshan almost once a week. Though late, I have a feeling that I must submit articles regarding *Sai Darshan-Nidarshan-Pradarshan*. In this way, I can purify myself inspite of pollution. First story is detailed below.

It was in June 1959 that I was required to make a sudden journey to Gulbarga for an interview for the post of Principal of S.B. College as my name was sponsored by then Vice-Chancellor Dr. D. Pawate. On my return journey by the train from Gulbarga to Hugti, I had to face the following strange dialogue with a strange young man dressed in white pant-shirt during the night from 8 p.m. to 11 p.m. etc., inside the moving train compartment (II-class).

He entered my compartment in a hurried manner just when the train started moving away from Gulbarga Station. I was sitting deeply thinking about my fate with no easy hope of settling with a comfortable job. I had just completed my experimental work for my Ph. D. Program in Karnataka University (1956-59) on three year study leave from R.L.Sc Institute Belgaum.

A small boy had brought a basket of fruits, along with the strange co-traveler, who had a bandage on one of his fingers of hand. He stood before me and asked me in loud voice: "There is lot of space with you. Why do you notu give me some space?" There were hardly two or three passengers in that compartment other than him and me. So I shouted back as though exhausting my internal agony.

"There is so much free space. Sit wherever you want. Why do you bother me?" He sat by my side and began talking to me and offered fruit while there was knife in his hand. Since I had just taken hot coffee, I could not receive the fruit (a gift which I am longing to receive now). He was moving his knife nearer my face. So in fear, I caught hold of his hand. He said, "Oh! You are afraid of the knife". I said, "No, there is already one bandage on your finger". Our dialogue continued:

He: I came in search of your compartment. I have not yet taken the ticket. I have told the T.C. to collect the charges at the next station.

The next station came within 15 minutes and the T.C. came and demanded Rs. 19.50). He took out one rupee bundle from his pocket. It was brand new bundle stitched with pins. He ordered me to take the bundle and to count the money to give to the T.C. But He went aside to the bathroom for a wash. My senses began to work faster to meet the strange situation. So I began to count the notes very loudly. He shouted from inside:- "I have faith in you". T.C. went away. He then began talking to me.

He: "You are not a rough man to manage the assignment at Gulbarga. Leave it. A safer place is being selected for you. Can you not keep your inner soul alive? Just wait for nine months more. That place is surrounded by water on all sides". (This prediction came true at the end of nine months.)

When he touched the actual current problems of my life, tears started rolling down from my eyes on to my face, uncontrolled; I was under His control by now.

Lo! Just then the other passengers were out of my sight. But they were seen again at Hutgi. During the entire journey, the dialogue continued as if 'He' & 'I' were left free for talks.

(He kept me engaged by telling the story of himself as an engineer working in Sahabad. But the entire story and its contents, were to be enacted in my future life from 1959 to 1987 etc.)

He: Do you know Gandhi-Ashram at Wardha? From here, I am going there. Do you think, I will go there in this dress, in pant etc. No, I will go there like a shepherd to talk to the persons in that *Ashram*.

(I was getting more and more puzzled about this strange person – He, His talk, ideas, motives etc.) As a good listener, I could restore my mental state at the level of calm with complete peace in mind.

He: Within the next two months say in November 1959. I am going to America not to see America but to see how Americans are now.

(It was around 11 P.M. Hutgi Station was nearing and I ordered for two cups of coffee, with the waiting attended of the railway Department). He made me drink both cups of coffee. He came nearer the exit as I was getting ready to get down at Hugti.

He said "OK! We will meet again."

I: How, when, what?

He: Just like this. [He continued the journey further and I moved to the other side of Platform to get into meter gauge train towards Dharwar.

Conclusion: His promise is kept up on several occasions of strange and fearful situation of danger to my life be but it train journey, bus journey, air-journey and in life journey.

Who is He; Is it His *Darshan* (visit) to be followed by Nidarshan (Logic of his ways; Words etc.) and waiting further *Pradarshan* i.e. exhibition. Year by year, His visiting cards reach me often awakening inner realization for pathway of God through kinetics of life cycle karmas while his cycle of *Darshan-Nidarshan*-Exhibition continues in every body's life circle.

Dr. D.R. Bagalkoti,
C/O, Dr. Ashok D. Bagalkoti,
Asst. Surgeon, Wenlock Hospital, Mangalore
(From: *Shri Sai Leela*, Jan. 1989)

28. WONDER OF WONDERS (1984)

"Nishta" and "*Saburi*" can only be understood when a person goes through the life history of Lord Sainath Mahaprabhu, in which He has revealed the significance of the dictum to the old lady, who earnestly awaited '*Upadesa*' from Him. Lord Sai explained to her in detail as to how He had been a disciple under His *Guru*. Devotees in the queue were moving slowly in the Sai Samadhi Mandir, shines I happened to see the big portraits of great saints hung on the walls of the Samadhi Mandir. The portrait of Sri Tajuddin Baba of Nagpur was also among them there.

Incidentally I had a talk with a devotee just before me in the queue and learnt that he was from Nagpur. Out of curiously, I requested him to let me know something about Sri Tajuddin Baba of Nagpur, about whom once Baba had said that he was His brother. I requested him also to kindly let me know, how he himself became a devotee of Sri Sainath.

On hearing this he immediately turned back and looked at me. I could then find an unimaginable love, dedicated devotion and implicit faith in Lord Sainath in his eyes.

He revealed that when he was once suffering from a severe stomach ache, he approached allopathic doctors for treatment, which only aggravated the disease instead of curing it. On the advice of his well-wishes, he approached an Ayurvedic doctor and took treatment, and the result was he developed swelling all over the body. Two days later the swelling subsided, but the body began to shrink a great deal. Due to the reaction of the drugs, the soles of his feet completely peeled off themselves and the nerves also became visible to the naked eye. In such a condition he was unable to stop on the ground. All the family members, not knowing what to do and in a helpless condition, were very much worried about his health. Having lost hope, but remembering the assurance of Lord Sainath he completely surrendered to Lord Sainath Mahaprabhu mentally and stopped taking any medicines except '*Udhi*' thrice a day with water, after duly chanting the Lord's name. During the above period, with prayers to Lord Sainath, he was daily applying butter to the soles of his feet covering it with cotton bandage and taking bed rest. For a long time he waited with unshakable implicit faith, *NISHAT*, and utmost patience, *SABURI*, with the confidence that Lord Sai would do certainly good to him. Within six months he became all right in all respects and then came to Shirdi to and express his gratitude to Lord Sainath Mahaprabhu.

When we are able to follow the instructions of our Lord Sri Sainath Mahaprabhu, Wonder of Wonders can be experienced by one and all. I am very sorry that I did not collect the address of the gentleman from Nagpur, but I remember that he was a railway employee at Nagpur.

"SRI SAMARTHA SADGURU SATCHIDANANDA SAINATH MAHAPRABHU KI JAI"

"JAI GURUDEVA DATTA"

-Mr. S. Sreenath M.I.E.,
Lecturer in Mechanical Engineering,
E.S.G. Government Polytechnic,
Nandyal 518 501,
Kurnool Dist., A.P.
(*Shree Sai Leela*, December 1987)

29. BABA SAVED SAI TEMPLE IN FLOOD (1961)

People of Pune can never forget its darkest day. The 13th of July 1961, when the Panchet Dam and Khadekvasla upstream burst and drowned Pune. Two eye witnesses and sufferers of the calamity were Sri B.V. Subba Rao and Sri S. Rama Krishnan. Gigantic columns of muddy water were seen spreading towards the town in no time. Police warning could hardly be followed. Bungalows and buildings collapsed, like pack of cards. With such devastation all round, the peoples anguish disappeared when they saw a small little Sai Baba temple in Shivajinagar. Pune intact. It was nothing short of a miracle. It was a lime mortar structure of 5 feet × 4 feet. The devotees were overcome with pleasure and decided to build a pucca temple. Soon a pucca temple was constructed. Sri Radha Krishna Swamiji consecrated the temple. He also presided over All India Sai Devotees Convention, held there.

30. HOW BABA TRANSFORMED A DEVOTEE (1965)

Upagrashta Sangamesan met an old Sage in 1941 who told him that Baba is a divine being, who would never let down His devotees, that he should do *Nitya Pooja* to Baba. He gave him a Baba photo. The sage also told him that in the beginning he would face mental worries, official problems, domestic worries etc., but not minding these difficulties, if he continued his devotion, Baba would take complete responsibility for his welfare, material and spiritual. As fore told by the sage, his troubles came from all sides and became unbearable. At this point of time, he even began to lose faith in the

Sage's words and in Sai Baba and in desperation sat on the steps leading to the temple. He found there a sign board "All India Sai Samaj". He went in and met Sri Narasimha Swamiji. Sangamesan bared himself before the Swamiji all his predicaments, doubts and misgivings Swamiji replied as under:

"No difficulties will come by having faith in Sai Baba and doing *pooja* to Him. One cannot escape the debts of *Poorva Karma*. Belief in Baba and Pooja to Him will help in liquidating the sins committed in *Poorva Janma* in course of time. You have so much dirt in your mind and on your soul. Hence the difficulties, that you are facing. When a seed is sown you cannot expect its fruit immediately. You have to wait patiently. It may take a short time or it may take some years. You should not cut the tree which is in the process of giving fruits. When the tree starts giving fruits, not only you, everybody in the locality will benefit."

Of course Sangamesan continued his Nitya Pooja to Baba and also met Swamiji several times thereafter. From 1965, Sai Baba began to speak to Sangamesan. Hundreds of people began to come to Sangamesan for solving their problems.

31 'SHRI SAI BABA OF SHIRDI *AVATAR* PAR EXCELLENCE (1964)

God is known to us in various forms or *avatars, Dasavatars*, Jesus Christ, Mohamed, Buddha and so on. The main purpose of so many avatars was the destruction of the wicked and protection of the virtuous, and in some preaching dharma and giving solace to those who look up to them and of course uplifting the spiritual aspirants. There are very few who would directly interfere and destroy Karma and give immediate relief to their devotees, which we call miracles. Shri Sai Baba of Shirdi, an avatar of Dattatreya i.e. Trinity (Brahma, Vishnu, Maheswara) in the form of *Samartha Sadguru* is the greatest, most powerful, merciful and munificent avatar in the Kaliyug. One has to have a pure mind and surrender to Him body, speech and mind and His immediate response and grace is forthcoming. As Sri Ramakrishna Paramahamsa said, when we invite our boss or a V.I.P. to our house we dust, clean and adorn the drawing room an make it fit to receive him. In the same manner when we invite the Lord into our heart we have to clean it of impurities and make it pure and fit for Him to reside. With a pure heart if we pray Shri Sai Baba, His grace and response is immediate as He is sure to hear our humble prayers. We are exposed to the vagarie of fate or rather our previous Karma and are tossed like a cork on the turbulent ocean of mundane existence. In this state we have no other recourse than the Lotus Feet of our all-powerful merciful *Samartha Sadguru* Shri Sai Baba. This does not mean that we pray Shri Sai for temporal benefits only. It is actually the other way round. Our main purpose and prayer to the Lord and for spiritual uplift and *moksha* in this very birth. But in our helpless state temporal relief is essential and as Baba Himself declared He gives His devotees what they want, so that they will ask Him what He wants to give them. I will give a couple of experiences we are having by His Grace since the time we become His devotees which ranges back to about 1943.

In the year 1964 my elder son, who was then 8 years old, suffered from acute and persistent headache. The headache used to start in the morning and last the whole day and was so unbearable that the poor boy who was brilliant in his studies just could not sit and write his exams. We consulted all specialist doctors. The ENT expert performed nasal puncture and the neuro surgeon lumbar puncture all to no avail. One Thursday night after our usual *bhajan* at home and before retiring in the night I prayed to Lord Shri Sai Nath, cast the entire burden on Him and invoked His Grace upon my son and applied His *udi* to his forehead. Next morning my son woke up shivering, went to my wife and narrated his dream to her. It seems in the dream he was playing with his younger brother when a butterfly past and diverted his attention. When he looked up he saw Lord Sri Sai Baba seated on the stone in His usual posture surrounded by blinding bluish light. My son gave his *namaskar* and asked that his headache he cured. Shri Sai Baba gave his *abhayam* and disappeared. When I was told his the next morning I said to my son that he would never get headache again. There was no headache from then onward. It just disappeared.

By Baba's grace myself along with my wife celebrate Shri Sai Nath's *Mahasamadhi* day on Vijayadasami day starting with Kakad arati in the morning, *Abhisheks*, *Astothras*, noon *arati*, *dhoop arati* at sunset and bhajan. Many Sai devotees attend the functions. In the year 1982 one Sri Kutumbarao came to our house at about 11 a.m. At the time of noon *arati* some other devotees also turned up bringing some fruits etc., as offering to the Lord. The arati commenced with me and my wife singing it. We reached the *Manthrapushpam* stage when Mr. Kutumbarao was sore with himself for having come empty handed and felt that he should have brought atleast a coconut. No soonerthan this thought passed through His mind an old man with a sack on His shoulder came in and asked Mr. Kutumbarao point blank "do you want a coconut? Here take this", and produced a coconut from His sack and handed over to Sri Kutumbarao. At this moment my wife was distributing flowers to be showered on Shri Sai Baba after the *Manthrapushpam*. The old man was nowhere to be seen. The old man gave the coconut, took the flower which was to be showered on Shri Sai Baba and disappeared. When the coconut was broken it resembled the ones we buy it Shirdi. This miracle was a turning point in Sri Kutumbarao's life, who became an ardent devotee of Shri Sai Baba and is so now, with Baba helping him at every step. The ways and *leelas* of The Almighty Sri Sai Baba are incomprehensible and inexplicable. He is everywhere at all times and can manifest Himself in any form and give darshan to His devotees. He blessed our house with His Divine Darshan which is all purifying and benevolent.

My humble *pranams* to His Holy Feet.

-Dr. K.V. Gopalakrishna,

D. No. 49-12/1/1, Lalitanagar,

(*Shri Sai Leela*, May, 1988,)

32. BABA'S HELP TO A DEVOTEE (1965-72)

1972; It was my first visit to Tirupathi, the abode of Lord Venkateshwara. I had read in the newspapers that there had been a great rush of devotees to see the Lord, resulting in stampede. I had also heard that one could get in for darshan on payment of a fee. My father had retired. We had built our house in Jayanagar, Bangalore and I had difficulties in my profession. We were experiencing financial constraints. To put if simply, I did not have money for making the trip as well as for payment for darshan. However, I felt the urge to go to Tirupathi.

So what else could I do than to appeal to my personal God Sri Sai Baba. Standing before His photo, I told him "Baba, you know my predicament and my financial condition. Can I not see the Lord without making payment and without any scuffle and stampede?" Having prayed thus, I transferred my problems to Sai Baba and left for Tirupathi.

The bus reached Tirumala at about 8 p.m. I could get an accommodation not for away from the temple. As I was coming out from my room a friend from Bangalore told me, "Go immediately, there is not much rush now". I went accordingly and saw Lord Venkateshwara for the first time. I had not thought while at Bangalore, that I could go and see Lord Venkateshwara, within half an hour of landing at Tirumala.

Between 8 p.m. and 8 p.m. the next day I had five darshan of the Lord to my heart's content.

The Lord was pleased to give me the fifth darshan, all exclusive to myself. At about 8 a.m. after my fourth darshan. I was sauntering around the sanctum sanctorum all alone, as all the other devotees had left. I was reminiscing about my good fortune in being able to see the Lord so effortlessly, when I saw the door leading to the sanctum sanctorum half-open. There was none around the place. I peeped in. A few *archakas* were preparing to give *abhishek* to the Lord. As they were busy with their work, they did not notice that the door was half open. I gingerly stepped in and saw Lord Venkateshwara once again, for full two minutes, undisturbed and all by myself. I quietly came out, feeling supremely happy.

Sai Baba of Shirdi and Lord Venkateshwara – the names are different; but in fact, they are one the same.

I had been suffering from a skin ailment called psoriasis for many years. It is a persistent and recurring skin condition. I had it on the covered portions of my body. Neither skin specialists of Madras, where I was living then, nor the skin specialists of the Christian Medical Hospital Vellore, could give my any relief, much less cure. A person suffering from a skin condition like psoriasis knows the misery and the suffering that has to be endured. I do now know if there is any remedy for this now. There was no cure at the time I suffered from it.

In the year 1965, I happened to come across the book *"The Incredible Sai Baba"* written by Arthur Osborne, Displayed at Higginbothams. Mount Road, Madras. I purchased the book and read it. My fascination for Sai Baba began from the reading of that book I came to know about Sai Baba His *Samadhi Mandir* and that He continues to give succor to the ailing and the troubled ones even after His *Mahasamadhi*. After reading that book, I very much wanted to go to Shirdi, to pray to Sai Baba to relieve me of my skin condition.

My wish could materialize only in December 1971, when I was settled at Bangalore. That was my first visit. At the end of December 1972. I happened to be at Bombay. From there I went to Shirdi. On my second visit. I prayed to Sai Baba, to cure me from the skin ailment. I returned to Bangalore by 1st January 1973.

Immediately thereafter things started to happen. While taking bath I noticed that the scaly crusts on eh skin were falling off. The next day, the same thing continued. On the third day, all the scaly crusts had come off, leaving red patches in their place. Within a week. I was completely free from psoriasis, which had troubled me for so many years. What a relief I felt at that time. I did not realize the profundity of the cure, a miracle you may call it. Having suffered at its hands for so long. I was apprehensive that it would reappear the next week, the next month, or the next year. But nothing of that sort happened. By Sai Baba's grace I am free from it.

33. SHRI SAI BABA'S DIVINE GRACE (1966)

On perusal of my diary, I am shocked to learn that my life would have ended nearly sixteen years back, but for the intervention of ever-vigilant and merciful Sri Sai, I am convinced that He is always guarding His devotees like an affectionate mother keeping a watch on her child which is playing in the park.

Here are the details:

Quite a number of trees plants have grown in our back yard which is vast in area. There we have observed a family of mongoose living happily for nearly two decades. Through the kitchen window, we have watched for hours the young ones playing nicely almost everyday. Hence we have never seen a snake in our compound at any time.

Kasthuribai Resident's Association is within a distance of about one km. from our house. It has a spacious hall suitable for *katha kalaakshepums*, *pravachanams* and meetings. On 20th Feb. 1966, we had arranged for a *Hair kathakalakshepam* by one famous Vidwan Sri Krishna Bhagavather of Bangalore. He was wellknown for a versatile presentation of Sri Rama Dasa Charitra in Kannada. The time fixed for the Harikartha was 6 p.m., but due to unforeseen circumstances, Bhagavathar arrived almost 2 hours late.

As my wife was having fever and the children fast asleep, I went alone walking to the Residents Association. The Kalakshepam ended by about 11 p.m. My eldest brother with his son had also come there from Gandhinagar in car. His house was more than 3 kilometers from the Association Hall. After the Harikatha was over, I went up to Sri Bhagavather to offer my respects. He was very happy to see me after a long time and blessed me with an affectionate embrace, he made enquiries about my wife and children. When I told him that my wife could not attend the evening programme on account of fever he was very sorry to hear the news. He expressed a desire to visit our house then itself. It was already 11:30 p.m. As such I thought within myself that if that Strothrey Brahmin came to our house at that odd hour, we might not be able to receive him properly. So I requested him to come to our house next day and also have food with us. Then I did not comprehend Sri Sai's *Leela* which is beyond human understanding. As he persisted that he would like to come then alone, there was no choice left and so I agreed to the proposal. I also told him that I would gladly take him and his accompanying musicians to Saidapet in my car which was in my garage. My brother was listening to our conversation. He asked me whether I had come in my car, when I told him that I had come walking, he immediately asked me to take his car along with the Bhagavathar to my house and then after our return to take the rest of the party to Saidapet. He would send his driver next day morning to collect his car. When he told me that he and his son was would walk home at that odd hour, I felt very unhappy because he was nearly ten years elder to me. I thought it would be cruel to accept his car to make them suffer for my sake, hence I flatly refused to accept his very kind offer. He again insisted that I should take his car without any mental reservations. So I accepted his generous offer. Mother Sai plans every movement meticulously carefully, but we fail to understand His divine will.

I took Sri Krishna Bhagavathar in my brother's car and reached our house within a short time. Both the gates were closed. When I got down from the driver's seat to open the gates, probably on account of the bright headlights, a big cobra suddenly got up hissing with its hood fully open from the middle where both gates meet. As I was taken aback, I called out Baba to save us and got back into the car at once. After a few minutes when I switched on the headlights, the cobra had disappeared from the scene. That was the first and the last time, I have ever seen a cobra in our compound. Then we entered the house. Bhagavathar enquired my wife about her health and after that straight went into our puja room, where he sat meditating for a few minutes. We offered him milk and fruits. He took only a little milk. Then he asked me to take him and the musicians immediately to Saidapet. He also expressed his inability to visit our house the next day on account of some prior engagements. I took him and his companions to the place where they were staying in Saidapet and returned home safely.

When I narrated all the details to my wife she shed tears of joy before Baba's photo and expressed her sincere gratitude to Him. I also joined her for offering my heartfelt thanks.

In retrospect while going through the events that occurred on that night, the following appear to me of utmost importance:

1. Because my wife was not well and children did not come, I did not go to the Association hall in my car. Instead I went there walking.
2. Because Sri Krishna Bhagavathar insisted that he would come to our house at that odd hour my brother forced me to take his car.

3. But for the event (2) in the ordinary course I would have walked back home, stepped on the cobra in the darkness with the consequent fatal end of my life.

4. So some higher power planned all the events meticulously to save me from an *akala maranam*. I believe and am sure you will all agree with me when I state that Shri Sai, our affectionate mother and all pervading Brahman, showered His divine Grace in extending my life for some time.

No logical or scientific explanation could adequately and satisfactorily answer the sequence of events.

With my *Sashtanga Namaskarams* and sincere gratitude to Shri Sai, I close this narration. I pray to Him to shower His divine grace on all the Sai devotees impartially.

-Dr. A.R. Govinda Rao,
M.B.B.S., M.S.
Padmalaya, 25, II Main Road,
Kasturba Nagar, Adyar, Madras – 600200
(*Shri Sai Leela*, Dec., 1988)

34. FIRST EXPERIENCE WITH SAI BABA (1966-1993)

During my last years of army service I was posted at Bombay. I was to retire on 29 Oct. 1968 and was planning to get re-employment for another 3-4 years in the same job. When suddenly during my annual medical examination in May 1967, the medical officer advised me to get my heart checked up sometime again as he had some doubts. I did not pay much attention to it but soon after during my official tour to Pune I felt very uneasy while going round a cadet camp in the hot sun. So on my return I went to the medical officer for a re-check and after an ECG he asked me to got admitted in the Naval Hospital. Nothing seemed seriously wrong and I was walking round the ward quite happily. But the diagnosis termed my case as IHD (Ischaemic Heart Disease) and I was low-categorized medically, Next one and half years or so I attended various up-grading medical boards but in the last board I was declared unfit to serve in the army. This closed my opportunity for re-employment in the Army. However luckily, before retirement I had attended a short Hotel Management course at the Institute of Hotel Management at Dadar (Bombay) which gave me some chance of working again as I was still 50 years of age.

During one of my above-mentioned hospitalizations, my co-patients in the room, happened to be an officer from my Regiment. He had kept on the dressing table between us a picture of Sri Sai Baba, whom he used to worship morning and evening, I was rather surprised, since the officer, as I remembered correctly, was a rich bachelor from a Royal Family in the South, and was a heavy drunkard and a hard smoker also. One day he told me that on getting discharge from the hospital, he would just visit Shirdi. Naturally I became inquisitive about Sai Baba about whom I hardly knew anything – although a Maharashtrian myself.

Luckily only a few days ago my daughter was engaged to a boy who happened to be a Sai devotee. So when he called on me in the evening I inquired from him if he had any literature on Sai Baba. He told me that he had a book 'Life of Sri Baba' but it was in Gujarati language. Although a Maharashtrian I was born and brought up at Vadodara in Gujarat State, hence there was no difficulty and I asked him to bring it the next day. As soon as I got it I started reading it and finished it during my stay in the hospital itself. On reading the book I was very much impressed and had a desire to visit Shirdi.

In the preface to the book, the author had mentioned that if the book is read within 7 days one is likely to get some wonderful experience. So on returning some from the hospital I again read it within seven days starting from a Thursday. On 3rd August 1968 (the next Thursday), as I looked at the morning issue of "SAKAL" (a Marathi daily), I saw a picture of silver *padukas* (sandals) of Shri Sai Baba of Shirdi. It was mentioned there in that they were being carried from Shirdi to London next day and were kept for devotees to visit at Shri Prenal Vithoda Temple at Fanaswadi in Girgaum. I was thrilled and left as if Baba said to me, "You may come to Shirdi whenever convenient in future, but I am available to you here at Bombay today and if you like you can come over and have my darshan".

Naturally I decided to go and in the evening along with the my wife and mother-in-law. At first, I wanted to take my car but then I changed my mind since I had just come out of the hospital. Luckily it turned out to be a good decision since later I realized that the location in which I thought the temple was situated was not correct. The taxi driver took us correctly to the area Fanaswadi and stopping the taxi said, "Here is Fanaswadi. Please inquire as to the exact location of the temple". I was about to get out of the taxi and inquire from somebody as to the location, when my mother-in-law, who had peeped out of the taxi on the other side, said "Look! The temple is here itself. See the sign-board" I was happily surprised and getting out paid the driver. The fare too turned out to be much less than expected.

As we entered the temple, I saw a life-size idol of Shri Sai Baba in front and two small idols of Shri Vithala (Krishna) and Rakhumai (Rukmini) on the right. As I saw the idol of Sai Baba, I was thrilled and forgot that I had come there for the silver *padukas* (sandals). I bowed down, placed my *dakshina* (cash) at Baba's feet and felt greatly satisfied. Then suddenly I heard my wife saying, "Look! Baba's *padukas* are here under Audumbar Tree. As I had my darshan with full contentment, I just got up mechanically, and without any excitement or emotion went behind the temple and bowed down to touch the silver sandals, and lo! what a thrill I had! My whole body quivered with great pleasure. The whole world around me was full of bliss and joy. My hands were almost glued to the rush of devotee visitors. I had to remove them and go round the tree along with other crowd. I again went to the *padukas* and touched them again and again. I felt as if I had found my solace, Guru's sacred feet, permanently never to be given up!

On returning home, I decided to study deeply all literature on Sai Baba and increase my devotion towards Him. I bought the original Marathi *"Shri Sai Satcharita"* on 13 Aug. '67 and read it completely. Immediately afterwards I decided to read one chapter every day whether at home, in travel and not to read anything. This vow of mine is going on with Baba's grace even till today (for the last 29 years) and I have had many a wonderful experiences thereof. In addition I started reading the same *"Sai Satcharita"* continuously in a week during the holy mouth of Shravan every year which also has given me rare experiences and blessing from Sai Baba.

As mentioned above, after retirement from the Army at the age of 50 with low medical category, I accepted a Manager's job in one of the top hotels in Pune. I was the top executive and had the liberty of attending to duties conveniently according to my wishes. However, after about six months I decided to leave it. Since my wonderful experience at Bombay on 4 Aug. 1967, I was drawn deep into Sai devotion and spiritually activities like Yoga, reading of religious books etc. I had married my daughter happily and out of my 4 sons, 3 had already hold got Class I appointments in service. The youngest was studying in college and my other sons had already taken up the responsibility of educating him further. So one day I suddenly realized that which person would have such relief from family responsibilities at such an early age! Why not make most of this rare opportunity to serve Sai Baba whole-heartedly to improve my spiritual prospects?

I started reading first Marathi religious literature – *jnaneshwari* (commentary on Geeta), *Dasbodha* (by Ramdas), *Eknathi Bhagvat* and *Tukaram Gatha*. As I had Sanskrit as my second language in school and college, I read *Ramayan* and *Mahabharat* in original Sanskrit and later the *Upanishadas* also. In the end with Baba's grace I dived deep into 4 *Vedas* also. Thus for 10 years Baba made me study the above-mentioned literature and then inspired me to write articles in *Sri Sai Leela* (official organ of Shri Sai Baba Sansthan of Shirdi) and other religious magazines. So far I have written more than 175 articles both in Marathi and English. I have also published a small book *"Guru-Geeta"* and English translation of Das Ganu's *Stavan Manjairi* in Marathi verse. As a *purinache*, Baba got from me a 700 page Marathi prose translation with detailed commentary and notes on the original *"Shri Sai Satcharita"* in verse, which written, about 60 years ago and full of the Sanskrit and archaic Marathi words, is not easily understood even by present day Maharashtrians. The book is beautifully printed with over 50 coloured and black-white pictures. The price is Rs. 200 + Rs. 30 packing & postage. It was published in 1993 and the first edition having been almost exhausted I have taken up publishing second edition having been almost exhausted I have taken up publishing second edition soon. I have also completed two books (one in Marathi & other in English) viz "Sai Baba's Philosophy and Teaching" consisting of 21 articles each. All this is Baba's grace for the benefit of Sai devotees and gives me intense satisfaction.

I shall be completing 78 years of age in October 1990 and hope Baba gets more service from me for Sai devotees till end of my life.

I am 77 old and suffering from Angina for the last 27 years. But it never got aggravated. Only while walking or on awakening from sleep during might, I used to get severe pain in the chest but by placing half sorbitrate tablet under the tongue I used to get relief. Naturally, therefore, I never dreamt that I would ever get on heart attack or I shall have to undergo a Bypass Surgery. Even the cardiologist who occasionally examined me and took ECG, found nothing seriously wrong with me.

However since September 1989, I suddenly started feeling very weak and in early October I started getting repeated pains in my chest during day as well as night, which would not easily subside even with more tablets of sorbitrate under the tongue. Hence my sons admitted me in N.M. India Institute of Cardiology at Pune for treatment. For almost the whole of October I was in the hospital and after carrying out Anagiography it was noticed that four of my cardiac arteries were blocked 70 to 100 p.c. and consequently a Bypass Surgery was carried out on my heart. By Sai Baba's grace the operation was successfully and safely performed and I am recovering. Now I would like to narrate how Sai Baba looked after me in all respects during my this illness.

Firstly on 8th November when my operation was to take place, somebody informed Shri Prabhakar Chandorkar (grand son of late Nanasaheb Chandorkar, the famous devotee of Sai Baba referred to repeatedly in *Shri Sai Satcharita*) about it, Shri Prabhakar stays in Pune on Pande Road opposite Vanaz Factory quite for away from the hospital, Situated near Pune Railway Station. But even then, Shri Prabhakar immediately rushed down at to place of my operation with *Udi* (holy ash) given to his grand father personality by Baba and stayed there with Baba's *Udi* for 6 long hours until my operation was successfully performed. Now, normally anybody who is not closely related to you would not come down immediately from such a long distance but would rather think of visiting the patient only next day at ease to inquire about his health but then, who must have prompted Shri Prabhakar to act thus abnormally? On hearing about this later, I was reminded of ch 33 of *"Shri Sai Satcharita"* wherein the late Shri Nanasaheb Chandorkar's daughter Maina Tai at Jamner was suffering from severe labour pains for 2-3 days without delivering and few Baba sent His *Udi* and *arati* with Ramgir Buva of Shirdi to effect Maina Tais delivery promptly. Indeed I was ever behind with Baba's similar grace to me – a very humble devotee compared to late Nanasaheb.

Secondly during my three week's stay at the hospital after the operation, inspite of being given 10 bottles of blood, I had gone, very weak, so much so that I could not lift my eyelids, I was scared of losing my eyesight had become very dejected. At that time one day, in my dream Baba Himself appeared before me and hitting my hand said, "Come! I will take you home." And really after 3-4 days I become perfectly alright and was discharged from the hospital also.

Finally, the correct timing for the operation. For the last 22 years after my retirement we both, myself and wife, are staying at Pune alone, and all our four sons being in service stay far away from us. Only recently 2-3 years ago our eldest son has taken premature retirement from Army and settled in Pune and during my recent aggravation of illness luckily all my sons, daughter and daughters-in-law were present due to the wedding of our grand-daughter. Consequently, the decision regarding the operation could be taken promptly without invitation and the problem regarding post-operation care was also easily solved. Actually this operation is very expensive – costly 1.50 lakhs to

1.75 lakhs of rupees. IN the Army at present, there is an insurance scheme for such expensive medical treatments. In our days this scheme was not in existence. But only one year before my operation, this scheme was extended to pensioners like me after paying certain subscription.

I paid the subscription of Rs. 2700/- immediately and thus became eligible to get Rs. 1 lakh for my operation next year. Just emagine the plight of myself and my wife, if my illness had aggravated 2-3 years earlier.

Thus I sincerely believe that during my this illness and consequent Bypass Surgery, Sai Baba was constantly looking after me.

"Those devotees who knowing no one else, constantly think of me and worship Me in a disinterested way, I bring full security and personally attend to their needs." (Ch 9 vol 22)

-Lt. Col. M. B. Nimbalkar, Pune
"Marathi Shri Baba Satcharita"
(Written in Sept. 95 and published
in SAI PREM of Calcutta)

35. BABA RELIEVED FINANCIAL TENSIONS OF A DEVOTEE (1970)

My family regards Baba as its Head and in turn we are blessed by Baba to the extent that whatever we pray to Him, He fulfills. There are good number of such experiences of His grace on us, which have been penned by me from time to time and published in different magazines and newspapers. I narrate one of them.

It was the decade 1970s when were financially tight but pulling on our livelihood somehow. I thought that whatever I get is with Baba's blessings, I owe a part of my earnings to Him. I started sending by money order or cheque a token amount to Shirdi Sai Baba Sansthan, which I still continue, you will be surprised to note that I never felt any financial crisis there after, and the cash box in our house is never empty, even on the last days of the month. I feel, Baba's saying, "...... The devotee, those who pay *dakshina* to Me, get 10 times more to whatever they offer and make their own ways in the spiritual life... "is 100 per cent true, and He takes care of him. "You look to me, I look to you." "You take one step forward, I will taken 10 steps forward for your welfare."

-Vijay Krishna Thakur, 55 years
Accounts Officer, M.P. Electircity Board,
'Sai Niketan', 152, Shantinagar, Jabalpur
482001 (M.P.)

36. BABA'S MIRACULOUS CURES IN PHYSICAL CALAMITIES

Sai Baba is a living presence. He manifests Himself in His own inscrutable ways and in different ways to different devotee according to their needs and evolution. He helped me both materially and spiritually in numerous occasions. And now He has made me desireless. There is an urge to become insignificant and unknown to people. Publicity, fame, lecturing, writing books and articles have all become tasteless to me. But at the same time, from a blade of grass to Maha Vishnu, and the Supreme power of the Supreme Ananda to me; all by the grace of Baba who is Omnipotent and Omnipresent!

On 14th Nov. 1971 my daughter Mrs. Aburi Prameela underwent operation for a delivery. After the operation the doctor found that so much blood had gone that it was necessary to infuse blood into her. She was praying to Baba since she got over the influence of Chloroform. As the doctor set up the necessary apparatus to infuse blood, she suddenly found that the patient had got back enough blood into her and there was no need to infuse it from outside. The doctor exclaimed, "It is a miracle". This happened at Hyderabad.

The same daughter at the age of three was bitten by a mad dog. Daily injections had to be given for 21 days. The doctor was surprised that the child did not cry when painful injections were given. When questioned the child would answer "Baba goes to the hospital along with me and holds my hand when injection is given. I never feel any pain". For 21 days the same thing happened.

Her frock caught fire when doing Puja. She was three years and a half then. She was seriously burnt. IN unconscious state, she saw Baba sitting by her side on the bed in the Hospital. She was discharged as it was a hopeless case. After taking home maggots appeared on her chest. The doctors said that there was no possible treatment. Suddenly a doctor from Anantapur who had come to see me saw the child. In half an hour, he went to the Traveller's Bungalow where he was temporarily residing, brought necessary instrument, removed all maggots by the aid of a battery light as it was already 8 P.M. From then for 3 months he treated her. Just on the day when she was able to sit up, he was again transferred to Medical College, Madras, as a lecturer.

At another time when she was five and quite well she had vision of Baba in a garden of Tulsi plants at Yerapedu.

Shri B.V. Narasimha Swami who invariably was my guest whenever he come to my p[lace had inspired in her heart devotion to Baba.

-C.S. Ramaswamy
C/II/4 Tata Housing Centre, Andheri,
Bombay – 400080
(Courtesy: T.R. Naidu, Hyderabad)

37. BABA HELPS DEBTOR (1971)

A Pleader's Clerk, not much of a devotee nor an ethical man, took a portrait of Baba from me. He used to put a garland of flowers over it and prostrate daily before it before going to office. This was all he did.

He was indebted. He creditor obtained a decree and brought his house for sale. Next day was the day for court auction. Highly in despair he went out of his house and sat on a culvert. It was nine in the night. His washerman was coming along the road fully drunk and with faltering steps. The washerman had something tied up in a towel. He said to the pleaders. "Sir, why are you here at this hour?" The Clerk narrated his circumstance. The drunken man said "Here is the money required. I had lent it to a co-worker. Just now he has returned it fully. Take this and pay back at your convenience." The Clerk paid it into court next day and the sale was stopped.

-C.S. Ramaswamy,
C/II/4 Tata Housing Centre, Andheri,
Bombay – 400080
(Courtesy: T.R. Naidu)
Hyderabad

38. BABA CURED A DUMB MAN IN MAURITIUS (1971)

May I, dear Sai brother, give you in a nutshell, the historic background of the Shirdi Sai Baba Mandir of Curepipe, Mauritius.

I had a son, Kumar by name (aged 14 years), who was dumb since his birth; in spite of all sorts of medical treatment, his dumbness persisted. So, I decided to go on pilgrimage to India and pray for the cure of my dear son. Thus I happened to visit the Sai Baba temple in Shirdi where I literally crept on all four towards Baba's Samadhi and entreated Bhagavan for the cure of my son. I guess Baba was moved by my very sincere and heart-felt prayers and He accorded me His Divine Grace. Shortly after my return to Mauritius and to my most pleasant surprise my dear son Kumar began talking normally. By

Baba's divine Grace he secured a good job later on, he got married and has two charming children. He spends most of his spare time in looking after the Mandir and conducting puja.

In gratitude to Shirdi Sai Baba and to the profuse Grace He showered on me, I made a *Sankalpa* to build a small Shirdi Sai Baba temple in my premises and to expound the glory, the grandeur and the divinity of Sai Baba among the people of Mauritius.

Thus it is that in 1971, the Sai Baba Mandir in Curepipe, Mauritius opened its doors with a very humble beginning. I worked very hard to make the Sai mission flourish; and to-day the Sai Baba Mandir and the Sai Baba Centre of Curepipe has become a place of pilgrimage for thousands of people from all over Mauritius as well as from the neighbouring countries.

By now I am 81 years old; I have been doing the Sai Baba Mission for some 30 years. By Baba's grace, I am healthy and in good shape, and I wish to continue this good work for many more years.

There have been innumerable instances of miraculous cures, of success, in enterprises, of childless couples blessed with a children, and several other such miracles for the devotees of the Shirdi Sai Baba temple of Mauritius. Sometimes on Sundays and public holidays, the crowd of devotees at Mandir is so dense that I have to have recourse to the local police to maintain order and discipline and to control the traffic. Baba's Glory is spreading far and wide and I am very happy that Baba has chosen me as His instrument to spread His Glory and Grace and this small country of Mauritius.

The Sai Baba Temple in Mauritius has become so famous and renowned that it is referred to as the little Shirdi in Mauritius.

Parsh cure pipe Mauritius Shri Baba,
(Sri Sai Leela, Sept.-Oct. 1996)

39. EIGHT THRILLING INCIDENTS OF SAI GRACE IN A PARSI DEVOTEE'S LIFE (1959-80)

Sri Jal Mani Chinoy, a Parsi devotee of Sri Shirdi Sai Baba, lives at B-3, Khullar Apartments, Byramji Town, Nagpur. He is aged 71 years and is a well-known and highly reputed Sai devotee of Nagpur. He is suffering from heart problem, loneliness and despondency after his dear wife Mani's death in 1992. He came in the fold of Sri Shirdi Sai Baba in October, 1956. ON my fervent request he wrote down and sent me the following thrilling experiences of his life wherein Sri Shirdi Sai Baba's grace descended on him and his family.

Then I visited Sri Jal M. Chinoy at Nagpur in November 1996 and had a very detailed discussion with him about Sri Shirdi Sai Baba and His grace on him.

-Editor

(1) In May 1959 I was serving as Office Manager, Office of the Deputy Accountant General, M.S. Nagpur. The D.A.G. Mr. Chawla was a very strict man. For every order he wanted compliance. One Saturday afternoon he called me and handed over his daughter's Admission Card for Matric Examination. He told me that he wanted her Examination centre to be shifted from Dhiran Kanya Shala to Bishop Cotton High School which was close to his Bungalow. It was Saturday, the next day was Sunday and the examination was on Monday. The task really seemed impossible. I went to my cabin and prayed to Sri Shirdi Sai Baba to help me in this job to beep myself in good terms with the top boss. I appealed to Sri Sai to show me the way how I should proceed and do this job. In an instant descended on me the divine guidance.

First I went and met the Secretary, High School Certificate Examination. After a good deal of persuasion, he endorsed on the Card. *"Change of centre permitted provided her name is struck off from the original centre and entered in Bishop Cotton School".* The entire task to be done by the girl's representative that is me. I again went and prayed to Sai. I went to Dhiran Kanya Shala and requested the Principal to delete her name from her centre. She said that the serial order of the tables arranged had to be rearranged, there was no peon available. I got hold of one peon and arranged the tables as desired by the Lady Principal. Then I approached the father Principal of Bishop Cotton School. He totally refused to disturb any arrangement already done. I appealed to beloved Sai Baba again to influence him. After a good deal of persuasive talk, he came round and asked me to fetch an extra table from a classroom. I managed to fetch the suitable table and got the job done as desired by the irritable Father Principal. Having obtained his signature I returned to the D.A.G's bungalow. He was anxious, as the job was really impossible and for which he had already tired with the officers of education Department. When I informed him that it had been done as desired by him he told me that he had put me to test. What cannot be achieved in the name of Sri Sai Baba!

(2) It was August 1960. My father was very fond of gardening. He used to grow big sized roses in the garden opposite our residence. One morning he had placed on Sri Sai's lap a very attractive rose. When I approached the

prayer alter, the rose captured my attention. I asked Sai Baba to give me that rose, but there was no response. It was Monday morning. On Tuesday and Wednesday there was the same craving in me. When the rose did not move I prayed to Sri Sai Baba, "Baba I am really sorry to ask you for something which I do not deserve now, but Baba whenever you consider me worthy to receive this rose through your own hands you put it right into my palms. Next day was Thursday, a special day for Sri Sai to give presents to his devotees. In the morning again there was no response, but I did not give up. As a History student at about 11 P.M. I was thick set in my study. I completed the book on Indian History by Prof. P. Sarkar and as per daily routine stood in front of the altar, praying, "Sri Sai, you have blessed me, and the day has passed off well. May tomorrow be better." As I was holding out my open palms to accept His blessings, the rose desired by me miraculously and gently came in my palms on Thursday. Thus my request of Monday was granted by Sai Sai on Thursday night before my going to bed. At that time I had such high spiritual feeling in me, as if I had personally met Sri Sai and He himself gave the desired rose personally to me. I have no words to record that feeling I experienced as it was just Super-divine. That is how our devotion towards Sri Sai Baba is rewarded. The petals that rose are still in my purse.

(3) In August 1961 after completing my Audit word at Kandri Mine I was returning home. The return bus had to be taken from Mansar Bus Stop. There was a big crowd of passengers on that day as it was *Bazaar* day. The Agent, Kandri Mine, insisted on me that he would take me in his jeep, I did not wish to accept any obligation. Three buses passed, I could not get in. The last bus to pass Munsar Bus Stop was due to arrive. The situation seemed very very difficult. It is at such times Sri Sai Baba instantly comes to help us. I earnestly prayed to Baba and with confidence on Baba I allowed the party to go back to Kandri. The bus arrived, but it was totally full. The driven stopped it at a little distance from the regular stop. I was standing at the stop. The Conductor shouted *"Sahab aap aa jayeeye"*. The crowd gave me way. Sai Leela!

After covering one kilometer it started raining so heavily that there was no visibility for the driver. In an attempt to clear off a cart the bus suddenly slided into a soft field filled with knee deep water. Women and children in the bus started screaming. The driver was a man of guts. He consoled everybody and requested the gents to get down and push back the bus on the main road. As there was no seat vacant, the Conductor had allowed me to occupy his seat, hence I was the first one to get down. My right hand was holding the door to let other gents get down. Suddenly, in that pitched darkness one man dressed in Sadhu's robes caught hold of my finger on which I had Sai Baba's ring. He said, "To save you today Sri Sai saved 40 lives of this bus". In the meantime, in hurry we all pushed the bus on the main road. The driver shouted and told us to occupy our seats. When I was seated, I wondered as to who that man could be in that pitched darkness who had held my finger and told me that Baba had rescued me. He was nowhere to be seen in the bus. I then presumed that he was Sri Sai Baba himself who had saved me and 40 other passengers from a ghastly disaster which could have happened.

(4) In February 1962, I, my wife Mani and my two sons decided to visit Sri Sai at Shirdi. Our friends and relatives gave us some amounts for *Aarti* and garlands etc. Our immediate neighbour Mr. Sapurjee, D.M., LIC, gave us Rs. 3/- and requested us to feed a poor man with a Thali. There was a long list of 27 requests. We reached Shirdi and very meticulously, according to list, fulfilled the requests of all the people. After doing very good Puja and receiving blessing of our beloved Sai, we stepped out of the Mandir on our way to our Hotel. Suddenly we were respectfully intercepted by an old bearded man. He asked us whether we had performed *Puja-Aarti* for us and done as desired by all those who had entrusted us money for *Aarti* etc. We confirmed that we had completed all that as per our list and we were returning to our Hotel. To our utter amazement he reminded us that a duty entrusted by a devotee had been overlooked by us. We looked askance at each other but for quite some time none of us could remember what we had missed. We were helpless, and finally, I requested that old bearded man to remind us what we had not fulfilled. He smiled at us affectionately and reminded us that one gentleman had paid Rs. 3/- for a *Thali* (meal plate) to a hungry man? Suddenly we remembered it. We all were so sorry to be reminded like that. That old man himself pointed out towards a man standing by and said, "Here is your man. Feed him. I immediately took him to a nearby canteen, got for him a *Thali*, then costing Rs. 3/-, waited till he dined, gave him a glass of water, and he went away. He was none else than Sri Shirdi Sai Baba himself in physical form. Before we could find him after doing our job, he had just vanished Strange are the ways of Sri Shirdi Sai!

(5) To add to my meagre income in Feb. 1963, I had taken up a job of an Insurance Agent, in addition to my principal job in an office. One day in May

1964 I felt my house on Sunday for my Insurance field – Defence Project about 20 K.M. from my house. Right from 8 A.M. till 3 P.M. I worked hard and could procure good business. At about 4 P.M., I returned home, very very tired. While others relaxed on Sundays and stayed at home I was so destined to move about from house to house to add to my petty income then. On return my two sons were very adamant to see the Circus on that day only. My wife tried to persuade them saying that I was very tired and needed rest but the young ones would not agree. They appealed to me. I told them that it was the first Sunday of that Circus in Nagpur and there were no chances of getting tickets. At last I had to agree. Knowing fully well that I would not get four tickets for us I stood before the altar of Sri Sai Baba and told Him. "Baba, these youngsters are very adamant and against all hopes I am taking them to see the Circus, kindly help me." When we reached the Circus Ground there was tremendous rush, no way to approach the Booking Office too.

But beside a true Sai devotee Sai Baba Himself is always present. He takes care of their interests. Strange are this ways, really. As we went a little further in the crowd, a well-dressed gentleman approached us and requested us to purchase four tickets of First Class from him without paying any extra amount. We accepted them readily and gratefully and proceeded for our entry inside the tent. I looked back. That man had vanished in thin air. That is how Sri Shirdi Sai Baba helps his devotees at the proper time in real difficulties and keeps them happy. This is what we call 'The true Sai Darshan'.

(6) In July 1969 my mother was under treatment of cardiologist Dr. Udwadia at Beach Candy Hospital. My brother at Bombay sent me a telegram that our mother was serious and keenly desired my presence. I was a petty Clerk in Nagpur office. By the Grace of Sri Sai the Administrative Officer placed Rs. 300/- in my hands and gave me Company's car to reach home and thence to Railway Station. All Sri Sai Leela! I had no time for reserving my berth, but on the train my school-time friend, who was T.C., arranged for a sleeper berth for me. Whole night I prayed to beloved Sai Baba that on reaching Bombay I must find my mother giving me a smile. Sai *Leela* again! When I reached her I found that aunty had told a joke to my mother and she was smiling. Sai Leela again! She insisted that she should be carried back to Nagpur. Dr. Udwadia when consulted got angry and told me that when she could not be made to sit up even in bed, the question of her travelling was just not possible. I left him and the taxi took me straight to my sister's shop HYGIEN STORES, at Forjett

Street opposite Sri Sai Mandir. She told me that it remained closed from 1 P.M. to 3 P.M. I told her that my devotion to Baba would take me right before Him just now. One old lady was cooking in the flat opposite Sai Mandir flat. I asked her for the key of Sai Mandir. Without turning towards me she said, "Take it from the self on your left." I took the lunch, and the very first key I tried worked to open Sri Sai Baba before me. I wept like a child there. I asked Baba whether I should take my mother in train against the doctor's advice and would take care. He prompted me to take mother to Nagpur. The same evening I could get two Sleeper berths. On one I allowed my mother to rest. Another one, the third on that berth, was for a passenger from Kalyan. By Sri Sai direction he failed to turn up at Kalyan. So the T.C. told me that I could utilize that berth also for my mother so that she could sleeping throughout the journey. Again Sai Leela! One MLA from Akola. stranger to us, occupied the front berth and boosted her up morally by touching her feet and offering her tea and breakfast. At Nagpur Station he himself waited but instructed his driver to take us first at our residence as it was close by. Can all this be other than Sai Leela? All his grace and blessing.

(7) In April 1969 on our way to Solapur, I with my wife, and two young children got down at Manmad at 10 A.M. We took the service bus to Shirdi after reserving our return trip from Shirdi to Manmad by 5.30 P.M. bus. Good Puja was performed there. On stepping out of the Sai Mandir we learnt that the 5.30 P.M. bus had been cancelled. We had our onward Railway reservation from Manmad by 8 P.M. Manmad – Dhond train. WE felt stranded. We had no option but to board the 6.30 P.M. bus from Shirdi to Manmad. The driver told us that it was impossible for us to reach Manmad for the 8 P.M. train. If we missed that then we would be required to spend full night at Manmad Station and we could the next day train at 5 A.M. We were in a fix. While in bus we prayed to Sri Sai to ensure our passage through. Strange are the ways of Sri Sai. The moment we opened our eyes after prayers we could see a taxi standing by the road side. We asked the driver to stop the bus; on enquiry we found that the taximan had brought our family to Shirdi and on his way back something went wrong with the engine of the taxi and the taxi would not start from Yeola. The driver told me, "Sir, I can take you anywhere before 8 P.M. if the taxi could start." Although himself a first class mechanic the driver was not able to get along till we reached there. The driver was a bearded old man with good nature. We left the bus. I put my hand on the bonnet of the taxi, prayed

to Sri Sai and what a surprise at the first shelf the taxi started. We hurried in and with a speed of 70-90 kms one hour we reached Manmad bridge at 8 P.M. and we could see our train ready to move. We hurried down the steps which the guard saw. He stopped the train and gestured us to come. He finally took us inside the compartment and allowed the train to leave. That taxi driver did not accept a single paisa from us. He was none other than our Sai Baba Himself. Strage are this ways for helping his devotees. Finally, we could reach Solapur in time as per railway reservations from Manmad and Dhond.

(8) In 1980, myself and Mrs. Chinoy had to rush to Solapur as my father-in-law was very seriously ill. We had to board Maharashtra Express from Nagpur at 10 A.M. A separate loggie of 75 passengers which was got detached at Dhond at 6 A.M. next day and attached to Sidheswar Express leaving Dhond at 6.30 A.M. Maharashtra Express left in time from Nagpur. After one mile or so the axle of the engine broke and on that spot we were detained for two hours and a half. The T.C., who was in our bogie, declared that under no circumstances we would be able to get Sidheswar Express from Dhond next day at 6.30 A.M. The difficulty arose. We both started praying to our beloved Sai Baba to ensure our transit onwards from Dhond. Sincere prayers were offered. At 4.30 A.M. I asked the T.C. whether there were any prospects of getting our bogie attached to Sidheswar Express, he emphatically replied in negative. We then were to reach Solapur at 7 P.M. instead of 9 A.M.

But our beloved Sai's ways are strange and miraculous. At 7 A.M. when we reached Dhond, the T.C. rushed to us and told us that if we were anxious to get into Sidheswar Express, we should hurry up! "Just roll up your beddings, and carry your luggage and on the opposite side of the same platform there is Sidheswar Express about to leave". "Hurry up. There is no room." Only two seats No. 30 and 31 were fixed by that T.C. with the T.C. of that express train which was also delayed just to take we two only out of 75, from Dhond. We rushed and the moment we entered the facing compartment the train left Dhond. This was Sai's Grace for a Sai devotee and his wife. We reached Solapur at 9.30 A.M. With intense appeal to Lord Sai we could achieve this His favour which is guaranteed to every true Sai devotee.

-Jal M. Chinoy
Nagpur

40. BABA'S MIRACULOUS HELP IN BIRTH OF SON (1997)

Sri Mayagonda, a Government Officer, had been praying to Jian Thirthankaras for a son for a long time but his prayer remained unfulfilled. He had two daughters. One day Sri Mayagonda came to Sri Kalyanpur's flat with his two daughters, and his wife and wanted to pray to Baba. "I need Baba's help" he said. My wife is expecting a third baby. The chromosome tests have revealed that the child will be again a daughter" Sri Kalyanpur conducted the prayer for the Mayagonda family and Sri Mayagonda promised that if a son were born, he would be taken to Shirdi and placed on Baba's holy *Samadhi*. As the prayer ended, the postman knocked on the door, with *udhi* packet which was being sent from Shirdi every month. The journalist assured his friend that this was Baba's answer to their prayer and a son would certainly be born, no matter what the chromosome tests might have indicated.

41. BABA'S BLESSING FOR TEMPLE (1997)

One Gummadalli Lakshminarayana of Secunderabad used to go to Shirdi when Baba was alive and had darshan of Baba many times. On one occasion, Baba told G.L. "You build a temple of Lakshminarayana". G.L. asked Baba what the cost would be. Baba said Rs. 6 lakhs. G.L. was aghast as he did not have that much money as he was an ordinary merchant. At that time G.L. thought it was a joke made by Baba. But within two years his business flourished to such an extent that he could spare Rs. 6 lakhs for the construction of their temple. By this time Baba had attained Mahasamadhi. G.L. obeyed the direction of Baba, and constructed a Lakshminarayana temple at Secunderbad costing about Rs. 6 lakhs. The temple is still maintained and managed by G.L.'s children.

42. A THANKS GIVING TO SHIRDI SAI BABA (1989)

Sai's Grace is spread over all His devotees. His wonderful leelas have been experienced by all, who have implicit faith in Him. I also consider myself as a humble devotee of our Shirdi Sai Baba, who has experienced many of His leelas. One of His kind act of Grace was bestowed on me recently. An unforeseen event took place in my brother's house – while he was away at work, his own servant took advantage of the empty house and broke open a cupboard removing a lot of valuables and money. We were all very upset as we had no means to trace the servant, who was just employed. My only recourse was to pray to our beloved Baba and ask for His guidance and help. There was no doubt in my mind that Baba would give me an answer in some way or other. My faith in Him * unshakable.

In a few days by Baba's guidance, we were able to trace the where abouts of the servant and as the police were alerted, it was not long before most of the valuables were traced.

For this, I wish to express my every grateful and sincere thanks to my Baba of Shirdi, who is always with us and within us at all times.

-Mrs. P.N. Davar,
41 A, Paradise Apt.,
44 Napeansea Road,
Bombay – 400006
(*Shri Sai Leela*, June 1983)

43. SHRI SAI BABA – THE FRIEND, PHILOSOPHER AND GUIDE (1990)

It is said that bhagvad Geeta is that great poem which provides solution to any kind of problem physical, psychological, political, economical. It is upto the reader and his approach to search out the solution from it.

For Sai Bhaktas *"Shri Sai Satcharita"* written by Shri Hemadpant is an identical treatise. There are many bhaktas who reach out to this book with faith and patience to get the guidance from Sri Sai Baba. I for one is never ever disappointed in my pursuit. Baba has guided me on many occasions through this great book. I would like to quote one such incident here.

Recently, my wife was taken very ill and had to be put in a hospital in a very serious condition. She was suffering of acute Gastroenteritis and some other complications. Doctors were trying out various medicines but the improvement was not at all satisfactory. It was a Sunday when she was admitted in the hospital and the loose motions and vomiting were not getting controlled till Wednesday evening. She had gone very weak and restless. I and our children were very much worried and anxious.

Thursday morning as I woke up I was feeling gloomy and sad. Somewhere within myself I was in anguish and in a disappointed mood with Baba. It has been observed that out Baba tests us to the farthest of *Shraddha* and *Saburi* before showering his grace and blessings on us. I felt that this was that particular moment and I was no more able to stand to this test.

In this dejected state of mind I picked up the Hindi version of *"Shri Sai Satcharita"* and intensely prayed to Baba for His help and guidance. I opened the book at random and lo! I found page no. 82 open before me and started reading.

There was no limit to my joy as soon as I read the paragraph. I knew Baba has heard my prayers. It appeared as if Baba was sitting before my wife and ordering her to get well. I felt assured that she was going to get well soon.

Subsequently, Shri Sai helped me in many ways through unseen and unexpected help and everything becoming well. Needless to say my wife came back home from the hospital and recovered fast from her illness.

-G.M. Bhunjibhoy

Bhopal 462 021

(*Shri Sai Leela*, Sept. 1990)

44. SAI BABA CLOSE BEHIND OUR THOUGHTS (1990)

My brother, Dr. G.R. Vijayakumar received a letter from Mr. Jal H. Chinoy, B-3, Khullar Apartments, Byramji Town, Nagpur, who was struggling with grief. "I am desperate for some advice and help". He wrote, "On 3rd July 1992 with no warning, my wife, Mrs. Mani Chinoy, collapsed and died. Cause: a sudden heart attack. We had been married for 38 years. Mani was so lovable; she was such a clean-living, talented person, devoted to our children, Sai Baba and to the society. Here are my questions:

"I worry about where she is now. How can we be sure where our loved ones go when they die? If Sai Baba is such a living God why would He take Mani away from me and children, who need her so much?

We are all devoted to Sai Baba, but this bereavement has shaken my faith and I cannot pray at all. I know that when you have lost your faith, you have lost everything. If only I could find my way back to Sai Baba instead of accusing and resenting Him, then may be I could find the will to go on.

For some people, time many heal the broken heart; for me each day opens the wound still further? Can you help me?"

Mr. Chinoy's problem is one of those common denominators of all mankind. We see widows and widowers all over. I have no final answers to these cries of the human heart. Yet I want so much to give a helping hand to Mr. Chinoy and to all others he represents. So I wrote to him as follows:

Dear Sai Brother Chinoyji, your letter to my brother touched my heart. I understand what you are going through because I have been there, too; my husband Dr. R.J. Ranganathan and I had been married for 12 years when he died in 1990 at the age of 44.

Let me begin by offering you this word of hope. While time alone does not heal, at three months after your wife's death, you have reached the lowest point of physical and spiritual agony. Mrs. Mani has gone from your side long enough for you to realize how large your loss really is. But hang on, there is light ahead.

Your ask where Mrs. Mani is *"Shri Sai Satcharita"* tells us that Sai Baba conquered this last enemy, 'Death', for us through His blessed assurance: "Though I be no more in flesh and blood, I shall be ever active and protect My devotees." His ringing assurance "You look to Me – I look to you".

But we are now pilling up experimental proof of this blessed assurance of Sai Baba that life goes right on after death. Not long ago we entertained in my brother's house, a Specialist in Heart diseases, who is also an ardent Sai Devotee. This doctor began his practice with the settled conviction that death is simply extinction. But then with modern resuscitation techniques, he witnessed what patient after patient saw and experienced as they were being resuscitated from clinical death, his thinking was turned around. It was exciting to hear a Physician as unequivocally convinced of immortality as any Sai-devotee I ever listened to. What the evidence points to, he asserts, is that there is not a Moment's gap between this life and the next; that beyond death's door we look and feel like ourselves and are recognizable to those who have preceded us. We have a spiritual body – perfect now – and no longer subject to the limitations of space and time. Even Sai Baba remarked to Shama that they had been together for seventy-two births.

Obviously, when we really believe in another life, we are forced to rethink our limited viewpoint of death as the ultimate tragedy. You should ask yourself whether you grief is not so much of Mrs. Mani Chinoy as for your own loss.

So what about you and your loneliness? You wrote that you can no longer pray and that you are accusing and resenting Sai Baba for her death. You should shut yourself in a room and tell Sai Baba as to how exactly you feel about Him in regard to your wife's death. To establish communion with Him, ruthless honesty is necessary. I have done this in moments of despair.

But then you need to go beyond bitterness and anger. Why? Because grief is a real wound in the human spirit. And that bitterness is effectively cutting you off from the only one who can heal that would and give you answers and a reason to go on living.

Let me share an experience with you. When my husband passed away, I was sunk down in my grief and asking "Why? Why?". My faith was shaken, too. And I stayed in my rebellion for almost six month. In desperation, a friend gave me a straight talk: "You are a child of God. He has promixed to supply your every need …you should not be grieving for ever."

That did me more good than a profusion of sympathy on could ever have! That day I learned that often the kindest thing we can do for the ill or sorrowing is to refuse to feed self-pity with large doses of sympathy. This jolted me into realizing that the solution lay in my own will. I was free to remain in my rebellion on if I wanted to, but if I chose that, I would be left hanging in limbo in a living death. So my prayer was, "Lord, I do not understand anything about your ways. But now, I want you and your blessings for ever."

The result? Suddenly, the world was green and beautiful again. And "the God of all comfort" as Sai Baba has promised to be, immediately began to pour His healing balm deep, deep into the wound in my spirit.

This is the answer to your second question. "If any one casts his burden on Me and thinks of Me, I look after all his concerns." I have never known this promise to fail. Over Sainath does this miracle of bringing something good and positive out of life's wrerckage.

Finally, I want to give you a prescription to restore zest to your life. It is based on one of the immutable laws at work in our world *we get back what we give away*. Figure out the number of hours you are awake each day. Then take at least one-tenth of those waking hours, and each day give unselfishly that much time to your own children or to others – as Sai Baba leads you. It is not an easy exercise at first, but day by day you will find life returning to you.

Sai Baba came into our life to make it purposeful. He is close behind our thoughts. Give your life and problem over to Him. I can guarantee that He has an answer tailor-made for your needs. He loves your personally and wants to see your laugh again.

-Mrs. Usha Ranganathan
(Courtesy: Jal M. Chinoy,
Personal letter of Jal. M. Chinoy

45. BABA'S GRACE SAVED LIFE (1990)

Once Sri Sai Baba said – "If a man utters My name with love I shall fulfil all his wishes, increase his devotion, and if he sings earnestly my life and My leelas. I shall beset in front and back and on all sides. I shall draw our My devotees from the jaws of death. The simple remembrance of my name as "Sai – Sai" will do away with sins of speech and hearing." Such is the greatness of

Namasankirtana in the view of Sri Sai Baba. He is still protecting His devotees and keeping up His promise in case of such devotees completely dedicated to Him.

Here is an extra-ordinary instance of extension of life-span of a devotee living before our eyes. That devotees is Bharam Umamaheswara Rao, Founder Editor of *Sai Prabha*. This miracle happened on 4ᵗʰ February 1990, when this devotee was then at Jubilee Hill, Hyderabad.

On 25ᵗʰ January 1990 Sai Baba told this devotee in his meditation that the end of the devotee had come near and it would be on 4-2-90 (Sunday). On 28-2-90 Sri Sai Baba instructed this devotee to chant His name always and to take the juice of bilva leaves from Sai-blessed devotee Pujya Sri K.V. Raghavarao Garu, till 4-2-90. Baba assured that there would be no fear of death to those who utter His name always. He pointed out that even God when born as a human being was subjected to death as it is inevitable to a human. Baba further said that He can remove the *'Prarabdha* (fate orFdestiny), but questioned how He could erase the writings on one's forehead. (Divine Law). Baba advised this devotee to remember His name at the moment of death and promised to be with such persons who chant His name at that moment. He instructed this devotee to invite all his close relations and Sai Bhaktas who were close to him to chant His name on 4ᵗʰ Feb. '90. On 30-1-90 Baba being a pure *Prema-swaroop* guided this devotee and gave some hope saying that if he survived on that day (4ᵗʰ Feb.), he should approach Sri Ratnapuri Swamiji at Bangalore and seek his guidance in knowing *'Dasa Manthra Rahasya'*, *'Sri Chakra Mahima'*, *'Sri Vidhya'* and get *Mantropadesham*.

As per instructions of Sri Sai Baba, Sri Umamaheswara Rao started chanting *'OM SAI SRI SAI JAYA JAYA SAI'* from 26ᵗʰ January onwards and as a hope was given on 30ᵗʰ January, it was intensified and the relatives of him came from different places. They also joined the bhajan programme. This news somehow reached many of Sai *bhaktas* of Hyderabad and Secunderabad and they all came to the house of Sri Umamaheswara Rao at Jubliee Hills, Hyderabad and joined in Namasankeertana on 3ʳᵈ night itself.

On 3ʳᵈ evening at about 7 P.M., Baba instructed Sri Umamaheswara Rao in the meditation to chant 9000 Sanskrit slokas of Dattatreya and complete the some by 6 a.m. the next day. It became a problem for us to secure that Sanskrit Sloka books and after so much effort we were able to secure that book and also two scholars to chant the slokas. We started at 9 a.m. and completed it by 6 a.m. on 4ᵗʰ.

To our surprise, Avadhuta Sri Bodhananda Saraswathi Swamiji came to Shri Maheswara Rao's house on 3rd night and in his presence the Datta *Saloka* Parayana was done.

The expected day had come. On 4-2-90 when the time was fast approaching, the number of Sai devotees had gone into hundreds and the chanting 'SAI NAM' was echoing the surrounding atmosphere. Everybody was anxious about the outcome "Will it be a mere drama or whether Sri Umamaheswra Rao will regain his life?" These were the questions lingering in the minds of many. But they had only one faith that Baba would never go back on His word and He would surely fight out the impending calamity.

On 4th morning, Baba instructed him to perform Datta Homa. The devotees who were present there conducted Datta Homa from 8 a.m. 12 noon.

The condition of Sri Umamaheswara Rao became serious and at about 2 P.M., the doctors who were present there certified that the pulse and breath had stopped. Pujya Sri Raghavarao Garu, an ardent devotee of Sri Sai Baba who was by the bed side of Umamaheswararao at the moment during that period of suffering, said the pulse of the devotee had fallen and the chanting of Baba 'Baba' was heard on the lips of the devotee on bed and he heard Baba saying that He had given the life to the devotee. The pulse rate began increasing.

All the prayers were heard b Sri Sai and Umamaheswara Rao came out of the trouble by 3 P.M. This all happened in the presence of about 400 devotees who had participated in *Namasankeertana*. Sri Raghavarao Garu who was on his bed-side said that he saw DEVI sitting by the side of Umamaheswararao at that time. The event turned into a joyful end. One and all gave arathi to Sri Sai Baba at 6 P.M. and prostrated before Baba in gratitude to His kindness.

By this incident, it is proved beyond doubt, that Lord Sai Nath takes care of His devotees who surrender to Him.

46. BABA – THE SAVIOUR (1991)

God, the Almighty we worship is the saviour of His devotees. He even rescues them from the jaws of death. The Lord incarnated Himself as Sai Baba in the Kalyuga to bring Divine Grace to the people.

Recently in the Ist Week of May 1991, Lord Sai saved my family in the house and me in my office. One day in the afternoon when my children were sleeping in the house, my wife, who was busy in the household work in the courtyard of the house, noticed due to short circuit. She immediately switched off the mains to control further damages. Baba thus saved my wife and the children, who otherwise could be victim of a major fire.

Similarly, next day while I was busy in getting the records checked by the auditors in the strong room of the bank. We were three persons inside the strong room and did not notice that the wire of the fan was hanging in between the door of the vault and the safe. One of the officers shut the vault door without noticing that the electric wire had got cut by shutting the door, thus passing electric current to the vault. However, the holder of the electric wier also got broken and the noise alerted the officers present, who saw what the electric wire had become naked. Instantaneously we thought of Baba; pulled the wire from the plug and thanked the Lord Sai for making us alert by the noise caused by the breaking of the holder, otherwise there would have been a major mishap. Lord Sai thus saved us all.

It is He, who knows and controls our actions and saves us even from the jaws of death. Please prey to Him, think of Him and surrender to Him, who is the saviour of all.

-G.K. Bhardwaj
STATE BANK OF PATIALA
27, WHITES ROAD
MADRAS – 600014

47. BABA'S GRACE ON A BABA WRITER (1993)

I have experienced many divine grace of Sri Shirdi Sai Baba. I have mentioned a number of them in my book 'SAI KRIPA KE PAVAN KISHAN' (In Hindi) published by me from Sai Prakashan, 12 Ashok Road, Sagar (M.P.) in November 1995. One of those incidents is as under:

A certain Bhatnagar family, my wife, my daughter and I – we fifteen people were going to Jabalpur in a Deluxe Coach in the night of 6th December 1993. The bus was running fast. An old man in the bus requested the conductor to stop the bus as he was getting desperate to urinate, but the driver ignored his request saying that the bus would stop after 5 kilometers at Damoh hotel stop. But before the bus could reach Damoh, the bus met a serious accident due to its sliding off the road in pitchy dark. However, no one in the bus was dead or hurt. In the form of that oldman Sri Shirdi Sai Baba was in the bus and therefore the lives of over 20 passengers in that ill-fated bus were saved. I still shudder to recall that incident. After that accident, that old man soon disappeared, no one knows where and how he went away in thin air. He was surely Baba who travelled with us in the bus to save our lives.

-Sushil Bharti,
Novelist & Writer of
Shirdi Sai Books in Hindi
Sai Prakashan, 15, Ashok Road,
Sagar (M.P.) – 470001

48. BABA'S MYSTERIOUS WAYS (1984)

In December, 1984, I had a problem in Uterus and underwent a major surgery in abdomen in January, 85. After the operation I grew weak as I was past fifty-five. I needed help for everything even to turn over or sit up in bed. It was very discouraging and uncomforting.

One day, feeling utterly helpless, I complained to my Sai-half, Sri R. Radhakrishnan: "Why do I keep on living? What good am I? I am just a nuisance. I can't do anything for anyone."

My beloved Sai-half was preparing himself to go to Shirdi for participating in the SAI LEELA MEET scheduled for 27th and 28th January, 85. He answered with a smile: "Oh, I don't know about it. I think there is something you can do. You can pray to Lord Sainath for the sake of others".

What a good timely medicine that was! There, flat on my back, I began t pray for my fellow-patients, for the Doctor and nurses, for Sai-bandhu, for anyone who came to my mind. And as I did that, I found I was moping less, and focusing more on the world outside. Without knowing it, I was getting out of myself, out into the world – if only in spirit. And eventually I was there physically too!

In fact, my health improved so much so that a year later, I could accompany my husband to Shirdi in February, '86 for the annual Gathering of Sai Leela Contributors and later to Vijayawada to participate in the Akhanda Sai-nama Saptha Sapthaham.

Today living at home, I am able to take care of myself and yet I am still following that excellent precaution for feeling myself useful to others.

-Mrs. Subbulakshmi,
W/o Sri R. Radhakrishnan,
78/B, Vijaynagar
Hubli – 580 032, Karnataka

49. A SAI-GIFT INDEED (1984)

This was a soul-stirring incident that I experienced when I was in U.S.A. in 1984-85. I was waiting for my husband in the Hospital, on a cold forenoon in December, 1984.

I noticed a young mother, about six months pregnant. She was holding a year-old child, a little girl in her arms. Squirming nearby was another little girl who had a brace on her foot. I thought to myself. 'Oh, she should not be having another child. She has too much to do now'.

'That is a pitiable family' I said to the nurse after they had gone into the Examination Room with the doctor.

"Not at all" the nurse answered: "Those children are the most fortunate I have even known. They are adopted. The parents thought they would never have children of their own, So they chose babies who needed love more than a normal child. They can well afford to give them the help that will overcome their handicaps in a few years." I was told that the one-year old in her arms was blind!

I really felt like adoring the couple. They had really understood God's love and they had gone the second mile. Now they would have an added blessing, what they had always hoped for a sister or brother for their two adopted children.

This was indeed a Sai-lesson for me. As I offered a short prayer: *"Om Jai Jagadeesa Hare, Sai Jai Jagadeesa Hare"* the young mother returned from the doctor's room. She smiled at me and as I returned her smile, I recalled Sainath's words: "Shri Hari will be certainly pleased if you give water to the thirsty, bread to the hungry, clothes to the naked and your verandah to strangers for sitting and resting."

I thanked Lord Sainath heartily for this first hand evidence of Sai-love!

-Mrs. Usha Ranganatha,
W/o, Dr. R.J. Ranganathan,
Belavady 577 146,
Chikmagalur Dust, Karnataka.
(Shri Sai Leela, March 1988)

50. HOW WE BECAME SAI DEVOTEES (1972)

After our marriage in 1972 we were going to Sinnar for some work. A friend of my husband told us to visit to Shirdi. Till then we had not known anything about Shirdi or Sri Sai Baba. After reaching Shirdi I was a bit hesitant to enter the temple because I am from an orthodox Roman Catholic family. But somehow I changed my mind and went to the temple. After the darshan of Baba's *Murthi* I was totally a changed person. Since then we are true believers in Sai Baba. We wanted our first child born on Sai Bab's day. We prayed to Baba and He blessed us with a boy on a Thursday.

When our second son was 5 years of age, he had an attack of severe jaundice. AT that time we both were out of the country and he was in a school hostel. What could we do being in a distant place? There also Baba came to our rescue. When we came back to our child, we learnt that Sri Baba had saved him and he was completely cured. Till now we have had a number of chances to visit our saviour and receive His blessings. Now we are settled in our small "SAI FARM" with the blessings of our saviour.

Last month my younger brother fainted and when he regained his consciousness he was paralysed on the left side of this body. In the hospital, after so many tests, doctors told that an operation was needed. On hearing the news I went straight to my pooja room, where I am having a small *'Murthi'* of Baba brought from Shirdi to do pooja. I stood there, weeping continuously. I couldn't even concentrate my mind to pray to Sri Baba. But Baba understood my condition. I had an inner feeling that Baba was speaking to me saying that "Child, why do you worry, have full faith in Me; leave the matter to Me and chant My name I'll do the rest" I did so. The next week the news I got was that my brother was discharged from the hospital. Only his left hand could not be moved freely, but that would be all right with physiotherapy. We thanked Sri Baba for all His blessings.

"OM SAI SREE SAI JAI JAI SAI".

Mrs. Lily K. Nair,
Sai Farm, Neelikunram,
Kinassery P.O.
PALGHAT-678 707 (Kerala)
(*Shri Sai Leela*, Nov. 87)

51. BABA CURED AN ASTHAMA PATIENT OF U.S.A. (1972)

Dr. C.C. Chang is a Professor of Mathematics Newhall, California. U.S.A He suffered from Asthma since childhood. In the early years, the problem would come and go with proper medication. From the time he was 30 years old, the Asthma became chronic. He depended on drugs and medicines to keep it in check. He used to carry a pressurized spray container, wherever he went, and would require to use it 3 or 4 times per day for inhalation. He tried prayers, Japa, meditation, fasts, exercises, diet etc. The maximum period of time, he would manage without medicines was 72 hours.

In the year 1982, while he was reading the book *'The Incredible Sai Baba'* a thought came to him and closing his eyes he prayed "Sai Baba, if you cure my asthma, I will agree that you are incarnation of God". At that moment, he had a small quantity of *udhi*, given to him by a friend, who had visited Shirdi. His problem was this. To put a pinch of *udhi* into his mouth every time he felt the on coming symptoms of Asthma, would have exhausted the *udhi* in his possession in no time. How was he to get a fresh supply of *udhi* from Shirdi? So Dr. Chang thought of an idea, that he should meditate on the *udhi*. So every time he felt an obstruction in his breathing, he meditated on the *udhi* he had with him. Strange to say, it worked! The obstruction in his breathing would gradually dissolve and sooner or later, normal breathing would be restored. He continued this method. His asthma came under check and he says it is almost eliminated.

52. EXPERIENCE OF R.S. CHITNIS AT SHIRDI (1973)

Sri R.S. Chitnis of Delhi is a well-known devotee of Sai Baba. In 1973, he left Delhi by car and reached Shirdi at 12.30 p.m. As he wanted to wash himself before going for darshan of Sai Baba, he made straight to one of the bathrooms. On the way some people accosted him and said that there was not a drop of water in any of the taps. Mr. Chitnis was non-plussed and thought that he should either go to the Receiver Saheb's residence of Sri Bhaghwe's residence both of whom he knew well.

At that time a well dressed young man came towards him. He had a piece of cloth round his head. He was fair and had very expressive eyes. He asked in full voice and in compassion, what the problem was. Sri Chitnis appraised him that the taps had gone dry and that he could not have his wash before darshan. They young man bade him to follow him and took him to a bathroom nearby, where water was gushing from the tap. Sri Chitnis had a good wash, and came out to thank the good Samaritan. But he had left!

Sri Chitnis purchased pooja material and visited the Samadhi Mandir, only to find himself at the far end of a long queue of Baba's devotees, who were all waiting for their turn for Baba's puja and darshan. The prospect of having to stand in the long queue after the tiresome journey, unnerved Sri Chitnis. But there was no other way.

Shri Chitnis felt that somebody was tugging at his arm. When he turned round, it was the same stranger again. Holding him by the arm, the stranger led him through the jostling crowd of devotees right upto Baba's Samadhi and he left him there. Sri Chitnis was, all the while, assailed by the fear that other devotees in the queue would take objection for jumping the queue. Not one devotee raised even as much as an eye brow in protest! Sri Chitnis handed over the puja materials and prasad, bowed and prayed to Baba. When Sri Chitnis turned back to thank the benefactor, he had disappeared again! He came out of the Samadhi Mandir and looked for the stranger but in vain.

He came back to the place where his car was parked, and found to his annoyance that his family members were still sitting under a tree. He asked them why they are idling away their time instead of going for Baba darshan and puja. They replied in chorus that there was not a drop of water in any of the bathrooms and taps.

Their reply surprised Sri Chitnis, only 20 minutes back he had as much water as he required. He confidently agreed to escort them to the room from which he had washed. He knocked about from bathroom to bathroom, but that "bathroom" eluded him. He was bewildered and confused. He began to enquire from the passersby where the particular bathroom was which had plenty of water. They all looked at him strangely and thought that something was wrong with him. They strangely with his family members that for about 1 1/2 hours there was no water in any of the taps.

Sri Chitnis in no time realized that it was all Baba's *leela*.

His people continued to ask him where the bathroom was from which he washed his hands and feet. There was no response he had gone speechless'

53. BABA CURED DEVOTEE'S PARALYTIC ATTACK (1973)

Sri G.S. Kalyanpur is a journalist by profession who lives in South Shivaji Park. Bombay. He is a staunch devotee of Sri Sai Baba of Shridi. On 12.5.1973 he woke up after midnight feeling quite ill. His right arm had gone out of commission. He could not lift it. He tried to move his fingers. They were immovable. He was running very high temperature. In his frenzied brain, he recalled that his mother was completely paralysed at the age of sixty. Her three sisters had also suffered paralytics strokes. Had he inherited the minus points of his mother's line? It was an unnerving thought. The journalist could ill afford to be ill with paralysis, as he was an old bachelor and dependent on an old house-keeper Yamunabai. He involuntarily turned his eyes in the direction of the little wooden mandir, in his room, in which he had installed a small idol of Sai Baba, he cried out, and in a few minutes dropped off to sleep. He woke up at 6 A.M. his usual time to wake up for his prayer and arathi.

As was customary, the house keeper, prepared the arathi with a wick and coconut oil and handed it to him. She did not notice that Sri Kalyanpur waved the arathi to Baba, with his left hand. The house keeper did not know of his predicament.

The only doctor nearby was an M.D. lady doctor, who was his friend's daughter. When he went to her residence she scolded him for coming out in that condition and examining him immediately recommended hospitalization. When Sri Kalyanpur was being taken to the hospital the old house keeper began to sob and asked him. "When will you be cured?" "In five days time" said the journalist involuntarily, though he knew that strokes sometimes prove incurable and sometimes fatal. In the hospital he was under the care of a very eminent Parsi physician. In the hospital, he used to start his day at A.M. with a prayer to Baba. It was 6 A.M. on Thursday, exactly the fifth day of his hospitalization. He experienced a vague sensation of new vigour in his right arm. But he was afraid of putting his arm to test, lest he should be disappointed. The physiotherapist arrived at 8 A.M. to give exercises to his arm. As on earlier days, he asked him to lift the arm. Sri Kalyanpur hesitated a little prayed to Baba, and lifted his right arm slowly. He found to his delight and to the physiotherapists's wonder, that he could stretch the arm to the full. He found no crippling sensations.

The Parsi specialist arrived at 9 A.M. and asked the journalist how he felts that day, Sri Kalyanpur could not keep back the flood of tears and thanked him for helping him to get back the power to his right arm.

The doctor asked, "Are you a believer in divine grace? It is the divine grace that has restored your arm, not I" said the doctor. The doctor advised further, "A sincere prayer can work miracles as in your case. Continue to have faith and all be well for the rest of your life". In 1985, Sri Kalyanpur was 81 years and in good health by the grace of Sai Baba.

Baba has come to Sri Kalyanpur's room in his flat in the form of an Ashirwad photo also. This has become a centre of attraction to his friends in distress. They come stand before the photo and tell Baba of their problems and seek His help.

54. SAI BABA, THE PROTECTOR AND SAVIOUR (1975)

Impelled by what I happened to read in 'Sri Sai Leela' (which I am reading only for last two months) I thought of writing some of Lord Sai Baba's miracles happened with me.

I am one of the innumerable devotees of Sri Baba who have experienced Baba's leelas in their daily life. My experiences of Sai miracles for the last 17 years of my married life are many but, I am giving a few out of them.

I was married in 1971 to Shri Sainath of Mysore. First time I saw Baba's life size photo in my husband's Pooja Room, till what day I had not heard of Baba's name, so personally I had no attraction or devotion towards Him. He is our family God. The very next year in Feb. 1972 I was in family was in the eighth month. Suddenly in the midnight I started getting labour pain. I had heard from my mother that children born in the eighth month generally do not survive, so we both were in panic. I was to go to my mother's house next month for delivery, since my mother's house was at Kalyan and I stayed at Sion. My husband applied some *udhi* on my abdomen and prayed to Baba, "Baba, after delivery we would visit Shirdi". ...Within half an hour the pain subsided and I went in sound sleep. On 2nd April I was blessed with a daughter. Somehow, we quite forget about our prayer.

In 1951 I was expecting my second child at Bhusaval. At 12 O'clock we were going to a friend's house for lunch. I was walking on the footpath, suddenly a scooter came on the wrong side and it was about to hit me straight on my stomach, someone told me to take a turn leftwards, I closed my eyes and waited due to it, to my utmost surprise the scooter hit me very slightly on the left side of my body and hit a lamppost which fell down and the scooterist was bleeding profusely. I could not keep balance and fell flat on the road; a small crowd gathered. Immediately I was taken to hospital. Every one expected an immediate abortion. After through examination the doctor confirmed that the child was quite safe, and I was discharged immediately after dressing on my bruises. After hearing the next all my relatives rushed to bhusaval from Bombay and were surprised to see me quite safe.

The next month I was going to my office (Bhusaval Railway Office) around 9.30 A.M. I saw a bull running and coming towards me and it wanted to hit me on my stomach. I was again worried, there was no time to cross the road or go to the other side. Something, told me, "Jump". I saw a small ditch near-by and jumped.

A devotee,
Shri Sai Leela, June 1989

55. My father was a Sai-devotee. He was wearing a silver locket of Sai Baba in his sacred thread. He passed away on 11th August 1977. When we cremated him we did not remove the locket and along with it consigned the body to flames. Next day when we went to collect the his ashes, that locket came into my hands. In spite of high temperature that reduced the body to ashes, the tiny Silver locket of Sai Baba remained untarnished and Unblemished, Sai Baba is Beyond The Panch Tattav of Fire Water Earth, Skey and Air.

I met with an accident in May 1985. My shoulder was fractured and dislocated. It was immobilized for over 1 1/2 months. When plaster was removed, these was no free movement of the shoulder. Physio therapy and exercises for over 3 months proved futile. Experts opined it as 'Frozen Shoulder' and said nothing could be done. I could not fold both hands for doing 'PRANAMS' to Sai Maharaj. In October '85. I went to Sai Spiritual Centre at Bangalore, wept in front of Sai Baba. I recited *Vishnu Sahsarnam* and unknowingly went forward I could move my right shoulder. Glory to Sai Maharaj His dictum worked where Doctor failed.

A devotee

56. HOW I WAS BLESSED WITH THE GRACE OF SAINATH

Before the year 1975, I didn't know anything about Sai Baba of Shirdi. While I was a lecturer in a degree college in early 1975, one of my friends who was very close to me had plucked in M.A. Examination. He, being frustrated due to many personal troubles including his results in the said examinations, met a gentleman who was known to be an astrologer, a Tantrika and a Sadhaka. Due to the magic-touch of the gentleman my friend had seen the face of success in various matters including his miraculous pass in the examination in which he had failed earlier after the expiry of six months from the date of the publication of the result earlier. Before this his personal experience, my friend did not believe in such type of religious or spiritual phenomenon but now gradually became a devotee of the gentleman.

Curiously my friend reported to me this miraculous incident. He also told me that the gentleman, after hearing about me, said, "I am very much eager to meet him and I have got some work with him". After hearing this, I was very eager to meet him, but due to some personal difficulties I didn't have time to do so. After a few days I had to face two or three serious problems which, I now believe, were created by the gentleman in order to attract me towards him. As these problems were insoluble by an ordinary man, I rushed towards him for the obvious reasons. After seeing me he had recognized and admitted that all the problems were created in order to attract me to him. At that time I noticed that the gentleman was of black complexion and had piercing vision and was wearing a garland of Tulsi with a locket on which I saw the picture of Sai Baba for the first time. On being asked about the picture, he replied that the picture was of Sri Sai Baba of Shridi who had given him darshan several times and continued to do so. He was found very much confident in saying that he could do everything depending on the grace of Sai Nath. He had narrated many miraculous incidents which evidenced his spiritual contact with Sai Baba as well as his deep devotion to Him. In course of my close connection with this gentleman for four years I had seen many miraculous incidents occurring in my presence. He said, "I am directed by Sai Baba to come over here in order to meet you and to convey to you the message of Him." It is needless to say that I became very much a devotee of the gentleman gradually. One night I had seen in a dream the vision of Sai Baba sitting by my side and fondling me with deep affection, and at that time. I was very much moved with the touch. What I had seen I am unable to describe here, but it is true that it was a thrilling experience in my life. As I was in a trouble at that time and sought Baba's help, Baba told me in a dram to have 'patience' and 'faith' in Him. Keeping Baba's advice in view I promised to act accordingly.

Since then I have tried many times to keep my promise to my Lord. He had put me in many hard situations in order to test whether I would strictly obey His advice with patience and faith. Sometimes I was successful in this test and sometimes failed. When I failed, I was spiritually rescued by way of giving courage and advised to have complete faith in Sai Baba by that gentleman whom I considered as my Master afterwards. After making me realize the glimpse of the mystic and spiritual power of Sai Baba and injecting the seed of devotion in me to Him, my Master in the form of that gentleman expired in the month of May, 1979. When I learnt that he might leave his mortal body, I wished to have a photograph of him for the purpose of worship. On hearing my request he told, "If you really want to worship, keep this photograph with you and worship it during the whole life." Saying this he gave me a photograph of Sri Sai Baba sitting on a stone and blessing with a raised hand. He said, "I shall be satisfied if you worship this photograph. Always remember that I am identical with Sai Baba." He affectionately used to address Sai Baba as *'Buro'* (a Bengali word meaning 'Old man'). From this incident I felt certain that Sai Baba had come to grace me in the guise of this gentleman, my Master.

After the expiry of my Master, I used to pass my days depending completely on the grace of Sai Baba who had shown His love and affection to me in various ways. Through His grace I have got all the necessary things, major and minor. In other words, He had made me what I am today. Till this day whenever I feel disturbed and I seek help of Baba, He directs me sometimes appearing in dream and sometimes staying in my heart.

A devotee

57. BABA GUIDED US ON OUR FIRST VISIT TO SHIRDI (1978)

In 1978 I and my family went to Nanded to see the famous Sikh Gurudwara there. From Aurangabad we went to Ajanta Ellora caves in a taxi. While returning from there at 7 P.M., we met one thin Sikh young with a little beard. He asked us, "Where are you going?" I replied, "We are going to Nanded from Manmad". He suggested that we should better go to Manmad and from there we should go to Shirdi Sai Baba's holy place, in bus. Buses were available every half an hour for Shirdi from there. He gave us detailed information about the places to be visited at Shirdi and also to visit the nearby Upasani Maharaj's Sakori ashram. We asked his name and address and he gave his address of a hotel in Manmad. As per his suggestions, we went to Shirdi and Sakori, stayed there for two days, and had very good pilgrimage of these two places. While returning from our visit to Nanded, we tried to meet that Sikh young man at the address given by him. We did find that Hotel but there was no person traced there like the unknown Sikh person whom we had meet and who had persuaded and guided us to visit Shirdi. It was only because of his suddenly appearing on the scene that we had decided to visit Shirdi and thereby we became devotees of Baba. I feel that it was Baba Himself who had met us in the form of a Sikh youngman speaking Punjabi, as we were Punjabi-speaking tourists.

-C.M. Sehgal, Excise Officer,
168, Sector 18, Faridabad

58. SHIRDI SAI BABA SPOKE TO ME (1978)

The name of Shirdi Sai Baba is known to me since my childhood. My grand parents were His devotees and also are parents. My father, a brilliant engineering student, with many gold medals of Bombay university to his credit, and later on an enterprising engineer of Bombay Government prior to Karnataka Maharashtra segregation in 1957, is a devotee. He has put Baba's photo in the sitting room with a bulb always lit. Baba's photo is found on his office table also.

It was in 1978 during my stay in Bombay that I came close to Shirdi Sai Baba. I was passing through difficult times when an elderly Parsi gentleman guided me to a Shirdi Sai Baba temple in Mahim. One gentleman had installed a marble statue of Baba in his house and he used to conduct puja on Thursday and Sunday for the benefit of public. He had the power of going in to trance and guide people in their problems by the grace of Baba. I used to go every Sunday to consult him about my problems. Every Sunday there used to be a long queue of devotees waiting to consult him. On a Sunday, I was waiting for my turn. The queue was quite long and it was getting late for me to attend my dispensary. I was getting impatient and restless. I was wondering whether there was a God. If so, then why all the sufferings. I was standing in the balcony and observing the side of the Baba's statue. I was wondering as to what He was doing when so many were suffering. I was losing my temper. All of a sudden, even though there were no people around me, I heard a voice which said *"Tere ko gussa bahuth hai beta! Aake mera charno me chod de"* meaning "Your temper is very bad son! come and leave it at my feet". By some unknown force I was drawn towards the statue and I touched my head to the feet of Shirdi Sai Baba's statue and I touched my head to His feet and promised to obey Him. After this incident my life started improving and many miracles of Baba have occurred in my life.

Thus, this was how Shirdi Sai Baba spoke to me.

Bow to SRI Sai Baba

Peace be us to all.
-Dr. Mahesh I. Magdum,
Lecturer in Ophthalmology,
Karnataka Medical College,
Hubli-580 022
(Shri Sai Leela), June 1988

59. BABA DECIDES (1979)

At the outset let me confess that I was never an ardent devotee of any deity till the day I visited Shirdi. My idea about Sai Baba was also vague till April, 1979. Before that I was on the mobile inspection team of my employer, a large Bank. During February, 1979 I was promoted and was asked to go back on permanent posting to Madhya Pradesh, to which circle of the Bank.

My transfer to Kerala, therefore, required the concurrence of both the circle authorities i.e. Madhya Pradesh and Madras. In normal course, it takes 5 to 10 years for such an inter-Circle transfer to materialize. The Bank has its main office at Bombay, under the control of which I was working before my promotion and subsequent posting to Madhya Pradesh, I therefore, as a last trial went to Bombay and persuaded my Department (Inspection) to consider my posting to Kerala. The decision, if any, in that connection was to be taken with the concurrence of the Circles concerned and such powers were vested only with a very higher level i.e. the Dy. Managing Director, who then happened to be on leave for a week when my representation reached his office.

Since I had no other engagement, I was sitting idly in the Department, waiting for the Dy. Managing Director's return from leave, when a senior officer there asked me whether I had ever been to Shirdi and said, "Better you go there and come back by which time the D.M.D. would be back." The same evening I left by Punjab Mail for Nasik and after an overnight stay there reached Shirdi the next day.

By the very first sight of Baba's *Moorthy*, I was overwhelmed by the pristine glory and I should say, I was taken in. I participated in various *Poojas* and *Abhishekams*, bought few Photos of Baba and a copy of the *"Shri Sai Satcharita"*. Later, when I decided to return and went to the Bus stand, no bus was available.

Thus, I had to stay one more night at Shirdi. The next day after morning Arati I returned to Bombay.

On reading the *'Shri Sai Satcharita'* later, I really felt like the vary same parrot which was pulled towards Baba with a string attached to its feet and also understood that one can visit and leave Shirdi only when Baba decides.

My senior officer was only an instrument prompted by Baba to connect the string on to me. And before my return, I was told that the most unusual decision, to transfer me to Kerala with a special mention to post me to a place of my choice in that area had been taken by the Dy. Managing Director without any further queries.

No words can adequately express my joy and I could only bow mentally to Baba for the kindness so explicitly showered on me. Since then I usually visit Shirdi every year, of course, when Baba decides.

My adorations unto Him.

-Radhakrishnan Punnakkal,
Cheruvaykara, P.O. Biyyam,
PONNANI, Kerala

60. BELIEVE IT OR NOT (1979)

I am not telling you a story, but I am just narrating an incident and it is upto the readers to draw their own conclusion.

Both my brothers are doctors, one is a cardiologist and the other is a children's specialist. Both are good and competent in their respective fields, so much so, even their colleagues often take advice from them in complicated cases. About three years back, my brother, the children's specialist got married and was blessed with a son in June, 1984, a boy, so to say, a lovely kid. We were all very happy and most of our relatives were wondering as to how and in what manner my brother would bring up that child. For two months, everything went on smoothly and afterwards the child started crying during night hours. My brother did not have belief in home remedies and hence treated his son himself with utmost care, but the child did not respond favorably. He consulted his brother Doctor who also treated him but in vain. Weeks after weeks were over, my brother and his wife became weak and most worried persons and were spending sleepless nights. Then he took the child to other doctors for their opinion. They also treated but failed to bring about the desired cure. Finally he yielded and started our house-hold remedies but even then with no positive results.

When we reached, there was not much crowd and we could stay in the Samadhi Mandir itself in a room attached to it. This enabled us to attend 3 *arties*, namely *kakad*, noon and night *arties* from that time onwards. I have been having full faith in the grace of Sai Baba.

After our return to Bombay, some times I have taken part in Sai Bhajans in the neighbourhood. A few years later. I visited Shirdi with my parents.

In 1979, I had the greatest blessings of Sri Baba through a dream.

My husband the late Sri K.P. layer, suffered from a severe. For about six months. Which made him feel very uncomfortable owing to the swelling both in the abdominal region and legs. Being himself a religious and God-fearing person, he suffered patiently with the realization that it was due to his past karma. At this hours of difficulty in the family, my daughter's marriage was somehow fixed to be celebrated on the 17th November, 1979, although I was least prepared on account of my husband's illness. As matters thus stood, one day my husband called me and affirmed that the daughter's marriage should be celebrated as fixed despite the odds in the family.

This desire and stand of his threw me into a state of confusion and dilemma as to what to do and where to proceed from without the husband's help in such an important matter. With worry deep set in my mind and prayers to the Almighty for his guidance and hope, I retired to bed one day and possibly would have slept a little. Suddenly, I had a dream in which I saw the Great Sri Sai Baba with a garland of white flowers in his hand, blessing me and assuring me that everything would pass off well.

I woke up immediately and felt a fresh energy in me and a great relief mentally.

Drawing strength from his blessings, I began the necessary preparations for the marriage and the happy function went off as scheduled. Surprisingly enough, my husband got better and even climbed up to the second floor to witness the holy function, with someone's assistance.

When the newly married couple was away from Bombay on their honeymoon trip, I took a vow that I would visit Shirdi along with my daughter and her husband for darshan. Despite our earnest wishes for the better, my husband's condition took a turn for the worse and he passed away peacefully with the contentment that his daughter's marriage was well celebrated with the blessings of Sri Baba. His soul actually departed on an Ekadashi day which fell on a Thursday, too. Who can escape the effect of past karma after all? But, yet, if we live a good and moral life and surrender ourselves to the gracious feet of Sadguru like our Baba, we can be quite sure of mental peace and contentment against all odds in our life.

In March the next year, we went to Shirdi again with my son Krishna, my daughter and her husband and performed *abhishekam* to Sri Baba's *moorthy* and adorned him with our humble *chaddar*. This gave us mental peace. I always felt over-whelmed whenever I looked at the statue of Sri Baba as he had appeared in the same positive in my dream to bless my daughter's marriage.

Again after my son's marriage, we visited Shirdi and obtained Sri Baba's blessings. My grand daughter, Sow. Jyothi too evinces keen interest in hearing the leelas of Sri Baba, which must be due to His Grace only, we believe.

May He continue to bless one and all for peace and bliss.

-Smt. Sita Iyer,
1/3, Durga Society,
Tilak Vidyalaya Road
Vile Parle (E) Bombay

61. HOW I BECAME BABA'S FOLLOWER (1986)

Dear Sai brothers and sister, Baba's miracles are many. We read in *Shri Sai Sat Charita* how He bestowed His showers of blessings, help and extended Abhaya-Hasta whenever the need of the ardent devotee arose. But we see in practical many more if you surrender to Him totally.

Before going in detail with His miracle, I would like to tell all our readers how I came into contact with Sai Baba. I was at Hyderabad for a decade by virtue of job from 1971-1982. During 1980 one of my friends, who runs kirana store gave one calendar (Baba's Asirwad-inscribed *(SAB KA MALIK EK)* and pasted it on a thick pad and did pooja daily. Added to this one of my Sai follower friends took me to a Thursday bhajan at Malakpet, Hyderabad (Then I did not know who was Baba and Bhajan etc.) where I was much inspired with the oneness of devotees and peace in chanting *"Om Sri Sai Ram"*. Later I attended a bhajan at another Sai devotees house. Apart from this my only first friend in 1971 at Hyderabad. A. Ranga Prasad who also happens to be a staunch follower of Baba gave one Baba's Asirwad galvanized metal photo and gave few *Shri Sai Leela* magazines through which I learnt much about His teachings and hence I subscribed for it and went through the magazines every month, I saw "Shirdi ke Sai Baba" film twice and sent Rs. 10/- every month to Shirdi. I was transferred to Tirupati in 1982 from Hyderabad, renewed subscription for the *Shri Sai Leela*. I experienced much problems at office and also at home just because of egoism. Then I realized much that without Baba's grace we can't do anything, gave up thinking much about self and started to change way of life i.e. chanting of Lord's name and doing whatever I did must be right. Just for this I had no tranquility and experienced day-in-day-out turbulences, upheaval task of solving problems. I met Sri P. Satyanarayana Garu, S.A.O. Tirumala-Tirupati Devasthanams who had many Baba's experiences in his life through my Sai friend. A Ranga Prasad who had given many books about Baba and made me to surrender totally. Through him only I came to know that there is a Satsang Nilayam in Tirupati, it is being run by few employees of Sri Venkateswara University and Mr. S.T. Narasimhulu, who had built and allowed devotees to have a room for Baba's Satsang Nilayam at his own cost. I used to go over their regularly and my problems vanished as morning dew. "Sai Ram" is my daily life's tonic and chanting whenever I am free. Baba had changed my wife's mind also, who had difference of opinion and she became a follower as and when we visited Mylapore All India Sai Samajam in February

5, 1987, where we had darshan of Baba's statue installed on 2nd February '87. Her devotion towards Baba rose very high and peace prevailed at home.

Meanwhile, my wife conceived and was ready for confinement, since it was third delivery I had to look after all the nursing expenditure. However, I was disturbed for the ceasarien operation whether to have it here in Tirupati or at Christian Medical College Hospital, Vellore, since we had lost the second baby after cesarian operation. Then at Satsang Nilayam along with friends there, we wrote two chits in which we had written Vellore and Tirupati separately. Asked my son Sai Karthik, 5-years-old, to pick one of the chits, accordingly order came from Baba to go over to Vellore. I had sent my wife to C.M.C. Vellore, where the doctors told my wife that if she underwent sterilization along with cesarien operation everything will be made free of cost. Since she had gone there little but early on 19.5.87 they asked her to come on 29th May '87. She was admitted for operation after my blood donation. First her operation was fixed for 6.7.87 morning and it is because of Baba's advice to doctors, they told us that it would be performed in the afternoon, as it was inauspicious in the morning. A healthy baby boy was born to her at 1405 hours. She opted for a girl but I wished for a boy only. This is all because of Baba's grace who showered His blessing to His staunch devotee. I gave one Asirwad photo and *udhi* to my wife who applied before going operation theatre. I sat near theatre and chanted "Om Sri Sai Ram". At 1430 hours we were shown baby boy. The doctors told us that there was no problem with baby and mother. I had a sigh of relief when we went to dispensary where they gave free medicine. Otherwise we would have to pay for everything. This is all because of Baba's timely advice which came to us through Satsang Nilayam. At the time of discharge we paid a paltry amount only. We hail from Paperi village, in North Arcot District of Tamil Nadu. It appears that the Tamil Nadu Government re-imburses the amount to Hospital to encourage Family planning. From this we see, Baba is omni present, omnipotent and resumes devotees from their turmoils. The sayings of Baba is proved "IF YOU LOOK TO ME I LOOK AFTER YOU". It is true that one who surrenders to Him will find that He will look after everything and there is no want of necessity felt at home.

-D. Bakthavatchalu,
18-3-57 A(I), Khadi Colony,
Tirupati-5177 507
(*Shri Sai Leela*, April 1989)

62. THE FENCE OF TRUST

It was on Highway 177 in the west coast that our car broke down on the 14th March, 1981. We were on our way to Mundakayam in Kottayam district of Kerala as my Sai-half Dr. G.R. Vijaya Kumar was transferred there. We had halted at the holy Guruvayoor the previous night and had continued our journey on the 14th morning. I hoped the trouble with our car was not bad because we had to be at Mundakayam that evening. But a look at the car's rear left wheel made my husband feel that the axle must have snapped. Even though I was worried, I did not want to talk. Instead I started reminding myself of the wonderful way Lord Sainath had led us during the thick and thin of our life and His sustained help. If Lord Sainath could do so much, I thought, surely. He could help us overcome the present situation also.

We were stranded at a small roadside village – 'Karukutty' – midway between Trichur and Cochin. What shall we do? I thought Knowing that we would never find a mechanic on a Sunday and with hardly Rs. 300/- in my purse, I had a sinking feeling of being hopelessly stranded.

I looked at my watch. It was 11.15 A.M. The sun was bright and it was very hot. Trust in Lord Sainath and He will care for all your needs! Surely we have a need now, I thought. Somewhat hesitatingly I prayed to Lord Sainath for help, wondering how He would get us out of this mess.

There was a small house closely. But we did not really expect to get any help from strangers. Feeling pessimistic, my husband went and knocked at the door anyway. When a man appeared, we told him of our problem. To our great surprise, he came near the car to have a look at it.

Right away he suspected the joint-star to be damaged and the axle broken. He said: "I can talk to my friend in the garage 1 km. away from here. Don't worry. Even if it is a holiday, I will ask him to help you." He added: "Where are you headed?"

My husband replied, "We have to be Mundakayam this evening. I have been transferred there."

"Mundakayam" he explained, "Why! that is my native town". Then he took my husband to his friend's garage one kilometer away.

I watched him with hesitancy. When we first came to Kerala in 1978, we had some bad experiences with strangers that had left me a bit wary and suspicious about future encounters. Why should this man want to help us? Or was he trying to fool us for some reason? Anyway I left everything to Lord Sainath.

Soon they returned with the person in charge of the Garage, he explained that he was not a professional mechanic but that he knew something about cars. After carefully examining our car, he gave us the bad news: a broken axle, a burnt bearing. In that village there was no shop to get the parts. Being Sunday the shops would be closed even in Cochin or Trichur. Even this man who had gone so far out of the way already, probably could not help us now.

"My friend at Chalukudy has a junk yard. Chalukudy is hardly 5 km. from here" the stranger said suddenly, "I am going to see if I can find the parts you need". I was stunned by his kindness, yet anxiety gnawed at me once more. Why should this man want to be so helpful? What would he want in return? In that hot noon the minutes passed slowly for me and my husband, but I had plenty to think about in the strange chain of events that brought us there. To find such a man, who has access to a garage, even to spare parts was a lot to think about.

At 1 p.m. the man returned. "I found a part, I think it will do" he said cheerfully. With the help of two boys of the garage he fitted it on the wheel after nearly an hour's efforts. "Drive her down the road and see how she runs", he said ultimately.

Again I had to wonder. What kind of a man is this? How does he know we won't drive off without paying?

The car ran beautifully and my husband returned to our friend. "How much do I owe you for all you have done, asked my husband."

-Mrs. Vijay Kumar
C/o Dr. Vijay Kumar (TW)

63. MIRACLES WORKED BY SHIRDI SAI BABA IN MY LIFE (1981)

The incident herein described bears ample testimony to the above-quoted assertion of Shri Meher Baba regarding Shirdi Sai Baba's absolute mastery over all creation, animate and inanimate, INdeed, we can realize that in reality the creator and the creation are one, the later being but the ocular demonstration of the former. This is in consonance with the latest discovery in the light of post-nuclear research in the frontiers of science according to which all manifested nature is only a phenomenon of thought behind which is the thinker. This in turn reflects and reiterates the Biblical enunciation regarding the origin of creation viz., 'Let there be light' said God, and there was light, and the Upanishadic axiom viz., "SWAYAM SAMKALPA SAM SIDDI" i.e., God's manifestation in concrete form according to His Will. It is as God's incarnation that Baba has repeatedly, both during His incarnate stay at Shirdi and after His Mahasamadhi, given recurring proofs of this divine aspect. As a direct corollary of this, forces of nature like rain, storm, lightning, fire, etc. bowed to His will. The present instance is an example of this. We celebrated the marriage of our youngest son Dr. V. Satyanarayana Sai, a life-member of the Sansthan, now a lecturer in A.P.S. University, Rewa, M.P. on April 5, 1981 at Rayagada in Orissa. We were returning to Rewa via Raipur by the morning passenger train from Waltainon the 7th of the month. We had not known that apart from the inconveniences incidental to travelling a long distance by passenger train, we were unwittingly in for an ordeal. We learnt later that people of the region avoid this train as a rule. The route traverses a tribal area more or less entirely dependent for sustenance on the internal sale and export of the forest product without any middlemen by the tribals themselves. The summer is the season for mangoes and the jack-fruits in unbelievable abundance of Nature's bounty which has to be seen to be believed. At every stop came an unending stream of the girijans carrying the maximum possible load of the above items and literally hurling themselves and their burdens helter-skelter through the doors and windows into the compartments nearest to them. No railway control even if tried could stem that onslaught, as it were, at any cost. The result was the compartments were literally jam-packed and choking. It was a frightful situation in which one did not have any space to move at all. Even the lavatories were full so that we were obliged with unshed tears to hold our souls in patience till we reached Raipur, a matter of twelve hours of torture since to detrain too was physically impossible.

However, that is not only anticipating things too soon but also overlooking the terrible ordeal of near annihilation of the compartment in the burst of flames before that. For, this is what happened all of a sudden without any one anticipating it.

One of our party consisting of my eldest son, the newly married couple and my wife besides myself, (I think it was the first) said that smoke was issuing from the tan above, from a few wisps at first, it suddenly swelled to clouds, slowly filling the compartment. It took a little time to realize the potential danger it portended. It was obvious, that there was spontaneous ignition in the wiring possibly due to a short circuit, which if not checked at once would prove dangerous. MY son Chi. Satyanarayan immediately tugged at the chain to stop the train. Unfortunately it gave way. We became frantic.

It is imperative to mention here that even in such a tense situation pregnant with danger, the girijans packing the compartment just continued sitting with their sphinx-like faces and far away looks, unmoved, unflappable, as if lost in contemplation like 'tapasvins' entrenched in their firm faith that "god is in his heaven and all is right with the world". It was an object lesson for us to understand that it is to trust god into what Baba meant when He beseeched his devotees to cast their burdens on Him and keep quiet letting Him take care and provide all we need. Indeed, it shamed me into knowing how much below their standard-in truth how hypocritical-my fickle faith was. Theirs was Resignation flowing from complete surrender.

Presently, the train stopped at a station and the Asst. Guard happened to pass by. When he was told of our predicament and requested for urgent readdress, he just remarked with the utmost callousness, "Marjao! and passed on as if he were Fate's own minion! He clearly smelt of liquor. We had no alternative except to fall back upon our Unfailing Source of Succor, Baba, and to pray. Rightly has Dr. Alexis carrel, the great medical scientist and savant, averred that it is not the atom that will provide the infinite source of power for the future for humanity but prayer, for when you pray with all your heart you are linked to that dynamo that spins the universe."

The All-merciful and solicitous Baba ever on the alert as Bhaktha Paraadina did come to the rescue in a most unexpected and dramatic manner before danger completely overwhelmed us. In a split second, the sloes darlemed with gathering clouds an there began a downpour which continued for over an hour, lashing on all sides, partly flooding the compartment and completely smothering out the smoke and the threatened comflagration!

Dr. P.S.R. Swami,
D-9, P&T Quarters,
Chikkadpally, Hyderabad-500 020
(*Shri Sai Leela*, Feb. 1988)

64. BABA'S HELP IN TRANSFER CASE (1981)

Sai Baba wanted two important principles for his devotion – faith and patience. (*"NISHTA AND SABURI"*).

I like to narrate my experience of first miracle of Baba. During the end of 1981, I was promoted and posted as Surgeon and R.M. O at Lady Goshan Hospital, Mangalore. I had been only left with 3 years of service. Due to my domestic problems I was unable to so above and work at on long distance from Bangalore. But the government forced me to obey the orders and resort for duty and work at Mangalore. As per Govt. order I had reported for duty at Mangalore and worked there for some time, I was unable to cope up there for a long time I applied for leave and returned to Bangalore. Though I was representing to the Government and explaining my difficulties the government never considered my request.

Later I prayed with faith to Lord Sainath. I took a vow that I would be visits Shirdi if Sainath helped me in getting my posting to Bangalore.

I observed Sabir and *Nista* which resulted in my posting to Bangalore. With Baba's grace, according to my vow reached SHIRDI during Aug. 1983 and prayed to Lord SAI BABA.

Dr. V. Balasundaram
Civil Surgeon
Bowring and Lady Curzon
Hospital, Bangalore 560001

65. BABA CURED A CATHOLIC PATIENT (1981)

Mrs. R. Femandez. of Namabhai Manji, No. 5, ALJ Road, Mahim, Bombay as a catholic who prays with devotion to Mary. Her son Anthony was in the II year B.Sc. in 1981. He started getting headache and fever. They tried several doctors but the fever did not subside. Even after two weeks he was getting fever on alternate days. The boy's urine, blood and chest X-ray showed a slight patch in the chest Medicine for this was taken, but there was no relief. The boy was afraid to take bath as that would result in shivering and more fever.

Then Mrs. Femadez remembered the homeopathy doctor, Mr. Chawdhry, a Sai devotee, who had cured her of an ailment earlier when no other doctor had done so. Mr. Chaudhuri examined all the reports and suggested to do sputum test to find out if there is a symptom of T.B. Mr. Chaudhury said, patting the boy, "Do the sputum test and show it to the doctor who examined you earlier, if he can not give you medicine for this, then I will give you medicine by invoking the name of Sai Baba", The little words "By the name of Sai Baba. I will give you medicine" was ringing in her ears, while she returned home with the boy. That very day she told her son to take bath by the name of Sai Baba. Though the boy was afraid to take bath he took it by invoking Sai Baba's name. Mrs. Fernadez feared that something terrible would happen to her son and that night she got up thrice to see his condition. But the boy was fast asleep. He got up the next morning feeling better and quite refreshed. They stopped all medicines and kept watch on him for the relapse of the fever. He was free from fever. On the fourth day there was a knock on their door. A poor man was at the door. A part of his sleeve was torn and he had blue shining eyes.

He asked her, "Sister give me one white shirt" Mrs. Fernadez had a white shirt with her which she thought was little too big for the poor man. So she thought of altering that shirt and giving it to the poor man. She said, "I shall give you next time when you visit us." She however went inside to give him some coins, but when she returned, he had left. He was not to be found anywhere in and around the place. The "poor man" could not be seen again.

After the sputum test the allopathic doctor had given Tony medicine for a week and had asked him to report to him after that. The medicines were not taken but Tony went to the doctor for examination. The doctor was surprised to find that the previous symptoms had disappeared and prescribed only B complex tablets. He even advised him not to take the earlier prescribed medicine.

Mrs. Fernadez went to Mr. Chaudhuri's clinic and related all that had happened. He told her "Mrs. Fernadez, Sai Baba can work lots of miracles; if you keep faith in Him."

66. BABA'S TIMES HELP IN AIR TRAVEL (1982)

As far as I am concerned, Baba appeared to me in Shirdi Sai Baba temple at Secunderabad on 5.8.1982 in 'ABHAYA MUDRA' of 6 feet height statue. During 1984, when I visited the same place, I found the statue which I had seen in 1982 was not there and a small statue of 3 feet height with two hands folded on the left knee was there. This gave me a surprise and I inquired about the statue. I was told this small statue is there since the installation of the temple at about 30 years back. The statue I have seen with my own eyes at 8 A.M. on 5.8.1982 was different one. With my Engineering background, I could not reconcile how and why Baba appeared in that 'ABHAYA MUDRA'. This is the beginning of my faith on Baba and subsequently, I have got innumerable Baba experiences at various places and times.

Recently, I had been to Kathmandu with my family and while coming back by Air, I was required to pay Rs. 1200/- in Nepalese coins for immigration fees. I had Indian currency of Rs. 500 notes which could not be accepted by Nepal banks. My ticket was confirmed and I was not able to get the boarding card. I was very much in trouble and sweating like anything. At this moment,

Baba appeared as a gentleman and gave me required Nepalese currency by accepting Indian currency of Rs. 500 notes. This happened on 4.6.96 at Kathmandu Airport. Thus, there are infinite number of instances happening more or less everyday.

-E.B. Pato

HIG-21, Sheela Nagar

Visakhapatnam-530012 (A.P.)

67. BABA'S GRACE IN A DEVOTEE'S LIFE (1982)

(1) Aurangabad, May 1982: I was very delighted to receive Shri N.M. Bhushan, Marketing Manager of 'the Malhotra House' reputed Razor Blades Mfg. Co. India, who was on a holiday with his family. He happened to be my ex-boss with utmost confidence in my work and usually happy with my gunshot results, for the decade long tenure with him. Though I was then working for Kerala soaps and oils Ltd. (a Govt. of Kerala enterprise) as Area Manager in charge of Maharashtra State, I still maintained the same regard for him. I applied for leave of couple of days and took time to take them around. After completing our visit to Ellora and Ajanta caves and other nearby places of interest, I requested them to extend their trip for one more day to pay a visit to Holy Shirdi, then Aurangabad, which of course was readily agreed unanimously with a great zeal and enthusiasm. However, it was decided to chalk out Programme-details of Shirdi, the next morning itself just a few hours before our leaving Aurangabad city.

At 7 O'clock morning of 19th May, I set out from my then residence (located at famous Printerwallah's building in Chawny area) in an authorickshaw to meet my guests staying in a suite at Hotel Aurangabad Ashoka. Sipping a cup of coffee pool side as their two young sons were enjoying a swim, the Bhushans couple finessed with me that our car would leave the city boundaries by 9.45 A.M. proceeding straight to Shirdi, before their finally motoring to Bombay. After my brief discussion, I was returning home to get ready for the trip. My family was away for summer vacation.

On my way back home in the same autorickshaw I was fully preoccupied in mind to arrange for the car, and thinking whether we would reach Shirdi in time to catch up with the afternoon-Aarthi. As my autorickshaw approached the small bridge, situated before Holy Gross High School, I suddenly noticed a fakir waking on the other parallel road that joins our high-way. My first impression was so magnetic that I could not take away my looks from Him, although in one way I was doubting that he could be another Muslim fakir hawking wayside. Somehow my inner-heart filled with a strong feeling that he was no other than our Lord Sai Baba Himself. I checked and rechecked again to confirm this fact. He appeared tall with similar white beared, wore a long Kafni and head gear while holding "satka" in his right hand. My hands, which were holding the long horizontal rod usually placed at the back of the driver, failed to function though I wanted to just tap the driver of the autorickshaw, my mouth failed to open to ask him to stop the vehicle for a moment, and everything looked as if I was in a fit of helplessness. So I had turned my head back only to see and have a darshan of Baba who in turn was smiling at me. Within seconds, the autorickshaw took a turn before the school and halted before my residence. Till then some inexplicable power converted my voluntary functions of the mind and body into uncontrollable system. Atleast to fold my hands in a posture of 'Namaskar' and pay my humble respects from a distance, it became impossible to act as per my wish!

No sooner the auto reached home, I was back to normalcy from that status of inexplicable divine fit. I just told the driver to turn back the vehicle at once and ride speedily the same route from which we came. I could stop the driver exactly at the same spot where Baba appeared to me, but this time only the place could be located not our Lord Baba. With a great curiosity, we went for about one kilometer's distance in a mission to find out if 'He' could be seen still walking that way but for no avail. My search for 'Him' failed me totally. Baba vanished into thin air. Yes, now I could confirm with firmness that it was not some ordinary human Muslim fakir but Sai Baba Himself! Had he not been so, it was just impossible to cross a distance of 1 km. within a couple of minutes, however fast he might have walked.

Thus disappointed I had to return to the same spot on that highway side and again addressed my mind in which the memory of the Holy Darshan of SAI MALIK was so fresh, knelt down and kissed that mud where he stepped (footprints remained undisturbed till then). Believe it or not, when I narrate this incident now after fourteen long years, I am full with ecstatic state of mind, as it is beyond words to express this 'Thrill'.

(2) Another miracle, That day not a single tourist taxi was available for me to go to Shirdi in that big city of Aurangabad, despite my frantic search till that noon. Of course I communicated telephonically the reason for delay to my

guests. Even my good friends who were owning Travel-agencies cut a sorry figure. Thus I was shunting from pillar to post to engage a car. Suddenly a friend of mine met me in the roadside coffee joint and asked me why I was so worried. After hearing my plight he offered his jeep and forced me to accept the same though I was modestly refusing. Unfortunately I did not want to trouble my beloved guests to travel by the typical M.S.R.T.C. bus that generally remains so crowded. Moreover, my guests were in a hurry to somehow return to Bombay the next day itself. Thus at 2 p.m. we proceeded to Shirdi in the jeep and had Sai-Darshan as well as well we attended the 'Evening *Aarthi*'. I once again heartily thanked Baba in my silent prayer before Samadhi Mandir for that great opportunity of seeing Him in flesh and blood at Aurangabad.

(3) I happened to be the Regional Sales Manager since 1992 mid-year headquartered at Hyderabad for M/s Swastik Vegetable Oil Products Ltd. My Marketing Director Mr. Rajgopal Bhangdia to whom I was reporting, was immensely impressed by my style of result-oriented functioning. One fine morning he entrusted the entire sales operation giving me the charge of almost the whole country wherever our product range was sold, like Maharashtra, Gujarat in West, Madhya Pradesh, Rajasthan in North, Orissa in East and all States of North-East region, in addition to souther region which I was looking after originally.

It was in May 1994 I was touring North-east zone camping at Guwahati. From midnight of 8th till 9 A.M. of 9th the telephone in my Hotel room (Hotel President) rang so often (all STD calls from Hyderabad) from my family and from my colleagues telling that I had lost my beloved father suddenly. Immediately I flew back home encountering lot of obstacles at Calcutta and Bombay Airports. All last rites were properly performed. Losing both my parents, being the only child I was badly depressed for some weeks. For a couple of months I vehemently refused to go to doctors inspite of continuous unabated fever, to the utter disappointment and anxiety of my family members. Atlast on July 21, I was forced to go to the doctors who asked me to go to Geetha Nursing Home, Secunderabad for necessary Medical investigations that very night of a Sunday.

Pending diagnosis, a series of tests and observations were continued for a couple of days. In the meanwhile on a Tuesday morning suddenly a mishap took place to the surprise of all. I started gasping for breath, Doctors rushed in pronouncing it to be a very serious about and put-up cylindered Oxygen supply and gave me some life-saving injections, but failed to bring it under control. The puzzled doctors informed my wife and others that they tried their best but to no avail, therefore, it was a matter of few hours only left for my survival. They after obtaining her consent, phoned up to other doctors concerned and shifted me (with the Oxygen mask still on) to MEDWIN Super Specially Hospitals. There I was rushed into the ICCU and was attended by a team of doctors headed by Chief Physician Dr. Dinakar. After some hours of efforts they declared that I was out of danger, informing my wife and others who were kept waiting outside till then. They all fervently prayed to Sai Baba to somehow save my life, and lo, they were replied positively by these doctors, as per their wish. What a wonderful God is SAI who blessed and takes care to avert our dangers. We all were relieved and conveyed to Him our hearty gratitude again and again from the core of our hearts.

Very often it is customary to feel that Sai pushes us to the brim and only after touching the climax of situations suddenly. He bestows a wonderful relief, perhaps as per the individual karma.

Let us see that happened again, after watching back the MEDWIN scenario. The same ICCU, the same Oxygen artificially being supplied and various investigations being kept on. They diagnosed that it was pneumonia complicated by high level diabetes and hypertension. They also suspected some cardiac-disorders and tuberculosis.

It was Thursday night. I was on drips drawing the Oxygen supply from the cylinder still from above my bed, there was also an electronic display of my ongoing cardio-graph for easy visibility of the doctor's team always present in that ICCU ward. One Dr. Ramana who came to wash his hands, suddenly looked at the cardiograph and ran to my bed calling his other colleagues and flashing messages to the 6th and 7th floors from where Cardiologists and other Specialists rushed to me in no time. Feeling very feeble and weak with my closed eyes, it was as if I was semi-conscious able to hear the surrounding doctors mutual talk and able to feel the packings of some injections etc. I could hear one doctor (a lady doctor of the team) commenting very crudely "This is a gone case. He may not survive", while all other doctors very seriously engaged in their concerned efforts, in a great haste. My crying wife was being consoled by her parents saying Sai Baba would not do her injustice and she was helplessly praying sincerely heart and soul to him to save my life. My mother-in-law could visualize Sri Sathya Sai Baba walking towards my bed, she thrilled and informed this to all. Lying on my bed, all the while, I was beholding a pocket size picture of Shirdi Sai folded in my closed right fist and mentally praying Him even when the doctors were busy with my body during the said mishap. One of them even opened my fist, saw Baba in my palm and quietly closed my fist as it was without any disturbance.

Faith is limitless power of God within us. Inspite of difficulties when we refuse to give it up and our mind becomes set, then we will find God responding to our soulfully call/prayer. God will answer every human-being irrespective of caste, creed, or colour. Suppose for any reason we fail to get His response, we must introspect our own intensity of worship, instead of blaming the God because we lacked the perfection and thus not deserved. As rightly said by a devout Poet Pandit Razda

"Jis Hall mein rakhe Sai – Yus hall mein rahte jao.
Thufanonon se kya ghabrana – Thufanonon mein bathe jao…"

There is nothing like surrounding to His will. When SAI hears our prayers and fulfils our wishes and overwhelming our heart throbs to gush out the emotion of gratefulness to Baba (to repeatedly quote the same above said Poet). As if yelling out

'Hukme Sai mein rahkar zara dekheye
Phir Kase ka khota hai zara dekhiye…"

I strongly believe the saying "Faith starts when reasoning fails". How nice it is for us to shed our 'Ego' and watch Sai's actions in everything we do. Of what use is a mere *nana* if ultimately it does not culminate into Bhakthi and selfless devotion surrendering all the resulting pros and cons to the almighty our Lord SAI BABA. 'Sarwam Sai *ayam*'.

-M. Narender Nath
No. 16, (Adjacent 24-79)
Near Little Buds School
Anand Bagh, Malkagivi,
Hyderabad-500047

68. SAI MIRACLE IN MY FAMILY (1982)

As a Sai-devotee you all might have read and heard of many wonders or what is called Sai's leelas. I would like to share the miracle that happened in my family. Dear, readers I have never stood before any idol or God nor I know what is meant by GOD, till I met my husband. When I came to know that my in-laws were devotees of Shirdi Sai Baba I didn't take it seriously. Once it so happened that when I and my mother-in-law were having a casual talk, she was telling me about her tragedy and miracle of Shri Sai Baba. I was so much emotionalized that what I felt in me as a result I could not express nor put in words, since then I was asking my husband to help me in writing this miracle for publication in Sai Leela. The faith my Mother-in-law has in Shri Sai Baba is wonder of wonders, that wonderful faith made some wonders in her life. It so happened in 1982 that my mother-in-law's the hairs on her head, eye-brow's and even eye-lids started falling, and these places became totally bald and therefore she was looking ugly, naturally, now you can very well visualize the appearance of a woman in such a condition. She was shown to the best doctors at Hydesafal. And they replied that my mother-in-law was the first case in their career, and they, had not known any remedy for the affliction. With this we can clearly say that medical science did not have an answer to this. But the faith in Sai Baba of my mother-in-law was unshaken and unstinted. Once she had a dream in which two persons came and stood before her, one man with a red cap on head and another, a old man in Kafni, head-gear, *satka* in his hand and jholi hanging by his side. The man with red cap was heard telling the old man who resembled Sri Sai Baba, "See that poor lady's hairs have gone, have pity on her *Deva*". The Baba raised his hand and blessed her and disappeared. When she wokeup, for her surprise, her scarf which she had tied around her head while retiring to bed had been removed, folded and kept under the pillow. Next morning she decided to go to Shirdi. After Shirdi's visit she started applying 'Udi' on her head and other places. Within a few weeks of application of Udi, the hairs began to re-grow and my mother-in-law now appears like a very normal woman. You have all now seen, that for an affliction for which the so-called medical experts could not prescribe a remedy nor they knew the basic reason, but Baba's *Udi* had answer.

Dear Sai Devotee, this wonder or miracle or karishma whatever name you may like to call it by. But one thing was in tact with my mother-in-law, is her faith in Shri Sai Baba and His sacred Udi.

At last I would only say that with this miracle in our family Sri Sai Baba has pulled me closer and I have learned to have more faith devotion and patience. So dear Sai devotees I pray for the good health of all Sai brothers and Sai sisters and last let us have a firm faith and patience in Sri Sai Baba, which brings us not only peace of mind and spiritual bliss which can not be had with all the wealth and power that one may have on earth.

Om Sai Shri Sai Jay Jay Sai.

-Mrs. Vijay Kumar,
A.B.L. Colony, SHAHABAD
(*Shri Sai Leela*, Sept., 1988)

69. *SHRADDA AND* SABURI (1983)

I became a Sai devotee in 1980 and from thence I used to visit Shridi every year during eth month of January with a group of devotees. Of all the visits those of 1983 and 1984 bear some importance in my life. I narrate how it happened. It was my long desire to obtain doctorate degree after my post graduation in 1964 but due to some unavoidable circumstances I could not succeed in my attempts and I had joined service as lecturer in a University. My quest for higher studies did not stop and I continued my efforts with a will to achieve the goal at any cost. At last I got the opportunity by the Grace of Lord Sai to do Ph.D. at Hyderabad itself from the same University from where I did my post graduation. Even though I had put in a long service of 18 years I was not granted study leave with full pay and as such I had to join on loss of pay as teacher candidate in July, 1983. I was thankful to the authorities that they agreed to relieve me to enable me to join Ph.D. programme on my own accord. Since I was having some leave to my credit I took a bold decision at the risk of foregoing my four figure salary and joined the doctorate programme. Before joining I visited Shirdi in January, 1983 and took His blessings. I prayed at Samadhi Mandir for Lord Sai to look after me and give me courage to face the situation financially and complete my studies without any hindrances.

As I have the research bent of mind from the beginning. I did not feel much difficulty in my new assignment and I started my research work with all faith and patience. Three months passed but my problem was not solved for want of certain materials and I tried my level best to procure it as per the instructions of my professor. I was very much frustrated and doubted whether I could complete my work within the stipulated period. At this juncture I prayed to Lord Sai to show a way and help me in the situation. Having heard my call, He appeared to me in my dream as an old man and said "Why are you worrying much? Your problem is solved. Do not be perturbed. You will get the material and you can start your work and complete the work" and disappeared. Immediately I woke up and saw the watch and it was 5 O'clock in the morning.

That day happened to be Thursday which is very auspicious to me. Lo! to the utter astonishment and surprise my professor called me to his chambers and said word by word the same what I heard the previous day. My problem was changed and I was provided all the required materials. Is it not the miracle of Sai Baba who rescued me from the distress? My joy knew no bounds and I was overwhelmed by his grace. After performing the *pooja* I started my research work with all His blessings. From that time onwards I did not look back and days were passing without any problems. The time clock did not run smoothly and troubles started from my domestic side. My wife became suddenly ill and she was bed-ridden and I was all alone in the house. I consulted almost all the leading gynecologists and they all advised me to get her operated without any further loss of time. Operation was a costly affair to me at that time as I was on loss of pay and moreover I was busy in research work. One doctor advised me to get the scanning done for correct diagnosis. Accordingly, I decided to get it done. We has to pass through Sai Baba temple on Sir Ronald Ross Road to go to the Institute for Scanning. We stopped at the temple and took *Udi* and Prasad and proceeded to hospital. We were chanting all the way *"Om Sai Sri Sai Jaya Jaya Sai"* till we reached our destination. After taking the report we consulted a Homeopath. He assured us to cure without any operation within a week. Accordingly he gave the medicine and she responded well. After a week there was some improvement and gradually she started recovering and attending her.

-Dr. P.S.R. Swami,
D-9, P&T Colony, Hyderabad 500 020

70. MIRACULOUS RECOVERY

I was not putting on weight and sometimes R.B. Cells were passing through my urine. To find out the reason, many types of urine and blood examination were done, X-rays were also taken, but everything was found to be normal. So the doctor advised me to do a test of renal-biopsy which takes 3 to 4 days. So I was admitted to hospital on 7.1.1983. On 12.1.83 biopsy was done. We were told that because of the 'biopsy' the colour of the urine may be a little reddish; but in my case, the urine continued to be red for 3 to 4 days. It was realized then, that while doing the biopsy, the testing needle must have injected on the wrong location, and it might have injured the blood vein, which was the cause of bleeding and so the urine was red.

We were frightened and praying to Lord Sai for His help. The doctor told that there was no medicine which could stop that bleeding, it would be healed on its own. Like that another fifteen days passed; but the urine was still red. Now the doctors were also worried. It was suggested that if it didn't get normal within two the three days, some more tests would be required to trace the exact place of the injury and after that if necessary, surgery should be done to stop the bleeding.

My mind was full of anxiety and tension. My parents were also much worried. We all prayed from the bottom of our heart to Shri Sai Baba to help us and do something, so we need not have to undergo the surgery.

It seemed that our prayers were answered and one day to our pleasant surprise the urine became normal. It was the day, just one day before when the other tests for the decision of surgery were to be done. The doctors were also surprised, and told that it couldn't possible, unless it is a miracle, after this the other test was conducted. Upto three to four days everything continued to be normal. So I was allowed to move. Unfortunately it was little too early and the injury was not bealed completely. So again the bleeding started.

It was a great shock for me and I thought that if bleeding could occur again, after everything was normal, it was very dangerous and what would happen in future if healing was not complete. I prayed once again, day and night, with full faith to Shri Sai Baba about 8 bottle of blood and more than 100 bottles of glucose-saline were given to me during the period of one month. Shri Sai Baba ultimately listened to our prayers and after a week the urine was once again quite clear: But this time, I we did not want to take a risk, so after 15 days of bed-rest, I started to move and when I was out of danger, I was discharged from the hospital.

I am working in a bank and to avoid the hardships of travelling, I applied for transfer to the breach near my house. By Shri Sai's grace, I got the transfer immediately, to the branch, which is very close to my house. By His grace I am now alright.

This incident has impressed me a lot and strengthened my faith in Sri Sai Baba even more. I strongly believe that if you have true faith and if you remember Him from the bottom of your heart, with patience, he will certainly come to your help and fulfil your wishes. May all have such faith towards Him and my Lord Sai Baba's grace be showered on them.

-Nita N. Parikh
12/432, Shraddhanand Road,
Kunj Vihar, 2nd Floor,
Matunga, Bombay-400 019

71. SAI THE SOURCE OF LIFE (1983)

During 1983, I had a severe problem. My own younger sister with her husband and a cousin brother scolded me and insulted me. I was thrown out of my parent's house. At night with my child and my husband I just prayed to God. The younger sister never shared late mother's and elder sister's jewels with me. I was totally left in the lurch.

At that time we were staying at Santa Cruz. I had two ladies as neighbours, who were always grumbling, insulting all tenants. I was jammed between them. They always stood for arguments, always refused t fight. It was not in my blood. I ignored it. My silence killed them and they started shouting and throwing rubbish in front of my house.

My sister's awkward behaviour, these old ladies tantrums and professional jealousy at my work made me suffer a miscarriage. Suddenly after that I became too emotional and lost self-confidence. But my belief in God's grace grew stronger. It was at that time I started reading 'Sri Sai-Sat-Charita' and started to do Sapthah. My husband had gone to visit his parents. I had gone out with my eight years old daughter. As I returned home I heard a loud noise. I went to the other room and saw the ceiling along with concrete had fallen on the bed. Sai saved us. Hed it been night we would have been killed!

But the neighbours wished we were dead. I completed my first 'Sapthah' of 'Sri Sai-Sat-Charita'. My husband decided to sell the house. I was doing the second 'Sapthah' of 'Sri-Sat-Charita'.

I went to Dadar Sansthan and prayed before of Baba, if he was pleased with my doing 'Sapthah' he must bless me with a particular white gajra, which had a red rose at its centre. It was a Thursday, lots of garlands adored Baba's neck. A man was standing near Baba's statue and was keeping his both hands in receiving posture. I thought he must be new to this place. He could have taken any prasad. Instead he was waiting for the office boy who was removing garlands from Baba's neck to give him. Suddenly the office boy turned and saw me. He came with the same gajra I had wished and gave it to me. My joy knew no bounds. The old man also came to me and said, "See the miracle of Baba. I brought it and I wanted it and you got it" I gave it to him as I had already known Baba's answer to my question. But the man refused, saying it is Baba's will and it is final. I gave him the *peda* as *prasad*! Thus my second Sapthah was completed.

Now I decided to do 7 Sapthahs! so while doing the third one, we happened to sell our Santacruz house. It fetched only 1.5 lakhs. But again Baba helped us by sending a Sai devotee to buy it. He bought it for 2.10 lakhs and gave us Shirdi prasad.

While doing my fourth Sapthah my father gave us some money for the new house, we had to pay for CIDCO. Our financial positions improved. My younger sister started visiting me. She had three miscarriages. One still born and one blue baby. Her husband had no job and she was also jobless. Selling the ornaments she was pulling on her days. As a Sai devotee she now says Baba taught her a lesson for her misbehaviour.

While doing the fifth Sapthah our new house was purchased from a Sai International Agent. The row is called T (It meant Thursday for me) and house number 14, i.e. 1+4=5. Five resembles 's' of Sai! various kinds of Shirdi *Prasad* started pouring from so many places. We shifted to our new house on Thursday. The first post to come to the house was from Shirdi with '*Udhi* and *Suntevada*' along with *Sai Leela* on a Thursday. Our financial position further improved. As Baba said, there was no scarcity for food and clothes in his devotee's house.

My husband had a slip-disc. He was asked not to go by scooter. So we planned to buy a car. Baba sent us money. My father financed for the car. We brought a second hand one and it came on a Thursday. We decided to visit Shirdi in that car. My sixth Sapthah completed.

All small tensions were borne successfully by me with grace of Baba. My father had a paralysis stroke. He stopped taking any food. He had lost interest in his life. He considered himself as a burden on us and often wept. His health started deteriorating. Seeing his condition I went to Dadar Sansthan on a Thursday and requested Baba, either to relieve him from his sickness or take him to His feet by next Thursday while admitting him in a *shushtrusha*, in his ward there was a 'Sai's photo'.

I left it to him. But father had premonition, On Tuesday he signaled saying "in another two days I will go up. Exactly on Thursday around 1.15 p.m. he passed away calmly during his sleep! I consoled, or rather Baba consoled me! Father was not allowed to suffer more! His calm face told us his death was peaceful.

My sister was again pregnant. By now she had sold all jewelries and was penniless. I went forward to help her financially in her delivery. She was insulted and treated badly by the cousin brother and his wife. But a live child even for the sixth time was doubtful. I prayed to Baba at least to give her one child. I gave her my '*Sai-Sat-Charita*' book and *Udhi*, asked her to read daily two chapters and apply *Udhi* on her stomach! She was a severe diabetic and blood pressure patient! Aged only 27 years she cried whenever the feudal moniter reports came as the foetus was dead! but I told her not to lose faith in Baba. Uttering Baba's name whenever I touched her belly the baby moved. She said it was a boy according to sonography tests. I prayed to Baba (generally in conditions like this the male child always died whereas the females survived). Baba heard our prayers! He changed the child to be a girl. Though she had serious problems, Baba gave her life. The baby has been named as 'Shraddha'. She is 15 months old now.

Baba has been always there. When we were in Shirdi I remembered my first visit which was not a pleasant one for me. We had accommodation problems. So I prayed next time kindly grant me a better accommodation. Next time we were able to stay at M.T.D.C. hotel. That much Baba had raised our financial position. I wanted to buy a big rose garland. Baba read my mind. My hubby who sometimes acts strangely bought the same to my surprise, he even agreed to donate the sum of rupees which I had in my mind.

We went to Shirdi this November in our car alongwith shraddha and her parents. It was a pleasant trip. Well, I am waiting for Baba to call me to do my seventh sapthah there.

Thank you Sai!

You are above us to bless us!

With in us to preserve us!

Before us to guide us!

After us to guard us!

So why worry!

-Mrs. Jaya Sree Ram

T-14, Ashirwad, Sector-6

Vashi, New Bombay – 400 703

(*Shri Sai Leela*, Oct. 1997, pp. 32-34)

72. *DARSHAN* OF SRI SAI BABA (1983)

This particular incident occurred to me and my daughter (11 yrs. old) in Oct./Nov. '83. I was on a visit to my parents in Delhi. We always go to Sai Temple at Lodhi Road, New Delhi, whenever we go to Delhi. This time I thought that with Sai's blessings I should offer a woolen blanket to a poor Fakir. So I purchased a blanket from a shop and went to another shop for buying chappals. Then suddenly a Sadhu, dressed in an immaculate red angarkha and a white dhoti appeared in that shop. He asked the shopkeeper, without looking at us, "Give me money as I want to buy a blanket because I am going to Vaishno Devi Temple." Now see the coincidence, I was having a blanket in my hand and I had already decided to offer it to a poor Fakir. So I thought why should not I offer it to this Sadhu, but the next instant I thought that as this Sadhu was so immaculately dressed, he did not seem to be poor, so it was better to give it to a really needy man. And so I didn't give the blanket to that Sadhu.

My daughter and myself saw clearly a bunch of nine rupees notes (5+2+2) in that Sadehu's hand. Then that shopkeeper told him to please go away as those were his business hours. Sadhu then left without asking anything from me. Later on I gave a second thought to this incident and asked myself that why at that particular time when I was having a blanket in my hand, somebody should suddenly appear and demand money for a blanket. Was he our Sai who wanted that blanket to be handed over to him! I could not find that particular Sadhu in the whole of market later on. I was convinced thus that Baba gave me darshan but I could not recognize Him in that guise. It was my egoism that I thought I would present the blanket to a Fakir but not to that Sadhu, which had prevented me from offering the blanket to the Sadhu who was none other than our Great Sai as was evident later.

In the evening I went to Sai mandir and with a heavy heart I offered it to Sai there. I told Him to give that blanket to whomsoever he wants. This incident proves that He still appears to His Devotees when a devotee livingly and devotionally calls him. He is omniscient, omni-present and omni-potent. We should simply remember and utter His name as 'Om Sai'. Such soul-stirring soul elevating experiences and incredible miracles of Shri Sai Baba proves that He is always there to bless His devotees and save them from any calamities, disease and disasters.

"BOW TO SHRI SAI AND PEACE BE TO ALL"

-Mrs. Madhur Mathur
A/8 ONGC Colony, Vidya Vihar (E),
Bombay-400 077
(*Shri Sai Leela*, Nov. 1987)

73. INCIDENTS OF SAI GRACE EXPERIENCED BY A PROMINENT SPIRITUALIST (1992-96)

Shri K.S. Jayaraman j-J

ji took me to the eminent saint Smt. Shivamma Thayee's *darshan* at her *ashram* in Bangalore. She was a real devotee of Shri Shirdi Sai Baba. Then she was 100 years old.

(1)   In July 1992 while I went on a pilgrimage tour to Shirdi Interred I prayed to the Sri Shirdi Sri Shirdi Baba universal teacher in front of our group of devotees and prophesized the beautiful literature would be coming-out in Sri Gurudev's name. They really wondered at my words.

Our group of devotees started the return journey from Shirdi to Bangalore, via Manmad and got into the Karnataka Express train. All of us occupied our respective seats. Soon after meditation, Japa and Thapa in the early morning, a divine person appeared sitting beside me. The spoke to me after doing *pranams*. He is the person who is well educated. We talked for about an hour. Thereafter, he expressed his desire to bring out. some books on Sri Shirdi Sai Baba. Our devotees wondered at this unexpected and wonderful incident and felt very very happy. They immediately said this is nothing but a miracle of Baba. Thus, Sri Shirdi Baba Ji created a holy miracle to his devotees on the spot to their surprise Shri Ruhela came to Bangalore on 24.7.92 my house and them met Shivamma Thayee. Whom he interviewed at length he proceeded thereafter to her native place Faridard and brought out a book about her in English, having gathered necessary detailed information on her family background, life experiences etc. He had wholeheartedly said that a literature would be brought out and he did so soon in 1992. Now, the great task of bringing out a vast literature on Sri Shirdi Sai Baba is being done by him at this moment.

(2)   In August 1992, while I was having my bath at Bhima river, I had *Sarpa Darshan* (Cobra *Darshan*). I saw really Sri Sai Baba in him and thereafter, we had darshan of Sri Dattatreya.

(3)   In September 1992 also I had *darshan* of Sri Sai Baba in the form of *Sarpa*, while I was taking bath at Godavari river and the same night we presented a garland containing 1008 Sphatika manis to Sri Shirdi Sai Baba.

(4) On one Thursday night in October 1992 a group of rowdies tried to trouble us at out residence. But we were saved by the divine grace miraculous power of Sri Sai Baba.

(5) In January 1993 on a Thursday, I was attending to my duties at my office. Some unknown person came to me and gave a big and beautiful flower garland saying that one of my student only had sent it. This incident took place to our surprise, that too in front of our training students. I placed the garland on Sri Sai Baba's photo.

(6) On one fine morning at 7.00 A.M. in February 1993, I was coming out from my house to attend the office. A young boy of about 16 years wearing torn clothes appeared in front of me and begged two rupees. I atonce realized that he was Sri Sai Baba and gave him the money.

(7) On some other day also, I was coming out of my house to attend my office. A middle aged man wearing torn clothes appeared and said that he had just come out of a jail. He begged two rupees from me. I searched my pocket for money, but unfortunately I could not find any money to give him. I realized that this was a test of Sri Sai Baba and proceeded further.

(8) I had *prerana* (inner instution) to proceed to Sri Shirdi and I was told that there would be only 54 devotees. Before our departure, their where people in excess. To our surprise, the four people who were in excess, went back to their houses taking back the amount paid by them for the journey and the same from persons were at Shirdi for Baba's darshan on Gurupoornima day. When the bus departed and we counted, there were 54 persons. In our said group, one fellow had darshan of Shri Baba in an aged man's form, at his feet. This miracle happened because of the said devotee.

(9) In November, 1993, a person called me for pooja at 5 p.m. On the way, I met a boy of 16 years who was like a mad person but he had luster on his face, in a low tone, he begged of me two rupees. I gave the money to him and came to the house where Babaji's pooja was going on. There was a surprise again. I saw a photo of the said boy in the pooja room of that house. It was nothing but Babaji's photo only. Then, I had sudden seating when I realized myself that this was Baba's miracle. Then I informed all these devotees who had come

for pooja there. It was the residence of a Manager of an Apex Bank of Bangalore namely Shri Muddabasave Gowda.

(10) One day, I went to a devotees house, for pooja. Thereafter, an aged man like a Fakir came to the same house, without looking at any other house. He came near the door, called the head of the family and blessed him. He also sent words for one more fellow and gave darshan to him. This miracle happened at the residence of Shri Krishnan, an employee of Hindustan Aeronautics Ltd. Bangalore.

(11) On a Thursday in January 1994, I had a sudden flash of a thought. I told my family members that some important person might come on that day, and he should be given some food. It thus happened that an aged man came and begged for some food. He was served food. My family members felt much surprise that this was the work of Sri Sai Baba.

(12) In February 1994 our group of devotees consisting of six persons viz., myself Sri Vasanthe Gowda, Sri B.V. Gnana Murthy, Sri K.R. Krishna Setty, Sri A.K. Ramanathan and Sri N. Ramu went to New Delhi to attend a Homeopathy Seminar that was arranged by M/s B. Jain Publications, New Delhi. Prof. S.P. Ruhela also had come at that time. Soon after the SEminar was over, we went to Shirdi for Babaji's darshan. Then, we left Shirdi for Bangalore by Karnataka Express. The train was moving via Gulbarga-Raichur. On the way, our train dashed against a lorry which was parked across the Railway line, smashing the lorry into small bits. The train's engine had derailed and had run nearly one K.M. after derailing. It was exactly 6.30 A.M. I was doing Japa and meditation when this accident took place. Even the Railway authorities who inspected the spot, expressed their surprise how none was hurt or injured inspite of such an accident, and said that some great Mahatma much there in this train. It was all a miraculous work of Sai Baba. But the driver of the lorry who was standing a little away from the railway lane, had to face a minor injury in his left arm. The train left that place an hour late after it was set right.

(13) It was at 7.30 p.m. of Friday, the 17th March 1995, One Smt. Anasuyadevi of Bombay brought an Officer to my house for Lord's Sai, darshan is. He was Sri Keri P. Taarapurewala, a Navy Officer. I prayed to Baba and presented a Rudrakashimala to him. Smt.

Anasuyadevi who was looking at me, was getting joyful tear. As she really saw Shridi Sai Baba, while I was handling over Japamala to Mr. Tharaporedwala. This is really an unforgettable incident for me.

(14) We had arranged a "Rudraksh Mala Yogna" from 15th to 17th December 1994. Then a great incident took place. From August 1994 to February 1995, I was doing all my work in the names of our Gurus and Lords. This Yagna work came through because of blessings of Shri Adi Shankaracharya. I was reiterating whenever we had meeting for this proposed Yagna, that all work would be done through Baba alone. We tried two or three places to carry on this yagna work. But at last, we got a place at Maratha hostel where we were able to put up a huge Shamiana in a spacious ground. That too, it was opposite to Sri Sai Baba Kalyana Mantapam, near Basavangudi, Gandhi Bazar, Bangalore. The Yagna took place very well. Everyone felt it was really wonderful. Thousands of people realized the power of Sai Babaji. It was, as though, all devotees were going to receive prasadams chanting *"Om Sai Sai"*.

(15) On a Thursday, 15th February 1996, I went to have darshan of the famous pilgrim place Sri Kshetra Akkalkot Maharaj. I had darshan and *prasadam*. I left for Bijapur by bus at 2 p.m. after getting a seat with great difficulty. I finished all pujas in a hurry, in Sri Gurudev name. It was all due t lack of time, the Bangalore Bus had to leave at 8.10 P.M. while I was travelling, the bus was stopped in the middle way, I got out and went in search of drinking water.

Before, I returned unfortunately, the bus had left for Jijapur, My kit bag was in that bus. My money, Reservation ticket for my travel to Bangalore and the Japamala used by me for the last 30 years including my official papers were in it. My mind became blank and I could not find a way to solve the problem. Then a miracle happened. Soon a tempo van came near me. A youth sat beside me in Babaji's form and filled my mind with full faith. I prayed to Babaji that all my things should reach me intact, safely, if I had really been Guruji's devotee. The boy took me to the control room of KSRTC where I found all of my luggage items intact, after giving them my identity. This was the real help done by Babaji I hope that Babaji is doing such to his true devotees even to-day, who believe him. One the same day when I was travelling to Bangalore, a conductor of KSRTC being a youth, demanded me a high luggage charge of Rs. 40/-. Somehow, I gave him without satisfaction. Though my neighbour's luggage was bigger, he had not charged for it. What he did to me was unjust. Then I prayed to Babaji. At 1.30 A.M. midnight, the bus stopped. The bus did not move an inch further inspite of much efforts, as it had an engine seizure. Somehow, I arrived Bangalore in other bus.

(16) In 1992 July on Shravana Gurupoornima and Bhadrapada Poornima in August, I had darshan of Babaji and Dattapanduranga. We did Gurupoornima in 1993, 1994 and 1995. But owing to some reason, it was not possible to go for Gurupoornima in 1996. I had requested Babaji that I would be coming to have his darshan and if 30 devotees could meet me. I waited for it. But it did not happen so. On 15th July 1996, I received a letter from Dr. Ruhela. Then I prayed Babaji for his *mahima*.

(17) Kumari Sakamma, aged 18 years came to me having an injury at her right leg caused by a sharp pointed firewood log after a lapse of seven years having consulted various doctors for medical treatment. She had already spent nearly Rs. 1000/- in the consulting famous doctors. Inspite of these efforts the doctors had opined that her leg had to be inputed. She had become weak and was convinced in her mind that she would surely die. I prayed Babaji and gave her Babaji's holy ash to consume it every day, after praying the Babaji. I also gave her Babaji's photo to perform pooja, together with certain medicines of Homeopathy. Her wound healed gradually and she was able to do tailoring job. She continued to pray Babaji and thereafter, her wound was healed totally. All this has happened by the divine grace of Sai Babaji.

(18) Shri Shreedhara Murthy, a 36 year aged man of Mysore, was suffering from Tuberulosis and had become much weak. He had severe cough, cold and Asthma, followed by different colours of phlem. He had undergone an operation and a few of his bones of his left chest had been removed. As the intensity of the problem was more, he had decided that he would die. His relatives brought him to me. The patient was in such a condition that it was much critical. Anyone would really feel afraid to look at him at that stage. However, I prayed to Sai Babaji and gave him Baba's holy ash with a photo of Babaji and told him to consume the ash daily. I also gave him a divine medicine of Homeopathy. Now, he is recovering from

such illness, gradually. His relatives who brought him to me here felt much surprised over this miraculous cure. Now, anyone can see luster on his face. Now they feel that normalcy may restore upto 80% in the instant case. This is all due to blessings of Babaji. He is really Almighty. Meditating on him is like Sanjeevini on hand. He cures all kinds of diseases and discomforts and grants total happiness and also longevity. It is his godly power that he will establish peace likewise, many patients have got cured miraculously by his grace.

(19) Smt. Subbalakshmamma aged 75 years of Ananthapur (Andhra Pradesh) came to me with a complaint of her stomach ulcer and blood vomiting. She had taken medical treatments from hospitals and Kidwai Cancer Institute, Bangalore, but returned home without any fruitful results. At her last stage, they brought her to me. She was lying on the ground. She had no consciousness. I prayed to Babaji and Banashakkari Devi and put holy water *(theertham)* and a little of Homopathy medicine. She gradually recovered consciousness. I continued to pray and gave her holy ash and medicines. To our surprise, she who was about to die survived due to the divine grace of Babaji. It was an impossible task done by Babaji.

(20) Like this, many people who were mentally ill have become well and such children who had left their homes, or had been lost have returned home safely. Such people who had no children have got issues, lost relationships have rejoined and children have come in close contact with their parents, lost properties have come back to them and people have been placed in better status. All these are happening in country cases due to the divine grace of Babaji. People who had come with the intention of committing murder have failed in making an attempt to murder and surrendered themselves. Babaji has been so much kind in safeguarding the interests of his devotees. He has been helpful to the whole mankind. There is nothing bogus here. These are the real facts which have already happened and are still happening like Baba's miracles. Babaji has been giving darshan to his devotees in many instances and in many forms. Sri Shirdi Baba is really universal and God Almighty.

Sri H.D. Lakshman Swamiji,
Spiritualist & Homeopathy
Bangalore-560086

74. BABA'S HELP IN DEVOTEES LIFE (1971-76)

In the year 1971 myself and my affectionate father Shri T.A. Ram Nathen were turning the pages of Late Dr. Baba Rao Patel (MP)'s *"Mother India"* in which we were carried away by the article on Shirdi Sai Baba. We were wonderstruck with Baba's simplicity and attachment towards poor and needy. We immediately decided to enroll ourselves into his list of innumerable Sai devotees. Our devotion to Shirdi Sai increased leaps and sounds. In the year 1976 my parents Sri T.A. Ram Nathen and Vijayem Ram Nathen's long cherished dream of Shirdi Sai's Darshan at Shirdi materialized. They were wonderstruck by Shirdi Sai's abode and the then monthly magazine *"Shri Sai Leela"* The sooner they returned back from the *TEERTH YATRA* in 1976, I was advised to visit Shirdi in August Mail (Via-Shirdi) and reached Bombay V.T. enroute to Shirdi by MSTC bus. The journey was pleasant. I stepped in Shirdi for the first time on an evening of August 1976. This inaugural "SAI MIRACLES" henceforth.

I stayed in "SHANTI NIWAS" aptly matching my future. On a Thursday I vehemently prayed Sai to bless me with a job in a Ltd. Concern as I was working in an ordinary company for a meagre salary. Then I also "vowed" to Sai that if He got me a good job of my liking I would visit Shirdi once a year from my yearly bonus received to recharge my "Spiritual Battery" again and again through Sai till I mixup with "Mother Eearth". Lo! wonder of wonder struck through my dear friend Mr. N.R. Chandran of M/s. Cutler Hammer Ltd. just after my return to Calcutta from Shirdi, I casually was disenssing with Mr. Chandran about his job, sooner he surprisedly asked me, if I was interested in the job. I immediately said "Yes" as because in 1976 getting into a LIMITED Concern of Cutler Hamer's standard at Rs. 400/- p.m. was a blessing of Sai indeed. Mr. Chandran appointed me as Sales Assistant in Cutler Hammer Ltd. Through his boss Mr. B.B. Chawla, then discerning Regional Managers. Since then I fully surrendered myself to Sai and followed his footsteps to the best of my efforts. With effect from 1976 August, my visits to Shridi are un-interrupted by Sai's grace. In October I may forget my office, home but not Shirdi. I had taken my dear parents Shri T.A. Ram Nathen, Mother Vijyem Ram Nathen, Sisters – Lakshmi Sitaraman, Geetha Venkataraman, Wife Lalitha Anand and daughters T.A. Sai Deepa and T.A. Sai Sudha thrice to Shirdi.

This year I will be making on my 12/10/96 23rd visit to Shirdi with my wife Mrs. Lalitha Anand and Sai Blessed son T.A. Sai Ram who is around four years of age now. I am anxious for my "Silver Jubilee" visit to Shridi Soon.

My friends relatives and colleagues of Bhartia Cutler Hammer are wonderstruck with Baba's blessings on me and my family.

Such "SPIRITUAL MIRACLES" can only happen with Shirdi Sai's grace. Never in my trip to Shirdi had I faced problem, but only Sai. Sai accompanies us everywhere. I and my family survive only through his grace. Being a Shirdi Sai *bhakta* I am grateful to him for showering everything in his fold on us. Today I am a sales officer, an executive of BHARTIA CUTLER HAMMER'S Calcutta office for a seizable salary with price through Shirdi Sai's grace. With this I conclude my till date.

Sai Baba Our Lamp Shirdi OUr Camp"

-T.R. Anand
Sales Officer,
Bhartia Cutler Hammer, 20B,
Abdul Hamid Street, Calcutta-700069

75. BABA'S GRACE ON A STUDENT (1986)

(1) I was doing my home-science course, from the South Delhi Polytechnic, in 1986, and in 1987, I was to go on their tour to Bangkok and Singapore. It was my first trip abroad. I was very excited about it and my parents had called two of my cousins from Allahabad to go with me. Everything was all set, but, I slipped and sprained my knee, just two days, before we were to leave, so I was left behind and my cousins, who were going for me, went without me. I was so angry with God that I flung all idols and photographs of God out of my room, I lost faith in God, I started cursing God. Then in January 1988, one day my mother came and told me that my father has arranged for some pooja for me at the Sai Temple at Lodhi Road at 6.30 A.M., the next day, and that I must take and accompany them. I agreed for fear of my father's wrath. I went to the temple full of anger and with the intention of shouting loudly (Amitabh Bachchan Style), at Baba, but the moment, I entered and saw Baba's *murti*, all my anger miraculously vanished and I did the pooja with genuine feelings. I came back home, wondering, *"Baba ki murti men aisa kya tha jise dekhte hi mera saara*

gussa shant ho gaya? Zaroor koi chamatkaari shakti hai, Baba mein". I became a Sai *Shakti* since then and in May 1988, I went to London and Birmingham for six months.

(2) This was in 1990, I had a massivemis-understanding with my most favourite uncle in May 1989, as a result of which he vowed never to talk to me, I was so much attached to my uncle, that I'd buy rings and lockets of Baba put them on his feet, get them, blessed, pray for my uncle's health (He's got severe asthma), and that, he cools down fast. They started making him melt, but he refused to show in. Then I fell seriously ill in September, 1990. I had to be hospitalized with high fever and black-coloured something. I was in hospital for three months, I had to undergo several painful tests drugs, etc. I asked my *mausi* (mother's sister) to pray to Baba, and get me a small statue of Baba, I used to firmly grip it in my hands and pray *"Baba, Shakti do, mujhe shakti do, Baba",* during all moments of pain, and endure it. MY kidneys and liver had all failed. I was in a Coma for three days. There were no chances of my survival. The doctors had last hope for me, but I suddenly revived. The doctors said that it was a miracle. I lost hope of ever being able t walk, I used to cry, helplessly, that I couldn't go to Baba's temple, and believe me, Baba used to come in my dreams, and say, *"Tu nahin aa Sakti to kya hua, meri bacchhi? Bilkul, theek ho jayegi".* I was brought home in the first week of November My uncle came to see me, then in November end, a childhood friend of my father started visiting me everyday to help me gain confidence in myself, by holding my hand and walking with me. *"Tab se main Baba ki our strong bhakt ho gayi".*

(3) My most favorite uncle lost his mother, in 1993, and it was such a set-back for him that he developed engina and started telling me that he won't live for more than four or five years. It upset me so much, that I started doing *nirjalaa* fast every Thursday, and praying to Baba for his long life, as a result of which Baba saved him from a near-fatal accident in 1994. The front portion of his car went down a cliff and he could feel a strong pull on the rear portion, much before people gathered to actually do so He said that the strong pull was that of my love, he called it his *raksha-kawach,* and Baba pulled him to Shirdi, ot personally bless him. He was in Bombay, for his balloon surgery, with aunts and kids, and through he never had faith in Baba, he had

a sudden urge to go to Shirdi, as though something was pulling him. There and once in front of Baba, he wept like a baby, he felt such strong vibes. *"Who meri jaan hain, mere Baba ne meri khaatir meri jaan ko apni taraf kheench ke khud unhein lambi umr ka aashirwaad de diya,* he's been better since then and I am utterly grateful to Baba for that. Baba *na bulaate to who yun, achaanak, Shirdi kyon jaate?"*

(4) This was in the last week of July last year, I was in Mussoorie, with my mother and my *naniji* (mother's mother). There is a woman there known as *'Sai Maa'*, she does miracles (I saw them, on a private video recording, last year), and I was wanting to meet her, but could not last year as she never comes down the steps of her house (Her house has been made into a Sai Darbar), and I am unable to climb steps. But this year Baba told her to step down at 7.00 A.M. on *Guru Purnima* day, take a *'prabhaat-pheri'* to his temple and bless people on the way. I was very excited, I got ready on time, and eagerly waited for the car to come and pick me up. Unfortunately, I reached the venue two minutes late *'Sai Maa'* had gone back upstairs. I was terribly disappointed and I was waiting for my mother to come down, when *'Sai Maa'* came down with her just to bless me. Honestly, I felt that it was Baba coming towards me, when I touched her feet and I felt that they were Baba's feet and like Baba's hand, when she touched my head. She said, the some words as Baba, aways says to me, *"Tere Sab kastha door honge, meri bacchhi",* and I could feel the vibes till much after I was back home.

(5) This was the day before Rakhi, the 27th August, last year, I was in Mussoorie, and like, every year, I'd made all my *rakhis* on my own this year as well. I have two brothers in Mussoorie, who I tie *rakhi* to them but unfortunately neither of them could make it this year, one of them was in Dehradun, with his newly born son, and the other one was down with conjunctivitis, so I was very depressed, but just, the day before Rakhi, a miracle happened. There's a cousin of mine, called Namrata, who's a very strong devotee of Baba, she ties him a rakhi every year. She came to see me a day before rakhi. I showed her my *rakhis* and when she appreciated them, I gave her one and insisted, on her keeping it as a moment from me as I'd made glass-painting ones (I think of some new idea, every year, I like mine to be unique and exclusive), and I didn't want to bring any back here, with me, Namrata did accept it, then, suddenly said "I just got a lovely idea, Anshoo, shall

I tie this to Baba, on your behalf, tomorrow? Would you mind if I do that? You know I tie him one every year, don't you? You want to tie him one this year? *"bolo"*. I was delighted, I knew that it was Baba, who'd asked for it through *didi*, I said excitely, "Sure, why not, *didi*? that's a fantastic idea". It was surely, Baba, who'd asked for my *rakhi*, he must have felt that, *'Bechaari bacchhi, bahut, udaas hai ke koi rakhi bandhwaane waala nahin hai main apni bacchhi ko dukhi nahin dekh sakta main, bandhwaa loonga, rakhi us se*, and got Namrata did, to ask for it. She tied it to Baba, early morning the next day, I was not at all sad and *'Sai Ma'* sent me prosaad of *kheer* and *gulab jamun*. Honestly, my faith in Baba has strengthened since then.

(6) We were supposed to return to Delhi on the 6th of September, but my father came on the 31st August and ruined our program, by insisting on our returning on the 4th. I got adamant, on staying till the 6th but, I have someone, whom I call *daadu*, in Delhi and whom I cannot dis-obey, and he gave me a call on the 2nd to say that he wanted me back on the 4th, so I agreed. I'm so attached to Mussoorie and my uncle (I call him, *papa*, *uncle*, he's a doctor snatched away, from my mother's arms, when it's time for us to leave. I wascrying, all the way, but Baba had a surprise waiting for me at Muzaffarnagar. We went to a cousin's house for lunch, and I saw my Karan *bhaiya* (The one, who had conjunctivitis) sitting there. *do maheene ek hi sheher mein hoke bhi mil nahin paaye, our jab jaa rahe the to yun mil gaye*, I was delighted. We reached back home by 8.00 P.M. on the 4th of September, and I was very bitter with my father and *daadu*, for having forced me to come back, but Satish (Sanju) contacted me on the 8th in response to my letter to him, through a friendship magazine, and we developed an instant rapport so I felt 'See? This is what Baba get you, forcefully, brought back to Delhi, for you fool, cool down, now, and forgave *Papa* and *daadu* for having brought me back against my wishes. Satish is, definitely, Baba's Rakhi-gift to me, I've become a new Anshoo, ever since I found him. *Joh, jitna bhi hai, mera hai, I love him beyond measure*. I know, he's Baba's gift to me, *phir bhi Satish ko khone ka khauf khaata rehta hai, mujhe*, because, I've always lost the ones I've loved, till now, *meri kismet, itni kharaab hai. Satish jitna bhi hai, utna hi mera rahe bas, aur kucchh nahin chaahiye mujhe.*

So these have been my miraculous experiences with Baba, I hope, I've jottled them down for you eligibly enough. Please do tell me, if I've gone wrong anywhere uncle.

Ashoo, NOIDA

(Courtesy: J.R. Laroriya)
NOIDA (U.P.) 17.1.1996

76 BABA'S GRACE EXPEREINCED BY A PROFESSOR (1989)

1. My wife Indu was keen to be appointed as a Lecturer or Research Associate after submitting her PH.D. Thesis in June 1989. She applied for these positions in several colleges but in vain. This had frustrated her and me very much. We both prayed to Sri Shirdi Sai Baba and ultimately He listened to our request and she was appointed as a Research Associate in April 1993.

2. In 1991, blood started coming out of my mouth. Despite several X-rays taken and treatments done at Amritsar, Delhi and elsewhere my condition become bad to worse. In November 1992 I visited Shirdi and prayed to Baba for my recovery. I started doing Baba's *aarti* regularly and stopped taking doctor's medicines.

   I started intensely praying to Baba to cure me. Soon Baba listened my request and cured me. On the basis of these two experiences of my life, I can empathetically say that Baba definitely saves his devotees in their calamities.

Prof. Pandeya Shashi Bhushan "Shitanshu"
Professor's Bungalow No. A-7
Guru Nanak Dev University
Amritsar – 143 005 (Punjab)

77. BABA VISITED DEVOTEE'S HOUSE (1989)

In year 1989, one day while I was coming home from local shopping centre in Sector 16, Faridabad, I saw a sadhu coming from a side road. He was wearing a black loose and long kurta and a black dhoti. He had covered his head with a cloth and was having a cloth bag hanging around his shoulder. Seeing him, the first thought came to any my mind was that he might be Shirdi Sai Baba. He saw me and came straight to me after crossing the road and said *'Beta chai peena hai pilaogey?'* I said, "Why not Baba"? Please come with me to my house which is only a few yards away". He followed me. Reaching home I told him to be seated on the floor outside the main gate and I went inside and asked my wife to make a cup tea for him. Since no tea leaf was available at home at that time I went out to a shop opposite our house to fetch a pocket. I requested the sadhu to wait for it! Again I requested him to stay and he agreed. Tea was served. He drank it very quickly, put the cup on the floor and stood up. When I bent to pick up the empty cup from the ground he put his hand on my head as if to bless me. But I did not like his touching my head with his five fingers. I was upset because I thought his hands might not be clean and could therefore, cause me some infection.

He said, "*Beta*, I am happy with you. Tell me if you have any desire?" I said "Baba we have God's blessing and we don't need anything." Then he said "I give you some prashad". He put his hand in the bag, took out some ash and wanted to give me I refused to accept it, saying, "I don't need it". He again asked me to have some but I declined. He said, "I am not angry". He then put the ash back in his 'bag'. A little power was still covering his fingers. He put his hand on his head. Some water appeared and he jirked his hand as if to wash it. Again he put the hand on his head and again some water drops oozed out on his fingers. I saw this magical production of water but was not much impressed. Before departing he said, "*Beta*, I am going to Badrinath, give me a blanket". Since my mind was still agitated I said, "I am sorry", you have had a cup of tea for which you came; now you please excuse me". He went away. After a few seconds I wanted to see where he was going but I could not find him anywhere. He had disappeared as if in the thin air. I could hardly have missed an ordinary human being in those few seconds.

The very next day I started feeling acute change on my head. A day later the place where his fingers had touched my head started wetting and oozing. This problem remained for more than a month. During this period I had consulted in physician who diagnosed it as wet eczema. Even after taking medicine there was hardly any sign of recovery. The feeling to scratch my head all the time made me very upset. Out of frustration one day I sat before aphoto of Bhagavan Shri Sathya Sai Baba and prayed thus "Baba, a sadhu asked me for a cup of tea and I served him. I have not done any wrong to him and have not committed any sin. In return I get this nasty problem. Please take care of me and rid me of this disease".

A week later I was to attend the marriage of my niece at Bombay. We thought it was a good occasion t break our journey and pay a visit to Shridi for a day. We reached there and were attending the evening aarthi. During *aarthi* I started feeling a great urge to put some vibhuti on my head. It was as if some hidden force was compelling me to do so. I could not resist this urge and physically ran to the place, where vibhuti pot is kept near Baba's Dhuni. I took some in my hand and sprinkled profusely on my head and come back to samadhi where aarthi was still being performed. Afterwards we stood in a line to bow our head at the Samadhi and offer pooja and put offering in the donation box lying near his lotus feet. I took out eleven rupees for the box but again that hidden force held my hand and wanted me to offer more. So I made up fifty-one, rupees put them in the box, bowed my head and came out. My eyes were wet. Next morning running eczema had dried and these was no more itching and I was perfectly normal to leave for Bombay to attend the marriage.

Thus appeared Baba to one of his imperfect devotee to relieve him of some past debts and leave him in pangs and prayers of meeting Him again. I pray Bhagwan Shirdi Baba, the incarnation of Bhagavan Shankar to visit me and take out gangajal out of his head once again.

-R.P. Bhalla, Sri Sathya devotee,
909, Sector 16 Faridabad – 121002 (Haryana)
Dt.: 4-10-1996 (Tel.: 286550)

78. BABA'S SAVED DEVOTEE'S LIFE IN ACCIDENTS (1988-94)

Sri Sai Baba in our Saviour and mother. I can say every moment of my life in regulated and guided by Baba. So I can not say about any particular incident.

My only daughter Kamini got married in 1988 to Sukh Dev Singh of merchant navy. They married in 27-5-88 and soon after the ceremony we took them to Nanded and Shirdi. They got the darshan of Baba. We took some photographs also. I asked my son-in-law to put *mangalsutra* in my daughter's neck before the Samadhi mandir. Baba witnessed the same. Soon after that they had to leave for Poone by a hire taxi. As per destiny they had to meet a deadly accident when the car was nearly swirled to the slope of the curve which was very narrow. But Baba's blessings averted the accident and they were thrilled by Baba's grace.

In the year 1994 I was not keeping good health. I was unable to walk properly and it was impossible for me to kneel down to pick up anything. But one day in my dream Baba with this musical troupe with bhajan, trumpet came to me and gave me vibhuti and asked me to apply it on my forehead sideways and then he gave me or rather put in my palm five small objects which I couldn't see properly as to what they are and disappeared without saying anything. When I woke up in the morning I found myself walking properly and able to sit and kneel down on the ground. Now by Baba's grace I can do my household jobs nicely. You know Baba helps me at every step.

My husband met with a deadly accident and each time he was saved by Baba and thus Baba saved my *Suhag*. Baba in always with me and our family.

In 1990 my daughter Kamini was suffering from H.B.P. and was admitted in the hospital. Doctors advised us that they would try to save my daughter rather her baby in the womb. Her condition was very critical. Her blood pressure was not coming down. But one night my daughter saw Baba on the well adjacent to her bed. Baba gave her assurance not to worry and of his presence near her. It is all Baba's grace. Of course the child couldn't survive but Baba gave second life to my daughter.

-Mrs. Sarojini Wicheni,
(61 years old Retired Teacher)
6-B, 320 phase, Adarsh Nagar,
Soneri, Jamshedpur – 831001 (Bihar)

79. HOW BABA SAVED A CANCER PATIENT IN KENYA (1990)

"Om Sri Sai Ram"

On 20ᵗʰ December 1990, our 21ˢᵗ Wedding Anniversary, my husband was diagnosed as having non-hodghing Lymphoma, a cancer of the glands. My husband had this swelling on his chest for almost a year and despite his frequent visits to the doctors, heart specialists included, they doctor could come up with nothing. Finally, when I was brave enough to ask my family doctor, if he had considered the possibility of cancer, he said, "Are you crazy?" I said "No, I'm realistic, please let us test him for cancer". I decided to take him to a chest specialist; As soon as Dr. Kavaki saw the lump, he said it reeded a gropsy. A few days later my husband was sheeled into the operation theatre. The doctor and the anesthetist, both friends of ours came out of the theatre sonbre-faced and my heart sank, when the doctor began by saying, "I'm sorry .... ORINO, I thought, it can't be! The doctor consoled me and said, "Mr. Desaja is o.k., but the cancer is too widespread. The inmount is on the heart, therefore we couldn't operate. It is lung cancer and in a very advanced stage. I was too dumbfounded to cry. I rushed out of the hospital and told my sister-in-law to look after my husband. I went home and called my mother-in-law in Bombay and my husband's sisters in Bombay and London. I just told them Dinesh was not too well & Mona should come since I too had fractured my leg, and she could help in looking after the kids. Thedoctor had given Dinesh 3 months survival chances and all I could think of was to get his treatment underway. The doctor had said that his condition was too serious. So it was agreed that the next day he would have an ultra sound and they would start the chemotherapy and a second opinion. That evening, an acquaintance of my husband, someone we had not heard from in 20 years, came to the hospital. He gave his sympathics concern about Dinesh's illness and asked me to go to his house for Sai Baba's *Vibhuti* and Amrit, which had been flowing out of Baba's photo for a few days. I had heard of Sai Baba and His miracles and at this junction when my husband's life was on a look, I could have done just about anything. Unfortunately, my husband's condition took a turn for the worse that evening, so I sent my daughter and my sister-in-law to get Baba's blessings. In the evening we all sat round my husband's bedside, while our family *pandit* held his hand and my sister-in-law Shree had not got back from our friends house and I was beginning to wonder what had happened. Just then, I saw a little girl peering through the door. As she stood, she stared at my husband and pointing towards him yield, "That's the man I saw in my dream. That's the man that Baba has sent me to help. "We were all astonished and didn't know what she was talking about. She walked into the room, took out some grey coloured ash and rubbed in on Dinesh's forehead and made him eat some. I had heard of Vibhuti, but I think this was the first time I was seeing it. The little girl had dreamt or had a vision of Baba, He told her that there was a men at Naubi Hospital in room 11, who was dying of cancer and needed Baba's help. Baba asked her to go to rub Vibhuti on his head and assure the family that in a few mouths. Dinesh is going to be sitting up hale and hearty. She left Vibhuti with us and left us with Baba's blessings. The next day, my husband had to have a CT Scan again basically to determine the extent and spread of the tumour, in order to start the treatment at the earliest. A couple of hours later, the surgeon and the amologist called me into their office. As I walked into the office, they were both nearby at blows at each other. The ancologist was saying that the scan didn't show a tumour in the lungs at all, whereas the surgeon said that he saw the tumour in the lungs with his own eyes. According to Dr. Kasinhi the tumour started from the lobe of the right lung, right into the lungs itself, emerging out to finally sit on the heart. The pathologist report showed it as lung cancer, but now suddenly, things had taken a turn for the better, with the scan showing so tumour in the lungs. This called for a re-assestment of the situation, and finally the conclusion was that it was not a lung cancer, but lymphoma, the progresses of which was 90% whereas lung cancer had 50% survival chances. The doctor asked me to fly out my husband to U.K. immediately. Yesterday Dinesh was too ill and too weak to be moved, and today the sun shone brightly and in a few days we would be on our way to London. I couldn't believe what had happened and how everything had changed. I was too excited, too overwhelmed to realize that this was one of the Baba's miracles. We stayed there for 9 months where Dinesh underwent chemo, as well as radio therapy. We had some very very trying moments. Initially after 4 shots my husband didn't respond and the last result seemed for him to have a bone marrow transport. This is a very painful procedure and the patient has to be in incubation during the whole period when his marrow is completely sucked out of his body, to be replaced by a bone marrow of a relative, son or daughter. I was so frightened and I prayed to Baba, not to let this happen. When we went to see to the doctor the next day, the doctor said he had decided against the bone marrow, and he would try another combination of chemotherapy. I was very relieved and with Baba's Grace, the new regime washed and within no time the tumour was in total remission. Today it is almost six years, Dinesh is well, with Baba's grace, and leads a normal life. In this time we have made Baba's temple at home, when we are both enjoying, spending a lot of time praying and meditating. Baba has become a part of our family. He is really there with us from morning till night. His blessings and grace are with us. I feel Baba's presence even so often. I know He is watching over us. I thank Baba, for He gave us all, including the children, strength to cope with a situation which could have totally thrown as all off our minds and wits. Our son, who was then 18 years old had to give up school and continue with our business. Baba guided him. Today he is married and with Baba's grace has just started a uniform business, which I pray will be a success. Thank you Baba for a new life for Dinesh.

Prof. Ruhela:- In 1993, I came across a person, to me a Divine, Enlightened soul, whose profile I'm sending you. This is Sai Sai Babaji, who is my Guru. If I start writing about him. I could write a book. I believe Mr. Arora has given you Babaji's contact. Dinesh I hoping to be in Delhi on 20th November for pooja in Jammu we'll contact you then and hope you can make it to Delhi and together we could have Babaji's interview. I've had experienced with Babaji as I've had with Bhagawan Shirdi Sai Baba and Swami. I see Babaji as a form of Sai Baba. For me Babaji is God sent. He has filled our lives with love, bless and regards.

-Rupi Dosajh
Nairobi (Kenya)

80. I SAW THEE HAND OF SAI (1964)

I have always believed in Lord Sainath. But over the years my beliefs about who Sainath is and what He can do have changed. It was not until my son was gravely ill two years ago that I learned that one can believe in Sainath while yet not knowing Him at all.

Know, knowledge, logic When I was young, those were the words I wanted to live by. I read great books of the western world and out of my reading formed my strongest beliefs. I believed in logic, in the mind's ability to put all creation into neat, rational categories.

At the same time I was growing up in a strongly orthodox Hindu family, and so I believed in God. But I insisted and my insistence caused a lot of arguments that God Himself was also a being bound by logic and His own natural laws. I guess I pictured God as a great scientist Miracles? No, God could not and would not break laws that way.

It was at this juncture, in the early fifties, that I came under the magnetic spell of Lord Sainath through that great apostle, H.H. Narasimha Swamiji, when I was a student at Mysore.

I turned to Lord SAINATH. His spirit answered. "I don't simply want belief that I exist. I want you, your will, your life, your dreams, your goals, your very being. And I want your faith, faith that I am sufficient for all your needs". My despair overcame my logics and I yielded all to Him. But just saying you have faith is not the same as having it. In my mind, I still had Lord Sainath in a box.

May be that is why I never thought to pray to Lord Sainath, when my eldest son, Chi. Nagaraj came home from his school one day in 1984 and said he did not feel well. What would Lord Sainath care about Flu?

Our local doctor who my wife Vimala and I had consulted was not very alarmed about Nagaraj's illness at first. "It is really not too serious" the doctor assured us, "just a bad case of flu complicated by a little acidosis, Give him this medicine and in a few days he will be fine".

But Nagaraj was not fine, not at all. The medicine worked for a day or so, but then his symptoms the gagging, choking, swollen face etc., came back more violently. His small frame started sinking and emaciation had set in. My cousin Dr. K.S. Srinivasan, who was then a Senior Scientist at Central Food Institute, Mysore and had come to our place, on seeing my son's grave illness, suggested that we take him to Mysore for further treatment.

The doctors at Mysore, after an initial examination and laboratory investigations told me; "...We think your son has Nephritis. It is a terminal kidney disease... "He paused, and I could feel the blood running from my face, "But we have found that in children there is a good chance of recovery. Your son has a fifty percent chance of being as good as new".

In the next couple of days we learnt that the X rays showed that my son's kidneys are badly infected. The odds were not in our favour. I looked at my wife Vimala, watching the tears well up in her eyes, as a huge lump formed in my throat. We were too shocked, too upset to even talk. All afternoon we sat at our son's bedside watching. I searched in the doctor's eyes for an answer, for some glimmer of hope, and got nothing. I could only cry in desperation.

Later in the evening, our cousins gave words of encouragement. And for a fleeting moment. I thought I saw in my wife's eyes the spark of hope that I had been looking for from the doctors.

By next day, that spark of hope had ignited a flame of confidence in her. "I turned Nagaraj's life over to Lord Sainath last night." She told me excitedly, before we were even out of bed. "I feel a real peace about what is going to happen, that Sai will is going to be done."

"Sainath's will?" ... I said angrily. "What kind of God makes little boys sick? He does not care." And I rolled over, Peace? Sai will? No. my little son would need more than that to get well.

But my anger did not stop me from trying to reason with Lord Sainath. The whole day I begged and pleaded and screamed at Lord Sainath, daring to ask Him to disprove my skepticism, trying to good Him into action.

"Who do you think you are?" I shouted once. "Why are you doing this to my son? He is only 12. Everybody says you are such a loving God, why don't you show it?" I yelled I was exhausted. Finally, convinced my arguments were falling on deaf ears, I headed to the hospital.

I was told that about a temple of Shirdi Sai Baba at Mysore. We went there and offered our respects. Suddenly this unjust God spoke to me. I felt His presence, soothing my still-hot anger. And I heard His voice, gentle, reassuring. He reminded me that I had made a commitment to Him, that I had promised to trust Him with my life, my all. And He had promised to take care of me, in all circumstances. "Take Me out of the box you have put Me in", He said: "and let Me work." By the time I left the Sai-temple my heart was beating wildly. I sat for a few moment longer and uttered but two words in reply to all that had happened: "Forgive me".

By the time I returned from the temple. I knew what I needed to do as clearly as if someone had given me written instructions. There had been no change in my son's condition. Placing my shaking hands on my son, I prayed to Lord Sainath as I never believed I would every pray: "Lord Sainath, forgive my ego, for trying to make you what I want you to be. If you will, heal my son and if you won't that is alright too. I will trust you. But, please, do either right now."

That was all. There are no lightening flashes, no glows, no surges of emotion, like the rushing mind. I calmly sat down and began to wait for Lord Sainath's answer. There was only one difference. For the first time in my life, I knew I was going to get one.

Over the next two weeks, my son underwent a battery of tests, consultations and sub—consultations with leading doctors of Mysore. But with every report. I could hear Lord Sainath saying to me: "I am, and I care."

A slow improvement came over my son. One regiment of drugs suited his system. Even the doctors were amazed to see the progress he made and one of them remarked: "I think we have been privileged to witness an act of God … it is a definite miracle".

And this time I was not about to argue. At last I fully believed in Lord Sainath whose love knows no bounds not the bounds of logic, not the hold of natural laws. FAITH that is what I know had that and the knowledge that one's belief in Lord Sainath is essentially hollow if the belief is not founded on faith.

-H.V. Srinivasan, Landlord
DEVARAYASAMUDRAM 563 127
Kolar District, Karnataka
(*Shri Sai Leela*, March 1988)

81. BABA SAVED LIFE IN HEART ATTACK (1997)

In the early morning of 28th February 1997 at about 4.30 A.M. suddenly I had sweating on my face and pain in the right hand side of the chest. I got up of the bed, and tired to sit in my study room to do Puja but I felt great weakness, so I lay down. I took Sri Shirdi Sai Baba's Vibhuti and after some time I felt well. In the forenoon I had to go to Union Public Service Commission New Delhi to attend a Selection Committee as an expert. I drove my car although I was much very fatigued. When I returned in the afternoon from there, I went to Appollo Hospital to see my sister's daughter-in-law who was admitted there. After returning home in the evening, my daughter-in-law from her house in Sector 16, Faridabad, inquired about my health on phone, and on her insistence I went with my son for a check up at a doctor's clinic in Sector 16, Faridabad. After the ECG and the Diabetes tests, the doctor told me that the ECG was normal but blood sugar level was very high and there was no heart problem. He gave me some capsules to take.

But again in the night, I had suddenly a great pain in the very centre of my chest for over six hours from midnight to 6 O'clock. I got up, drank water many times, took Sri Shirdi Sai Baba Vibhuti and kept on chanting his Mahamantra *"Om Sai, Sri Sai, Jaya Jaya Sai"* throughout this period of painful agony. I didn't think of doctor or of any of my three sons and did not even awaken my wife sleeping in the some room, but only prayed to Sri Shirdi Sai Baba for saving my life as I had still some more books to be written and many unfinished things in this life to complete. By 6 O'clock Avg. the pain subsided then I slept for almost an hour.

Around 10 A.M., I dictated about 5 pages of Hindi translation of my book *"Sri Shirdi Sai Baba – The Universal Master"* to a writer for about one hour and a half and then took rest. I did not realize that any heart attack had already taken place – I thought that I had pain due to Diabetes and I would get myself checked up in Delhi at the University dispensary the next day which was Monday.

I did not take my ailment seriously then. Again around 1 p.m. my daughter-in-law Sarya again telephoned me to inquire about my health. I told her that I had in the pain which was tearing apart the centre of my chest for about six hours but I was O.K. at that time. She immediately rang Dr. Rakesh Gupta, who had checked last evening and described my ailment to him. He asked her to tell me to come to his clinic at once, or he would himself visit me if I was unable to do so. Immediately, I took my meals and drove my car to the doctor's clinic. He took my ECG and immediately told me that I had indeed suffered heart attach and that I must be immediately admitted in a nearby hospital. When I told him that I had come to his clinic in my car, he was surprised. I told him that I had not come with much money to be able to get admitted in a hospital. He told me not to be worried. He sent for my daughter-in-law on phone and in about an hour and a half I was admitted to the Sun Flag Hospital,

Faridabad and immediately kept in the intensive care unit. The doctor gave we a very costly injection and told my family members that it I would respond well to the injection in 12 hours, then they could hope for survival further treatment. Then I and they all realized the gravity of my health situation. I remained in that hospital for about two weeks and was the referred to Escort Heart Institute, New Delhi. Angiography test was done there.

While this was being done, when the doctor told me that heart operation Angiography or illumining would have to be done, which would involve on expenditure of about Rs. 1.5 lakhs or so, I was very much disturbed and shocked to hear it, as I didn't have any funds as much. Already more than Rs. 45,000/- I had been spent by my family with great difficulty. I prayed to Lord Sai Nath to spare we from the burden and agony of undergoing any heart operation or ballooning. After a few days when I visited the doctor in the Escort Heart Institute to get the Angiography test report, I was greatly relieved to hear from him that there was blessing no need for me to undergo heart operation and that wished I should depend on medicines and fat-free and sugar-free food as per the dictición's prescription. Since then I am following his prescription only and am keeping well.

I am convinced that it was only Sri Shridi Sai Baba who had saved my life when I had twice heart attack on the nights of 27th and 28th February. Since then He alone has saving my self, dispite my having to do a lot of hard work in order to prepare the manuscripts of a member of books and articles during all these six months. I am now perfectly alright, quite active and quite optimistic due to Baba's grace on me.

-S.P. Ruhela
Professor of Education,
'Sai Kripa' 126, Sector 37,
Faridabad – 121003

82. BABA HAS FULFILLED DEVOTEE'S WISH OM SRI SAI (1996)

The *slokas* in *"Sri Sai Ashtotharasatha Namavali"* composed by HH Brahmasri H.H. Narasimha Swamiji, the apostle of Sadguru Sri Sai Baba, are true to every word of the holy *stotram*, e.g. *'Bhaktha Paradhaenaya Namah Bhaktha Abhaya Pradaya Namah Sulabha Durlabhaya Namah Bhaktha Anugraha Gataraya Namah'.*

Believe me or not, recently one day a company representative came to my office and while in discussion he took out his ball-point pen to note something which was fixed with a Puttaparthi Sai Babaji's locket in its clip, I could not stop my eagerness and I asked him if he could get me a smaller ball-point pen fixed with Shirdi Sai Baba locket in the clip. He told me that it might be available, but he had not it seen and he would get me one when he would come across the same anywhere in future and then the left our office after discussion. Just after a few days I went to Calcutta to see my daughter who had come back from Madras. Soon after reaching there, she brought some ball-point pens, all fixed with Sri Sai Baba locket in the clips which were given to her by one of my co-brothers at Madras to be handed over to me. There was no communication at all between us about the ball-point pen fixed with Sri Sai Baba locket. I was only wondering how mysteriously Baba fulfils even the smallest devotional desires of his devotees showering His abundant blessings! This is only just an example to cite how true are the words of Sri Sai Ashtotharasatha Namavali Stotram of Guru Dev Sri Narasimha Swamiji on the glories of Divine Sadguru Sai Baba. Bow to Baba and peace be with all. Jai Sai Ram.

13.3.1996

-K.N. Narayananswamy
SAI HOME, 7/87, OCL Colony
P.O. Rajgangpur 770017
Dist. Sundargarh. (Orissa)

83. MIRACLES OF SHIRDI SAI BABA (1985)

In June, 1985, both my wife and myself went to U.S.A. to meet our two sons living there. My younger son V.C. Kansal was having problems after problems. He was not having job satisfaction as his qualifications were higher for the job he was doing. He was a M.Sc. in Chemical Engineering. But the job he was doing was at the most fit for M.Sc. only and therefore his qualification of Chemical Engineering was not of use and he felt disappointed and frustrated on this score. We stayed with him in Paterson (New Jersey) U.S.A. and came to know of his dissatisfaction. We prayed to Sai Baba daily in the night requesting Him to grant him a better job so that he might have job satisfaction. We opened our heart to Sai Baba in the prayer and pleaded with him for our son's sake.

Further, he was having an apartment in 100 Hospital Plaza which was too small and my daughter-in-law was very anxious to purchase a good house. We prayed to Sai Baba for this also. We prayed to Sai Baba to help them and remove their difficulties. On 14th December, 1986, we received a trunk call from U.S.A. around 11.30 P.M., that he had been interviewed and selected for better job commensurate with his qualifications, merit and ability. Nearly six months earlier he also purchased a good house with lawns, 3 bed rooms, very well-furnished, basement and living room with wall to wall carpet and 2 garages.

Although, it took more than a year, his desires ultimately were fulfilled. With folded hands and salutations to Sai Baba, we went to Sai Baba temple in New Delhi and thanked Him for all these mercies and kindness for us all. Sai Baba always listens to the sincere and honest prayers of his devotees and solves them at the proper time. If there is any delay in granting your prayers then keep *"Sharddha"* and *"Saburi"* (Faith and Patience) and do not lose heart. Baba has said "Cast all your burdens on me and I will bear them". We realized the truth of these words of Sai Baba that he would always fulfil his promise, at any cost.

-R.R. Kansal,
13, Bank Enclave,
Laxmi Nagar,
Delhi – 110 092
(*Shri Sai Leela*, Oct. 1987)

84. SAI BABA – *KARUNASAGAR* (Oean of compassion,1985)

Man is not in a position to know what would happen the next minute. Although he may be the most intelligent of the created beings, he can not predict his own future accurately. But at the same time a person who has unshakable faith in our Sadguru will always enjoy his constant protection, and his calamities would be somehow averted by our Sadguru Sai Baba, the *Karuna Sagar*, before the devotee even realizes it.

Two incidents, which took place in our family, are worth-mentioning here. The first incident was when Baba got the negotiation done for us in purchasing a car of our choice. The second incident was when Baba saved my husband's life at Devalali Railway Station on 3rd January, 1986. I would like to express my gratitude to our Sadguru who is always with us in solving our problems.

In October 1985, my husband had applied for Government loan to buy a car. The loan materialized during the month of December 1985. As we planned to buy a second-hand car in good condition, the hunt was a prolonged one. The prices quoted by the owners were quite exorbitant. As per rules and instructions on the subject, the car had to be purchased within a period of one month failing which the loan amount would have to be returned to be Government with interest. The first car seen by my husband was of 1980 model 'Premier Padmini' with all the latest gadgets fitted in it and in a very good condition. The owner initially asked for Rs. 64,000/- which was beyond our means. My husband quoted a price of Rs. 54,000/-. On hearing this, the owner was so annoyed that he asked my husband to leave his place and never come to him again for bargaining. This was because, the man had been looking after this car very well and it was in perfect condition. My husband did not lose hope but told him that the car would come to him with the blessings of our Sadguru Sai Nath.

After the above incident and placing the matter at our Sadguru's lotus feet, my husband went in search of other offers. Somehow, he was not satisfied with the performance of any other car compared to the one which he saw initially. He was intensely praying to our Sadguru to help get us the same car.

A week after this incident, my husband got a telephone call from the owner of this car to confirm whether he was still interested in buying the car. My husband was surprised to receive this call as he had not expected such a response from the owner for the same price quoted by us. We therefore had our suspicious as to how and why he could agree to the price which was Rs. 10,000-less than what he earlier wanted. We wildly presumed that it had possibly met with an accident in the meantime and that was why he wanted to dispose it off. However it was not so, The reason was, the day my husband was turned out of the owner's premises, in the evening on the very day he had a mild heart attack and was hospitalized for a week. The doctors had imposed restriction on his movements including driving. This incident naturally had an impact on his family members who persuaded him to sell the vehicle for the price quoted by my husband. Curiously, he told my husband to take the car and pay later as we would have to get the draft from our bankers at Madras. Thus Sri Sai saved the owner's life also, while at the same time blessing us with the car of our choice.

The car came to our house on 5th Dec., '85 (Thursday) and we went straight to Mukti Dham and placed it at the lotus feet of our Sadguru Sai Baba and our Cosmic Mother Bhawani.

On 8th December, 1985 (Sunday) morning we drove the car to Shirdi and placed the same at our Sadguru's lotus feet. We thanked Him for concluding the purchase and giving us the very same car which we wanted to possess. My husband prayed to Baba to accept the car as His property and keep us only its custodians. After this incident many a time we had been to Shirdi and with

Baba's grace, we were always in time for this morning or noon arati. This blessing is a perennial flow of love from our Sadguru Sai Baba, the *Karuna Sagar* (ocean of compassion) to us his devotees.

The second incident took place in June '86 when we were to move to Pathankot on my husband's transfer from Nasik. We got our car booked in a motor van of the Central Railway for Pathankot from Devalali. This husband had gone to the Railway station to see that the bogie was attached to the train. The electric engine came and towed this bogie to attach it to the main train. My husband was at the Railway platform holding on to the iron railings and watching the bogie getting towed.

Very near this railing there was a tree whose one branch was slanting and was touching the high tension wire over head car rying 11,000 volts of current. As the engine was hauling the bogie, the overhead bracket of the engine which was sliding alongwith the over-head wire, touched the slanting branch which at once caught fire being wet. Had the branch been dry, it would not have caught fire being a non-conductor of electricity. My husband was shocked of the tree and watching the bogie being hauled. Had he continued to hold on to the same, the out-come would have been fatal. Baba, the *Karuna Sagar* had moved him from that place and made him hold the railing instead and thus saved my husband's life.

Dear brothers and sisters, my husband did not know the least of the danger whereas our Sadguru being Omnipresenet is always vigilant in protecting His devotees. Hence, if we surrender ourselves to our *Sadguru*, we can rest assured that we will always be under His care. Didn't Baba say "Look to me and I will look after you?"

What more guarantee do we need of Baba's assurance that even after his disappearance from His mortal body, His bones still continue to protect us and fulfill our desire?

Let us, therefore, surrender ourselves to our Sadguru Sai Baba, the Karuna Sagar and leave the rest to him to decide.

With crores of *Pranams* to our Sadguru.

-Mrs. Shanta Rajamani
W/o., Lt. Col. R. Rajamani
HQ 39 Mountain Artillery Bridge
C/o, 56 APO
(*Shri Sai Leela*, Feb. 1987)

85. EXPERIENCE OF A DEVOTEE (1997)

I had been having loose motions for a couple of months and despite medication I could not control it. I was very much worried because of it. I was having disturbing thoughts about my health. One night I took a pinch of *udhi*, touched it with Baba's feet, mixed it in a glass of water and drank it. When I was going to bed I heard Baba saying that next morning I would be having the last loose motion and thereafter I would be cured. Next morning I indeed had a loose motion in a big way, and thereafter it has been almost three months onward and I never had a loose motion and I am completely cured or my disease.

May Sai Baba continue to pour His Blessings on all of His devotees.

JAI SAI BABA

-DR. ALOKE KALLA
Anjli Niwas, 2153, Gali Sudama,
Bazar Sita Ram, Delhi – 110006
(From: *Sri Kripa*)

86. MY ENCOUNTERS WITH SHIRDI SAI BABA (1997)

It was 1991, I had lost my mother all of a sudden and was gried-sticken. I knew not where to turn. Where had Mother gone? Was she alright? I kept wondering. I desperation my sister and I sought an answer to our pain in astrology. One elderly astrologer, a Devi Upaasaka, who could see into other dimension intuitively, chided us, asked us to stop crying and to go home as Mother had merged with Krishna. What he said sounded re-assuring but I wanted to know for sure. I turned to spiritual books. I read Yogananda. I re-read Howard Murphel's books on Bhagawan Sathya Sai Baba. I read about Shirdi Sai Baba and Sathya Sai Baba; and my gut feeling was that I had at last stumbled on the Truth!

One day, lost in thoughts about Mother, I was singing my heart out, sitting in front of a small mud-statue of Shirdi Baba that a Muslim friend had given me years ago while at college. I mentally asked Bhagawan Sri Sathya Sai Baba, "If you are truly Omniscient Omnipresent and Omnipotent and mummy is with you, then why can't some *Vibhuthi* come on this Shirdi Baba form of yours?" But as I sang I wondered how I would honour the Presence of the Lord should Vibhoothi appear; I knew no puja or worship; and so I said, "No, No, Baba! better it doesn't come!" But when I finished singing – lo! Shirdi Baba had a shower of *Vibhuthi* on Him! Later, the Lord in His infinite kindness indicated that Mother was indeed with Him for after a while when *Vibhuthi* appeared on the pictures of various deities it appeared on the photo of my dear late mother too. Then I remembered what that old astrologer had said "Mother is with Krishna". Well Rama, Krishna, Sai they are all but One. I have never since worried about Mother.

Some time later, while we had gone to our village. *The Paadukas* of Baba, from Shirdi, were brought to Madras and they were brought to our neighbour's house too. As soon as we reached back our neighbour told us about it and I felt very sad that I had missed Darshan of Baba's Paadukas. When I went to the Puja Room I was dismayed to find a pile of mud like stuff on my small silver Naagdev's peetham; earlier a pile of *Vibhuthi* had appeared on the other side but what was this? Since it was in a cupboard there was no way something could have fallen into it. That evening an elderly Sai devotee came. I showed her the "mud" and asked her what she thought it was where upon she exclaimed excitedly, "This is *"udhi"* We were all so thrilled. Though we missed seeing His Paadukas Bhagawan Baba had kindly left some Prasad for us ... How very loving and thoughtful Baba is!

This *Udhi* was to serve another purpose too. During our stay in the village an uncle who was an ardent Shirdi Sai devotee had visited us. He had been happy to learn that we had turned Sai devotees, however his faith had been narrow; while Shirdi Sai was God to him, he had berated Bhagawan Sathya Sai needlessly. I had felt hurt but since he was an elder said nothing. Some time later he came to Madras. He came to the Puja room and saw Baba's Leelas. He saw the little Naagdev's Peetham and instantly recognized the *Udhi*. I then gently told him that the pile of grayish ash just next to the pile of *Udhi* was *Vibhuthi*. Some chord deep within was struck and he prostrated. Today he sees Ram, Allah, Jesus, Krishna, Shirdi Sai, Sathya Sai – all as the One God who takes various forms.

Though we had become Sai devotees, I hadn't been to a Sai Mandir yet. Somewhere along the line I heard that there was a Sai Baba Temple in Madras called Sundaram where doctors did free service on Sunday. One Sunday I resolved to go there and find out. I was new to Madras and did not know my way around. But trusting in Baba I set out' I kept stopping and asking for directions. Everyone was helpful but instead of reaching Sundaram, I reached the Shirdi Sai Mandir at Mylapore! I went in, I was thrilled to see Baba from the entrance itself. I flower girl pressed a garland into my hands. I took it and quickly walked in; the priest beckoned me to come in; I gave him the garland but he returned it saying I could garland Baba myself. I was delighted; it was the first time I was garlanding a deity in a temple myself! As I garlanded Baba, I felt it was no vigraha; it was Baba Himself! What joy I felt! After some time, stethoscope and bag unused, I returned home. I had missed the medical camp but I had found Baba!

I planned to take my husband and children t Baba's Mandir but somehow we never made it. One day as we were driving along the Beach Road to Santhome to a friend's place, to my amazemet, I found Shirdi Baba sitting in His characteristic pose just outside my car-window i.e., the front passenger window travelling at the same speed as the car and He said to me, "Come, come to my Mandir to see Me." I did not know how to react whereupon he repeated the same. I wanted to straightway follow His orders but I was a bit worried about whether my husband would agree to it. You see, my husband was in those days one of those people who didn't take kindly to people changing their minds while halfway to a destination! So I said to Baba, "Swami! I'd love to come but you must tackle him". And then I said gently to my husband. "Why don't we go to the Shirdi Sai Mandir instead?" He seemed to be in a good mood and said, "Why not? What do you say, you children?" The little ones in the back-seat chimed in "Yes! Yes!" Just in time we turned into Edward Elliot's Road.

I was so happy. Thereafter I could not see Baba outside the windows. Presently thanks to the heavy traffic we were crawling along the road to Luz. We were in front of the Luz Hanuman Temple. I longed to get down but I dared not ask my husband to make another change! So I bowed to Hanumaanji from the car itself and said, "Swami, if I was driving the car I would have surely stopped; but now you know I can't; so please accept my *namaskarams* from the car itself!" Soon we reached the Shirdi Sai Mandir.

As we got down all the bells began to chime. It was some very auspicious day. Somehow we were swept into the sanctum sanctorum. We had a divine Darshan and got lots of Prasad too. But Baba had yet another surprise in store. As we came out we bumped into my sister's husband. He and my husband got talking and then suddenly for no reason my brother-in-law said, "There is a lovely Hanuman temple nearby; let me take you there." My heart leapt with joy! We went to the Hanumaan temple also and we all sang the Hanumaan Chalisa and returned home. What a lovely evening Baba arranged thus!

Some time later, Baba arranged for us to reach the feet of our Gurudev; a Fakir from Shirdi who used to live under a neem tree there using a brick for a pillow, just like Baba. He considered Himself a Das of Sai. A *Trikaalajnani*, He had instantly recognized with a soul-sight that Bhagavan Sathya Sai was Bhagavan Shirdi Sai come again. He used to say that His mission was to spread the word that – Sai is God; that Sai is One. Shirdi Sai who was, Sathya Sai who is and Prema Sai who is to come are all but One; Divinity is one; and finally His aim was to give Sai Prema to all. And it was this overwhelming Prema that drew all of us to Him. We received Guru Mantra from Him on January the 23rd 1995. On the first monthly anniversary i.e., Feb. 23rd, we decided to go to both the Sathya Sai Mandir on Pugh's Road and to the Shirdi Sai Mandir at Mylapore. On the way to Mylapore a thought came, "Today Baba will give me a sweet".

We reached the Mandir only to find that as it was a Thursday it was jam-packed. The crowd pushed and showed us and we found ourselves near that easy-chair in the mainhall. Presently the priests began their *aarathi* rounds form that point. We joined them. We went to the Dhuni. Gurusthaan etc., and finally reached the sanctum. At that point I hesitated to go in because we were really not part of the official group; we had just tagged on. But the priest suddenly turned and beckoned us. So in we went. I marveled at the turn of events. "O Swami! Your Grace is such! We came late and were wondering how to come in and by your grace here we are next to you!" my eyes filled. But the next minute my monkey-mind began working. "But where is my sweet, Bapu?" my monkey mind was at its worst. I chided myself and said, "The *Darshan* of Baba that you are having is the sweet, now shut up and pray." Aarathi over, I did *pranaam* at Baba's feet and moved to the marble *charan* of Baba. As it was Thursday there were so many garlands and flowers. One priest was standing near the *Simhaasan* (Throne) and throwing down flowers to people a rose here, some jasmine there, some *tulsi leave* here and so on. He threw at me also something, a *Peda*! I was stunned! So Baba gave me my sweet after all!

For four or five visits thereafter, each time I went to the Mandir somehow I would get something sweet to eat! But around the sixth time or so I did not get a sweet. I felt a trifle disappointed. But I told myself, "Now come on. Baba has better things to do than to keep giving you sweets each time you come." From the Mandir I went to Prashanthi Jewellers where our Gurudev had placed an order for a pair of *Padukaas* of Bhagawan Sathya Sai Baba for a Sai Mandir. The Paadukas were not ready yet, informed the jewelers. "But wait a minute, Doctor", said he, "I went to Puttaparthi last week and Swami gave me these sweets."

So saying, he handed me two sweets blessed and given to him by BHagawan Sathya Sai Baba. Preoccupied with the thoughts of the Paadukas, its significance did not strike me immediately. But a few minutes later it dawned – Baba had not given me sweets at the Mandir as usual but He had now given me sweets consecrated and blessed by the Divine Touch of His Sathya Sai Form! What a wonderful *leela*!

Our desire to go to Shirdi materialized when our Gurudev took us there. I had a secret wish. I wanted to sing at Dwarakamayi I made enquiries at Madras whereupon I was told that to sing at the Shirdi Mandir one had to correspond with the Shirdi Sansthan and get special permission etc. It all seemed so complicated that I dropped the idea.

When we went to Dwarakamaayi, an old Englishman with a walking-stick was there, just as Shirdi Sai is pictured in paintings, next to the wooden railings there. He smiled at us. We sat near him and I sang a Bhajan softly. He liked it and said, "Do sing some more." And soon before we knew it we were having a regular Bhajan session at Dwarakamayee. The other pilgrims also joined in. The air was surcharged with *Bhakthi* and *Aananda*. We felt Baba Himself was sitting there and we sang to our heart's content! Finally we did Pranaams to the old man – our one man audience – and got up to go. As I got up, a sign board just above our heads caught my eye. It read, "Silence Please!" That area was meant to be an area of silence! And we had been merrily singing. Yet no one had stopped us; what was more everyone had joined in. We chuckled at this charming *leela* of the Lord; I came out pleased as plum thrilled that I could sing my heart out at Dwarakamayi!

By Bhagavan Baba's grace a lot of music has been flowing in. The compositions are mostly on Karnatic classical style sand they come complete with *Sahitya-Swara-Raaga* and *Thaala*. By Baba's grace small Sai *Kriti* group has been constituted and we give recitals of these *kritis* wherever He sends us. The year 1996 marked the fifth anniversary of my dear late mother. I thought that it was high time we came out of our grief; high time that we celebrated her life and thanked the Lord for creating one such as her who brought joy to all who came her way in life. She had been responsible for my learning music and for my reading Baba too. I prayed to Baba and then He arranged it all. A concert in memory of mother was held at the Travancore Palace, Madras. The Travancore Royal Family had been very close to mother and Baba arranged for them to be the hosts. What a perfect evening it was! We paid a tribute to mother first and then sang. The ambience was divine; Bhagavan Shridi Sai Baba, Bhagavan Sathya Sai Baba and Gurudev Saidas Babaji were present in the form of their pictures on the dais while Padmanabhaswami, the deity to whom the Travancore Royal Family owed allegiance, presided over the function. The late Maharaja's picture and the picture of my mother next to her dear Bhagavan Krishna, completed the alter. The grand Durbar Hall of the Palace provided the perfect backdrop and we all felt Sai's Presence when the garland on Padmanabhaswami fell as the kirtan on Sai Padmanabha was sung. But the most remarkable event of the day occurred just before the function; let me share it with you.

I always take my Bapu's i.e., Shirdi Baba's blessings before doing anything. So that day also, en route to the Palace, I went to the Mylapore Shridi Sai Mandir. My thoughts were all about Mother, Krishna, Sai ... Mother had been named Meera; how appropriate, I reminisced, remembering her total devotion to Bhagavan Krishna. "O Sai! please bring Mother and Krishna with you and come for the concert and bless us all". I prayed. With these thoughts I entered the Mylapore Shirdi Sai Mandir. The sight that greeted my eyes stunned me – for there, in the hall, in front of the sanctum door was a large, freshly anointed and decorated life-size picture of Bhagavan Krishna and Radha Rani! I had been praying to Baba to please bring Bhagavan Krishna and mother and it seemed to me that He had instantly answered my please! To me Radha Raniji represented mother and Beloved Bhagawan Krishna was there too and of course Bapu Sai Baba! It was just too much. "The Radha Krishna Moorthy was installed just this morning, here at the Mandir", the priest informed me. As I left for the Palace after praying I truly felt that Baba, Krishna Bhagavan and mother were coming along to Bless us. The divine bliss that we all experienced later on only went to prove it.

-Dr. Hira Malini, Madras
Sai Chetna, July 1996

87. THRILLING SAI GRACE ON A SCIENTIST (1989-92)

(i) I am working as a Scientific Officer in the Department of Atomic Energy, Hyderabad.

Till 1989 I was not knowing about Sri Shirdi Sai Baba. Somebody gave me the photo of Sri Sai Baba in the month of January, 1989. Whenever I looked at that photo I felt Sri Sai Baba was smiling towards me. It was a magnetic effect and I felt I must visit Shridi. In the month of July 1989 my neighbours Sri Bhonslay invited me to visit Shirdi along with him. I visited Shirdi and it was the turning point of my life. From 7ᵗʰ June 1990, daily I started reading *Shri Sai Satcharita*, written by Sri Nagesh Vasudev Gunaji, and my life style totally changed. Prior to 1989 I was living like a vagabond. The day I started reading *Sri Sai Satcharita* I felt my responsibility in family life and Official life. It was on 11ᵗʰ April 1991 that I was reading Chapter 21, of *Sri Sai Satcharita* and the following lines on page 111 attracted me, "You should study this book and if you do so, your desire will be fulfilled; and when you go to the North in the discharge of your duties in future, you will come across a great Saint by your good luck, and then he will show you the future path, and give rest to your mind and make you happy,.

In the month of March 1991 there was a talk in the Office that some officers would be sent on official duty to Sweden and South Korea. On 11ᵗʰ April 1991 at 7.30 a.m. I prayed to Baba to give me a chance to go abroad. When I reached my office on 11-4-91 I was asked to sign the Passport papers. On that day I came to know that the Chief Executive had recommended my name along with another name to visit South Korea. When I signed the passport papers I felt happy and bowed my head on the Lotus feet of Lord SAINATH, and offered my "PRANAMS". I got my official passport and Visa on 1ˢᵗ May 1991 in my hand. Myself and my co-officer left Hyderabad on 5ᵗʰ May 1991 for South Korea.

It was on 6ᵗʰ May 1991 (the time was 1.00 a.m.) and my security check was over at the Bombay International Airport and I was waiting to board the aircraft of SWISS AIR, (FLIGHT from ZURICH – BOMBAY – HONGKONG – SEOUL). I felt I must pray to Sai Baba before entering the aircraft. I was going by the side of all the *duty free shops* in the airport and felt happy to see the photo of Sai Baba in one shop. The time was 1 a.m. and the departure time of flight was 1.20 a.m. I prayed in front of that photo for two minutes and entered the aircraft. The time was 1.20 a.m. the air craft was moving on the runway. The time was 1.30 a.m. and the air craft was with full speed flying in the air. That was my first experience to travel in the international flight, and my heart-beat was fast. I closed my eyes for ten minutes and started chanting OM SAI – SRI SAI – JAYA JAYA SAI. I felt very happy when the pilot of the aircraft announced that the passenger could remove the bells and relax. At that time the aircraft was moving at a speed of 900 miles per hour at an attitude of 40,000 feet. Just before the take off of the flight, one tall gentleman with a fair completion entered the aircraft and sat by my side. When the airhostess started serving cold drinks, in a friendly talk I asked that gentlemen who was sitting by the side of me who he was and whence he had come. He told that he was Raj I. Mirpuri and he was coming from Shirdi and going to Hongkong. On learning that he came from Shirdi. I was overpowered with love and talked about *Sai Leelas* with him. We were talking up to 3.00 a.m. and I set my alarm at 5.00 a.m. to read the Kakada Arati of Sai Baba and went to sleep. When the alarm was ringing I got up and I saw bright Sun light in the aircraft and the airhostess was serving morning breakfast. I asked about the time she told it was 8.00 a.m. (local time). I washed my face and started reading Kakada Arati. The gentleman sitting by the side of me (Mr. Raj I. Mirpuri) asked me to read the Kakada Arati little loudly so that he can listen to it. I completed reading the Kakada Arati and offered the morning breakfast itself as Naividyam to Sai, and offered the Prasad to that gentlemen. He questioned what was the guarantee that it is Sai's Prasad. I felt I must answer to his question and I prayed to Sai about my position. When I looked to the break-fast plate cover I found letter Sai on it. It was actually printed as Swissair on it and I underlined the letters Sai with my pen and showed to that gentlemen the word Sai. I told him *Annam* (Food) is *Parabrahma Swarupam* and Sai *Parabrahma*. He congratulated me for the feelings I had about SAI, and he purchased a sweets packet from the Sky Shop in the aircraft and presented to me. It was around 9.00 a.m. (local time) the plane landed at Hongkong. I asked that gentlemen to give his visiting card so that I could drop a letter to him when I got back to India. With a smile he gave me his visiting card and left the aircraft. After Hong Kong the plane landed in SEOUL (1.00 p.m local time). From Sroul I and my co-officer took domestic flight to Pusan. In Pusan our host received us at the airport and took as to Changwon City in the Car. It was evening 6.30 (local time) I reached the Hotel and relaxed.

It was night 8.00 p.m. and my host came to my room and asked me to join for the dinner. I requested him to wait for about half-an-hour so that I could complete the night prayer. He agreed to wait and I completed Sej Arati of Sai Baba. During Arati I prayed to Sai to give me a feeling that he was in the Changwon City also. After the Arati my host took me to balcony of my hotel room and started showing me the Changwon City in lights. To my surprise I could see big Neon letters SAI on a nearby hotel. I asked my host about the Nwon letters SAI, he could not explain about word SAI, but he promised me to take to that place. He took me to that hotel and I could see Neon letters SAI clearly and other letters not glowing.

When I gone near the Neon letters I found it as Saloon. I asked my host what was meant by Saloon, he explained me the meaning of Saloon as Bar where cone can relax and drink Beer etcTo fulfil my wish SAI appeared in the form of Neon lights (SAI) and proved that he is everywhere on earth.

After completing my official work in South Korea, I returned to Hyderabad on 21st May 1991 wrote and two letters to that gentlemen of Hongkong. I could not get any reply from him. When I could not get any reply I felt he was Sai and I checked the visiting card and I could see small size emblem of Globe on the card and felt Sai is everywhere in this universe.

During the year 1991 I was trying for a good marriage alliance for my daughter but I could not succeed. I had been to various places and invited bridegrooms parents to visit my house and see my daughter. Inspite of various requests no one turned up to see my daughter. It was on 1st January 1992, New Year's day morning, I prayed to Sri Sai Baba of Shridi and asked for a message regarding the marriage of my daughter. I closed my eyes and opened a page in the *Sai Satcharita* written by Sri Nagesh Vasudev Gunaji. To my surprise on page 241 chapter 47 the message

I was very happy as the message indicates marriage of my daughter would takes place in the year 1992. In the month of January 1992, One of my friends Sri Sree Ramachandra Murthy asked me the bio-data and horoscope of my daughter so that he would give it to his friend Sri Somayajulu who is a social worker and match maker. Infact I was not much associated with Sri Somayajulu. On 17th February, 1992 when I reached my office at 9.00 a.m., telephone on my table was ringing and I lifted the phone when I asked who was speaking at the other end, the answer was, He was a prospective bridegroom who had come from Visakapatnam to see my daughter.

The marriage was fixed on 10th May 1992, at 6.58 a.m. in Hyderabad. I prayed to Baba to help me in the marriage activities and for the success of the marriage. On 22nd March 1992, in the afternoon sleep Sri Sai Baba appeared to me in the dream in the form of my father (Late Sri R.V. Rao) and promised me that he would help me in my daughter's marriage and he would attend the marriage also. I was surprised how a dead person (my father) could attend the marriage and help me in the marriage. In *Sri Sai Satcharita*, chapter 40 page 212, Sri Sai Baba says "I always think of him who remembers Me, I require no conveyance, carriage, *tonga*, train or aeroplane. I run and manifest Myself to him, who lovingly calls me". I felt Sri Sai Baba might not attend the marriage of my daughter in the form of my father. Sri Sai says in the *Sai Satcharita* Page 151 Chapter 28. "I have no form nor any extension – I always live everywhere" Sri Sai Baba told in chapter 40 page 213 "See, to keep My words I would sacrifice my life, I would never be untrue to my words."

I totally believed in Sri Sai Baba and started the marriage arrangements. In the month of March 92 wedding cards were printed and as per the directions of Sri Sai I posted first card to Ganesh Temple Ranathambhor, second card to Balaji temple, Tirupathi, Third card to Sri Sai Baba at Shridi.

Then I posted five cards to abroad and prayed Baba to see that at least one family from abroad attended the marriage. I was surprised to see that my well wishers Smt. and Sri V. Surya Rao from U.S.A. came to Hyderabad on 9th May 1992 to attend the marriage. On 9th May 1992, I prayed to Baba to help me in the marriage function and see that it was successful.

Finally the marriage day i.e. 10th May 1992, I was very busy in the morning as the Muhurat was at 06.58 a.m. I could not spare even five minutes time for the *Sai Satcharita Parayana*. I was having *Ahankar* (Pride) that I could spare daily time for *Satcharita Parayana*. Sri Sai made me so much busy that I could not touch the *Sai Satcharita* on that day, and he removed my *Ahankar*. I totally forgot Sri Sai in the marriage and I was talking to my friends and bridegrooms relatives. It was around 11.45 a.m. the Pandit of Bridegroom and come to me along with a Brahmin and asked me to give some *Dakshina* to Brahmin. I thought the Brahmin must be his relative, and I gave Rs. 21/- as *Dakshina*. Then the Brahmin was asking about food. The *Pandit* sent him to the dining Hall to take the food along with other guests. When I entered dining hall to talk with the guests and relatives, I found that Brahmin who took Dakshina from me was smiling towards me. I felt he might ask more money so I left that place. I was fully busy in attending the needs of the Bridegrooms party. The time was 4.30 p.m. and the *Doli* started. I could not take food even at 6.30 p.m. I was having some misunderstandings with some relatives and was upset. Because of the misunderstandings I could not take food in the night also. After the *Muhurat* in the morning my well wisher Sri V. Surya Rao who came to the marriage from U.S.A. offered the break-fast and told me "You will be very busy today and you will not get time to take food, so have this break-fast". Had I not taken the break-fast it would have become a fasting day to me.

Sri Sai is against fasting and He never allowed his devotees to observe fasting. (Ref. Chapter 32, Page 173). In the night before I was going to bed I prayed t Sri Sai Baba and conveyed my thanks to him for the success of the marriage. I felt Sri Sai Baba had not attended the marriage and it was Baba's breach of promise. Sri Sai had promised me on 22nd March 1992, that He would attend the marriage. If Sri Sai Baba attended the marriage in which from he attended? It was a question t me and I asked Sri Sai to kindly clear my doubts. Sri Sai Baba appeared to me in the dream in the form of the Brahmin (who took Rs. 21/- from me as *Dakshina*) and was smiling. I got up from my bed and stood in front of Sai's photo and blamed myself for not recognizing Sai who attended my daughter's marriage. Next day to cross check I asked Bridegroom's Pandit about the Brahmin who took Rs. 21/- as Pandit Dakshina from me. He informed that the Brahmin was a stranger to him who happened to come to the marriage. I felt that stranger was none other than Sai.

HOW TO SHRI SAI PEACE BE TO ALL

-SAI BA.NI.SA. RAVADA GOPALA RAO,
PLOT NO. 15, H.NO. 1-7-204,
E.C.I.L., 'X' ROAD,
HYDERABAD – 500 062
Aug. 1986

88. INCREDIBLE SAI LEELAS (1996)

I was in Calcutta on a short visit on 8th April, 1996. My host introduced his son-in-law, who is an Officer in the Telephone Department. I offered him *'udhi'* prasad along with a photo of Sai Baba. He requested me to put both of them in his bag myself. Then he took leave of me and went to his office.

When he reached his office, he discovered that he had forgotten his wallet in the taxi itself. It was indeed a rude shock to him as he had kept a cash of Rs. 15,0000/- and some important official documents. He was more worried about the documents than the loss of Rs. 15,000/-.

He made a fervent appeal to Sai Maharaj. Within seconds the telephone bell rang and the taxi driver was at the other end. He told the Officer that his wallet was safe and he could come and collect it from a specified point.

While handing over the wallet, taxi, driver brought his attention to the picture of Sai Baba and told him: "On opening this wallet, the old man is this picture beckoned me not to touch any of its contents but return it to you." Overwhelmed at this gesture, our friend offered Rs. 1000/- to the taxi driver but he refused to accept the gift saying "Pray to Sai Baba for my welfare".

When he narrated the above incident at my host's residence later in the evening, tears rolled down from our eyes and we were wonderstruck at the ever vigilant eyes of Sai Baba.

-Sai Narsimha Baba of Karur
Sai Prabha

89. SAI MIRACLE (1987)

In the house of my uncle, who happens to be an ardent Sai devotee, there were many Sai photos. My uncle's daughter was recently blessed with a daughter. As soon as the new-born baby was out of labour room my aunt put a little of Baba's *Udi* in her mouth.

When she was brought home, her cot was fully covered with mosquito net and rope was tied to nails on the wall. On one side there was Baba's photo hanging from a nail and the mosquito net was tied to that nail. Just below that photo there was cradle in which the baby was kept.

Suddenly, the nail from which the mosquito net and Baba's photo were hanging came out, but to every-body's surprise, Baba's photo did not fall down, had it fallen, it would have fallen right on the head of the baby. The photo was hanging on the wall without any support, till somebody noticed it. So the great Baba, knowing if that photo falls down, it would be a threat to the life of the baby had not allowed it to fall.

So our almighty Sai Baba is Saviour and always protects His children.

-A.V.V. Kumar,
A-63, Fertilizer Town,
ROURKELA 729 007
(*Shri Sai Leela*, Nov. 1987)

90. HOW SAI BABA LOVES THE DEVOTEE (1987)

It was at 6 p.m. on the 14th May 1987, Thursday, when my 8 year old son Ashish was busy in making a big jasmine garland for BABA, the needle was 3 inches long and thread used was 3 feet long. For fastening the flowers by the thread he had kept the needle aside for a while and forgetting the place, where he had kept, he started searching the needle. When he could not locate it he asked the mother as to where was the needle? When his mother searched for it, it was noticed that the thread was falling and showing out from his ankle and 2 inches long needle was outside the ankle and 1 inch inside.

Just see the greatness of Baba that there was no pain at all and even the body did not know it got inside. When his mother started weeping at the sight of this, I rushed to him and felt dumbfounded. He was silently sitting and saying that ... *"Muze dard nahi hai Papa, muze nahi maloom ye kaisa chub gayi. Mai to Baba ke liye mala bana raha tha."*

Within a minute a doctor friend of mine came to my house for showing a horoscope. Perhaps Baba might have sent him and we took the boy to the hospital. He gave two injections and while taking out the needle broke in the middle with 1" inside the ankle. Now it became more of a problem to locate the place. Immediately we got the X-ray done and the broken needle was taken out by a minor operation. The doctor advised the boy 3 days rest and not to walk. But the next day he started walking and the wound was fully cured within 2 days.

See how kindly the Baba takes care of devotee – may Lord Sai bless every body. BLESS EVERY BODY.

-Omprakash S. Mehta,
Sirpur – Kaghaznagar
(*Shri Sai Leela*, April 1989)

91. I AM PROSTEGE (1961)

I came to know about Sri Baba in late fifties i.e. 1958 or so. One Leela Sai came to Trivandrum and was staying at Dr. Narayan Nair's house. She used to predict the future of the people who visited her, with Baba's blessings. My mother, a young widow with five children, also went to her for her help and guidance. Slowly she brought a photograph of Baba and kept it in her pooja room. That is how I started worshipping Sri Baba. Then I read many books and as a result was completely drawn to Him!

In 1961, I got married to an army officer, and left my home town to stay with him in the North. As soon as we reached there, my husband got orders to move to Goa for military operation. I was left all alone in that hill station. That was my first time to be away from home. I stayed all alone in that huge building, our house, with no neighbours near-by. Then came the 1962 Chinese aggression. It was a very bad experience for me. Silently I prayed to Sri Baba to give me enough strength to go through all these crises. Things were happening so suddenly that we did not have time to think about anything else. My husband was posted from his original battalion to another battalion. Sri Baba knew what was going to happen to that battalion. When I now look back I can see so clearly all His love and protection for me, nay for us.

We came to the new place Hyderabad, and the preparation for the move was going on. In the mean time I fell sick and underwent some treatment. As a newly married and sick person, I was very much upset about the whole thing.

271

On top of it, my mother-in-law wrote to my husband saying that astrologically there was a possibility of early widowhood to me. I started crying and did not know what to do except praying to Sri Baba. Somehow my husband was left back in the 'Rear Party'. Otherwise I don't think he would be alive to-day. I was so overjoyed by His Kindness and grace and thanked Him immensely.

I have an innate feeling that He always protects me. As a young girl I have seen a person like Sri Baba with the headgear etc. He used to come to our house for alms. The same person came to my house after so many years when I was in distress. Again it was connected with my husband. He was in the field area and I was not getting any letters from him. So many days passed but no news, whatsoever, I was naturally worried. That was the time Sri Baba came to our door step. I gave him some money and He disappeared. After few hours the postman delivered my husband's letter to me. See, how Gracious my Baba is!

I can narrate so many incidents. When I was a young woman my parents, grand parents and other members of the family were staying in a double-story terraced building. One day my kind and myself and sister were playing near the terrace. The minute we moved out of that place the whole terrace collapsed where we had been playing a little ago. Thank God we both were saved by Baba's Grace. I remember my mother saying, "She has got some protection, otherwise see what would have happened to her". I was so shocked at the sudden event that I could not imagine what would have been our fate had the terrace collapsed while we were in its neighbourhood! Sri Baba only saved us from that calamity.

As the years rolled on I began and continue to leave everything to Him. I have complete faith in Him. After my marriage most of the time I was in and out of the hospital. I had three major operations. During those times only Sri Baba helped me to keep calm and quiet. With His blessings I always came out of the hospital without any damage to my health.

Then we came to Bangalore t settle down. To get a site in Bangalore is very difficult for obvious reasons. As soon as we reached there we started applying to B.D.A.; 3 or 4 times we applied and afterwards we completely forgot about it. In the mean time I was involved in collecting some money for a Sai Baba temple there. I did collect some money and handed over to the persons concerned. During that time in 1983 on a Sri Ramanavmi day the post-man brought a better for me. When I opened it I was overjoyed by the contents. It was an allotment letter for a site from B.D.A. authorities. See, how kind and helpful Sri Baba is! So friends, have complete faith in Him. He will look after you, not only here in this world but hereafter too.

OM SRI SAI RAM

Mrs. Lalita Nair,
44, Kodehally Layout,
Bhimanagar P.O., Bangalore
(*Shri Sai Leela*, March 1988)

92. BABA CURED STOMACH OF A DEVOTEE (190)

Sri M. Nemchand Jain, Post Market, Secunderabad 3, remembers that it was a Tuesday of June 190. A tall well built Fakir, stood with joli, (bag) near their jewelry shop. He had to wait for more than half an hour, as Sri Jain was busy with his customers. Later, Sri Jain asked the Fakir, "What do you want?" "Five annas" was the reply, Jain searched for five annas in his cash box, but he could find only four annas. The Fakir refused to accept one anna less or one anna more. "Are you not suffering from severe stomach pain?" asked the Fakir. Sri Jain was shocked and wondered as to how a stranger could know about his physical condition. It was true that he suffered from stomach pain, which did not cure inspite of all medical treatment. The Fakir advised that he would be relieved of all stomach pain, if he started doing puja to Shirdi Sai Baba from Thursday, and stopped taking all medicines. The Fakir put his hand into his joli, took out *udhi*, and put some *udhi* into Sri Jain's hand and instructed him to put a pinch of *udhi* in his mouth, and also apply on his forehead. The treatment was to be for two days, and that complete cure would take place by Thursday. True to what the Fakir said, Sri Jain's stomach pain disappeared from the third day.

In the meantime, the Fakir who was standing in the shop, while Sri Jain was searching for five annas, now enhanced his "fees" to one rupee four annas. He would not accept anything less or anything more. While Sri Jain was again searching for the exact change, the Fakir disappeared. He could not be found inspite of hectic search.

The Jian family were devout persons doing regular pooja to their family deities. Sai Baba did not find a place in their Pooja Mandir till this incident. In the month of August 190, the Jain family visited Shirdi for the first time. The Fakir who came to the Jain jewelry shop was found sitting on the throne of the Samadhi Mandir. As if to confirm that the Fakir was none else than Sai Baba, He continued to sit on the throne till one rupee five annas were put into the hundi. Soon after, in the place of Fakir, they saw a beautiful marble statue of Sai Baba.

93. *VIBHUTI* MATERIALIZED ON BABA'S PHOTO (1995)

Sai Samaj was established in my own house. *Abhishekam* and *puja*, *Lalitha* and *Vishnu Sahasranama shastrs prayers, Arathi* and *Nama Parayana* are performed daily.

On 1th April 1995, suddenly I saw Vibhuthi on the feet of Sri Sai Nath's photo and the statue saw. I wanted to know how it happened on the lotus feet of Sri SAi. On the nextday Vibhuti grew up like bubbles on the left, feet of Sai and it gradually covered the whole body. ON the 49th day Baba's voice came out and asked me to remove the Vibhuthi. But I prayed and asked permission to remove the same on the Gurupurnima day, the 12th July 1995.

On that day we removed Vibhuthi from Baba's photo it was distributed among all devotees. Abhishekam was made with *panchamruthas*. From that day onwards no Vibhuthi came out of his body. It is a great miracle of Sri SAi Nath experienced by us here in Rajmundari.

28.11.1995

Sri V. Narasimha Swamiji

Secretary

SRI SHIRDI SAI BABA NAMA JAPA YAGNA

SAMAJANRAJMUNDARY

94. HOW BABA'S GRACE SHOWERED ON ME (1996)

Last year in 199 I had the fortune of visiting Shridi with my brother. At Ajmer Railway Station a Faqir attaired as Sai Baba, had met we and gave we a *tabeej* (talisman). Heshowed we the miracle of materializing Ganga and Yamuna waters just from his hands and My visit to Shirdi was the more memorable visit of my life. During the last one year and half so many incidents of Sai Baba's grace have taken where in my life. I have taken to the daily reading to 'Shri Sai Satcharita' solely which gives me undescriable bliss.

Prabhash Chandra Srivastava,

Enforcement Officer,

Food & Civil Supplies Department,

Government of Rajasthan,

M.G. Mansion, Rahul Marg,

Abhay Colony, Neem Ka Thana Contt.

95. BABA'S HELP IN MARRIAGE AND EXAMINATION (1996)

It is not easy for an ordinary and ignorant person like me to write about the greatness of Sri Baba. It is very difficult to describe His Leelas or actions but I am making a small attempt to share my experiences with all the other devotees.

About 5 or 6 years back I came to know of Baba and His greatness. Slowly I started developing an immense faith in Him.

Let me share my first experience of Sai Leela. This is about my daughter's marriage. My daughter had been studying in the USA for the last 7 years. About three years back, she fell in love with a foreigner over there and decided to marry him. We had not seen him. It was a difficult time; for us to say 'yes' to her was tough. I kept on praying to Baba and completely surrendered to Him. Finally, by Baba's Grace the boy and my daughter come to India and got married in the traditional Hindu way. We found the bridegroom a very nice man and we performed the marriage happily. It is all due to Baba's grace.

My second experience is with my son. He is studying Engineering in Karnataka and he came home for vacation last July/August. He had to appear for an examination on 4th August and on 3rd was our daughter marriage. He had to attend the examination and at the same time he could not miss his sister's marriage. We booked a plane ticket for him on 3rd to Bangalore Via Madras. But the flight get delayed and he missed his flight to Bangalore. We were getting panicky and kept on praying to Baba. This boy suddenly managed to get a ticket to Mangalore by next morning flight and finally reached his college in time for his examination. Not only that, he even passed that examination with good marks. Baba gave my son the courage he needed in that difficult solution and sent him to his college in time for his examination. But for Baba's blessing and grace, we donot know could have happened.

Let us all bow to SAI.

Mrs. ANASUYA
54, Vayupuri
Secunderabad (AP) 500014

96. EXPERIENCE OF A PUBLISHER (1997)

(1) Baba appeared in my dream and taught we a *mantra* for *Japam*.
(2) Baba appeared in a dream and asked for Rs. 80, I gave it to him for book publication.

(3) Baba appeared in a dream and cheerfully touched my hand and told me "The whole universe is our unit".

(4) Baba appeared in a dream and told me "*Sadhaka*, who is in enjoyment with family shall not feel worry."

(5) In 197 I went to Shirdi to do special *pooja* along with my wife, daughter and son in law and requested the authorities to give me permission to do puja ourselves at Samadhi Mandir in my own way. NO body heard our request. I sat for the grace of Baba from A.M. to 11 A.M. There were about 100 devotees waiting in the hall for their round of call. I simply prayed to Baba to show HIS KINDNESS. At 11 A.M. an *archaka* came forward and told us: "You four persons can do your puja as your like. Take sufficient time." That was the Grace of Baba! He is great.

B.V. Pardhasaradhy
Sri Sai Nilayam,
Cheruyu 22113

97. PERSONAL PROBLEMS SOLVED BY BABA (1996)

There was a time when I did not know anything about Shirdi Sai Baba. One of my friends who was a devotee of Sai Baba insisted that I should visit Baba's Mandir at Lodhi Road, New Delhi with her. Since she was my best friend I went to Baba's Mandir with her one day. That was the day of total transformation of my mind. I entered Baba's Mandir and was face to face with Baba's marble statue. I touched his feet and stood near the entrance gate, By that time I had not much faith in Baba. Suddenly, I heard a voice which to me appeared to be echocing in eh hall. I thought someone was talking loudly. I started looking here and there but nobody else seemed to have heard the sound and all were standing quietly in eh queue. The voice again echoed. "Why are you looking here and there, I am talking to you. You are having basket in your hand. Don't worry. I will take care of your problems; your wishes will be fulfilled." Then I realized that Baba was talking to me as only I was having basket in my hand.

It could not be an ordinary human voice. I left the temple with total sense of satisfaction. Surprisingly, my problems were solved within few days. Above all, I am now keenly attached with Baba and find tranquility sitting in his feet.

After personally talking face to face with Baba in Lodhi Road Temple I was proud of being Baba's devotee. All my problems were being solved by Baba.

ONce we were having Satyanarayan Pooja in our house. After Pooja, when Baba was being offered Bhog, Baba came out of his picture and said, "I am going" and walked out of the wall. I gave a silent cry "What will happened to me without you." But he did not turn his back and disappeared. I wonder when will I meet Him again. I feel very sad without Baba. Baba please come back to me.

-Vimal Sobti
A-370, Sector 19,
NOIDA (U.P.) 201301

98. BABA REVEALED A WOMAN DEVOTEE SHE WAS A DOG FED BY HIM AT SHIRDI IN HER PREVIOUS LIFE (1996)

I met one Sudhakar Reddy, an Andhrite, at Mamlam (Madras). He told me that his father was a great devotee of Sri Shirdi Sai Baba and his mother was a devotee of Lord Rama. When she was asked by him to visit Shirdi with him she refused, but later she said she would visit Shirdi if she were shown some incident which would make her believe in Baba. Once they went to take the *darshan* of Sri Rama in Bhadrachalam, holy place of the famous saint Ramdass. There she was surprised to see only the form of Sri Shirdi Sai Baba and not Rama in the temple of Rama. From that time she became Sri Shirdi Sai Baba's devotee.

She started offering *Naivaidhya* (food offering) to Sri Shirdi Sai Baba and every day Baba came and accepted it. Once she asked Baba, "Baba, how is it that you come and accept food from me; but it is not the case with many others who are also your devotees? "To this Baba replied appearing in his full physical form?" In your previous life, you were a dog at Shirdi who used to come to Me daily and take food from Me in Dwarkamai *masjid*. Such being the case, how can I forget you?"

27th Nov. 199

-Sri M.G. Bavanarayanan,
Secretar Correspondent, Bhairav Sai Temple Trust,
IOA, Gopala Krishna Iyer Street,
T. Nagar, Madras 600017

99. BABA SAVED HIS DEVOTEES FROM ACCIDENT IN TRAIN (1995)

1. Sri G. Meenakshisundaram Sai Dasan', Founder President of Bhairav Sai Temple, Plot No. 6, Door 15B, Bharat Nagar, Keelakkattalai Road,

Madipakkam, Madras, and I, as the Secretary and Correspondents of this Temple Trust, in 1996 went to Bombay to purchase *apanchdatu* (five metal) statue of Sri Shirdi Sai Baba for installation in our newly established Bhairav Sai Temple. By 9.30 in night we slept in the train. Sri Sundaram was on the middle berth and I was on the lower berth. Early morning at 4 O'clock, Sri Sundaram got awakened and saw that his middle berth was slowing going down. He discovered that both the chains had been separated from the plank of his berth; when it had separated he did not know. One chain was completely away from the plank and the other chain was just touching the plank. I was on the lower berth. I am a heart patient; I have had three heart attacks. He frantically called me to get up. I got up atone and was surprised how Baba had saved my life. Had the berth fallen on me, being without chains, I would certainly have been crushed to death. We at once got down and prayed to Baba for saving both of us from the accident which would have been fatal for both.

2. We had purchased tickets upto Kalyan suburb station only in this journey. We were requesting the TTE (Travailing Ticket Examiner) to give us extension up to Bombay VT but he did not give it. At Bombay VT Station the TT Squad was on the platform. They were heavily charging the passengers without tickets and those having any deficiency in their tickets. One TTE came and caught hold of both of us and demanded nearly Rs. 200 per ticket from both of us as reservation charges plus penalty charges from Kalyan to Bombay VT. We said to him "We came to Bombay in connection with the purchase of a Sai Baba statue for our Bhairav Sai Temple at Madras." Even then, he was adamant and he was about to hand both us over to the Station Superintendent for collection of excess fare, reservation charges and penalty. When we reached the Exit Gate, he greeted us and then handed over our tickets and allowed us to go out freely without getting us charged by the Sqaud. Out mental agony and tension during the early hours of the period of 10 minutes from the Station Platform to the Exit Gate cannot be described. It was only Sri Shirdi Sai Baba's grace that he was forced to change his mind and he allowed us to move out freely without any entanglement.

3. Last year in July 199 I had heart attack for the third time in my life. I was admitted in the hospital and the date for the bypass surgery

had also been fixed for Tuesday. But my friend and well-wisher Sri G. Meenakshisundaram Sai Dasan prayee to Sri Shirdi Sai Baba and as a result no operation was done on Tuesday. Then the same bypass surgery was fixed for Saturday morning against my wishes. I was praying to Sri Shridi Sai Baba all along to bless me without operation. On Thursday night, Baba patted me on my shoulder in the dream and asked me to go home.

In the morning the team of doctors who were nominated to do my operation informed me that I had only a minor blockage in the vessel and as such there was no need for immediate operation. So saying, they discharged me on Friday evening itself. I sincerely felt that when all arrangements had been done by my sons and relatives for my bypass operation at the cost of Rs. 1.20 lakhs, they borrowed this huge amount from different people, Baba gave His grace; He gave us relief and saved my life and the family without causing any debt to be paid by my children. While I was in the Intensive Care Unit of the Maller Hospital, Madras, Baba showed through my relatives a B.E. (Civil) boy and fixed the marriage of my daughter aged 19 years months. Previously I was not aware of the betrothal function that took place in the presence of my co-brother and his wife at my native place Tanjavour.

When I came home after discharge from the hospital, I learnt of it. I was never having any ready cash so I was lying on the bed deeply worried about the cash needed for marriage. Then one of my classmates, a retired officer in the LIC (life Insurance Corporation) came to see me casually. On my request he arranged a sum of Rs. 25,000/- as LIC loan against my Insurance Policy within a matter of 48 hours.

Then secondly, a Brahmin boy who was working in Sundaram Finance Co., arranged to release my deposit of Rs. 50,000/- within 4 hours and handed over the cheque in person although the date of maturity for the Fixed Deposit was six months ahead, after the Company deducting6 months interest. He had himself brought the application from for me and got my signatures on it, and within 4 hours he got me the cheque. I did not know him earlier. The bridegroom's parents agreed to do the marriage and purchase all the things and requested me only to pay the amount and accordingly I paid Rs. 48,000/- for arranging the marriage, purchase of TV, sofa and all household articles and they very gladly accepted all that and performed the marriage in a very decent manner. My daughter is happy. In the dream I was performing Kumbhakesam ceremony and then delivering a speech about the services of Sri Meenakshisundaram Sai dasan and the greatness of Sri Shirdi Sai Baba in Thursday night. of the 28th Nov. 1996

-M.G. Bavanarayanan,
10A, Gopala Krishna Iyer Street,
T. Nagar, Madras – 600017

100. BABA SAVED DEVOTEE'S HUSBAND' IN CAR ACCIDENT (1995)

On Monday, 19th June 1995 my husband was travailing in DCM Toyota car from Mussoorie to Dehradun to go to his office. On the way, a truck coming from the opposite direction hit the Toyota car violently. At that time my husband was wearing a Sai Baba pendent given to my husband by Sai Ma (Mrs. Mehta of Sai Darbar, 2 Garden Reach, Kulri, Mussorie). That pendent saved my husband's life by coming out his neck and getting suddenly between him and the broken pieces of glass. It was, of course, undamaged. Only Baba thus miraculously saved my husband's life with his pendent's helped in it.

-Mrs. Madhuri Srivastava
C/o Mrs. Om Prakash Srivastava
Based on her experience published in 'Sai Ma Ki Kripa Vrishti',
(1997) a publication of Sai Darbar, 2 Garden Reach, Kulri,
Mussoorie – 248179

101. BABA'S MIRACULOUS HELP IN JOURNEY (1993)

My father and my younger brother went to Bombay in 1993 for an interview of my brother. My father is a sugar patient and my brother of age 20 years was visiting Bombay for the first time. Few days after they left for Bombay, I came to know that there was some political disturbance in Bombay. I rang up to one of our relatives and I was told that the interviews were over and my father and brother had been held up at Bombay as they could not get even general ticket since railway computer was showing 'No Room' and for two weeks all trains were full. I was also told that my father was not doing well and the money with them was almost exhausted. As I heard this news I was very much worried about them and I could not understand what to do.

Suddenly my sight fell on the Shirdi Sai Baba's photo and I closed my eyes and prayed Baba with whole heart to help my father and brother to reach

Hyderabad with safely. I said in Hindi *"Baba rahem nazar karna, mere pitaji aur bhai ki raksha karna."* In the evening I went to Baba's temple at Nailagutta and sat there for about half an hour praying Baba with words "OM SAI SRI SAI JAYA JAYA SAI".

"JAI GURU DATTA". I could not sleep in the night because of the worry. Next day I went to my office in a bad mood and in the evening when I returned to my home from my office, to my surprise I found my father and brother reached home safe and it was all the work surprising when I was told by my father that, every day they were going to V.T. Station to try to get ticket and on the last day at V.T. Station as my father and brother were talking in Telugu, a stranger wished them in Telugu and told that he was having two space confirmed tickets since two of his relatives and dropped their journey. He allowed my father and brother to travel on the same tickets and during journey he gave them good food and also he did not take the train fair deposit them reveal request. As I heard this news in joy mood I could not stop myself from uttering the word "Sai Baba Aap Mahan Hain". I always feel that Baba had come as the stranger and helped my father and brother to reach home safely.

-N.V. Chenneshwar,
HMT Lamps, Hyderabad – 500054

102. BABA'S INSTANT RESPONSE TO HIS DEVOTEE'S PRAYER (1996)

On a particular day I was travailing by an express night bus from Bangalore to Bombay on official duty. On the mid-way the driver had stopped the bus and informed the passengers to relax themselves for a few minutes. I got down from the bus and after finishing the call of nature took two small coconuts to quench my thirst at midnight, short in level of time the bus again started the journey, peering its all passengers made their efforts to sleep in their sitting posture closing their cycloids. The water of two coconuts went into my stomach started its function and made my bladders inside to swell. I felt uneasy and uncomfortable as I had the sever urge for nature call again. Any amount of my controlling that urge became useless and the discomfort in the lower abdomen was unbearable due to the swelling of the blodder with the accumulation of fresh stock there in. No words could describe my agony in that situation. I was afraid and felt ashamed of myself to request the driver to stop the bus for a while for enabling me to get down for nature call when all other co-passengers were in their deep slumber. I was looking out eagerly for the approach of my destination stop so that I could get down to ease myself but there was no such symptoms as two more hours of journey was still left to reach my destination stop.

When the pain become extremely unbearable. I cried out to our Swami Sai Samarath and prayed in my heart of heart to stop the bus on some pretext or other so that I could get down and ease myself. What I wonder it was! My humble prayer reached our Lord Sainath, the Onipresent and indweller of the heart, instantly as Dranpad's prayer had reached Lord Krishna when her saree was pulled in the court hall by Dushasana. The speeding bus suddenly stopped to my surprise and astonishment. The driver of the bus simply got down on his own from the bus with a tin full of water and disappeared in the darkness of the night. The omnipresent Sai Samarath on hearing my prayer had created a similar urge in the bus driver in order to relieve the sufferings of His deer devotee. Who can understand His Leelas!

I whole heartedly thanked our Lord and got down from the bus to ease myself without any loss of time. I rushed myself to a nearby bush to ease but to my dismay, I couldn't ease myself at all: perhaps due to contraction for a long time as well as anxiety I was afraid whether I might have to board the bus again without getting myself relieved of my problem and continue to undergo the torture again in the bus. Though several minutes passed, there was no relief for me. Again I turned to our Lord Sainath and prayed to save me from my critical position. Relief came instantly as my prayer was answered by the all providing benefit or Sai Samarth and I was completely relieved of my problem in the next few minutes. What a joy it was for me at that moment! It can't be expressed in word. I prostrated to our Lord Sainath in my heart for coming to my help in a miraculous manner in that midnight and then boarded the bus. The bus driver unaware of the miracle of our Swami returned to the bus with his empty tin and resumed his driving.

When the bus came to destination stop after some hours of journey. I got down from the bus and expressed my gratitude to the driver in whom our Lord Samarth Sai had manifested Himself and enacted His divine drama in His own way to relieve the suffering of His deer devotee. My humble pranams at the Lotus Feet of our Lord Samarth Sainath Prabhu.

JAI SAI RAM

-D. T.HIRUGNANAM

1450, Sri Sai Laxmi Nivas,

13 Main II Stage West of Chord Road,

Bangalore-560086

103. BABA'S TIMELY HELP (1996)

On 27th June 1996 Thursday night at about 8 PM I was quietly resting in my home reading some magazine and the only other person in the house at that time was my daughter-in-law who was carrying by three months. My wife had gone to Madras on that same day to attend some marriage ceremony and my two sons who were in the station were not available at home since they had gone to some movies.

At 8 PM on 27th June 1996 suddenly my daughter-in-law started crying due to severe pain due to bleeding and desperately she called me and told that her husband (one of my sons) should be called to take her to the hospital. What a test for me, where could I go searching for my son in the big city like Bangalore? My son had not told me or his wife to which theatre he is going to see the movie. Since he has taken the car with him the car also was not available for me to take my daughter-in-law to any hospital in that emergency.

All that I could do was go to our Pooja Room, look at our Lord Shridi Sai Baba and plead with him for his mercy. I took a pinch of Baba's Vibhooti from our Pooja Room and mixed it with little water and gave to my daughter-in-law to drink and only told her to pacity herself and mutter Lord Sai's name in her lips. She did the same with all the devotion. Believe me, Sir, the severe pain subsided and the she slowly went for sleep. My two sons came home at about 12 night and by then my daughter-in-law was peaceful and joyful and with smile on her face.

Next day we took her to our family doctor and got her thoroughly tested, as usual.

But who is this greatest Doctor who has attended to my daughter-in-law in the night? Is it not our beloved Lord Shirdi Sai Nath? Once again our Lord Sai Baba proved his promise that he is devotee of his devotees readily available whenever we need Him.

-K. Vasudev, "Krishna",
No. 19, I Main III Cross,
KHB Colony, I stage,
Bavareswar Nagar, Bangalore – 500079

104. BABA HELPS HIS DEVOTEE IN SHIRDI TRAVEL (1996)

One night at 11.30 I received a phone call from Guruji Sathpathy Ji who told me, "I am going to Shirdi tonight. I was ill for 2-3 days, my temperature was 101 degree. I am not in position to do train travel. You also come to Shirdi taking morning train." I had then Rs. 1500/- in cash in my house. Immediately in the morning taking that amount I reached New Delhi railway station. No railway ticket was available for the same day. With great difficulty I got a II class ticket in Goa Express and sat in a three tier compartment. A Sai devotee family was sitting on the front seats. In the night we were talking about Baba. Then one passenger, a boy, told me, "One berth of mine is booked in AC Compartment. You may please go there and occupy that berth." When Baba calls anyone to Shirdi He himself arranges his journey. No one asked me my ticket among the 74 passengers of the compartment.

S.C. Srivastava,
Manager, Sri Shirdi Sai Baba Temple,
Chattarpur, Mehrauli, Delhi

105. THE DOWN-ROW PULLER (1985)

I am from an agriculturist's family. Being short in stature, during the harvest, I was given the task of gathering the 'down row'. This was the row of corn that was straddled by the tractor and flattened to the ground.

Every year I fussed and fumed; it was not fair that others in the family got other important jobs – driving the Tractor or gathering the proud, straight stalks – while I walked behind.

We should learn to be neither attached to pleasure not fearful of pain. As Sai-devotees, we should accept what life gives without being too much elated or too much discouraged. This should be the state for a true Sai-devotee. It is not some great strength that we can gather suddenly when we need it to face a big problem. This Sai consciousness has to be built up gradually within us, by training ourselves to react properly to everyday problems and occurrences.

In May 1986, I developed pain and a swelling in my groin area. When I went for a checkup at the Karnataka Medical College Hospital at Hubli, the doctors diagnosed the conditions as 'Direct Inguinal Hernia' and suggested an immediate operation. I was nearing seventy and naturally was afraid to face a major operation at this age. Moreover my wife had undergone an operation of her uterus in January 1985 and her suffering were still fresh in my memory. So I was in a dilemma as to whether to undergo an operation or just carry-on.

Usually in such doubtful circumstances I cast lots before the holy feet of Lord Sainath. In this case, Sainath commanded me not undergo right them but to wait for sometime. I abided by the Sai-will. My wife and children chided me up for my blind faith and insisted on my undergoing immediate surgery. Somehow Sai prompted me not to head to their advice.

As the days went on, the swelling increased and so the pain, I was even wondering if Sai's decision to postpone my operation was wise. I had difficulty even to walk around and lead a normal life. I patiently bore this suffering and prayed to Sai Baba: "Lord, I am suffering on account of my bad karma. I am unable to bear this pain. You have healed Sri Bhimaji Patil, Dr. Pillay, Khaparde and so many others by your spiritual powers. Am I not eligible for your grace? Kindly bestow your grace on me or if the inevitable has to happen, kindly allow me die in the consciousness of yourself."

This silent suffering went on for a few months. In October 1986, my brother, R. Subramanian of Madras came to Hubli to join in the performance of the annual ceremony for our late mother. When he saw my agony he suggested that I should make a trip to Madras and consult Sai-brother Dr. Vira Reddy who was an expert in surgery. Earlier, I had the good fortune of meeting Dr. Reddy at the holy soil of Shirdi on the Guru Purnima day in July 1985 and was really impressed by his humility and sense of deep dedication to Lord Sainath.

I was in Madras in the third week of November, 1986 on yet another Sai-mission of participating in the wedding of Sai-brother M.V. Venkatesam's daughter. I extended my stay at Madras to participate in the 'Aardhana' celebrations of Swami Gnananda Giri of Tapovanam. My brother was persistent in taking me to Dr. Vira Reddy.

So on the 6th December, 1986, I went to Dr. Vira Reddy at his Nursing Home. This Sai-brother was delighted to see me. He conducted a detailed check-up and all relevant laboratory tests. He advised me to get it operated as soon as possible as the hernia might get strangulated which is a very dangerous condition leading to instant death. Accordingly, I was operated on the 11th December, 1986 by Dr. Reddy himself at his Nursing Home.

Just the day prior to my operation, I received the November, 1986 issue of 'Sri Sai Leela' and Sai-udhi from Shirdi through my brother, Sri R. Subramanian, at the Nursing Home itself. What a great blessing? Sai's dictum: "WHY FEAR WHEN I AM HERE" flashed across my mind.

The post-operative period was quite eventless. Dr. Reddy and his Sai-half, Dr. Mrs. Saraswathi Reddy and their colleagues looked after me very well. The whole hospital vibrates with Sai consciousness. Every where one can see Sai Baba's portraits. Verily Sai Baba was with all the patients in that Nursing Home.

Two weeks after my operation. I was able to go home. Dr. Reddy refused to accept any money from me either for the operation or for my stay in the nursing Home. He just smiled and told me to put whatever I wished to give him in the 'HUNDI' at Shirdi on my next visit there. What a magnanimous heart that I came across? My eyes shed tears of Sai-joy. May Lord Sainath bless him and Mrs. Saraswathi Reddy with many more years of Sai-seva.

Dear Sai-brothers and Sai-sister: Become anchored in Sai and you will find it very easy to cope with life with its problems.

BOW TO SRI SAI, PEACE BE TO ALL

-R. Radhakrishna,
78, Vijaynagar,
Hubli 580 032 Karnataka

106. *GURU*'S GRACE (1986)

Sai-Brother Chandranath Laha of Standard Chartered Bank, and I drew up an itinerary early June, 86 to pay a visit to Shirdi on the auspicious day of 68th Mahasamadhi of Shirdi Sai. It struck us later that it would be a day with great crowds and we revised our itinerary to visit Shirdi in Sept. '86. This was Chandranath's first visit to that place. We booked our tickets from 2 Up Bombay Mail scheduled to steam off Howrah on 27.9.86. Little did we realize then that it was Sai who prompted us to revise our itinerary.

Three days before the scheduled date of departure, our "City of Joy" was hit by torrential rains for 3 days continuously leaving the city temporarily a "City of Sorrow". Naturally I could not contact Mr. Chandranath to know from him if we were to leave Howrah on the scheduled date at all and if so how to reach Howrah without conveyance. On Friday the 26.9.86 our City was submerged under 3 feet of water. Hope of or departure the next day became fainter and fainter as, after a lull, it again rained cats and dogs.

But to our surprise, 27th Sept. '86 began with a sunny morning and the water level receded to a great extent letting a few transport operators to venture out after 3 full day's lack of business. This revived our spirit and we both met on 27th morning at State Bank of India (Netaji Sunhash Road Branch) to get a few Travellers Cheques. The counter clerk hesitated to issue the tickets on the ground of trails not having plied for the last three days. But Mr. Chandranath requested him to issue us the cheques at our own risk.

Because we felt that the trains would be cancelled or perhaps would depart from outer station of Howrah, we left early at 4.30 p.m. By Sai grace there was no rain at all during the day save for a brief but light shower in the afternoon.

At howrah, we found that several trains were not plying and frequent announcements over the mike also confirmed that. However, only two traisn were scheduled to depart on that day on the S.E.R. Route – the 9 UP Jagannath Express and 2 Up Bombay Mail. Sai-Grace manifested itself on that occasion and we were relieved that Baba did want us to visit His Mausoleum at Shirdi.

Though the train departed an hour late at 9 p.m. we reached Nasik on the scheduled time of 3.40 a.m. the next day and stayed there for a day and by Sai-Grace could visit many important pilgrim spots in the town.

On the morning of Tuesday, the 30th October, we found ourselves safe and sound at Shirdi and at once I dashed off a letter at Sai-Baba International Hotel to Mr. Ram Nathenji who I thought would be anxious about us as to our safe and timely arrival. I had already posted a letter to my own family members from Nasik giving them an account of the safe journey.

During the two and a half days we stayed at Shirdi, we performed most comfortably the *abhishek* to Baba's Holy Samadhi and met many resident devotees notable among them being late Martand Baba.

JAI SAI RAM

-Sanjay M. Padia,
P.O. Box No. 2566,
Calcutta – 700 001
(*Shri Sai Leela*, September 1987)

107. *SADGURU* SAINATH IS IMMORTAL HIS MIRACLES ARE INCREDIBLE & INFINITE (1985)

To be frank, I knew nothing about Sri Shirdi Sai Baba earlier. One Mr. Rao, a retired Engineer has been staying in our colony for the past nearly two years with his family. They worship Sai on all days and conduct Bhajans on Thursdays. We, as neighbours, took part in all bhajans and thus became aware of Sai Baba and His Leelas.

It is said that Chy. Syamala, daughter of Mrs. Rao, is a gifted child and would sit in meditation for hours together during which Baba talks to her. When she puts forth any of the problems of the devotees, Baba gives the solution to them. During Bhajans, the spirit of Baba speaks through Syamala, blesses all the devotees and answers their questions. Only with His grace and kind blessings we could perform the marriage of our daughter in May, 1985.

One night, in the month of December, 1985, while I was sleeping close to the window in my bedroom, at about 2.00 A.M., I saw Sadguru Sainath inserting His hand through the window and showing His *'Abhayashastha'* to me. On seeing this remarkable manifestation of His Omnipresence, I woke up with great pleasure and surprise and prayed to Him with folded hands. Meanwhile, I heard a big sound of breaking of the doors of the rear room of my house. Immediately I got up from my bed and switched on the lights. Then I saw three thieves throwing away the crow-bar and taking to their heels by jumping over the compound wall. Then only in understood that Baba had come to my room to wake me and to save me from the possible theft. Baba has thus proved His saying, 'Even when you sleep, I will be awake and watchful". It is literally true that Baba always protects His devotees, who have full faith in Him.

Beginning from the last Datta Jayanthi day (26-12-85), *Nama Saptah Sapthaham* was performed in Shirdi Sai Mandir at Vijayawada. I used to attend and participate in all Arthis throughout and receive *tirtha prasadams* with the kind blessing and promptitude of Lord Sainath, I could visit the Holy Shirdi and have His darshan. The Blissful form of all pervading Sainath is indescribable. On return from Shirdi, as usual I have been attending the Thursday Bhajans in our colony and spending the spare time in reading Shri Sai Satcharita etc.

Chy. Syamala has not been keeping well for the past four days. I have been attending on her both morning and evening, enquiring about her health etc. On Monday 24-2-'86 afternoon, I was stunned to see the situation there and I was shaken to my bones. I could not control my agony – tears rolled down. Chy. Syamala, a beloved child of Baba, was in bed with a paralytic attack, unable to move her right hand and right leg. I could not even speak for some time. I could not understand how this beloved child of Baba becdame a victim to this deadly disease. On enquiry, I came to know that Chy. Syamala was all right in the morning. At 9.30 A.M., it appears she complained of headache and heaviness in the head and went to bed to have some rest. After a while she became practically unconscious and continued to be like that for about four hours. No one could wake her up by any means. At 1.30 P.M. she opened her eyes by herself and expressed, in a very low voice, to her father, who was helplessly sitting by her bedside, that she was feeling very heavy and painful in the left half of her head, as though all the blood veins and nerves in that part were twisted and bundled up and also that she was not able to move the right leg and right hand and they were also heavy. It was considered by her father as a case of Cerebral Thrombosis and paralytic stroke of the right side.

Immediately he tried to get the help of his cousin brother to secure a doctor. They were all in confused mind and grief-stricken. I was helpless and unable to see her condition. I went back to my house and was eagerly awaiting my husband. As soon as he came back home, I explained the situation and we both came to see Syamala with the intention of taking her to a doctor.

In the meantime, thinking that Sadguru Sainath, the protector of all, alone could help them in that crisis, and with firm faith in Him, Mr. Rao took Syamala to Pooja mandir and made her sit there. She was asked to pray and meditate on Baba. On this occasion she was in meditation for 40 minutes. During this period, it appears Baba gave darshan to her, rubbed her head with His hand and said "Why fear when I am here". He also said that her paralytic condition would disappear within five days, but wanted her to attend the Sai Mandir and do *pradakshinas* for three days – 21 times each day. He also wanted her to take His *Udi* both morning and evening mixed in milk. After Baba's touch over the head, she felt a great relief in the head. Syamala's father then said that there was no need to take her to any doctor, but requested our help in taking her to the Sai Mandir.

In the evening 7.30 P.M. myself along with my husband and Mr. Rao took her to Sai Baba's temple with great difficulty. Devotees present in the mandir felt very sad for the girl's pitiable condition. With great difficulty, I could manage and made her complete 21 *pradakshinas*. After this we noticed a slight movement in the fingers of the right hand. The whole of the night, she was suffering with severe pain in the right leg and hand. She could not sleep.

On the second day again myself and my husband together with Mr. Rao took Syamala to the temple and started doing *pradakshinas*. As I did on the previous day, I had to hold her and somehow drag her with difficulty to go round the idol. After completing eleven *pradakshinas*, when the 12th was about to begin, by the grace of Baba, suddenly her right leg got released and she could freely walk around, without any assistance. She jogged like a child with quick spacings and made more than forty *pradakshinas*. As arathi bell rang, she stopped and stood near one of the pillars. After *arathi* to Baba, she asked to fetch some water near Dwarakamai portrait. It appears the *poojari* used to keep that tumbler of water near Baba during nights. Without any thinking or hesitation, I brought that tumbler of water and gave it to Syamala. Lo! Baba's grace! Surprisingly Syamala held the glass tumbler with her right hand and quickly drank the water fully. Earlier the right leg and right hand were just like hanging snake-gourds without any control of movement. In the middle of the second day *pradakshinas*, the leg got released and at the end, the hand started moving. It sent thrills of joy in me and I thanked Lord Sainath mentally. All those present in the mandir were struck with wonder and gazed steadily at her for some time. They all praised Baba for this miraculous *leela*. On the third day I was able to make Syamala do 21 pradakshinas without any difficulty.

Fourth day being Thursday, while Bhajan was going on as usual in their house, Baba entered the spirit of Syamala and blessed all the devotees. Baba said that Syamala would be completely relieved of the trouble by the next day i.e. 5th day (28.2.1986). He further wanted us to do Bhajan in Sai Mandir on 28-2-1986. We all left very happy for Syamala ebing very fortunate. As a result of her *poorvajanma sukrutam* (good deeds of past life) sand good deeds she has always been with Sainath, the Perfect Master and Personification of all knowledge, the God-state. In that Bhajan, Baba called one Mr. Sreenivasamurthy, a devotee, and said, "You are suffering – is it not? Come tomorrow to Mandir, I shall get some *Udi* for you."

On the 5th day, as ordained by Baba, Bhajan was going on in Sai Mandir. In the middle, Syamala could see Baba smiling and standing on the steps in the front with a stick in his hand. To bring Him in, Syamala went up to the steps. She did not know what had happened afterwards. Baba possesses Syamala and put *Udi* in her hand. She then walked in to the hall slowly, gave some *Udi* to Sreenivasamurthy as intimated on the previous day, and applied *Udi* to the foreheads of all the devotees present there. The good fortune of all of us in the Mandir on that day is indescribable.

Mr. Srinivasamurthy, an asthma patient suffering for a long time says, he is now free from the trouble after using the *Udi* for three days. The two difficult cases – Paralysis and Asthma were easily cured by Baba's Udi. Thus His leelas are incredible, Infinite and beyond our limited understanding. Baba is an ocean of love and kindness and bears the sufferings of his devotees patiently as his own. He is the Divine effulgence that offers His hand of protection to the devotees with all the cheerfulness. He is the personification of Rama, Krishna, Siva, Maruthi and all other deities. Our two hands are not enough to raise in His worship. Our voices are *incapable of singing His praise adequately. Jai* Sadguru Sainath Maharaj ki jai

-Lingamsetti Sita Ravamma,
W/o Sri L.K. Rao,
H. 8, State Bank Colony, No. 2,
Vijayawada – 10
(*Shri Sai Leela*, January 1987)

108. BELIEVE IT OR NOT (1986)

I would like to narrate my experience to Sai brothers and sisters. Since I happened to be the eldest son of our family, the burden of responsibilities is on my shoulders. After getting my degree, I had made many friends. One of them Sri K. Radha Krishna asked me to pray to Sri Sai Baba for getting rid of my worries. From that day onwards, I have been worshipping Sri Sai with utmost devotion.

As necessary, I was appearing for different competitive examination including the ones by Banking Service Recruitment Board, Railways, etc., etc., I passed the bank test at last though, earlier. I had not succeeded in three attempts. After a few days, I received a letter from B.S.R.B., Hyderabad, asking me to appear before the interviewing Board at Vijayawada on March 11, 1986.

Before the receipt of this letter, I had decided to visit Shirdi on March 3, 1986. At this stage, I could not decide whether to put off my visit or to prepare for the interview and visit Shirdi afterwards. My friends advised me to cancel the visit at least for the time being. Even the members of my family suggested to me to first prepare for the interview. I was in a dilemma as to what to do. Then I approached my friend R. Radha Krishnaji, for his advice. He said that if I cast my burden on Sri. Sai, He would get the things done smoothly. I did as he said and fixed the 3rd March, 1986 as the date for my journey to Shirdi.

I reached Shirdi safely on March 4, 1986 and had the darshan of Sri Sai Baba. After staying for three days there, I came back to my place. Masulipatnam, on the 9th morning with bounteous blessings of the Master Sri Sai.

And now there was only one day for me to prepare for the interview to be held on March 11, 1986. I attended the interview and answered all the simple questions put to me. By the grace of Sai, I did my best in the interview. My friends and relatives did not expect my selection to come through as I had not prepared for it well enough. Just my luck! I was selected as a clerk in Andhra Bank and posted at Tanuku. That is how Sri Sai helped me to get an employment, I firmly believe.

If you earn the grace of Sai, you are reinforced with so much strength that you can carry out the most difficult tasks, successfully.

May Sai bless us all!

-J. Raghuram,
D/o. No. 5/5-4, Inugudurupet,
Machilipatnam (Andhra Pradesh)
(*Shri Sai Leela*, March 1988)

109. LORD SAI NATH: HIS OMNIPRESENCE AND OMNISCIENCE (1986)

My *Sadguru* Sai Sainath has prompted me to communicate this small but miraculous experience. This clearly proves His omnipresence and omniscience for the protection of His devotees as and when the same in needed.

During the middle of 1982 while I was in Ranchi, Baba arranged to offer me a very important and responsible assignment in New Delhi in the Ministry of Education, Government of India I was so much excited that I never thought that at our Ranchi establishment Baba resides and He became a part and parcel of our family. Right from morning coffee till night meals, Baba should be offered first and then we would partake. The house was being looked after by Baba as our Sadguru and guardian. So I left immediately for New Delhi, handing over the residence to someone to look after it. I did not even realize the consequences. In between I had to settle down in Pune for some years and was hardly interested about Shirdi Niwas, where our Baba resides.

Around middle of 1986, when I was in Delhi and my husband was in Manipur, suddenly the thought come to my mind about the Shirdi Niwas and I could foresee that it was now high time that I should be back to Ranchi and re-organize the abode of Baba. My husband met one Sai devotee in Pune who was also having his house at Ranchi and who was an ardent devotee of Baba. My husband narrated him the recent development related to our house at Ranchi that the care taker was about to grab the house and it was no longer an abode of Sainath. The Sai devotee assured my husband of all possible help. I was informed accordingly.

I came to Ranchi around middle of 1986 and stayed with the family for two days. I collected news that it would be extremely difficult to recover Shirdi Niwas without the help of any miracle or Baba's direct influence.

The house was in a most pitiable and wretched condition with the fencing removed, the articles of great importance missing and the amount of damage that was made by the care taker and his associated. My heart snubbed seeing the condition of Shirdi Niwas and I could realize the great blunder I had made by neglecting our Lord Sainath.

I came to Ranchi with two days at my disposal. The first day was entirely spent in collecting news about the house and the persons who could possibly help me in getting the same restored. The second or the last day ultimately appeared before me and I was absolutely shivering when I went on thinking about my forthcoming programme. Before starting for the work, I prayed to strength. I visited the Commissioner of Chotanagpur division, who fortunately was a lady and met District officials and all of them started helping me as if they all were instructed by someone to complete the work on that very day itself. Ultimately, with His help and guidance I could succeed in getting back my Shirdi Niwas after full five years. I could guess that Baba was all along looking after me and at my movements.

It was because of His desire that we have set up a Centre for Environmental and Developmental Research, an autonomous non-profit educational centre, to serve the grassroot community and organizations. We have been contemplating to construct a temple where His *Abhishek, Puja, Arati* etc., would be conducted every day as it is done in Delhi and Shirdi. I am absolutely hopeful and determined that this will also be granted by Him.

-Dr. Smt. Rama Chakravartti,
Shirdi Niwas 6/3,
University Colony,
Bariatu, Ranchi 834009 Bihar
(*Shri Sai Leela*, November 1988)

110. THE GRACE OF *SADGURU* (1986)

Sairam Saikalyan, the second son of my eldest nephew S.V. Ramakrishna Sai Sadan, Sri rama Nagar, Kakinada had suddenly went into coma on 9-12-86. He was admitted in a private nursing home at Kakinada. Five expert doctors were attending on him. The doctors declared that his condition was critical and advised that all the relations might be informed. As I was away at Visakhapatnam I was informed and telephone and was summoned to return to Kakinada immediately when I placed down the telephone receiver.

On my return the next day, I found Mr. Saikalyan in coma and the doctor told me that the condition of the patient was most critical and the end might call at any moment. But Sainath was informing me that Mr. Saikalyan would be O.K. Mr. Ramakrishna, my nephew caught hold of my hands and began crying like a child saying "Please pray to Sai Baba to come here to save my son". I told him "Sainath is standing beside the bed of Mr. Saikalyan and He has blessed him. So Saikalyan will be allright before Thursday."

On Tuesday slight movements were observed. In early hours of Wednesday, by 3 A.M. Mr. Saikalyan suddenly got up from his bed and began to walk. Everybody watching day and night for the four days were stunned. Mr. Saikalyan told everybody that a ray resembling a lightening approached him followed by Sri Sai Baba in pure white robes. Sri Sai Baba struck him with a small stick on his chest and told him that he would be allright.

-K.V. Ramana Murthy,
Opp. Bajee Fire Works,
Sriramanagar, Rajahmundry
(*Shri Sai Leela*, April, 1988)

111. BABA HELPS THOSE WHO CAN NOT HELP THEMSELVES (1988)

While posted to Indore as Pay & Accounts Officer, Central Excise & Customs, I had an occasion to go to Delhi on some official work. I stayed in a newly developed colony with my son, Anil Laroiya, who had recently shifted there. In the very first night, at about 12.30 p.m. I felt a severe stomach trouble. The patent medicines as available in the house were taken but to no avail. On the contrary, the pain increased and became rather unbearable. In that colony, to find a doctor, especially during those odd hours was a big problem. However, my son went out to call a doctor known to him who was practicing in his residence itself. He rang and rang his door bell but nobody responded. Finally, a boy servant turned up simply to tell that the doctor was not available. Anil, my son, returned home disappointed and was naturally very much perturbed. On the one hand I was crying with severe pains and on the other hand no doctor was available. Shifting to a hospital was also not possible as no transport could be available in that locality. All of us were thus absolutely helpless and entirely at the mercy of BABA and, if any case we had to wait for the morning. Meanwhile, the pain was increasing more and more. About an hour passed in his way.

Suddenly, somebody knocked at our doors. On opening the doors we found an old man who wanted to know about our problem. He told us that he was an old non-practicing doctor living in the locality and would like to examine me. My son agreed with some initial hesitation. The old man, after examining me, took out some tiny pills from his pocket and made them into 5-6 small packets and directed me to take them one by one after every half an hour. The first dose was given by him. Miraculously, the very first dose gave me much relief. The old man then went away and I took the medicines as per his directions. Needless to say that I was perfectly O.K. by the next morning.

My son went out to see the old man at the address given by him to thank him for his timely help at the most crucial hour but to his astonishment, there was no such house and no such old man.

No doubt, it was BABA who had come to help his helpless devotees.

-J.R. Laroiya,
A-475, Sector-19,
Noida 201 301
(*Shri Sai Leela*, July 1988)

112. A THURSDAY SAI MESSAGE (1988)

I had the privilege of having 'Darshan' of Lord Sainath in the Sai temple at New York when we went to the U.S.A. in 1984. I came across an unforgettable incident on a Thursday evening.

An elderly white-haired Gujarat-born Sai-brother was next to me. After the worship, I noticed that he put a small slip of paper, but no money in the *'Arathi'* plate. Just then, a gust of wind from the open window blew the paper on to the floor. Bending over to retrieve it, I could not help but see these words printed in large letter: "I will pray one hour a day".

I became curious and as such requested him to explain the message he had put in the *'Arathi'* plate. What he told me was quite moving.

His wife had died following a long and very expensive illness and he had been forced to sell his home to pay medical bills. Now he lived with his married daughter. "I am too old to work and I have no money" he said: "But I can pray. Lord Sainath has assured, "If you spread your palms with devotion before Me, I am with you day and night. So He is taking care of me."

His story brought to my mind Sai Baba's assurance "I always think of him who remembers Me" and reminded me once again that when we give sincerely what we have, no gift brought before Lord Sainath is too small or insignificant.

-Mrs. Usha Ranganathan
W/o Dr. R.J. Ranganathan
BELAVADI-577 146
Chikmagalur Dist. Karnataka
(*Shri Sai Leela*, March 1988)

113. "HOW LORD SAINATH PROMPTLY RESPONDED TO THE ARDENT PRAYER OF MY BROTHER-IN-LAW (1988)

My brother-in-law, who is an ardent Sai devotee, is very regular in observing Thursday as the day of fasting and abstinence, offering incense and camphor before the portrait of Lord Sai. On one occasion Lord Sai appeared in his dream and assured of His ever presence and continued protection of our devoted humble family. I used to send *Udi* and other Prasadams to my brother-in-law by post parcel. All of my close relatives thus became very faithful devotees of Lord Sai Nath.

In one of his recent letters, my brother-in-law, who is 86 years old, has narrated an interesting incident evidencing Baba's unseen presence with our family. His right eye had developed a severe ache during the forenoon leading to more painful throbbing sensation inside the skull. This was unbearable and my brother-in-law appealed to Lord Sai thus:

"Oh! Lord Sai, Why This New ailment to me while I have been praying for revieving me from the ailments already existing." Then soon the painwasover.

114. SHRI SAI KNOWS THE DESIRE OF HIS DEVOTEES (1986)

My wife D. Padnavathy and I are the devotee of Shri Sai since twenty years. We have visited Shirdi many times for having darshan of our Sadguru Shri Sai's "MAHASAMADHI" with our family members, and have had many experiences of His miracles during our visits.

On 2nd February, 1986 being the first day of the 12th Annual Gathering of Sai writers & poets my wife and myself participated in it. Before attending the gathering, we visited Gurusthan, Dwarakamai, Chavadi and Shri *'Sai Mahasamadhi' Mandir*. While entering 'Dwarakamai' a thought-provoking idea entered my mind, about the great Shri Sai's devotee Kushabhabhave, who had a prasad of Shri Sai direct from his mouth on Ekadashi Day.

At once an impressive idea entered my heart: "That why should not I have such prasad from Baba." Immediately I approached Baba's big size photo and touched the sweet lips of Baba and kept my fingers in my mouth. So as to satisfy myself that I too got Shri Sai's Prasad. The next day (Monday) when I entered Dwaraka Mai my wife I was embarrassed to see that "Peda was sticking to the lips of Baba. My enthusiasm and happiness had no bounds. Without noticing what was happening around with Shri Sai's Photo. As soon as I went near Shri Sai's Photo, the Peda fell on his lotus feet. I proceeded and look the Peda *(prasad)* with reverence. We both took the Prasad with reverence which was really a boon to us.

An another wonderful experience was also on this Annual gathering. A visitor came to us and asked us whether we had the keys either with me or my wife. We made vain search and lost our hopes. My wife could not even control her tears. She sat near Gurusthan and was moving in the crowd aimlessly. At once the same gentleman came near me and said "why are you worried for the keys! They are in the office safe custody." I ran to the office side of Gurusthan and found our keys. The officer gave the keys to me. Suddenly I told him to see the miracle of Shri Sai. Who else could have come as a gentleman except Shri Sai? Oh Lord Sai, how kind you are towards your devotees! What a wonderful Leela of Shri Sai".

-Shri D. Satyanarayana,
Shri Sai Bharat Watch Co., Road,
Hanamkonda P.O.,
Warangal 560 011 (A.P.)
(Shri Sai Leela, December, 1987)

115. BABA'S GRACE ON A FEMALE DEVOTEE (1996)

My grand father was a devotee of Sri Shirdi Sai Baba. As a child years I had first gone to Shirdi. During 1979-80 I had lots of problems in my married life. Then someone gave me a photo of Shirdi Sai Baba. One night I dreamt that I was travelling in the bus. An old man like Baba, wearing white torn clothes, touched my hand in the bus window and told me, "You don't worry daughter." He saw a something unique in his face. From that day, my problems started vanishing. Within a month I got a DDA flat. I got Baba's Pooja done as suggested by a visiting Sadhu. I had not much funds, but with Baba's blessings I was able to get a good pooja done in my flat. A three hour programme of bhajans was arranged by a music party. All I went well. Then I sold the DDA flat and purchased a Society flat. In 1994 I went to Shirdi and offered my gratitude to Baba there. In the train I fell it. A thin girl in jeans sitting on the front seat me shivering in fever; she told me, "I am a doctor. I have some medicines. I will give you some tablets right now." I took the tablets from her and was soon cured. I could return to Delhi from Shirdi without train reservation. All these were Baba's acts of grace on me.

-Mrs. Revathi Madhusudan Bhattathiripad,
Administrative Officer,
Jagjit Industries, Delhi

116. BABA SAVED LIVES IN HEADLONG CAR ACCIDENT (1996)

Once I and my son-in-law had gone to Punjab. While returning from there, we passed by Chandigarh. Before Chandigarh we stopped at a wayside tea shop. A Sadhu met us there. He asked me for some money for food which I readily gave him. He told me, "After some time you are likely to meet an accident with us. I told him, "I always start from my place after taking Baba's name. He will help us even if there is any problem on the way."

After driving some distance when we were about to reach Karnal, suddenly we saw a tractor rushing on the road from the opposite direction. Suddenly its right hand side wheel was broken. In an effort to stop the car frantically my foot wrongly pressed the hit the tractor. It tossed up in air thrice and fell down trice on the ground. I was laid down under the upturned car and my son-in-law was also hurt badly. By this time many people assembled there on the spot. They lifted the broken car and removed me and my son-in-law. The car got totally damaged, but I and my son-in-law did not get even a scratch on our bodies. The car was so much damaged that later on we got Rs. 75,000/- as damage claim from the Insurance Company. Sri Shirdi Sai Baba alone had saved us. We reached our house in Delhi safely by bus after this harrowing car accident.

Baba saved the life of my son-in-law at another time also some time back. An astrologer on reading his palm had told him that he would fall seriously ill after a few days and the chances of his survival were very less. After a few days, he had so much High Blood Pressure that a vein in his brain got burst and he suffered paralytic attack on one side of his body. We took him to the Apollo Hospital. There the doctors examined his and told us that the chances of his recovery were very remote, as he had very High Blood Pressure and a vein had burst and blood clot was there. I then decided to take him home and sought Sri Shirdi Baba's blessings for his recovery. Despite the strong protests of the doctors we brought him back to his house. We gave him Sai Baba's *udi* (Holy Ash) in water to drink twice a day for one month and thus his condition improved. Then we took him to a hospital. The doctors examined him and found that the blood clot had vanished and his paralysis had also cured without any medical treatment. This was all due to Sai Baba's grace alone. I strongly feel that by remembering Him, He definitely helps his devotees in distress."

Darya Ganj, New Delhi – 110002

117. SAI BABA RESCUED A DEVOTEE FROM DISTRESS (1994)

I know a Sai devotee for eight years, who is a frequent visitor to Sri Sai Spiritual Centre, Bangalore, He had met me many times to talk about Sri Sai.

Although we were meeting often, may be after 1993, I did not see him for quite some time. When I did meet him on the road. I enquired about his health as he looked very pale and run down. He told me that he had been suspended by his office a year back on some false allegations and no enquiry had been conducted till them. He also added that he had a 88 year old mother, wife and a daughter of marriageable age and that he was struggling for existence.

I told him: "Have patience. Sai is always with you to help you. He is more concerned about you than you are about your family. Have firm faith in Him." He did not seem be convinced and continued to look dejected.

Meanwhile, in spite of his repeated representations, his office never cared to conduct an enquiry even after two years. I had thought he might not meet me again. Surprising, he turned up one day to convey the information that he was able to get his daughter married with his brother's help. However, Sai was not helpful, he remarked in his reinstatement.

I told him that it was only by Sai's grace that he could get his daughter married in the midst of his hardships and in the same way his other problem would also be solved by Baba. Only he should wait patiently for His help. He countered by saying that he had no faith in God and it had become a hand-to-mouth existence for him and that he had decided to end his life. I told him it was unwise to take such a sinful decision, and reminded him about Sai's words that by suicide one's problems would not get solved as one had to be reborn again to suffer hardship. I also gave him Sai *udhi*, suggesting his chanting Sri Sai Ashtothra daily after bath, taking a little *udhi* mixed in water as Sai 'threertha'.

Meanwhile, I came to know that his benefactor, his brother, suddenly passed away.

In July, 1996, a miracle happened. The devotee came to tell me that through a well-wisher, he had approached an M.P. who, after listening to his pathetic condition, promised to take up his case with the Minister concerned. Within a week, he came back again to inform me that the M.P. had asked him to meet the Minister personally. But he could meet the Minister after an unsuccessful attempt, a week later. When he met the Minister, the later told him that he had studied his case file and as he had no time to spare, he should answer 'yes' or 'no' the following questions:

A: Have you misappropriate Government money? B: Have you ever misbehaved with your superiors? C: Have you stolen anything from the office?

The devotee answered 'no' to the queries. When the Minister asked him how he could believe him. The devotee answered politely: "Sir, in the name of Guru, Shirdi Sai Baba, I can swear that I am telling you the truth only. I am undergoing great hardships. Sir, believe me, my wife and aged mother have no food to eat and I am almost begging from my well-wishers. However, permit me to say that I cannot satisfy human beings, but, if you take me to Shirdi, my *Gurusthan*, there I will swear at the Samadhi of my Sadguru that I am speaking the truth only and nothing but the truth. Believe me Sir, I have sent back my pregnant daughter to her in-laws, as I cannot attend to he (Puttanna) told me: "I was not myself when I was talking to the Minister. I could see the Minister's eyes welling up with tears. Nay, I was seeing Baba Him-self in the guise of the Minister, showering His grace on His down-trodden devotee."

On hearing me, the Minister without any further words, noted on the case file: "Reinstate and report atonce."

Within a week, he got a letter from his office asking him to report for duty immediately. Later, he came to convey the joyous news, but was unable as he was overwhelmed by emotion. With tears rolling down his cheeks, he prostrated before Sai Baba's photo and then getting up slowly cried out loudly: Sai, Sai, Sai... for a while, Regaining his composure, he whispered to me: "Through Sai's ever-merciful grace. I have reported for duty yesterday. Sai is really great."

This narration is a very recent saga of a humble devotee, who is his own way responded faith in the Loka Guru, Sai, who under any conditions, will not let down his devotees. Sai He is ever with us. Only when we look at Him, He will look at us. To get at Him, as Sai Himself has said, no elaborate worship is required. Simply uttering His sweet name "Sai" or chanting *"Om Sai Sri Sai Jaya Jaya Sai"*. One is sure to cross the ocean of *samsara* and reunite with Him. So, wherever you may be, in whatever condition you be, remember Sai, Sai and Sai alone and be happy.

Sri Putanna

(Reproduced from: *Sai Padananda*)

(Bangalore) Sri Sai Spiritual Centre, Bangalore

Courtesy: Editor

118. HOW SAI NATH PROTECTS HELPS US

Generally people look for big events to occur wherein they feel divine had of God is at work, I have experienced that Baba guards His wards all the time. His watchful eyes ever look to the worries, troubles and difficulties of His children.

I daily go for a morning walk at about 6 A.M. in the nearby park. As usual I had just gone a few steps ahead that abruptly three full-sized alsation dogs rushed out of the nearby 'Kothi' and surrounded me. They howled in a terrific voice. In normal course I should have tried to run but instead of doing so I stood firm by and the only sound that come out of me was 'NO-NO'. The dog instead of charging me just kept on howling. Their master came out of the house and called them back. I got into argument with him that he was a highly irresponsible person: instead of feeling sorry he started defending himself. He was off his head, foul smell was coming, out of his mouth, he appeared still under effect of drinks. I told him that his animals were more sensible than him and I would report the matter to the police. Who saved me? In no time I would have been produced to pieces Lord Sai of course, otherwise this R.S. Sharma would have been no more in this world today.

Once Electricity failed. It was summer season's The electrician was called. Just after repairs, he put, the main switch on. There was a cry instantaneously, "fire-fire". the electrical put the main switch off I rushed into the side room. The fridge in the room had caught sparks. The room was dark, full of smoke. But the fire had extinguished. Who had saved the three storeyed building and the inmates from being reduced to ash? Lord Sai no doubt.

In the year 1956 I had gone to Amritsar with Shri G.L. Nanda then Cabinet Minister for Planning. I was working with him. Shri Nanda had gone to Khalsa College in Amritsar to address a large gathering I had accompanied him. I went in the big hall & sat with other persons there. Shri Nanda called me. I was asked to go to the Camp and speak on phone to Secretary, Planning Commission at New Delhi in connection with an office matter. In the morning after saying my prayers I discovered I had dropped the Home Minister's Identity Card. I knew I had lost it for all times. Just then a thought passed my mind, "Baba if I get this card now, I will be further convinced you are really wonderful." Soon a colleague of mine asked me to accompany him to the exhibition ground to deliver Five Year Plan Volumes there Just when on arrived, at the Exhibition ground and came out of the car a young man came near me and said "You are Mr. Sharma. This is your card, your photograph is these? You had dropped it in the Hall. I was sitting near you I picked it. I thought I shall give it to you, when you came back, but you never come back. "Yes this was my card. Lord Sai has His own ways of winning over peoples hearts.

-R.S. Sharma Secretary,
Sai Bhakta Samaj,
Editor, *Sai Kripa*, New Delhi

119. A SAI-RENDEZVOUS! (1988)

"Unless there is some relationship or connection nobody goes anywhere."

The Ootty bus bumped along, shivering in the cold of a Nilgiris winter. I sat dejectedly near the exit door, watching the passengers get off one; by now only the driver and two other persons were left, one near the front and the other at the very back.

I stared unseemingly out of the window, watching the buildings and people flit past like pages in a familiar, dusty book. The Nilgiris, we had been here for almost a year now and things were not going as expected. So many people, so many dreams, and everyone fighting to get the top. Did I really have it in me? Sometimes the ever-green estates seemed huge, terrifying people eating, lonely. Goals that had been clear when we came here seemed to be falling apart.

The old man at the front of the bus was shivering in the cold, and the woman at the back was staring out of the window in a distracted way. Oh, well…we all have our problems, I thought.

We had our own problems; problems of setting down, the change from Karnataka to Tamil Nadu, kids had to learn Tamil. Somehow I had a chunk of despair in the pit of my stomach. The thought of my kids struggling through their studies made the pain in my stomach worse.

The bus lurched to a stop at a red light. I glanced at the woman sitting on the rear seat. She was tall, well-dressed, middle-aged and intelligent-looking, yet there was something about her…I guardedly stole another glance. She turned her face and the look of naked pain in her eyes shot through me with the force of a physical punch, hitting me in the stomach, right where it hurt.

I looked away, feeling I had seen something forbidden, something too private.

Then it came over me, strong and appealing, the urge to go and sit beside her. It was Lord Sainath's command to me.

I can not go and sit beside a stranger in an empty bus, I reasoned. She will think I am out of my mind.

Again Lord Sainath's urge came, stronger and more irresistible; "Go and sit beside her. Show her that you identify with her."

I got up, went to the back of the bus and sat next to her.

"Excuse me" I said, to my surprise, "but I wanted to come over and sit with you. You seem to be so sad".

She turned and looked me full into the face, her dark eyes wide with astonishment. Then she covered her face with her hand and began to cry quietly.

I felt her pain welling up in me and spilling out of my eyes. Gently, I took her hand and we sat without a word, tears spilling down both of our faces on to our clasped hands.

"I just wanted to tell you that it is going to be all right" I began, "I don't know what the problem is, and you don't need to tell me, but it is going to be all right".

She was shaking her head.

"I can't believe this" she said, "I have never had anything like this happening to me in my life."

I put my other arm around the back of the seat and gripped her shoulders in a sisterly hug. She was so much like me, I had to strengthen her, or in some way we would all be weaker.

"It's Okay" I said, "You have a lot of strength inside you."

"No" she said miserably, "I don't have any strength."

"Yes" I said, "it is there inside you...and God is with you."

She looked at me, half-smiling, half-crying.

"This is incredible", she said, "I have never felt so horribly shattered and alone in all my life...and you, a perfect stranger I can't believe this is happening to me. Who are you? Would you give me yhour name and address?"

I fumbled for a pen and paper, and in my purse found a copy of the booklet. "THUS SPARE SAI BABA". Just a few days earlier, my husband, Dr. Vijayakumar had received 25 copies of the booklet "THUS SPARE SAI BABA" from Sai-uncle S. Krishna Murthy of Shirdi Sai Bhakta Samajam, 4-3-111, 4th Cross, Ramannapet, Guntur (Andhra Pradesh). I had kept a copy of this booklet and since I could not get a paper, I wrote my name and address on this booklet and gave it to her, realizing how strange a real name and address looked in the middle of an experience like this. She put this booklet in her purse and glanced out of the bus window.

"Oh, my goodness" she said, "I am going to miss my stop, Bless you, I will never forget this as long as I live. I will write to you."

She bid me good-bye, and was off the bus, I sat with my head in an absolute whirl until I realized it was my stop and got off.

The pavement seemed carpeted under my feet, and a curious sense of discovery raced through me. What had I said to that woman! "It is going to be all-right. You have a lot of strength down inside you and God is with you." Had I said that, or had she said it to me?

Somehow in my busy schedule I forgot this incident. Three days later I had a letter with an unfamiliar name and address. I had not asked her name, allowing her to remain anonymous if she wanted to, but there it was, in a bold clear script. I opened the envelope slowly, feeling I was treading on hallowed ground.

"Dear friend: This was a holy experience for me. Today when you came and sat beside me."

The rest of the letter blurred in front of me, a jumble of words explaining a maze of human suffering. Eagerly my eyes went back to the first line – a holy experience. That was what it had been for me as well; and unexpected moment when two human beings had dared to fully accept each other and found themselves face to face with God.

She was happy to be introduced to Sai Baba through the small booklet "THUS SPARE SAI BABA". She wanted to read more about Sai and had sought information about Him. She had in particular liked Sai Maharaj's advice. "Be calm and quiet. *Uge Muge Chup Karo.* Everything will come to you by His will. God is the Master. *Allah Malik.*"

I folded the letter reventially and thanked Lord Sainath for this unique experience. After this experience whenever I travel in a bus, I sit surrounded by a cloud of awe, wondering what is inside each of those faces staring impassively into space, absorbed in worlds within worlds, and within each of them the breath of the Eternal – allmightly Lord Sainath.

As I pen these lines, Sainath is close behind my thoughts. The new position and place that Sainath has brought us! We could take it. And whatever was good to do here, I had it in me to do I was not alone.

-Mrs. Seetha Vijay Kumar
W/o Dr. G.R. Vijay Kumar,
Kil-Kotagiri Estate
Kil-Kotagiri 643 216
Nilgiris, Tamil Nadu

120. SAI, THE GUARDIAN (1988)

Whenever my husband had t be away overnight on a business trip, I used to be nervous about staying in the house with only our two small children for company.

Then came the time when we were stationed at Guntur and my husband was on a week-long trip. Once again I dreaded the nights ahead until the afternoon our six-year old Karthik showed me crayon drawing he had made in the school, for my inspection. Yes, it had the right shape. It really did look like our house. But what was that strange object on the top?

"It is very nice", I complimented him, "You did a good job. But what is this?" I pointed to the odd, man-like thing perched on the roof.

Looking at me as if he thought me a little stupid, he causally answered, "Why, Mummy, don't you know? That is Sai Baba taking care of us."

'Oh, Lord Sainath.' I thought: "Thank you for the faith of this little child in you." Karthik knew and remembered and I had forgotten, that Lord Sainath had promised: 'Why fear when I am here'.

That evening, as I tucked the picture away with Karthik's other school mentors, my fear of the dark night was tucked away too-buried forever.

-Mrs. Niveditha Kishore,
W/o Sri B. Krishna Kishore,
10-5-63/5/A, Sri Rama Nagar Colony,
Masab Tank, Hyderabad 500 028
(*Shri Sai Leela*, January, 1988)

121. BABA'S ANSWER TO MY PRAYER (1988)

I am a humble devote of Sri Sai Baba. I was travelling from Miami (USA) to Tokyo (Japan). The flight from Miami reached Los Angeles (USA) late by nearly 90 minutes. So I missed the connecting flight at Los Angeless. I was in a fix. So I prayed to Sai to help me. I had written to a friend in Japan to meet me at Tokyo airport, who had to travel nearly 800 kms. I wrote to him that I would be travelling by that flight which I missed. So I thought I would face difficulties if my friend was not there. I approached the airlines through which I was booked, and requested them to put me in some flight on that day so that I could reach Tokyo. They pleaded inability and asked me to try with one flight which was about to leave. I rushed to that gate and requested the lady at the gate to help me. She was about to close the doors. She anyway asked me to go in without formalities and occupy any vacant seat. I went in and sat down in a vacant seat. I was praying to Sai to keep my friend in the airport at Tokyo, so that I might not have any problem. I kissed the Sai Baba ring on my finger and prayed for a few minutes. When I landed at Tokyo airport and went out I saw my friend waiting though he need not have waited for more than two hours, after my scheduled flight reached Tokyo. If he had not been there I would have had many problems.

So it was Sri Sai who answered my prayer and helped me. This is Sai's way of helping his devotees.

-Prof. P. Varadaraju,
73/1, Guest House Rd.,
Nazarbad, Mysore
(*Shri Sai Leela*, September, 1988)

122. SAI-LOVE FOR THE DEVOTEES (1988)

Once after I had a *darshan* at *Samadhi Mandir* in Shirdi, I completely forgot to take the *prasad* offered by the *pujari*. It came to my notice only afterwards, I had sat with folded hands and concentrating on the *Murthi* of Sri Sai. In my heart of hearts, I prayed to Sai to forgive me, for not taking the prasad as there was a long queue for taking the darshan of Lord Sainath. But to my utter surprise an old lady around 80 years of age came and tapped my shoulder and said "brother, have some prasad in Marathi. To my entire satisfaction, tears rolled down my eyes and I thanked Lord Sainath for an on the spot miracle.

During one of my visits to Shirdi, I had a new motorcycle brought for the blessing of Shri Sainath. After having his *darshan* I wanted a good *mala* flower-garland to be placed on the motorcycle. I asked the Pujari to give me one nice garland, but he gave me a very small garland, with hardly any flowers. I was a little disappointed, since I wanted a big garland. After having my *darshan* at Samadhi Mandir and Dwarkamai, I went near the motorcycle to put the garland which Pujari had given me.

But here Sai devotees, to my utter surprise a beautiful garland of yellow marigold and white flowers was already, there on my motorcycle. I inquired with the persons standing next to the motorcycle if it belonged to them. But they all refused. I was so much pleased that I again remembered Baba and prayed to Him for fulfilling my wish. Hence by these two experiences. I think that if a person has implicit faith and patience then Baba can do miracles even today.

I bow to the Lotus feet of Sai.

Om Sai Sri Sai Jai Jai Sai.

-R.N. Unwalla,
Hendripada, Kulgaon,
Badlapur, Dist.-Thane
(*Shri Sai Leela*, April, 1988)

123. SRI SAI *LEELA* (1988)

I am Sai Bhaktha for the last 14 years. I come across many miracles of Sai Baba who is always with his devotees and comes for help as and when are pray whole-heartedly. I have been to Shirdi many times and got the blessing of Lord Sai. There are so many events when my Lord Sai helped me and guided me on the right path.

It was the morning of Thursday, the 11th June '88. I had to offer something to some poor money or sweet meat etc. in memory of my descesed wife. Since I was quite new in Bombay and was thinking over where to find out a deserving person on that particular day. As usual I was on morning walk and my mind was only thinking about this problem, in the meantime I saw one sadhu who was coming from the opposite side and as he came near to me I gave him Rs. 10/- which he gladly accepted I told him for which reason the money was given to him and further he asked me how many sons I had. I told him, "Only one. He blessed me saying Your son will look after you nicely in your old age." Though I had got more money in my hand but he did not ask any more money from me and within no time he disappeared. I have never come across any sadhu on this road, where daily I go for morning walk. It was definitely Sai Baba who had solved even my minor problem.

How lucky I am that BABA appeared physically on Thursday early morning.

JAI GURU DATTA SAI

-Lieut Devi Sharan Kohli (Retd.)
K-51/206, Ekasar Road,
Yoginagar, Borivli (W)
Bombay 400 092
(<i>Shri Sai Leela</i>, Nov., 1988)</div>

124. BABA'S LOVING AND BENEVOLENT SUPERVISION (1988)

I was travelling in the first class compartment of a train from Delhi to Jodhpur, where I had to change to another train bound for Barmer. Strangely, I was the lone occupant of a four berth compartment and was therefore in a very carefree and relaxed mood. The train left Delhi at 10 p.m. and soon I spread my bed with a clean white bed sheet and myself changed into glistening white Kurta and pyjama. I lied down on the bed and started reading *"Sri Sai Sat-Charita"* under the bedlamp having switched off all other lights of the compartment. It must have been after an hour or so that I dozed off with the open book on my chest. A1 4 a.m. during my sleep I saw Sai Baba appear before me and He told me that I had mad e serious mistake in not handing over the keys of the office almirah to my assistant Director, totally forgetting that an important meeting was fixed for a date on which I would be out on tour, and that all the files and connected samples of products etc. were lying in that particular almirah. Sri Sai also reminded me that the keys were lying in my portfolio bag, which in turn was kept in my almirah at home. On hearing this from Baba, I became totally nervous, but immediately He advised not to panic, but to send a telegram to my son from Jodhpur telegraph office, which He alone told me was just outside the gate of the Railway Station, to the effect that he (my son) should take the keys and hand them over to the particular officer whose name I was to mention in the telegram, for doing the needful. After guiding me fully, Sri Sai disappeared from my vision, and I woke up from my slumber. The first thing I did was to see my watch, it was exactly 4 a.m. and then I looked around to make sure where was I and what had happened I could understand, it was not a mere dream but something more real and concrete. The implications were so profound that it could certainly not be a mere dream but something different. I could soon understand and to this day I believe that our Lord Sai Sai did appear before me to help me out of a predictment which, but for His help and guidance, would have had serious repercussions on my career as a senior Government officer. Needless to say, I followed His advice meticulously and proceeded on my journey as planned. Sri Sai Baba has said that He will continue to exercise benevolent and loving supervision over the actions of His devotees and this incident is just one of the innumerable proofs, if any proof is needed at all, for the truth of His promises.

This indeed was my very first experience of Sri Sai's abundant love and *Kripa*, but certainly not the last. I and my family members continue to get His help at every step and miracles do happen whenever we are in any trouble or grief, to give us solace and peace.

-S.B. Mathur
157, Sector XII
R.K. Puram, New Delhi – 110 022

126. BABA – SOLVER OF PROBLEMS" (1988)

When I got married I was serving at a place about 900 kms. away from the place my husband was working. I had no intention of resigning from the job on marriage and I had to wait till I got a transfer to my husband's place of work.

I applied for the request transfer and to my surprise, within a fort night's time I got the transfer orders to my place of choice. My joy was very much short-lived because the management was not prepared to relive me without the substitute joining the place, where I was swerving. So I went on leave for nearly two months. Meanwhile, I tried my best to get an early relief through many sources and channels but of no use. So I lost all hopes of early relief and was depressed to such an extent that I lost interest in everything. I was questioning Baba, where I had gone wrong in my prayers to Him. I thought all my sufferings were falling on the deaf ears of Sai Baba. Then I came to realize that it was a testing time for me in the life.

With a heavy heart, I returned to the place of work after the leave and again pleaded with the management to relieve me in view of the problems I was facing. This fell on the deaf ears of the management. So I finally decided to go on loss of pay leave as the landlord of the house where I was staying had asked me to vacate the house in view of his son's marriage. Now I had no other alternative but to go on indefinite leave till the substitute joined. Then I questioned Baba "If you are really great then see that I am relieved from the place without a substitute".

Just a day after this, the management announced that I was going to be relieved without a substitute. My heart overflowed with a million thanks to the Baba who had heard my agonized cry and thus proved to be the "Solver of solutions".

-A Devotee
(*Shri Sai Leela*, April 1986)

127. An American woman took a photo of the statue of Sri Shirdi Sai Babaat his *Samadhi Mandir* in Shirdi in March 1999, but in place of the face of theBaba's statue, his real image as Shirdi Sai Baba came in the print. She gave copies of this photo to the principal of Sai Baba school, Bamanpalli, near Puttaparthi (Andhra Pradesh), who is an ardent Shirdi Sai devotee. He gave it to Mrs. MariaAragoues, an ardent devotee of Sri Shirdi Sai Baba from Spain (who is a Spanishpublisher of books on Shirdi Sai Baba: Ed. I'Ermita, *Travessera De Deit*, 62,

Barcelona, 08024, Spain) in September 1999. Mrs. Maria Aragoues, who hastranslated my book into Spanish '*Sri Shirdi Sai Baba: The Universal Master*', senta photo copy that rare and minaculous photo to me, in mid-November, 1999.

-S.P.Ruhela

128. An old Zorastrian Mr. Dinshaw J. Buxey, who introducing himself as a close acquaintance of Yogi M.K. Spencer and his cousin brother Homi S. Spencer's family in Mumbay had sent the following Sai miracles known to him for my information and publication.:

H.S. Spencer's father was captain of Parsi cricket team in 1900. Here is a Sai miracle of ashes in Bandra (Bombay) where also Spencer lived. I used to visit (his) house during 1955-1980.

There was a burnt photo of Sai. I could never ask. We were too busy with his Zoroastrian books, which have not seen the light of day. Someone wrote from Europe, books are with Brill, you can't do better than that. The books went to 100 Universities, but Zoroastrian centres have not heard of it. Now he was ill. I was on his bed, got on opportunity to ask his most devoted sister Putlibai, and this is the story she told me.

I will try to put it in her own words—may Sai help me:"A friend brought the photo. I never believed, but kept it. I heard about ashes . . . and then . . .(I interrupted—when did the photo get burnt? How?—and why kept?)"I am coming to it, dear boy . . . have patience . . ." she said.

"We had a big shepherd dog . . . devoted to us . . . year 1946 or 1948 (I don't remember exact year she said) . . ." he was dying on this very bed in pain. I was touching him, patting him—my eyes fell on photo . . . small lamp beneath . . ." I said, can you, Sai Baba, do something? The light shot up . . . photo caught fire . . . I screamed. I left dog, put out flames with bare hands (now ashes on her hands) dog whined as she left him. She rushed did not think even as she petted him . . . that Sai ashes are on her hand . . . and now on dog . . . pain left . . . dog passed away peacefully. and Homi, on other bed, in pain . . . echoed Meher Baba's words (I saw him as a child in 1937 at Sunderbai hall took stool, put on stage-crossed legs-looked at him as evotees greated him, he'd give me a wink)—"You cannoi understand Ari Shirsi Sai Baba's greatness.

- Dinshaw J. Buxey., Mumbai

129. Sai Baba's second miracle in my life

I am not a liar. Ever since, as child, I read Sri Ramakrishna, that truth, is our support—I have clung to it. I was cheated in business, (perhaps past *Karma*, perhaps not knowing how to do business—*Karmic* reaction). I had no money for plumber, and removing 100 times, up and down, toilet marble heavy top-got hernia. Dr. Bhamgara of NatureCure Institute, Marine Drive (now closed) diagnosed it. Having no money, Iwant to Charak Clinic where Dr. Telang confirmed it operation means death. I phoned to my ex-office, Dr. Beck & Co. Ltd. (a Mahindra and Mahindra concern then, later bought by BASF group, now part of multinational Schenectady group of USA), which I helped started. The operator Ludi couldnot believe her ears, that it was me. (I had found a brilliant chemist, and competed with them—with disastrous financial results, as I was told I have tostudy character in the business partner or boss, not chemistry; I had to look upthe word, "character" in son's dictionary).I heard her say, "Bane, Buxey on line." "Impossible". I heard him say. "I tellyou it is he . . ." Pause . . . silence . . . "yes, sir." timid voice replied. I gave him straight: "Bane, take me to Shirdi". Please Silence. Perhaps he was being tactful. I was no longer his boss, and I was asking forthe company car—my old car. "Sir" he said, "you are in no position to travel", and then knowing my attachment to him (since childhood) he gave it to mestraight: "Pray mentally." I put phone down. Later, I went to Dr. Kriplani downstairs. "Who told you you hadhernia? . . ." To cross-check—I went to Dr. Telang and asked him "How you canmake such a mistake . . . ?" "I never do . . ." "Take out your clothes . . . Who cured?" He sereamed, "This is NOT the condition in which you came." I breathed a sigh of relief and one word, Thanks. It was Sai Baba's miracle that I was cured at that time.

- Dinshaw J. Buxey., Mumbai

130. Miraclous acts of Sri Shirdi in my life (S.P.Ruhels)

(1) Sri Shidi Sai Baba saved my life in 1997:

On 28th February 1997, I felt great pain in my chest from midnight to 6 A.M. I intensely prayed to Sri Shirdi Sai Baba, "Baba, kindly save my life as I have still several pressing family responsibilities to discharge and I wish to write some more books on You." I took Baba's Holy *udi* and sipped water many times and slept at 6 A,M. I got up after four hours feeling very weak. After some time my daughter-in-law Saryu from her house in Sector 16 in the same citty rang me. I told her of my chest pain. She said that it could be heart problem and so I must get it checked at once. She asked me to reach Sarvodaya Hospital atonce nd meet ou fsmily doctor Rskesh Gupta. She assured me that she would be reaching there soon to see me. I at once drove to the hospital. The doctor examied me and said that I had suffered two heart attacks in the night, so I must immediately be shifted to Sun Flag Hospital for cardioogical treatmnt. I was admiited there and after sometime I was taken to Escorts Heart Institure, New Delhi for Angiography. The doctor there did the Angiograpghy and asked me to come after a weekfor examination. I was very afraid of heart operation. I prayed to Sai Baba that I should not be operarted yoon as I did not have money foroperation id the doctorwould prescribe for meonthe next date. I was worried thaty I mighh die during operation leaving my family in helpless condition. On the next date I went to the docor and reuested him not to suggestfor heart operatiionas far as possible. The doctor examined my Angiography film again and its report very carefully and then reassuringly said, "Heart operation is not done in all cases. Do not worry; you need not undergo heart operation. I am prescribing certain medicines, dietary precautions and daily walk for you. Follow this course. You will be O.K. in some months." By these words of the doctor, I was greatlyrelieved and felt indebted to Shirdi Sai Baba for this miracle and then I solemnlypromised to Him in my heart that I would like to devote the remaining years of my life in His service by writing and editing books on Sai Baba in the rest of my life. Since tren I have been doing so.

131. I unexpectedly met an unknown spiritualist Swami H.D Lakshmanaof Bangalore in an evening of July 1992 in the second class compartment of K.K. Express train, in which I was traveling to ach Puttaparthi—Sri Sathya SaiBaba's famous *ashram*. Swami Lakshmana boarded it from Manmad and entered the same bogey and sat on the seat just near me. He was then returning from his pilgrimage to Shirdi with a small band of his close devotees to his home town Bangalore. After silently watching me for some hours he started conversin with me. In course of our conversation he suddenly closed his eyes for a few minutes and then opeing them he said to intuitively in a low voice: "Just now I have got the divine intuition that you are the blessed son of Saraswati— the Goddess of Learning. You are presently thinking of writing a book on Sri Shirdi Sai Baba. In it you should highlight Sri Shirdi Baba's unique status and role as the'Universal Master.' which aspect has not been projected by most of the writers on him so far. *Sadguru* Sai Baba's wishes so and this is his divine assignmentfor you. Would you accept it with pleasure?" I readily accepted it with great pleasure. Then he said to me," Please meet me at my home-cum-temple of Banashankari Devi (Goddess Parvati—the Consort of Lord Shiva) in Bangalore..

My address is:

Aadi Shankara and Dattatreya Adhyathmik Bhakti Mandali,

No.52," Sri Manjunatha Degula".

14th "B' Main Road, 2nd Stage, 2nd Phase,

(Behind Nandini Theatre) West of Chord Road,

Mahalakshmipura, Bangalore—5000860)

When you will be coming to Bangalore from Puttaparthi after some dayson your return journey to New Delhi in order to take the K.K. Express from Bangalore Jn, please come my place and stay with me for the night. I shall then perform special worship of Goddess Banashankari Devi for obtaining her blessings on you for the successful completion of this new project of writing this book. Then you should return to your place and there you should preparethe tentative Table of Contents and then bring it to Shirdi on the mutuallyagreed auspicious day in the next month (August}. I would reach there and we both shall together pray at the Sai Baba's *Gurusthan* and Sai *Samadhi Mandir* to seek Sai Baba's blessings on your book project."

Thus I travelled to Bangalore and reached Swami Lakshmana's place—in the noon of 24thJuly. he was very glad to receive me. In course of our talks, he casually mentioned about a great local woman *sanyasin* saint Shivmma Thayee who was then 102 year old and was then known to be the only surviving ardent and oldest devotee of Shirdi Sai Baba. She had been privileged to see Sai Baba as early as in 1906 when she was only 15 year old. She had visited Shirdi many times till 1917 i.e., one year before He shed His mortal coil. He had given her the new name Shivamma Thayee when she had been left alone and deeply frustrated by great tragedies in her life—her husband had deserted her due to her being highly spiritual and unworldly and he soon remarried, and then her only adult son along with his wife and son unfortunately died in motor cycle accident and thus she was rendered totally homeless and helpless. In 1917 Sai Baba instructed her to go and settle downin Banalore. For many years she was just homeless with no acquaintance with any body, confined to a deserted corner spot in Bangalore and survived on begging alms till in 1944 one pious soul donated his surplus cremation ground land to her and built for her a modest "Sai Baba *Ashram*' in Roopen Agraham, Madiwala locality in Bangalore.

Hearing this, I became very impatient to go to meet her immediately and so Lakshamana Swami asked one of his devotees to take me on his motor cycle to meet her in the afternoon before 5 P.M. to seek her blessings for the successof the project of writing the book *"Sri Shirdi Sai Baba: The Universal Master"*. I was greatly impressed and fascinated by her her highly advanced age andspirituality and simplicity. I wished to interview her and for that she asked me to come next day at 10 A.M. She very graciously allowed me to interview her indepth for over four hours. Swami Lakshman and two local Tamil devotees, who were luckily present there, acted as Tamil interpreters. She spoke her mothertongue Tamil fluently and they translated her narrations into English for me and my queries in English into Tamil for her to reply. Thus I was privileged to write and bring out the book *'My Life with Sri Shirdi Sai Baba—Thrilling memories of Shivamma Thayee"* in 1992. It has been translated and published in Japanese, Hindi and Tamil languages subsequently and the glory of Shirdi Sai Baba Shivamma Thayee has been spread world wide. so I was greatly impressed and fascinated by her her highly advanced age and spirituality and simplicity. I wished to interview her and for that she asked meto come next day at 10 A.M. She very graciously allowed me to interview her in depth for over four hours. Swami Lakshman and two local Tamil devotees, who were luckily present there, acted as Tamil interpreters. She spoke her mothertongue Tamil fluently, they ranslated her narrations into English for me and my queries in English into Tamil for her to reply. Thus I was privileged to writeand bring out the book *'My Life with Sri Shirdi Sai Baba—Thrilling memoriesof Shivamma Thayee"* in 1992. It has been ranslated and published in Japanese, Hindi and Tamil languages subsequently and the glory of Shirdi Sai Baba Shivamma Thayee has spread world wide. As bessed by her, I was able to write my book *'Sri Shirdi SaiBaba: The Universal Master"* and gebyer t it published in 1995 and republished in2007 by another publisher and it has been selling all over the world Thus by Sai Baba's miraculous grace I was privileged to write these two importent books in1994-95.

132. On 27th July, 1995 I received a letter dated from an unknown Saidevotee M.R. Raghunathen, a retired clerk from the Madras informing me thathe had discovered Shirdi Sai Baba's rare horoscope from the renowned over 2000years old palm leaf *naadi* book of fure predictions in the lives of individuals bythe ancient sage Agastya, which was in the possession of Dr Karunakaran, *Naadi* Astrologer of Sughar Agastyar Naadi yothida Nilayam, 14, Mannar (Reddy) Street, T. Nagar, Madras. That rare ancient *naadi* revealed that his (Sai Baba's) mother Devagiriamma had re-incarnated as Tamil Brahmin lady Seethamma, then popularly known as Baba Patti (84 year old) and Sai Baba's

elder sisterBalwant Bai had slso incarnated as P.Rajeswari (54 year old) ass the onlydaughter of Baba Patti, who was married but childless and they both were thenliving in Rajeswari's Rajeswari's retired husband A.V.Padnabhan's House Nno.22, III Trust Cross Street, Mandavallikam, Madras—600026. This horoscope written by Sage Agastya thousands of year back also reveaedthat Raghunathan had been Shirdi Sai Baba's elder brother Ambadass in hispast birth. It further showed that Sai Baba was born on Thursday, the 27thSeptember, 1838 in the Tamil year of *Vilabhi, Vikram samvat* 1895, in the Tamilmonth of *Pruattassi*, His Rasi was *Dhanus* (Sagittarius) at 12.05 and 25 secondsin the noon of that day. His parents were Ganga Bhavadia and Devagiriammaof Pathri village. The Horoscope of Sri Shirdi Baba has been given in an earlierchapter of this book. Shri Raghunath sent me these thrilling highlights of Sai Baba's horoscopeand urged me to travel to Madras to personally verify these rare fact by meetingthe famous *naadi* astrologer Jyothda Ratna Dr.Karunakaran and them—Baba Patty and Rajeswari, if I wanted to do so as an earnest researcher and committed writer on Sai Baba. His letter was very motivating to me as I was really eagerto collect these rare facts which were thereto unknown to the Sai devotees all over the world; they are still not known to over 99% Sai devotees. I soon reached Madras and met Raghunath and the naadi reade Dr,Karunakatran andthen interviewed Baba Patti and her daughter Rajeswari at their house on 27t hNovember, 1995. Later on i wrote a small pocket size beautifully illustratedbook '*Shirdi Sai Baba's Moter and her Re—incarnation*' reporting the fullinterview, which was lpublished in 1998 by Aravali International (P) Ltd, New Delhi-110020. This again was Sai Baba's unique miraculous privilege granted tome. I consider it to be my pious duty to apprise these rare facts about Sri Shirdi Sai Avatar to all His devotees before my death. Wither anyone believes inthem or not, it does not bother me. I am grateful to Sai Baba for givin1343.

133. By Sai Baba's miraculous grace, blessings and help only that I could write/edit these books on Shirdi Sai Baba in spite of my ill health and severe and financial and agonizing family problems in the last 21 years without any body'sfinancial support:

- Sri Shirdi Sai Baba Avatar,1992.
- My Life with Sri Shirdi Sai Baba (Shivamma Thayee), 1992.
- What Researchers say on Sri Shirdi Sai Baba,1994.

- Sri Shirdi Sai Baba: The Universal Master: First published in 1994.
- Sri Shirdi Sai Baba: El Maetro Universal (in Spanish), 1994.
- Shirdi Sai: The Supreme, 1997.
- Thus Spoke Sri Shirdi Sai Baba (Compiler: B.Uma Maheswar Rao of Guntur,1997.
- Divine Grace of Sri Shirdi Sai Baba, 1997.
- Divine Grace and Recent Predictions (Spiritual experiences and utterances of Prof. P.S. Varma),1999.
- Divine Revelations of a Sai devotee (Spiritual experiences and utterances Prof. P.S,Varma, 2000.
- Communications from the Spirit of Shri Shirdi Sai Baba—Unique messages received by the compiler in meditation from Sri Shirdi Sai Baba from the Spiritual Plane (Compiler B. Uma Maheswar Rao of Guntur, A.P.),1998.
- New Light on Sri Shirdi Sai Baba, pp.159: 1999.
- *Sri Shirdi Sai Baba Bhajan-mala* (in Roman, 1998.
- Sai Ideal and the Sai World, (containing also the 41 unique postings of eminent Sai devotee Ram Nathan of Sarangpur (West Bengal) in his unique 'The Sai Graph Mail'. pp.96),: 1999.
- The Divine Glory of Sri Shirdi Sai Baba, pp. 126: 1998.
- Hamre pyare Sri Shirdi Sai Baba, (in Hindi) 1999.
- The Immortal Fakir of Shirdi—Sai Baba as seen by His contemporary devotees, 2000.
- The Spiritual Philosophy of Sri Shirdi Sai Baba (Complied by B.Uma Maheswar Rao of Guntur),1998.
- Shirdi Sai Speaks to Yogi Spencer in Vision., 1998.
- Divine Revelations of a Sai devotee (Spiritual experiences and utterancesProf.P.S.,Varma) pp.270:2000.
- The Eternal Sai (Compiier Maneey of Banglore),2001.
- Sri Shirdi Sai Baba: The Unique Prophet of Integration, 2004.
- Sri Shirdi Sai Baba: The Universal Master, 2007.
- *Divya Sai Sandesh* (Rare Discourses of Sri Shirdi Sai Baba as God received by Yogi M.K.Spencer (in Hindi), 2007.
- Sri *Shirdi Sai Baba ke Divya Chamatka*r, 2007
- How I Found God (Ed.)1002.2013
- Maine Ishwar ko Kaise paya (In Hindi). 2015.

And some books on Sri Sathya Sai Baba who was the second Sai incarnation-
(134) BY BABA'S GRACE ONLY MY 30 YEARS OLD PENSION CASE
WAS DECIDED:

Since I was the son of a poor school teacher who did not have the means to send
me to a college, he got me appointed as untrained Matriculate temporary teacher
on 19,7.52 (when I was only 17½ years old) in Govt. Darbar High School,
Sambhar Lake. (from which school I had passed my High School exam. two
years back) on the poor pay of just Rs.70/- (Rs.50/-Basic pay+Rs.20/-Dearness
Allowance, Later on I was confirmed in service. As teachers were permitted
to pursue higher education as private candidates. I passed the Intermediate,
B.A.and M.A.(Sociology) examinations privately and then became a lecturer in
Sociogy in a Govt. College in Rajasthan. I did Ph.D. in Sociology as a private
candidate and served the NCERT (National Council of Educational Training
& Research in New Delhi for over 5 years on deputation and then was selecte.
My resignation from Rajasthan Govt. service for 17 ½ years was not accepted
in 1971 even when I had been confirmed in Jamia illlia Islamia in 197, it was
accepted much later and I was not even informed of it. I was denied my due
pension benefit by the Govt. of Rajasthan. I failed in my long struggle to get
pensionary dues for my 17 ½ years service from the Govt. of Rajasthan for
over 25 years and failed.. I had even retired from the Jamia Millia Islamia
university but had failed in my struggle to getpensionary dues from the Govt.
of Rajasthan for over 25 years. Then only by grace of Sri Shirdi Sai Baba. A
retired High Court judge who was Shirdi Sai Baba devotee whom I never knew,
suddenly came to my help. He examined all my case papers and then advised
me how I could in my ongoing case. He ssured me that the Rajasthan Govt.
was bound to give pensionary benefits as they had accepted my resignation
after 20 years service, not when I had submitted it in 1971. It was their lapse.
Till the regnatiion was actually accepted bynthem, I was deemed to be inntheir
serviceand it could notne dened. This argument was placed before the Chief
Justice by my advocate and it was immediately accepted and thus I ultimately
won the case. Had Sai Baba not given His divine help and my family wound
not have been able to even survive in these very hard times when costs of all
commodities have been drastically rising every day. I am now getting more
than 7 times of that pension amount sanctioned by Jamia Millia Islamia
University in 1995 on compleion of my 25 years servce under them. By Sai

Baba's grace my earler Rajasthan Covt. service of 17 1/2cyears was added and I became eligible for full pension.

135. *BABA'S UDI* CURED SCORPION BITE CASE (1997) The clinic was located at the ground floor of their residence. She had read in *Sai Satcharita* of Baba's *udhi* working a cure in the case of corpion bites also. A case of scorpion bite came to her husband's clinic and she and her usband were tempted to try the same, with all apologies to Sri Sai Baba. A Muslim lady had brought her 11 years old daughter to the clinic whose right index finger had been bitten by scorpion. The girl was tossing and howling in pain. Three ligatures were also tied by her parents. One at the base of the finger second over the wrist and the third over her arm. After necessary examination the doctor intentionally avoided giving the patient any drug or anesthesia. Only *udhi* was tried. The *udhi* was rubbed on the index finger, forearm and arm, and a pinch of *udhi* in water was also iven for drinking. The girl and her mother were asked to remain in the clinic for some time. The doctor and his wife were wonder-struck to see the girl completely relieved of pain in a short ime, the girl and her mother went home happily.

136. BABA PULLS THE CHAIN (1987)

It was my 42nd visit to Shirdi via Puttaparthi. I reached Shirdi on 26th November, 1987, and left it in the evening of 27th instant. It is mentioned in *Shri Sai Satcharita*, (Chapter 8 on the last page) same that those devotees, who sought the permission of Sri Sai Baba before leaving Shirdi and followed his directions, they reached their homes safe, but those, who did not abide by His commands had suffer a lot and had to face adversities of various types. Again in the beginning of Chapter 9, it is mentioned that if Baba asked someone to return home, he was bound to leave Shirdi. While going back to their native place, the devotees used to go to Baba to prostrate before Him and at the moment Baba gave a few instructions to them that was inevitable to observe. If someone returned back disobeying His instructions, then he has to face misfortune certainly. In this Chapter, Tatya Kote Patil and an European gentleman's incidents are mentioned in detail. In Chapter 12, it is mentioned in respect of Kaka Mahajani that when he reached Shirdi with an intention to stay there for atleast a week and wished to participate in Gokul Asthami functions, Baba asked him immediately, when he was going back? Kaka Mahajani answered, "When Baba orders me to go back?" Bbaa asked him to go the following day. Baba's words were law and to comply them was a necessity. So Kaka proceeded for Bombay the very next day. Bahu Saheb Dhumal came to Shirdi and after Baba's darshan, proceeded to Niphad to attend a court case thee, but Baba did not permit him to leave and so he was detained for seven days altogether. Ofcourse the result of this detention was profitable enough. In Chapter 30, it is written that no one can have darshan of a Saint unless He himself wills. In chapter 18, 19 and 36, it is mentioned that due to some pious deads of past birth, a person can reach to Shridi.

Being aware of all these narrations, it has been my practice to go to Chawadi, Dwarkamai, Samadhi Mandir, Gurusthan and Lendibagh and seek Baba's kind permission before leaving Shirdi. But I don't know why and how this time I sought Baba's permission to leave as usual but I also asked Baba to accompany me upto my residence at Betul and to take me safely to my home. Perhaps it was the first chance when I asked Baba to go with me.

This time my acute Asthma trouble of 22 years old had put me to an unbearable state, yet by Baba's grace, I could be present at Shirdi in September, October and then in November 26th of that year. So I boarded three tier compartment at Manmad without obtaining reservation to it. The train might have covered hardly 40 KM. distance from Manmad when the Conductor of the three tier compartment told me to get down at Bhussawal and try to get a place in general compartment. I requested him about my asthma trouble and submitted to him that under such acute trouble, it would not b epossible for me to get down at Bhusawal and again board the train in general compartment which was generally choked by the passengers who serve at Bombay for their livelihood. I knew when the train stopped at Jalgaon and again at Bhusawal, but neither I got down the compartment nor the conductor disturbed me. It all was Baba's game. But after Bhusawal, though I had no sound sleep at all, but only Baba knows how I could not know the following stations of Burhanpur, Nepanagar, Khandwa, Khirakiya, Harda, Banapur, Hoshangabad etc., because before reaching the train at some stations, I had a small sleep. I was to get down at Itarsi Junction in the night at about 3.00 A.M. because the train was running very late. After getting down at Itarsi Junction, I had to go to Itarsi Bus Stand to catch the Bus scheduled for Betul. At such odd hours in Itarsi, unsocial elements finding someone alone with bag and baggage, stop him and start snatching the belongings and to save one's life, it is only the remedial course to surrender each and every belongings, i.e. money, watch, ring etc.

Probably the luck had destined me to be a victim of such a happening that day at Itarsi, so Baba blessed me with such a sound sleep that the train halted at Itarsi Junction for half an hour but I could not be aware that the train has touched Itarsi. There was one youngman in my compartment who was going to Orai near Kanpur and he was aware of this fact that I am to get down at Itarsi. All of a sudden I heard a long whistle of the train which awakened me, I got up and started enquiring with the young co-passenger of Orai if the Itarsi station had come. He, said, "Please get down immediately". When I came to the door of the compartment with both hands holding the handbag etc., I saw the train settled and giving long whistles. After getting down in quite lonely and at a dark place, I saw two scootermen on the road, because the halting train had blocked their way. Railway authorities were trying to find out the defaulter who might have pulled the chain to stop the train, but no-body else except myself was found getting down from the said train. So, the conductor inquired of me whether I had pulled the chain. I replied humbly that upto this old age, I never dared even to touch the chain, what of say of pulling it. Then he asked about my occupation? I told him that I was a Professor in a Government College of Betul. I had slept and could not guess that the train was halting at Itarsi Junction. So I failed to get down there. They might have handed me over to Railway Police any anything indecent could have happened to me but they spared me. The train was still awaiting. Thus I inquired with those two scooterwalas to give me a lift upto Itarsi Station. They asked my destination where I had to go. I told them that I had to go to Betul. They told me that a Bus right in front of me was going to Betul. "Please get in and catch the bus immediately." And so I had a seat in the bus going to Betul. It was 3.30 A.M. then I reached Betul safely in the morning of 28th November at 5.15 A.M. I spread over the bed-sheets in Baba's room, put a jug of water to drink, set up a big framed photo of Sai Baba, garlanded it with Samadhi garland, which I had brought from Shirdi and weepingly asked Baba to please take a bit rest as He might be feeling tired in pulling the chain and stopping the from before the bus for Betul for my sake.

Dear Sai brothers, if you have firm faith and belief in our Lord of Lords Bhagawan Sainath, rest assure that he is always behind you for your safety of life and to save you from incoming calamities. He is Lord Shankar, Omnipresent, Omniscient and Omnipotent and not less than it. May Lord Sainath ever shower His blessings on all those who have completely surrendered to His Lotus Feet. Om Shri Sai Yashahkaya Shirdivasime Namah.

-Prof. A.P. Tripathi,
Government Girl's College, BETUL
(*Shri Sai Leela*, Nov. 1988)

136. BA'S MIRACLES

(1) Once, a young couple highly educated with qualifications of M.Tech. and B.E., came from Andhra Pradesh. They were rich also The youth was suffering from severe pain due to Kidney stones. The scan report revealed that there were eight such stones, Of course, he had already undergone an operation and got some stones removed, but the same problem had recurred, before he approached me.

As usual, I prayed to Sai Baba and gave him holy ash with Babaji's photo. I told him to trust Babaji and advised him to consume it after offering prayers to Babaji. To our surprise, all the eight stones were dissolved within a fortnight. The youth fully got rid of his problem without any operation and felt very happy. Then full faith dawned on him about Babaji's miraculous cures.

-Sri H.D. Lakshmana Swamiji,

(2) This is an incident which took place during March 1966. A couple was very much worried about their children's progress. After regular prayer to Babaji, they found better character and behaviour of their children and now there is much progress in their education. Actually, the parents had never thought of this improvement in their dreams even. Now they are free from worries and have much faith in Babaji. I had advised them to meditate on Babaji when their children come. Now they have found alround development in their family. This is all due to blessings and miraculous grace of Babaji, and their strong belief in him.

-Sri H.D. Lakshmana Swamiji,
No. 52 "BANASHANKARI DEVI MANDIRA"
14th "B", Main, II Cross, II phase,
Mahalakshmipuram,
BANGALORE-560 086

137. BABA'S MIRACULOUS MESSAGES (1995-96) (Experiences of. Umamaheswar Rao

Sri Sai Baba has been giving his messages since 28-5-87 while I sit in meditation. The first message was given when I was in meditation in Dwarakamai at Shirdi. Since then I have been getting these messages regularly. All are in Telugu only as I am a Telugu man. Baba did not give permission to me to publish these messages upto 1.1.90. Following His direction, the first 35

Messages covering the period upto 19.2.1989 were published in Telugu under the caption *'SRI SAI TATWA SANDESHAMS'* and the English version of a total of 77 Messages upto 28.1.90 was published subsequently under the caption *'SAT SANDESH'*.

The Messages covering the period upto 17.11.91 were published as Vol. I under the caption *'SAI TATWA SANDESHAMS'* in Telugu. Subsequent Messages received from 17.11.1991 upto 9.3.95 were published as Vol. II under the same caption. The messages after this period are yet to be printed. I have received more than 300 Messages uptill now.

Sri Sai Baba gave The Following Message While I was in meditation on 5.1.95 at 10.30 P.M.:

"Death is inevitable to every one. Life and death are tied down by the results of your past actions. Death means the Jiva leaving one body and taking another. Whatever the person thinks at the time of death, that thought will persist and will make Jiva to enter into a subtle body. The thought persisting at the time of death will lead to similar future life. The persons living in sensual pleasures are ignorant and can not understand this truth.

When one leaves the body, his relations or his friends should not worry about death. One has to experience his own *karma*. If a person gets a disease due to his past karma, even if he gets relief of the ailment with the aid of doctors and medicines, he has to suffer from that remaining trouble in the next birth. Karma can not be dissolved or removed by others. One has to suffer the results of his *Prarabdha Karma*. Knowing that your body is impermanent and unreal you will take more care for your *'Deha'* Shake off you *'Deha-abhimana'*.

The Jiva resides in the water present in the heart. At the time of Jiva leaving the body, the water in the heart gets gradually reduced and the area below the tongue gets dried up. Knowing this, think that death is fast approaching and think of *Bhagavanama*.

2. Message Received from Lord Sainath on 16.1.1995

"If you do not become a servant of your body and its senses, if you lead simple life, if you do not get attached to caste and creed, body, or beauty, money or momentary pleasures, you will have peaceful death at the end of life. However much you may take trouble in protecting your body, it is bound to perish one day. Do not waste your time in giving pleasures to the body. Know that the ultimate aim of your life is to know and receive the effulgent truth of yourself".

"Your death depends on your past actions. If you are in God Consciousness, your death will take easy stride. Soul is not body and one should not fear death. When the result of all past accumulated karmas, whether they are good or bad, get destroyed, then *Jivatma* leaves its attachment to the body consisting of five primary elements and get merged with Supreme (*Parmatma.*)"

3. Sri Sai Sandesh on 17.1.1995 at 9.30 P.M.

"Leaving the worldly attractions and aiming the Universal spirit as the ultimate goal of Supreme pleasure and peace, lead your life in meditation on Atman. Do not depend on the body which is made up of five elements. The accumulated sinful acts of many past lives get stored in *chitta* and project a thick wall of obstruction in the spiritual path. Treat them with devotional activities and get rid of them before the death engulfs you. In the same way, get rid of your doubts and go beyond pleasures and pains. Do not encourage ignorance which is the cause of 'Samsara' resulting in routine life and death cycle. Even though you are bound by actions of previous lives, by the steadfast devotion on Supreme Divinity you can get over the resultant ties of those karmas. With staunch devotion and meditation, destroy the six enemies residing in you before the disappearance of very transient body. Get firm hold of effluent Divine Spirit, leave the worldly matters which are very transient and always troublesome. When death approaches you, welcome it with open hands, merging entire attention of you mind in Me. With such powerful medicine you will get peace of mind."

Message Given by Sri Sai Baba on 21.1.95 at 8.40 P.M.

"I am omniscient, Controller of the whole Universe, support of the whole world and the prime cause of all activities. Without diverting your mind on worldly affairs, fix it in your heart where I am residing, If you constantly think of Me, you will be eligible for my Grace, otherwise with doubtful mind you go hither and thither without my Grace; no one can eliminate your troubles. Except Myself nobody can erase the prints on your fore-head. Know that body is an abode of unhappiness and is transient, and when such a body goes off, why should you all weep?"

Sri Sai Baba's Message Received on 25.1.95 at 1.30 A.M.

"First know who I am and then if you meditate on Me, you can reach Me. Whatever form you think at the end of your life, you will attain that form only in the next life. If you meditate on *'Ananta Paramatma'*, you will attain Him only. In the Universe know which is permanent *(Ananta)* and which is impermanent. Except the Supreme God, all other lives and matters have to end one day or other."

"I am indestructible and ever present. So if you meditate on Me, you can reach the permanent abode in Me. If you take this as your unquivering aim in your life, you can reach the goal safely. Never aspire at impermanent affairs. To attain My mercy and to reach Me, devotion with pure heart is very essential. Whatever ideas you have during your life time, they only project in your mind at the end of your life. So to eliminate all other thoughts, think of Me always."

"Fill your mind with Divine Wisdom. If you are having such wisdom at the end of your life, you will not have rebirth. To attain such wisdom of Truth at the end of your life, you must meditate on Me, thinking of my divine attributes etc. throughout your life and then you are sure to attain Me."

Sri Sai Baba's Message *(Sandesh)* received on 28.1.95 at 11.30 P.M.

"Happiness and grief are imaginations. Know that worldly happiness is not real. *Kama, Krodha, Lobha, Moha, Mada, Matsara* are all false impressions. Always remember that death may reach you at any moment and be prepared to continue the journey of 'Jiva'. Then you will attain the blessed state."

"Without depending on friends and relations and without leaving your philosophical activities on them, keep your aim on Me. Death may snatch your life without previous notice. Then your relatives and friends may not be able to remind you about God and there may not be any one by your side to pray God for your future welfare. Understand this and surrendering all your thoughts to Me, meditate on Me and be peaceful."

Message given by Sri Sai Baba on 31.1.95 at 8.10 P.M.

"As you have carried on the load of miseries and some happiness from the previews lives to this life, you have made this life an abode of miseries with less of happiness."

"Know what is Supreme State which gives immense peace and try hard to attain that state. Then you will not have next birth and even if you have another life, it will give you happiness only. Divert your attention in search of God. Fix your mind in Divine path. Know what is *'ATMA'* and what is *'ANATMA'* what is 'Jhana' (Knowledge) and what is *'AJNANA'* (ignorance);

what is bound state and what is freedom. Knowing that constant Divine rememberence alone, can take you to deathless state, try for God's mercy and you will attain the state of Godhood which is beyond 'Gunas'."

"The main cause for life activity is presence of 'JIVA' in the body. When the Jiva leaves the body, the life will extinguish and the person dies. At the time of death speech etc. will get merged in Mind, the activities of mind get merged in 'PRANA', the 'Prana' gets merged in 'TEJAS'. When the man is about to die, you observe the heat of the body and that heat itself, is 'Tejas'. To every living being at the time of birth itself the time of death is fixed. No one can escape this. Every born being must die and this is the open secret of life. Try hard to attain Supreme Godhood."

Sri Sai Baba's *sandesh* (message) given on 6.2.95 at 8.00 P.M.

"One gets spiritual inclination by God's Grace. All worldly matters are like images in a mirror. Earnestly pray the Supreme God to lead you from untruth to truthful state and to eternal peaceful state."

"Believe firmly that except God, no one gives any helping hand to you and the attachment to the forms and associations of your so called relatives is useless. Always try hard to reach God who has no beginning and no end, and who is always blissful and unbound."

Sri Sai Baba's Divine Sandesh Given on Sivaratri day, Monday, 27.2.1995, at 9.10 P.M.

"Uncontrolled mind leads one into dark paths of 'ignorance' and one gets rid of this unruly mind, he will get knowledge about God. Until that time, your old impressions of mind remain as they are unless one gets rid of the *vasanas*, he will be immersed in pleasures and pains of life."

"There are two birds in you – they are 'PARAMATMA' and 'JIVATMA'. The 'Jivatma' thinks that it consists of body organs (*Indriyas*) and thinks that pleasures and pain of these belong to it and get immersed in them. The other bird 'PARAMATMA' will not get perturbed with either pleasures or pains and remain calm as a witness. 'JIVA' gets ego feeling and thinks that every act is done by him only. When *Jiva* gets rid of this egoism, then he understands that he is not the cause of pains and pleasures of the body. Otherwise with bodily attachments '*Jiva*' goes on in the cycle of births and deaths."

"Death means that the Jiva leaves the gross body and with subtle body goes to other worlds. '*Jiva*' when he is egoless, becomes a witness of pleasures and pains of the body and contemplates always that he is *'PARABRAHMA'*, then the results of all actions drop off and he becomes *'Paramatma'*. That is the Supreme goal and so all of you should do meditation on Atma always."

Sri Sai Baba's Message Given on Thursday, 2.3.1995, at 7.45 P.M.

"As you are immersed in the sea of *'Samsara'*, you are not able to get rid of the desires of the body and this is leading you to have very many lives in which you accumulate the results of good and bad acts you do in those lives. If you learn and separate what is gross and what is subtle body and if you learn the activities of ten types of airs *(Vayus)*, then you can know the relationship of *'Jivatma'* and *'Paramatma'*. Till you know that you are *'Brahman'*, the cycle of births and deaths are inevitable. Try to attain that ever blissful state. Know what is body and what is soul. The association of five sense organs and five motor organs *(Pancha Karmendriyas)* is body. in that body the *'Jivatma'* is residing. If you understand this, you can visualize *'Paramatma'*."

"Merger of *'Jivatma'* in *'Parmatma'* is *'MUKTI'*. To attain this, meditate on Me always. If you do this, you need not go anywhere to get My Grace. I am Omnipresent. Meditate on Me with the firm idea that I lead you in the way of salvation and you will attain better state in next life."

"Now I will show you the way how the mind can merge in *'Atma'* during meditation. Without any fear all of you meditate on Me. I am like *'Kalpavriksha'*. I am *'Adi Sakti'*; I am *'Jagan Mata'*; I am in all forms. All forms are mine."

"Do not fear when your mind gets merge din *'Atma'*. Take *'Udhi'* and that will protect your body. When your mind gets merged in *'Atma'*, chant my name. Sit on dear skin, close your eyes, keep your back, chest, neck and head in straight position and sit like a status and meditate on Me. Then only you can know how your body and mind merge in *'ATMA'*."

"Keep faith in Me and whatever action you take it as being done by Me. Whatever you or your wife write, know that they are written by Me. Let not the ego ever enter in your minds that you are writing all these."

"Whenever you get My philosophical Messages or any books on my philosophy and Tatwa are printed, let introductions to those books be written by well-known Sai Sevaks. Let them write elaborately who I am, what are My *leelas*; what is importance of My Avatar, why I have come on to the earth etc. I will protect such people always."

Sri Sai Baba's Message Receive don 9.4.95 at 9 P.M.

"Constantly think of *'Atma'*. 'Atma' is indivisible. Cause and effect are not concerned with 'Atma'. 'Atma' is not bound by good or bad results of action. When the mind gets purification by doing duty bound actions, then one can attain *'Jnana'*. Then only one can realize the pure *'Paramatma'* residing in all animate and inanimate objects. When you are performing actions which are ordained to you as your duties in selfless manner, you will get purity of mind. If you do not do this, you will be wasting your time in pleasures of life. Try to become good aspirant of *'Brahma Jnani'*.

"You must first of all know what is 'Atma'? The 'Atma' that is present every where is MYSELF. There is nothing except Me. Know this clearly. If you are constant in meditation, you can visualize 'Atma'.

"Know that the entire Universe is seen in self-effulgent Atma. The whole world is a mirage. It is a projection of 'MAYA'. As you are not having real knowledge of *"Atma Swaroopa"*, you will see the tricks of Maya as real. When you attain real knowledge the *'Maya'* gets dissolved."

"Pray for *Nitya-Anitya*, *Viveka*, and *'Vairagya'*, turning your mind inside towards Me. With full faith on Me, offer your prayers. Bookish knowledge without practice leads you nowhere. Leaving your vanity of body completely, offer yourself at My feet. Leave the idea of 'I' and 'Mine', without aspiring for worldly pleasures, worship Me for My Grace. If you chant My name always, you can attain the Supreme State."

Sri Sai Baba's Message received on 5.5.95 at 7 A.M.

"You are getting immersed in acquiring wealth and thus wasting your time. Without worshipping God you will not attain purity of mind. Without purity of mind, you cannot get *Jnana*. So to attain God-knowledge, do your fixed duties without fear. Thus *Antah Karma* will be purified. By doing actions without aspiring for fruits of action and with single minded devotion, surrendering yourself completely to Me, you will become get one pointed devotion and *Jnana* and thus become great personifications of wisdom."

"Your ignorance is the cause for your increasing interest in Samsara. When you attain *Atma-Jnana*, then you will get rid of your egoism and you will get disassociated from Samsara. At that state you will not have friends or foes, you do not aspire for body pleasures and you can face any amount of painful and sorrowful events."

Message given by Sri Sai Baba on 25.5.1995 at 9.15 P.M.

"To attain Godhood one need not become an ascetic and go into the forest. A *grahasta* who performs his duty-bound actions without aspiring for the results is a true Sanasi and the person who leaves his bounded duties is not a Sanyasi. Leading a life of Grahasta if one strives hard to practice Divine activity he will get rid of all bad-thoughts, impurities and other defects and attains salvation. More than Sanyasis, these who mediate on God always are great persons. He who does not allow his mind to go towards worldly pleasures, who with one pointed concentration meditates on Atma, who is not moved by any tribulations, who thinks that god is dwelling in God, who feels that pleasures and pains of others are equal to his pleasures and pains, such a person is greater than a Sanyasi and he becomes a great Yogi. Mind is fickle, not steady and is as difficult as controlling the air. But just because it is difficult to control the mind, taking up Sanyasa is not good. By constant practice, you can attain *Vairagya*. If you donot have *Raga* and *Dwesha*, the mind will not run towards any object. If the mind goes on any object, divert it from that object and surrender it to Atma. If you practice like this, your mind will get fixed, and even without attaining Sanyasa, you can get salvation."

"Taking up sanyasa without one-pointed mind is useless. So by staying in Grahastha Ashram, if you perform your duty in proper way, you will become eligible for *'Moksha'*."

Sri Sai Baba's Message given on 28.5.95 Sunday 9.30 P.M.

"Know *'Brahma Satyam, Jagan MIthya'* Every being who is born is bound to die. However beautiful and energetic one may be, he is bound to die, at one moment or the other. So why do you have grief for the transient things. As long as you are immersed in ignorance, you will not have peace of mind."

"Ignorant person will always have impermanent mind. When he gets light of Knowledge, he will see his own self every where. When one gets Jnana. The veil of ignorance vanishes, then you will know your real state, and you will know the worldly existence is impermanent."

"The action performed with *Karma-Indriyas* can be obstructed by others but the thinking process cannot be obstructed by others. So you yourself have to remove the bad ideas of your mind with the firm attitude of your buddhi. Others can not change them. Unless your mind, speech and action are uniform and single-minded it is impossible to prosper in the philosophical line."

"You are responsible for your present state. The ideas and actions of the previous lives are responsible for the present state of life. So if you want to have good life in future, your present thoughts and actions must be good."

"To whichever form of God you worship, and in whichever way you do worship, it all reaches Me only. In whatever manner one worships Me, I will bless them in the same way. I am the Father, good advisor, and support of all beings in this world. I am the permanent seal of the whole Universe. I do not have likes and dislikes. I am the Father of Saints and sinners, *Jnanis* and *Ajnanis* also."

"Thinking of Me always, surrender all your actions to Me. Those who do have such firm faith, do not have any obstructions, troubles, difficulties, grief or mental worries at all.

Message given by Sri Sai Baba on 13.6.96

"I am personified love. All of you are involve din bad thoughts due to ignorance. I have come in human form to lift all of you from ignorance. I convert those who approach Me into high philosophical Bhaktas. I will grant you much philosophical power to lift yourself to higher state of experience.

My prime purpose is to keep my devotees in high state of *'Atma-Sandhna'* *Sadhan*. Depending on the devotion and philosophical attitude of the Bhaktas, they get the results accordingly. I will submerge the human weaknesses and bad habits with my teachings and make them pure and fit to attain the philosophical heights. Nobody can understand the real meaning of My teachings and do not give importance to them. My sayings are essences of Vedanta and the essence of all religious philosophical books. Those who understand the essence of my preachings and digest them, they will get rid of their lethargy, body consciousness and their tickle mindedness and keep their aim on Me only."

"When I was in human form I preached the same teachings and gospels but nobody has propagated them. That is why for the benefit of all my bhaktas, I am once again expressing same old teachings through you but not preaching any new ones."

-B. Uma Meshware Rao,
Guntur (A.P.)

135. BABA COMES TO THE RESCUE OF THE INNOCENT DEVOTEES (1996)

Wherever I go through the various chapters of *'Shri Sai Satcharita'* and read Baba's miracles galore how he saved an innocent child of a black-smith, how he saved innocent residents from cholera, etc. etc., I recollect how he had come to rescue me from the clutches of the wicked persons. I shudder to think of the consequences if the merciful Baba had not been so gracious and kind enough to help the poor and helpless devotee like me. It would have meant total misery which could have easily taken my life even.

While posted at Kathmandu under India Embassy Nepal, I was abruptly transferred to a District Hqrs. far away from Kathmandu to head a small office there. A brand new jeep was placed at my disposal with strict instructions to ply it for our own official purposes only. The driver, a Nepali youngman had to take orders from me before taking out the vehicle from the garrage.

The facility of the jeep was available only to me. No other officer functioning at the station had its privilege. Many a time, the local officers approached me for it but had to return disappointed. this made me an unpopular official.

Everything went on well when suddenly one day I fell ill and was advised by the doctor for bed rest for a week or ten days. During my absence, my Nepali Head Clerk was looking after my duties in the office. It was during that period that the local Superintendent of Police wished to send his children to a town across the Indian border. He contacted my head clerk for the jeep. Taking advantage of my absence and wishing to oblige the S.P., he directed the driver (ofcourse, verbally) to take away the vehicle to the S.P. and act as per his direction. I was blissfully kept ignorant of the whole matter.

As the ill luck would have it, the jeep while on return journey after leaving the children at their destination, met with a serious accident, practically smashing the body. The driver was seriously injured and had to be removed to the civil hospital unconscious in a precarious condition.

As soon as this sad news reached my office, the head clerk taking advantage of the driver's critical condition, cooked false story with the connivance of the S.P. that the vehicle moved under my orders. Obviously, this was done to get me implicated in the serious matter.

I was immediately summoned to Kathmandu to face the fury of my senior officers. A count of enquiry was immediately held and an Inquiry Officer from Delhi was asked to submit a prima-facie charge sheet against me. All evidences were against me. In the meanwhile, the driver was still fighting with life and death in the hospital. I was sure to be held personally responsible for the mishap and likely to be sacked from service alongwith any other punishment including immediate repatriation to India, for no fault of mine. My only helpful witness could be the driver who was so serious that he could expire any time.

Till then, I was a Sai devotee of a modest nature. We had a large mounted photograph of Baba hanging in our drawing room but I had never seriously or regularly prayed before Him. On that fateful night, I bowed before Him touching His lotus feet every now and then begging Him emotionally to save an innocent fellow from disaster.

Next morning, I was about to leave for the final session of the Inquiry. Some unknown and complete stranger knocked at my door to tell me that the driver had come to senses and was fit to give his statement. Before I could leave for the hospital, the man was gone and untraced. In the hospital, I found the police men had already taken his brief but to the point statement. He looked a time with a quiet and smiling glance and breathed his last, as if his death was waiting just for my arrival. With the factual last-minute statement of the driver, the inquiry concluded in my favour, fully exonerating me for the charges. Surely, Baba and himself come to inform me about the decision. Since then, Baba's saviour hand has been on me in every walk of my life.

"BOW TO SHRI SAI, PEACE BE TO ALL."

JANAKRAJ LAROIYA
Noida (U.P.)

136. BABA'S UNIQUE *LEELA* (1996)

Shirdi sai Baba's ways are mysterious inscrutable, inconceivable and beyond the ken of our mind and thought.

Once a devotee comes under his fold, he (Baba) strengthen his Devotion by giving him such experiences and he ultimately realizes that Baba is no other than God (*Parabrahma*) and manifested in this world as '*Avatara Purusha*' (Divine Incarnation) to elevate mankind by removing their ignorance (*Avidya* or Nescience) and bestowing knowledge (*Jyana*) in them to realize the truth (Self-Realization). Now, I shall relate a recent experience (Miracle of Baba) for the benefit of the Devotees.

On 8th October 1996 (Tuesday) early morning while I was still sleeping on the bed in one of the Sai Bandhu's Home at Benson Town, Bangalore, I heard A distinct voice as follows", I will come along with you for '*Bhiksha*' (Food) today" I immediately woke up from my bed and, to my surprise, there was none in the room. I was reminded of a similar instance in '*Sai Satcharita*' chapter 40, in which Baba told Hemadpant (Anna Saheb Dabholkar) that he would go to his house for meals on the full noon day morning in 1917.

I did not reveal this message to anybody. But kept quiet. It is my usual practice, whenever I go to Bangalore, I used to visit Sai Spiritual Centre in Thyagarajanagar to pay my obeisance to Lord Sai and his Apostles, Poojya Narasimha Swamiji and Pooja Sai Padananda Radhakrishna Swamiji (Trinity) whose idols are installed in the Sai Mandir.

I attended the noon arathi at 12 noon (sung on Shirdi Lines), took 'Tirtha' and 'Udi Prasadam' and was about to go to a Sai Bandhu's House at Bansankari (3 Kms from the Sai Mandir) for food as pre-arranged. But, in the meantime Shri D.V. Krishnamurthy, a personal attendant and a great disciple of (late) Shri Radhakrishna Swamiji and now chief priest at Sai Spiritual Centre, whom I know very well, having acquainted with him for more than 15 years, accosted me thus:

"Radhakrishna, you are Sai blessed (lucky). Today, six Devotees are invited by a great Sai devotee in N.R. Colony to 'Vishnu Sahasramma', 'Parayanam' and 'Arathi' to Bab and to have 'Prasadum' (Food) in his house. We are now five available and one devotee sent word that he could not come due to some reason. Please come along with us, their car is waiting to take us to their house."

So saying, Shri Krishnamurthy took me to his house. We did 'Vishnu Sahasranama' Parayana followed by 'Sai Nama Japa' chanting of Baba's Taraka Mantra, Om Sai Sri Sai Jaya Jaya Sai' for half an hour in the Sindhi gentleman's house. The Sindhi gentleman's wife narrated to us their Sai Leelas (miracles), How Baba got them back their lost business account book (credit book) in which lakhs of rupees due from creditors were recorded, the same way as Baba got back Chand Bhai's lost mare to him.

I always carry Baba's Udhi' and photos with me and Baba prompted me to give them all of them. When I took Baba's photo from my bag to present is to the pious lady, lo! Baba's photo in 'Bikshadana' (begging Food) pose came in my hand and I was overwhelmed with Sai joy and Sai bliss and tears gushed out of my eyes. I was wonder-struck at this leela of Baba. then I remembered Baba's uttering early morning in Benson Town on that day, "I will come along with you for 'Biksha' (Food) today. I am also reminded of how Baba fulfilled his promise to Shri Hemadpant by visiting his house at the nick of time in the form of a beautiful photo presented to him by two Muslim gentlemen (Shri Sai Sai Charita – Chapter 40).

To conclude, Let us always chant Baba's Taraka Mantra, 'Om Sai Sri Sai Jaya Jaya Sai', constantly and enjoy Sai bliss for ever.

Sree Satchidananda Sadguru Sainath Maharaj Ki Jai.
OM TAT SAT.

-Radhakrishnan 'Sai Jeevi'
President,
Akhanda Sai Nama Saptaha Trust,
Benson Town,
Bangalore – 560 046

139. BABA'S GRACE (1989)

In the first week of November, 1986 I received a letter from Sai-brother Sri S. Krishna Murthy, a retired Deputy Collector who is also the Secretary of Om Sri Sai Ram Committee at 4-3-5, Ramanapet, Guntur – 522 007, seeking my assistance in getting their Sai magazine registered with the Government of India. It seems he was advised by Sai-brother Dr. G.R. vijayakumar of Kil-Kotagiri (Tamil Nadu) to contact me, as I might know the authorities concerned. I was really happy that Lord Sainath provided me an opportunity to serve his children in Andhra Pradesh. Sri Krishna Murthy had sent to me all the relevant documents, from which I could make out that it had been in 'cold storage' for sometime.

I prayed to Lord Sainath to enable me to get this registration done. I contacted the department concerned over the telephone. Sri Surender Kumar of the office of the Registrar of Newspapers gave me an appointment on Thursday the 13th November, 1986 and directed me to call on him personally with all the relevant papers for registration.

When I went to the Registration office I was told that the matter was pending due to non-receipt of a document from the Sub-Divisional Magistrate at Guntur. It looked as if I had to return without getting the work done. In fact when I was waiting for the officer concerned, I came to know of several instances of pending matters.

I prayed to Lord Sainath, who gave me an intuition to search the papers sent by Sri Krishna Murthy. Sai directed me to give the photo-stat copy of the document signed by the Sub-Divisional Magistrate, Guntur. Immediately I took it and showed to the Registration Officer. (Perhaps the original communication from the Magistrate of Guntur might have been lost somewhere in the transit). I sincerely prayed to Lord Sainath to make the Officer accept the Photostat copy.

Yes, Lord Sainath responded to my prayer. The Officer accepted the photostat copy and accorded the necessary sanction then and there. He chose one of the names sent – *'Ninnu Parkshinthuna'* for the Telugu Sai magazine. Right in my presence, the Officer signed the necessary communication to the Guntur authorities registering the Sai-magazine. This is indeed a great *'Sai Leela'* in truth, Sai Himself did it.

-P.K. Kapoor,
1121, Chah Rahat,
Delhi-110 006
(*Shri Sai Leela*, April 1989)

140. SHIRDI SAI BABA – THE UNIVERSAL GOD (1986)

I would like to narrate here a recent *leela* of Baba which averted a serious train accident and saved hundreds of passengers from the jaws of imminent death on 5.11.1986.

My second daughter-in-law was delivered of her first child, a female on 22.10.86 at Kanchipuram (Tamil Nadu) and her parents sent to us invitation to attend the cradle ceremony, which is usually celebrated on the 11th day after brith i.e. on 1.11.86 in our case. I could not attend due to some domestic circumstances but sent my wife and son Chi. Shankar for the function. They left Hubli on 29.10.86 and after staying for a couple of days at my eldest son's place at Bangalore left for Kanchipuram on 31.10.86 afternoon by 'Brindavan Express' and reached there on the same day at 9.30 P.M.

My son was working in the Workshops of South Central Railway, Hubli, and he was granted only 6 days leave from 30.10.86 to 4.11.86. He had to be back to duty on 5.11.86 morning at 7.00 a.m. My wife and son were expected to return to Hubli in the night of 4.11.86 at 9.45 p.m. by 'Golgumbaz Express'. But, they did not arrive. I satisfied myself thinking they might be arriving the next day morning i.e. on 5.11.86 by 'Kittur Express' from Bangalore scheduled to arrive at Hubli at 6.15 a.m. But, alas! there was no trace of the train and the station authorities at Hubli were unable to explain the cause immediately to the waiting passengers. I was very much perturbed. I did not know what to do. Under such circumstances, the only refuge was our Mother Sai. I prayed to Sai Baba with all my heart for their safe return. After doing Sai Nama Japam silently with love and devotion for more than an hour, I prostrated before Baba's photo in the pooja room. Wonder of Wonders! Two flowers, one from Baba's photo and the other from Lord Venkateswara's photo simultaneously fell on my head. I took them as blessings both from Shri Venkateswara and Samartha Sadguru Sai Baba. Peace was restored to my mind and I was feeling Sai Bliss and Joy.

At 6.30 p.m. on 5.11.86 my wife and son arrive d engaging an auto rickshaw from the station, went straight to the Pooja room with tears in their eyes, reverently prostrated before Baba and then told me that Baba only saved them in the morning on that day and related what happened on the way, as follows:

They missed the train (Golgumbaz Express) at Bangalore on 4.11.86 which leaves Bangalore at 11.05 a.m. So they, boarded 'Kittur Express' on the same day which leaves Bangalore at 7.35 p.m. and is scheduled to arrive at Hubli next day morning at 6.15 a.m. On that dya it was running late by 2 hours and it passed through Kodaganuru station at 6.00 a.m. (5.11.86). After passing hardly one KM from this station, the Driver of the Engine examined the 'Line clear', picked up at Kodaganura and found the 'TOKEN' missing and he immediately stopped the train and brought back the train to Kodaganuru and traced the missing 'TOKEN' on the platform. IN the meanwhile the Gangman from the opposite direction came running and reported to the Station Master, the Driver and the Guard of the train that the Railway Bridge near the next station was found breached due to heavy floods and therefore it was unsafe to pass through the bridge. Messages were given to all concerned and trans-shipment of passengers from Kodaganuru to Davangree by State Transport buses was arranged from where they arrived at Hubli by a special train at 5.45 p.m. on 5.11.86.

Dear Sai Bandhus, please imagine what would have happened to all the passengers travelling in that train if the Driver had not backed the train to Kodaganuru to pick the lost token in the 'Line Clear'. Certainly, he would have passed through the damaged bridge in a few minutes which would have resulted in a great human tragedy in which hundreds of passengers would have perished and their limbs broken for life including my wife and son. It is our Bhagavan Sai who had saved them all in a dramatic and wonderful way as stated above.

-Mr. R. Radhakrishnan,
C/o Shri C.V. Mugali,
Bilgi Plot, Nagashetty Koppa,
Hubli-580023
(*Shri Sai Leela*, September 1987)

141. PURE DEVOTION PAYS (1986)

I learnt this at the tender age of 13, and it has only made my love for and faith in Baba all the more strong. Since then Sai Baba is inscribed indelibly in letters of gold in my young mind.

It was just 7 or 8 months since we had returned from Zambia and with much difficulty I had got myself admitted in a good school in the 8th standard. Accommodation had been a problem, but soon, by the grace of Baba, we managed to get comfortable accommodation. From the new residence my school was about 22 kms. away and I had to travel by the local trains, and during the typical Bombay monsoons, it was obviously a great problem. Almost every other day I took ill. In the middle of the scholastic year, it was impossible to secure admission in any of the nearby schools were I to escape the incessant down-pour. Moreover, my 2nd language being French, it was necessary to get admission in a school that offered French. As far as our knowledge would go, there were no such schools in our area. It therefore was really an issue engaging the mind of all at home. But my parents did not lose hope. They kept on saying that Baba would find a way out for us.

On one fine day, my father's colleague told him of a school, quite close to our house, that offered French. But he also warned that admission should be a problem, since it was one of the best schools in the area, and a very strict one at that. It was indeed a thrilling news for us. We made inquiries here and there, but got the same reply, "It is futile to seek admission there".

Unexpectedly, all our relatives planned to make a week end trip to Shirdi. We also joined them. I was pretty young then and I do not now recall the details of the trip. But one thing I remember very vividly. I remember sitting in the main Mandir and becoming oblivious of all around me while I concentrated only on the statue of Baba. Well, I did not have to tell Him my problem, it seemed as if He knew everything. I just sat there, and for the first time in my life, I experienced something new – something that I can not define in words even today. I must have sat there for an hour or so and all the time there was Baba in my mind. Since that day, each time I want to think of Him, I just have to close my eyes and right in the centre of forehead between my eyes, I can see Baba clearly. Sometimes I can see Him walking around in Shirdi, sometimes seated on the stone.

The very next day after returning home, my father and I went to the school and in a matter of fifteen minutes, I was enrolled as a student. No more details are required as every thing speaks for itself. Baba has become so much a part of me that I do not do anything without a thought of him. Since that event, I have been to Shirdi 4 to 5 times. A fortnight ago too, I had been to Him. Actually, there is no need to pray. He knows all that we need. You just have to look into those love filled eyes with devotion and all your problems and worries melt away. I am almost 19 now and all these years have only strengthened 'our relationship'!! My prostrations to SAI BABA.

-Miss. Lata Balasubramanian,
A-1, Shivaji Park
Telephone Exchange Quarters,
Anant Patil Marg, Dadar (W),
Bombay 400 028
(*Shri Sai Leela*, 1987)

142. THE MIRACLE OF MY REACHING HOME AT 11 A.M. IN A DARK AND DREADED NIGHT (1986)

I had been to Madras in connection with the proposed installation of the Life size marble statue of Sri Sai Baba, at the All India Sai Samaj, Mylapore, Madras.

I returned to Bangalore on 19.9.1986 by Bangalore Express, which unfortunately arrived at Bangalore City at 10 P.M. being late by one and half hours. It was drizzling and partially a dark night.

At Bangalore City Station, all auto drivers refused to ply for me upto Malleswaram. I felt disappointed as I was hungry, exhausted, tired and sleepy after nearly 10 hours of journey, sitting all along and did not know what to do. It was about 10.45 p.m. and no buses also were available. No police man or Railway Staff was around to help me.

In such a predicament, a miracle happened. All of a sudden from nowhere, one Muslim automan appeared before me and asked me on his own, where I wanted to go. I replied with no hope "to Malleswaram". But no sooner I replied than he was off with me to my house at Malleswaram.

For a Sai Bhakta, who else can this Muslim be, except Lord Sri Sai Baba Himself! The rescuer of His devotee in distress!

Had not this Muslim appeared, what would have been my lot that night, as neither I could go home nor stay at the Station, safely.

To emphasize that Sri Sai Baba alone came and none else I should say, that this Muslim appeared exactly like Sai Baba with the same features of beard and dress. He came only because, I am His possessed bhakta. He came in that predicament and critical situation for my rescue, as Lord Krishna rushed towards Gajendra and Lord Shiva towards Markandeya, in their perilous hour.

That Sri Sai Baba will not allow his Bhaktas to suffer, is well proved and illustrated here.

The only qualification is that one should have deep-rooted faith in HIM, for HIM to help us, as HIS slogan goes "When I am here, why do you fear".

"Bow to Sri Sai – Peace unto all."

-Mr. B. Ramanadha Rao,
Sri Sai Kutir, Bangalore – 23
(*Shri Sai Leela*, August 1987)

143. SRI SAI'S GRACE (1986)

During Oct., 1986 I developed severe abdominal pain; my husband gave me homeopathic medicines, but they did not give relief, and as the pain persisted he consulted the family physician. The doctor diagnosed my pain as due to 'acidity' and prescribed a treatment, but the pain continued for next two days despite the intake of medicines. On the third day the pain became unbearable and hence another physician was consulted for a second opinion; his diagnosis was also the same i.e. 'acidity'. Now the fourth day the pain again became unbearable. It happened to be a Sunday, the time was 9.30 p.m. and no doctor was available. My husband who is a great devotee of Baba immediately gave me *Udi* mixed with water it worked like a miracle and the pain stopped. However, my husband consulted a doctor, a family friend. He was the third physician prescribed by them. He decided to examine me on Monday the fifth day and proposed Barium Meal and Ultra sound of Gall Bladder, stomach and the kidneys. Now the fear of surgery started haunting me. However before going to the radiologist we decided to go to Sai Baba Mandir, Lodhi Road, for the blessings of Baba and put some *Udi* on my tongue. After this we proceeded to the Radiologist. IN two hours, the X-Ray was over. My prayers were answered in a miraculous way. Believe it or not, the specialist declared "all clear". I think even now that it is Baba's blessings and kindness that saved me from surgery etc.

I close this with a short prayer begging Sri Baba always to protect us, forgive us for our trespasses, and correct and guide us at every stage. Bow to Shri Sai, Peace be to all.

-Smt. K. Sayal,
J-1, Green Park Exten.
New Delhi-11 0016
(*Shri Sai Leela*, Dec. 1987)

144. BABA DRWS OUT HIS DEVOTEES FROM THE JAWS OF DEATH (1986)

Sri Sai Baba of Shirdi, the refuge and saviour of His devotees, is ever active and more so, even after Mahasamadhi. We are fortunate to be His devotees from early 40's i.e. from about 1943.

On 6th November, 1986 at Kakinada (AP), my nephew's son, aged 20 had an acute attack of Jaundice (Hepatic) affecting the brain. He became violent and lapsed into Coma in a matter of a how hours. He was immediately admitted to hospital. We came to know that his condition was critical and given up by the doctors, on 7th night. My niece's daughter's marriage had been fixed for the 12th November, '86. Upon hearing this shocking news we were flabbiergasted. As per habit I immediately concentrated on Sri Sai Baba and received a reply to say that he would be all right. My wife during concentration received a vision of the boy on bed with Sri Sai Baba sitting on a stool beside the bed with His hands on him. On receiving Baba's message and assurance we were relieved of anxiety and were sure that the boy would recover completely. We went to Kakinada on 9th morning and found the boy in an isolated room in a private hospital, with my nephew, his wife and all our relations in utter gloom and despair. His condition was very critical and the doctors had practically given up all hopes and pronounced that lung failure was setting in.

Being a qualified homeopathic doctor (R.M. P.), I started homeo-treatment right from 9th noon as per Baba's will. It was only Baba's grace and miracle that could save him. Because of Baba's word and assurance to us we were confident and had no doubt in fact as Baba's word is the decree of the Almighty. I told my niece to go ahead with the marriage schedule as planned. The patient looked better on 9th evening, but the doctors pronounced status quo. On 10th morning the boy started to get a little involuntary movement. In the evening he began focusing his eyes and seeing things. On 11th morning he spoke slowly to the utter surprise of the doctors. In the beginning, his words were dragging and slowly he was set right. He said he got a vision of Lord Sri Sai Nath who came to him and hit him with His Satka (small stick which Baba carried) and from that moment the pain in his chest was gone and that he felt better. Baba by that hit with His Satka evidently drove away death and cured him of all his physiological ailments like lung failure etc. The boy began improving without any complication whatsoever rapidly and he was taken home a few days later for convalescence.

The marriage of my niece's daughter went through as scheduled with my nephew and his wife attending all functions happily. Baba's saying "I will draw out my devotees from the jaws of death" has been proved here and it is another of the millions of confirmations that Sri Sai Baba is ever active and more so even after His Mahasamadhi which is only a biological formality for an avatar.

-K.V. Gopala Krishna,
49-II-I/1, Lalithanagar,
Visakhapatnam 530 016
(Andhra Pradesh)
(*Shri Sai Leela*, Sept. 1987)

145. CUSTOM DUTY WAIVED BY BABA'S GRACE (1986)

Sri R. Subramaniam, Lakshmipuram Colony, Villivakam Madras, and his friends visited holy places of North India and Nepal in March 1986. The group comprising ladies and gentleman purchased sarees, electronic goods, other items at Nepal which were cheaper than in India. On the way back from Nepal at Sownali, Gorakhpur District, the customs authorities, verifying the purchases made charged a dut of Rs. 4000/- on the items. Sri Subramaniam who happened to be the only Hindi-knowing person in the group pleaded with the authorities to reduce the duty, which was reduced to Rs. 1000/-. But the group members out of greediness or out of ignorance of law, said that they could pay only Rs. 500/- in total. Sri Subramaniam who had not made any purchases, but was only pleading for his friends was aghast at the adamance of his group. Unless the duty was paid, the customs authorities would not allow the bus to proceed. Sri Subramaniam was embarrassed to meet the customs officer to say that the group would pay only Rs. 500/- as duty Sri Subramaniam silently prayed to Sai Baba to get him out of this embarrassing predicament.

At this point of time, an officer arrived in a jeep and entered the customs office, Sri Subramaniam was called inside the customs office. This officer told him that he was a supervisory customs officer for Gorakhpur District, that he was a Sai-devotee and that he had seen Sri Subramaniam in the Shrine at Shirdi, on 2nd and 3rd of February 1986. The officer apprised of the predicament being faced by Sri Subramaniam, suddenly produced Rs. 500/- from his pocket, asked him to pay the customs duty and obtain receipt. He even said "This Rs. 500/- is your money, you had given me earlier." Sri Subramaniam, was perplexed, as he had not meet this gentleman earlier, much less paid him Rs. 500/-. The officer on special duty got into his jeep and was off. The customs officer now became very cordial and said that his boss usually did not visit on Sundays!

When Sri Subramaniam reached Madras at the conclusion of the trip his landlord handed over to him an envelope from Sri D. Shankariah of Hyderabad, which contained receipt for Rs. 500/- which money was earlier collected by Sri Subramaniam and sent to Sri Shankariah for *Akhanda Sai Nama Saptaham*, Sri Shankariah had mentioned that since he did not know the addresses of the individual contributors, he had requested Sri Subramaniam to pass on the receipts on his behalf. At this it flashed to him "Remember you had given me Rs. 500/-. This is your own money".

146. UNIQUE SAINT OF *KALIYUG* (1986)

I wish to express my heart-felt gratitude with tears at Sai's feet. There are no words to describe and to praise the kindness he has shown towards me.

There was a misunderstanding between me and my close friend, following which I was altogether unable to trace my friend. I was then totally unhappy, with a very painful heart. The grief was so much, I even thought of suicide.

One day while travelling in a bus, I saw a person wearing a ring with Shirdi Baba's picture engraved. I casually enquired about it, He explained to me that the ring was from Shirdi and narrated miracles experienced by his devotees. I then expressed my feelings to him. I also told him that I did not want to ask any one who was very close to my friend. He suggested that I pray to Baba with a pure heart to find my friend out. I started praying to Baba from 14.8.1986.

One evening I went to Baba's temple and poured out my feelings at His feet and looked at his eyes which shine like the moon. At the same time I thought that "Baba if your existence is true, show me some good sign indicating that my prayer has reached your heart pervading the universe". The *archaka* of that temple gave some flowers, which were at Baba's feet, to a lady. She wore those flowers in her hair knot and when she was leaving the temple she passed in front of me. Suddenly the flowers which were in her hairs fell in front of me. Immediately my heart felt the bliss of Baba's grace and I started dancing in the shades of Lotus feet of Baba. I offered my *Sashtanganamaskar* at his feet and with full happiness and confidence I came out from the temple.

Three days later, I met my friend who was missing for two months. It was significant of Baba's mercy cast upon me for my sincere prayers.

Though I am a Christian I believe Him and have always succeeded by praying to Him.

-A.R. Kumar,
138830, S.T.A.,
Technical Literature Deptt.
B.E.L. Bangalore – 13

147. SAI *NAAM MAHAAN* (1986)

I narrate here under the Sai miracle experienced by me during my visit to Shirdi on 9th of October 1986.

I was as usual arranging to purchase a railway ticket to Manmad station for 9th October, 1986 and return ticket for 14th October. One of my colleagues Mr. Jagbandhu Parida requested me to book a ticket for him also along with mine. I was glad to note that Sai was adding one more devotee in his list of innumerable devotees.

By Sai's grace both our tickets were booked, duly confirmed with reservation by Bombay Mail (via Nagpur). On the 9th I took Rs. 350/- and Mr. Parida took Rs. 600/- as pocket money. We spent our day in train on 10th joyfully. We alighted at Manmad station on 11th at 2 A.M. We took coffee at the canteen for refreshment. A couple from Bhilai was sitting in front of us. They were enquiring about bus to Shirdi from the canteen owner. I volunteered myself and answered their question. They felt happy and left.

When we reached Manmad Bus Stand we found the couple not to be seen. As we were waiting for the bus to come they also arrived safely. The bus for Shirdi came at 3.30 A.M. and soon a huge crowd gathered near the door and were fighting to enter the bus. We too tried our luck and got proper sitting accommodation. Lo! I lost my wallet containing Rs. 250/- in it, I was perplexed. I searched the whole of the bus and then complained to the police there, but with no result. I felt it was Sai's wish and the needy got it. I re-collected last year's incident on the same date that my beloved father Shri T.A. Ram Nathen lost his shawl while entering the bus and thus consoled myself.

The couple Mr. Shailendera Kumar Rant and Anjali Sathey voluntarily offered me Rs. 250/- as loan, to be returned as and when I could. I could not believe my own ears because in these days of Kali Yug who will offer money to a stranger. I refused stating that I would live penniless and if Baba wills he would feed me at Shirdi. I lived exactly as Baba lived in his days of stay at Shirdi till the year 1918. I controlled all my desires and took food when offered. We took leave of the couple on 17th morning on our way to Bombay for a short stay.

In Bombay we stayed at Chembur Guest House in a double bed room on the rent Rs. 125/- per day. All expenses were to the account of Mr. Nagbandhu Parida, my colleague. On the day of our leaving Bombay we felt short of Rs. 250/- to clear the dues of the hotel. Lo! it struck me now that my bosom friend Mr. V. Sunder of 10A, Jatindas Road had given me a sum of Rs. 250/- as advance money for purchase of "SHIRDI KE SAI BABA" Video-Cassette from Bombay. I thanked Sai for making my friend give me this amount as Sai Baba knew beforehand that such a contingency was to arise.

I thanked profusely and felt in myself that Sai helps his devotees from drowning but does not change his Karma. It is cent percent true as it happened to me.

He also kept Mr. Md. Hamsa at V.T. Station on 14th October the day of our departure by Bombay Mail on our way back to Howrah. He helped us in train and we paid him off next day at our office.

-Mr. T.R. Anand,
Ground Floor, IA, Wedderburn Road,
Calcutta 700 029
(Shri Sai Leela, August 1987)

148. WHEN TRUTH IS STRANGER THAN FICTION (1986)

Yes, there He stood at the gate, with His serene indulgent face and benevolent eyes, clothed in 'Kafri' with the cloth over the head falling loosely over the shoulders, the *'Biksha-paatra'* held in the right hand with the left folded and resting over the right shoulder, exactly as in the portrait facing P. 112 of the *Satcharita* (Eng. edn.) I was stunned with amazement it was INCREDIBLE!

Only a moment before, in my frenzied despair at the passing away of my first-born son aged 10 years, I had denied Him. His Divinity and His Omnipresence testified again and again by His devotees experiences both before and after His 'Maha Samadhi. I had declared Him to be a false deity and beseeched my wife to throw His portrait on the dung-hill. But here He stood to prove the truth of his eternal existence.

You see, the medicine I poured into the mouth of my semiconscious son remained there. I shouted to him to swallow it but the mouth remained open. I became frantic and tried to close it. No, the jaws had become rigid. I checked the pulse. It too had stopped. It was then that I called out my wife from the kitchen and spoke those blasphemous words. She just sat by the bed, head bent and tears trickling down, as much hurt by my profanity no doubt as by the bereavement.

I had come to the tether end of my spiritually. I was not myself. Thus I had the brutal impudence to ask my grieving wife whether she had cooked adding, "He has anyway gone. I don't want to die, too. I shall go and eat."

Imagine the father, however forlorn, to be so devoid of all feeling as to put such an inhuman question to the mother just bereaved.

There is no limit to which human nature can sink though, thank God, it can also soar to Elysian heights. Here I must say that my wife's faith unlike mine has throughout been unflickering, standing foursquare to all the winds that blow. Whenever my mind barks back to that scene, I can not help wondering how I escaped her righteous indignation for my frenzied out-burst. Where else except in this land hallowed by Sita and Savitri, Damayanti and Mandodhari, Nalayhini and Renuka Devi can one meet with such phenomenal forbearance? It is not far fetched to say that it is for such paragons of virtue that the sun Shines, it rains and Mother Earth continues to yield her bounty. It has been said that the greatness of a man does not consist in never falling but rising every time he falls. Indeed, it is by the magnetic charm of their devotion the 'homo sapiens' are not completely debased.

In her own gentle manner she said, "I just finished cooking rice for the children. Pray, serve yourself for this once", and lapsed into what I know now in retrospect to have been prayer to Baba.

You see, there were four younger children, two of them twins hardly six months old. But my mind and heart had become dry, no thought or feeling for any one, not even Baba!

So I betook myself to the kitchen to eat. I sat with a 'thali' before me and mechanically served myself some rice. Before I could bring myself to eat, while sitting and staring at the rice vacantly, I became schizophrenic, as it were, one part of me questioning the other, "Look, what are you trying to do? There lies your first born son dead and you are going to gorge your self." This shocked me into realizing how perfectly horrid of me it was. I turned to look in the direction of the bed in the front-room which was in line with the kitchen. It was then that my eyes behold the wonderful, form of Baba. Was it a mere vision, a figment of my imagination? I shouted to my wife with head still bent, "Kamu, look out and see who has come". Reacting t the frantic urgency in

344

my voice, she looked up and glanced at the gate. At once, as if touched by a live wire, she sprang up and as if that was the consummation she was devoutly praying for the exclaimed, *"Amma Naayana Baba Vachycherul"* (Oh! at long last Baba has come!)

Actually, neither of us had seen the *Satcharita* portrait of Baba by then. Our puja portrait showed Him sitting cross-legged. However, in His inscrutable Wisdom, He had led us into buying at a *'mela'* a few months earlier a wood-cut portraying Him in five different poses including this one. Thus we were able to recognize Him at once.

Now I felt sure it was indeed HE. I was back in my senses. My heart was full of gratitude to Him for coming in the nick of time, and saving the situation. Else, in my forsaken condition, with no thought of Him or for Him I might have polluted the food before me. In this new found happiness, I reverentially took the *thali* up to Him and put the rice in the lifted *"Biksha-paatra"*. He received it with His beatific face and went away. No word was spoken indeed there was no need for any. My heart was too full for it, too. There was 'peace that passeth understanding'.

As I stepped into the house, my son opened his eyes and said, "Father, I am thirsty. Give me some water." This occurred in March 1944, twenty six years after Baba's Mahasamadhi.

-Dr. P.S.R. Swami
100/2Rt, Vijayanagar Colony,
Hyderabad – 500 457
(*Shri Sri Sai Leela*, Sept. 1986)

149. MY EXPERIENCE OF THE BLESSINGS OF SRI SAI BABA (1986)

Approximately30 years ago, I had an opportunity of visiting Shirdi and having darshan of Sai Baba. A Gujarati lady, who happened to be a friend, took me along with her relatives. Earlier I had absolutely no idea at all of the great saint of Shridi.

I wanted to utilize my L.T.C. during April, 1996. My wife insisted on our going to Shirdi since it was the first time I was availing of L.T.C. and since also she had not visited Shirdi earlier. I readily agreed. The day before my departure, I received a letter from my brother asking me to bring with me some ash (*Udhi*) from Shirdi on my return. We visited Shirdi without any problem whatsoever and returned to our place safely, with the sacred ash, the *Udhi*. I sent it to my brother accordingly. The next time when I met him, I asked him what for he had wanted the sacred ash from Shirdi. He replied, "I tried all method, consulted many eminent doctors but yet I was not able to find out the reason for baby's crying at all. Finally I put the sacred ash in a talisman and tied around the baby's waist, Believe it or not, a miracle happened, the crying stopped right from that day and the child continues to be well ever since."

"My fervent prostrations unto Him, the Ruler of the Universe".

-S. Sainath, B.E. (Mech.)

D.I.S.D-1/338, 8th Block

Paper Town, Bhadravathi 577 302

150. THE SUPREME MASTER (1986)

I brought a small statue of Sai Nath from Shirdi after perform Pooja at the Samadhi Mandir. The statue was kept in a small shelf and continues to be there even now. I was very much surprised to see *Udhi* around the statue on 20.3.1986, with a sweet aroma covering the entire the house. After some days, the *Udhi* started coming from the statue itself and it was like the *Udhi* from the Dhuni of Dwarakamai. The *Udhi* continues to come for the last two years.

We are doing sankeertan daily in the evening. Surprisingly enough we noted two small pieces of sugar candy before Baba's feet in time. The sugar candy also comes from the statue only. We do not know the exact time of coming of *Udhi* nad Sugar candy from the statue.

But the important thing to note is the *udhi* comes from statue only after the earlier ones has already been distributed to his devotees. I believe that Sai Baba wants to teach us that nothing is ours in this world. Sweet aroma spreads around statue during prayers. *Abishekam* is conducted on every Thursday.

Devotees attend *abishekams* and *bhajans*. Many diseases are being cured with the application of this *Udhi*. Sai Baba, our Supreme Master, is guiding, 'teaching and protecting his devotees from Samadhi showing that He is everywhere. Where His devotees totally surrender to Him.

Interested devotees can have this *Udhi* from Sri Sai Baba's statue at the following address:

-K. Ranha Rajeswara Prasad,

Clerk, State Bank of India,

H. No. 2-4-12, Maruthi Nilayam,

New Badvel Road, Giddalur – 523 357

Prakasam Dist. (A.P.)

346

151. BREAST CANCER CURED BY BABA'S *UDHI* (1986)

A Sai Sevika of Maitri Park. ST Road, Chembur Bombay developed a big lump on her right breast in the year 1986. After the necessary medical examination, the doctor advised removal of the breast lump by surgery. the lady was very much afraid. She would partake of any medicine, but agree for not surgery. A date for operation was fixed. In the meanwhile the lady told her sisters that she would try Baba's *udhi* and prayer instead of operation. Her relatives said, "If you have so much faith in Sai Baba, then we will also join in praying for your health". They all went to Panvel Sai Baba Temple and handed over the surgeon's letter to Sri Narayan Baba and expressed their predicament. Sri Narayan Baba said that there was no need for operation, but to have complete faith in Sai Baba, and apply *udhi* paste (vibhuti mixed with water) five times a day after reading 'Sai Mahima'. He also suggested Til oil massage on Monday. Tuesday and Thursday, after chanting 'Om Sai Ram' 108 Times.

The lady carried out the instructions and also visited Sai Baba Mandir at Shirdi. On return from Shirdi, she noticed that the lump had started reducing. On 12.10.1986 (Dussera day). She was completely relieved of the lump.

152. SRI SAI BABA: THE GREATEST OF SAINTS (1986)

I have been a small and humble devotee of Sri Sai Baba of Shirdi for quite a few years how and I have always been observing Thursdays as days for darshan and special puja to this indescribable Avatar Purushe.

And it is only by way of observing this custom of mine. I motored to Matunga on 2nd January, 1988, a Thursday, for purchase of some fruits and flowers to offer to the Lord during the puja at home in the evening.

I parked my car near the Matunga Railway Station and locked all the doors before going out for purchase. My brief-case containing very important official papers and Rs. 12,000/- was left behind in the car itself near the driver's seat covered with a duster to deceive the eyes of wary thieves.

Finishing the purchase in about half-an-hour's time. I returned to the car. I was shocked at the theft of the brief-case. The next few minutes were of nervousness and confusion, for the theft was so deftly carried out during the broad day while the bazaar itself was busy and active. Enquiries of the shop-keepers nearby only revealed their ignorance of the incident and no clue was forth coming from any quarter. Thereupon, I phoned up to the Matunga Police Station and lodged a verbal complaint and requested the Inspector to visit the spot for the first hand information. The Inspector opined that there was absolutely no use in his visiting the place of theft as no useful clue could be obtained in such cases of robbery as the robbers employed very shrewd methods to leave no mark or impression which could expose them to the police. On the contrary, he advised me to call at the Police station with the car and lodge a written complaint. I did so and while returning home, I asked the Inspector if there was at all any chance of tracing the brief-case to which he replied that there was only the least possibility to that end as almost every person, rich or poor, educated or ignorant, carried a briefcase now a days. He further added that if I were lucky and if God would come to my rescue, I might be able to get the brief-case back intact. These his last words sent into me a strong feeling of hope and confidence.

I reached home, took my bath, collected some flowers from the garden around my house and began the worship of the Lord Sainath with all my heart. I, literally uttered to Him, "O Lord, I am not worried about the loss of cash and papers, but what would the devotees and people in general think if and when they come to know that the theft took place on a Thursday, most sacred for you, and when I had gone out into the bazzar only to purchase things for offering to you. Won't they not begin to have two opinions of the worship of you and of your super-natural powers. Please do not turn a deaf ear to my prayers but quickly manifest your Godly power so that the lost brief-case be recovered by me." Saying these words, I was showing the desparathana with tears in my eyes.

Just then, the door bell also rang and I, my self, ran and opened the door, I saw two young men.

I saws utterly surprised to learn from the Station Master that the thief was caught red-handed on the platform itself by one of the ticket checking inspectors. The culprit not being in possession of valid ticket, left the box on the floor and ran away lest he should be roughed and charged. Before the development the Station Master had asked to phone up all the stations station. V.T. to Kalyan to ascertain if any complain of a theft of a briefcase was lodged with them by any to which he only received the negative reply.

Hence under a strong assumption that the brief-case was picked by the thief elsewhere and that he must have travelled by the local electric train, he had a *panchanama* held to record the contents of the brief-case and to find out, if possible, the owner of the same. And in the process, he could lay his hand on my visiting card with the help of which his peon came to call me from my house.

My dear and learned devotees, it is thus transparently clear that our Sai Nath, the *Kaliyuga Avatara Purusha*, runs to the rescue and safety of those who are dear to him only because of their sincere devotion and surrender to His will. Hence let us all be pure and moral in our daily lives and become eligible to receive His Grace.

SAI NATH MAHARAJ KI JAI.

-Muthu Pillai, 103/3534, Nehru Nagar,

S.G. Barve Marg, Kurla East,

Bombay – 400 024

153. DRAGGED THE SPARROW TO THE DESTINATION (1987)

My brother-in-law, Mr. Mohan, aged 26 is an educated man. I was unemployed while writing this. Because of the unemployment, he was in a desperate condition. One night his father came to me to inform that Mr. Mohan had left his house not informing anybody, in the morning the previous day with no money. Since he did not return home till 10 P.M., feeling much distressed he informed, about the disappearance of his son. Immediately we searched for him at all the places of Nandyal town and other surrounding areas, including tanks, wells etc., throughout night, but could not find him anywhere. In a distressed and helpless mood and not knowing what to do next we returned home. Every member of the family was under severe mental agony and strain. Since I am fortunate to have contacts with Sri Sri Sri Shyam Charan Baba Gurudev, I took my father-in-law to him, with the hope that the problem might be solved. At that time he was observing a vow of silence. We wrote on a paper the sorrowful incident that took place and placed it before him. At 8 A.M. he opened his eyes and looked into the eyes of the portrait of Lord Sri Sainatha Mahaprabhu and prayed and wrote in a corner of the same paper that the boy was alright and would return soon. He advised us to pray to the Lord with whole-hearted sincere devotion. As per his advice, we prayed to our Lord Sadguru Sainatha Mahaprabhu and kept quiet. By His grace, suddenly my brother-in-law came to the house by 11.00 a.m. on the same day; our joy knew no bounds.

After enquiry, my brother-in-law revealed that, he had decided to leave the house once for all, because of lack of peace of mind, and unknowingly went to the holy shrine Mahanandi, 10 miles from Nandyal on foot, and stayed there that night. The next morning, he returned to Nandyal by 7.30 A.M. on foot and was proceeding to the railway station, with no aim but with a determined mind not to return home. Exactly at 8.00 A.M. (the time our Gurudev opened his eyes) some unknown voice directed him to go home soon, and he felt that some force wad dragging him home. After some time he also informed us, that the voice which directed him was of our Sri Shyam Charan Gurudev.

At present he is an employee at Hyderabad and is relieved of the earlier mental agony. In this connection, we must remember, the assurance to its destination at the appropriate time, where-ever it is. Like wise, Lora Sainatha Mahaprabhu showered His grace for the sincere prayer, made to him and dragged my brother-in-law safely to the house and also provided him an employment, making everybody happy.

"Jai Bolo Sri Samartha Sadguru Satchidananda
Sainatha Mahaprabhu Ki Jai!"
"JAI GURUDEVA DATTA"

-Mr. S. Sreenath, M.I.E.,
Lecturer in Mech. Engineering,
E.S.C. Govt. Polytechnic,
Nandyal 518 501, Kurnool Dt., A.P.

154. SAI'S MIRACLE (1987)

Last year I was trying to sell my plot in Chandanagar, Ramachandrapuram, but in vain, Nobody came forward to offer a reasonable price. I wanted to buy a flat in the city. As for first installment for flat I pledged ornaments and paid off. Unless I sold my plot I could not pay off the remaining installments. I prayed to Baba "Lord Sainath I need money badly, I can not sell my plot at throwaway price. If I get a hand-some amount I will offer Rs. 101/- to you."

On 06.07.1987, Guru Purnima celebrations were started in Sri Venkateswara temple premises at B.H.E.L., Ramachandrapuram, Hyderabad. In the morning I went and took *darshan* and *Kakad* Arati in the evening I went and listened to the discourse by a Swamiji Sri Vitthal Baba of Vanasthalipuram.

On 7.7.1987 I went and again listened to the discourses of Sri Vitthal Maharaj. After that I took *prasadam* and went home by 8.30 p.m. My wife informed me that two persons had come to buy the plot. They wanted to see me. "You had gone to the temple. They offered Rs. 38,000/- and said they would come again". I wanted Rs. 40,000/- now there was a difference of Rs. 2,000/- What a miracle See the work of Sai.

On 8.7.1987 in the evening I was sitting in the Bhajan Hall listening to the *Upanyasam* by Sri Vitthal Baba. There my son came and said, "Daddy, the same people here come. They want to see you". I got up in the middle and went home. Ninety-nine per cent of the transaction was talked over.

On 9th, 10th and 11th July, 1987 as usual I attended the celebrations and witnessed Arati.

On 12.07.1987 it was the concluding day of Guru Purnima celebrations. I went in the morning, had darshan of Baba and returned home. Five persons came to my house at about 8.30 a.m. Two were the buyers, two others were their friends and the fifth one was one more man who is my friend and a Sai Devotee. They examined the documents, went to visit the plot and came back around 11.30 A.M. They gave me Rs. 2,000/- as advance and agreed to pay the balance Rs. 36,000/- on or before 5th August '87. I made out a receipt for them for the amount paid to me.

See how quickly things were executed by Shirdi Sai's Grace. By 12.30 noon on 12.07.87 I went to attend Sai celebrations. The *Annadanam* was taking place under the supervision of Sri Vitthal Maharaj. It was later learnt that nearly thousand people took food. I happily joined the volunteers in serving the food.

By the By I must acknowledge my debt of gratitude to Sri Vitthal Baba of Vanasthalipuram.

In 1986, during Sai's Gurupurnima celebrations at BHEL heard his discourse for the first time and he said to the audience "Look at Sai's eyes and pray three times. Glance at Sai's photo from feet to head and back and then meditate. Your prayer will be answered. Not matter what you eat, no matter whether you take bath or not."

These words of Vitthal Maharaj penetrated into my heart, from that day I have been doing as the Swamiji said. My faith in Sai has been increasing.

-E. Parameswara Iyer,
Personnel Department,
The Aluminium Industries Ltd.
Lingampally Post, Hyderabad – 500 133
(Shri Sai Leela)

155. SAI'S GRACIOUS MIRACLES TO FORCE MY RE-ADMISSION IN HIS BLISSFUL FOLD (1987)

The year 1982 is a year to be reminisced and a year to reckon with for me as it was during that year I was re-admitted to Sai Parivar like a failed old student getting re-admitted to an educational institution.

I had known about Shri Sai Baba of Shirdi earlier from my boyhood days. When I was studying in a High School at Chitradurga during 1964-65. I chanced to visit Shri Sai Mandir every Thursday along with my dear mother in one Dr. Rama Rao's house nearby.

Being a young lad of only 13 years, I was greatly impressed by the conspicuous, intense devotion of Dr. Rama Rao and his family and other visiting devotees there. Ironically, my visits to Sai Mandir were not borne out of any real piety on my part to Sai Baba the Great as by my boyish inquisitiveness to listen to the sweet melody of the devout bhajans and to pamper my palate, with the sweeter still, Baba's Prasad distributed invariably at the close of the function everyday.

And at home it came my way perchance to conduct Sai Pooja as and when my father, a State level Officer in the Education Department of the Karnataka State, happened to be out of station on official tours. And in deference to the wishes of my father I did the Pooja not with the necessary devotion or *Shradhdha* but mechanically as a matter of daily routine in the family.

When all was thus well, before long as irony of fate would have it, to our utter and unbearable shock my father was snatched away from our midst as a result of an acute heart attack. The untimely and premature death of the only earning member and the head of the family deprived us all of his august and imposing presence amidst us, his ever affectionate touch and loving care. My young widowed mother and we, her five children, were thrown to suffer the consequential lonliness in this world and were bereft of the sense of security and the comforts of a well-looked after and disciplined family.

Despite being young but not so young, I knew to the best of my knowledge and belief that my father was all along enjoying the unanimous and unsolicited admiration of not only the entire officialdom but also of the public outside for his honesty and uprightness in service till his passing away. After his disappearance from the face of the material world, the so-called entire circle of friends and colleagues and also our close relations who were hitherto crowding at my father's office and residence for favour of all kinds now began to exhibit, unashamedly though, an uncanny indifference and disregard. With tears in my eyes I had to be a passive and helpless witness to the pinching sigh of grief and anguish of my mother and the pitiable condition of the youngsters, the youngest of whom was still on the lap of the indulgent mother. The egoism and the basic selfishness of man perhaps has no limits or remedy. As one of the direct and immediate consequences of the abrupt cessation of income to the family, sizable as it was, I had to discontinue my high school studies just to save a few coins and to be of help to my mother in her daily routine.

Under the circumstances, with no prospect of any immediate relief to the deprived family, it was thought wise and expedient to leave Chitradurga and shift to Bangalore where my father had managed to erect a small and modest house, which was our only asset.

And yes! we moved to Bangalore and occupied our house with a view to settling down once and for all. Life became really miserable to us with no monetary income; but with an unflinching faith in the Omni-potent and All-merciful God, my mother and I struggled on and on to keep our body and soul together. Imagine the pathetic condition of a middle class family in a city like Bangalore when cost of living was shooting up almost every day. As we, the children were growing up in age, the demands of the family were also naturally growing more and more. And what would the young helpless mother do except console and pacify us with soothing words while praying inwardly for better days to dawn. Upon her fond and persuasive goading I began to put in efforts in a small measure to resume my interrupted studies and by His Grace came out successful in my S.S.L.C. Examinations in due course. It should be called the most trying and difficult period for our family as a whole. Feeling desolate and dejected and unable to bear up the seemingly insunnountable financial difficulties and the plight of our family, many a time I wished to attempt to commit suicide myself or to desert the house. But on every such occasion an unseen power held me back and advised me to face life as it came to me boldly.

On the advice of my mother and other elders I approached the Government for employment as the legitimate ward of a deceased Government servant and was fortunately offered the post of a second division clerk on compassionate grounds. In the Education Department, I joined duty in the year 1974 and have since been working.

My first younger sister who had already come of age was married to an M.D. in the year 1973 and the couple are now settled in Princeton, U.S.A. and reported to be happy and peaceful. Gentlemen, this is another concrete proof of the unfailing protection and Mercy of God, for can we, by any stretch of imagination expect a Doctor of Medicine willing to wed a girl from a comparatively poorer family when mounting demands of dowry are so rampant in our society? No, we can never But had not god willed otherwise in our favour?

Subsequently in the year 1977. God blessed me with a loving and understanding wife and I am a father of three children now.

My first younger brother got his B.D.S. Degree from the Bangalore Dental College and is now prosecuting his higher studies in U.S.A. My youngest brother is flourishing with a lucrative business of his own using his ambassador car. My youngest sister has also been recently married to a businessman in Bangalore itself and the couple is well off.

I was often driven to wonder as to how all the above mentioned good things took place in my family at the proper time while the family itself was passing through hard days with a very meager income. It thrills me and shakes to the nerve whenever I happen to compare the happenings in the family following my father's demise to the condition now obtaining in which we are looked upon by the society with respect and love. Of course, we are self-sufficient in every way.

Although my material and worldly life was apparently satisfactory and there was nothing to feel aggrieved about personally I was restless and there was constantly a sense of emptiness in me. I could not possibly find out what was wanting in me innately. Had I been with my father at his beside, I could have in all probability sought his mature guidance and advice as I would do from a Guru. This state of mind then made me wander about visiting Ashrams in quest of peace and tranquility that would keep me steady in the household.

Not too long after, I was invited to attend the marriage of a good friend of mine at Brindavan, White Field, Bangalore. When I reached the place of the function at 9 A.M. I witnessed a large number of devotees, both Indians and Foreigners, eagerly waiting for the gracious darshan of Shri Sathya a Sai Baba while some others were rendering devoutly melodious bhajans.

In the atmosphere surcharged with divine vibrations. When I was watching the goings-on o fthe function in the Kalyana Mantapa, my eyes accidently fell on a book with a gentleman on my left. Curiously I dared to ask him much against my wont as to what book it was and if I may please see it. When the gentleman, obviously a devotee of Shri Sai Baba, handed me the book in his inimitable humble manner I was taken by utter surprise, to find that it was 'Shri Sai Sat Charitra' in kannada version, with a majestic and magnanimous picture of Sai Baba on the outer cover. I felt overwhelmed with an inexplicable joy and surprise at the very sight of this wonderful good old man after a long lapse and a sense of gratification and fulfillment were felt running through my veins. I felt elated and exalted for an unknown reason. Where was this old prophet all these years? And from where has he now come to my sight, that too so unexpectedly? It would be no exaggeration to state that I felt I was back again with my own father infusing in me a sense of security and bliss. I could not withhold my tears of joy and weapingly condition. He said that he would do it only it Baba assured him that Vitthal would appear on the seventh day. Baba assured him of this, saying that the Pandhari of Vitthal and Dwarka of Lord Krishna was also in Shirdi and that no one need come from outside. Vitthal would very much manifest himself and all that was required was devotee's earnestness to have the darshan. After the *saptaha* was over and when Kakasahib Dixit was sitting in meditation, he saw Vitthal in a vision. At noon, in the Darbar, Baba asked him if he had seen Vitthal. This was before all and in the evening a hawker came to the Masjid for selling the pictures of Vitthal, which tallied exactly with the figure which Kaka Saheb had seen in the vision. This showed what Baba would do for his Bhaktas and how much he cared for them.

Sai Baba was an apostle of Hindu-Muslim unity, a beacon light to show us the way in life. It is on record that He guaranteed the welfare of his Bhaktas, announcing clearly that there would never be any dearth or scarcity of food and clothes in the homes of his devotees. "It is my special characteristic that I look always to and provide for the welfare of those devotees who worship me whole-hearted with their minds fixed on me. Fix your mind in remembering always, so that it will not wander elsewhere, towards body, wealth and home. Then you will be calm, peaceful and carefree." It is unfortunate that even after this clear exposition, we suffer in various ways because of our ignorance. It is high-time we took Baba's words to heart and without consideration of faith and religion, colour or region, love each other as brothers from the same family and raise this nation to the same heights to which it once belonged.

-N.N. Shalla
104/15, C.P.W.D. Qr. Saket,
New Delhi – 17
(*Shri Sai Leela*, Jan. 1987)

156. MIGHTINESS OF THE ALMIGHTY – "SAI"

One day when we were casually discussing worldly matters, the marriage issue of my brother-in-law, Chi, Chandra Sekhar also came up for discussion. By Baba's grace, miraculously and automatically further developments took place and the *muhurtham* was also fixed.

At that time the grandfather of the bridegroom aged 86 years, was on death bed. Besides this, the uncle of the bride aged 70 years was suffering from high blood pressure and was bed-ridden. The sister-in-law of the bride was in an advanced state of pregnancy.

Generally, Hindu marriages are not celebrated in such circumstances. This situation caused anxiety to all of us, about the celebration of the marriage on the day fixed by the pandits.

At that crucial time, our Gurudev, Sri Shyam Charan Baba informed was that our Lord Sai Sadguru Sainath Mahaprabhu was responsible for the fixation of *muhurtham* by pandits and hence it could be taken as assured that the marriage would be celebrated as scheduled by His grace, because Lord Sainath Mahaprabhu is always merciful to His children, and will never allow them to suffer in any way at any time.

Accordingly the marriage was celebrated happily. Prior to the *muhurtham*, Sri Shyam Charan Baba spent four hours in devotional bhajans and songs which made the audience forget themselves. Only half an hour prior to muhurtham we were reminded about the same by the purohit, duly initiated by our Lord Sai Sainatha Mahaprabhu. Everything went on happily.

By His grace the uncle of the bride left his body sixteen days before the marriage and the grandfather of the bride-groom left his body sixteen days after the marriage, without causing any inconvenience to the concerned. The sister-in-law of the bride was delivered of a child three days after the marriage.

When we decide our matters with our limited knowledge and intellect, we will be held responsible for results. When He decides the matters, everything will end in happiness and satisfaction to one and all.

Casting off the burdens on the shoulders of our Lord Sri Sadguru Sainath Mahaprabhu, gives us peace of mind and happiness, which we must cherish throughout our life.

-S. Sreenath, M.I.E.,
Lecturer in Mechanical Engineering,
E.S.C. Government Polytechnic,
NANDYAL-518 501, Karnool (Dt.) A.P.
(*Shri Sai Leela*, Sept. 1987)

157. FAITH IS SUPREME, FAITH IS ALL (1987)

I was suffering with unbearable cough from September 1987. In the early stages, I neglected it, presuming it to be some infection which would be alright in a few days. But, as the days passed, the problem started getting severe, especially in journey.

I was married on Ist October 1987, i.e. on Thursday. My wife is also an ardent devotee of Sai Baba. She too started worrying as it had almost become difficult for me to breathe and I was feeling exertion if I walked a few yards. Then, I consulted a doctor at Hyderabad At first, he too thought that it may be due to infection and prescribed some medicines. But after a week, there were no signs of relief. Then, I approached him again. He advised some tests, like Blood test, X-ray etc. On receiving the reports, he said, it was Bronchitis and prescribed some medicines and said, there is no permanent cure, as it is due to some kind of allergy. Then I consulted another doctor for the second opinion. He too expressed the same, and prescribed some medicines for timely relief. Then, I had to come back to Bangalore for joining the duty after leave. I was told, the problem might get aggravated, as Bangalore is in cold atmospheric zone. But as there was no leave for me, I came to Bangalore, joined the duty, and was continuing with the medicines given by the doctor, but they were of no avail. At last, I stopped all the medicines and totally submitted myself to the mercy of Lord Sainath. I used to take Baba's *Udhi* everyday with little water and was praying Baba for cure, with full faith and confidence in him. Sai's *Udhi* worked like Sanjeevani on my illness. Within a week, I was free from cough and flum.

-K.V.R. Sastry,
Language Officer, Dena Bank,
Zonal Office, Sona Towers,
1 Floor, 71 Millers Road,
Bangalore – 560 052

158. BABA'S TIMELY HELP AND BLESSINGS (1987)

Devotion to Sri Sai Baba was granted to me through my late beloved mother, which has saved me through every difficult situation.

After eight years of one married life, we got an opportunity to buy a flat ready for eseapation on out-right payment basis. We had to pay half the amount in block to enter into an agreement. My father helped us with his provident fund loan amount. With his and my husband's savings, we somehow managed to pay the initial amount. The agreement was signed and within two months the balance amount had to be paid.

We tried all over resources t dispose of our existing flat but in vain. During this period my husband because a devotee of Sri Sai Baba, and he was dragged to Shirdi every month. I myself and my family members daily prayed whole-heartedly to Baba to help us to finalize the deal. With every sun rise, we used to get hope only to vanish with sun-set the same day. Two months thus passed.

The vendor gave us one more month as grace period.

Finally, the day came when Sai Baba came to our rescue, and the deal was finalized within a week's time. We made the payment and took possession of the flat. We were worried again by the increased expenses in the new flat, which was however taken care of by Sai Baba by blessing my husband with a much better job in the same concern.

The points I would like to emphatically state here are:

1.   The seller or the party disposing of the flat was also a Sai Devotee.
2.   Each and every deal took place on a Thursday without any design or special effort by us.

Who has been behind all these? I leave it to the readers to conclude.

-Mangala Karjodkar,
New Trishul, Cooperative Housing Society
Bhavaninagar, Marol,
Maroshi Rd., Andheri,
Bombay – 400 059
(*Shri Sai Leela*, May 1987)

159. HOW BABA PREVENTED A MAJOR ACCIDENT (1987)

We were travelling to Shirdi from Thane on 20th Feb. 1987. I was accompanied by my husband and his uncle's family. We are travelling along the Nasik Highway in a jeep. It was a very hot noon and we were all in a sleepy mood as the jeep was moving at a great speed.

We noticed that to our left a lorry was parked and another lorry was coming towards our direction in a great speed. Suddenly the driver of our jeep realized that in order to avoid a collusion with the oncoming lorry he had to take a turn to the left. When he turned the jeep to the left, it hit the lorry which was stationed. So the inevitable happened. the jeep hit the lorry. The impact was so great that the jeep's left door was ripped open and the glass window was broken in pieces in no minute. It took us only a few seconds to realize what had happened.

My husband who had so long kept his left hand resting on the door had luckily withdrawn his hand at the 11th minute before the accident. Had my husband not kept the hand inside, one can imagine what would have happened. Thousand thanks to Sai Baba for the signal he gave beforehand. One more thing which saved my husband's eyes from being hit by broken glass pieces was the goggle he was wearing. To tell the readers about the miracle, he had worn the goggle only a few minutes back. All this was nothing but the signal given by the Baba in the hour of great crisis. I thank the Lord for saving the catastrophe that would have cost my husband's hand.

This incident only enhances my existing *Shradha* and *Saburi* in Sai Baba and here are my salutations to the Great Saviour.

-A Devotee
(*Shri Sai Leela*, April, 1988)

160. SAI'S MIRACLE IN THE REBIRTH OF MY CHILD

It was in the year 1983 I first visited Shirdi along with my close friend Mr. D.P. Rao and his family and friends.

My trip to Shirdi was unexpectedly arranged all of a sudden by my friend, who was a distributor at that time for the company for which I was working. Till that time I was not aware of Baba's *Leelas* and it was my first visit to Shirdi. Mr. Rao, my friend, already had reserved the tickets for his family and friends. When I made a courtesy call at his place in the afternoon on the day, he was leaving for Shirdi by the evening train from Hyderabad. My friend asked me also to join them. I wanted to take my wife and a one year old son Vikram also with me. As my wife was working in a private organization, she could not get permission from her Superiors and therefore did not accompany me.

I went to Shirdi along with my friends and had a nice and satisfying stay by the grace of Lord Sainath.

I was married in the year 1981 and was blessed with a son on March 16, 1982. We named our son Vikram as Baba Vikram and he was a sweet looking child and was precocious, always had a smiling face and showering his love and affection to one and all. He was liked by everyone in the family and also by all in our building complex.

When I took up a new assignment in the year 1983, I developed hypertension and I was mentally and physically unwell. In the year 1984 I had to quit my job. In May, 1984 my wife went to stay with her elder sister at Secunderabad along with my son who was 2 years and 3 months old by then.

On the morning of 4th June, 1984 my parents received a phone call from my wife informing that my son had an accident falling in hot water in a neighbour's house. My father and myself rushed to the Government Hospital, Secunderabd. When we reached there we saw the little soul brunt from abondmen to knees on both legs and was in a dazed condition and no medical treatment was given to him for nearly one hour and my wife was running from pillar to post to complete the hospital formalities for nearly an hour. Doctors assured us not to worry saying the child would be alright soon.

The child was also speaking and recognizing every one. On the night of June 6, 1984 the child began to breath heavily We wamted to complain to the nurse incharge of the ward but there was no one available immediately. By the time my wife could run to other block and bring a doctor the little soul was no more in world.

This came as a very rude shock to everyone in our family of course birth and death are not solely out of our will and therefore, not in our hands. If proper medical care would have been given, the child could have been saved. My wife and myself were totally depressed, demoralized and went on a pilgrimage to South India in July, 1984. Our prayers in all the temples were only to give our son. I also did not take up any job for nearly 3 months as I was totally depressed and upset. In this period, I do not now exactly remember the month and date, wehtehr it was September or October around midnight in my dream I saw that I was waiting for Baba's darshan along with some devotees. Suddenly Baba appeared in front of me like a flash; I looked at him for a few seconds and prostrated at his lotus feet and holding them I conversed him in English asking about my son. Baba spoke to me in English saying "You will get back your Son". Then I asked Baba about job, for which He replied "You will get one soon" and he immediately vanished. I woke up immediately, and woke up my wife and told her about the dream that our son Vikram was coming back. At that time my wife was in the family way.

I got a job within a month without much difficulty and I told about my dream to my family members and friends. My wife and myself went to Shirdi when she was in her seventh month of pregnancy to take Sri Baba's blessings.

On March 10, 1984, my wife was blessed with a son. There was some difficulty during delivery but by the grace of our am Sainath, everything went on well. This child was born exactly nine months after we lost our first child.

My second child Sai Karti has a very close resemblance of my our earlier son. This was noticed by many people and his movements and acts are like my first child. This is nothing but Baba's miracle. In January 1986 I went with my wife and child to Shirdi to show my gratitude for blessing me and my son.

May we live with abiding faith in Him.

-T.T. Vijay Kumar
B-4, Meera Apartments,
Basheerbagh, Hyderabad – 500 029

161. SAI BABA'S GRACE (1987)

Though I have been hearing regarding the Saint of Shirdi Sri Sai Baba, I had no opportunity, either to visit any of His Temples or visit Shirdi.

It was on the 16th July 87, as I had some work with a Cabinet Minister, I had taken with me the Prominent and well-known social worker of Karnataka Sri S.R. Chandrasekhar and after we met the Minister, as we were about to return, Mr. S.R. Chandrasekhar, suggested to me that we should visit Sai Baba Temple at Thyagajanagar.

As a marriage alliance was to be talked over for my daughter and they had come from Keveripakam. Tamil Nadu, I was in a hurry to return home. But I valued the advice and went to Sai Baba Mandir and prayed. It was a first visit for all of us. There Mr. S.R. Chandrasekhar said "Baba has blessed you and certainly marriage will click". In fact I was not at all willing, but by the time I reached home, my wife and children had spoken to them, it was almost settled. So, I also agreed and this is how Sainath has blessed us.

Again on 21st July 87, we sent to the same Ministers house and again Mr. S.R. Chandrasekhar, suggested that we should go to Baba Mandir. We all agreed and this time, Deenabandhu Sri V.R. Naidu, President, All India Sreenivasa Mission, was also with us.

We visited the Mandir, prayed and prostrated before Sainath and when we were about to return, Mr. Seshadri, Chairman of the centre, Secretary and others invited Mr. Naidu, took us round, showed and explained all the activities and also presented fine books and we were all very happy.

The same night, myself and my wife Smt. Ayammal, sons altogether 13 perosns, travelled from Bangalore to Kancheepuram in a Karnataka Government bus.

In between Krishnagiri and Natrampol, there is Farakur and it is here a giant lory dashed against our bus, damaging heavily. We were all in a shock, but by the grace of God no passenger was hurt. We were all extremely happy that there was not even a simple scratch on us. Immediately we thought of Baba who blessed us at this critical juncture.

So, I feel, a true devotee will definitely be blessed if he has immense faith in Him.

-P. Venkataswamy,
General Secretary,
Gandhi Vidyashala Educational Society,
Sri Ramapuram, Bangalore-21
(*Shri Sai Leela*, December, 1988)

162. "SAI GREETS NEW YEAR" (1987

On the morning of December 31, 1986 while taking morning tea, I was wondering and telling my wife and children casually, that how lucky we would be – if we receive "NEW YEAR GREETINGS" from Sri BABA Himself. They also agreed with me.

I returned home from office as usual at 6.30 p.m. My wife handed over to me a cover, addressed to me and told me that we had received New Year Greetings from 'BABA' as desired by us in the morning. There was no indication on the cover from where and by whom it was sent. I then opened the cover and found the 'BABA' photo with some sacred sayings inside. There was no indication even on the photo by whom the cover was sent. I could see only my residential address written by hand on the cover.

Out of curiosity, I examined the place of posting of the cover to my utter surprise, I found that the cover was posted at 'SHIRDI' on 23.12.1986. This I found out from the Post Office date stamp on the envelope.

We can assume from the above that 'BABA' Himself appeared in our house as desired by us, on the eve of New Year. We felt very happy. We have kept the photo for our daily puja.

From this, one of the Eleven Saying of Baba i.e. "IF YOU LOOK TO ME, I WILL LOOK AFTER YOU" is proved.

-G. Nagaraja Rao,
H. No. 14/11/806
Begum Bazar, Hyderabad 500 012

163. SAI'S MIRACLES (1987)

My family i.e. my husband, daughter and myself are staunch believers of "God Sai Baba". For this we thank with respect my sister Lata A. Rang who showed us the way to believe in God Sai Baba. For us Sai Baba is our God and Protector.

My daughter Meenakshi, now 8 yrs old, was suffering from skin allergy since her birth. At the age of six it took a turn for worse. I told this to my sister Lata who advised me to have faith in God Sai Baba. She sent to me *Udi* from Bombay and he condition used to get better. Again she had the same all over the body, and with *Udi* it would become better. So my entire family i.e. all the three of us with my sister Lata visited Shirdi in Dec. 86. Sicne then her allergy has become much less. Now the summer was approaching and my daughter wanted to go to my-in-law's place for horse riding. I was not so sure if she could go as she was allergic to animals and during this time also pollen allergic. So I asked her in April 87 to write a letter to God Sai Baba to help her. She wrote a letter in German to God Sai Baba. This she wrote from the heart to put an end to her allergic condition and asked the priest at Shridi to place this letter on God Sai Baba's Samadhi. I translated the letter in English. By end of May '87 she received *Udi* and Prasad from Shirdi. She was so happy, she immediately put it in her mouth. She prayed at night to Sai Baba to help her nad cure her from this ailment so she could go for horse-riding.

Wonder of Wonders, my daughter Meenakshi's allergy disappeared and she now is completely cured, In July '87, which was the summer vacation in Germany, she went to my-in-laws house enjoyed herself with contact with animals and pollen times without suffering any skin reaction. Nobody would now be able to say that this child had suffered from allergy. The letter from Meenakshi placed at the Samadhi of God Sai Baba, shows that God Sai Baba always looks after His dear ones who have full faith in Him.

This miracle shows that Sai Baba never leaves his devotees alone, no matter how far one is still He is everywhere. Therefore, we should have full faith and patience in God Sai Baba. God sai Baba always helps those who lay body and Soul in His Hands.

Bow to God Sai Baba-Peace unto all.

-Vimla Kaiser,
Hoffmann Str. 20, 6100 Darmstadt,
West Germany
(*Shri Sai Leela*, Dec., 1988)

164. A MIRACLE OF SHRI SAINATH

I am an employee of a Public Sector Undertaking. I was assigned with the job on 22.2.87 of arranging visas for our Engineers within a scheduled date, as they were required to proceed to U.S.S.R., on urgent work by 10.3.87. Being a staunch believer in Sai Nath I left everything to Him, because it was the first time I had to attend to such a type of job as also it was my first visit to New Delhi. With my usual devotion to Him I had prayed 'SAINATH' and accepted the assignment. On 23.2.87, I went to Secunderabad Rly. Station for arranging my reservation to New Delhi by A.P. Express on 24.2.1987, solely depending on 'BABA' because it was very difficult to get reservation, even a week in advance. Baba sent a person (whom I used to meet once in a year during Sri Swamy Ayyappa Pooja) to reservation counter and arranged for A.C. Chair Car reservation. I left my house with Baba's *Udhi* and boarded A.P. Express for New Delhi on 24.2.87. Being my first visit to Delhi, I was afraid as to how to go to our Guest House at Asiad Village. By the grace of Sainath I was guided by one of the co-passengers. Accordingly I got down at Hazarat Nizamuddin Rly. Station and went to Guest House by auto. The Guest House incharge received me with a smile and allotted a room without any delay, even though it used to be difficult to find a vacant room in our guest House, since all the rooms used to be normally occupied by our top officials. I could get a room on this occasion only by the grace of Baba. I proceeded to Russian Embassy for submission of visa applications, where I was guided by the concerned, the procedures for obtaining visas by the grace of 'SAINATH'. The visa authority refused to accept the application for want of one copy each of photographs, whereas I was having only two copies. I was very much disappointed, because I had to go back to Hyderabad/Secunderabad for bringing another copy of photograph. Again, I prayed for the help of 'SAINATH' who gave me a thought to get Photostat copy of photographs, the concerned officer also accepted the same only by the grace of Baba, because generally they do not accept. The next day i.e. on 26.2.87 I proceeded to the Embassy to complete other formalities; they agreed to give me visa on 2.3.87 i.e. within 6 days, whereas it takes 25 days, normally. On 28.2.87 I proceeded to Haridwar, since I had a desire to do *'Pindapradhanam'* to my late father at Brahma Khund of Haridwar. I requested Baba to lead me as I was not knowing anything. On reaching the Bus stand I was surprised to find a bus which was ready to leave for Haridwar and it started immediately on my boarding, as if, it was waiting for me. At Haridwar, a Purohit came to me and completed all the formalities to my satisfaction without demanding abnormal payment and accepted whatever I offered to him. It was a surprise to me, because, at such places mostly the demand is heavy. I returned to Delhi on 1.3.87 evening.

I was also proud of myself thinking that I could complete the work on my own and approached Embassy for collection of visas on 2.3.87. I also forgot 'SAINATH' entirely on this day and not even carried *Udhi* of Baba with me, which causes a lot of miracles. But when I was enroute to the embassy somebody hinted to me that I would be failing in getting visas, because I had neglected and did not carry Baba's *Udhi*. Accordingly, I was disappointed at Embassy, when the concerned officer refused to give me appointment upto 3.30 p.m. and even at 3.30 p.m. he expressed his inability to issue the visas, since no clearance was received from their Government. He also expressed that it might take 5 to 6 more days for receiving the clearance. This completely upset my programme, because I was holding firast class confirmed ticket for Secunderabad by A.P. Express of 4.3.87 and our engineers are scheduled to leave on 10.3.87 after obtaining foreign exchange etc., on my return Apart from this I was asked to be at Secunderabad by 5.3.87 with visas. I was in a disturbed mood and realized that this might have happened, because I had neglected to carry Baba's *Udhi* and realized my mistake. Immediately I started chanting the name of 'SAIRAM' and prayed Him to help me in this critical juncture. Then again I approached the officer for his help in getting the visas, Now he was a completely changed man. He asked me to see him on the next day. I came to my room and chanted the name of 'SAIRAM' and prayed Him to come to my rescue after fully surrendering myself to Him. On 3.3.87 I got up early and appealed 'SAIRAM' having full confidence, to guide me in the work and proceeded to Embassy. I was informed that the concerned officer was on sick leave and other officers asked me to come the next day since it was not possible to issue visas in his absence. But having full confidence in 'BABA' I explained the urgency and requested him for the needful. But they expressed their helplessness. It was a surprise that on the last minute an officer who was unknown to me and not connected with the visa section appeared there stating that he would try to help me. He took all the particulars of Engineers, enquired from visa section, and confirmed that the visas were ready and collected by the officer who was on leave. He even took the trouble of searching the visas from his drawer and handed them over to me. Who knows, it might have been Sainath Himself who appeared on the scene to render His helping hand to me? Because, Sainath has said to Shama (Madhava Rao Deshpande) (Sat-Charita

III Chapter) that if a man utter Baba's name with love, He shall fulfil all his wishes.

Here I proudly would like to inform all of you that I am very much grateful/ indebted to Shri Ch. Sambamurthy, R/o H.No. 1, 8-426, Chikkadpally, Hyderabad-500 020, who iniated me into 'SAI'S CULT' during 1963-64. He is in the service of Sainath for the last 50 years, and having dedicated his life to this cause, he performs poojas on every Thursday, and about 50 to 100 devotees attend. He tells Sai Leelas to every devotee. He also celebrates the festivals of Sainath i.e., Mahasivarathri, Sriramanavami and Gurupoornima on a grand level by arranging Harikatas, Bhajans, Laksha Archana etc. Distributes clothes to the physically handicapped, Fakirs and other deserving people and concludes the celebrations with poor feeding.

He is known to most of the Sai devotees in Andhra Pradesh, Madras etc. He visits Shirdi every year. He is generally calledby devotees as Baba or Guruji.

Here I would like to affirm that I could succeed in my assignment only the grace of 'SAINATH'. Sainath has also proved His words "IF YOU LOOK UP TO ME, I WILL LOOK AFTER YOU".

-A. Veeraiah,
'Sai Nilayam',
Plot No. 93, Vasavinagar,
SECUNDERABAD 500 003

166. Sai Baba cured a Dumb Man in Mauritius (1971)-Pandit Shiv Prasad

May I, dear Sai brothers, give you in a nutshell, the historic background of the Shirdi Sai Baba Mandir of Curepipe, Mauritius.

I had a son, Kumar by name (aged 14 years), who was dumb since his birth; in spite of all sorts of medical treatment, his dumbness persisted.

So, I decided to go on pilgrimage to India and pray for the cure of my dear son; thus it is that I happened to visit the Sai Baba temple in Shirdi where I literally crept on all floors, towards Baba's *Samadhi* and entreated Bhagawan for the cure of my son.

I guess Baba was moved by my very sincere and heart-felt prayers and He accorded me His Divine Grace.

Shortly after my return to Mauritius and to my most agreeable surprise my dear son Kumar began talking normally, by Baba's Divine Grace he secured a good job later on, he got married and has tow charming children.

He spends most of his spare time in looking after the Mandir and conducting *puja*.

In gratitude to Shirdi Sai Baba and to the profuse Grace He showered on me, I made a *Sankalpa* to build a small Shirdi Sai Baba temple in my premises * to expound the glory, the grandeur and the * of Sai Baba among the people of Mauritius.

Thus it is that in 1971, the Sai Baba Mandir in Curepipe, Mauritius opened its doors with a very humble beginning. I worked very hard to make the Sai mission flourish; and today the Sai Baba Mandir and the Sai Baba Centre of Curepipe has become a place of pilgrimage for thousands and thousands of people from all over Mauritius as well as from the neighbouring countries.

By now I am 81 years old; I have been doing the Sai Baba Mission for some 30 years; I am, by Baba's grace, healthy and in good shape, and I wish to continue this good work for many more years.

There have been innumerable instances of miraculous cures, of success in enterprises, of childless couples graced with a child, and several other such miracles for the devotees of the Shirdi Sai Baba temple of Mauritius.

Sometimes on Sundays and public holidays, the crowd of devotees at the Mandir is so dense that I have to have recourse to the local police to maintain order and discipline and to control the traffic.

Baba's Glory is spreading far and wide and I am very happy (but very humble also) that Baba has chosen me as His instrument to spread His Glory and Grace in this small country of Mauritius.

The Sai Baba temple in Mauritius has become so famous and renowned that it is referred to as the little Shirdi in Mauritius.

-Pandit Shiv Prasad
Curepipe, Mauritius
(Courtesy: *Sri Sai Leela*, Sept.-Oct,. 1990)

166. A Miraclem of Dharma Sai

My wife committed suicide. I was really innocent in this mater. But her people including her parents started blaming me in this regard. I was really disgusted and afraid of this blame and ran away from my place. As I am a staunch believer of Lord Sri Shirdi Sainath, I started *Akhandanama Japa* and left everything to him. One Thursday a very old lady with a common Balance in her hands appeared in my dream and she said, "My name is Dharma Sai. I am staying in Dharmagiri Kshethra. I have given you to justice; immediately come t me and donate some amount towards making the *Pratima* of Sri Dharma Sai in marble stone and disappeared. Next day morning I sold my gold chain which was in my neck since 20 years and rushed to Lord Sri Dharma Sai of Dharmagiri Kshetra, Shamshabad, R.R. District-509218 (14 Kms. from Zoo Park), Hyderabda-509 218 and I dropped some amount in Hundi. At the same moment I saw my in-laws in that place as they come over there to have the *darshan* of Sri DharmaSai. Immediately all of them apologized for their mistake in front of Sri Dharma Sai. They offered me to get married with their second daughter. I married her and I am leading a very happy life with her. Grateful thanks to Sri Dharma Sai for favours received.

Vinod Kumar Jain,
Mulund, Bombay
(Courtesy: *The Hindustan times*, June 16, 1994)

167. Another Miracle of Sri Dharma Sai

My land located in Madras City was in court for the last 20 years due to disputes. One day I happened to see the advertisement given by Sri Govind Singh in *Hindustan Times* about the Miracles Sri Dharma Sai and about "Siddi Yantram". I immediately went to Sri Dharmagiri Kshetra 14 Kms. from Zoo Park, Hyderabad and had *darshan* of Sri Dharma Sai and took to Siddi Yantram. Within one week after taking Siddi Yantram I got back my property worth several crores of rupees which was in disputes.

-K. Ram Nadham, Tambaram, Madras
Dharmagiri Kshetram, Shamshabad,
Ranga Reddy Dist., Hyderabad (A.P.)
(Courtesy: *The Hindustan times*, July 6, 1995)

168. *Udhi*, A Unique Remedy

My friend and I are great believers of Sai and remember always the saying of Sri Sai, "If you chant my name 'Sai' will be with you".

Recently in the month of Sept. '86 my friend's mother went to an eye specialist for eye check-up. The specialist checked up her eyes and asked her to be ready for cataract operation of the right eye. Being an old lady she was much worried of this and was not willing for operation. My friend advised her to have faith in Sri Sai Baba and apply *Udhi* daily on the affected eye. In the month of November '86, she went to the same eye specialist to undergo the operation. But to the surprise of the doctor and others, her vision was found to be clean. The doctor now opined that there was no need for the operation.

The above incident surprised us all, beyond words. With prostrations to Sai Baba.

S. Sarojini,
2-2-1164/15/3, Tilak Nagar,
New Nallakunta
(Courtesy: *Shri Sai Leela*, Aug., 1997)

169. Sai Miracles Experienced by A Film Editor (1960-1996)

I am a devotee of Sri Shirdi Sai Baba for the last 40 years.

To think about, to speak about, and to write about the glories of Shri Samartha Satguru Sai Baba of Shirdi, is a blessing. It gives inner strength to man and facilitate his all-round advancement. The deepest experience one has is incapable of utterances. As you are keen after any bit of information I shall mention some of such facts.

In the year 1960, I was with my family suffering all of a sudden for a morsel of food due to a big break in my film career. One day in the middle of the night I was crying and scolding God not withstanding His tests. I stubbornly made a vow to myself unless He appears immediately in person and saves me from the horrible situation. I will never have faith in his existence. Sometime passed in blank. The test of time came to reveal His presence. All of a sudden there was blinding light of flash lighting my place for a fraction of a second. I thought that there would be rain. I thought as if it was summer and there was no possibility of rain coming. Then what was the flasti for? As my mind was pondering over suddenly and more distinctly I heard the sound of the *Padukas* coming forward me and going into my *pooja* room. This happened for a moment. My hair stood still. I immediately realized the presence of the Almighty Shirdi Sai Baba. I am reminded about a photo of His given to me in my studenthood by my principal who was an ardent devotee of Baba, who used to make a trip to Shirdi every year.

Next day I made a search, and got it. I kept it beside the other photos of the Gods in my *pooja* room. I bathed and sat on my sofa dressed as if ready to go to the studio. I heard the sound of a car stopping in front of my house. My friend came inside and told me that he was in search in me from the last night for an editing job which must be started immediately. As Baba said, "Look up to me and I will look after you. Not vain is my promise that I shall ever lighten your burden." One begins to understand much better the way in which Sai Baba was approached and He operated upon those contacting him. in 1962 I was going through some books in an old book stall. I saw one old book in the shelf that attracted my attention. Though there was KD name written on it, still my mind was for it. I took the book and saw inside it the name *"Sri Sai Baba's Charters and Sayings"* by His Holiness Shri Narasimha Swamiji. After going through it, I was very much keen to know much more about Samartha Satguru Sai Baba of Shirdi. After sometime I was returning from the church which is at Armenian street at Madras and I happened to stop near soiled Second hand books kept on the platform for sale. As it happened before, I saw a black soiled book without any name. I eagerly took *Sayings"* by His Holiness Shri Narasimha Swamiji. After going through it, I was very much keen to know much more about Samartha Satguru Sai Baba of Shirdi. After sometime I was returning from the church which is at Armenian street at Madras and I happened to stop near soiled Second hand books kept on the platform for sale. As it happened before, I saw a black soiled book without any name. I eagerly took *

170. I am Vishwanathan from Mauritius. I am 26 ears old. I am so in love with Baba for being with me every single second. I work as Director in a company based in security Fence. On the 6th February 2014, there was a cyclone in Mauritius and so it was a day off for all citizens. It happened to be a Thursday. After the noon *Aarti*, I bowed as usual to the Divine picture of Shri Shirdi Sai Baba in my room with an oil lamp that is always kept burning. Then I went downstairs to have lunch with my family after offering *Naivedam* (holy food) to our saviour Shri Sai Baba first. My mom had cooked special food as we were all at home at this time of the day. After the sumptuous lunch I went back up again.

To my surprise the door of my room was closed, when I went inside I noticed the curtain was wet by rain through the window that was slightly opened. As a result, the lamp in front of the Divine Picture of Shri Sainath was no more burning ll. I was about to light it again with the match box in my hands, when I noticed that the small orange colour shawl that used to be on the picture had caught on fire in my absence. I immediately begged my adorable mother Sai to kindly forgive my carelessness as it was my fault of not closing the window during cyclonic weather that the wind went in, blew the shawl on the lampand caught fire. The picture frame was burnt on the edge too. I started cleaning the burnin shawl particles by moving slightly the picture of adorable Sai to the left & then My Goodness- wonder of wonders. I clearly felt my heart beat and breathing stopped for 3-5 seconds due to what I saw. The burning flames stopped by the picture of Sainath and the divine picture image of adorable Shri Shirdi Sai Samartha Sat Guru was behind on the wall. I bowed in reverence in my mind & immediately called out my family who came very fast as my tone of calling was still under the shock effect.

The wall of my room is custard yellow in colour & still the silvery white beard of my Baba Sai can be seen clearly. Still now by His loving grace, every time the *Aarti* is being sung with devotion, the beard along with holy image of *Sadguru* Baba glitters with amazing brightness. *Still* I cannot enough say" Thank You my Baba Sai." I just wash His holy feet with my tears of gratitude., I have begged the divine permission of our All- powerful Sai Nath to allow me to take pictures of this divine experience- miracle image that has appeared on the wall just next to the picture of Shri Sai Baba while the fire was spreading and lateron stopped by His divine presence. I will update more pictures shortly & kindly share it with other devotees also. I am aware of the fact that we are all instruments in the divine hands of Shri Samartha Sat Guru Sai Natha Deva & His love is unlimited & matchless. I would consider myself even more blessed if you could kindly post this divine experience along with the pictures for the devotees to see. I confirm my resence on this earth as living testimonial that everything is indeed ordained by our God Sai's wil. - Vishwanathan, Mauritius

171. Baba helped me to clear my exam

I am a student and i completed my post graduation recently. My exams were in the month of July, but there was some time constraint for the preparation of exams but somehow i managed. For our syllabus there was a subject considered a bit difficult. For this particular subject before the exam I tried to revise the entire subject so that I do not find it difficult during the exam, I had studied the entire night, completed revising the subject and was a bit relaxed that I will be able to attempt the exam. Now when i was sitting in the examination hall I was just praying Baba that the paper should go well. After I received the question paper I read all the questions and felt that I could answer them but when I started writing I got confused and I was not able to work out the problems, I forgot the formulas which I had studied thoroughly, though the questions were easy I do not know what happened at that time and after the exam I was feeling that I wouldl not be able to pass in this subject due to this I was feeling very low. After this exam there was one more subject left for which I had to prepare so I left everything to Baba's wishsaying" let Him do what He wants. Later when the results were out Iwas sj ocked as well as happy. The passi mark for the subject was 40 and I had got 41, finally I had cleared that paper. This was possible only because of our beloved Baba.

172. My first cousin was tracked with hepatitis-c and had this virus for couple of years. 2 weeks back my cousin underwent Hepatitis-C test by the doctor. But Sai Baba Baba helped our family byhis miraculous grace. We received medical reports and result is there is no virus in her body and doctor told to forget about this virus and it will not be there in her body in future also. I sincerely bow to Shri Sai Baba for listening to our prayers and concerns. Sai Baba is amazing.

173. *BABA'S UDI* CURED SCORPION BITE CASE (1997) Dr. B.G. Das was running a clinic in Kanpur. Mrs. Das used to visit the clinic in her leisure time. The clinic was located at the ground floor of their residence. She had read in *Sai Satcharita* of Baba's *udhi* working a cure in the case of scorpion bites also. A case of scorpion bite came to her husband's clinic and she and her husband were tempted to try the same, with all apologies to Sri Sai Baba. A Muslim lady had brought her 11 years old daughter to the clinic whose right index finger had been bitten by scorpion. The girl was tossing and howling in pain. Three ligatures were tied by her arents. One at the base of the finger second over the wrist and the third over her arm.

After necessary examination the doctor intentionally avoided giving the patient any drug or anesthesia. Only *udhi* was tried. The *udhi* was rubbed on the index finger, forearm and arm, and a pinch of *udhi* in water was also given for drinking. The girl and her mother were asked to remain in the clinic for some time. The doctor and his wife were wonder-struck to see the girl completely relieved of pain in a short time, the girl and her mother went home happily.

174. BABA PULIS THE CHAIN (1987)

It was my 42nd visit to Shirdi via Puttaparthi. I reached Shirdi on 26th November, 1987, and left it in the evening of 27th instant. It is mentioned in *Shri Sai Satcharita*, (Chapter 8 on the last page) same that those devotees, who sought the permission of Sri Sai Baba before leaving Shirdi and followed his directions, they reached their homes safe, but those, who did not abide by

His commands had suffer a lot and had to face adversities of various types. Again in the beginning of Chapter 9, it is mentioned that if Baba asked someone to return home, he was bound to leave Shirdi. While going back to their native place, the devotees used to go to Baba to prostrate before Him and at the moment Baba gave a few instructions to them that was inevitable to observe. If someone returned back disobeying His instructions, then he has to face misfortune certainly. In this Chapter, Tatya Kote Patil and an European gentleman's incidents are mentioned in detail. In Chapter 12, it is mentioned in respect of Kaka Mahajani that when he reached Shirdi with an intention to stay there for atleast a week and wished to participate in Gokul Asthami functions, Baba asked him immediately, when he was going back? Kaka Mahajani answered, "When Baba orders me to go back?" Bbaa asked him to go the following day. Baba's words were law and to comply them was a necessity. So Kaka proceeded for Bombay the very next day. Bahu Saheb Dhumal came to Shirdi and after Baba's darshan, proceeded to Niphad to attend a court case thee, but Baba did not permit him to leave and so he was detained for seven days altogether. Ofcourse the result of this detention was profitable enough. In Chapter 30, it is written that no one can have darshan of a Saint unless He himself wills. In chapter 18, 19 and 36, it is mentioned that due to some pious deads of past birth, a person can reach to Shridi.

Being aware of all these narrations, it has been my practice to go to Chawadi, Dwarkamai, Samadhi Mandir, Gurusthan and Lendibagh and seek Baba's kind permission before leaving Shirdi. But I don't know why and how this time I sought Baba's permission to leave as usual but I also asked Baba to accompany me upto my residence at Betul and to take me safely to my home. Perhaps it was the first chance when I asked Baba to go with me.

This time my acute Asthma trouble of 22 years old had put me to an unbearable state, yet by Baba's grace, I could be present at Shirdi in September, October and then in November 26th of that year. So I boarded three tier compartment at Manmad without obtaining reservation to it. The train might have covered hardly 40 KM. distance from Manmad when the Conductor of the three tier compartment told me to get down at Bhussawal and try to get a place in general compartment. I requested him about my asthma trouble and submitted to him that under such acute trouble, it would not b epossible for me to get down at Bhusawal and again board the train in general compartment which was generally choked by the passengers who serve at Bombay for their livelihood. I knew when the train stopped at Jalgaon and again at Bhusawal, but neither I got down the compartment nor the conductor disturbed me. It all was Baba's game. But after Bhusawal, though I had no sound sleep at all, but only Baba knows how I could not know the following stations of Burhanpur, Nepanagar, Khandwa, Khirakiya, Harda, Banapur, Hoshangabad etc., because before reaching the train at some stations, I had a small sleep. I was to get down at Itarsi Junction in the night at about 3.00 A.M. because the train was running very late. After getting down at Itarsi Junction, I had to go to Itarsi Bus Stand to catch the Bus scheduled for Betul. At such odd hours in Itarsi, unsocial elements finding someone alone with bag and baggage, stop him and start snatching the belongings and to save one's life, it is only the remedial course to surrender each and every belongings, i.e. money, watch, ring etc.

Probably the luck had destined me to be a victim of such a happening that day at Itarsi, so Baba blessed me with such a sound sleep that the train halted at Itarsi Junction for half an hour but I could not be aware that the train has touched Itarsi. There was one youngman in my compartment who was going to Orai near Kanpur and he was aware of this fact that I am to get down at Itarsi. All of a sudden I heard a long whistle of the train which awakened me, I got up and started enquiring with the young co-passenger of Orai if the Itarsi station had come. He, said, "Please get down immediately". When I came to the door of the compartment with both hands holding the handbag etc., I saw the train settled and giving long whistles. After getting down in quite lonely and at a dark place, I saw two scootermen on the road, because the halting train had blocked their way. Railway authorities were trying to find out the defaulter who might have pulled the chain to stop the train, but no-body else except myself was found getting down from the said train. So, the conductor inquired of me whether I had pulled the chain. I replied humbly that upto this old age, I never dared even to touch the chain, what of say of pulling it. Then he asked about my occupation? I told him that I was a Professor in a Government College of Betul. I had slept and could not guess that the train was halting at Itarsi Junction. So I failed to get down there. They might have handed me over to Railway Police any anything indecent could have happened to me but they spared me. The train was still awaiting. Thus I inquired with those two scooterwalas to give me a lift upto Itarsi Station. They asked my destination where I had to go. I told them that I had to go to Betul. They told me that a Bus right in front of me was going to Betul. "Please get in and catch the bus immediately." And so I had a seat in the bus going to Betul. It was 3.30 A.M. then I reached Betul safely in the morning of 28th November at 5.15 A.M. I spread over the bed-sheets in Baba's room, put a jug of water to drink, set up a big framed photo of Sai Baba, garlanded it with Samadhi garland, which I had brought from Shirdi and weepingly asked Baba to please take a bit rest as He might be feeling tired in pulling the chain and stopping the from before the bus for Betul for my sake.

Dear Sai brothers, if you have firm faith and belief in our Lord of Lords Bhagawan Sainath, rest assure that he is always behind you for your safety of life and to save you from incoming calamities. He is Lord Shankar, Omnipresent, Omniscient and Omnipotent and not less than it. May Lord Sainath ever shower His blessings on all those who have completely surrendered to His Lotus Feet.

Om Shri Sai Yashahkaya Shirdivasime Namah.

-(Late) Prof. A.P. Tripathi,
Head of the Department of Hindi,
Sri Sathya Sai Institute of Higher Learning,
Prasanthi Nilayam (A.P.)

175. BABA'S MIRACLES

Once, a young couple highly educated with qualifications of M.Tech. and B.E., came from Andhra Pradesh. They were rich also The youth was suffering from severe pain due to Kidney stones. The scan report revealed that there were eight such stones, Of course, he had already undergone an operation and got some stones removed, but the same problem had recurred, before he approached me. As usual, I prayed to Sai Baba and gave him holy ash with Babaji's photo. I told him to trust Babaji and advised him to consume it after offering prayers to Babaji. To our surprise, all the eight stones were dissolved within a fortnight. The youth fully got rid of his problem without any operation and felt very happy. Then full faith dawned on him about Babaji's miraculous cures.

-Sri H.D. Lakshmana Swamiji

1376 This is an incident which took place during March 1966. A couple was very much worried about their children's progress. After regular prayer to Babaji, they found better character and behaviour of their children and now there is much progress in their education. Actually, the parents had never thought of this improvement in their dreams even. Now they are free from worries and have much faith in Babaji. I had advised them to meditate on

Babaji when their children come. Now they have found alround development in their family. This is all due to blessings and miraculous grace of Babaji, and their strong belief in him.

-Sri H.D. Lakshmana Swamiji,
No. 52 "BANASHANKARI DEVI MANDIRA"
14th "B", Main, II Cross, II phase,
Mahalakshmipuram,
BANGALORE-560 086

176. BABA'S MIRACULOUS MESSAGES (1995-96)

Sri Sai Baba has been giving his messages since 28-5-87 while I sit in meditation. The first message was given when I was in meditation in Dwarakamai at Shirdi. Since then I have been getting these messages regularly. All are in Telugu only as I am a Telugu man. Baba did not give permission to me to publish these messages upto 1.1.90. Following His direction, the first 35 Messages covering the period upto 19.2.1989 were published in Telugu under the caption 'SRI SAI TATWA SANDESHAMS' and the English version of a total of 77 Messages upto 28.1.90 was published subsequently under the caption 'SAT SANDESH'.

The Messages covering the period upto 17.11.91 were published as Vol. I under the caption 'SAI TATWA SANDESHAMS' in Telugu. Subsequent Messages received from 17.11.1991 upto 9.3.95 were published as Vol. II under the same caption. The messages after this period are yet to be printed. I have received more than 300 Messages uptill now.

Sri Sai Baba gave The Following Message While I was in meditation on 5.1.95 at 10.30 P.M.:

"Death is inevitable to every one. Life and death are tied down by the results of your past actions. Death means the Jiva leaving one body and taking another. Whatever the person thinks at the time of death, that thought will persist and will make Jiva to enter into a subtle body. The thought persisting at the time of death will lead to similar future life. The persons living in sensual pleasures are ignorant and can not understand this truth.

When one leaves the body, his relations or his friends should not worry about death. One has to experience his own *karma*. If a person gets a disease due to his past karma, even if he gets relief of the ailment with the aid of doctors and medicines, he has to suffer from that remaining trouble in the next birth. Karma can not be dissolved or removed by others. One has to suffer the results of his *Prarabdha Karma*. Knowing that your body is impermanent and unreal you will take more care for your *'Deha'* Shake off you *'Deha-abhimana'*.

The Jiva resides in the water present in the heart. At the time of Jiva leaving the body, the water in the heart gets gradually reduced and the area below the tongue gets dried up. Knowing this, think that death is fast approaching and think of *Bhagavanama*.

2. Message Received from Lord Sainath on 16.1.1995

"If you do not become a servant of your body and its senses, if you lead simple life, if you do not get attached to caste and creed, body, or beauty, money or momentary pleasures, you will have peaceful death at the end of life. However much you may take trouble in protecting your body, it is bound to perish one day. Do not waste your time in giving pleasures to the body. Know that the ultimate aim of your life is to know and receive the effulgent truth of yourself".

"Your death depends on your past actions. If you are in God Consciousness, your death will take easy stride. Soul is not body and one should not fear death. When the result of all past accumulated karmas, whether they are good or bad, get destroyed, then *'Jivatma'* leaves its *attachment to the body consisting of five primary elements and get merged with Supreme (Paramatma.)* Those who surrender to God completely without even a trace of ego, they only can get the Supreme-Godhood."

3. Sri Sai Sandesh on 17.1.1995 at 9.30 P.M.

"Leaving the worldly attractions and aiming the Universal spirit as the ultimate goal of Supreme pleasure and peace, lead your life in meditation on Atman. Do not depend on the body which is made up of five elements. The accumulated sinful acts of many past lives get stored in *chitta* and project a thick wall of obstruction in the spiritual path. Treat them with devotional activities and get rid of them before the death engulfs you. In the same way, get rid of your doubts and go beyond pleasures and pains. Do not encourage ignorance which is the cause of *'Samsara'* resulting in routine life and death cycle. Even though you are bound by actions of previous lives, by the steadfast devotion on Supreme Divinity you can get over the resultant ties of those karmas. With staunch devotion and meditation, destroy the six enemies residing in you before the disappearance of very transient body. Get firm hold of effluent Divine Spirit, leave the worldly matters which are very transient and always troublesome. When death approaches you, welcome it with open hands, merging entire attention of you mind in Me. With such powerful medicine you will get peace of mind."

Message Given by Sri Sai Baba on 21.1.95 at 8.40 P.M.

"I am omniscient, Controller of the whole Universe, support of the whole world and the prime cause of all activities. Without diverting your mind on worldly affairs, fix it in your heart where I am residing, If you constantly think of Me, you will be eligible for my Grace, otherwise with doubtful mind you go hither and thither without my Grace; no one can eliminate your troubles. Except Myself nobody can erase the prints on your fore-head. Know that body is an abode of unhappiness and is transient, and when such a body goes off, why should you all weep?"

Sri Sai Baba's Message Received on 25.1.95 at 1.30 A.M.

"First know who I am and then if you meditate on Me, you can reach Me. Whatever form you think at the end of your life, you will attain that form only in the next life. If you meditate on 'Ananta Paramatma', you will attain Him only. In the Universe know which is permanent (Ananta) and which is impermanent. Except the Supreme God, all other lives and matters have to end one day or other."

"I am indestructible and ever present. So if you meditate on Me, you can reach the permanent abode in Me. If you take this as your unquivering aim in your life, you can reach the goal safely. Never aspire at impermanent affairs. To attain My mercy and to reach Me, devotion with pure heart is very essential. Whatever ideas you have during your life time, they only project in your mind at the end of your life. So to eliminate all other thoughts, think of Me always."

"Fill your mind with Divine Wisdom. If you are having such wisdom at the end of your life, you will not have rebirth. To attain such wisdom of Truth at the end of your life, you must meditate on Me, thinking of my divine attributes etc. throughout your life and then you are sure to attain Me."

Sri Sai Baba's Message (Sandesh) received on 28.1.95 at 11.30 P.M.

"Happiness and grief are imaginations. Know that worldly happiness is not real. Kama, Krodha, Lobha, Moha, Mada, Matsara are all false impressions. Always remember that death may reach you at any moment and be prepared to continue the journey of 'Jiva'. Then you will attain the blessed state."

"Without depending on friends and relations and without leaving your philosophical activities on them, keep your aim on Me. Death may snatch your life without previous notice. Then your relatives and friends may not be able to remind you about God and there may not be any one by your side to pray God for your future welfare. Understand this and surrendering all your thoughts to Me, meditate on Me and be peaceful."

Message given by Sri Sai Baba on 31.1.95 at 8.10 P.M.

"As you have carried on the load of miseries and some happiness from the previews lives to this life, you have made this life an abode of miseries with less of happiness."

"Know what is Supreme State which gives immense peace and try hard to attain that state. Then you will not have next birth and even if you have another life, it will give you happiness only. Divert your attention in search of God. Fix your mind in Divine path. Know what is 'ATMA' and what is 'ANATMA' what is 'Jhana' (Knowledge) and what is 'AJNANA' (ignorance); what is bound state and what is freedom. Knowing that constant Divine rememberence alone, can take you to deathless state, try for God's mercy and you will attain the state of Godhood which is beyond 'Gunas'."

"The main cause for life activity is presence of 'JIVA' in the body. When the Jiva leaves the body, the life will extinguish and the person dies. At the time of death speech etc. will get merged in Mind, the activities of mind get merged in 'PRANA', the 'Prana' gets merged in 'TEJAS'. When the man is about to die, you observe the heat of the body and that heat itself, is 'Tejas'. To every living being at the time of birth itself the time of death is fixed. No one can escape this. Every born being must die and this is the open secret of life. Try hard to attain Supreme Godhood."

Sri Sai Baba's Sandesh Given on 6.2.95 at 8.00 P.M.

"One gets spiritual inclination by God's Grace. All worldly matters are like images in a mirror. Earnestly pray the Supreme God to lead you from untruth to truthful state and to eternal peaceful state."

"Believe firmly that except God, no one gives any helping hand to you and the attachment to the forms and associations of your so called relatives is useless. Always try hard to reach God who has no beginning and no end, and who is always blissful and unbound."

Sri Sai Baba's Divine Sandesh Given on Sivaratri day, Monday, 27.2.1995, at 9.10 P.M.

"Uncontrolled mind leads one into dark paths of 'ignorance' and one gets rid of this unruly mind, he will get knowledge about God. Until that time, your old impressions of mind remain as they are unless one gets rid of the *vasanas*, he will be immersed in pleasures and pains of life."

"There are two birds in you – they are *'PARAMATMA'* and *'JIVATMA'*. The 'Jivatma' thinks that it consists of body organs *(Indriyas)* and thinks that pleasures and pain of these belong to it and get immersed in them. The other bird *'PARAMATMA'* will not get perturbed with either pleasures or pains and remain calm as a witness. *'JIVA'* gets ego feeling and thinks that every act is done by him only. When *Jiva* gets rid of this egoism, then he understands that he is not the cause of pains and pleasures of the body. Otherwise with bodily attachments *'Jiva'* goes on in the cycle of births and deaths."

"Death means that the Jiva leaves the gross body and with subtle body goes to other worlds. *'Jiva'* when he is egoless, becomes a witness of pleasures and pains of the body and contemplates always that he is *'PARABRAHMA'*, then the results of all actions drop off and he becomes *'Paramatma'*. That is the Supreme goal and so all of you should do meditation on Atma always."

Sri Sai Baba's Message Given on Thursday, 2.3.1995, at 7.45 P.M.

"As you are immersed in the sea of *'Samsara'*, you are not able to get rid of the desires of the body and this is leading you to have very many lives in which you accumulate the results of good and bad acts you do in those lives. If you learn and separate what is gross and what is subtle body and if you learn the activities of ten types of airs *(Vayus)*, then you can know the relationship of *'Jivatma'* and *'Paramatma'*. Till you know that you are *'Brahman'*, the cycle of births and deaths are inevitable. Try to attain that ever blissful state. Know what is body and what is soul. The association of five sense organs and five motor organs *(Pancha Karmendriyas)* is body. in that body the *'Jivatma'* is residing. If you understand this, you can visualize *'Paramatma'*."

"Merger of *'Jivatma'* in *'Parmatma'* is *'MUKTI'*. To attain this, meditate on Me always. If you do this, you need not go anywhere to get My Grace. I am Omnipresent. Meditate on Me with the firm idea that I lead you in the way of salvation and you will attain better state in next life."

"Now I will show you the way how the mind can merge in *'Atma'* during meditation. Without any fear all of you meditate on Me. I am like *'Kalpavriksha'*. I am *'Adi Sakti'*; I am *'Jagan Mata'*; I am in all forms. All forms are mine."

"Do not fear when your mind gets merge din *'Atma'*. Take *'Udhi'* and that will protect your body. When your mind gets merged in *'Atma'*, chant my name. Sit on dear skin, close your eyes, keep your back, chest, neck and head in straight position and sit like a status and meditate on Me. Then only you can know how your body and mind merge in 'ATMA'.

"Keep faith in Me and whatever action you take it as being done by Me. Whatever you or your wife write, know that they are written by Me. Let not the ego ever enter in your minds that you are writing all these."

"Whenever you get My philosophical Messages or any books on my philosophy and Tatwa are printed, let introductions to those books be written by well-known Sai Sevaks. Let them write elaborately who I am, what are My *leelas*; what is importance of My Avatar, why I have come on to the earth etc. I will protect such people always."

Sri Sai Baba's Message Receive don 9.4.95 at 9 P.M.

"Constantly think of *'Atma'*. 'Atma' is indivisible. Cause and effect are not concerned with 'Atma'. 'Atma' is not bound by good or bad results of action. When the mind gets purification by doing duty bound actions, then one can attain *'Jnana'*. Then only one can realize the pure *'Paramatma'* residing in all animate and inanimate objects. When you are performing actions which are ordained to you as your duties in selfless manner, you will get purity of mind. If you do not do this, you will be wasting your time in pleasures of life. Try to become good aspirant of *'Brahma Jnani'*.

"You must first of all know what is 'Atma'? The 'Atma' that is present every where is MYSELF. There is nothing except Me. Know this clearly. If you are constant in meditation, you can visualize 'Atma'.

"Know that the entire Universe is seen in self-effulgent Atma. The whole world is a mirage. It is a projection of 'MAYA'. As you are not having real knowledge of *"Atma Swaroopa"*, you will see the tricks of Maya as real. When you attain real knowledge the *'Maya'* gets dissolved."

"Pray for *Nitya-Anitya*, *Viveka*, and *'Vairagya'*, turning your mind inside towards Me. With full faith on Me, offer your prayers. Bookish knowledge without practice leads you nowhere. Leaving your vanity of body completely, offer yourself at My feet. Leave the idea of 'I' and 'Mine', without aspiring for worldly pleasures, worship Me for My Grace. If you chant My name always, you can attain the Supreme State."

Sri Sai Baba's Message received on 5.5.95 at 7 A.M.

"You are getting immersed in acquiring wealth and thus wasting your time. Without worshipping God you will not attain purity of mind. Without purity of mind, you cannot get *Jnana*. So to attain God-knowledge, do your fixed duties without fear. Thus *Antah Karma* will be purified. By doing actions without aspiring for fruits of action and with single minded devotion, surrendering yourself completely to Me, you will become get one pointed devotion and *Jnana* and thus become great personifications of wisdom."

"Your ignorance is the cause for your increasing interest in Samsara. When you attain *Atma-Jnana*, then you will get rid of your egoism and you will get disassociated from Samsara. At that state you will not have friends or foes, you do not aspire for body pleasures and you can face any amount of painful and sorrowful events."

Message given by Sri Sai Baba on 25.5.1995 at 9.15 P.M.

"To attain Godhood one need not become an ascetic and go into the forest. A *grahasta* who performs his duty-bound actions without aspiring for the results is a true Sanasi and the person who leaves his bounded duties is not a Sanyasi. Leading a life of Grahasta if one strives hard to practice Divine activity he will get rid of all bad-thoughts, impurities and other defects and attains salvation. More than Sanyasis, these who mediate on God always are great persons. He who does not allow his mind to go towards worldly pleasures, who with one pointed concentration meditates on Atma, who is not moved by any tribulations, who thinks that god is dwelling in God, who feels that pleasures and pains of others are equal to his pleasures and pains, such a person is greater than a Sanyasi and he becomes a great Yogi. Mind is fickle, not steady and is as difficult as controlling the air. But just because it is difficult to control the mind, taking up Sanyasa is not good. By constant practice, you can attain *Vairagya*. If you donot have *Raga* and *Dwesha*, the mind will not run towards any object. If the mind goes on any object, divert it from that object and surrender it to Atma. If you practice like this, your mind will get fixed, and even without attaining Sanyasa, you can get salvation."

"Taking up sanyasa without one-pointed mind is useless. So by staying in Grahastha Ashram, if you perform your duty in proper way, you will become eligible for *'Moksha'*."

Sri Sai Baba's Message given on 28.5.95 Sunday 9.30 P.M.

"Know *'Brahma Satyam, Jagan MIthya'* Every being who is born is bound to die. However beautiful and energetic one may be, he is bound to die, at one moment or the other. So why do you have grief for the transient things. As long as you are immersed in ignorance, you will not have peace of mind."

"Ignorant person will always have impermanent mind. When he gets light of Knowledge, he will see his own self every where. When one gets Jnana. The veil of ignorance vanishes, then you will know your real state, and you will know the worldly existence is impermanent."

"The action performed with *Karma-Indriyas* can be obstructed by others but the thinking process cannot be obstructed by others. So you yourself have to remove the bad ideas of your mind with the firm attitude of your buddhi. Others can not change them. Unless your mind, speech and action are uniform and single-minded it is impossible to prosper in the philosophical line."

"You are responsible for your present state. The ideas and actions of the previous lives are responsible for the present state of life. So if you want to have good life in future, your present thoughts and actions must be good."

"To whichever form of God you worship, and in whichever way you do worship, it all reaches Me only. In whatever manner one worships Me, I will bless them in the same way. I am the Father, good advisor, and support of all beings in this world. I am the permanent seal of the whole Universe. I do not have likes and dislikes. I am the Father of Saints and sinners, *Jnanis* and *Ajnanis* also."

"Thinking of Me always, surrender all your actions to Me. Those who do have such firm faith, do not have any obstructions, troubles, difficulties, grief or mental worries at all.

Message given by Sri Sai Baba on 13.6.96

"I am personified love. All of you are involve din bad thoughts due to ignorance. I have come in human form to lift all of you from ignorance. I convert those who approach Me into high philosophical Bhaktas. I will grant you much philosophical power to lift yourself to higher state of experience.

My prime purpose is to keep my devotees in high state of *'Atma-Sandhna'* *Sadhan*. Depending on the devotion and philosophical attitude of the Bhaktas, they get the results accordingly. I will submerge the human weaknesses and bad habits with my teachings and make them pure and fit to attain the philosophical heights. Nobody can understand the real meaning of My teachings and do not give importance to them. My sayings are essences of Vedanta and the essence of all religious philosophical books. Those who understand the essence of my preachings and digest them, they will get rid of their lethargy, body consciousness and their tickle mindedness and keep their aim on Me only."

"When I was in human form I preached the same teachings and gospels but nobody has propagated them. That is why for the benefit of all my bhaktas, I am once again expressing same old teachings through you but not preaching any new ones."

-B. Uma Mahesware Rao,
Guntur (A.P.)

174. BABA COMES TO THE RESCUE OF THE INNOCENT DEVOTEES (1996)

Wherever I go through the various chapters of *'Shri Sai Satcharita'* and read Baba's miracles galore how he saved an innocent child of a black-smith, how he saved innocent residents from cholera, etc. etc., I recollect how he had come to rescue me from the clutches of the wicked persons. I shudder to think of the consequences if the merciful Baba had not been so gracious and kind enough to help the poor and helpless devotee like me. It would have meant total misery which could have easily taken my life even.

While posted at Kathmandu under India Embassy Nepal, I was abruptly transferred to a District Hqrs. far away from Kathmandu to head a small office there. A brand new jeep was placed at my disposal with strict instructions to ply it for our own official purposes only. The driver, a Nepali youngman had to take orders from me before taking out the vehicle from the garrage.

The facility of the jeep was available only to me. No other officer functioning at the station had its privilege. Many a time, the local officers approached me for it but had to return disappointed. this made me an unpopular official.

Everything went on well when suddenly one day I fell ill and was advised by the doctor for bed rest for a week or ten days. During my absence, my Nepali Head Clerk was looking after my duties in the office. It was during that period that the local Superintendent of Police wished to send his children to a town across the Indian border. He contacted my head clerk for the jeep. Taking advantage of my absence and wishing to oblige the S.P., he directed the driver (ofcourse, verbally) to take away the vehicle to the S.P. and act as per his direction. I was blissfully kept ignorant of the whole matter.

As the ill luck would have it, the jeep while on return journey after leaving the children at their destination, met with a serious accident, practically smashing the body. The driver was seriously injured and had to be removed to the civil hospital unconscious in a precarious condition.

As soon as this sad news reached my office, the head clerk taking advantage of the driver's critical condition, cooked false story with the connivance of the S.P. that the vehicle moved under my orders. Obviously, this was done to get me implicated in the serious matter.

I was immediately summoned to Kathmandu to face the fury of my senior officers. A count of enquiry was immediately held and an Inquiry Officer from Delhi was asked to submit a prima-facie charge sheet against me. All evidences were against me. In the meanwhile, the driver was still fighting with life and death in the hospital. I was sure to be held personally responsible for the mishap and likely to be sacked from service alongwith any other punishment including immediate repatriation to India, for no fault of mine. My only helpful witness could be the driver who was so serious that he could expire any time.

Till then, I was a Sai devotee of a modest nature. We had a large mounted photograph of Baba hanging in our drawing room but I had never seriously or regularly prayed before Him. On that fateful night, I bowed before Him touching His lotus feet every now and then begging Him emotionally to save an innocent fellow from disaster.

Next morning, I was about to leave for the final session of the Inquiry. Some unknown and complete stranger knocked at my door to tell me that the driver had come to senses and was fit to give his statement. Before I could leave for the hospital, the man was gone and untraced.

In the hospital, I found the police men had already taken his brief but to the point statement. He looked a time with a quiet and smiling glance and breathed his last, as if his death was waiting just for my arrival.

With the factual last-minute statement of the driver, the inquiry concluded in my favour, fully exonerating me for the charges. Surely, Baba and himself come to inform me about the decision.

Since then, Baba's saviour hand has been on me in every walk of my life.

"BOW TO SHRI SAI, PEACE BE TO ALL."

JANAKRAJ LAROIYA
Noida (U.P.)

177. BABA'S UNIQUE *LEELA* (1996)

Shirdi sai Baba's ways are mysterious inscrutable, inconceivable and beyond the ken of our mind and thought.

Once a devotee comes under his fold, he (Baba) strengthen his Devotion by giving him such experiences and he ultimately realizes that Baba is no other than God *(Parabrahma)* and manifested in this world as *'Avatara Purusha'* (Divine Incarnation) to elevate mankind by removing their ignorance (*Avidya* or Nescience) and bestowing knowledge *(Jyana)* in them to realize the truth (Self-Realization). Now, I shall relate a recent experience (Miracle of Baba) for the benefit of the Devotees.

On 8ᵗʰ October 1996 (Tuesday) early morning while I was still sleeping on the bed in one of the Sai Bandhu's Home at Benson Town, Bangalore, I heard A distinct voice as follows", I will come along with you for *'Bhiksha'* (Food) today" I immediately woke up from my bed and, to my surprise, there was none in the room. I was reminded of a similar instance in *'Sai Satcharita'* chapter 40, in which Baba told Hemadpant (Anna Saheb Dabholkar) that he would go to his house for meals on the full noon day morning in 1917.

I did not reveal this message to anybody. But kept quiet. It is my usual practice, whenever I go to Bangalore, I used to visit Sai Spiritual Centre in Thyagarajanagar to pay my obeisance to Lord Sai and his Apostles, Poojya Narasimha Swamiji and Pooja Sai Padananda Radhakrishna Swamiji (Trinity) whose idols are installed in the Sai Mandir.

I attended the noon arathi at 12 noon (sung on Shirdi Lines), took *'Tirtha'* and *'Udi Prasadam'* and was about to go to a Sai Bandhu's House at Bansankari (3 Kms from the Sai Mandir) for food as pre-arranged. But, in the meantime Shri D.V. Krishnamurthy, a personal attendant and a great disciple of (late) Shri Radhakrishna Swamiji and now chief priest at Sai Spiritual Centre, whom I know very well, having acquainted with him for more than 15 years, accosted me thus:

"Radhakrishna, you are Sai blessed (lucky). Today, six Devotees are invited by a great Sai devotee in N.R. Colony to *'Vishnu Sahasramma'*, *'Parayanam'* and *'Arathi'* to Bab and to have *'Prasadum'* (Food) in his house. We are now five available and one devotee sent word that he could not come due to some reason. Please come along with us, their car is waiting to take us to their house."

So saying, Shri Krishnamurthy took me to his house. We did *'Vishnu Sahasranama'* Parayana followed by *'Sai Nama Japa'* chanting of Baba's *Taraka Mantra, Om Sai Sri Sai Jaya Jaya Sai'* for half an hour in the Sindhi gentleman's house. The Sindhi gentleman's wife narrated to us their *Sai Leelas* (miracles), How Baba got them back their lost business account book (credit book) in which lakhs of rupees due from creditors were recorded, the same way as Baba got back Chand Bhai's lost mare to him.

I always carry Baba's *Udhi*' and photos with me and Baba prompted me to give them all of them. When I took Baba's photo from my bag to present is to the pious lady, lo! Baba's photo in *'Bikshadana'* (begging Food) pose came in my hand and I was overwhelmed with Sai joy and Sai bliss and tears gushed out of my eyes. I was wonder-struck at this leela of Baba. then I remembered Baba's uttering early morning in Benson Town on that day, "I will come along with you for *'Biksha'* (Food) today. I am also reminded of how Baba fulfilled his promise to Shri Hemadpant by visiting his house at the nick of time in the form of a beautiful photo presented to him by two Muslim gentlemen (*Shri Sai Sai Charita* – Chapter 40).

To conclude, Let us always chant Baba's Taraka Mantra, *'Om Sai Sri Sai Jaya Jaya Sai'*, constantly and enjoy Sai bliss for ever.

Sree Satchidananda Sadguru Sainath Maharaj Ki Jai.

OM TAT SAT.

-Radhakrishnan 'Sai Jeevi' President,
Akhanda Sai Nama Saptaha Trust,
Benson Town,
Bangalore – 560 046

146. BABA'S GRACE (1989)

In the first week of November, 1986 I received a letter from Sai-brother Sri S. Krishna Murthy, a retired Deputy Collector who is also the Secretary of Om Sri Sai Ram Committee at 4-3-5, Ramanapet, Guntur – 522 007, seeking my assistance in getting their Sai magazine registered with the Government of India. It seems he was advised by Sai-brother Dr. G.R. vijayakumar of Kil-Kotagiri (Tamil Nadu) to contact me, as I might know the authorities concerned. I was really happy that Lord Sainath provided me an opportunity to serve his children in Andhra Pradesh. Sri Krishna Murthy had sent to me all the relevant documents, from which I could make out that it had been in 'cold storage' for sometime.

I prayed to Lord Sainath to enable me to get this registration done. I contacted the department concerned over the telephone. Sri Surender Kumar of the office of the Registrar of Newspapers gave me an appointment on

Thursday the 13th November, 1986 and directed me to call on him personally with all the relevant papers for registration.

When I went to the Registration office I was told that the matter was pending due to non-receipt of a document from the Sub-Divisional Magistrate at Guntur. It looked as if I had to return without getting the work done. In fact when I was waiting for the officer concerned, I came to know of several instances of pending matters.

I prayed to Lord Sainath, who gave me an intuition to search the papers sent by Sri Krishna Murthy. Sai directed me to give the photo-stat copy of the document signed by the Sub-Divisional Magistrate, Guntur. Immediately I took it and showed to the Registration Officer. (Perhaps the original communication from the Magistrate of Guntur might have been lost somewhere in the transit). I sincerely prayed to Lord Sainath to make the Officer accept the Photostat copy.

Yes, Lord Sainath responded to my prayer. The Officer accepted the photostat copy and accorded the necessary sanction then and there. He chose one of the names sent – '*Ninnu Parkshinthuna*' for the Telugu Sai magazine. Right in my presence, the Officer signed the necessary communication to the Guntur authorities registering the Sai-magazine. This is indeed a great '*Sai Leela*' in truth, Sai Himself did it.

-P.K. Kapoor,
1121, Chah Rahat,
Delhi-110 006
(*Shri Sai Leela*, April 1989)

178. SHIRDI SAI BABA – THE UNIVERSAL GOD (1986)

I would like to narrate here a recent *leela* of Baba which averted a serious train accident and saved hundreds of passengers from the jaws of imminent death on 5.11.1986.

My second daughter-in-law was delivered of her first child, a female on 22.10.86 at Kanchipuram (Tamil Nadu) and her parents sent to us invitation to attend the cradle ceremony, which is usually celebrated on the 11th day after brith i.e. on 1.11.86 in our case. I could not attend due to some domestic circumstances but sent my wife and son Chi. Shankar for the function. They left Hubli on 29.10.86 and after staying for a couple of days at my eldest son's place at Bangalore left for Kanchipuram on 31.10.86 afternoon by 'Brindavan Express' and reached there on the same day at 9.30 P.M.

My son was working in the Workshops of South Central Railway, Hubli, and he was granted only 6 days leave from 30.10.86 to 4.11.86. He had to be back to duty on 5.11.86 morning at 7.00 a.m. My wife and son were expected to return to Hubli in the night of 4.11.86 at 9.45 p.m. by 'Golgumbaz Express'. But, they did not arrive. I satisfied myself thinking they might be arriving the next day morning i.e. on 5.11.86 by 'Kittur Express' from Bangalore scheduled to arrive at Hubli at 6.15 a.m. But, alas! there was no trace of the train and the station authorities at Hubli were unable to explain the cause immediately to the waiting passengers. I was very much perturbed. I did not know what to do. Under such circumstances, the only refuge was our Mother Sai. I prayed to Sai Baba with all my heart for their safe return. After doing Sai Nama Japam silently with love and devotion for more than an hour, I prostrated before Baba's photo in the pooja room. Wonder of Wonders! Two flowers, one from Baba's photo and the other from Lord Venkateswara's photo simultaneously fell on my head. I took them as blessings both from Shri Venkateswara and Samartha Sadguru Sai Baba. Peace was restored to my mind and I was feeling Sai Bliss and Joy.

At 6.30 p.m. on 5.11.86 my wife and son arrive d engaging an auto rickshaw from the station, went straight to the Pooja room with tears in their eyes, reverently prostrated before Baba and then told me that Baba only saved them in the morning on that day and related what happened on the way, as follows:

They missed the train (Golgumbaz Express) at Bangalore on 4.11.86 which leaves Bangalore at 11.05 a.m. So they, boarded 'Kittur Express' on the same day which leaves Bangalore at 7.35 p.m. and is scheduled to arrive at Hubli next day morning at 6.15 a.m. On that dya it was running late by 2 hours and it passed through Kodaganuru station at 6.00 a.m. (5.11.86). After passing hardly one KM from this station, the Driver of the Engine examined the 'Line clear', picked up at Kodaganura and found the 'TOKEN' missing and he immediately stopped the train and brought back the train to Kodaganuru and traced the missing 'TOKEN' on the platform. IN the meanwhile the Gangman from the opposite direction came running and reported to the Station Master, the Driver and the Guard of the train that the Railway Bridge near the next station was found breached due to heavy floods and therefore it was unsafe to pass through the bridge. Messages were given to all concerned and trans-shipment of passengers from Kodaganuru to Davangree by State Transport buses was arranged from where they arrived at Hubli by a special train at 5.45 p.m. on 5.11.86.

Dear Sai Bandhus, please imagine what would have happened to all the passengers travelling in that train if the Driver had not backed the train to Kodaganuru to pick the lost token in the 'Line Clear'. Certainly, he would have passed through the damaged bridge in a few minutes which would have resulted in a great human tragedy in which hundreds of passengers would have perished and their limbs broken for life including my wife and son. It is our Bhagavan Sai who had saved them all in a dramatic and wonderful way as stated above.

-Mr. R. Radhakrishnan,
C/o Shri C.V. Mugali,
Bilgi Plot, Nagashetty Koppa,
Hubli-580023
(*Shri Sai Leela*, September 1987)

179. PURE DEVOTION PAYS (1986)

I learnt this at the tender age of 13, and it has only made my love for and faith in Baba all the more strong. Since then Sai Baba is inscribed indelibly in letters of gold in my young mind.

It was just 7 or 8 months since we had returned from Zambia and with much difficulty I had got myself admitted in a good school in the 8th standard. Accommodation had been a problem, but soon, by the grace of Baba, we managed to get comfortable accommodation. From the new residence my school was about 22 kms. away and I had to travel by the local trains, and during the typical Bombay monsoons, it was obviously a great problem. Almost every other day I took ill. In the middle of the scholastic year, it was impossible to secure admission in any of the nearby schools were I to escape the incessant down-pour. Moreover, my 2nd language being French, it was necessary to get admission in a school that offered French. As far as our knowledge would go, there were no such schools in our area. It therefore was really an issue engaging the mind of all at home. But my parents did not lose hope. They kept on saying that Baba would find a way out for us.

On one fine day, my father's colleague told him of a school, quite close to our house, that offered French. But he also warned that admission should be a problem, since it was one of the best schools in the area, and a very strict one at that. It was indeed a thrilling news for us. We made inquiries here and there, but got the same reply, "It is futile to seek admission there".

Unexpectedly, all our relatives planned to make a week end trip to Shirdi. We also joined them. I was pretty young then and I do not now recall the details of the trip. But one thing I remember very vividly. I remember sitting in the main Mandir and becoming oblivious of all around me while I concentrated only on the statue of Baba. Well, I did not have to tell Him my problem, it seemed as if He knew everything. I just sat there, and for the first time in my life, I experienced something new – something that I can not define in words even today. I must have sat there for an hour or so and all the time there was Baba in my mind. Since that day, each time I want to think of Him, I just have to close my eyes and right in the centre of forehead between my eyes, I can see Baba clearly. Sometimes I can see Him walking around in Shirdi, sometimes seated on the stone.

The very next day after returning home, my father and I went to the school and in a matter of fifteen minutes, I was enrolled as a student. No more details are required as every thing speaks for itself. Baba has become so much a part of me that I do not do anything without a thought of him. Since that event, I have been to Shirdi 4 to 5 times. A fortnight ago too, I had been to Him. Actually, there is no need to pray. He knows all that we need. You just have to look into those love filled eyes with devotion and all your problems and worries melt away. I am almost 19 now and all these years have only strengthened 'our relationship'!!

My prostrations to SAI BABA.

-Miss. Lata Balasubramanian,
A-1, Shivaji Park
Telephone Exchange Quarters,
Anant Patil Marg, Dadar (W),
Bombay 400 028
(*Shri Sai Leela*, 1987)

180. THE MIRACLE OF MY REACHING HOME AT 11 A.M. IN A DARK AND DREADED NIGHT (1986)

I had been to Madras in connection with the proposed installation of the Life size marble statue of Sri Sai Baba, at the All India Sai Samaj, Mylapore, Madras.

I returned to Bangalore on 19.9.1986 by Bangalore Express, which unfortunately arrived at Bangalore City at 10 P.M. being late by one and half hours. It was drizzling and partially a dark night.

At Bangalore City Station, all auto drivers refused to ply for me upto Malleswaram. I felt disappointed as I was hungry, exhausted, tired and sleepy after nearly 10 hours of journey, sitting all along and did not know what to do. It was about 10.45 p.m. and no buses also were available. No police man or Railway Staff was around to help me.

In such a predicament, a miracle happened. All of a sudden from nowhere, one Muslim automan appeared before me and asked me on his own, where I wanted to go. I replied with no hope "to Malleswaram". But no sooner I replied than he was off with me to my house at Malleswaram.

For a Sai Bhakta, who else can this Muslim be, except Lord Sri Sai Baba Himself! The rescuer of His devotee in distress!

Had not this Muslim appeared, what would have been my lot that night, as neither I could go home nor stay at the Station, safely.

To emphasize that Sri Sai Baba alone came and none else I should say, that this Muslim appeared exactly like Sai Baba with the same features of beard and dress. He came only because, I am His possessed bhakta. He came in that predicament and critical situation for my rescue, as Lord Krishna rushed towards Gajendra and Lord Shiva towards Markandeya, in their perilous hour.

That Sri Sai Baba will not allow his Bhaktas to suffer, is well proved and illustrated here.

The only qualification is that one should have deep-rooted faith in HIM, for HIM to help us, as HIS slogan goes "When I am here, why do you fear".
"Bow to Sri Sai – Peace unto all."

-Mr. B. Ramanadha Rao,
Sri Sai Kutir, Bangalore – 23
(*Shri Sai Leela*, August 1987)

181. SRI SAI'S GRACE (1986)

During Oct., 1986 I developed severe abdominal pain; my husband gave me homeopathic medicines, but they did not give relief, and as the pain persisted he consulted the family physician. The doctor diagnosed my pain as due to 'acidity' and prescribed a treatment, but the pain continued for next two days despite the intake of medicines. On the third day the pain became unbearable and hence another physician was consulted for a second opinion; his diagnosis was also the same i.e. 'acidity'. Now the fourth day the pain again became unbearable. It happened to be a Sunday, the time was 9.30 p.m. and no doctor was available. My husband who is a great devotee of Baba immediately gave me *Udi* mixed with water it worked like a miracle and the pain stopped. However, my husband consulted a doctor, a family friend. He was the third physician prescribed by them. He decided to examine me on Monday the fifth day and proposed Barium Meal and Ultra sound of Gall Bladder, stomach and the kidneys. Now the fear of surgery started haunting me. However before going to the radiologist we decided to go to Sai Baba Mandir, Lodhi Road, for the blessings of Baba and put some *Udi* on my tongue. After this we proceeded to the Radiologist. IN two hours, the X-Ray was over. My prayers were answered in a miraculous way. Believe it or not, the specialist declared "all clear". I think even now that it is Baba's blessings and kindness that saved me from surgery etc.

I close this with a short prayer begging Sri Baba always to protect us, forgive us for our trespasses, and correct and guide us at every stage. Bow to Shri Sai, Peace be to all.

-Smt. K. Sayal,
J-1, Green Park Exten.
New Delhi-11 0016
(*Shri Sai Leela*, Dec. 1987)

182. BABA DRWS OUT HIS DEVOTEES FROM THE JAWS OF DEATH (1986)

Sri Sai Baba of Shirdi, the refuge and saviour of His devotees, is ever active and more so, even after Mahasamadhi. We are fortunate to be His devotees from early 40's i.e. from about 1943.

On 6th November, 1986 at Kakinada (AP), my nephew's son, aged 20 had an acute attack of Jaundice (Hepatic) affecting the brain. He became violent and lapsed into Coma in a matter of a how hours. He was immediately admitted to hospital. We came to know that his condition was critical and given up by the doctors, on 7th night. My niece's daughter's marriage had been fixed for the 12th November, '86. Upon hearing this shocking news we were flabbiergasted. As per habit I immediately concentrated on Sri Sai Baba and received a reply to say that he would be all right. My wife during concentration received a vision of the boy on bed with Sri Sai Baba sitting on a stool beside the bed with His hands on him. On receiving Baba's message and assurance we were relieved of anxiety and were sure that the boy would recover completely. We went to Kakinada on 9th morning and found the boy in an isolated room in a private hospital, with my nephew, his wife and all our relations in utter gloom and despair. His condition was very critical and the doctors had practically given up all hopes and pronounced that lung failure was setting in.

Being a qualified homeopathic doctor (R.M. P.), I started homeo-treatment right from 9th noon as per Baba's will. It was only Baba's grace and miracle that could save him. Because of Baba's word and assurance to us we were confident and had no doubt in fact as Baba's word is the decree of the Almighty. I told my niece to go ahead with the marriage schedule as planned. The patient looked better on 9th evening, but the doctors pronounced status quo. On 10th morning the boy started to get a little involuntary movement. In the evening he began focusing his eyes and seeing things. On 11th morning he spoke slowly to the utter surprise of the doctors. In the beginning, his words were dragging and slowly he was set right. He said he got a vision of Lord Sri Sai Nath who came to him and hit him with His Satka (small stick which Baba carried) and from that moment the pain in his chest was gone and that he felt better. Baba by that hit with His Satka evidently drove away death and cured him of all his physiological ailments like lung failure etc. The boy began improving without any complication whatsoever rapidly and he was taken home a few days later for convalescence.

The marriage of my niece's daughter went through as scheduled with my nephew and his wife attending all functions happily. Baba's saying "I will draw out my devotees from the jaws of death" has been proved here and it is another of the millions of confirmations that Sri Sai Baba is ever active and more so even after His Mahasamadhi which is only a biological formality for an avatar.

-K.V. Gopala Krishna,
49-II-I/1, Lalithanagar,
Visakhapatnam 530 016
(Andhra Pradesh)
(*Shri Sai Leela*, Sept. 1987)

182. CUSTOM DUTY WAIVED BY BABA'S GRACE (1986)

Sri R. Subramaniam, Lakshmipuram Colony, Villivakam Madras, and his friends visited holy places of North India and Nepal in March 1986. The group comprising ladies and gentleman purchased sarees, electronic goods, other items at Nepal which were cheaper than in India. On the way back from Nepal at Sownali, Gorakhpur District, the customs authorities, verifying the purchases made charged a dut of Rs. 4000/- on the items. Sri Subramaniam who happened to be the only Hindi-knowing person in the group pleaded with the authorities to reduce the duty, which was reduced to Rs. 1000/-. But the group members out of greediness or out of ignorance of law, said that they could pay only Rs. 500/- in total. Sri Subramaniam who had not made any purchases, but was only pleading for his friends was aghast at the adamance of his group. Unless the duty was paid, the customs authorities would not allow the bus to proceed. Sri Subramaniam was embarrassed to meet the customs officer to say that the group would pay only Rs. 500/- as duty Sri Subramaniam silently prayed to Sai Baba to get him out of this embarrassing predicament.

At this point of time, an officer arrived in a jeep and entered the customs office, Sri Subramaniam was called inside the customs office. This officer told him that he was a supervisory customs officer for Gorakhpur District, that he was a Sai-devotee and that he had seen Sri Subramaniam in the Shrine at Shirdi, on 2nd and 3rd of February 1986. The officer apprised of the predicament being faced by Sri Subramaniam, suddenly produced Rs. 500/- from his pocket, asked him to pay the customs duty and obtain receipt. He even said "This Rs. 500/- is your money, you had given me earlier." Sri Subramaniam, was perplexed, as he had not meet this gentleman earlier, much less paid him Rs. 500/-. The officer on special duty got into his jeep and was off. The customs officer now became very cordial and said that his boss usually did not visit on Sundays!

When Sri Subramaniam reached Madras at the conclusion of the trip his landlord handed over to him an envelope from Sri D. Shankariah of Hyderabad, which contained receipt for Rs. 500/- which money was earlier collected by Sri Subramaniam and sent to Sri Shankariah for *Akhanda Sai Nama Saptaham*, Sri Shankariah had mentioned that since he did not know the addresses of the individual contributors, he had requested Sri Subramaniam to pass on the receipts on his behalf. At this it flashed to him "Remember you had given me Rs. 500/-. This is your own money".

183. UNIQUE SAINT OF KALIYUG (1986)

I wish to express my heart-felt gratitude with tears at Sai's feet. There are no words to describe and to praise the kindness he has shown towards me.

There was a misunderstanding between me and my close friend, following which I was altogether unable to trace my friend. I was then totally unhappy, with a very painful heart. The grief was so much, I even thought of suicide.

One day while travelling in a bus, I saw a person wearing a ring with Shirdi Baba's picture engraved. I casually enquired about it, He explained to me that the ring was from Shirdi and narrated miracles experienced by his devotees. I then expressed my feelings to him. I also told him that I did not want to ask any one who was very close to my friend. He suggested that I pray to Baba with a pure heart to find my friend out. I started praying to Baba from 14.8.1986.

One evening I went to Baba's temple and poured out my feelings at His feet and looked at his eyes which shine like the moon. At the same time I thought that "Baba if your existence is true, show me some good sign indicating that my prayer has reached your heart pervading the universe". The *archaka* of that temple gave some flowers, which were at Baba's feet, to a lady. She wore those flowers in her hair knot and when she was leaving the temple she passed in front of me. Suddenly the flowers which were in her hairs fell in front of me. Immediately my heart felt the bliss of Baba's grace and I started dancing in the shades of Lotus feet of Baba. I offered my *Sashtanganamaskar* at his feet and with full happiness and confidence I came out from the temple.

Three days later, I met my friend who was missing for two months. It was significant of Baba's mercy cast upon me for my sincere prayers.

Though I am a Christian I believe Him and have always succeeded by praying to Him.

-A.R. Kumar,
138830, S.T.A.,
Technical Literature Deptt.
B.E.L. Bangalore – 13

184. *SAI NAAM MAHAAN* (1986)

I narrate here under the Sai miracle experienced by me during my visit to Shirdi on 9th of October 1986.

I was as usual arranging to purchase a railway ticket to Manmad station for 9th October, 1986 and return ticket for 14th October. One of my colleagues Mr. Jagbandhu Parida requested me to book a ticket for him also along with mine. I was glad to note that Sai was adding one more devotee in his list of innumerable devotees.

By Sai's grace both our tickets were booked, duly confirmed with reservation by Bombay Mail (via Nagpur). On the 9th I took Rs. 350/- and Mr. Parida took Rs. 600/- as pocket money. We spent our day in train on 10th joyfully. We alighted at Manmad station on 11th at 2 A.M. We took coffee at the canteen for refreshment. A couple from Bhilai was sitting in front of us.

They were enquiring about bus to Shirdi from the canteen owner. I volunteered myself and answered their question. They felt happy and left.

When we reached Manmad Bus Stand we found the couple not to be seen. As we were waiting for the bus to come they also arrived safely. The bus for Shirdi came at 3.30 A.M. and soon a huge crowd gathered near the door and were fighting to enter the bus. We too tried our luck and got proper sitting accommodation. Lo! I lost my wallet containing Rs. 250/- in it, I was perplexed. I searched the whole of the bus and then complained to the police there, but with no result. I felt it was Sai's wish and the needy got it. I re-collected last year's incident on the same date that my beloved father Shri T.A. Ram Nathen lost his shawl while entering the bus and thus consoled myself.

The couple Mr. Shailendera Kumar Rant and Anjali Sathey voluntarily offered me Rs. 250/- as loan, to be returned as and when I could. I could not believe my own ears because in these days of Kali Yug who will offer money to a stranger. I refused stating that I would live penniless and if Baba wills he would feed me at Shirdi. I lived exactly as Baba lived in his days of stay at Shirdi till the year 1918. I controlled all my desires and took food when offered. We took leave of the couple on 17th morning on our way to Bombay for a short stay.

In Bombay we stayed at Chembur Guest House in a double bed room on the rent Rs. 125/- per day. All expenses were to the account of Mr. Nagbandhu Parida, my colleague. On the day of our leaving Bombay we felt short of Rs. 250/- to clear the dues of the hotel. Lo! it struck me now that my bosom friend Mr. V. Sunder of 10A, Jatindas Road had given me a sum of Rs. 250/- as advance money for purchase of "SHIRDI KE SAI BABA" Video-Cassette from Bombay. I thanked Sai for making my friend give me this amount as Sai Baba knew beforehand that such a contingency was to arise.

I thanked profusely and felt in myself that Sai helps his devotees from drowning but does not change his Karma. It is cent percent true as it happened to me.

He also kept Mr. Md. Hamsa at V.T. Station on 14th October the day of our departure by Bombay Mail on our way back to Howrah. He helped us in train and we paid him off next day at our office.

-Mr. T.R. Anand,
Ground Floor, IA, Wedderburn Road,
Calcutta 700 029
(*Shri Sai Leela*, August 1987)

185. WHEN TRUTH IS STRANGER THAN FICTION (1986)

Yes, there He stood at the gate, with His serene indulgent face and benevolent eyes, clothed in 'Kafri' with the cloth over the head falling loosely over the shoulders, the *'Biksha-paatra'* held in the right hand with the left folded and resting over the right shoulder, exactly as in the portrait facing P. 112 of the *Satcharita* (Eng. edn.) I was stunned with amazement it was INCREDIBLE!

Only a moment before, in my frenzied despair at the passing away of my first-born son aged 10 years, I had denied Him. His Divinity and His Omnipresence testified again and again by His devotees experiences both before and after His 'Maha Samadhi. I had declared Him to be a false deity and beseeched my wife to throw His portrait on the dung-hill. But here He stood to prove the truth of his eternal existence.

You see, the medicine I poured into the mouth of my semiconscious son remained there. I shouted to him to swallow it but the mouth remained open. I became frantic and tried to close it. No, the jaws had become rigid. I checked the pulse. It too had stopped. It was then that I called out my wife from the kitchen and spoke those blasphemous words. She just sat by the bed, head bent and tears trickling down, as much hurt by my profanity no doubt as by the bereavement.

I had come to the tether end of my spiritually. I was not myself. Thus I had the brutal impudence to ask my grieving wife whether she had cooked adding, "He has anyway gone. I don't want to die, too. I shall go and eat."

Imagine the father, however forlorn, to be so devoid of all feeling as to put such an inhuman question to the mother just bereaved.

There is no limit to which human nature can sink though, thank God, it can also soar to Elysian heights. Here I must say that my wife's faith unlike mine has throughout been unflickering, standing foursquare to all the winds that blow. Whenever my mind barks back to that scene, I can not help wondering how I escaped her righteous indignation for my frenzied out-burst. Where else except in this land hallowed by Sita and Savitri, Damayanti and Mandodhari, Nalayhini and Renuka Devi can one meet with such phenomenal forbearance? It is not far fetched to say that it is for such paragons of virtue that the sun Shines, it rains and Mother Earth continues to yield her bounty. It has been said that the greatness of a man does not consist in never falling but rising every time he falls. Indeed, it is by the magnetic charm of their devotion the 'homo sapiens' are not completely debased.

In her own gentle manner she said, "I just finished cooking rice for the children. Pray, serve yourself for this once", and lapsed into what I know now in retrospect to have been prayer to Baba.

You see, there were four younger children, two of them twins hardly six months old. But my mind and heart had become dry, no thought or feeling for any one, not even Baba!

So I betook myself to the kitchen to eat. I sat with a 'thali' before me and mechanically served myself some rice. Before I could bring myself to eat, while sitting and staring at the rice vacantly, I became schizophrenic, as it were, one part of me questioning the other, "Look, what are you trying to do? There lies your first born son dead and you are going to gorge your self." This shocked me into realizing how perfectly horrid of me it was. I turned to look in the direction of the bed in the front-room which was in line with the kitchen. It was then that my eyes behold the wonderful, form of Baba. Was it a mere vision, a figment of my imagination? I shouted to my wife with head still bent, "Kamu, look out and see who has come". Reacting t the frantic urgency in my voice, she looked up and glanced at the gate. At once, as if touched by a live wire, she sprang up and as if that was the consummation she was devoutly praying for the exclaimed, *"Amma Naayana Baba Vachycherul"* (Oh! at long last Baba has come!)

Actually, neither of us had seen the *Satcharita* portrait of Baba by then. Our puja portrait showed Him sitting cross-legged. However, in His inscrutable Wisdom, He had led us into buying at a *'mela'* a few months earlier a wood-cut portraying Him in five different poses including this one. Thus we were able to recognize Him at once.

Now I felt sure it was indeed HE. I was back in my senses. My heart was full of gratitude to Him for coming in the nick of time, and saving the situation. Else, in my forsaken condition, with no thought of Him or for Him I might have polluted the food before me. In this new found happiness, I reverentially took the *thali* up to Him and put the rice in the lifted *"Biksha-paatra"*. He received it with His beatific face and went away. No word was spoken indeed there was no need for any. My heart was too full for it, too. There was 'peace that passeth understanding'.

As I stepped into the house, my son opened his eyes and said, "Father, I am thirsty. Give me some water." This occurred in March 1944, twenty six years after Baba's Mahasamadhi.

-Dr. P.S.R. Swami
100/2Rt, Vijayanagar Colony,
Hyderabad – 500 457
(*Shri Sri Sai Leela*, Sept. 1986)

186. MY EXPERIENCE OF THE BLESSINGS OF SRI SAI BABA (1986)

Approximately30 years ago, I had an opportunity of visiting Shirdi and having darshan of Sai Baba. A Gujarati lady, who happened to be a friend, took me along with her relatives. Earlier I had absolutely no idea at all of the great saint of Shridi.

I wanted to utilize my L.T.C. during April, 1996. My wife insisted on our going to Shirdi since it was the first time I was availing of L.T.C. and since also she had not visited Shirdi earlier. I readily agreed. The day before my departure, I received a letter from my brother asking me to bring with me some ash (*Udhi*) from Shirdi on my return. We visited Shirdi without any problem whatsoever and returned to our place safely, with the sacred ash, the *Udhi*. I sent it to my brother accordingly. The next time when I met him, I asked him what for he had wanted the sacred ash from Shirdi. He replied, "I tried all method, consulted many eminent doctors but yet I was not able to find out the reason for baby's crying at all. Finally I put the sacred ash in a talisman and tied around the baby's waist, Believe it or not, a miracle happened, the crying stopped right from that day and the child continues to be well ever since."

"My fervent prostrations unto Him, the Ruler of the Universe".

-S. Sainath, B.E. (Mech.)
D.I.S.D-1/338, 8th Block
Paper Town, Bhadravathi 577 302
(*Shri Sai Leela*, April 1987)

187. THE SUPREME MASTER (1986)

I brought a small statue of Sai Nath from Shirdi after perform Pooja at the Samadhi Mandir. The statue was kept in a small shelf and continues to be there even now. I was very much surprised to see *Udhi* around the statue on 20.3.1986, with a sweet aroma covering the entire the house. After some days, the *Udhi* started coming from the statue itself and it was like the *Udhi* from the Dhuni of Dwarakamai. The *Udhi* continues to come for the last two years.

We are doing sankeertan daily in the evening. Surprisingly enough we noted two small pieces of sugar candy before Baba's feet in time. The sugar candy also comes from the statue only. We do not know the exact time of coming of *Udhi* nad Sugar candy from the statue.

But the important thing to note is the *udhi* comes from statue only after the earlier ones has already been distributed to his devotees. I believe that Sai Baba wants to teach us that nothing is ours in this world. Sweet aroma spreads around statue during prayers. *Abishekam* is conducted on every Thursday.

Devotees attend *abishekams* and *bhajans*. Many diseases are being cured with the application of this *Udhi*. Sai Baba, our Supreme Master, is guiding, 'teaching and protecting his devotees from Samadhi showing that He is everywhere. Where His devotees totally surrender to Him.

Interested devotees can have this *Udhi* from Sri Sai Baba's statue at the following address:

-K. Ranha Rajeswara Prasad,
Clerk, State Bank of India,
H. No. 2-4-12, Maruthi Nilayam,
New Badvel Road, Giddalur – 523 357
Prakasam Dist. (A.P.)

188. BREAST CANCER CURED BY BABA'S *UDHI* (1986)

A Sai Sevika of Maitri Park. ST Road, Chembur Bombay developed a big lump on her right breast in the year 1986. After the necessary medical examination, the doctor advised removal of the breast lump by surgery. the lady was very much afraid. She would partake of any medicine, but agree for not surgery. A date for operation was fixed. In the meanwhile the lady told her sisters that she would try Baba's *udhi* and prayer instead of operation. Her relatives said, "If you have so much faith in Sai Baba, then we will also join in praying for your health". They all went to Panvel Sai Baba Temple and handed over the surgeon's letter to Sri Narayan Baba and expressed their predicament. Sri Narayan Baba said that there was no need for operation, but to have complete faith in Sai Baba, and apply *udhi* paste (vibhuti mixed with water) five times a day after reading 'Sai Mahima'. He also suggested Til oil massage on Monday. Tuesday and Thursday, after chanting 'Om Sai Ram' 108 Times.

The lady carried out the instructions and also visited Sai Baba Mandir at Shirdi. On return from Shirdi, she noticed that the lump had started reducing. On 12.10.1986 (Dussera day). She was comp

189. SRI SAI BABA: THE GREATEST OF SAINTS (1986)

I have been a small and humble devotee of Sri Sai Baba of Shirdi for quite a few years how and I have always been observing Thursdays as days for darshan and special puja to this indescribable Avatar Purushe.

And it is only by way of observing this custom of mine. I motored to Matunga on 2nd January, 1988, a Thursday, for purchase of some fruits and flowers to offer to the Lord during the puja at home in the evening.

I parked my car near the Matunga Railway Station and locked all the doors before going out for purchase. My brief-case containing very important official papers and Rs. 12,000/- was left behind in the car itself near the driver's seat covered with a duster to deceive the eyes of wary thieves.

Finishing the purchase in about half-an-hour's time. I returned to the car. I was shocked at the theft of the brief-case. The next few minutes were of nervousness and confusion, for the theft was so deftly carried out during the broad day while the bazaar itself was busy and active. Enquiries of the shop-keepers nearby only revealed their ignorance of the incident and no clue was forth coming from any quarter. Thereupon, I phoned up to the Matunga Police Station and lodged a verbal complaint and requested the Inspector to visit the spot for the first hand information. The Inspector opined that there was absolutely no use in his visiting the place of theft as no useful clue could be obtained in such cases of robbery as the robbers employed very shrewd methods to leave no mark or impression which could expose them to the police. On the contrary, he advised me to call at the Police station with the car and lodge a written complaint. I did so and while returning home, I asked the Inspector if there was at all any chance of tracing the brief-case to which he replied that there was only the least possibility to that end as almost every person, rich or poor, educated or ignorant, carried a briefcase now a days. He further added that if I were lucky and if God would come to my rescue, I might be able to get the brief-case back intact. These his last words sent into me a strong feeling of hope and confidence.

I reached home, took my bath, collected some flowers from the garden around my house and began the worship of the Lord Sainath with all my heart. I, literally uttered to Him, "O Lord, I am not worried about the loss of cash and papers, but what would the devotees and people in general think if and when they come to know that the theft took place on a Thursday, most sacred for you, and when I had gone out into the bazzar only to purchase things for offering to you. Won't they not begin to have two opinions of the worship of you and of your super-natural powers. Please do not turn a deaf ear to my prayers but quickly manifest your Godly power so that the lost brief-case be recovered by me." Saying these words, I was showing the desparathana with tears in my eyes.

Just then, the door bell also rang and I, my self, ran and opened the door, I saw two young men.

I saws utterly surprised to learn from the Station Master that the thief was caught red-handed on the platform itself by one of the ticket checking inspectors. The culprit not being in possession of valid ticket, left the box on the floor and ran away lest he should be roughed and charged. Before the development the Station Master had asked to phone up all the stations station. V.T. to Kalyan to ascertain if any complain of a theft of a briefcase was lodged with them by any to which he only received the negative reply.

Hence under a strong assumption that the brief-case was picked by the thief elsewhere and that he must have travelled by the local electric train, he had a *panchanama* held to record the contents of the brief-case and to find out, if possible, the owner of the same. And in the process, he could lay his hand on my visiting card with the help of which his peon came to call me from my house.

My dear and learned devotees, it is thus transparently clear that our Sai Nath, the *Kaliyuga Avatara Purusha*, runs to the rescue and safety of those who are dear to him only because of their sincere devotion and surrender to His will. Hence let us all be pure and moral in our daily lives and become eligible to receive His Grace.

SAI NATH MAHARAJ KI JAI.

-Muthu Pillai, 103/3534, Nehru Nagar,

S.G. Barve Marg, Kurla East,

Bombay – 400 024

(*Shri Sai Leela*, May 1987)

190. DRAGGED THE SPARROW TO THE DESTINATION (1987)

My brother-in-law, Mr. Mohan, aged 26 is an educated man. I was unemployed while writing this. Because of the unemployment, he was in a desperate condition. One night his father came to me to inform that Mr. Mohan had left his house not informing anybody, in the morning the previous day with no money. Since he did not return home till 10 P.M., feeling much distressed he informed, about the disappearance of his son. Immediately we searched for him at all the places of Nandyal town and other surrounding areas, including tanks, wells etc., throughout night, but could not find him anywhere. In a distressed and helpless mood and not knowing what to do next we returned home. Every member of the family was under severe mental agony and strain. Since I am fortunate to have contacts with Sri Sri Sri Shyam Charan Baba Gurudev, I took my father-in-law to him, with the hope that the problem might be solved. At that time he was observing a vow of silence. We wrote on a paper the sorrowful incident that took place and placed it before him. At 8 A.M. he opened his eyes and looked into the eyes of the portrait of Lord Sri Sainatha Mahaprabhu and prayed and wrote in a corner of the same paper that the boy was alright and would return soon. He advised us to pray to the Lord with whole-hearted sincere devotion. As per his advice, we prayed to our Lord Sadguru Sainatha Mahaprabhu and kept quiet. By His grace, suddenly my brother-in-law came to the house by 11.00 a.m. on the same day; our joy knew no bounds.

After enquiry, my brother-in-law revealed that, he had decided to leave the house once for all, because of lack of peace of mind, and unknowingly went to the holy shrine Mahanandi, 10 miles from Nandyal on foot, and stayed there that night. The next morning, he returned to Nandyal by 7.30 A.M. on foot and was proceeding to the railway station, with no aim but with a determined mind not to return home. Exactly at 8.00 A.M. (the time our Gurudev opened his eyes) some unknown voice directed him to go home soon, and he felt that some force wad dragging him home. After some time he also informed us, that the voice which directed him was of our Sri Shyam Charan Gurudev.

At present he is an employee at Hyderabad and is relieved of the earlier mental agony. In this connection, we must remember, the assurance to its destination at the appropriate time, where-ever it is. Like wise, Lora Sainatha Mahaprabhu showered His grace for the sincere prayer, made to him and dragged my brother-in-law safely to the house and also provided him an employment, making everybody happy.

"Jai Bolo Sri Samartha Sadguru Satchidananda Sainatha Mahaprabhu Ki Jai!"
"JAI GURUDEVA DATTA"

-Mr. S. Sreenath, M.I.E.,
Lecturer in Mech. Engineering,
E.S.C. Govt. Polytechnic,
Nandyal 518 501, Kurnool Dt., A.P.

191. SAI'S MIRACLE (1987)

Last year I was trying to sell my plot in Chandanagar, Ramachandrapuram, but in vain, Nobody came forward to offer a reasonable price. I wanted to buy a flat in the city. As for first installment for flat I pledged ornaments and paid off. Unless I sold my plot I could not pay off the remaining installments. I prayed to Baba "Lord Sainath I need money badly, I can not sell my plot at throwaway price. If I get a hand-some amount I will offer Rs. 101/- to you."

On 06.07.1987, Guru Purnima celebrations were started in Sri Venkateswara temple premises at B.H.E.L., Ramachandrapuram, Hyderabad. In the morning I went and took *darshan* and *Kakad* Arati in the evening I went and listened to the discourse by a Swamiji Sri Vitthal Baba of Vanasthalipuram.

On 7.7.1987 I went and again listened to the discourses of Sri Vitthal Maharaj. After that I took *prasadam* and went home by 8.30 p.m. My wife informed me that two persons had come to buy the plot. They wanted to see me. "You had gone to the temple. They offered Rs. 38,000/- and said they would come again". I wanted Rs. 40,000/- now there was a difference of Rs. 2,000/- What a miracle See the work of Sai.

On 8.7.1987 in the evening I was sitting in the Bhajan Hall listening to the *Upanyasam* by Sri Vitthal Baba. There my son came and said, "Daddy, the same people here come. They want to see you". I got up in the middle and went home. Ninety-nine per cent of the transaction was talked over.

On 9th, 10th and 11th July, 1987 as usual I attended the celebrations and witnessed Arati.

On 12.07.1987 it was the concluding day of Guru Purnima celebrations. I went in the morning, had darshan of Baba and returned home. Five persons came to my house at about 8.30 a.m. Two were the buyers, two others were their friends and the fifth one was one more man who is my friend and a Sai Devotee. They examined the documents, went to visit the plot and came back around 11.30 A.M. They gave me Rs. 2,000/- as advance and agreed to pay the balance Rs. 36,000/- on or before 5th August '87. I made out a receipt for them for the amount paid to me.

See how quickly things were executed by Shirdi Sai's Grace. By 12.30 noon on 12.07.87 I went to attend Sai celebrations. The *Annadanam* was taking place under the supervision of Sri Vitthal Maharaj. It was later learnt that nearly thousand people took food. I happily joined the volunteers in serving the food.

By the By I must acknowledge my debt of gratitude to Sri Vitthal Baba of Vanasthalipuram.

In 1986, during Sai's Gurupurnima celebrations at BHEL heard his discourse for the first time and he said to the audience "Look at Sai's eyes and pray three times. Glance at Sai's photo from feet to head and back and then meditate. Your prayer will be answered. Not matter what you eat, no matter whether you take bath or not."

These words of Vitthal Maharaj penetrated into my heart, from that day I have been doing as the Swamiji said. My faith in Sai has been increasing.

-E. Parameswara Iyer,
Personnel Department,
The Aluminium Industries Ltd.
Lingampally Post, Hyderabad – 500 133
(Shri Sai Leela)

192. SAI'S GRACIOUS MIRACLES TO FORCE MY RE-ADMISSION IN HIS BLISSFUL FOLD (1987)

The year 1982 is a year to be reminisced and a year to reckon with for me as it was during that year I was re-admitted to Sai Parivar like a failed old student getting re-admitted to an educational institution.

I had known about Shri Sai Baba of Shirdi earlier from my boyhood days. When I was studying in a High School at Chitradurga during 1964-65. I chanced to visit Shri Sai Mandir every Thursday along with my dear mother in one Dr. Rama Rao's house nearby.

Being a young lad of only 13 years, I was greatly impressed by the conspicuous, intense devotion of Dr. Rama Rao and his family and other visiting devotees there. Ironically, my visits to Sai Mandir were not borne out of any real piety on my part to Sai Baba the Great as by my boyish inquisitiveness to listen to the sweet melody of the devout bhajans and to pamper my palate, with the sweeter still, Baba's Prasad distributed invariably at the close of the function everyday.

And at home it came my way perchance to conduct Sai Pooja as and when my father, a State level Officer in the Education Department of the Karnataka State, happened to be out of station on official tours. And in deference to the wishes of my father I did the Pooja not with the necessary devotion or *Shradhdha* but mechanically as a matter of daily routine in the family.

When all was thus well, before long as irony of fate would have it, to our utter and unbearable shock my father was snatched away from our midst as a result of an acute heart attack. The untimely and premature death of the only earning member and the head of the family deprived us all of his august and imposing presence amidst us, his ever affectionate touch and loving care. My young widowed mother and we, her five children, were thrown to suffer the consequential lonliness in this world and were bereft of the sense of security and the comforts of a well-looked after and disciplined family.

Despite being young but not so young, I knew to the best of my knowledge and belief that my father was all along enjoying the unanimous and unsolicited admiration of not only the entire officialdom but also of the public outside for his honesty and uprighteness in service till his passing away. After his disappearance from the face of the material world, the so-called entire circle of friends and colleagues and also our close relations who were hitherto crowding at my father's office and residence for favour of all kinds now began to exhibit, unashamedly though, an uncanny indifference and disregard. With tears in my eyes I had to be a passive and helpless witness to the pinching sigh of grief and anguish of my mother and the pitiable condition of the youngsters, the youngest of whom was still on the lap of the indulgent mother. The egoism and the basic selfishness of man perhaps has no limits or remedy. As one of the direct and immediate consequences of the abrupt cessation of income to the family, sizable as it was, I had to discontinue my high school studies just to save a few coins and to be of help to my mother in her daily routine.

Under the circumstances, with no prospect of any immediate relief to the deprived family, it was thought wise and expedient to leave Chitradurga and shift to Bangalore where my father had managed to erect a small and modest house, which was our only asset.

And yes! we moved to Bangalore and occupied our house with a view to settling down once and for all. Life became really miserable to us with no monetary income; but with an unflinching faith in the Omni-potent and All-merciful God, my mother and I struggled on and on to keep our body and soul together. Imagine the pathetic condition of a middle class family in a city like Bangalore when cost of living was shooting up almost every day. As we, the children were growing up in age, the demands of the family were also naturally growing more and more. And what would the young helpless mother do except console and pacify us with soothing words while praying inwardly for better days to dawn. Upon her fond and persuasive goading I began to put in efforts in a small measure to resume my interrupted studies and by His Grace came out successful in my S.S.L.C. Examinations in due course. It should be called the most trying and difficult period for our family as a whole. Feeling desolate and dejected and unable to bear up the seemingly insunnountable financial difficulties and the plight of our family, many a time I wished to attempt to commit suicide myself or to desert the house. But on every such occasion an unseen power held me back and advised me to face life as it came to me boldly.

On the advice of my mother and other elders I approached the Government for employment as the legitimate ward of a deceased Government servant and was fortunately offered the post of a second division clerk on compassionate grounds. In the Education Department, I joined duty in the year 1974 and have since been working.

My first younger sister who had already come of age was married to an M.D. in the year 1973 and the couple are now settled in Princeton, U.S.A. and reported to be happy and peaceful. Gentlemen, this is another concrete proof of the unfailing protection and Mercy of God, for can we, by any stretch of imagination expect a Doctor of Medicine willing to wed a girl from a comparatively poorer family when mounting demands of dowry are so rampant in our society? No, we can never But had not god willed otherwise in our favour?

Subsequently in the year 1977. God blessed me with a loving and understanding wife and I am a father of three children now.

My first younger brother got his B.D.S. Degree from the Bangalore Dental College and is now prosecuting his higher studies in U.S.A. My youngest brother is flourishing with a lucrative business of his own using his ambassador car. My youngest sister has also been recently married to a businessman in Bangalore itself and the couple is well off.

I was often driven to wonder as to how all the above mentioned good things took place in my family at the proper time while the family itself was passing through hard days with a very meager income. It thrills me and shakes to the nerve whenever I happen to compare the happenings in the family following my father's demise to the condition now obtaining in which we are looked upon by the society with respect and love. Of course, we are self-sufficient in every way.

Although my material and worldly life was apparently satisfactory and there was nothing to feel aggrieved about personally I was restless and there was constantly a sense of emptiness in me. I could not possibly find out what was wanting in me innately. Had I been with my father at his beside, I could have in all probability sought his mature guidance and advice as I would do from a *Guru*. This state of mind then made me wander about visiting Ashrams in quest of peace and tranquility that would keep me steady in the household.

Not too long after, I was invited to attend the marriage of a good friend of mine at Brindavan, White Field, Bangalore. When I reached the place of the function at 9 A.M. I witnessed a large number of devotees, both Indians and Foreigners, eagerly waiting for the gracious darshan of Shri Sathya a Sai Baba while some others were rendering devoutly melodious bhajans.

In the atmosphere surcharged with divine vibrations. When I was watching the goings-on o fthe function in the Kalyana Mantapa, my eyes accidently fell on a book with a gentleman on my left. Curiously I dared to ask him much against my wont as to what book it was and if I may please see it. When the gentleman, obviously a devotee of Shri Sai Baba, handed me the book in his inimitable humble manner I was taken by utter surprise, to find that it was 'Shri Sai Sat Charitra' in kannada version, with a majestic and magnanimous picture of Sai Baba on the outer cover. I felt overwhelmed with an inexplicable joy and surprise at the very sight of this wonderful good old man after a long lapse and a sense of gratification and fulfillment were felt running through my veins. I felt elated and exalted for an unknown reason. Where was this old prophet all these years? And from where has he now come to my sight, that too so unexpectedly? It would be no exaggeration to state that I felt I was back again with my own father infusing in me a sense of security and bliss. I could not withhold my tears of joy and weapingly condition. He said that he would do it only it Baba assured him that Vitthal would appear on the seventh day. Baba assured him of this, saying that the Pandhari of Vitthal and Dwarka of Lord Krishna was also in Shirdi and that no one need come from outside. Vitthal would very much manifest himself and all that was required was devotee's earnestness to have the darshan. After the *saptaha* was over and when Kakasahib Dixit was sitting in meditation, he saw Vitthal in a vision. At noon, in the Darbar, Baba asked him if he had seen Vitthal. This was before all and in the evening a hawker came to the Masjid for selling the pictures of Vitthal, which tallied exactly with the figure which Kaka Saheb had seen in the vision. This showed what Baba would do for his Bhaktas and how much he cared for them.

Sai Baba was an apostle of Hindu-Muslim unity, a beacon light to show us the way in life. It is on record that He guaranteed the welfare of his Bhaktas, announcing clearly that there would never be any dearth or scarcity of food and clothes in the homes of his devotees. "It is my special characteristic that I look always to and provide for the welfare of those devotees who worship me whole-hearted with their minds fixed on me. Fix your mind in remembering always, so that it will not wander elsewhere, towards body, wealth and home. Then you will be calm, peaceful and carefree." It is unfortunate that even after this clear exposition, we suffer in various ways because of our ignorance. It is high-time we took Baba's words to heart and without consideration of faith and religion, colour or region, love each other as brothers from the same family and raise this nation to the same heights to which it once belonged.

-N.N. Shalla
104/15, C.P.W.D. Qr. Saket,
New Delhi – 17
(*Shri Sai Leela*, Jan. 1987)

193. MIGHTINESS OF THE ALMIGHTY – "SAI"

One day when we were casually discussing worldly matters, the marriage issue of my brother-in-law, Chi, Chandra Sekhar also came up for discussion. By Baba's grace, miraculously and automatically further developments took place and the *muhurtham* was also fixed.

At that time the grandfather of the bridegroom aged 86 years, was on death bed. Besides this, the uncle of the bride aged 70 years was suffering from high blood pressure and was bed-ridden. The sister-in-law of the bride was in an advanced state of pregnancy.

Generally, Hindu marriages are not celebrated in such circumstances. This situation caused anxiety to all of us, about the celebration of the marriage on the day fixed by the pandits.

At that crucial time, our Gurudev, Sri Shyam Charan Baba informed was that our Lord Sai Sadguru Sainath Mahaprabhu was responsible for the fixation of *muhurtham* by pandits and hence it could be taken as assured that the marriage would be celebrated as scheduled by His grace, because Lord Sainath Mahaprabhu is always merciful to His children, and will never allow them to suffer in any way at any time.

Accordingly the marriage was celebrated happily. Prior to the *muhurtham*, Sri Shyam Charan Baba spent four hours in devotional bhajans and songs which made the audience forget themselves. Only half an hour prior to muhurtham we were reminded about the same by the purohit, duly initiated by our Lord Sai Sainatha Mahaprabhu. Everything went on happily.

By His grace the uncle of the bride left his body sixteen days before the marriage and the grandfather of the bride-groom left his body sixteen days after the marriage, without causing any inconvenience to the concerned. The sister-in-law of the bride was delivered of a child three days after the marriage.

When we decide our matters with our limited knowledge and intellect, we will be held responsible for results. When He decides the matters, everything will end in happiness and satisfaction to one and all.

Casting off the burdens on the shoulders of our Lord Sri Sadguru Sainath Mahaprabhu, gives us peace of mind and happiness, which we must cherish throughout our life.

-S. Sreenath, M.I.E.,
Lecturer in Mechanical Engineering,
E.S.C. Government Polytechnic,
NANDYAL-518 501, Karnool (Dt.) A.P.
(*Shri Sai Leela*, Sept. 1987)

194. FAITH IS SUPREME, FAITH IS ALL (1987)

I was suffering with unbearable cough from September 1987. In the early stages, I neglected it, presuming it to be some infection which would be alright in a few days. But, as the days passed, the problem started getting severe, especially in journey.

I was married on Ist October 1987, i.e. on Thursday. My wife is also an ardent devotee of Sai Baba. She too started worrying as it had almost become difficult for me to breathe and I was feeling exertion if I walked a few yards. Then, I consulted a doctor at Hyderabad At first, he too thought that it may be due to infection and prescribed some medicines. But after a week, there were no signs of relief. Then, I approached him again. He advised some tests, like Blood test, X-ray etc. On receiving the reports, he said, it was Bronchitis and prescribed some medicines and said, there is no permanent cure, as it is due to some kind of allergy. Then I consulted another doctor for the second opinion. He too expressed the same, and prescribed some medicines for timely relief. Then, I had to come back to Bangalore for joining the duty after leave. I was told, the problem might get aggravated, as Bangalore is in cold atmospheric zone. But as there was no leave for me, I came to Bangalore, joined the duty, and was continuing with the medicines given by the doctor, but they were of no avail. At last, I stopped all the medicines and totally submitted myself to the mercy of Lord Sainath. I used to take Baba's *Udhi* everyday with little water and was praying Baba for cure, with full faith and confidence in him. Sai's *Udhi* worked like Sanjeevani on my illness. Within a week, I was free from cough and flum.

-K.V.R. Sastry,
Language Officer, Dena Bank,
Zonal Office, Sona Towers,
1 Floor, 71 Millers Road,
Bangalore – 560 052

195. BABA'S TIMELY HELP AND BLESSINGS (1987)

Devotion to Sri Sai Baba was granted to me through my late beloved mother, which has saved me through every difficult situation.

After eight years of one married life, we got an opportunity to buy a flat ready for eseapation on out-right payment basis. We had to pay half the amount in block to enter into an agreement. My father helped us with his provident fund loan amount. With his and my husband's savings, we somehow managed to pay the initial amount. The agreement was signed and within two months the balance amount had to be paid.

We tried all over resources t dispose of our existing flat but in vain. During this period my husband because a devotee of Sri Sai Baba, and he was dragged to Shirdi every month. I myself and my family members daily prayed whole-heartedly to Baba to help us to finalize the deal. With every sun rise, we used to get hope only to vanish with sun-set the same day. Two months thus passed.

The vendor gave us one more month as grace period.

Finally, the day came when Sai Baba came to our rescue, and the deal was finalized within a week's time. We made the payment and took possession of the flat. We were worried again by the increased expenses in the new flat, which was however taken care of by Sai Baba by blessing my husband with a much better job in the same concern.

The points I would like to emphatically state here are:

1. The seller or the party disposing of the flat was also a Sai Devotee
2. Each and every deal took place on a Thursday without any design or special effort by us

Who has been behind all these? I leave it to the readers to conclude.

-Mangala Karjodkar,
New Trishul, Cooperative Housing Society
Bhavaninagar, Marol,
Maroshi Rd., Andheri,
Bombay – 400 059
(*Shri Sai Leela*, May 1987)

196. HOW BABA PREVENTED A MAJOR ACCIDENT (1987)

We were travelling to Shirdi from Thane on 20th Feb. 1987. I was accompanied by my husband and his uncle's family. We are travelling along the Nasik Highway in a jeep. It was a very hot noon and we were all in a sleepy mood as the jeep was moving at a great speed.

We noticed that to our left a lorry was parked and another lorry was coming towards our direction in a great speed. Suddenly the driver of our jeep realized that in order to avoid a collusion with the oncoming lorry he had to take a turn to the left. When he turned the jeep to the left, it hit the lorry which was stationed. So the inevitable happened. the jeep hit the lorry. The impact was so great that the jeep's left door was ripped open and the glass window was broken in pieces in no minute. It took us only a few seconds to realize what had happened.

My husband who had so long kept his left hand resting on the door had luckily withdrawn his hand at the 11th minute before the accident. Had my husband not kept the hand inside, one can imagine what would have happened. Thousand thanks to Sai Baba for the signal he gave beforehand. One more thing which saved my husband's eyes from being hit by broken glass pieces was the goggle he was wearing. To tell the readers about the miracle, he had worn the goggle only a few minutes back. All this was nothing but the signal given by the Baba in the hour of great crisis. I thank the Lord for saving the catastrophe that would have cost my husband's hand. This incident only enhances my existing *Shradha* and *Saburi* in Sai Baba and here are my salutations to the Great Saviour.

-A devotee
(*Shri Sai Leela*, April, 1988)

197. SAI'S MIRACLE IN THE REBIRTH OF MY CHILD

It was in the year 1983 I first visited Shirdi along with my close friend Mr. D.P. Rao and his family and friends.

My trip to Shirdi was unexpectedly arranged all of a sudden by my friend, who was a distributor at that time for the company for which I was working. Till that time I was not aware of Baba's *Leelas* and it was my first visit to Shirdi. Mr. Rao, my friend, already had reserved the tickets for his family and friends. When I made a courtesy call at his place in the afternoon on the day, he was leaving for Shirdi by the evening train from Hyderabad. My friend asked me also to join them. I wanted to take my wife and a one year old son Vikram also with me. As my wife was working in a private organization, she could not get permission from her Superiors and therefore did not accompany me.

I went to Shirdi along with my friends and had a nice and satisfying stay by the grace of Lord Sainath.

I was married in the year 1981 and was blessed with a son on March 16, 1982. We named our son Vikram as Baba Vikram and he was a sweet looking child and was precocious, always had a smiling face and showering his love and affection to one and all. He was liked by everyone in the family and also by all in our building complex.

When I took up a new assignment in the year 1983, I developed hypertension and I was mentally and physically unwell. In the year 1984 I had to quit my job. In May, 1984 my wife went to stay with her elder sister at Secunderabad along with my son who was 2 years and 3 months old by then.

On the morning of 4th June, 1984 my parents received a phone call from my wife informing that my son had an accident falling in hot water in a neighbour's house. My father and myself rushed to the Government Hospital, Secunderabd. When we reached there we saw the little soul brunt from abondmen to knees on both legs and was in a dazed condition and no medical treatment was given to him for nearly one hour and my wife was running from pillar to post to complete the hospital formalities for nearly an hour. Doctors assured us not to worry saying the child would be alright soon.

The child was also speaking and recognizing every one. On the night of June 6, 1984 the child began to breath heavily We wamted to complain to the nurse incharge of the ward but there was no one available immediately. By the time my wife could run to other block and bring a doctor the little soul was no more in world.

This came as a very rude shock to everyone in our family of course birth and death are not solely out of our will and therefore, not in our hands. If proper medical care would have been given, the child could have been saved. My wife and myself were totally depressed, demoralized and went on a pilgrimage to South India in July, 1984. Our prayers in all the temples were only to give our son. I also did not take up any job for nearly 3 months as I was totally depressed and upset. In this period, I do not now exactly remember the month and date, wehtehr it was September or October around midnight in my dream I saw that I was waiting for Baba's darshan along with some devotees. Suddenly Baba appeared in front of me like a flash; I looked at him for a few seconds and prostrated at his lotus feet and holding them I conversed him in English asking about my son. Baba spoke to me in English saying "You will get back your Son". Then I asked Baba about job, for which He replied "You will get one soon" and he immediately vanished. I woke up immediately, and woke up my wife and told her about the dream that our son Vikram was coming back. At that time my wife was in the family way.

I got a job within a month without much difficulty and I told about my dream to my family members and friends. My wife and myself went to Shirdi when she was in her seventh month of pregnancy to take Sri Baba's blessings.

On March 10, 1984, my wife was blessed with a son. There was some difficulty during delivery but by the grace of our am Sainath, everything went on well. This child was born exactly nine months after we lost our first child.

My second child Sai Karti has a very close resemblance of my our earlier son. This was noticed by many people and his movements and acts are like my first child. This is nothing but Baba's miracle. In January 1986 I went with my wife and child to Shirdi to show my gratitude for blessing me and my son.

May we live with abiding faith in Him.

-T.T. Vijay Kumar
B-4, Meera Apartments,
Basheerbagh, Hyderabad – 500 029

198. SAI BABA'S GRACE (1987)

Though I have been hearing regarding the Saint of Shirdi Sri Sai Baba, I had no opportunity, either to visit any of His Temples or visit Shirdi.

It was on the 16th July 87, as I had some work with a Cabinet Minister, I had taken with me the Prominent and well-known social worker of Karnataka

Sri S.R. Chandrasekhar and after we met the Minister, as we were about to return, Mr. S.R. Chandrasekhar, suggested to me that we should visit Sai Baba Temple at Thyagajanagar.

As a marriage alliance was to be talked over for my daughter and they had come from Keveripakam. Tamil Nadu, I was in a hurry to return home. But I valued the advice and went to Sai Baba Mandir and prayed. It was a first visit for all of us. There Mr. S.R. Chandrasekhar said "Baba has blessed you and certainly marriage will click". In fact I was not at all willing, but by the time I reached home, my wife and children had spoken to them, it was almost settled. So, I also agreed and this is how Sainath has blessed us.

Again on 21st July 87, we sent to the same Ministers house and again Mr. S.R. Chandrasekhar, suggested that we should go to Baba Mandir. We all agreed and this time, Deenabandhu Sri V.R. Naidu, President, All India Sreenivasa Mission, was also with us.

We visited the Mandir, prayed and prostrated before Sainath and when we were about to return, Mr. Seshadri, Chairman of the centre, Secretary and others invited Mr. Naidu, took us round, showed and explained all the activities and also presented fine books and we were all very happy.

The same night, myself and my wife Smt. Ayammal, sons altogether 13 perosns, travelled from Bangalore to Kancheepuram in a Karnataka Government bus.

In between Krishnagiri and Natrampol, there is Farakur and it is here a giant lory dashed against our bus, damaging heavily. We were all in a shock, but by the grace of God no passenger was hurt. We were all extremely happy that there was not even a simple scratch on us. Immediately we thought of Baba who blessed us at this critical juncture.

So, I feel, a true devotee will definitely be blessed if he has immense faith in Him.

-P. Venkataswamy,
General Secretary,
Gandhi Vidyashala Educational Society,
Sri Ramapuram, Bangalore-21
(*Shri Sai Leela*, December, 1988)

199. "SAI GREETS NEW YEAR" (1987

On the morning of December 31, 1986 while taking morning tea, I was wondering and telling my wife and children casually, that how lucky we would be – if we receive "NEW YEAR GREETINGS" from Sri BABA Himself. They also agreed with me.

I returned home from office as usual at 6.30 p.m. My wife handed over to me a cover, addressed to me and told me that we had received New Year Greetings from 'BABA' as desired by us in the morning. There was no indication on the cover from where and by whom it was sent. I then opened the cover and found the 'BABA' photo with some sacred sayings inside. There was no indication even on the photo by whom the cover was sent. I could see only my residential address written by hand on the cover.

Out of curiosity, I examined the place of posting of the cover to my utter surprise, I found that the cover was posted at 'SHIRDI' on 23.12.1986. This I found out from the Post Office date stamp on the envelope.

We can assume from the above that 'BABA' Himself appeared in our house as desired by us, on the eve of New Year. We felt very happy. We have kept the photo for our daily puja.

From this, one of the Eleven Saying of Baba i.e. "IF YOU LOOK TO ME, I WILL LOOK AFTER YOU" is proved.

-G. Nagaraja Rao,
H. No. 14/11/806
Begum Bazar, Hyderabad 500 012

200. SAI'S MIRACLES (1987)

My family i.e. my husband, daughter and myself are staunch believers of "God Sai Baba". For this we thank with respect my sister Lata A. Rang who showed us the way to believe in God Sai Baba. For us Sai Baba is our God and Protector.

My daughter Meenakshi, now 8 yrs old, was suffering from skin allergy since her birth. At the age of six it took a turn for worse. I told this to my sister Lata who advised me to have faith in God Sai Baba. She sent to me *Udi* from Bombay and he condition used to get better. Again she had the same all over the body, and with *Udi* it would become better. So my entire family i.e. all the three of us with my sister Lata visited Shirdi in Dec. 86. Sicne then her allergy has become much less. Now the summer was approaching and my daughter wanted to go to my-in-law's place for horse riding. I was not so sure if she could go as she was allergic to animals and during this time also pollen allergic. So I asked her in April 87 to write a letter to God Sai Baba to help her. She wrote a letter in German to God Sai Baba. This she wrote from the heart to put an end to her allergic condition and asked the priest at Shridi to place this letter on God Sai Baba's Samadhi. I translated the letter in English. By end of May '87 she received *Udi* and Prasad from Shirdi. She was so happy, she immediately put it in her mouth. She prayed at night to Sai Baba to help her nad cure her from this ailment so she could go for horse-riding.

Wonder of Wonders, my daughter Meenakshi's allergy disappeared and she now is completely cured, In July '87, which was the summer vacation in Germany, she went to my-in-laws house enjoyed herself with contact with animals and pollen times without suffering any skin reaction. Nobody would now be able to say that this child had suffered from allergy. The letter from Meenakshi placed at the Samadhi of God Sai Baba, shows that God Sai Baba always looks after His dear ones who have full faith in Him.

This miracle shows that Sai Baba never leaves his devotees alone, no matter how far one is still He is everywhere. Therefore, we should have full faith and patience in God Sai Baba. God sai Baba always helps those who lay body and Soul in His Hands.

Bow to God Sai Baba-Peace unto all.

-Vimla Kaiser,
Hoffmann Str. 20, 6100 Darmstadt,
West Germany
(Shri Sai Leela, Dec., 1988)

201. A MIRACLE OF SHRI SAINATH

I am an employee of a Public Sector Undertaking. I was assigned with the job on 22.2.87 of arranging visas for our Engineers within a scheduled date, as they were required to proceed to U.S.S.R., on urgent work by 10.3.87. Being a staunch believer in Sai Nath I left everything to Him, because it was the first time I had to attend to such a type of job as also it was my first visit to New Delhi. With my usual devotion to Him I had prayed 'SAINATH' and accepted the assignment. On 23.2.87, I went to Secunderabad Rly. Station for arranging my reservation to New Delhi by A.P. Express on 24.2.1987, solely depending on 'BABA' because it was very difficult to get reservation, even a week in advance. Baba sent a person (whom I used to meet once in a year during Sri Swamy Ayyappa Pooja) to reservation counter and arranged for A.C. Chair Car reservation. I left my house with Baba's *Udhi* and boarded A.P. Express for New Delhi on 24.2.87. Being my first visit to Delhi, I was afraid as to how to go to our Guest House at Asiad Village. By the grace of Sainath I was guided by one of the co-passengers.

Accordingly I got down at Hazarat Nizamuddin Rly. Station and went to Guest House by auto. The Guest House incharge received me with a smile and allotted a room without any delay, even though it used to be difficult to find a vacant room in our guest House, since all the rooms used to be normally occupied by our top officials. I could get a room on this occasion only by the grace of Baba. I proceeded to Russian Embassy for submission of visa applications, where I was guided by the concerned, the procedures for obtaining visas by the grace of 'SAINATH'. The visa authority refused to accept the application for want of one copy each of photographs, whereas I was having only two copies. I was very much disappointed, because I had to go back to Hyderabad/Secunderabad for bringing another copy of photograph. Again, I prayed for the help of 'SAINATH' who gave me a thought to get Photostat copy of photographs, the concerned officer also accepted the same only by the grace of Baba, because generally they do not accept. The next day i.e. on 26.2.87 I proceeded to the Embassy to complete other formalities; they agreed to give me visa on 2.3.87 i.e. within 6 days, whereas it takes 25 days, normally. On 28.2.87 I proceeded to Haridwar, since I had a desire to do 'Pindapradhanam' to my late father at Brahma Khund of Haridwar. I requested Baba to lead me as I was not knowing anything. On reaching the Bus stand I was surprised to find a bus which was ready to leave for Haridwar and it started immediately on my boarding, as if, it was waiting for me. At Haridwar, a Purohit came to me and completed all the formalities to my satisfaction without demanding abnormal payment and accepted whatever I offered to him. It was a surprise to me, because, at such places mostly the demand is heavy. I returned to Delhi on 1.3.87 evening.

Sri Shirdi Sai Baba (1838-1918), the first one in the trinity of Sai Baba *Avatars* (incarnations) was the incarnation of Lord Shiva. He led the life of an ideal Sufi saint - begging for alms, helping all, teaching the basics of morality and spirituality in His typical rural, rustic, simple, and lively manner telling true stories of many births of His devotees and other creatures, and by His very brief and heart penetrating comments, and pieces of advice.

He taught all to believe in God who is omnipotent, omnipresent and omniscient and the One *Malik* (Master) of all and who is present in every creature. God's grace can be achieved by anyone by earnestly remembering Him, by being moral, kind and loving to all creatures, and by doing one's duties honestly and sincerely. Sai Baba always gave genuine assurances to those who called upon Him for His miraculous grace and helped the distressed ones instantly. It is a well known fact that Sri Shirdi Sai Baba's grace is being experienced by countless people throughout the world but only a few of such incidents are published in Sai journals and on internet..

This book is a collection of invaluable articles on Sri Shirdi Sai Baba's legendary grace and thrilling record of over 200 testimonies of post-*Samadhi* period (after 1918till now) beneficiaries of His grace. His temples are in India, U.S.A., U.K., Canada, China, South Africa, Mauritius, and many countries. Thousands of pilgrim daily visit His *Dwarka Mai Masjid* and Samadhi Mandir Inn Shirdi (India) and Sai temples in their countries daily to obtain His gracious help.

All those who are eager to receive Sri Shirdi Baba's divine grace for getting instant solution of and relief in their problems and seek proper guidance shall find this book a boon.

I was also proud of myself thinking that I could complete the work on my own and approached Embassy for collection of visas on 2.3.87. I also forgot 'SAINATH' entirely on this day and not even carried *Udhi* of Baba with me, which causes a lot of miracles. But when I was enroute to the embassy somebody hinted to me that I would be failing in getting visas, because I had neglected and did not carry Baba's *Udhi*. Accordingly, I was disappointed at Embassy, when the concerned officer refused to give me appointment upto 3.30 p.m. and even at 3.30 p.m. he expressed his inability to issue the visas, since no clearance was received from their Government. He also expressed that it might take 5 to 6 more days for receiving the clearance. This completely upset my programme, because I was holding firast class confirmed ticket for Secunderabad by A.P. Express of 4.3.87 and our engineers are scheduled to leave on 10.3.87 after obtaining foreign exchange etc., on my return Apart from this I was asked to be at Secunderabad by 5.3.87 with visas. I was in a disturbed mood and realized that this might have happened, because I had neglected to carry Baba's *Udhi* and realized my mistake. Immediately I started chanting the name of 'SAIRAM' and prayed Him to help me in this critical juncture. Then again I approached the officer for his help in getting the visas, Now he was a completely changed man. He asked me to see him on the next day. I came to my room and chanted the name of 'SAIRAM' and prayed Him to come to my rescue after fully surrendering myself to Him. On 3.3.87 I got up early and appealed 'SAIRAM' having full confidence, to guide me in the work and proceeded to Embassy. I was informed that the concerned officer was on sick leave and other officers asked me to come the next day since it was not possible to issue visas in his absence. But having full confidence in 'BABA'

I explained the urgency and requested him for the needful. But they expressed their helplessness. It was a surprise that on the last minute an officer who was unknown to me and not connected with the visa section appeared there stating that he would try to help me. He took all the particulars of Engineers, enquired from visa section, and confirmed that the visas were ready and collected by the officer who was on leave. He even took the trouble of searching the visas from his drawer and handed them over to me. Who knows, it might have been Sainath Himself who appeared on the scene to render His helping hand to me? Because, Sainath has said to Shama (Madhava Rao Deshpande) (Sat-Charita III Chapter) that if a man utter Baba's name with love, He shall fulfil all his wishes.

Here I proudly would like to inform all of you that I am very much grateful/ indebted to Shri Ch. Sambamurthy, R/o H.No. 1, 8-426, Chikkadpally, Hyderabad-500 020, who iniated me into 'SAI'S CULT' during 1963-64. He is in the service of Sainath for the last 50 years, and having dedicated his life to this cause, he performs poojas on every Thursday, and about 50 to 100 devotees attend. He tells Sai Leelas to every devotee. He also celebrates the festivals of Sainath i.e., Mahasivarathri, Sriramanavami and Gurupoornima on a grand level by arranging Harikatas, Bhajans, Laksha Archana etc. Distributes clothes to the physically handicapped, Fakirs and other deserving people and concludes the celebrations with poor feeding.

He is known to most of the Sai devotees in Andhra Pradesh, Madras etc. He visits Shirdi every year. He is generally calledby devotees as Baba or Guruji.

Here I would like to affirm that I could succeed in my assignment only the grace of 'SAINATH'. Sainath has also proved His words "IF YOU LOOK UP TO ME, I WILL LOOK AFTER YOU".

-A. Veeraiah,
'Sai Nilayam',
Plot No. 93, Vasavinagar,
SECUNDERABAD 500 003

202. Baba cured a Dumb Man in Mauritius (1971)

-Pandit Shiv Prasad

May I, dear Sai brothers, give you in a nutshell, the historic background of the Shirdi Sai Baba Mandir of Curepipe, Mauritius.

I had a son, Kumar by name (aged 14 years), who was dumb since his birth; in spite of all sorts of medical treatment, his dumbness persisted.

So, I decided to go on pilgrimage to India and pray for the cure of my dear son; thus it is that I happened to visit the Sai Baba temple in Shirdi where I literally crept on all floors, towards Baba's *Samadhi* and entreated Bhagawan for the cure of my son.

I guess Baba was moved by my very sincere and heart-felt prayers and He accorded me His Divine Grace.

Shortly after my return to Mauritius and to my most agreeable surprise my dear son Kumar began talking normally, by Baba's Divine Grace he secured a good job later on, he got married and has tow charming children.

He spends most of his spare time in looking after the Mandir and conducting *puja*.

In gratitude to Shirdi Sai Baba and to the profuse Grace He showered on me, I made a *Sankalpa* to build a small Shirdi Sai Baba temple in my premises * to expound the glory, the grandeur and the * of Sai Baba among the people of Mauritius.

Thus it is that in 1971, the Sai Baba Mandir in Curepipe, Mauritius opened its doors with a very humble beginning. I worked very hard to make the Sai mission flourish; and today the Sai Baba Mandir and the Sai Baba Centre of Curepipe has become a place of pilgrimage for thousands and thousands of people from all over Mauritius as well as from the neighbouring countries.

By now I am 81 years old; I have been doing the Sai Baba Mission for some 30 years; I am, by Baba's grace, healthy and in good shape, and I wish to continue this good work for many more years.

There have been innumerable instances of miraculous cures, of success in enterprises, of childless couples graced with a child, and several other such miracles for the devotees of the Shirdi Sai Baba temple of Mauritius.

Sometimes on Sundays and public holidays, the crowd of devotees at the Mandir is so dense that I have to have recourse to the local police to maintain order and discipline and to control the traffic.

Baba's Glory is spreading far and wide and I am very happy (but very humble also) that Baba has chosen me as His instrument to spread His Glory and Grace in this small country of Mauritius.

The Sai Baba temple in Mauritius has become so famous and renowned that it is referred to as the little Shirdi in Mauritius.

-Pandit Shiv Prasad
Curepipe, Mauritius
(Courtesy: *Sri Sai Leela*, Sept.-Oct. 1990)

203. A Miracleof Dharma Sai

My wife committed suicide. I was really innocent in this mater. But her people including her parents started blaming me in this regard. I was really disgusted and afraid of this blame and ran away from my place. As I am a staunch believer of Lord Sri Shirdi Sainath, I started *Akhandanama Japa* and left everything to him. One Thursday a very old lady with a common Balance in her hands appeared in my dream and she said, "My name is Dharma Sai. I am staying in Dharmagiri Kshethra. I have given you to justice; immediately come t me and donate some amount towards making the *Pratima* of Sri Dharma Sai in marble stone and disappeared. Next day morning I sold my gold chain which was in my neck since 20 years and rushed to **Lord Sri** Dharma Sai of Dharmagiri Kshetra, Shamshabad, R.R. District-509218 (14 Kms. from Zoo Park), Hyderabda-509 218 and I dropped some amount in Hundi. At the same moment I saw my in-laws in that place as they come over there to have the *darshan* of Sri DharmaSai. Immediately all of them apologized for their mistake in front of Sri Dharma Sai. They offered me to get married with their second daughter. I married her and I am leading a very happy life with her. Grateful thanks to Sri Dharma Sai for favours received.

Vinod Kumar Jain,
Mulund, Bombay
(Courtesy: *The Hindustan times*, June 16, 1994)

204. Another Miracle of Sri Dharma Sai

My land located in Madras City was in court for the last 20 years due to disputes. One day I happened to see the advertisement given by Sri Govind Singh in *Hindustan Times* about the Miracles Sri Dharma Sai and about "Siddi Yantram". I immediately went to Sri Dharmagiri Kshetra 14 Kms. from Zoo Park, Hyderabad and had *darshan* of Sri Dharma Sai and took to Siddi Yantram. Within one week after taking Siddi Yantram I got back my property worth several crores of rupees which was in disputes.

-K. Ram Nadham, Tambaram, Madras

SRI DHARMA SAI SEVA TRUST
Dharmagiri Kshetram, Shamshabad,
Ranga Reddy Dist., Hyderabad (A.P.)
(Courtesy: *The Hindustan times*, July 6, 1995)

205. *Udhi*, A Unique Remedy

My friend and I are great believers of Sai and remember always the saying of Sri Sai, "If you chant my name 'Sai' will be with you".

Recently in the month of Sept. '86 my friend's mother went to an eye specialist for eye check-up. The specialist checked up her eyes and asked her to be ready for cataract operation of the right eye. Being an old lady she was much worried of this and was not willing for operation. My friend advised her to have faith in Sri Sai Baba and apply *Udhi* daily on the affected eye. In the month of November '86, she went to the same eye specialist to undergo the operation. But to the surprise of the doctor and others, her vision was found to be clean. The doctor now opined that there was no need for the operation.

The above incident surprised us all, beyond words. With prostrations to Sai Baba.

S. Sarojini,
2-2-1164/15/3, Tilak Nagar,
New Nallakunta
(Courtesy: *Shri Sai Leela*, Aug., 1997)

206. Sai Miracles Experienced by A Film Editor (1960-1996)

I am a devotee of Sri Shirdi Sai Baba for the last 40 years.

To think about, to speak about, and to write about the glories of Shri Samartha Satguru Sai Baba of Shirdi, is a blessing. It gives inner strength to man and facilitate his all-round advancement. The deepest experience one has is incapable of utterances. As you are keen after any bit of information I shall mention some of such facts.

1. In the year 1960, I was with my family suffering all of a sudden for a morsel of food due to a big break in my film career. One day in the middle of the night I was crying and scolding God not withstanding His tests. I stubbornly made a vow to myself unless He appears immediately in person and saves me from the horrible situation. I will never have faith in his existence. Sometime passed in blank. The test of time came to reveal His presence. All of a sudden there was blinding light of flash lighting my place for a fraction of a second. I thought that there would be rain. I thought as if it was summer and there was no possibility of rain coming. Then what was the flasti for? As my mind was pondering over suddenly and more distinctly I heard

the sound of the *Padukas* coming forward me and going into my *pooja* room. This happened for a moment. My hair stood still. I immediately realized the presence of the Almighty Shirdi Sai Baba. I am reminded about a photo of His given to me in my studenthood by my principal who was an ardent devotee of Baba, who used to make a trip to Shirdi every year.

Next day I made a search, and got it. I kept it beside the other photos of the Gods in my *pooja* room. I bathed and sat on my sofa dressed as if ready to go to the studio. I heard the sound of a car stopping in front of my house. My friend came inside and told me that he was in search in me from the last night for an editing job which must be started immediately. My mind turned toward the pooja room searching for the photo of Shirdi Sai Baba.

As Baba said, "Look up to me and I will look after you. Not vain is my promise that I shall ever lighten your burden."

One begins to understand much better the way in which Sai Baba was approached and He operated upon those contacting him.

2. In 1962 I was going through some books in an old book stall. I saw one old book in the shelf that attracted my attention. Though there was KD name written on it, still my mind was for it. I took the book and saw inside it the name *"Sri Sai Baba's Charters and Sayings"* by His Holiness Shri Narasimha Swamiji. After going through it, I was very much keen to know much more about Samartha Satguru Sai Baba of Shirdi.

After sometime I was returning from the church which is at Armenian street at Madras and I happened to stop near soiled Second hand books kept on the platform for sale. As it happened before, I saw a black soiled book without any name. I eagerly took *

SOME DEVOTEES' EXPERIENCES REPORTED ON THE INTERNET

April 12,2015 - December 28, 2009

1. **Shirdi Sai Baba blessings to get job**
    April 28, 2013
2. **Sai inspires to do _Parayan_ of Sundarakandam and blessed devotee to get pregnant**
    April 7, 2013
3. **Shirdi Sai Baba Leela healing child with good skin and blessing her dad with good job**,
    February 3, 2013
4. **Lord Ganesha and Shirdi Sai Baba blessings for happy married life**
    January 7,
5. Sai Baba will come with you in your pilgrimage to Shirdi
    February 18, 2012
6. Fakir accepting blanket – Sai Baba helps whenever we wish to do a good deed.
    January 29, 2012
7. **Sai Baba graciously showing His lotus feet to do _pada pooja_ – a _pooja_ from heart**
    January 21, 2012
8. **Writing Sai Sai Sai one crore times**.
    December 25, 2011
9. **Shirdi Saibaba Photos – let light of Sai Baba glow everywhere**.
    December 24, 2011
10. **God is listening because Sai Baba blessed us with a beautiful house**
11. **Yearly Shirdi trip experiences from my best Sai friends family**
    October 15, 2011

12. **A dream of "Shri Vidya" – Goddess Durga and Shirdi Sai baba leela**
    June 17, 2011
13. **Shirdi Sai baba's guidance to make a Job website**
    March 29, 2011
14. **Shirdi Sai baba helps a Devotee for a good married life**
    February 18, 2011
15. When Sai calls you to Shirdi Go Shirdi. Try not to change Travel plans
    December 19, 2010
16. **Shirdi Sai baba blessings to renew Visa**
    October 4, 2010
17. **Sai *Leela* – Lost money during Shirdi trip but Sai blessed for safe journey**
    August 17, 2010
18. Sai blessings to a devotee who called him a human being
    August 4, 2010
19. Shirdi Sai Baba temples Miracles experiences by sai devotees living in USA cities and towns
    July 3, 2010
20. **Give up what you like, Shirdi Sai baba will bless your family**
    May 20, 2010
21. **Shirdi Sai Baba miracle curing mother's health**
    February 27, 2010
22. **A friend's help to get Job and call to *Samadhi mandir* of Shirdi Sai Baba**
    February 24, 2010
23. **Sai *leela* under the *neem* tree at Shirdi**
    January 9, 2010
24. Saibaba assured "Doctors have nothing to tell about your health"
    December 28, 2009

Printed in the United States
By Bookmasters